THE
- QUICK AND EASY MEALS FOR THE BUSY COOK
- **200** 20-MINUTE RECIPES & **200** 30-MINUTE RECIPES

HALF HOUR

OVER **1600** PHOTOGRAPHS ILLUSTRATE
HUNDREDS OF SIMPLE STEP-BY-STEP IDEAS

COOK

CONTRIBUTING EDITOR: JENNI FLEETWOOD

LORENZ BOOKS

This edition is published by Lorenz Books
an imprint of Anness Publishing Ltd
Hermes House, 88–89 Blackfriars Road,
London SE1 8HA
tel. 020 7401 2077; fax 020 7633 9499
www.lorenzbooks.com; www.annesspublishing.com

If you like the images in this book and would like to investigate
using them for publishing, promotions or advertising, please visit
our website www. practicalpictures.com for more information.

UK agent: The Manning Partnership Ltd; tel. 01225 478444;
fax 01225 478440; sales@manning-partnership.co.uk
UK distributor: Grantham Book Services Ltd; tel. 01476 541080;
fax 01476 541061; orders@gbs.tbs-ltd.co.uk
North American agent/distributor: National Book Network;
tel. 301 459 3366; fax 301 429 5746; www.nbnbooks.com
Australian agent/distributor: Pan Macmillan Australia; tel. 1300 135
113; fax 1300 135 103; customer.service@macmillan.com.au
New Zealand agent/distributor: David Bateman Ltd; tel. (09) 415 7664;
fax (09) 415 8892

Publisher: Joanna Lorenz
Editorial Director: Helen Sudell
Project Editors: Doreen Gillon, Molly Perham
Production Manager: Steve Lang
Book Design: Ian Sandom
Contributors: Pepita Aris, Mridula Baljekar, Jane Bamforth,
Alex Barker, Judy Bastyra, Georgina Campbell, Coralie Dorman,
Matthew Drennan, Joanna Farrow, Maria Filippelli, Jenni Fleetwood,
Christine France, Brian Glover, Juliet Harbutt, Simona Hill,
Becky Johnson, Bridget Jones, Lucy Knox, Jane Milton,
Suzannah Olivier, Keith Richmond, Rena Salaman, Marlena Spieler, Liz
Trigg, Linda Tubby, Sunil Vijayakar, Jenny White, Biddy White-Lennon,
Kate Whiteman, Rosemary Wilkinson, Jeni Wright
Photography: Karl Adamson, Edward Allwright, Caroline Barty,
Steve Baxter, Martin Brigdale, Nicki Dowey, James Duncan,
Michelle Garrett, John Heseltine, Amanda Heywood, Janine Hosegood,
Don Last, William Lingwood, Craig Robertson and Sam Stowell

ETHICAL TRADING POLICY
At Anness Publishing we believe that business should be conducted
in an ethical and ecologically sustainable way, with respect for the
environment and a proper regard to the replacement of the natural
resources we employ.

As a publisher, we use a lot of wood pulp to make high-quality paper
for printing, and that wood commonly comes from spruce trees. We
are therefore currently growing more than 500,000 trees in two
Scottish forest plantations near Aberdeen – Berrymoss (130
hectares/320 acres) and West Touxhill (125 hectares/305 acres). The
forests we manage contain twice the number of trees employed each
year in paper-making for our books.
Because of this ongoing ecological investment programme, you, as
our customer, can have the pleasure and reassurance of knowing that
a tree is being cultivated on your behalf to naturally replace the
materials used to make the book you are holding.
Our forestry programme is run in accordance with the UK Woodland
Assurance Scheme (UKWAS) and will be certified by the
internationally recognized Forest Stewardship Council (FSC). The FSC
is a non-government organization dedicated to promoting responsible
management of the world's forests. Certification ensures forests are
managed in an environmentally sustainable and socially responsible
basis. For further information about this scheme, go to
www.annesspublishing.com/trees

A CIP catalogue record for this book is available from the British Library.

NOTES
Bracketed terms are intended for American readers.
For all recipes, quantities are given in both metric and imperial measures and,
where appropriate, in standard cups and spoons. Follow one set of measures,
but not a mixture, because they are not interchangeable.
Standard spoon and cup measures are level. 1 tsp = 5ml, 1 tbsp = 15ml,
1 cup = 250ml/8fl oz.
Australian standard tablespoons are 20ml. Australian readers should use 3 tsp in
place of 1 tbsp for measuring small quantities.
American pints are 16fl oz/2 cups. American readers should use 20fl oz/2.5 cups
in place of 1 pint when measuring liquids.
Electric oven temperatures in this book are for conventional ovens. When using a
fan oven, the temperature will probably need to be reduced by about
10–20°C/20–40°F. Since ovens vary, check with your manufacturer's instruction
book for guidance.
The nutritional analysis given for each recipe is calculated per portion (i.e. serving
or item), unless otherwise stated. If the recipe gives a range, such as Serves 4–6,
then the nutritional analysis will be for the smaller portion size, i.e. 6 servings.
Measurements for sodium do not include salt added to taste.
Medium (US large) eggs are used unless otherwise stated.

CONTENTS

GREAT FOOD FAST

Half an hour isn't very long. You can easily spend that amount of time puzzling over a crossword clue, or trying to telephone a company determined to leave you on hold, or having a cup of coffee in a busy restaurant. So can you cook a meal in half an hour? Yes you can, and this is the book to tell you how to do it.

When you want great food fast, what you need in your repertoire are easy, no-fuss recipes: breakfasts you can blitz in a blender; lunches you can prepare and pack in next to no time and suppers that raise your spirits without sapping any of the energy you have left at the end of the day. You want food that looks as good as it tastes, but doesn't require you to carve a rose out of a radish. If you are entertaining, you want to do so in style, but without missing more than a few moments of your guests' company.

You can achieve these aims – after a fashion – by frequenting the ready meal section of your favourite supermarket. Some days you'll do just that, but it is much more rewarding and nutritious to serve something you've cooked yourself. Dishing up a ready meal is rather like reading a raunchy novel; satisfying as far as it goes, but sadly lacking as a sensory experience.

AN EXPERIENCE WORTH HAVING

Food isn't just fuel and providing it need not be seen as a chore. When you prepare a meal you engage all your senses. The glowing colours of ingredients – a bunch of basil, a bowl of tomatoes, a basket of blueberries – are a delight to see. When you prepare them, your sense of touch comes into play. You cut a lemon or a lime, and immediately a lovely citrus aroma permeates the room. The pleasure continues with other satisfying smells: onions sizzling in a pan, apples and cloves simmering on the stove. With cooking smells come cooking sounds, and all help to stimulate the appetite. Before you take a single bite, you've already experienced a range of remarkable sensory experiences, and taste, the final food frontier, is still to come. Looked at that way, it isn't surprising that many of us love to cook, and would do much more of it if only we had the time.

PRESSING PRIORITIES

Time. There's the rub. We never seem to have enough of it. Whether you are a student trying to balance study with a hectic social life, a single person trying to carve out a career or a parent with a different but equally pressing set of

Above: Ready-made dips and pâtés are always on the supermarket shopping list, but it's so easy to produce your own with just a few ingredients.

priorities, time is a precious luxury. We're all riding the rollercoaster, rushing from home to work to home to sport to parents' evening to home to sleep. Putting good food on the table should be in there somewhere, but sometimes it is difficult to achieve. That's why this book takes a pragmatic approach. Preparing your own vegetables is ideal, but if buying a bag of shake-it-out salad or some ready trimmed beans means you can eat well and still get to your night class, go for it. Look out for quick-cook versions of favourite ingredients, like polenta and rice, and don't be afraid of mixing bought items like pesto or tapenade with home-cooked pasta.

There is no longer any rule about precisely what constitutes a meal. You can have soup and a toasted sandwich one day, a stir-fry the next and a sophisticated treat like pan-fried steaks with whisky and cream on a Friday night. A simple one-pot dish like pork and pineapple coconut curry can be served solo, or with noodles that only take a minute or so to prepare. There will be some occasions when you will want to offer a vegetable side dish and others when the dish is so complete in itself that a chunk of bread is all that is required. What matters is that you cook

Left: This melt-in-the-mouth dish of honey-glazed aubergines is just one of many innovative recipes that can be turned around in a few simple steps, and will never fail to impress.

Right: A tight time frame doesn't mean you can't experiment – a vegetarian version of this Spiced Chicken Risotto is just as easily prepared as its meaty counterpart. Many other recipes in the book offer useful tips and variations.

what you know you can cope with in the time available and serve up something which everyone will enjoy.

THE RECIPES

The aim of this book is to provide a wide-ranging selection of recipes that can be cooked in thirty minutes or less. That's assuming the cook is reasonably experienced. If you've never chopped an onion in your life, it is likely to take you a little longer. Efficient cooking is all about organization, so do read through your chosen recipe carefully, assemble your ingredients and give some thought to strategy. If something has to go in the oven, switch it on to heat up before you do anything else; if you need to add grated cheese in Step 4, grate it straight away. Recipe methods reflect this, but you need to work within the bounds of

Below: A sudden craving for your favourite dessert – like this glorious Baked Pineapple Alaska – can be answered in twenty minutes or less.

your own ability and the confines of your own kitchen. If a recipe calls for a slotted spoon and you need to rummage under the sink for one, you could lose valuable time, so be as well prepared as possible. If you are inexperienced, the best way to start is by choosing the shortest recipes of 10 minutes or less, or opt for something that needs no cooking at all, such as a salad. Also, enlist aid when you can.

Something as simple as getting a partner to line up ingredients can be a huge help.

Some of the recipes in this book require some advance preparation – for example, marinating, soaking or chilling. The timeline at the top of the recipe will make it clear when this is required and there will probably be some mention of the fact in the recipe introduction, so do watch out for this. In most cases, the recipe still won't take more than 30 minutes in all, but the preparation will be in stages and not all at the same time. There are times when advance preparation is an advantage – when you want to get some dinner party cooking out of the way early, for instance.

When you have extra time on your hands, consider making stock or a few sauces that can be frozen for later use. Then, when you are in a rush, you'll have the means to make a simple speedy meal that tastes great. You'll find recipes for these, and ideas for quick and easy accompaniments, in the opening chapter. Also in this section are some suggested menus for special occasions. These show how easy it is to mix and match three or four courses and produce a meal that is stunningly simple and tastes delicious.

THE ART OF QUICK COOKING

Although having the right recipes gives you the best start, when it comes to producing great food in the shortest possible time there are some other criteria to consider. Every workman needs decent tools and having a well-equipped kitchen will help you to make more efficient use of your time. This doesn't mean owning every new gadget on the market, but it is sensible to invest in good-quality knives and pans, accurate measuring equipment, spoons and spatulas and a few well-chosen appliances. A food processor is just about essential these days, particularly when speed is a prime consideration and you will also benefit from having a good hand-held electric beater. The quick cook also needs a heavy griddle pan — for cooking items like salmon, duck and Mediterranean vegetables — and a wok for the stir-fries that are central to swift cooking. It also helps to have a repertoire of simple sauces and stocks, which can be made in advance and kept in the freezer. Some of the recipes in this book suggest suitable accompaniments, but if you need more inspiration, you'll find it right here.

EQUIPMENT: PANS, CUTTING AND MEASURING

You don't need a kitchen full of equipment to be a spontaneous and versatile cook. It is quality, not quantity, that counts when you're preparing and cooking food, particularly when choosing essential pieces of equipment such as pans and knives. As long as you look after them, these items should last for many years so are well worth the investment. The following section guides you through the essential items that make cooking as simple and enjoyable as possible, and also offers suggestions on how to improvise if you don't have the right piece of equipment.

PANS AND BAKEWARE

Always choose good-quality pans with a solid, heavy base because they retain heat better and are less likely to warp or buckle. Heatproof glass lids are useful because they allow you to check cooking progress without having to uncover the pan repeatedly.

Pans: small, medium and large

When cooking large quantities of food, such as pasta or rice that need to be boiled in a large amount of water, the bigger the pan the better. It does not matter whether the pan is non-stick, but it is useful to have heatproof handles and lids so that the pan can double as a large ovenproof pot. A medium pan is ideal for cooking sauces and similar mixtures. For these a non-stick pan is best; it will help to prevent thickened sauces sticking and burning. Washing up will also be easier. The same guidelines apply to a small pan, which is ideal for small quantities.

Frying pan

Select a non-stick pan that is shallow enough, so that it is easy to slide a metal spatula into it. A pan with an ovenproof handle and lid can be placed in the oven as a shallow casserole dish and under the grill (broiler).

Baking sheets

Having one or two non-stick baking sheets on hand in the kitchen is invaluable to the busy cook. They can be used for a multitude of tasks such as roasting hazelnuts, or they can be placed under full dishes in the oven to catch any drips if the mixture overflows. Choose good-quality heavy baking sheets that will not buckle in the oven.

Roasting pan

As a quick cook you may only roast meat or vegetables occasionally, but when you do, a good, heavy roasting pan is essential. Choose a large pan; you will achieve better results if there is room for heat to circulate as the food cooks. Potatoes, for example, will not crisp well if they are crammed together in a small pan. Treat all pans with care to get maximum usage from them.

Below: Baking sheets are essential to the half-hour kitchen – having more than one will mean several things can be cooked at the same time.

CUTTING AND GRINDING

Chopping, slicing, cutting, peeling and grinding are all essential aspects of food preparation so it's important to have the right tools for the job.

Chopping boards

Essential in every kitchen, these can be made of wood or plastic. Wooden boards tend to be heavier and more stable, but they must be thoroughly scrubbed in hot soapy water and properly dried. Plastic boards are easier to clean and better for cutting meat, poultry and fish.

Knives: cook's, vegetable and serrated

When buying knives, choose the best ones you can afford. They should feel comfortable in your hand, so try several different types and practise a cutting action before you buy. You will need

Left: It is wise to invest in three good quality pans of different sizes.

three different knives. A cook's knife is a good multi-purpose knife. The blade is usually about 18cm/7in long, but you may find that you prefer a slightly longer or shorter blade. A vegetable knife is a small version of the cook's knife and is used for finer cutting. A large serrated knife is essential for slicing bread and ingredients such as tomatoes, which have a hard-to-cut skin compared to the soft flesh underneath. Store knives safely and securely, out of reach of young children.

Vegetable peelers

These can have a fixed or swivel blade. Both types will make quick work of peeling vegetables and fruit, with less waste than a small knife.

Graters

These come in various shapes and sizes. Box graters have several different cutting blades and are easy to handle. Microplane graters have razor-sharp blades that retain their sharp edges. It is worth investing in several of these, with different grating surfaces.

MEASURING EQUIPMENT

Accurate measuring equipment is essential, particularly when making breads and cakes, which need very precise quantities of ingredients.

Weighing scales

These are good for measuring dry ingredients. Digital scales are the most accurate but balance scales that use weights or a sliding weight are also a good choice. Spring scales with a scoop and dial are not usually as precise.

Measuring cups

Suitable for dry or liquid ingredients, these standard measures usually come in a set of separate cups for different fractions or portions of a full cup.

Measuring jug/pitcher

This is essential for liquids. A heatproof glass jug is useful because it allows hot liquids to be measured and makes it easy to check the quantity.

Measuring spoons

Table cutlery varies in size, so a set of standard measuring spoons is extremely useful for measuring small quantities.

Left: The traditional box grater is solid, reliable and easy to handle – with several different grating blades.

Looking after knives

Although it might seem contradictory, the sharper the knife, the safer it is to use. It takes far more effort to use a blunt knife and this often results in accidents. Try to get into the habit of sharpening your knives regularly, because the blunter they become, the more difficult they are to use and the longer it will take to sharpen them. Always wash knives carefully after use and dry them thoroughly to prevent discolouring or rusting.

Below: Compact kitchen utensils such as measuring jugs and cups are vital to the art of successful quick cooking.

EQUIPMENT: BLENDING, BAKING, GRIDDLING AND WOK-FRYING

MIXING, ROLLING AND DRAINING

Bowls, spoons, whisks and strainers are vital to the half-hour kitchen. Establish suitable places to store the equipment, so that you always know where to find it in a hurry. Having essentials to hand is one of the golden rules of successful quick cooking.

Mixing bowls

You will need one large and one small bowl. Heatproof glass bowls are a good choice because they can be placed over a pan of simmering water to heat delicate sauces and to melt chocolate.

Wooden spoons

Inexpensive and essential for stirring and beating, every kitchen should have two or three wooden spoons.

Metal slotted spoon

This large spoon with draining holes is very useful for lifting small pieces of food out of cooking liquid.

Fish slice/metal spatula

This is invaluable for lifting delicate fish fillets and other foods out of a pan.

Rolling pin

A heavy wooden or marble rolling pin is useful for rolling out pastry. If you don't have one, use a clean, dry, tall glass bottle (such as a wine bottle) instead.

Balloon whisk

A metal balloon whisk is great for softly whipping cream and whisking sauces to a smooth consistency. Whisks are available in all shapes and sizes. Do not buy an enormous whisk that is difficult to use and will not fit into pans. Mini-whisks are not essential – you can always use a fork instead.

Sieve/strainer

For sifting flour, icing (confectioners') sugar, cocoa and other dry ingredients, a stainless-steel sieve is essential. It can also be used for straining small quantities of cooked vegetables, pasta and rice. Wash and dry a sieve well after use to prevent it becoming heavily clogged and damp.

Colander

Choose a free-standing metal colander with feet on the base. This has the advantage of leaving both hands free to empty heavy pans, and will keep the base of the colander above the liquid that is being drained off.

ELECTRICAL APPLIANCES

Although not always essential, these can speed up preparation.

Food processor

This fabulous invention can make life a lot easier. It is perfect for processing soft and hard foods and is more versatile than a blender, which is best suited to puréeing very soft foods or liquids.

Hand-held electric whisk

A small, hand-held electric whisk or beater is very useful for making cakes, whipping cream and whisking egg whites. Choose an appliance with sturdy beaters and a powerful motor that will last.

Above: Wooden spoons and spatulas are essential for stirring, beating and lifting.

Below: A food processor is the quick cook's best friend, especially if it has a mini bowl – perfect for grinding nuts or making breadcrumbs for toppings.

Above: Cookie cutters come in all kinds of shapes and sizes.

Above: A pastry brush is useful when baking or grilling (broiling).

EXTRA EQUIPMENT

As well as the essential items, some recipes require other items such as tart tins (pans) and cookie cutters. The following are some items you may find useful, whether you are putting together a speedy snack or attempting something more elaborate.

Cookie cutters

These make quick work of cutting out pastry and cookie dough. Metal ones have a sharper cutting edge so are usually preferable to plastic ones. If you don't have cutters, you can use a glass which is much quicker.

Pastry brush

Made of bristle, with a wooden or plastic handle, this is useful for brushing food lightly with liquid – for example, brushing meat or fish with oil or marinade while grilling (broiling).

CAKE TINS/PANS

These can have loose bottoms or spring-clip sides to allow easy removal of the cake. Be sure to use the size specified in the recipe.

Tartlet tins/muffin pans

These consist of six or twelve fairly deep cups in a tray. They can be used for baking tartlets, muffins, cupcakes, buns and bread rolls.

Tart tins/pans

Available with straight or fluted sides, these are not as deep as tartlet tins (muffin pans). They come in a variety of sizes, from individual containers to very large tins. They are useful for baking all kinds of sweet and savoury tarts. Loose-bottomed tins are best because they allow you to remove the contents more easily.

Skewers

These are used for kebabs and other skewered foods. Metal skewers are reusable and practical if you cook over the barbecue frequently, or cook kebabs that need lengthy cooking. Bamboo skewers are disposable and useful for foods that cook quickly – soak them in cold water before use to stop them burning.

Palette knife/metal spatula

Use this large, flat, round-bladed, blunt knife for spreading or flipping pancakes.

Griddle pan

A good quality, heavy griddle pan is useful for cooking meat and fish. The pan should be very hot before food is placed on it and you should brush the surface of the food with a little oil to prevent it from sticking, rather than adding oil to the pan. To clean, hot soapy water can be used but make sure the pan has cooled before washing, and then rinse and dry thoroughly. Do not plunge into water for soaking.

Above: A heavy griddle pan is a boon to the quick cook.

Wok

Larger and deeper than a frying pan, often with a rounded base, a wok has high sides and a large surface area, which make it ideal for stir-frying, steaming and simmering. Clean with hot water (no soap) and wipe with kitchen paper until the paper comes away clean.

Below: Woks come with one or two handles. The two-handled variety makes a good table centrepiece when dishing up a sizzling supper from wok to plate during a dinner party or family meal.

SIMPLE WAYS <u>TO</u> FLAVOUR FOOD

As well as selecting the cooking method best suited to the ingredients, there are several quick and simple methods of adding flavour using herbs, spices and aromatics. Match the seasoning to the ingredient and go for simple techniques such as marinating, stuffing or coating with a dry spice rub, which will help to intensify the flavours. The longer you leave food in a marinade or with a rub, the more the flavours will penetrate, so if you want to incorporate these techniques in a quick meal, you need to do a bit of forward planning.

FLAVOURS FOR FISH

Classic aromatics used for flavouring fish and shellfish include lemon, lime, parsley, dill, fennel and bay leaves. These flavours all have a fresh, intense quality that complements the delicate taste of fish and shellfish without overpowering it. All work well added before, during or after cooking, either as a filling or a marinade.

• To flavour whole fish, such as trout or mackerel, stuff a few lemon slices and some fresh parsley or basil into the body cavity before cooking. Season with plenty of salt and freshly ground black pepper, then wrap the fish in foil or baking parchment, ensuring the packet is well sealed. Place the fish in an ovenproof dish or on a baking tray and bake until cooked through.
• To make an unusual, yet delicious, marinade for salmon, arrange the salmon fillets in a single layer in an overproof dish. Drizzle the fillets with a little light olive oil and add a split vanilla pod (bean). Cover and chill for a couple of hours before cooking.

• To marinate chunky fillets of fish, such as cod or salmon, arrange the fish fillets in a dish in a single layer. Drizzle the fish with olive oil, then sprinkle over a little crushed garlic and grated lime rind and squeeze over lime juice. Cover the dish in clear film (plastic wrap) and leave to marinate in the refrigerator for at least 30 minutes. Grill (broil) lightly until just cooked through.

PEPPING UP MEAT AND POULTRY

Meat and poultry can take both delicate and punchy seasonings. Dry rubs, marinades and sticky glazes are all perfect ways to introduce flavour into the food. Marinating the tougher cuts, such as stewing steak, also helps to make the meat more tender. A quick way of introducing flavour to meat is to inject it with marinade using a veterinary syringe.

• To make a fragrant Cajun spice rub for pork chops, steaks and chicken, mix together 5ml/1 tsp each dried thyme, dried oregano, finely crushed black peppercorns, salt, crushed cumin seeds and hot paprika. Rub the Cajun spice mix into the raw meat or poultry, then barbecue or bake until cooked.

• To marinate red meat, such as beef, lamb or venison, prepare a mixture of two-thirds red wine to one-third olive oil in a shallow non-metallic dish. Stir in some chopped garlic and bruised fresh rosemary sprigs. Add the meat and turn to coat it in the marinade. Cover and chill for at least 2 hours or overnight before cooking.
• To make a mildly-spiced sticky mustard glaze for chicken, pork or red meat, mix 45ml/3 tbsp each Dijon mustard, clear honey and demerara (raw) sugar, 2.5ml/½ tsp chilli powder, 1.5ml/¼ tsp ground cloves, and salt and ground black pepper. Cook the poultry or meat over the barbecue or under the grill (broiler) and brush with the glaze about 10 minutes before the end of the cooking time.
• A lemon grass and ginger marinade that can be whizzed up in the food processor is quick and easy and works well with chicken or pork. Chop the lower half of two lemon grass stalks and put them in the bowl of a food processor with 30ml/2 tbsp sliced fresh root ginger, 6 chopped garlic cloves, 4 chopped shallots, ½ bunch chopped coriander (cilantro) roots, 30ml/2 tbsp each Thai fish sauce and light soy sauce, 120ml/4fl oz/½ cup coconut milk and 1 tbsp palm sugar. Process until smooth, pour over 8 chicken portions and marinate for at least 4 hours. Bake the chicken pieces in the oven or cook over a barbecue, brushing them with the marinade once or twice during cooking.

Below: Brush on sticky glazes towards the end of the cooking time; if the glaze is cooked for too long, it will burn.

Above: Adding a drizzle of sesame oil to stir-fried vegetables gives them a wonderfully rich, smoky, nutty flavour.

VIBRANT VEGETABLES

Most fresh vegetables have a subtle flavour that needs to be brought out and enhanced. When using speedy cooking methods such as steaming and stir-frying, go for light, fresh flavourings that will enhance the taste of the vegetables. When using more robust cooking methods, such as roasting, choose richer flavours such as garlic and spices.

• To make fragrant, Asian-style steamed vegetables, add a bruised stalk of lemon grass and/or a few kaffir lime leaves to the steaming water, then cook vegetables such as pak choi (bok choy) over the water until just tender. Alternatively, place the aromatics in the steamer under the vegetables and steam as before until just tender.
• To add a rich flavour to stir-fried vegetables, add a splash of sesame oil just before the end of cooking time. (Do not use more than 5ml/1 tsp because sesame oil has a very strong flavour and can be overpowering.)

• To enhance the taste of naturally sweet vegetables, such as parsnips and carrots, glaze them with honey and mustard before roasting. Mix together 30ml/2 tbsp wholegrain mustard and 45ml/3 tbsp clear honey, and season with salt and ground black pepper. Brush the glaze over the prepared vegetables to coat completely, then roast until sweet and tender. To cut the roasting time, par-boil the vegetables first.

FRAGRANT RICE AND GRAINS

Classic accompaniments, such as rice and couscous, can be enhanced by the addition of simple flavourings. Adding herbs, spices and aromatics can help to perk up the rice and grains' subtle flavour without overpowering them. Always choose flavourings that will complement the dish with which the rice or grains will be served.

• To make exotic fragrant rice to serve with Asian-style stir-fries and braised dishes, add a whole star anise or a few cardamom pods to a pan of rice before cooking. The rice will absorb the flavour during cooking. Remove the spices from the pan using a slotted spoon just before serving the rice.

• To make zesty herb rice or couscous, heat a little chopped fresh tarragon and grated lemon rind in olive oil or melted butter until warm, then drizzle the flavoured oil and herbs over freshly cooked rice or couscous.

• To make simple fresh herb rice or couscous, fork plenty of chopped fresh parsley and chives through the cooked grains and drizzle over a little oil just before serving.

• Add roasted seeds to rice for a delicious flavour. Place 50g/2oz/6 tbsp mixed pumpkin seeds and sunflower seeds in a non-stick frying pan over a medium heat. Toss until golden, cool, and mix into cooked long grain rice.

BASICS: OILS, STOCKS, MARINADES AND DRESSINGS

A few ready-made basics, such as stocks, pasta sauces and flavoured oils, can really speed up everyday cooking. They can all be bought ready-made in the supermarket, but they are easy to make at home. Stocks take time to prepare, but they can be stored in the freezer for several months. Flavoured oils are straightforward and keep in the same way as ordinary oils so it's well worth having a few in the cupboard. All the basic sauces, dressings, marinades and flavoured creams on the following pages are simple to prepare and can either be made fresh or in advance.

FLAVOURED OILS

Good-quality olive oil can be flavoured with herbs, spices and aromatics for drizzling, dressing and cooking.

Herb-infused oil

Half fill a jar with washed and dried fresh herbs such as rosemary or basil. Pour over olive oil to cover, then seal the jar and place in a cool, dark place for three days. Strain the oil into a clean jar or bottle and discard the herbs.

Lemon oil

Finely pare the rind from one lemon, place on kitchen paper, and leave to dry for one day. Add the dried rind to a bottle of olive oil and leave to infuse for up to three days. Strain the oil into a clean bottle and discard the rind.

Chilli oil

Add several dried chillies to a bottle of olive oil and leave to infuse for about two weeks before using. If the flavour is

not sufficiently pronounced, leave for another week. The chillies can be left in the bottle and give a very decorative and colourful effect.

Garlic oil

Add several whole garlic cloves to a bottle of olive oil and leave to infuse for about two weeks before using. If the flavour is not sufficiently pronounced, leave the oil to infuse for another week, then strain the oil into a clean bottle and store in a cool, dark place.

STOCKS

When you have a little time on your hands, make stock. A supply of home-made stock in the freezer gives you the basis of dozens of quick and easy dishes, including risotto and a range of sauces. It's also a great way of using up leftover chicken, meat and fish, or a surplus of vegetables. To freeze, pour the cooled stock into 600ml/1 pint/ 2½ cup containers and freeze for up to two months.

Chicken stock

Put a 1.3kg/3lb chicken carcass into a large pan with 2 peeled and quartered onions, 2 halved carrots, 2 roughly chopped celery sticks, 1 bouquet garni, 1 peeled garlic clove and 5 black peppercorns. Pour in 1.2 litres/2 pints/ 5 cups cold water and bring to the boil. Reduce the heat, cover and simmer for 4–5 hours, regularly skimming off any scum from the surface and adding more water if needed. Strain the stock through a sieve (strainer) lined with kitchen paper and leave to cool.

Beef stock

Preheat the oven to 230°C/450°F/Gas 8. Put 1.8kg/4lb beef bones in a roasting pan and roast for 40 minutes, until browned, turning occasionally. Transfer the bones and vegetables to a large pan. Cover with water, add 2 chopped tomatoes and cook as for chicken stock.

Fish stock

Put 2 chopped onions, 1.3kg/3lb fish bones and heads, 300ml/½ pint/1¼ cups white wine, 5 black peppercorns and 1 bouquet garni in a large pan. Pour in 2 litres/3½ pints/9 cups water. Bring to the boil and simmer for 20 minutes, skimming often. Strain.

Vegetable stock

Put 900g/2lb chopped vegetables, including onions, leeks, tomatoes, carrots, parsnips and cabbage, in a large pan. Pour in 1.5 litres/2½ pints/ 6¼ cups water. Bring to the boil and simmer for 30 minutes, then strain.

MARINADES

These strong-tasting mixes are perfect for adding flavour to meat, poultry, fish and vegetables. Most ingredients should be marinated for at least 30 minutes.

Ginger and soy marinade

This is perfect for use with chicken and beef. Peel and grate a 2.5cm/1in piece of fresh root ginger and peel and finely chop a large garlic clove. In a small bowl, whisk 60ml/4 tbsp olive oil with 75ml/5 tbsp dark soy sauce. Season with ground black pepper and stir in the ginger and garlic.

Rosemary and garlic marinade

This is ideal for robust fish, lamb and chicken. Roughly chop the leaves from 3 fresh rosemary sprigs. Finely chop 2 garlic cloves and whisk with the rosemary, 75ml/5 tbsp olive oil and the juice of 1 lemon. Add the grated rind of the lemon too, if you like.

Lemon grass and lime marinade

Use this delicately flavoured marinade with pieces of fish and chicken. Finely chop 1 lemon grass stalk. Whisk the grated rind and juice of 1 lime with 75ml/5 tbsp olive oil, salt and black pepper to taste, and the lemon grass.

Red wine and bay marinade

This easy-to-learn marinade is ideal for flavouring red meat, particularly if you want to soften the texture of tougher cuts. Whisk together 150ml/¼ pint/⅔ cup red wine, 1 finely chopped garlic clove, 2 torn fresh bay leaves and 45ml/3 tbsp olive oil. Season to taste with black pepper.

Below: Marinades containing red wine are particularly good for tenderizing tougher cuts of meat such as stewing steak.

DRESSINGS

Freshly made dressings are delicious drizzled over salads but are also tasty served with cooked vegetables and simply cooked fish, meat and poultry. You can make these dressings a few hours in advance and store them in a sealed container in the refrigerator until ready to use. Give them a quick whisk before drizzling over the food.

Honey and wholegrain mustard dressing

Drizzle this sweet, peppery dressing over leafy salads, fish, chicken and red meat dishes or toss with warm new potatoes. Whisk together 15ml/1 tbsp wholegrain mustard, 30ml/2 tbsp white wine vinegar, 15ml/1 tbsp honey and 75ml/5 tbsp extra virgin olive oil and season generously with salt and ground black pepper.

Orange and tarragon dressing

Serve this fresh, tangy dressing with salads and grilled (broiled) fish. In a small bowl, whisk the rind and juice of 1 large orange with 45ml/3 tbsp olive oil and 15ml/1 tbsp chopped fresh tarragon. Season with salt and plenty of ground black pepper to taste and chill before use if possible.

Toasted coriander and cumin dressing

Drizzle this warm, spicy dressing over grilled (broiled) chicken, lamb or beef. Heat a small frying pan and sprinkle in 15ml/1 tbsp each coriander and cumin seeds. Dry-fry until the seeds release their aromas and start to pop, then crush the seeds using a mortar and pestle. Add 45ml/3 tbsp olive oil, whisk to combine, then leave to infuse for 20 minutes. Season with salt and pepper to taste.

Lemon and horseradish dressing

This tangy dressing is particularly good with cooked beetroot. For a quick and easy lunch, serve it with smoked mackerel and a herb salad. There is no need to dress the salad – this delight-fully creamy relish will do very nicely sitting on the side of the plate. In a small bowl, combine 30ml/2 tbsp freshly squeezed lemon juice and 30ml/2 tbsp mirin or dry sherry. Whisk well, then add 120ml/4fl oz/½ cup olive oil, continuing to whisk the dressing until it emulsifies. Whisk in 30ml/2 tbsp creamed horseradish. Taste the dressing, and add a little salt and black pepper, if you think it needs it. The dressing should be smooth in texture.

BASICS: SAVOURY SAUCES AND DIPS

A repertoire of simple savoury sauce recipes is a must for the versatile quick cook. The following suggestions can be stirred through pasta and grains, heaped on baked potatoes, used to add interest to simple grilled (broiled) meats or fish, or served as savoury dips.

SAVOURY SAUCES

The following classic sauces can be made in a matter of minutes and are so much nicer than their ready-bought counterparts. You'll need a blender for the pesto variations.

Easy tomato sauce

Toss with pasta, top a pizza or serve with fish and chicken. Heat 15ml/1 tbsp olive oil in a pan, add 1 chopped onion and fry for 2–3 minutes until soft. Add 1 chopped garlic clove and cook for 1 minute more. Pour in 400g/14oz chopped canned tomatoes and stir in 15ml/1 tbsp tomato purée (paste). Add 30ml/2 tbsp dried oregano and simmer for 15 minutes, until thickened. Season.

Quick satay sauce

Serve this spicy Asian-style sauce with grilled (broiled) chicken, beef or prawns (shrimp), or toss with freshly cooked

egg noodles. Put 30ml/2 tbsp crunchy peanut butter in a pan and stir in 150ml/¼ pint/⅔ cup coconut milk, 45ml/3 tbsp hot water, a pinch of chilli powder and 30ml/2 tbsp light soy sauce. Heat gently, stirring until the peanut butter has melted and the mixture is well blended. Simmer for about a minute and serve immediately, while still hot.

Mustard cheese sauce

Stir this sauce through pasta, or serve with vegetables or baked white fish. Melt around 25g/1oz/2 tbsp butter in a medium pan and stir in 25g/1oz/ ¼ cup plain (all-purpose) flour. Remove the pan from the heat and stir in 5ml/ 1 tsp prepared English mustard.

Gradually add 200ml/7fl oz/scant 1 cup milk, stirring well to remove any lumps. (If the sauce becomes lumpy, whisk until smooth.) Return the pan to the heat and bring to the boil, stirring constantly. Remove from the heat and stir in 115g/4oz/1 cup grated Gruyère or Cheddar cheese. Continue to blend, away from the heat, until the cheese has melted and the texture is smooth. Season to taste.

Traditional pesto

This classic Italian sauce is made with basil, garlic, pine nuts and Parmesan cheese but there are many variations. Toss with pasta, stir into mashed potatoes or plain boiled rice, or use to flavour sauces and dressings. Put 50g/ 2oz fresh basil leaves in a food processor and blend to a paste with 25g/1oz/ ¼ cup toasted pine nuts and 2 peeled garlic cloves. With the motor still running, drizzle in 120ml/4fl oz/½ cup extra virgin olive oil until the mixture forms a paste. Spoon the pesto into a bowl and stir in 25g/1oz/⅓ cup freshly grated Parmesan cheese. Season to taste with salt and ground black pepper.

Parsley and walnut pesto

Put 50g/2oz fresh parsley leaves in a food processor and blend to a paste with 25g/1oz/¼ cup walnuts and 2 peeled garlic cloves. With the motor still running, drizzle in 120ml/ 4fl oz/ ½ cup extra virgin olive oil until the mixture forms a paste. Spoon the pesto into a bowl and stir in 25g/1oz/⅓ cup freshly grated Parmesan cheese. Season to taste with salt and ground black pepper.

Rocket pesto

Put 50g/2oz fresh rocket (arugula) leaves into a food processor and blend to a paste with 25g/1oz/¼ cup toasted pine nuts and 2 peeled garlic cloves. With the motor still running, drizzle in 120ml/4fl oz/½ cup extra virgin olive oil until the mixture forms a paste. Spoon the pesto into a bowl and stir in 25g/ 1oz/⅓ cup freshly grated Parmesan cheese. Season to taste with salt and ground black pepper.

Asian-style pesto

Try this Asian version of Italian pesto tossed with freshly cooked egg noodles. Put 50g/2oz fresh coriander (cilantro) leaves into a food processor and add 25g/1oz/¼ cup toasted pine nuts, 2 peeled garlic cloves and 1 seeded and roughly chopped green chilli. Blend until smooth. With the motor still running, drizzle in 120ml/4fl oz/½ cup extra virgin olive oil until the mixture forms a paste. Spoon the pesto into a bowl and season to taste with salt and ground black pepper.

Coriander and pistachio pesto

This aromatic pesto is delicious over fish or chicken. Put 50g/2oz fresh coriander (cilantro) leaves in a food processor. Add 15g/½oz fresh parsley and process until finely chopped. Add 2 seeded and chopped fresh red chillies, and 1 garlic clove. Process until finely chopped.

Add 50g/2oz/⅓ cup shelled pistachio nuts and pulse until roughly chopped. Stir in 25g/1oz/⅓ cup grated Parmesan cheese, 90ml/6 tbsp olive oil and the juice of 2 limes. Season with salt and pepper to taste.

SAVOURY DIPS

These richly flavoured dips are delicious served with tortilla chips, crudités or small savoury crackers, but can also be served as an accompaniment to grilled (broiled) or poached chicken and fish. The creamy dips also make flavourful dressings for salads; you may need to thin them slightly with a squeeze of lemon juice or a little cold water.

Blue cheese dip

This sharp, tangy mixture is best served with crudités. Put 200ml/7fl oz/scant 1 cup crème fraîche in a large bowl and add 115g/4oz/1 cup crumbled blue cheese such as Stilton. Stir well until the mixture is smooth and creamy. Season with salt and ground black pepper and fold in about 30ml/2 tbsp chopped fresh chives.

Sour cream and chive dip

This tasty dip is a classic combination and goes particularly well with crudités and savoury crackers. Put 200ml/7fl oz/scant 1 cup sour cream in a bowl and add 30ml/2 tbsp chopped fresh chives and a pinch of caster (superfine) sugar. Stir well to mix, then season with salt and ground black pepper.

Classic mayonnaise

There are some excellent makes of mayonnaise on the market and these are what you'll reach for when time is short. However, for that special-occasion meal, nothing beats home-made mayonnaise. Surprisingly, it doesn't take much longer to make than spooning the bought stuff out of the jar. Put 2 egg yolks, 10ml/2 tsp lemon juice, 5ml/1 tsp Dijon mustard and some salt and ground black pepper in a food processor. Process briefly to combine, then, with the motor running, drizzle in about 350ml/12fl oz/1½ cups olive oil. The mayonnaise will become thick and pale. Scrape the mayonnaise into a bowl, taste and add more lemon juice and salt and pepper if necessary.

Aioli

This classic French garlic mayonnaise is particularly good served with piping hot chips (French fries). Make the mayonnaise as described above, adding 2 peeled garlic cloves to the food processor with the egg yolks.

Lemon or caper mayonnaise

A tangy mayonnnaise complements cold poached fish perfectly. Make the mayonnaise as described above, adding the grated rind of 1 lemon to the food processor with the egg yolks. For caper mayonnaise, simply add 15ml/1 tbsp rinsed capers instead of the lemon zest.

Herb mayonnaise

Finely chop a handful of fresh herbs, such as basil, coriander (cilantro) and tarragon, and stir into freshly made plain mayonnaise.

BASICS: FRUIT RELISHES, SWEET SAUCES AND FLAVOURED CREAMS

Tart fruit sauces and relishes are the perfect foil to fish, poultry and pork, as they nicely offset rich flavours and oily textures. The avocado salsa, laced with the juice of a lime, works well as an accompaniment to corn snacks, but is also delicious served on the side with pork, poultry or steak. After sampling these fruity flavours, move on to sheer indulgence with an irresistible selection of dessert sauces and creams. Sweetness is supplied by spices, syrups, soft fruits, chocolate and fortified wines.

Apple sauce

Serve with pork. Peel, core and slice 450g/1lb cooking apples and place in a pan. Add a splash of water, 15ml/1 tbsp caster (superfine) sugar and a few whole cloves. Cook the apples over a gentle heat, stirring occasionally, until the fruit becomes pulpy.

Quick cranberry sauce

Serve with roast chicken or turkey. Put 225g/8oz/2 cups cranberries in a pan with about 75g/3oz/scant ½ cup light muscovado (brown) sugar, 45ml/3 tbsp port and 45ml/3 tbsp orange juice. Bring to the boil, then simmer, uncovered, for 10 minutes, or until the cranberries are tender. Stir occasionally to stop the fruit from sticking.

Gooseberry relish

Serve this tart relish with oily fish, such as mackerel, or fatty meat such as pork. Put 225g/8oz fresh or frozen gooseberries in a pan with 225g/8oz/ generous 1 cup caster (superfine) sugar and 1 star anise. Add a splash of water

and a little white wine if you like. Bring to the boil and simmer, uncovered, for 10 minutes, stirring occasionally, until the fruit has broken down and the texture is soft and pulpy.

Avocado and cumin salsa

Serve this spicy Mexican-style salsa as an unusual accompaniment to a meat meal, or solo, with a large bowl of tortilla chips. They're the perfect shape for scooping up the chunky salsa. Peel, stone (pit) and roughly chop 1 ripe avocado. Transfer to a bowl and gently stir in 1 finely chopped fresh red chilli, 15ml/1 tbsp toasted crushed cumin seeds, 1 chopped ripe tomato, the juice of 1 lime, 45ml/3 tbsp olive oil and 30ml/2 tbsp chopped fresh coriander (cilantro). Season and serve.

SWEET SAUCES

These luscious sauces are perfect spooned over ice cream and can turn a store-bought dessert or slice of sponge cake into an indulgent treat.

White chocolate sauce

Break 150g/5oz white chocolate into squares. Heat 150ml/¼ pint/⅔ cup double (heavy) cream in a heavy pan. When almost boiling, stir in the white chocolate, a few pieces at a time, until melted and smooth. Remove from the heat and stir in 30ml/2 tbsp brandy or Cointreau. Serve the sauce hot.

Toffee chocolate sauce

This is perhaps the simplest sweet sauce to make of all. Roughly chop 2 Mars bars (chocolate toffee bars) and

put the pieces in a pan with 300ml/ ½ pint/1¼ cups double (heavy) cream. Stir over a gentle heat until the chocolate bars have melted. Serve hot with ice cream, or combine with 50g/2oz/1 cup corn flakes to make chocolate crispy cakes.

Raspberry and vanilla sauce

Scrape the seeds from a vanilla pod (bean) into a food processor. Add 175g/ 6oz/1 cup raspberries and 30ml/2 tbsp icing (confectioners') sugar. Process to a purée, adding a little water to thin, if necessary.

Chocolate fudge sauce

Put 175ml/6fl oz/¾ cup double (heavy) cream in a small pan with 45ml/3 tbsp golden (light corn) syrup, 200g/7oz/ scant 1 cup light muscovado (brown) sugar and a pinch of salt. Heat gently, stirring, until the sugar has dissolved. Add 75g/3oz/½ cup chopped plain (semisweet) chocolate and stir until melted. Simmer the sauce gently for about 20 minutes, stirring occasionally, until thickened. Keep warm in a heatproof bowl until ready to use.

FLAVOURED CREAMS

Cream is the perfect accompaniment for any dessert – whether it's a healthy fruit salad, a sumptuous plum tart or a warming baked apple. Flavoured creams are even better and can transform a tasty dessert into a truly luscious one.

Rosemary and almond cream

This fragrant cream has a lovely texture and is good served with fruit compotes, pies and tarts. Pour 300ml/½ pint/1¼ cups double (heavy) cream into a pan and add 2 fresh rosemary sprigs. Heat the mixture until just about to boil, then remove the pan from the heat and leave the mixture to infuse for 20 minutes. Remove the rosemary from the pan and discard. Pour the cream into a bowl and chill until cold. Whip the cold cream into soft peaks and stir in 30ml/2 tbsp chopped toasted almonds.

Rum and cinnamon cream

You can serve this versatile cream with most desserts. It goes particularly well with coffee, chocolate and fruit. Pour 300ml/½ pint/1¼ cups double (heavy) cream into a pan and add a cinnamon stick. Heat the mixture until it is just about to boil, then remove the pan from the heat and leave to infuse for about 20 minutes. Strain the cream through a fine sieve (strainer) and place in the refrigerator until cold. Whip the cold cream until it stands in soft peaks, then stir in 30ml/2 tbsp rum and 15ml/1 tbsp icing (confectioners') sugar, sifted if necessary, until thoroughly combined. Try a variation with 30ml/2 tbsp advocaat liqueur and 15ml/1 tbsp ginger conserve, too.

Marsala mascarpone

This sweet cream, based on a rich Italian cheese, is perfect for serving with grilled (broiled) fruit, tarts and hot desserts. Spoon 200g/7oz/scant 1 cup mascarpone into a large bowl and add 30ml/2 tbsp icing (confectioners') sugar and 45ml/3 tbsp Marsala. Beat the mixture until smooth. Another alcohol and sweet cream combo uses 45ml/3 tbsp Amaretto to 300ml/½ pint/1¼ cups whipped cream. Stir in 15ml/1 tbsp icing (confectioner's) sugar.

Cardamom cream

Warm, spicy cardamom pods make a wonderfully subtle, aromatic cream that is delicious served with fruit salads, compôtes, tarts and pies. It goes particularly well with tropical fruits such as mango. Pour 300ml/½ pint/1¼ cups double (heavy) cream into a pan and add 3 green cardamom pods. Heat the mixture gently until just about to boil, then remove the pan from the heat and leave to infuse for about 20 minutes. Pour the cream through a fine sieve (strainer) and place in the refrigerator until cold. Whip the cold cream until it stands in soft peaks, spoon it into a bowl and serve.

Praline cream

What could be more delicious than golden almond nut brittle, tasting of toffee but with a hint of bitterness from the nuts, blended with whipped cream? This is a wonderful accompaniment to poached apricots.

1 Put 115g/4oz/½ cup sugar and 75ml/5 tbsp water in a small, heavy pan. Stir over a gentle heat until the sugar has dissolved, then boil without stirring until the syrup is golden.

2 Remove from the heat, stir in 50g/2oz/⅓ cup whole blanched almonds and spread out on a lightly oiled baking sheet. Leave the nut syrup to cool until it turns glassy.

3 Scrape the hardened nut mixture off the surface of the baking tray and break into smaller pieces using your fingers, then put in a food processor. Process for about 1 minute, until finely chopped with the appearance of ground nuts.

4 In a large bowl, whip 300ml/½ pint/1¼ cups double (heavy) cream into soft peaks, then stir in the praline and serve immediately.

MAKING SIMPLE ACCOMPANIMENTS

When you've made a delicious main dish, you need to serve it with equally tasty accompaniments. The following section is full of simple, speedy ideas for fabulous side dishes – from creamy mashed potatoes, fragrant rice and spicy noodles to Italian-style polenta and simple, healthy vegetables.

MASHED POTATOES

Potatoes go well with just about any main dish. They can be cooked simply – boiled, steamed, fried or baked – but they are even better mashed with milk and butter.

Perfect mashed potatoes

Peel 675g/1½lb floury potatoes and cut them into large chunks. Place in a pan of salted boiling water. Return to the boil, then simmer for 15–20 minutes, or until completely tender. Drain the potatoes and return to the pan. Leave over a low heat for a couple of minutes, shaking the pan to drive off any excess moisture. Take the pan off the heat and, using a potato masher, mash the potatoes until smooth. Beat in 45–60ml/ 3–4 tbsp warm milk and a large knob (pat) of butter, then season with salt and pepper to taste.

Mustard mash

Make the mashed potatoes as directed above, then stir in 15–30ml/1–2 tbsp wholegrain mustard just before seasoning, and beat until smooth.

Parmesan and parsley mash

Make mashed potatoes as above, then stir in 30ml/2 tbsp freshly grated Parmesan and 15ml/1 tbsp chopped fresh flat leaf parsley.

Apple and thyme mash

Serve with pork. Make mashed potatoes as above. Heat 25g/1oz/2 tbsp butter in a pan and add 2 peeled, cored and sliced eating apples. Fry for 4–5 minutes, turning them often. Roughly mash, then fold into the potatoes, with 15ml/1 tbsp fresh thyme leaves.

Pesto mash

This is a simple way to dress up plain mashed potatoes. They have real bite and a lovely green-specked appearance. Make mashed potatoes as described above, then stir in 30ml/2 tbsp pesto sauce until thoroughly combined.

Masala mash

This tastes great with grilled (broiled) duck or pork. Put 15ml/1 tbsp mixed chopped fresh mint and coriander (cilantro) in a bowl. Add 5ml/1 tsp mango chutney, then stir in 5ml/1 tsp salt and 5ml/1 tsp crushed black peppercorns. Finely chop 1 fresh red and 1 fresh green chilli, removing the seeds if you like, and add to the mixture. Beat in 50g/2oz/¼ cup softened butter. Beat most of the herb mixture into the mashed potatoes and spoon the rest on top.

CRUSHED POTATOES

This chunky, modern version of mashed potatoes tastes fabulous. For all variations, simply crush the potatoes roughly, using the back of a fork.

Crushed potatoes with parsley and lemon

Cook 675g/1½lb new potatoes in salted boiling water for 15–20 minutes, until tender. Drain the potatoes and crush. Stir in 30ml/2 tbsp extra virgin olive oil, the grated rind and juice of 1 lemon and 30ml/2 tbsp chopped fresh flat leaf parsley. Season to taste.

Crushed potatoes with garlic and basil

Cook 675g/1½lb new potatoes in a pan of boiling salted water for 15–20 minutes until tender. Drain and crush. Stir in 30ml/2 tbsp extra virgin olive oil, 2 finely chopped garlic cloves and a handful of torn basil leaves. Season.

Crushed potatoes with pine nuts and Parmesan

Cook 675g/1½lb new potatoes in boiling salted water for 15–20 minutes until tender. Drain and crush. Stir in 30ml/ 2 tbsp extra virgin olive oil, 30ml/2 tbsp grated Parmesan cheese and 30ml/ 2 tbsp toasted pine nuts.

RICE

This versatile grain can be served simply – either boiled or steamed – or can be flavoured or stir-fried with different ingredients to make tasty, exciting accompaniments.

Easy egg-fried rice

Cook 115g/4oz/generous ½ cup long grain rice in a large pan of boiling water for 10–12 minutes, until tender. Drain well and refresh under cold running water. Spread out on a baking sheet and leave until completely cold. Heat 30ml/2 tbsp sunflower oil in a large frying pan and add 1 finely chopped garlic clove. Cook for 1 minute, then add the rice and stir-fry for 1 minute. Push the rice to the side of the pan and pour 1 beaten egg into the pan. Cook the egg until set, then break up with a fork and stir into the rice. Add a splash of soy sauce, and mix well.

Coconut rice

Put 225g/8oz/generous 1 cup basmati rice in a pan and pour in a 400ml/14oz can coconut milk. Cover with water, add some salt and bring to the boil. Simmer for 12 minutes, or until the rice is tender. Drain well and serve.

Coriander and spring onion rice

Cook 225g/8oz/generous 1 cup basmati rice in a large pan of salted boiling water for about 12 minutes, or until tender. Drain the rice well and return to the pan. Stir in 3 finely sliced spring onions (scallions) and a roughly chopped bunch of fresh coriander (cilantro) until well mixed, then serve.

NOODLES

There are many different types of noodles, all of which are quick to cook and make the perfect accompaniment to Chinese- and Asian-style stir-fries and curries. Serve them on their own, or toss them with a few simple flavourings. They can also be served cold as a simple salad.

Soy and sesame egg noodles

Cook a 250g/9oz packet of egg noodles according to the instructions on the packet. Drain well and tip the noodles into a large bowl. Drizzle over 30ml/ 2 tbsp dark soy sauce and 10ml/2 tsp sesame oil, then sprinkle over 15ml/ 1 tbsp toasted sesame seeds and toss well until thoroughly combined. These noodles will be delicious whether served hot, or cold as a salad.

Spicy peanut noodles

This simple and very tasty dish takes only minutes to make and is good on its own or with grilled (broiled) chicken. Cook a 250g/9oz packet of egg noodles according to the instructions on the packet, then drain. Heat 15ml/1 tbsp sunflower oil in a wok and add 30ml/ 2 tbsp crunchy peanut butter. Add a splash of cold water and a dash of soy sauce and stir the mixture over a gentle heat until thoroughly combined. Add the noodles to the pan and toss to coat in the peanut mixture. Sprinkle with fresh coriander (cilantro) to serve.

Chilli and spring onion noodles

Soak 115g/4oz flat rice noodles in cold water for 30 minutes, until softened. Tip into a colander and drain well. Heat 30ml/2 tbsp olive oil in a wok or large frying pan. Add 2 finely chopped garlic cloves and 1 seeded and finely chopped fresh red chilli and fry gently for 2 minutes. Slice a bunch of spring onions (scallions) and add to the pan. Cook for a minute or so, then stir in the rice noodles, combining them with the other ingredients until heated through. Season with salt and ground black pepper before serving.

POLENTA

This classic Italian dish made from cornmeal makes a swift and delicious accompaniment to many dishes and is a useful alternative to the usual potatoes, bread or pasta. It can be served in two ways – either soft, or set and cut into wedges and grilled (broiled) or fried. Soft polenta is rather like mashed potato, and like mashed potato, it can be layered with other ingredients and baked, or used as a topping. Grilled or fried polenta has a much firmer texture and a lovely crisp shell. Both types can be enjoyed plain, if you choose, or flavoured with other ingredients such as cheese, herbs and spices. Traditional polenta requires lengthy boiling and constant attention during cooking, but the quick-cook varieties, which are widely available in most large supermarkets, give excellent results and are much simpler and quicker to prepare.

Soft polenta

Cook 225g/8oz/2 cups quick-cook polenta according to the instructions on the packet. As soon as the polenta is cooked, stir in about 50g/2oz/¼ cup butter. Season with salt and black pepper to taste, then serve immediately.

Soft polenta with Parmesan and sage

Cook 225g/8oz/2 cups quick-cook polenta according to the instructions on the packet. As soon as the polenta is cooked, stir in 115g/4oz/1⅓ cups freshly grated Parmesan cheese and a handful of chopped fresh sage. Stir in a large knob (pat) of butter and season with salt and ground black pepper to taste before serving.

Soft polenta with Cheddar cheese and thyme

Cook 225g/8oz/2 cups quick-cook polenta according to the instructions on the packet. As soon as the polenta is cooked, stir in 50g/2oz/½ cups grated Cheddar cheese and 30ml/2 tbsp chopped fresh thyme until thoroughly combined. Stir a large knob (pat) of butter into the cheesy polenta and season with salt and plenty of ground black pepper to taste before serving.

Fried chilli polenta triangles

Cook 225g/8oz/2 cups quick-cook polenta according to the instructions on the packet. Stir in 5ml/1 tsp dried chilli flakes, check the seasoning, adding more if necessary, and spread the mixture out on an oiled baking sheet to a thickness of about 1cm/½in. Leave the polenta until cold and completely set, then chill for about 20 minutes. Turn the polenta out on to a board and cut it into large squares, then cut each square into 2 triangles. Heat 30ml/2 tbsp olive oil in a large frying pan. Fry the triangles in the olive oil for 2–3 minutes on each side, until golden, then lift out and drain briefly on kitchen paper before serving.

Grilled polenta with Gorgonzola

Cook 225g/8oz/2 cups quick-cook polenta according to the instructions on the packet. Check the seasoning, adding more if necessary, and spread the mixture out on an oiled baking sheet to a thickness of about 1cm/½in. Leave the polenta until cold and completely set, then chill for about 20 minutes. Turn the polenta out on to a board and cut it into large squares, then cut each square into 2 triangles. Pre-heat the grill (broiler) and arrange the polenta triangles on the grill pan. Cook for about 5 minutes, or until golden brown, then turn over and top each triangle with a sliver of Gorgonzola. Grill (broil) for a further 5 minutes, or until bubbling.

Baked polenta with two cheeses

Serve this simple bake with slices of prosciutto and a simple leaf and herb salad tossed with a lemon and honey dressing. Preheat the oven to 200°C/400°F/Gas 6. Grate 115g/4oz Cheddar cheese and crumble 115g/4oz soft Dolcelatte cheese. Mix the cheeses together in a bowl, using your fingers to combine them thoroughly. Cook 225g/8oz/2 cups quick-cook polenta according to the instructions on the packet. Spoon half the polenta into a baking dish and level the surface. Cover with half the cheese mixture, spoon the remaining polenta on top and sprinkle with the remaining cheese. Melt 50g/2oz/¼ cup butter in a pan and fry 2 chopped garlic cloves and a few chopped fresh sage leaves until golden. Drizzle over the polenta and grind black pepper over the top. Bake for 5 minutes until the cheese topping is bubbling.

QUICK AND SIMPLE VEGETABLES

Fresh vegetables are an essential part of our diet. They are delicious cooked on their own but they can also be combined with other ingredients.

Stir-fried cabbage with nuts and smoky bacon

Heat 30ml/2 tbsp sunflower oil in a wok or large frying pan and add 4 roughly chopped rashers (strips) smoked streaky (fatty) bacon. Stir-fry for about 3 minutes, until the bacon starts to turn golden, then add ½ shredded green cabbage to the pan. Stir-fry for 3–4 minutes, until the cabbage is just tender. Season with salt and ground black pepper, and stir in 25g/1oz/¼ cup roughly chopped toasted hazelnuts or almonds just before serving.

Creamy stir-fried Brussels sprouts

Shred 450g/1lb Brussels sprouts and add to the pan. Heat 15ml/1 tbsp sunflower oil in a wok or large frying pan. Add 1 chopped garlic clove and stir-fry for about 30 seconds. Stir-fry for 3–4 minutes, until just tender. Season with salt and black pepper and stir in 30ml/2 tbsp crème fraîche. Warm through for 1 minute.

Honey-fried parsnips and celeriac

Peel 225g/8oz parsnips and 115g/4oz celeriac. Cut both into matchsticks. Heat 30ml/2 tbsp olive oil in a wok or large frying pan and add the parsnips and celeriac. Fry over a gentle heat for 6–7 minutes, stirring occasionally, until golden and tender. Season with salt and ground black pepper and stir in 15ml/1 tbsp clear honey. Allow to bubble for 1 minute before serving.

Glazed carrots

Clear honey is the magic ingredient to use with this carrot side dish too. Cut three large carrots into matchsticks. Steam them over a pan of boiling water for 2–4 minutes until just tender. Meanwhile, heat 25g/1oz/2 tbsp butter in a heavy pan, add 1 crushed garlic clove and 15ml/1 tbsp chopped fresh rosemary leaves and cook for 1 minute or until the garlic is golden brown. Add 5ml/1 tsp Dijon mustard and 10ml/2 tsp clear honey. Stir over the heat until the honey has melted into the buttery sauce, then add the carrots. Cook, tossing the carrots to coat them with the mixture, for 2 minutes until the carrots are glazed. Season lightly with salt, if needed, and serve immediately.

SPECIALIST BREADS

Bread makes a simple accompaniment to many meals and is the perfect ready-made side dish when time is short. Look out for part-baked breads that you can finish off in the oven, so you can enjoy the taste of freshly baked bread in just a few minutes.

Ciabatta This chewy Italian bread is long and oval in shape and is commonly available in ready-to-bake form. Look out for ciabatta with added sun-dried tomatoes or olives.

Focaccia This flat, dimpled Italian bread is made with olive oil and has a softer texture than ciabatta. It is available plain but is also often flavoured with fresh rosemary and garlic.

Naan Traditionally cooked in a clay oven, this Indian bread is easy to find in supermarkets and makes a tasty accompaniment to curries. It is available plain, and also flavoured with spices.

Chapati This Indian flatbread is less heavy than naan and makes a good alternative. The small, round breads can be a little more difficult to find but are worth searching for.

Soda bread This traditional Irish bread is made using buttermilk and bicarbonate of soda (baking soda). It has a delicious flavour and is great for mopping up sauces or serving with soups.

Above: Rosemary focaccia has a crumbly texture and is perfect for sandwiches and for serving with a whole range of Italian-style dishes.

PLANNING A MENU: TIPS FOR THE COOK

Quick cooking does not necessarily mean throwing all your effort into a single dish. In fact, the bigger and better the meal, the more time you'll have to share food and swap news with family and friends. If you're planning a evening out, on the other hand, you'll need some light but nourishing fare to fuel the night ahead, A multi-faceted meal, full of different flavours, will remind you just how good food can be when you put in the effort. These well crafted menus will enable the quick cook to throw together memorable meals, each course complementing the other, without spending hours slaving in the kitchen. Cooking and preparation times given here are approximate, assuming one is making all the menus at the same time. Above all, remember that the key to successful quick cooking is always to plan ahead.

• Make a list of all those you are cooking for to work out exactly how much food you will need. Check if anyone is vegetarian or has special dietary requirements such as an allergy to nuts or dairy products. If it's a special occasion, and there will be children present, remember to supply a range of drinks suitable for everyone.

• Decide what you are going to make, then be sure you have all the necessary equipment to hand. Choose courses that complement each other, and dishes you can cook with confidence. As you are short on time, it's best to stick to familiar techniques – few of us get a new recipe right the first go, and a group of hungry guests in the next room will only increase the pressure!

• Ensure you have enough space in the refrigerator for drinks, ingredients and dishes that need to be chilled. If necessary, have a clear-out beforehand to remove any unnecessary items.

• If you are serving up lots of courses, try to have as much as possible ready in advance. If some dishes can be made or part-prepared the day before, this is well worth doing.

• If possible, try to shop in advance for meals – it'll give you just that bit more energy when you come to cook.

• Recipes may need to be increased or reduced in quantity – sometimes at the last minute – depending on how many you are feeding. Dishes that can be most easily adapted in this way include soups, sauces for pasta and individual portions (such as a specific number of chicken portions).

• Accompanying sauces for hot dishes and dressings for salads do not have to be multiplied up as much as the main ingredients. Similarly, do not multiply up herbs, spices and garlic as they may become overpowering.

• When eating *alfresco* with friends, remember to select dishes that are practical to serve and eat as well as easy to prepare.

ENERGY-BOOSTING BREAKFAST
Preparation: 10 minutes; Cooking: 7 minutes

A healthy breakfast is a good start to the day and will see you right through the morning to lunchtime. This menu is easy to make and can't fail to put a spring in your step.

VITALITY JUICE (PAGE 39)

The slightly peppery flavour of watercress blends well with pear, wheatgerm and yogurt in this juice that really lives up to its name in boosting your morning energy levels.

ZINGY PAPAYA FRUIT SALAD (PAGE 48)

This refreshing tropical fruit salad is so simple to make. The addition of a little stem ginger will stimulate your taste buds. Adapt the ingredients for one person.

SCRAMBLED EGGS WITH ANCHOVIES (PAGE 60)

Creamy scrambled eggs take on a new dimension with the addition of tangy anchovies and a generous sprinkling of spicy paprika. Halve the ingredients for one person.

SUNDAY BRUNCH
Preparation: 8 minutes; Cooking: 12 minutes

After a well-earned lie-in, indulge yourself and your guests with a delicious brunch of traditional crunchy oat cereal and kippers, teamed with a melon and strawberry salad.

CRANACHAN CRUNCH (PAGE 47)

Based on a traditional Scottish recipe, this version is made more luxurious with the additional of fresh raspberries and creamy Greek (strained plain) yogurt.

JUGGED KIPPERS (PAGE 68)

A long-established favourite, choose kippers that have been naturally smoked, if possible. Serve them with a pat of butter, a wedge of lemon, and some fresh crusty bread.

CANTELOUPE MELON SALAD (PAGE 49)

Spoil everyone with this colourful dish, in which the lightly caramelized strawberries look really pretty teamed with the canteloupe melon.

QUICK LUNCH WITH FRIENDS
Preparation: 10 minutes; Cooking: 4 minutes

Shortage of time need not be a problem when preparing a quick lunch for friends. Try this fresh and unusual menu next time you invite friends home for an impromptu meal.

AVOCADO SOUP (PAGE 78)

This soup couldn't be quicker and is just the thing to impress your friends. Its fresh delicate flavour can be enhanced by a squeeze of lime or lemon juice just before serving.

LEMONY COUSCOUS WITH OLIVES AND ALMONDS (PAGE 346)

This delicious salad mixes olives, almonds and courgettes with fluffy couscous. Leave the couscous to soak while you are making the soup and preparing the trifles.

RHUBARB AND GINGER TRIFLES (PAGE 466)

Use good quality rhubarb compote with chunky pieces of fruit – your own or a bought jar – for this recipe. Whole-fruit apricot jam works equally well.

WORKING LUNCH
Preparation: 12 minutes; Cooking: 8 minutes

There's no need to stint yourself just because you are on your own for lunch. This menu can be easily fitted into a working day as it takes so little time to prepare.

PINEAPPLE, GINGER AND CARROT JUICE (PAGE 40)

Ginger adds a zing to this sweet, scented mixture of pineapple and carrot. It tastes best served very cold. You can use prepared pineapple to cut down on preparation time.

SMOKED SALMON AND CHIVE OMELETTE (PAGE 62)

For one person, halve the ingredients given in the recipe on page 62. Serve the omelette with some fresh crusty bread and, if you like, a green salad.

COOL CHOCOLATE FLOAT (PAGE 469)

Spoil yourself with this meltingly delicious dessert drink of chocolate milkshake and scoops of chocolate and vanilla ice cream. Don't forget to halve the ingredients!

SIMPLE SUMMER LUNCH
Preparation: 15 minutes; Cooking: 15 minutes

On warm summer days, you may want to invite friends or family for lunch in the garden. This menu of fresh and flavourful dishes requires very little in the way of preparation.

CHILLED TOMATO SOUP WITH ROCKET PESTO (PAGE 76)

Prepare this refreshing soup ahead of time and chill for a few hours in the refrigerator. Make the pesto just before serving. Sun-dried tomato bread is a good accompaniment.

GRILLED SOLE WITH CHIVE BUTTER (PAGE 160)

Make the chive butter early in the morning, and you'll have very little to do after your guests arrive. Sole cooks quickly, so don't leave it unattended while it is under the grill (broiler).

SUMMER BERRIES IN WARM SABAYON GLAZE (PAGE 476)

Eating berries that have been coated in warm sabayon is like tasting freshly picked fruit you have picked yourself on a sunny day. The warmth seems to bring out their flavour.

WINTER WARMER
Preparation: 8 minutes; Cooking: 20 minutes

Keep out the cold with a warming soup and a substantial main dish. Finish the meal with a dried fruit salad, which needs to be made beforehand and will save you time on the day.

BUTTER BEAN AND SUN-DRIED TOMATO SOUP (PAGE 81)

Cook this soup ahead of time while you are preparing the dried fruit salad. When you are ready to eat, reheat the soup and serve with warm crusty bread or breadsticks.

PAN-FRIED STEAKS WITH WHISKY AND CREAM (PAGE 252)

With the soup and fruit salad made in advance, this is the only cooking you will need to do just before the meal. The whisky and cream turns an ordinary steak into a luxurious treat.

DRIED FRUIT SALAD (PAGE 458)

This dessert needs to be made ahead of time to allow the dried fruit to plump up and the flavours to blend. Serve it with a dollop of cream, fromage frais or créme fraîche.

FAMILY WEEKEND LUNCH (1)
Preparation: 11 minutes; Cooking: 12 minutes

Choosing dishes that everyone will enjoy is the key to harmonious family lunches. This menu cannot fail to please even the youngest member, and will have them all coming back for more.

CRUMBED CHICKEN WITH GREEN MAYONNAISE (PAGE 211)

Crisp-crumbed chicken is always popular, but it's the tangy caper mayonnaise that really rounds off this fine family main course. A lightly-spiced speciality, suitable for all palates.

CAULIFLOWER WITH EGG AND LEMON (PAGE 426)

Even the kids will enjoy cauliflower when it is cooked like this. It goes beautifully with the crumbed chicken, and you could add some baby new potatoes for extra bulk.

BLUEBERRY MERINGUE FOOL (PAGE 467)

Combining healthy fresh fruit with a treat of vanilla-flavoured cream and the surprise crunch of meringue, this wonderful dessert will delight family members of all ages.

FAMILY WEEKEND LUNCH (2)
Preparation: 16 minutes; Cooking: 14 minutes

This menu offers an alternative to the ubiquitous fish and chips and provides plenty of fresh fruit and vegetables. The kids won't even notice that they are eating healthy food.

FRIED PLAICE WITH TOMATO SAUCE (PAGE 163)

A fish dish that is perennially popular with children, this recipe works equally well with fillets of haddock or whiting. Serve the tomato sauce and lemon wedges separately.

WILTED SPINACH WITH RICE AND DILL (PAGE 416)

This spinach and rice dish flavoured with dill goes particularly well with fish. If you like, add some baby broad (fava) beans to the rice for the final 5 minutes or so.

FRESH FRUIT SALAD (PAGE 458)

Make sure the children eat enough fresh fruit by serving them this delicious salad. You can use any fruits that are in season, but oranges are an essential ingredient.

SUNDAY LUNCH
Preparation: 15 minutes; Cooking 20 minutes
On Sundays, it's something of a novelty to have a main meal in the middle of the day.
But there's no need to spend the whole morning slaving over a hot stove.

GOAT'S CHEESE SALAD (PAGE 130)

Start the meal with this tasty salad, for which you need a goat's cheese with plenty of flavour.
Almonds or walnuts would work just as well as hazelnuts.

CALF'S LIVER WITH CRISP ONIONS (PAGE 265)

Sautéed or mashed potatoes go well with this main dish and can be cooked at the same time.
Take care not to cook the liver for too long as this may cause it to toughen.

PINEAPPLE AND RUM CREAM (PAGE 475)

This fruity alcoholic dessert is sumptuous enough already, but you could make it even more
decadent by spooning it over vanilla or rum-and-raisin ice cream.

VEGETARIAN SUNDAY LUNCH
Preparation: 15 minutes; Cooking: 15 minutes
If your family and friends are vegetarian this menu is sure to please as it is as colourful as it is good
to eat. Use a combination of red, orange and yellow peppers to make it even more colourful.

STUFFED SWEET PEPPERS (PAGE 328)

In this unusual recipe the stuffed peppers need to be steamed for 15 minutes, so fill them
ahead of time and put them on to steam before making the pasta dish.

PASTA WITH SUN-DRIED TOMATOES (PAGE 370)

A pasta dish that is not only quick and easy to prepare, but looks stunning too. You can serve it in
individual bowls for people to toss themselves, or in a large bowl already mixed.

CLEMENTINES WITH STAR ANISE (PAGE 463)

Depending on the time available, you can make this dessert at the same time as the rest of the meal
and leave it to cool, or prepare it beforehand so that you can chill it in the refrigerator.

HOME LATE AND HUNGRY

Preparation: 8 minutes; Cooking: 12 minutes

When you are home late and feeling weary, what you want is something quick and easy to prepare that is also light and will not keep you awake at night. This menu is just that.

FETTUCINE ALL'ALFREDO (PAGE 372)

This simple pasta recipe is delicious but will not lay too heavily in the stomach. Adjust the amount of ingredients given on page 372 according to how many people there are to feed.

BRAISED LETTUCE AND PEAS (PAGE 420)

A light vegetable dish to eat with the pasta, this can be cooked at the same time as the pasta, as it takes the same amount of cooking time. Again, adjust the ingredients for the number of people.

MUESLI SMOOTHIE (PAGE 42)

Perhaps you eat it for breakfast, but muesli is just as good at bedtime, too. In this recipe muesli is mixed with dried apricots and a little ginger into a soothing drink to help you sleep.

SOPHISTICATED SUPPER

Preparation: 15 minutes; Cooking: 20 minutes

Whether it is a romantic supper for two, or entertaining a group of colleagues or friends, this fish-based menu will be sure to impress but will not take all evening to prepare. Provide plenty of French bread.

SIZZLING PRAWNS (PAGE 145)

This is a great way of cooking prawns, but eating them can make a bit of a mess. Provide a plate for the heads and shells, and plenty of napkins for wiping fingers.

SEARED TUNA WITH SPICY WATERCRESS SALAD (PAGE 194)

In this recipe the tuna steaks are rubbed with a punchy mixture of harissa, olive oil and honey before being cooked slightly rare. They look very attractive on a bed of watercress salad.

WARM ZABAGLIONE (PAGE 484)

Light as air and highly alcoholic, this much-loved Italian dessert is always popular. It can be made with Madeira or sweet sherry instead of Marsala. Serve it with amaretti for dipping.

LIGHT BITES BEFORE A NIGHT OUT
Preparation: 5 minutes; Cooking 5 minutes (for each dish)

If you are going to the theatre or a concert, here are some ideas to keep you sustained between lunch and dining late. You will probably want just one of these dishes rather than all three.

EGGS BENEDICT (PAGE 70)

For speed, use a good-quality hollandaise sauce rather than making your own. English muffins are used in this recipe, but you could substitute toast.

GRIDDLED TOMATOES ON SODA BREAD (PAGE 64)

Simple tomatoes on toast is transformed by adding a drizzle of olive oil, balsamic vinegar and shavings of Parmesan cheese. Adjust the amount of ingredients according to the number of people.

LOX WITH BAGELS AND CREAM CHEESE (PAGE 67)

Perfect for a quick snack, you can save even more time by toasting the bagels instead of waiting for the oven to heat up. Full-fat cream cheese tastes better than the low-fat version.

QUICK SUPPER TO SHARE WITH FRIENDS
Preparation: 18 minutes; Cooking 22 minutes

When friends drop by for supper, you don't want to miss all the conversation by being cooped up in the kitchen. This menu will make sure you don't miss too much of the action.

SPICY FRIED NOODLES WITH CHICKEN (PAGE 229)

This versatile dish can be adjusted to include your favourite ingredients, or whatever you have in the refrigerator. The important thing is to keep a balance of flavours, textures and colours.

WARM PANCAKES WITH CARAMELIZED PEARS (PAGE 52)

Use ready-made pancakes – either bought or made yourself and frozen – to speed up the cooking process. Other fruits can be used instead of pears.

VANILLA CAFE LATTE (PAGE 44)

Make this classic coffee drink more luxurious by topping it with whipped cream and offering cinnamon sticks to stir it with. Vanilla sugar adds a special flavour.

DINNER PARTY
Preparation: 10 minutes; Cooking: 4 minutes

To keep your guests happy while you are putting the finishing touches to the meal, serve a selection of tapas (see page 88) with the pre-dinner drinks. Provide plenty of cocktail sticks.

CHICKEN LIVER AND BRANDY PATÉ (PAGE 95)

Paté is always a good bet for a dinner party because it can be made ahead of time. A couple of tablespoons of brandy gives this recipe an extra punch. Serve it with crispy Melba toast.

ESCALOPES OF VEAL WITH CREAM SAUCE (PAGE 261)

Serve this main course with buttered tagliatelli and lightly steamed vegetables, such as broccoli, mangetouts (snow peas) or French beans. The cream sauce is nicely flavoured with fresh tarragon.

HONEY BAKED FIGS WITH HAZELNUT ICE CREAM (PAGE 481)

The figs for this luscious dessert can be baking in the oven while you are cooking the main course. The lemon grass and cinnamon stick impart a wonderful flavour.

VEGETARIAN DINNER PARTY
Preparation: 10 minutes; Cooking: 4 minutes

If some of your dinner party guests are vegetarian, why not choose a menu like this – which is interesting enough for those who normally eat meat – to save you cooking different dishes.

PEARS WITH BLUE CHEESE AND WALNUTS (PAGE 107)

Pears filled with blue cheese and walnut look pretty on colourful leaves and make a great appetizer. Choose small ripe pears, such as Comice or Bartlett.

MUSHROOM STROGANOFF (PAGE 330)

This creamy mixed mushroom sauce tastes great and is ideal for a dinner party. Serve it with toasted buckwheat, brown rice or a mixture of wild rices.

CHOCOLATE AND BANANA FOOL (PAGE 464)

This is quite a rich dessert, so serve it with some dessert cookies, such as shortbread or biscotti. Make it the day before the dinner party and chill in the refrigerator.

PICNIC LUNCH
Preparation: 15 minutes; Cooking: 10 minutes
Food for the perfect picnic needs to be portable, easy to eat, filling enough for hearty outdoor appetites and sufficiently varied to appeal to everyone. Pack everything into a cool bag.

SIMPLE RICE SALAD (PAGE 333)

This brightly coloured rice salad with chopped vegetables has a flavoursome oil and vinegar dressing. Pack into a plastic container and chill well before taking on the picnic.

MEXICAN TORTAS (PAGE 124)

This version uses roast pork and refried beans, but you can experiment with other ingredients. To keep the filling in place, wrap each torta in clingfilm (plastic wrap) or tinfoil.

CHOCOLATE AND PRUNE REFRIGERATOR BARS (PAGE 500)

These delicious fruity chocolate bars can be made a couple of days in advance and stored in the refrigerator until needed. Make sure you keep them cool on hot summer days.

BARBECUE SUPPER
Preparation: 10 minutes; Cooking: 15 minutes
There's more to a barbecue than plain sausages and burgers. Try these enticing recipes for a meal to remember. Serve them with rice or couscous, crusty bread and a bowl of salad.

BARBECUED LAMB WITH RED PEPPER SALSA (PAGE 293)

Vibrant red pepper salsa brings out the best in succulent lamb steaks to make a dish that looks as good as it tastes. Marinate the meat in the refrigerator for 24 hours beforehand.

HOT SMOKED SALMON (PAGE 192)

Everyone – particularly those who don't eat meat – will enjoy this fantastic barbecue-smoked salmon with its mildly spicy mojo sauce. Use fresh pineapple if available.

SWEET PEPPERS STUFFED WITH TWO CHEESES (PAGE 327)

Start these peppers cooking before the grill tastes too strongly of meat and fish, which would spoil their delicate flavour. Blanch them in boiling water before filling to give them a headstart.

BREAKFASTS
AND BRUNCHES

Very few people have time to cook a lengthy breakfast, especially during the week. But this does

not mean that you have to resort to nothing more exciting than a bowl of cereal or a piece of

toast. With just a little imagination and often no more than five minutes' work, you can enjoy

a tasty and imaginative breakfast that will wake up your tastebuds and set you up for the day.

If you like your breakfast in liquid form, then a smoothie is ideal. Packed with flavours and

vitamins, Pineapple, Ginger and Carrot Juice or Muesli Smoothie make a healthy start to the

day. Alternatively, keep the fruit whole in dishes such as Zingy Papaya Fruit Salad. For a

crunchy breakfast, opt for Cranachan Crunch or Cinnamon Toast; or find comfort in Warm

Pancakes with Caramelized Pears. If you need protein to get you going, try a Smoked Salmon

and Chive Omelette, the classic Kedgeree, Kidney and Mushroom Toasts or, for a special treat,

Egg and Bacon Muffins Hollandaise. Finally, if you really aren't a morning person and seek

only a comforting drink, try Frothy Hot Chocolate made with real chocolate – delicious!

BIG BREAKFAST

EASY TO PREPARE, THIS ENERGY-PACKED SMOOTHIE MAKES A GREAT START TO THE DAY. BANANAS AND SESAME SEEDS PROVIDE SLOW-RELEASE CARBOHYDRATE THAT WILL KEEP YOU GOING ALL MORNING, WHILE FRESH AND ZESTY ORANGE JUICE AND SWEET, SCENTED MANGO WILL SET YOUR TASTEBUDS TINGLING.

Preparation: 6 minutes; Cooking: 0 minutes

MAKES TWO GLASSES

INGREDIENTS
   ½ mango
   1 banana
   1 large orange
   30ml/2 tbsp wheatbran
   15ml/1 tbsp sesame seeds
   10–15ml/2–3 tsp honey

COOK'S TIP
Mango juice is naturally very sweet so you may wish to add less honey or leave it out altogether. Taste the drink to decide how much you need.

1 Using a small, sharp knife, skin the mango, then slice the flesh off the stone (pit). Peel the banana and break it into short lengths, then place it in a blender or food processor with the mango.

2 Squeeze the juice from the orange and add to the blender or food processor along with the bran, sesame seeds and honey. Whizz until the mixture is smooth and creamy, then pour into glasses.

Energy 172kcal/726kJ; Protein 4.9g; Carbohydrate 27.6g, of which sugars 23.1g; Fat 5.5g, of which saturates 0.9g; Cholesterol 0mg; Calcium 102mg; Fibre 8.5g; Sodium 11mg.

VITALITY JUICE

THE CLUE IS IN THE NAME. THIS SPEEDY JUICE REALLY DOES PUT A SPRING IN YOUR STEP. WATERCRESS HAS A SLIGHTLY PEPPERY FLAVOUR WHEN EATEN ON ITS OWN, BUT BLENDING IT WITH PEAR, WHEATGERM AND YOGURT TAMES THE TASTE WHILE BOOSTING YOUR MORNING ENERGY LEVELS.

Preparation: 4 minutes; Cooking: 0 minutes

SERVES ONE

INGREDIENTS
  25g/1oz watercress
  1 large ripe pear
  30ml/2 tbsp wheatgerm
  150ml/¼ pint/⅔ cup natural
   (plain) yogurt
  15ml/1 tbsp linseeds (flax seeds)
  10ml/2 tsp lemon juice
  mineral water (optional)
  ice cubes

1 Roughly chop the watercress (you do not need to remove the tough stalks). Peel, core and roughly chop the pear.

2 Put the watercress and pear in a blender or food processor with the wheatgerm and blend until smooth. Scrape the mixture down from the side of the bowl if necessary.

3 Add the yogurt, seeds and lemon juice and blend until combined. Thin with a little mineral water if too thick.

4 Put several ice cubes in the bottom of a tall glass. Fill the glass to just below the brim with the Vitality Juice, leaving enough room to decorate with a few sprigs of chopped watercress on top.

VARIATIONS
For a non-dairy version of this delicious, refreshing drink, use yogurt made from goat's milk, sheep's milk or soya. A large apple can be used instead of the pear.

Energy 287kcal/1207kJ; Protein 17.8g; Carbohydrate 39.8g, of which sugars 31.2g; Fat 7.6g, of which saturates 1.6g; Cholesterol 2mg; Calcium 394mg; Fibre 8.8g; Sodium 144mg

PINEAPPLE, GINGER AND CARROT JUICE

YOU'RE NEVER TOO BUSY FOR BREAKFAST WHEN YOU HAVE RECIPES LIKE THIS ONE IN YOUR REPERTOIRE. GINGER ADDS A ZING TO THE SWEET, SCENTED MIXTURE OF FRESH PINEAPPLE AND CARROT.

Preparation: 5 minutes; Cooking: 0 minutes

MAKES ONE GLASS

INGREDIENTS
½ small pineapple
25g/1oz fresh root ginger
1 carrot
ice cubes

COOK'S TIP
This is one of the speediest breakfast snacks there is, but you can prepare it even more quickly if you buy ready-sliced fresh pineapple. This is sold in tubs and you will often find it in the chiller at the local supermarket.

1 Using a sharp knife, cut away the skin from the pineapple, then cut it into quarters and remove the core from each piece. Roughly slice the pineapple flesh and then chop into portions small enough to fit in the juicer.

2 Thinly peel the ginger, using a sharp knife or vegetable peeler, then chop the flesh roughly. Scrape or peel the carrot and cut it into rounds or chunks.

3 Push the carrot, ginger and pineapple through a juicer and pour into a glass. Add ice cubes and serve immediately.

Energy 108kcal/462kJ; Protein 1.3g; Carbohydrate 26.1g, of which sugars 25.8g; Fat 0.6g, of which saturates 0.1g; Cholesterol 0mg; Calcium 55mg; Fibre 4.2g; Sodium 23mg

BREAKFAST IN A GLASS

THIS ENERGIZING BLEND IS SIMPLY BURSTING WITH GOODNESS — JUST WHAT YOU NEED WHEN YOU WAKE UP WISHING YOU COULD STAY IN YOUR COMFY BED FOR JUST AN HOUR OR SO LONGER.

Preparation: 5 minutes; Cooking: 0 minutes

SERVES TWO

INGREDIENTS

250g/9oz firm tofu
200g/7oz/1¾ cups strawberries
45ml/3 tbsp pumpkin or
  sunflower seeds, plus extra
  for sprinkling
30–45ml/2–3 tbsp clear honey
juice of 2 large oranges
juice of 1 lemon

VARIATION
Almost any other fruit can be used instead of the strawberries. Those with textures that blend well, such as mangoes, bananas, peaches, plums and raspberries, work particularly well as single variety substitutes, or you could try a mixture according to your taste. The juicy sweetness of mangoes and slightly tart tang of raspberries are a winning combination.

1 Roughly chop the tofu, then hull and roughly chop the strawberries. Reserve a few strawberry chunks.

2 Put all the ingredients in a blender or food processor and blend until completely smooth, scraping the mixture down from the side of the bowl, if necessary.

3 Pour into tumblers and sprinkle with extra seeds and strawberry chunks.

Energy 259kcal/1087kJ; Protein 13.3g; Carbohydrate 30.4g, of which sugars 28.2g; Fat 10.2g, of which saturates 1.1g; Cholesterol 0mg; Calcium 671mg; Fibre 1.8g; Sodium 19mg

MUESLI SMOOTHIE

LOVE MUESLI BUT DON'T LIKE THE TEXTURE? THIS DIVINELY SMOOTH DRINK HAS ALL THE GOODNESS BUT NONE OF THE LUMPY BITS. PURÉED APRICOTS AND STEM GINGER JUST ADD TO THE FLAVOUR.

Preparation: 4 minutes; Cooking: 0 minutes

SERVES TWO

INGREDIENTS

50g/2oz/¼ cup ready-to-eat
dried apricots
1 piece preserved stem ginger,
plus 30ml/2 tbsp syrup from the
ginger jar
40g/1½oz/scant ½ cup natural
muesli (granola)
about 200ml/7fl oz/scant 1 cup
semi-skimmed (low-fat) milk

COOK'S TIP

Apricot and ginger are perfect partners in this divine drink. It makes an incredibly healthy, tasty breakfast, but is so delicious and indulgent that you could even serve it as a dessert after a summer meal. If serving it as a dessert, partner it with poached apricots.

1 Using a sharp knife, chop the dried apricots into slices or chunks. Chop the preserved ginger.

2 Put the apricots and ginger in a blender or food processor and add the syrup from the ginger jar with the muesli and milk.

3 Process until smooth, adding more milk if necessary, to make a creamy drink. Serve in wide glasses.

Energy 204kcal/865kJ; Protein 6.6g; Carbohydrate 39.1g, of which sugars 28.8g; Fat 3.4g, of which saturates 1.4g; Cholesterol 6mg; Calcium 150mg; Fibre 3.1g; Sodium 97mg

BANANA AND MAPLE FLIP

THIS SATISFYING DRINK IS PACKED WITH SO MUCH GOODNESS THAT IT MAKES A COMPLETE BREAKFAST IN A GLASS — GREAT FOR WHEN YOU'RE IN A HURRY. BE SURE TO USE A REALLY FRESH FREE-RANGE EGG.

Preparation: 4 minutes; Cooking: 0 minutes

SERVES ONE

INGREDIENTS

1 small banana, peeled and halved
50ml/2fl oz/¼ cup thick Greek
   (US strained plain) yogurt
1 egg
30ml/2 tbsp maple syrup

1 Put the peeled and halved banana, thick Greek yogurt, egg and maple syrup in a food processor or blender. Add 30ml/2 tbsp chilled water or an ice cube.

2 Process the ingredients constantly for about 2 minutes, or until the mixture turns a really pale, creamy colour and has a nice frothy texture.

3 Pour the drink into a tall, chilled glass and serve immediately.

WARNING
The very young, the elderly and pregnant women are advised against consuming raw eggs or drinks containing raw eggs.

Energy 376Kcal/1573kJ; Protein 12g; Carbohydrate 58g, of which sugars 52g; Fat 12g, of which saturates 5g; Cholesterol 240mg; Calcium 141mg; Fibre 0.9g; Sodium 100mg

VANILLA CAFFÉ LATTE

THIS LUXURIOUS VANILLA AND CHOCOLATE VERSION OF THE CLASSIC COFFEE DRINK CAN BE SERVED AT ANY TIME OF DAY TOPPED WITH WHIPPED CREAM, WITH CINNAMON STICKS TO STIR AND FLAVOUR IT.

Preparation: 3 minutes; Cooking: 8 minutes

SERVES TWO

INGREDIENTS
700ml/24fl oz/scant 3 cups milk
250ml/8fl oz/1 cup espresso or very
strong coffee
45ml/3 tbsp vanilla sugar, plus extra
to taste
115g/4oz dark (bittersweet)
chocolate, grated

1 Pour the milk into a small pan and bring to the boil, then remove from the heat. Mix the espresso or very strong coffee with 500ml/16fl oz/2 cups of the boiled milk in a large heatproof jug (pitcher). Sweeten with vanilla sugar to taste.

2 Return the remaining boiled milk in the pan to the heat and add the 45ml/3 tbsp vanilla sugar. Stir constantly until dissolved. Bring to the boil, then reduce the heat.

3 Add the dark chocolate and continue to heat, stirring constantly until all the chocolate has melted and the mixture is smooth and glossy.

4 Pour the chocolate milk into the jug of coffee and whisk thoroughly. Serve in mugs or glasses.

Energy 545Kcal/2299kJ; Protein 15g; Carbohydrate 77g, of which sugars 76g; Fat 22g, of which saturates 13g; Cholesterol 24mg; Calcium 445mg; Fibre 1.4g; Sodium 200mg

FROTHY HOT CHOCOLATE

REAL HOT CHOCOLATE DOESN'T COME AS A POWDER IN A PACKET — IT IS MADE WITH THE BEST CHOCOLATE YOU CAN AFFORD, WHISKED IN HOT MILK UNTIL REALLY FROTHY.

Preparation: 3 minutes; Cooking: 4 minutes

SERVES FOUR

INGREDIENTS
  1 litre/1¾ pints/4 cups milk
  1 vanilla pod (bean)
  50–115g/2–4oz dark (bittersweet)
    chocolate, grated

VARIATION
You could use Mexican chocolate, which is flavoured with almonds, cinnamon and vanilla, and sweetened with sugar. All the ingredients are crushed together in a special mortar, and heated over coals. The powdered mixture is then shaped into discs, which can be bought in specialist stores.

1 Pour the milk into a pan. Split the vanilla pod lengthways using a sharp knife to reveal the seeds, and add it to the milk; the vanilla seeds and the pod will flavour the milk.

2 Add the chocolate. The amount to use depends on personal taste – start with a smaller amount if you are unsure of the flavour and taste at the beginning of step 3, adding more if necessary.

3 Heat the chocolate milk gently, stirring until all the chocolate has melted and the mixture is smooth, then whisk with a wire whisk until the mixture boils. Remove the vanilla pod from the pan and divide the drink among four mugs or heatproof glasses. Serve the hot chocolate immediately.

Energy 223Kcal/942kJ; Protein 10g; Carbohydrate 25g, of which sugars 25g; Fat 10g, of which saturates 6g; Cholesterol 16mg; Calcium 307mg; Fibre 0.5g; Sodium 100mg

BANANA SMOOTHIE <u>WITH</u> CHOCOLATE SAUCE

THE SECRET OF A GOOD SMOOTHIE IS TO SERVE IT ICE-COLD AND WHIZZING IT UP WITH ICE IS THE PERFECT WAY TO ENSURE THIS. KEEP AN ICE TRAY OF FROZEN ORANGE JUICE AT THE READY.

Preparation: 5 minutes; Cooking: 10–12 minutes

SERVES TWO GENEROUSLY

INGREDIENTS

For the smoothie
   3 ripe bananas
   200ml/7fl oz/scant 1 cup natural
      (plain) yogurt
   30ml/2 tbsp mild honey
   350ml/12fl oz/1½ cups orange juice
      ice cubes, crushed
For the hot chocolate sauce
   175g/6oz plain (semisweet) chocolate
      with more than 60% cocoa solids
   60ml/4 tbsp water
   15ml/1 tbsp golden (light corn) syrup
   15g/½oz/1 tbsp butter

COOK'S TIP
Pouring chocolate sauce like this cools it slightly on the way down, so that it thickens on contact with the cold smoothie.

1 Peel and chop the bananas, then mash them with a fork.

2 For the sauce, break up the chocolate and put into a bowl over a pan of barely simmering water. Leave undisturbed for 10 minutes until the chocolate has melted, then add the water, syrup and butter and stir until smooth.

3 Place all the smoothie ingredients in a blender or food processor and blend until smooth.

4 Pour into big, tall glasses, then pour in some chocolate sauce from a height. The sauce will swirl around the glasses to give a marbled effect.

Energy 901kcal/3790kJ; Protein 13.2g; Carbohydrate 148.1g, of which sugars 142.2g; Fat 32.5g, of which saturates 19.4g; Cholesterol 23mg; Calcium 253mg; Fibre 4.9g; Sodium 176mg.

CRANACHAN CRUNCH

THIS TASTY BREAKFAST DISH IS BASED ON A TRADITIONAL SCOTTISH RECIPE. THE TOASTED CEREAL
TASTES DELICIOUS WITH YOGURT AND A GENEROUS DRIZZLE OF HEATHER HONEY.

Preparation: 2 minutes; Cooking: 3−4 minutes

SERVES FOUR

INGREDIENTS
75g/3oz crunchy oat cereal
600ml/1 pint/2½ cups Greek
  (US strained plain) yogurt
250g/9oz/1½ cups raspberries

1 Preheat the grill (broiler) to high.
Spread the oat cereal on a baking
sheet and place under the hot grill for
3–4 minutes until lightly toasted, stirring
regularly. Set aside to cool.

2 When the oat cereal has cooled
completely, fold it into the Greek yogurt,
then gently fold in 200g/7oz/generous
1 cup of the raspberries, being careful
not to crush the berries too much.

3 Spoon the yogurt mixture into four
serving glasses or dishes, top with the
remaining raspberries and serve
immediately.

Energy 222kcal/935kJ; Protein 10.1g; Carbohydrate 23g, of which sugars 13.3g; Fat 10.7g, of which saturates 6.7g; Cholesterol 21mg; Calcium 250mg; Fibre 3g; Sodium 236mg

ZINGY PAPAYA FRUIT SALAD

THIS REFRESHING, FRUITY SALAD MAKES A LOVELY LIGHT BREAKFAST, PERFECT FOR THE SUMMER MONTHS. CHOOSE REALLY RIPE, FRAGRANT PAPAYAS AND JUICY LIMES FOR THE BEST FLAVOUR.

Preparation: 5 minutes; Cooking: 0 minutes

SERVES FOUR

INGREDIENTS
   2 large ripe papayas
   juice of 1 fresh lime
   2 pieces preserved stem ginger,
      finely sliced

VARIATION
This fruit salad is delicious made with other tropical fruit. Try using passion fruit pulp instead of the ginger, or substitute two ripe, peeled and stoned (pitted) mangoes for the papaya.

1 Cut the papayas in half lengthways. Scoop out the seeds, using a teaspoon. With a sharp knife, cut the flesh into neat, thin slices.

2 Arrange the papaya slices on a platter. Squeeze the lime juice over the papaya and sprinkle with the sliced stem ginger. Serve immediately.

Energy 112kcal/475kJ; Protein 1.6g; Carbohydrate 27.3g, of which sugars 27.3g; Fat 0.3g, of which saturates 0g; Cholesterol 0mg; Calcium 72mg; Fibre 6.8g; Sodium 16mg

CANTALOUPE MELON SALAD

LIGHTLY CARAMELIZED STRAWBERRIES LOOK PRETTY AND TASTE DIVINE IN THIS SIMPLEST OF SALADS.
SERVE IT WITH A GLASS OF CHAMPAGNE TO WELCOME GUESTS AT A SOPHISTICATED SUMMER BRUNCH.
Preparation: 3 minutes; Cooking: 4–5 minutes

SERVES FOUR

INGREDIENTS
   115g/4oz/1 cup strawberries
   15ml/1 tbsp icing (confectioners')
      sugar, plus extra for dusting
   ½ cantaloupe melon

COOK'S TIP
When you need just a small amount of sifted icing (confectioners') sugar, use a tea strainer. Spoon the sugar into the strainer, then lightly tap the side with the spoon so that the sifted sugar drifts down evenly. Though tempting when you're in a hurry, mashing the sugar in the strainer with the spoon will not quicken the time it takes to sift through!

1 Preheat the grill (broiler) to high. Hull the strawberries and cut them in half. Arrange the fruit in a single layer, cut side up, on a baking sheet or in an ovenproof dish and dust with the icing sugar.

2 Grill (broil) the strawberries for 4–5 minutes, or until the sugar starts to bubble and turn golden.

3 Meanwhile, scoop out the seeds from the half melon using a spoon. Using a sharp knife, remove the skin, then cut the flesh into wedges.

4 Arrange the melon wedges attractively on a serving plate and sprinkle the lightly caramelized strawberries on top. Dust the salad with icing sugar and serve immediately.

Energy 34kcal/144kJ; Protein 0.7g; Carbohydrate 8g, of which sugars 8g; Fat 0.1g, of which saturates 0g; Cholesterol 0mg; Calcium 21mg; Fibre 1.1g; Sodium 8mg

PANETTONE FRENCH TOAST

THICKLY SLICED STALE WHITE BREAD IS USUALLY USED FOR FRENCH TOAST, BUT THE SLIGHTLY DRY TEXTURE OF PANETTONE MAKES A GREAT ALTERNATIVE. SERVE WITH FRESH SUMMER BERRIES.

Preparation: 2 minutes; Cooking: 4–6 minutes

SERVES FOUR

INGREDIENTS
   2 large (US extra large) eggs
   50g/2oz/¼ cup butter or 30ml/2 tbsp
      sunflower oil
   4 large slices panettone, halved
   30ml/2 tbsp caster (superfine) sugar
   fresh berries, to serve

COOK'S TIP
A generous portion of chilled mixed
berry fruits such as raspberries,
blackberries, morello cherries and
blueberries perfectly complements
the richness of this snack.

1 Break the eggs into a bowl and whisk
lightly, then tip them into a shallow
dish. Heat the butter or oil in a large
non-stick frying pan.

2 Dip the panettone slices in the egg
and fry for 2–3 minutes on each side,
until golden brown. Drain, dust with
sugar and serve with the berries.

Energy 369kcal/1550kJ; Protein 9.2g; Carbohydrate 47.4g, of which sugars 19.9g; Fat 17.3g, of which saturates 8.7g; Cholesterol 123mg; Calcium 103mg; Fibre 1.7g; Sodium 349mg

CINNAMON TOAST

THIS IS AN OLD-FASHIONED SNACK THAT IS WARMING AND COMFORTING ON A COLD DAY. CINNAMON TOAST IS PERFECT WITH A SPICY HOT CHOCOLATE DRINK OR WITH A FEW SLICES OF FRESH FRUIT.

Preparation: 2 minutes; Cooking: 2–3 minutes

SERVES TWO

INGREDIENTS

    75g/3oz/6 tbsp butter, softened
    10ml/2 tsp ground cinnamon
    30ml/2 tbsp caster (superfine) sugar,
      plus extra to serve
    4 slices bread
    prepared fresh fruit, such as
      peaches, plums, nectarines or
      mango (optional)

1 Place the softened butter in a bowl. Beat with a spoon until soft and creamy, then mix in the ground cinnamon and most of the sugar.

2 Toast the bread on both sides. Spread with the butter and sprinkle with a little remaining sugar. Serve at once, with pieces of fresh fruit, if you like.

COOK'S TIP

To round off this winter warmer, serve a quick cardamom hot chocolate with the cinnamon toast. Put 900ml/1½ pints/ 3¾ cups milk in a pan with two bruised cardamom pods and bring to the boil. Add 200g/7oz plain (semisweet) chocolate and whisk until melted. Using a slotted spoon, remove the cardamom pods just before serving.

Energy 461kcal/1921kJ; Protein 4.7g; Carbohydrate 41.6g, of which sugars 17.3g; Fat 31.8g, of which saturates 19.6g; Cholesterol 80mg; Calcium 72mg; Fibre 0.8g; Sodium 499mg

WARM PANCAKES WITH CARAMELIZED PEARS

IF YOU CAN FIND THEM, USE WILLIAMS PEARS FOR THIS RECIPE BECAUSE THEY ARE SO JUICY. FOR A REALLY INDULGENT BREAKFAST, TOP WITH A SPOONFUL OF CRÈME FRAÎCHE OR FROMAGE FRAIS.

Preparation: 5 minutes; Cooking: 6 minutes

SERVES FOUR

INGREDIENTS

8 ready-made pancakes
50g/2oz/¼ cup butter
4 ripe pears, peeled, cored and
   thickly sliced
30ml/2 tbsp light muscovado
   (brown) sugar
crème fraîche or fromage frais,
   to serve

1 Preheat the oven to 150°C/300°F/ Gas 2. Tightly wrap the pancakes in foil and place in the oven to warm through.

2 Meanwhile, heat the butter in a large frying pan and add the pears. Fry for 2–3 minutes, until the undersides are golden. Turn the pears over and sprinkle with sugar. Cook for a further 2–3 minutes, or until the sugar dissolves and the pan juices become sticky.

3 Remove the pancakes from the oven and take them out of the foil. Divide the pears among them, placing them in one quarter. Fold each pancake in half over the filling, then into quarters and place two folded pancakes on each plate. Drizzle the pan juices over and serve with crème fraîche or fromage frais.

VARIATION
This tastes just as good with sliced nectarines instead of pears.

Energy 544kcal/2274kJ; Protein 7.7g; Carbohydrate 64.9g, of which sugars 42.4g; Fat 29.9g, of which saturates 6.5g; Cholesterol 27mg; Calcium 155mg; Fibre 4.3g; Sodium 144mg

BUTTERMILK PANCAKES

IT IS TRADITIONAL TO HAVE THESE PLUMP PANCAKES ON THEIR OWN, WITH HONEY, BUT THEY ALSO TASTE GOOD AMERICAN-STYLE, WITH CRISP FRIED BACON AND A GENEROUS DRIZZLE OF MAPLE SYRUP.

Preparation: 2 minutes; Cooking: 12–18 minutes

MAKES ABOUT TWELVE

INGREDIENTS
225g/8oz/2 cups plain
   (all-purpose) flour
7.5ml/1½ tsp bicarbonate of
   soda (baking soda)
25–50g/1–2oz/2–4 tbsp sugar
1 egg
about 300ml/½ pint/1¼ cups
   buttermilk
butter and oil, mixed, or white
   vegetable fat (shortening), for frying
honey, to serve

COOK'S TIP
You will need to cook the pancakes in batches, so keep warm on a low oven temperature, tightly wrapped in foil.

1 In a food processor or a large mixing bowl, mix together the plain flour, the bicarbonate of soda and enough sugar to taste. Add the egg, blend or stir to mix, then gradually pour in just enough of the buttermilk to make a thick, smooth batter.

2 Heat a heavy pan and add the butter and oil, or fat. Place spoonfuls of the batter on to the hot pan and cook for 2–3 minutes until bubbles rise to the surface. Flip the pancakes over and cook for a further 2–3 minutes. Remove from the pan and serve warm with honey.

Energy 90kcal/380kJ; Protein 3.2g; Carbohydrate 18.7g, of which sugars 4.4g; Fat 0.8g, of which saturates 0.2g; Cholesterol 17mg; Calcium 61mg; Fibre 0.6g; Sodium 18mg

CINNAMON RINGS

THESE SPICY LITTLE PUFFS, AUTHENTICALLY CALLED BUÑUELOS, *RESEMBLE TINY DOUGHNUTS AND TASTE SO GOOD IT IS HARD NOT TO OVER-INDULGE. MAKE THEM FOR A SNACK OR TO SERVE WITH COFFEE.*

Preparation: 25 minutes; Cooking: 6 minutes

MAKES TWELVE

INGREDIENTS

225g/8oz/2 cups plain (all-purpose)
   flour
pinch of salt
5ml/1 tsp baking powder
2.5ml/$\frac{1}{2}$ tsp ground anise
115g/4oz/$\frac{1}{2}$ cup caster
   (superfine) sugar
1 large (US extra large) egg
120ml/4fl oz/$\frac{1}{2}$ cup milk
50g/2oz/$\frac{1}{4}$ cup butter
oil, for deep frying
10ml/2 tsp ground cinnamon
cinnamon sticks, to decorate

1 Sift the flour, salt, baking powder and ground anise into a mixing bowl. Add 30ml/2 tbsp of the sugar.

2 Place the egg and milk in a small jug (pitcher) and whisk well with a fork. Melt the butter in a small pan.

COOK'S TIP
Buñuelos are sometimes served with syrup for dunking, which is just right when you need cheering up. For a syrup, heat 175g/6oz/$\frac{3}{4}$ cup soft dark brown sugar and 450ml/$\frac{3}{4}$ pint/scant 2 cups water. Add a cinnamon stick and stir until the sugar dissolves, then boil and simmer for 15 minutes without stirring. Cool slightly before serving.

3 Pour the egg mixture and milk gradually into the flour, stirring all the time, until well blended, then add the melted butter. Mix first with a wooden spoon and then with your hands to make a soft dough.

4 Lightly flour a work surface, tip the dough out on to it and knead for about 10 minutes, until smooth.

5 Divide the dough into 12 pieces and roll into balls. Slightly flatten each ball with your hand and make a hole with the floured handle of a wooden spoon.

6 Heat the oil for deep-frying to a temperature of 190ºC/375ºF, or until a cube of dried bread, added to the oil, floats and then turns a golden colour in 30–60 seconds. Fry the *buñuelos* in batches until they are puffy and golden brown, turning them once or twice during cooking. As soon as they are golden, lift them out of the oil using a slotted spoon and lie them on a double layer of kitchen paper to drain.

7 Mix the remaining sugar with the ground cinnamon in a small bowl. Add the *buñuelos*, one at a time, while they are still warm. Toss them in the mixture until they are lightly coated and either serve at once or leave to cool. Decorate with cinnamon sticks.

Energy 195Kcal/818kJ; Protein 2.6g; Carbohydrate 23.5g, of which sugars 10.8g; Fat 10.8g, of which saturates 3.2g; Cholesterol 29mg; Calcium 44mg; Fibre 0.5g; Sodium 38mg

BLUEBERRY MUFFINS

LIGHT AND FRUITY, THESE WELL-KNOWN AMERICAN MUFFINS ARE DELICIOUS AT ANY TIME OF DAY.
THEY TASTE TERRIFIC AND THE BLUEBERRIES MAKE A USEFUL CONTRIBUTION TO A HEALTHY DIET.

Preparation: 10 minutes; Cooking: 20–25 minutes

MAKES TWELVE

INGREDIENTS

180g/6¼oz/generous 1½ cups plain
(all-purpose) flour
60g/2¼oz/generous ¼ cup caster
(superfine) sugar
10ml/2 tsp baking powder
1.5ml/¼ tsp salt
2 eggs
50g/2oz/4 tbsp butter, melted
175ml/6fl oz/¾ cup milk
5ml/1 tsp vanilla extract
5ml/1 tsp grated lemon rind
175g/6oz/1½ cups fresh blueberries

1 Preheat the oven to 200ºC/400ºF/
Gas 6. Arrange 12 paper muffin cases
on a baking tray or grease a 12-cup
patty tin (muffin pan).

2 Sift the flour, sugar, baking powder
and salt into a large mixing bowl. In
another bowl, whisk the eggs until
blended. Add the melted butter, milk,
vanilla and lemon rind to the eggs and
stir thoroughly to combine.

COOK'S TIP
If you want to serve these muffins for
breakfast, prepare the dry ingredients the
night before to save time.

3 Make a well in the dry ingredients and
pour in the egg mixture. With a large
metal spoon, stir until the flour is just
moistened, but not smooth.

4 Add the blueberries to the muffin
mixture and gently fold in, being careful
not to crush the berries.

5 Spoon the batter into the paper cases
or patty tin, leaving enough room for the
muffins to rise.

6 Bake for 20–25 minutes, until the
tops spring back when touched lightly.
Turn out on to a wire rack to cool a little
before serving. (If using a tin, leave for
6 minutes before turning them out.)

VARIATION
Muffins are delicious with all kinds of
different fruits. Try out some variations
using this basic muffin recipe. Replace
the blueberries with the same weight of
bilberries, blackcurrants, pitted cherries
or raspberries.

Energy 127Kcal/536kJ; Protein 3.3g; Carbohydrate 18.6g, of which sugars 7.1g; Fat 5g, of which saturates 2.7g; Cholesterol 48mg; Calcium 56mg; Fibre 1g; Sodium 96mg

APRICOT TURNOVERS

*THESE SWEET AND SUCCULENT PASTRIES ARE DELICIOUS SERVED WITH A BIG CUP OF MILKY COFFEE
FOR A LATE BREAKFAST OR A WELL-EARNED MID-MORNING TREAT.*

Preparation: 10 minutes; Cooking: 15–20 minutes

SERVES FOUR

INGREDIENTS
  225g/8oz ready-made puff pastry,
    thawed if frozen
  60ml/4 tbsp apricot conserve
  30ml/2 tbsp icing
    (confectioners') sugar, for dusting

VARIATION
Other varieties of fruit may be used
instead of apricots. These turnovers are
equally delicious made with strawberry or
raspberry conserve.

1 Preheat the oven to 190°C/375°F/
Gas 5. Roll out the pastry on a lightly
floured surface to a 25cm/10in square.
Using a sharp knife, cut the pastry
into four 13cm/5in squares. Place a
tablespoon of the apricot conserve in
the middle of each square of pastry.

2 Brush the edges of the pastry with
cold water and fold each square over to
form a triangle. Press the edges together
to seal. Transfer to a baking sheet and
bake for 15–20 minutes, or until risen
and golden. Remove to a wire rack to
cool, then dust with icing sugar.

Energy 291Kcal/1225kJ; Protein 3g; Carbohydrate 43g, of which sugars 22g; Fat 14g, of which saturates 0g; Cholesterol 0mg; Calcium 35mg; Fibre 0g; Sodium 200mg

CLASSIC PORRIDGE

PORRIDGE REMAINS A FAVOURITE WAY TO START THE DAY, ESPECIALLY DURING WINTER. BROWN SUGAR OR HONEY, SYRUP, CREAM AND EVEN A TOT OF WHISKY CAN BE ADDED FOR THE WEEKEND.

Preparation: 1 minute; Cooking: 28 minutes

SERVES FOUR

INGREDIENTS
 1 litre/1¾ pints/4 cups water
 115g/4oz/1 cup pinhead oatmeal
 good pinch of salt

VARIATION
Modern rolled oats can be used, in the proportion of 115g/4oz/1 cup rolled oats to 750ml/1¼ pints/3 cups water, plus a sprinkling of salt. They cook more quickly than pinhead oatmeal. Bring to the boil then simmer, stirring to prevent sticking, for about 5 minutes. Either type of oatmeal can be left to cook overnight in the slow oven of a range.

1 Put the water, pinhead oatmeal and salt into a heavy pan and bring to the boil over a medium heat, stirring with a wooden spatula. When the porridge is smooth and beginning to thicken, reduce the heat to a simmer.

2 Cook gently for about 25 minutes, stirring occasionally, until the oatmeal is cooked and the consistency smooth.

3 Serve hot with cold milk and extra salt, if required.

Energy 460kcal/1952kJ; Protein 14.4g; Carbohydrate 83.6g, of which sugars 0g; Fat 10g, of which saturates 0g; Cholesterol 0mg; Calcium 64mg; Fibre 8g; Sodium 1216mg

SWEET BREAKFAST OMELETTE

*FOR A HEARTY START TO A DAY WHEN YOU KNOW YOU'RE GOING TO BE TOO RUSHED TO HAVE MUCH
MORE THAN AN APPLE FOR LUNCH, TRY THIS SWEET OMELETTE WITH A SPOONFUL OF JAM.*

Preparation: 3 minutes; Cooking: 5 minutes

SERVES ONE

INGREDIENTS
   3 eggs
   10ml/2 tsp caster (superfine) sugar
   5ml/1 tsp plain (all-purpose) flour
   10g/¼oz/½ tbsp unsalted
    (sweet) butter
   bread and jam, to serve

COOK'S TIP
Although this recipe is stated to serve
one, it is substantial enough for two not-
very-hungry people. Omelettes are best
eaten the moment they emerge from
the pan, so if you are cooking for a
crowd, get each to make their own and
eat in relays.

1 Break the eggs into a large bowl, add
the sugar and flour and beat until really
frothy. Heat the butter in an omelette
pan until it begins to bubble, then pour
in the egg mixture and cook, without
stirring, until it begins to set.

2 Run a wooden spatula around the
edge of the omelette, then carefully turn
it over and cook the second side for
1–2 minutes until golden. Serve hot or
warm with thick slices of fresh bread
and a bowlful of fruity jam.

Energy 351kcal/1465kJ; Protein 19.3g; Carbohydrate 14.4g, of which sugars 10.6g; Fat 24.9g, of which saturates 9.9g; Cholesterol 592mg; Calcium 100mg; Fibre 0.2g; Sodium 271mg

SCRAMBLED EGGS WITH ANCHOVIES

LIFTING THE SPIRITS ON THE DULLEST OF DAYS, SCRAMBLED EGGS ARE TRUE COMFORT FOOD.
THIS VERSION COMBINES WITH ANCHOVIES, WHOSE SALTY TANG IS SUPERB WITH THE CREAMY EGG.

Preparation: 2–3 minutes; Cooking: 7 minutes

SERVES TWO

INGREDIENTS
2 slices bread
40g/1½oz/3 tbsp butter, plus
   extra for spreading
anchovy paste, such as
   Gentleman's Relish, for spreading
2 eggs and 2 egg yolks, beaten
60–90ml/4–6 tbsp single (light)
   cream or milk
ground black pepper
anchovy fillets, cut into strips,
   and paprika, to garnish

COOK'S TIP
These creamy scrambled eggs are
delicious in baked potatoes instead of
on toast. Serve with a salad and a glass
of crisp white wine for a tasty lunch.

1 Toast the bread, spread with butter
and anchovy paste, then remove the
crusts and cut into triangles. Keep warm.

2 Melt the rest of the butter in a
medium non-stick pan, then stir in the
beaten eggs, cream or milk, and a little
ground pepper. Heat very gently, stirring
constantly, until the mixture begins
to thicken.

3 Remove the pan from the heat and
continue to stir until the mixture
becomes very creamy, but do not allow
it to harden.

4 Divide the scrambled eggs among the
triangles of toast and garnish each one
with strips of anchovy fillet and a
generous sprinkling of paprika. Serve
immediately, while still hot.

Energy 405kcal/1680kJ; Protein 12.6g; Carbohydrate 14.1g, of which sugars 1.5g; Fat 33.7g, of which saturates 17.2g; Cholesterol 451mg; Calcium 112mg; Fibre 0.4g; Sodium 350mg

CHIVE SCRAMBLED EGGS <u>IN</u> BRIOCHES

THESE CREAMY SCRAMBLED EGGS ARE DELICIOUS AT ANY TIME OF DAY BUT, WHEN SERVED WITH FRANCE'S FAVOURITE BREAKFAST BREAD, THEY BECOME THE ULTIMATE BREAKFAST OR BRUNCH TREAT.

Preparation: 6 minutes; Cooking: 7 minutes

SERVES FOUR

INGREDIENTS
4 individual brioches
6 eggs, beaten
45ml/3 tbsp chopped fresh chives,
   plus extra to serve
25g/1oz/2 tbsp butter
45ml/3 tbsp cottage cheese
60–75ml/4–5 tbsp double
   (heavy) cream
salt and ground black pepper

3 Stir in the cottage cheese, cream and half the remaining chives. Cook for 1–2 minutes more, making sure that the eggs remain soft and creamy.

COOK'S TIP
Save the scooped-out brioche centres and freeze them in an airtight container. Partly defrost and blend or grate them to make crumbs for coating fish or pieces of chicken before frying.

4 To serve, spoon the eggs into the crisp brioche shells and sprinkle with the remaining chives.

VARIATION
If you do not happen to have brioches to hand, these wonderful herby eggs taste delicious on top of thick slices of toasted bread. Try them piled high on warm focaccia, or on toasted ciabatta, Granary (whole-wheat) bread or muffins.

1 Preheat the oven to 180°C/350°F/ Gas 4. Cut the tops off the brioches and set to one side. Carefully scoop out the centre of each brioche, leaving a bread case. Put the brioche cases and lids on a baking sheet and bake for 5 minutes until hot and crisp.

2 Meanwhile, beat the eggs lightly and season to taste. Add about one-third of the chopped chives. Heat the butter in a medium pan until it begins to foam, then add the eggs and cook, stirring constantly with a wooden spoon until semi-solid.

Energy 414kcal/1731kJ; Protein 16.2g; Carbohydrate 32.5g, of which sugars 10.5g; Fat 25.5g, of which saturates 12g; Cholesterol 322mg; Calcium 154mg; Fibre 1.9g; Sodium 374mg

SMOKED SALMON <u>AND</u> CHIVE OMELETTE

THE ADDITION OF A GENEROUS PORTION OF CHOPPED SMOKED SALMON GIVES A REALLY LUXURIOUS FINISH TO THIS SIMPLE, CLASSIC DISH, WHICH IS AN IDEAL QUICK LUNCH FOR TWO PEOPLE.

Preparation: 2–3 minutes; Cooking: 5–6 minutes

SERVES TWO

INGREDIENTS

4 eggs
15ml/1 tbsp chopped fresh chives or
    spring onions (scallions)
a knob (pat) of butter
50g/2oz smoked salmon,
    roughly chopped
salt and ground black pepper

1 Break the eggs into a bowl. Beat with a fork until just combined, then stir in the chopped fresh chives or spring onions. Season with salt and a generous sprinkling of freshly ground black pepper, and set aside.

2 Heat the butter in a medium frying pan until foamy. Pour in the eggs and cook over a medium heat for 3–4 minutes, drawing the cooked egg from around the edge into the centre of the pan from time to time.

3 At this stage, you can either leave the top of the omelette slightly soft or finish it off under the grill (broiler), depending on how you like your omelette. Top with the smoked salmon, fold the omelette over and cut in half to serve.

Energy 221kcal/920kJ; Protein 19g; Carbohydrate 0.2g, of which sugars 0.2g; Fat 16.4g, of which saturates 5.9g; Cholesterol 400mg; Calcium 65mg; Fibre 0.1g; Sodium 641mg

KEDGEREE

IMPRESS HOUSE GUESTS BY RUSTLING UP THIS DELECTABLE DISH IN LESS TIME THAN IT TAKES THEM TO TAKE A SHOWER. KEDGEREE IS GREAT FOR BREAKFAST, BRUNCH OR SUPPER.

Preparation: 2–3 minutes; Cooking: 16 minutes

SERVES FOUR

INGREDIENTS
   350g/12oz/1½ cups basmati rice
   225g/8oz undyed smoked
    haddock fillet
   4 eggs
   25g/1oz/2 tbsp butter
   30ml/2 tbsp garam masala
   ground black pepper

1 Preheat the grill (broiler) to medium. Place the smoked haddock on a baking sheet and grill (broil) for 10 minutes, or until cooked through.

2 Meanwhile, place the eggs in a pan of cold water and bring to the boil. Cook for 6–7 minutes. At the same time as the eggs and haddock are cooking, cook the rice in a pan of boiling water for 10–12 minutes.

3 When the eggs are cooked, drain and place under cold running water until cool enough to handle. Shell the eggs and cut into halves or quarters.

4 Remove the baking sheet from under the grill and transfer the smoked haddock to a board. Remove the skin when cool enough to handle.

5 Using a fork, ease the flesh apart so that it separates into large flakes. Remove any remaining bones.

6 Drain the rice and tip it into a bowl. Melt the butter in a pan, stir in the garam masala and add the fish. When it has warmed through, add it to the rice with the smoked fish and eggs. Mix gently, taking care not to mash the eggs. Season and serve immediately.

Energy 480kcal/2006kJ; Protein 23.5g; Carbohydrate 69.9g, of which sugars 0g; Fat 11.5g, of which saturates 4.9g; Cholesterol 224mg; Calcium 59mg; Fibre 0g; Sodium 536mg

GRIDDLED TOMATOES ON SODA BREAD

NOTHING COULD BE SIMPLER THAN THIS BASIC DISH, TRANSFORMED INTO SOMETHING SPECIAL BY ADDING A DRIZZLE OF OLIVE OIL, BALSAMIC VINEGAR AND SHAVINGS OF PARMESAN CHEESE.

Preparation: 2 minutes; Cooking: 4–6 minutes

SERVES FOUR

INGREDIENTS

olive oil, for brushing and drizzling
6 tomatoes, thickly sliced
4 thick slices soda bread
balsamic vinegar, for drizzling
salt and ground black pepper
shavings of Parmesan cheese,
  to serve

COOK'S TIP

Using a griddle pan reduces the amount of oil required for cooking the tomatoes and gives them a barbecued flavour. The ridges on the pan brand the tomatoes, which look very attractive.

1 Brush a griddle pan with olive oil and heat. Add the tomato slices and cook for 4–6 minutes, turning once, until softened and slightly blackened. Alternatively, heat a grill (broiler) to high and line the rack with foil. Grill (broil) the tomato slices for 4–6 minutes, turning once, until softened.

2 While the tomatoes are cooking, lightly toast the soda bread. Place the tomatoes on top of the toast and drizzle each portion with a little olive oil and vinegar. Season to taste and serve immediately with thin shavings of Parmesan.

Energy 178kcal/751kJ; Protein 4.2g; Carbohydrate 26.3g, of which sugars 6.9g; Fat 7g, of which saturates 1g; Cholesterol 0mg; Calcium 66mg; Fibre 2.7g; Sodium 175mg

MUSHROOMS ON SPICY TOAST

*DRY-PANNING IS A QUICK WAY OF COOKING MUSHROOMS THAT MAKES THE MOST OF THEIR FLAVOUR.
THE JUICES RUN WHEN THE MUSHROOMS ARE HEATED, SO THEY BECOME REALLY MOIST AND TENDER.*

Preparation: 2–3 minutes; Cooking: 4–5 minutes

SERVES FOUR

INGREDIENTS

8–12 large flat field (portabello)
  mushrooms
50g/1oz/2 tbsp butter
5ml/1 tsp curry paste
salt
4 slices thickly-sliced white bread,
  toasted, to serve

1 Preheat the oven to 200°C/400°F/
Gas 6. Peel the mushrooms, if
necessary, and remove the stalks. Heat
a dry frying pan until very hot.

2 Place the mushrooms in the hot frying
pan, with the gills on top. Using half
the butter, add a piece the size of a
hazelnut to each one, then sprinkle all
the mushrooms lightly with salt.

3 Cook over a medium heat until the
butter begins to bubble and the
mushrooms are juicy and tender.

4 Meanwhile, mix the remaining butter
with the curry powder. Spread on the
bread. Bake in the oven for 10 minutes,
pile the mushrooms on top and serve.

VARIATIONS
• Using a flavoured butter makes these
mushrooms even more special. Try one of
the following.
• **Herb butter** Mix softened butter with
chopped fresh herbs such as parsley and
thyme, or marjoram and chopped chives.
• **Olive butter** Mix softened butter with diced
green olives and spring onions (scallions).
• **Tomato butter** Mix softened butter with
sun-dried tomato purée (paste).
• **Garlic butter** Mix softened butter with
finely chopped garlic.
• **Pepper and paprika butter** Mix softened
butter with 2.5ml/½ tsp paprika and
2.5ml/½ tsp black pepper.

Energy 230kcal/966kJ; Protein 6.1g; Carbohydrate 25.1g, of which sugars 1.6g; Fat 12.5g, of which saturates 6.7g; Cholesterol 27mg; Calcium 63mg; Fibre 1.9g; Sodium 341mg

CHEESE TOASTIES

ALSO KNOWN AS BUBBLY CHEESE TOAST, BECAUSE OF THE WAY THE EGG AND CHEESE MIXTURE PUFFS UP DURING BAKING, THIS IS A NUTRITIOUS AND EASY SNACK THAT EVERYONE ENJOYS.

Preparation: 3–4 minutes; Cooking: 10–15 minutes

SERVES FOUR

INGREDIENTS

2 eggs
175–225g/6–8oz/1½–2 cups grated
  Cheddar cheese
5–10ml/1–2 tsp wholegrain mustard
4 slices bread, buttered
2–4 halved tomatoes (optional)
ground black pepper
watercress or fresh parsley,
  to serve (optional)

COOK'S TIP

For the best flavour, use a mature (sharp) Cheddar cheese or a mixture of Cheddar and Leicester. To save time, buy packets of ready-grated cheese from the supermarket.

1 Preheat the oven to 230°C/450°F/ Gas 8 (the top oven of a range-type stove is ideal for this recipe). Whisk the eggs lightly and stir in the grated cheese, mustard and pepper.

2 Lay the buttered bread face down in a shallow baking dish.

3 Divide the cheese mixture among the slices of bread, spreading it out evenly.

4 Bake in the oven for 10–15 minutes, or until well risen and golden brown, adding the halved tomatoes for a few minutes, if using. Serve immediately, with the tomatoes, and garnish with sprigs of watercress or parsley.

Energy 357kcal/1484kJ; Protein 16.6g; Carbohydrate 13.4g, of which sugars 0.8g; Fat 25.8g, of which saturates 15.5g; Cholesterol 159mg; Calcium 369mg; Fibre 0.4g; Sodium 552mg

LOX WITH BAGELS AND CREAM CHEESE

THIS SOPHISTICATED DISH IS PERFECT FOR A WEEKEND BREAKFAST OR BRUNCH WITH FRIENDS. LOX IS THE JEWISH WORD FOR SMOKED SALMON AND THIS DELI CLASSIC IS EASY TO MAKE AT HOME.

Preparation: 3 minutes; Cooking: 4–5 minutes

SERVES TWO

INGREDIENTS

2 bagels
115–175g/4–6oz/½–¾ cup full-fat
cream cheese
150g/5oz sliced best smoked salmon
ground black pepper
lemon wedges, to serve

1 Preheat the oven to 200°C/400°F/Gas 6. Put the bagels on a large baking sheet and warm them in the oven for 4–5 minutes.

2 Remove the bagels from the oven, split them in two and spread each half generously with cream cheese. Pile the salmon on top of the bagel bases and grind over plenty of black pepper.

3 Squeeze over some lemon juice, then add the bagel tops, at an angle.

4 Place on serving plates with the lemon wedges. If you have time, wrap each lemon wedge in a small square of muslin (cheesecloth), tie with fine string and put it on the plate.

COOK'S TIP
It is essential to be generous with the smoked salmon and to use the best cream cheese you can find – absolutely not a low-fat version.

Energy 496kcal/2068kJ; Protein 25.9g; Carbohydrate 28.9g, of which sugars 3.3g; Fat 31.6g, of which saturates 17.7g; Cholesterol 81mg; Calcium 71mg; Fibre 1.2g; Sodium 1858mg

JUGGED KIPPERS

THE DEMAND FOR NATURALLY SMOKED KIPPERS IS EVER INCREASING. THEY ARE MOST POPULAR FOR BREAKFAST, WITH BUTTER, LEMON JUICE AND CRUSTY BREAD AND ARE PREPARED IN MINUTES.

Preparation: 2–3 minutes; Cooking: 5–6 minutes

SERVES FOUR

INGREDIENTS
   4 kippers (smoked herrings),
    preferably naturally smoked,
    whole or filleted
   25g/1oz/2 tbsp butter
   ground black pepper
   lemon wedges, to serve

1 Select a heatproof glass jug (pitcher) tall enough for the kippers to be immersed when the water is added. If the heads are still on the kippers, remove them.

2 Put the fish into the jug, tails up, and then cover them with boiling water. Leave for about 5 minutes, until tender.

3 Drain well and serve on warmed plates with butter, a little black pepper and the lemon wedges.

Energy 248kcal/1025kJ; Protein 15.9g; Carbohydrate 0g, of which sugars 0g; Fat 20.4g, of which saturates 5.8g; Cholesterol 68mg; Calcium 49mg; Fibre 0g; Sodium 776mg

KIDNEY AND MUSHROOM TOASTS

MELTINGLY TENDER LAMB'S KIDNEYS ARE A TRADITIONAL BREAKFAST TREAT. COOKING THEM WITH MUSHROOMS IN MUSTARD BUTTER FLATTERS THEIR FLAVOUR AND THEY TASTE GREAT ON TOAST.

Preparation: 5 minutes; Cooking: 4–6 minutes

SERVES TWO TO FOUR

INGREDIENTS
    4 large, flat field (portabello)
    mushrooms, stalks trimmed
    75g/3oz/6 tbsp butter, softened
    10ml/2 tsp wholegrain mustard
    15ml/1 tbsp chopped fresh parsley
    4 lamb's kidneys, skinned, halved
    and cored
    4 thick slices of brown bread, cut
    into rounds and toasted
    sprig of parsley, to garnish
    tomato wedges, to serve

COOK'S TIPS
• Kidneys are best served when they are
still pink in the centre.
• Serve the mixture on halved, warm
scones, if you prefer.

1 Wash the mushrooms, pat dry with kitchen paper and remove the stalks.

2 Mix the butter, wholegrain mustard and fresh parsley together.

3 Rinse the prepared lamb's kidneys well under cold running water and pat dry with kitchen paper.

4 Melt about two-thirds of the butter mixture in a large frying pan and fry the mushrooms and kidneys for 2–3 minutes on each side.

5 When the kidneys are cooked to your liking, spread with the remaining herb butter. Pile on the hot toast and serve with the tomato, garnished with parsley.

Energy 379kcal/1580kJ; Protein 20.1g; Carbohydrate 14.9g, of which sugars 1g; Fat 27.1g, of which saturates 15.9g; Cholesterol 353mg; Calcium 59mg; Fibre 1.7g; Sodium 560mg

CROQUE MONSIEUR

THIS CLASSIC FRENCH TOASTIE IS DELICIOUS SERVED AT ANY TIME OF DAY, BUT WITH A FOAMING CUP OF MILKY COFFEE IT MAKES A PARTICULARLY ENJOYABLE BRUNCH DISH.

Preparation: 5 minutes; Cooking: 5 minutes

SERVES FOUR

INGREDIENTS
    8 slices white bread
    softened butter
    4 large lean ham slices
    175g/6oz Gruyère or
      mild Cheddar cheese
    ground black pepper

1 Preheat the grill (broiler) to the highest setting. Arrange the bread on the grill rack and toast four slices on both sides and the other four slices on one side only.

2 Slice the cheese thinly. Butter the slices of bread that have been toasted on both sides and top with the ham, then the cheese. Season with plenty of ground black pepper. Transfer the topped bread slices to the grill pan.

3 Lay the remaining, half-toasted bread slices on top of the cheese, with the untoasted side uppermost. Grill (broil) the tops of the sandwiches until golden brown, then cut them in half using a sharp knife and serve.

Energy 336kcal/1409kJ; Protein 20.3g; Carbohydrate 26.9g, of which sugars 1.7g; Fat 16.2g, of which saturates 9.8g; Cholesterol 57mg; Calcium 385mg; Fibre 0.8g; Sodium 897mg.

EGGS BENEDICT

USING A GOOD-QUALITY BOUGHT HOLLANDAISE FOR THIS RECIPE SAVES TIME AND MAKES ALL THE DIFFERENCE TO THE RESULT. EGGS BENEDICT ARE DELICIOUS SERVED ON TOASTED ENGLISH MUFFINS.

Preparation: 2–3 minutes; Cooking: 4–6 minutes

SERVES FOUR

INGREDIENTS
    4 large (US extra large) eggs
    4 lean ham slices
    60ml/4 tbsp warm hollandaise sauce
    2 English muffins, split
    salt and ground black pepper

3 Meanwhile, toast the muffin halves. Place on four serving plates and arrange the ham slices on top. Remove the eggs from the pan using a slotted spoon and place on top of the ham on two of the plates. Poach two more eggs and top the remaining muffins.

COOK'S TIP
Many people complain that it's near impossible to poach a perfectly round egg – too often the edges of the cooked whites look a bit ragged. You can try swirling the simmering water with a spoon just before adding the eggs – the little currents of water help to cement the shape of the whites. Failing this, simply use a sharp knife point to trim around the edges just before serving.

1 Pour cold water into a medium pan to a depth of about 5cm/2in and bring to a gentle simmer. Crack an egg into a saucer. Swirl the water in the pan with a spoon, then slide the egg carefully into the centre of the swirl.

2 Add the second egg to the pan. Simmer both eggs for 2–3 minutes, until the whites are set, but the yolks are still soft.

4 Spoon the hollandaise sauce over the eggs, season and serve immediately.

Energy 276kcal/1154kJ; Protein 14.9g; Carbohydrate 15.9g, of which sugars 1.6g; Fat 17.7g, of which saturates 3.7g; Cholesterol 258mg; Calcium 81mg; Fibre 0.7g; Sodium 520mg

OATMEAL PANCAKES WITH BACON

WRAP AN OATMEAL PANCAKE AROUND A CRISP SLICE OF BEST BACON AND SAMPLE A NEW TASTE SENSATION WITH YOUR TRADITIONAL COOKED BREAKFAST. IT MAKES A GREAT EGG DIPPER, TOO.

Preparation: 2–3 minutes; Cooking: 12 minutes

MAKES FOUR PANCAKES

INGREDIENTS
50g/2oz/½ cup fine wholemeal (whole-wheat) flour
30ml/2 tbsp fine pinhead oatmeal
pinch of salt
1 egg
about 150ml/¼ pint/⅔ cup buttermilk or milk
butter or oil, for greasing
4 rashers (strips) bacon

COOK'S TIP
The oatmeal in the batter gives it texture, so these pancakes are firmer than conventional crêpes. You can easily double or treble the mixture and even make it ahead of time. It will thicken on standing, though, so thin it with buttermilk or milk before use.

1 Mix the flour, oatmeal and salt in a bowl, beat in the egg and add enough buttermilk or milk to make a creamy batter of the same consistency as that used for ordinary pancakes.

2 Thoroughly heat a griddle or cast-iron frying pan over a medium-hot heat. When very hot, grease the surface lightly with butter or oil.

3 Pour in the batter, about a ladleful at a time. Tilt the frying pan to spread evenly and cook the pancake for about 2 minutes until set and the underside is browned. Turn over and cook for 1 minute until browned.

4 Keep the pancake warm while you cook the others and fry the bacon. Roll the pancakes around the bacon to serve.

Energy 148kcal/621kJ; Protein 9.7g; Carbohydrate 13.1g, of which sugars 2g; Fat 6.7g, of which saturates 2.2g; Cholesterol 64mg; Calcium 62mg; Fibre 1.5g; Sodium 469mg

BACON AND EGG MUFFINS HOLLANDAISE

THIS TASTY BREAKFAST IS IDEAL FOR BIRTHDAYS, ANNIVERSARIES OR OTHER DAYS WHEN YOU WANT TO TREAT FAMILY OR FRIENDS TO AN EXTRA-SPECIAL START TO THE DAY.

Preparation: 5 minutes; Cooking: 8–12 minutes

SERVES FOUR

INGREDIENTS

350g/12oz rindless back (lean) bacon
rashers (strips)
dash of white wine vinegar
4 eggs
4 English muffins
butter, for spreading
ground black pepper
For the hollandaise sauce
2 egg yolks
5ml/1 tsp white wine vinegar
75g/3oz/6 tbsp butter

1 Preheat the grill (broiler) and cook the bacon for 5–8 minutes, turning once, or until crisp on both sides. Keep warm.

2 Fill a large frying pan with water and bring to the boil. Add the vinegar and regulate the heat so that the water simmers. Crack the eggs into the water and poach them for 3–4 minutes, or slightly longer for firm eggs.

3 Split and toast the muffins while the eggs are cooking. Spread with butter and place on warmed plates.

VARIATIONS
• Replace the bacon with smoked salmon for a luxurious touch.
• Add some sliced grilled mushrooms for a more substantial breakfast.

4 To make the hollandaise sauce, process the egg yolks and white wine vinegar in a blender or food processor. Melt the butter. With the motor still running, very gradually add the hot melted butter through the feeder tube. The hot butter will cook the yolks to make a thick, glossy sauce. Switch off the machine as soon as all the butter has been added and the sauce has thickened. Season to taste.

5 Arrange the bacon on the muffins and add a poached egg to each. Top with a spoonful of sauce and grind over some black pepper. Serve immediately.

COOK'S TIPS
• Making the hollandaise sauce in a food processor or blender rather than by hand turns it from a slightly difficult recipe into an easy option.
• Eggs that are a week or more old will not keep their shape when poached so, for the best results, use very fresh eggs.
• Use the best eggs you can afford – ideally free-range organic ones.
• To make sure that you don't break the yolk, crack the eggs into a cup before carefully adding them to the gently simmering water.

Energy 612Kcal/2549kJ; Protein 32.6g; Carbohydrate 30.2g, of which sugars 2.4g; Fat 41.1g, of which saturates 18.3g; Cholesterol 429mg; Calcium 143mg; Fibre 1.3g; Sodium 1880mg

SOUPS
AND APPETIZERS

Soup is a highly versatile dish that can often be extremely quick to make — just 6–7 minutes in the case of Avocado Soup. It can be served chilled (Gazpacho) or hot (Avgolemono); it can be a fine, thin liquid fit for a dinner party (Chilled Tomato Soup with Rocket Pesto) or a chunky bowlful for a sustaining lunch (Tuscan Bean Soup or Clam Chowder); and it can contain what may seem unlikely ingredients (Curried Cauliflower Soup or Parsnip Soup). Dips are very popular appetizers, encouraging casual sharing of bowls and items to dip, rather than individual appetizers. In addition to the old favourites such as Guacamole and Hummus, try Artichoke and Cumin Dip or Melting Cheese Dip. For dinner party appetizers, consider Chicken Liver and Brandy Paté, Figs with Prosciutto and Roquefort or Pears with Blue Cheese and Walnuts, or for the calorie-conscious Melon, Pineapple and Grape Cocktail or Sweet and Sour Cucumber with Fresh Dill. Whatever you choose, there are plenty of dishes here that can be made in less than half an hour while still tasting delicious.

CHILLED TOMATO SOUP WITH ROCKET PESTO

THIS SOUP TAKES HARDLY ANY TIME TO MAKE, BUT MUST BE CHILLED, SO BEAR THAT IN MIND WHEN PLANNING YOUR MENU. WHIZZ IT UP WHEN YOU WAKE, AND MAKE THE PESTO JUST BEFORE SERVING.

Preparation: 10 minutes; Cooking: 4–5 minutes; Chilling: 4–8 hours

SERVES FOUR

INGREDIENTS
    225g/8oz cherry tomatoes, halved
    225g/8oz baby plum
      tomatoes, halved
    225g/8oz vine-ripened
      tomatoes, halved
    2 shallots, roughly chopped
    25ml/1½ tbsp sun-dried
      tomato purée (paste)
    600ml/1 pint/2½ cups
      vegetable stock
    salt and ground black pepper
    ice cubes, to serve
For the rocket pesto
    15g/½oz rocket (arugula) leaves
    75ml/5 tbsp olive oil
    15g/½oz/2 tbsp pine nuts
    1 garlic clove
    25g/1oz/⅓ cup freshly grated
      Parmesan cheese

1 Purée all the tomatoes and the shallots in a food processor or blender. Add the sun-dried tomato paste and process until smooth. Press the purée through a sieve (strainer) into a pan.

2 Add the vegetable stock and heat gently for 4–5 minutes. Season well. Pour into a bowl, leave to cool, then chill for at least 4 hours.

3 For the rocket pesto, put the rocket, oil, pine nuts and garlic in a food processor or blender and process to form a paste. Transfer to a bowl and stir in the Parmesan cheese. (This can also be prepared using a mortar and pestle.)

4 Ladle the soup into bowls and add a few ice cubes to each. Spoon some of the rocket pesto into the centre of each portion and serve.

Energy 218kcal/902kJ; Protein 4.8g; Carbohydrate 7.5g, of which sugars 7.2g; Fat 19g, of which saturates 3.6g; Cholesterol 6mg; Calcium 100mg; Fibre 2.2g; Sodium 104mg

GAZPACHO

PROBABLY THE MOST FAMOUS CHILLED SOUP IN THE WORLD, THIS ORIGINATED IN SPAIN BUT NOW
APPEARS ON MENUS EVERYWHERE. IT IS PERFECT FOR A SUMMER LUNCH IN THE GARDEN.
Preparation: 12 minutes; Cooking: 5–6 minutes; Chilling: 4–8 hours

SERVES SIX

INGREDIENTS
    900g/2lb ripe tomatoes, peeled
    and seeded
    1 cucumber, peeled and
    roughly chopped
    2 red (bell) peppers, seeded and
    roughly chopped
    2 garlic cloves, crushed
    1 large onion, roughly chopped
    30ml/2 tbsp white wine vinegar
    120ml/4fl oz/½ cup olive oil
    250g/9oz/4½ cups fresh white
    breadcrumbs
    450ml/¾ pint/scant 2 cups iced water
    salt and ground black pepper
    ice cubes, to serve
For the garnish
    30–45ml/2–3 tbsp olive oil
    4 thick slices bread, crusts removed,
    cut into small cubes
    2 tomatoes, peeled, seeded and
    finely diced
    1 small green (bell) pepper, seeded
    and finely diced
    1 small onion, very finely sliced
    a small bunch of fresh flat leaf
    parsley, chopped

1 In a large bowl, mix the tomatoes, cucumber, peppers, garlic and onion. Stir in the vinegar, oil, breadcrumbs and water until well mixed. Purée the mixture in a food processor or blender until almost smooth, and pour into a large bowl. Stir in salt and pepper to taste and chill for at least 4 hours.

2 To make the garnish, heat the oil in a frying pan and add the bread cubes.

3 Fry over a medium heat for 5–6 minutes, stirring occasionally to brown evenly. Lift out the cubes with a slotted spoon, drain on kitchen paper and put into a small bowl. Place the remaining garnishing ingredients in separate bowls or on a serving plate.

COOK'S TIP
If the vegetable and vinegar mixture seems very thick after puréeing, stir in a little water. Cover the bowl with clear film before chilling the soup.

4 Ladle the gazpacho into bowls and add ice cubes to each portion. Serve at once. Pass around the bowls of garnishing ingredients with the soup so that they can be added to taste.

Energy 412kcal/1730kJ; Protein 9.1g; Carbohydrate 55.6g, of which sugars 14.7g; Fat 18.6g, of which saturates 2.6g; Cholesterol 0mg; Calcium 109mg; Fibre 5g; Sodium 431mg

AVOCADO SOUP

THIS DELICIOUS SOUP HAS A FRESH, DELICATE FLAVOUR AND A WONDERFUL COLOUR. FOR ADDED
ZEST, ADD A GENEROUS SQUEEZE OF LIME OR LEMON JUICE JUST BEFORE SERVING.

Preparation: 3 minutes; Cooking: 3–4 minutes

SERVES FOUR

INGREDIENTS
    2 large ripe avocados
    300ml/½ pint/1¼ cups sour cream
    1 litre/1¾ pints/4 cups
        well-flavoured chicken stock
    a small bunch of fresh coriander
        (cilantro), chopped
    salt and ground black pepper

COOK'S TIP
Choose ripe avocados for this soup –
they should feel soft when gently
pressed. Keep very firm avocados at
room temperature for 3–4 days until
they soften. To speed ripening, place
in a brown paper bag.

1 Cut the avocados in half, remove the
peel and lift out the stones (pits). Chop
the flesh coarsely and place it in a food
processor with 45–60ml/3–4 tbsp of the
sour cream. Process until smooth.

2 Heat the chicken stock in a pan.
When it is hot, but still below simmering
point, add the rest of the sour cream
and stir gently to mix.

3 Gradually stir the avocado mixture
into the hot stock. Heat gently but do
not let the mixture approach boiling
point. Add salt to taste.

4 Ladle the soup into heated bowls and
sprinkle each portion with chopped
coriander and black pepper. Serve
immediately, as it will discolour
on standing.

Energy 343kcal/1416kJ; Protein 4.4g; Carbohydrate 5.1g, of which sugars 3.6g; Fat 33.9g, of which saturates 13.4g; Cholesterol 45mg; Calcium 106mg; Fibre 4g; Sodium 41mg

AVGOLEMONO

THIS IS A GREAT FAVOURITE IN GREECE AND IS A FINE EXAMPLE OF HOW A FEW INGREDIENTS CAN MAKE A MARVELLOUS DISH IN A SHORT SPACE OF TIME. ADD AS LITTLE OR AS MUCH RICE AS YOU LIKE.

Preparation: 10 minutes; Cooking: 12 minutes

SERVES FOUR

INGREDIENTS
900ml/1½ pints/3¾ cups well-
  flavoured chicken stock, preferably
  home-made
50g/2oz/generous ⅓ cup long grain
  rice
3 egg yolks
30–60ml/2–4 tbsp lemon juice
30ml/2 tbsp finely chopped
  fresh parsley
salt and freshly ground black pepper
lemon slices and parsley sprigs,
  to garnish

1 Pour the stock into a pan, bring to simmering point, then add the drained rice. Half cover and cook for about 12 minutes until the rice is just tender. Season with salt and pepper

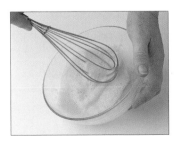

2 Whisk the egg yolks in a bowl, then add about 30ml/2 tbsp of the lemon juice, whisking constantly until the mixture is smooth and bubbly. Add a ladleful of soup and whisk again.

3 Remove the soup from the heat and slowly add the egg mixture, whisking all the time. The soup will turn a pretty lemon colour and will thicken slightly.

4 Taste and add more lemon juice if necessary. Stir in the parsley. Serve at once, without reheating, garnished with lemon slices and parsley sprigs.

COOK'S TIP
The trick here is to add the egg mixture to the soup without it curdling. Avoid whisking the mixture into boiling liquid. It is safest to remove the soup from the heat entirely and then whisk in the mixture in a slow but steady stream. Do not reheat, because curdling would be almost inevitable.

Energy 96Kcal/404kJ; Protein 3.3g; Carbohydrate 10.9g, of which sugars 0.2g; Fat 4.7g, of which saturates 1.2g; Cholesterol 151mg; Calcium 39mg; Fibre 0.4g; Sodium 10mg

GARLIC AND CORIANDER SOUP

THIS RECIPE IS BASED ON THE WONDERFUL BREAD SOUPS OR AÇORDAS OF PORTUGAL. BEING A SIMPLE SOUP, IT SHOULD BE MADE WITH THE BEST INGREDIENTS, SUCH AS FRESH CORIANDER AND PLUMP GARLIC.

Preparation: 8 minutes; Cooking: 15 minutes

SERVES SIX

INGREDIENTS
    25g/1oz fresh coriander (cilantro),
      leaves and stalks chopped separately
    1.5 litres/2½ pints/6¼ cups
      vegetable or chicken stock, or water
    5–6 plump garlic cloves, peeled
    6 eggs
    275g/10oz day-old bread, most of the
      crust removed and torn into bitesize
      pieces
    salt and ground black pepper
    90ml/6 tbsp extra virgin olive oil,
      plus extra to serve

1 Place the coriander stalks in a pan. Add the stock or water and bring to the boil. Lower the heat and simmer for 10 minutes, then process in a blender or food processor and sieve back into the pan.

2 Crush the garlic with 5ml/1 tsp salt, then stir in 120ml/4fl oz/½ cup hot soup. Return the mixture to the pan.

3 Meanwhile, poach the eggs in a frying pan of simmering water for about 3–4 minutes, until just set. Use a draining spoon to remove them from the pan and transfer to a warmed plate. Trim off any untidy bits of white.

4 Bring the soup back to the boil and add seasoning. Stir in the chopped coriander leaves and remove the pan from the heat.

5 Place the bread in six soup plates or bowls and drizzle the oil over it. Ladle in the soup and stir. Add a poached egg to each bowl and serve immediately, offering olive oil at the table so that it can be drizzled over the soup to taste.

Energy 290kcal/1212kJ; Protein 10.9g; Carbohydrate 24.1g, of which sugars 1.4g; Fat 17.5g, of which saturates 3.1g; Cholesterol 190mg; Calcium 89mg; Fibre 1.2g; Sodium 310mg.

BUTTER BEAN AND SUN-DRIED TOMATO SOUP

THIS SOUP IS QUICK AND EASY TO MAKE. THE KEY IS TO USE A GOOD-QUALITY HOME-MADE OR BOUGHT FRESH STOCK WITH PLENTY OF PESTO AND SUN-DRIED TOMATO PURÉE.

Preparation: 2 minutes; Cooking: 12 minutes

SERVES FOUR

INGREDIENTS

2 x 400g/14oz cans butter (lima) beans, drained and rinsed
900ml/1½ pints/3¾ cups chicken or vegetable stock
60ml/4 tbsp sun-dried tomato purée (paste)
75ml/5 tbsp pesto

COOK'S TIP

For the busy cook, good-quality bought stocks are a blessing. Most large supermarkets now sell fresh stock in tubs. Another good product is concentrated liquid stock, sold in bottles. However, if you cannot find any of the above, a good-quality stock cube will do the job.

1 Put the butter beans in a pan. Pour in the stock and bring to the boil over a medium heat, stirring once or twice.

2 Stir in the tomato purée and pesto. Lower the heat and cook gently for 5 minutes.

3 Transfer six ladlefuls of the soup to a blender or food processor, scooping up plenty of the beans. Process until smooth, then return the purée to the pan.

4 Heat gently, stirring frequently, for 5 minutes, then season if necessary. Ladle into four warmed soup bowls and serve with warm crusty bread or breadsticks.

Energy 269kcal/1130kJ; Protein 15.6g; Carbohydrate 28.3g, of which sugars 4.5g; Fat 11.2g, of which saturates 2.5g; Cholesterol 6mg; Calcium 111mg; Fibre 9.7g; Sodium 944mg

CURRIED CAULIFLOWER SOUP

THIS SPICY, CREAMY, COMFORTING SOUP IS PERFECT FOR LUNCH ON A COLD WINTER'S DAY SERVED WITH CRUSTY BREAD AND GARNISHED WITH FRESH CORIANDER.

Preparation: 5 minutes; Cooking: 20 minutes

SERVES FOUR

INGREDIENTS
750ml/1¼ pints/3 cups milk
1 large cauliflower
15ml/1 tbsp garam masala
salt and ground black pepper
fresh coriander (cilantro), to garnish

VARIATION
You can also make broccoli soup in the same way, using the same weight of broccoli in place of the cauliflower. For a slightly different flavour, experiment with different spices or try adding creamed coconut.

1 Pour the milk into a large pan and place over a medium heat. Break the cauliflower into florets, add to the milk with the garam masala and season.

2 Bring the milk to the boil, then reduce the heat, partially cover the pan with a lid and simmer for about 20 minutes, or until the cauliflower is tender.

3 Let the mixture cool for a few minutes, then transfer to a blender and process until smooth (you may have to do this in two batches). Return the purée to the pan and heat through gently, checking and adjusting the seasoning, and serve immediately, garnished with coriander.

Energy 137Kcal/579kJ; Protein 11g; Carbohydrate 14g, of which sugars 12g; Fat 5g, of which saturates 2g; Cholesterol 11mg; Calcium 268mg; Fibre 2.3g; Sodium 200mg

TUSCAN BEAN SOUP

CAVOLO NERO, A VERY DARK GREEN CABBAGE WITH A NUTTY FLAVOUR FROM TUSCANY AND SOUTHERN ITALY, IS IDEAL FOR THIS TRADITIONAL RECIPE. IF YOU CAN'T GET IT, USE SAVOY CABBAGE INSTEAD.

Preparation: 5 minutes; Cooking: 20 minutes

SERVES FOUR

INGREDIENTS

2 x 400g/14oz cans chopped
  tomatoes with herbs
250g/9oz cavolo nero leaves
400g/14oz can cannellini beans
salt and ground black pepper
60ml/4 tbsp extra virgin
  olive oil, to serve

1 Pour the tomatoes into a large pan and add a can of cold water. Season with salt and pepper and bring to the boil, then reduce the heat to a simmer.

2 Roughly shred the cabbage leaves and add them to the pan. Partially cover the pan and simmer gently for about 15 minutes, or until the cabbage is tender.

3 Drain and rinse the cannellini beans, add to the pan and warm through for a few minutes. Check and adjust the seasoning, then ladle the soup into bowls and drizzle each one with a little olive oil and serve.

Energy 209Kcal/877kJ; Protein 8g; Carbohydrate 19g, of which sugars 9g; Fat 12g, of which saturates 2g; Cholesterol 0mg; Calcium 79mg; Fibre 6.6g; Sodium 500mg

PARSNIP SOUP

THIS LIGHTLY SPICED SOUP HAS BECOME POPULAR IN RECENT YEARS AND VARIATIONS ABOUND,
INCLUDING A TRADITIONAL COMBINATION OF PARSNIP AND APPLE IN EQUAL PROPORTIONS.

Preparation: 5 minutes; Cooking: 25 minutes

SERVES SIX

INGREDIENTS
900g/2lb parsnips
50g/2oz/¼ cup butter
1 onion, chopped
2 garlic cloves, crushed
10ml/2 tsp ground cumin
5ml/1 tsp ground coriander
about 1.2 litres/2 pints/5 cups hot
   chicken stock
150ml/¼ pint/¾ cup single (light)
   cream
salt and ground black pepper
chopped fresh chives or parsley
   and/or croutons, to garnish

COOK'S TIP
If the parsnips are very large and have a
dense, woody core, discard this and use
only the outer flesh.

1 Peel and thinly slice the parsnips.
Heat the butter in a large heavy pan
and add the sliced parsnips and
chopped onion with the crushed garlic.
Cook until softened but not coloured,
stirring occasionally. Add the ground
cumin and ground coriander to the
vegetable mixture and cook, stirring, for
1–2 minutes, and then gradually blend
in the hot chicken stock and mix well.

2 Cover and simmer for about 20
minutes, or until the parsnip is soft.
Purée the soup, adjust the texture with
extra stock or water if it seems too
thick, and check the seasoning. Add
the cream and reheat without boiling.

3 Serve immediately, sprinkled with
chopped chives or parsley and/or
croutons, to garnish.

Energy 325Kcal/1355kJ; Protein 5.9g; Carbohydrate 32.1g, of which sugars 15.9g; Fat 20.1g, of which saturates 11.5g; Cholesterol 47mg; Calcium 138mg; Fibre 10.9g; Sodium 233mg

STILTON AND WATERCRESS SOUP

*A GOOD CREAMY STILTON AND PLENTY OF PEPPERY WATERCRESS BRING MAXIMUM FLAVOUR TO THIS
RICH, SMOOTH SOUP, WHICH IS SUPERLATIVE IN SMALL PORTIONS AND VERY QUICK TO PREPARE.*
Preparation: 6 minutes; Cooking: 8 minutes

SERVES FOUR TO SIX

INGREDIENTS
600ml/1 pint/2½ cups chicken or
  vegetable stock
225g/8oz watercress
150g/5oz Stilton or other blue cheese
150ml/¼ pint/⅔ cup single
  (light) cream

1 Pour the stock into a pan and bring almost to the boil. Remove and discard any very large stalks from the watercress. Add the watercress to the pan and simmer gently for 2–3 minutes, until tender.

2 Crumble the cheese into the pan and simmer for 1 minute more, until the cheese has started to melt. Process the soup in a blender or food processor, in batches if necessary, until very smooth. Return the soup to the pan.

3 Stir in the cream and check the seasoning. The soup will probably not need any extra salt, as the blue cheese is already quite salty. Heat the soup gently, without boiling, then ladle it into warm bowls.

COOK'S TIP
Rocket (arugula) can be used as an alternative to watercress – both leaves are an excellent source of iron. When choosing any salad leaves, look for crisp, fresh leaves and reject any wilted or discoloured greens.

Energy 162Kcal/671kJ; Protein 8g; Carbohydrate 1g, of which sugars 1g; Fat 14g, of which saturates 9g; Cholesterol 38mg; Calcium 169mg; Fibre 0.6g; Sodium 400mg

CLAM CHOWDER

IF FRESH CLAMS ARE HARD TO FIND, USE FROZEN OR CANNED CLAMS FOR THIS CLASSIC RECIPE FROM NEW ENGLAND. RESERVE A FEW CLAMS IN THEIR SHELLS FOR GARNISH, IF YOU LIKE.

Preparation: 5 minutes; Cooking: 25 minutes

SERVES FOUR

INGREDIENTS
100g/3¾ oz salt pork or thinly sliced
   unsmoked bacon, diced
1 large onion, chopped
2 potatoes, peeled and cut into
   1cm/½in cubes
1 bay leaf
1 fresh thyme sprig
300ml/½ pint/1¼ cups milk
400g/14oz cooked clams, cooking
   liquid reserved, cut up if large
150ml/¼ pint/⅔ cup double (heavy)
   cream
salt, ground white pepper and
   cayenne pepper
chopped fresh parsley, to garnish

1 Put the salt pork or unsmoked bacon in a pan, and heat gently, stirring frequently, until the fat runs and the meat is starting to brown. Add the chopped onion and fry over a low heat until softened but not browned.

2 Add the cubed potatoes, the bay leaf and thyme sprig, stir well to coat with fat, then pour in the milk and reserved clam liquid and bring to the boil. Lower the heat and simmer for about 10 minutes, until the potatoes are tender but still firm. Lift out the bay leaf and thyme sprig and discard.

3 Remove the shells from most of the clams. Add all the clams to the pan and season to taste with salt, pepper and cayenne. Simmer gently for 5 minutes more, then stir in the cream. Heat until the soup is very hot, but do not allow it to boil. Pour into a tureen, garnish with the chopped parsley and serve.

Energy 374kcal/1557kJ; Protein 23.9g; Carbohydrate 11.3g, of which sugars 5.3g; Fat 26.3g, of which saturates 15.1g; Cholesterol 136mg; Calcium 189mg; Fibre 0.5g; Sodium 1629mg.

CHINESE CRAB AND CORN SOUP

FROZEN WHITE CRAB MEAT WORKS AS WELL AS FRESH IN THIS DELICATELY FLAVOURED SOUP.

Preparation: 6 minutes; Cooking: 10 minutes

SERVES FOUR

INGREDIENTS
600ml/1 pint/2½ cups fish or
   chicken stock
2.5cm/1in piece fresh root ginger,
   peeled and very finely sliced
400g/14oz can creamed corn
150g/5oz cooked white crab meat
15ml/1 tbsp arrowroot or cornflour
   (cornstarch)
15ml/1 tbsp rice wine or dry sherry
15–30ml/1–2 tbsp light soy sauce
1 egg white
salt and ground white pepper
shredded spring onions (scallions),
   to garnish

1 Put the stock and ginger in a large saucepan and bring to the boil. Stir in the creamed sweetcorn and bring back to the boil.

2 Switch off the heat and add the crab meat. Put the arrowroot or cornflour in a cup and stir in the rice wine or sherry to make a smooth paste; stir this into the soup. Cook over a low heat for about 4 minutes until the soup has thickened and is slightly glutinous in consistency. Add light soy sauce, salt and white pepper to taste.

3 In a bowl, whisk the egg white to a stiff foam. Gradually fold it into the soup. Ladle the soup into heated bowls, garnish each portion with spring onions and serve.

COOK'S TIP
This soup is sometimes made with whole kernel corn, but creamed corn gives a better texture. If you can't find it in a can, use thawed frozen creamed corn.

Energy 194kcal/821kJ; Protein 10.5g; Carbohydrate 30.1g, of which sugars 9.7g; Fat 3.9g, of which saturates 0.6g; Cholesterol 27mg; Calcium 50mg; Fibre 1.4g; Sodium 494mg.

TAPAS OF ALMONDS, OLIVES AND CHEESE

SERVING A FEW CHOICE NIBBLES WITH DRINKS IS THE PERFECT WAY TO GET AN EVENING OFF TO A GOOD START, AND WHEN YOU CAN GET EVERYTHING READY AHEAD OF TIME, LIFE'S EASIER ALL ROUND.

Preparation: 10–15 minutes; Cooking: 5 minutes; Make ahead

SERVES SIX TO EIGHT

INGREDIENTS

For the marinated olives
2.5ml/½ tsp coriander seeds
2.5ml/½ tsp fennel seeds
2 garlic cloves, crushed
5ml/1 tsp chopped fresh rosemary
10ml/2 tsp chopped fresh parsley
15ml/1 tbsp sherry vinegar
30ml/2 tbsp olive oil
115g/4oz/⅔ cup black olives
115g/4oz/⅔ cup green olives

For the marinated cheese
150g/5oz Manchego or other
   firm cheese
90ml/6 tbsp olive oil
15ml/1 tbsp white wine vinegar
5ml/1 tsp black peppercorns
1 garlic clove, sliced
fresh thyme or tarragon sprigs
fresh flat leaf parsley or tarragon
   sprigs, to garnish (optional)

For the salted almonds
1.5ml/¼ tsp cayenne pepper
30ml/2 tbsp sea salt
25g/1oz/2 tbsp butter
60ml/4 tbsp olive oil
200g/7oz/1¾ cups blanched
   almonds
extra salt for sprinkling (optional)

1 To make the marinated olives, crush the coriander and fennel seeds in a mortar with a pestle. Work in the garlic, then add the rosemary, parsley, vinegar and olive oil. Mix well. Put the olives in a small bowl and pour over the marinade. Cover with clear film (plastic wrap) and chill for up to 1 week.

2 To make the marinated cheese, cut the Manchego or other firm cheese into bitesize pieces, removing any rind, and put in a small bowl. Combine the oil, vinegar, peppercorns, garlic, thyme or tarragon and pour over the cheese. Cover with clear film and chill for up to 3 days.

3 To make the salted almonds, combine the cayenne pepper and salt in a bowl. Melt the butter with the oil in a frying pan. Add the almonds and fry them, stirring, for 5 minutes, or until golden.

4 Tip the almonds into the salt mixture and toss until the almonds are coated. Leave to cool, then store in an airtight container for up to 1 week.

5 To serve, arrange the almonds, olives and cheese in three separate small, shallow dishes. Garnish the cheese with fresh herbs if you like and sprinkle the almonds with a little more salt, to taste. Provide cocktail sticks (toothpicks) so that guests can pick up the cheese and olives easily.

COOK'S TIPS
• Whole olives, sold with the stone, invariably taste better than pitted ones. Don't serve them directly from the brine, but drain and rinse them, then pat dry with kitchen paper. Put the olives in a jar and pour over extra virgin olive oil to cover. Seal and store in the refrigerator for 1–2 months; the flavour of the olives will become richer. Serve the olives as a tapas dish, or add to salads. When the olives have been eaten, the fruity oil can be used as a dressing for hot food, or made into flavoursome salad dressings.
• A number of exotic stuffed olives are exported from Spain and are widely available in most large supermarkets. Popular varieties include pimiento-stuffed olives, which have been in existence for more than half a century; olives stuffed with salted anchovies; and olives filled with roast garlic.

Energy 383kcal/1580kJ; Protein 10.3g; Carbohydrate 1.8g, of which sugars 1.1g; Fat 36.8g, of which saturates 8.9g; Cholesterol 25mg; Calcium 217mg; Fibre 2.7g; Sodium 1051mg

ARTICHOKE AND CUMIN DIP

THIS DIP IS SO EASY TO MAKE AND IS UNBELIEVABLY TASTY. SERVE WITH OLIVES, HUMMUS AND WEDGES OF PITTA BREAD AS AN INFORMAL SUMMERY SNACK SELECTION.

Preparation: 2 minutes; Cooking: 0 minutes

SERVES FOUR

INGREDIENTS

 2 x 400g/14oz cans artichoke
  hearts, drained
 2 garlic cloves, peeled
 2.5ml/½ tsp ground cumin
 olive oil
 salt and ground black pepper

VARIATIONS
Grilled (broiled) artichokes bottled in oil have a fabulous flavour and can be used instead of canned artichokes. Try adding a handful of basil leaves to the artichokes before blending.

1 Put the artichoke hearts in a food processor with the garlic and ground cumin, and add a generous drizzle of olive oil. Process to a smooth purée and season with plenty of salt and ground black pepper to taste.

2 Spoon the purée into a serving bowl and serve with an extra drizzle of olive oil swirled on the top and slices of warm pitta bread or wholemeal (wholewheat) toast fingers and carrot sticks for dipping.

Energy 76kcal/315kJ; Protein 1.6g; Carbohydrate 3.9g, of which sugars 3.5g; Fat 6.2g, of which saturates 1g; Cholesterol 0mg; Calcium 18mg; Fibre 3.5g; Sodium 4mg

GUACAMOLE

NACHOS OR TORTILLA CHIPS ARE THE PERFECT ACCOMPANIMENT FOR THIS CLASSIC MEXICAN DIP,
WHICH NOT ONLY TASTES DELICIOUSLY FRESH BUT ALSO TAKES JUST MINUTES TO PREPARE.

Preparation: 5 minutes; Cooking: 0 minutes

SERVES FOUR

INGREDIENTS
2 ripe avocados
2 red chillies, seeded
1 garlic clove
1 shallot
30ml/2 tbsp olive oil,
  plus extra to serve
juice of 1 lemon
salt
flat leaf parsley leaves, to garnish

1 Halve the avocados, remove their stones (pits) and, using a spoon, scoop out their flesh into a bowl.

2 Mash the flesh well with a large fork or a potato masher.

COOK'S TIP
The lemon juice prevents the avocado flesh from discolouring once it is exposed to the air. However, even with lemon juice in a recipe, it is still sensible to prepare avocado dishes shortly before they are to be eaten rather than hours in advance.

3 Finely chop the chillies, garlic and shallot, then stir into the mashed avocado with the olive oil and lemon juice. Add salt to taste.

4 Spoon the mixture into a small serving bowl. Drizzle over a little olive oil and scatter with a few flat leaf parsley leaves. Serve.

Energy 151kcal/623kJ; Protein 1.2g; Carbohydrate 2.4g, of which sugars 1.3g; Fat 15.2g, of which saturates 2.9g; Cholesterol 0mg; Calcium 10mg; Fibre 2g; Sodium 4mg.

MUHAMMARA

THIS THICK, ROASTED RED PEPPER AND WALNUT PURÉE IS BELOVED IN THE MIDDLE EAST. SERVE IT AS A DIP WITH SPEARS OF COS OR ROMAINE LETTUCE, WEDGES OF PITTA BREAD AND CHUNKS OF TOMATO.

Preparation: 8 minutes; Cooking: 0 minutes

SERVES FOUR

INGREDIENTS

1½ slices Granary (whole-wheat) bread, day-old or toasted
3 red (bell) peppers, roasted, skinned and chopped
2 very mild chillies, roasted, skinned and chopped
115g/4oz/1 cup walnut pieces
3–4 garlic cloves, chopped
15–30ml/1–2 tbsp balsamic vinegar or pomegranate molasses
juice of ½ lemon
2.5–5ml/½–1 tsp ground cumin
2.5ml/½ tsp sugar, or to taste
105ml/7 tbsp extra virgin olive oil
salt

1 Break the Granary bread into small pieces and place in a food processor or blender with all the remaining ingredients except the extra virgin olive oil. Blend together until the ingredients are finely chopped.

2 With the motor running, slowly drizzle the extra virgin olive oil into the food processor or blender and process until the mixture forms a smooth paste. Tip the muhammara into a serving dish. Serve at room temperature.

Energy 444kcal/1833kJ; Protein 6.8g; Carbohydrate 15.5g, of which sugars 9.9g; Fat 39.8g, of which saturates 4.6g; Cholesterol 0mg; Calcium 62mg; Fibre 3.7g; Sodium 69mg.

HUMMUS

THIS CLASSIC MIDDLE EASTERN DISH IS MADE FROM COOKED CHICKPEAS, GROUND TO A PASTE AND FLAVOURED WITH GARLIC, LEMON JUICE, TAHINI, OLIVE OIL AND CUMIN. SERVE WITH PITTA WEDGES.

Preparation: 5 minutes; Cooking: 0 minutes

SERVES FOUR TO SIX

INGREDIENTS

400g/14oz can chickpeas, drained
60ml/4 tbsp tahini
2–3 garlic cloves, chopped
juice of ½–1 lemon
cayenne pepper to taste
small pinch to 1.5ml/¼ tsp ground
  cumin, or more to taste
salt and ground black pepper

VARIATION
Process 2 roasted red (bell) peppers with the chickpeas, then continue as above. Serve sprinkled with lightly toasted pine nuts and paprika mixed with olive oil.

1 Using a potato masher or food processor, coarsely mash the chickpeas. If you prefer a smoother purée, process them in a food processor or blender until smooth.

2 Mix the tahini into the chickpeas, then stir in the garlic, lemon juice, cayenne, cumin and salt and pepper to taste. If needed, add a little water. Serve at room temperature.

Energy 140kcal/586kJ; Protein 6.9g; Carbohydrate 11.2g, of which sugars 0.4g; Fat 7.8g, of which saturates 1.1g; Cholesterol 0mg; Calcium 97mg; Fibre 3.6g; Sodium 149mg.

SMOKED MACKEREL PATÉ

THIS TASTY PATÉ BENEFITS FROM BEING CHILLED FOR A COUPLE OF HOURS, BUT IF YOU HAVEN'T GOT TIME FOR THAT, SERVE IT RIGHT AWAY. IT WON'T BE AS FIRM, BUT WILL TASTE JUST AS DELICIOUS.

Preparation: 2–3 minutes; Cooking: 20 minutes; Chilling: 1–2 hours (optional)

SERVES SIX

INGREDIENTS
  4 smoked mackerel fillets, skinned
  225g/8oz/1 cup cream cheese
  1–2 garlic cloves, finely chopped
  juice of 1 lemon
  30ml/2 tbsp chopped fresh chervil,
    parsley or chives
  15ml/1 tbsp Worcestershire sauce
  salt and cayenne pepper
  fresh chives, to garnish
  warmed Melba toast, to serve

VARIATION
Use peppered mackerel fillets for a more piquant flavour. This pâté is also delicious when prepared using smoked haddock or kipper (smoked herring) fillets.

1 Break up the smoked mackerel fillets and put them in a food processor. Add the cream cheese, chopped garlic and lemon juice.

2 Process the mixture for a few seconds, just long enough to mix the ingredients, then add the chopped chervil, parsley or chives.

3 Process the mixture until it is fairly smooth but still slightly chunky, then add Worcestershire sauce, salt and cayenne pepper to taste. Process again to mix.

4 Spoon the pâté into a dish, cover with clear film (plastic wrap) and chill. Garnish with chives and serve with Melba toast.

Energy 344kcal/1421kJ; Protein 10.7g; Carbohydrate 0.5g, of which sugars 0.4g; Fat 33.3g, of which saturates 14.3g; Cholesterol 88mg; Calcium 57mg; Fibre 0.1g; Sodium 518mg

CHICKEN LIVER <u>AND</u> BRANDY PATÉ

THIS PATÉ REALLY COULD NOT BE SIMPLER TO PUT TOGETHER, AND TASTES SO MUCH BETTER THAN ANYTHING YOU CAN BUY READY-MADE IN THE SUPERMARKETS. SERVE WITH CRISPY MELBA TOAST.

Preparation: 3 minutes; Cooking: 5–6 minutes; Make ahead

SERVES FOUR

INGREDIENTS

50g/2oz/¼ cup butter
350g/12oz chicken livers, trimmed
  and roughly chopped
30ml/2 tbsp brandy
30ml/2 tbsp double (heavy) cream
salt and ground black pepper

1 Heat the butter in a large frying pan. Add the chicken livers. Cook over a medium heat for 3–4 minutes, or until browned and cooked through.

2 Add the brandy and allow to bubble for a few minutes. Let the mixture cool slightly, then place in a food processor with the cream and some salt and pepper.

3 Process the mixture until smooth and spoon into ramekin dishes. Level the surface and chill overnight to set. If making more than 1 day ahead, seal the surface of each portion with a layer of melted butter. Serve garnished with sprigs of parsley to add a little colour.

Energy 227kcal/942kJ; Protein 15.7g; Carbohydrate 0.2g, of which sugars 0.2g; Fat 16.3g, of which saturates 9.6g; Cholesterol 369mg; Calcium 13mg; Fibre 0g; Sodium 144mg

MELTING CHEESE DIP

THIS IS A CLASSIC FONDUE IN TRUE SWISS STYLE. IT SHOULD BE SERVED WITH CUBES OF CRUSTY,
DAY-OLD BREAD, BUT IT IS ALSO GOOD WITH CHUNKS OF SPICY, CURED SAUSAGE SUCH AS CHORIZO.

Preparation: 3 minutes; Cooking: 7 minutes

SERVES TWO

INGREDIENTS

1 garlic clove, finely chopped
150ml/¼ pint/⅔ cup dry white wine
150g/5oz Gruyère cheese
5ml/1 tsp cornflour (cornstarch)
15ml/1 tbsp Kirsch
salt and ground black pepper
bread or chorizo cubes, to serve

COOK'S TIP
Gruyére is a tasty cheese that melts
incredibly well. Don't substitute other
cheeses in this dip.

1 Place the garlic and wine in a small
pan and bring gently to the boil. Lower
the heat and simmer for 3–4 minutes.

2 Coarsely grate the cheese and stir it
into the wine. Continue to stir as the
cheese melts.

3 Blend the cornflour to a smooth paste
with the Kirsch and pour into the pan,
stirring. Bring to the boil, stirring
continuously until the sauce is smooth
and thickened.

4 Add salt and pepper to taste. Serve
immediately in heated bowls or transfer
to a fondue pan and keep hot over a
spirit burner. Garnish with black pepper
and serve with bread or chorizo cubes.

Energy 390kcal/1617kJ; Protein 19.4g; Carbohydrate 3.3g, of which sugars 0.6g; Fat 24.6g, of which saturates 16.3g; Cholesterol 73mg; Calcium 562mg; Fibre 0.1g; Sodium 547mg.

FIGS <u>WITH</u> PROSCIUTTO <u>AND</u> ROQUEFORT

IN THIS EASY, STYLISH DISH, FIGS AND HONEY BALANCE THE RICHNESS OF THE HAM AND CHEESE.
SERVE WITH WARM BREAD FOR A SIMPLE APPETIZER BEFORE ANY RICH MAIN COURSE.
Preparation: 2–3 minutes; Cooking: 4–5 minutes

SERVES FOUR

INGREDIENTS
    8 fresh figs
    75g/3oz prosciutto
    45ml/3 tbsp clear honey
    75g/3oz Roquefort cheese
    ground black pepper

COOK'S TIP
Fresh figs are a delicious treat, whether you choose dark purple, yellow green or green-skinned varieties. When they are ripe, you can split them open with your fingers to reveal the soft, sweet flesh full of edible seeds. They also taste great stuffed with goat's cheese.

1 Preheat the grill (broiler). Quarter the figs and place on a foil-lined grill rack. Tear each slice of prosciutto into two or three pieces. Crumple the pieces of prosciutto and place them on the foil beside the figs. Brush the figs with 15ml/1 tbsp of the clear honey and cook under the grill until lightly browned.

2 Crumble the Roquefort cheese and divide among four plates, setting it to one side. Add the honey-grilled figs and ham and pour over any cooking juices caught on the foil. Drizzle the remaining honey over the figs, ham and cheese, and serve seasoned with plenty of ground black pepper.

Energy 326kcal/1378kJ; Protein 10.7g; Carbohydrate 57.4g, of which sugars 57.4g; Fat 7.5g, of which saturates 3.8g; Cholesterol 25mg; Calcium 324mg; Fibre 6.9g; Sodium 512mg

WHITE BEANS IN A SPICY DRESSING

TENDER WHITE BEANS ARE DELICIOUS IN THIS SPICY SAUCE WITH THE BITE OF FRESH, CRUNCHY GREEN PEPPER AND THE FLAVOUR OF JUICY TOMATOES. IT IS PERFECT FOR PREPARING AHEAD OF TIME.

Preparation: 7 minutes; Cooking: 0 minutes

SERVES FOUR

INGREDIENTS

750g/1⅔lb tomatoes, diced
1 onion, finely chopped
½–1 mild fresh chilli, finely chopped
1 green (bell) pepper, seeded
  and chopped
pinch of sugar
4 garlic cloves, chopped
400g/14oz can cannellini beans,
  drained
45–60ml/3–4 tbsp olive oil
grated rind and juice of 1 lemon
15ml/1 tbsp cider vinegar or
  wine vinegar
salt and ground black pepper
chopped fresh parsley, to garnish

1 Put the tomatoes, onion, chilli, green pepper, sugar, garlic, cannellini beans, salt and plenty of ground black pepper in a large bowl and toss together until well combined.

2 Add the olive oil, grated lemon rind, lemon juice and vinegar to the salad and toss lightly to combine. Chill. Garnish with chopped parsley and serve with toasted pitta breads.

Energy 391kcal/1654kJ; Protein 24g; Carbohydrate 53.8g, of which sugars 11.8g; Fat 10.4g, of which saturates 1.6g; Cholesterol 0mg; Calcium 120mg; Fibre 18.5g; Sodium 37mg.

VEGETARIAN CHOPPED LIVER

THIS MIXTURE OF BROWNED ONIONS, CHOPPED VEGETABLES, HARD-BOILED EGG AND WALNUTS LOOKS AND TASTES SURPRISINGLY LIKE CHOPPED LIVER BUT IS LIGHTER AND FRESHER.

Preparation: 7–8 minutes; Cooking: 8 minutes

SERVES SIX

INGREDIENTS

90ml/6 tbsp vegetable oil, plus extra
  if necessary
3 onions, chopped
175–200g/6–7oz/1½–scant 1¾ cups
  frozen peas
115–150g/4–5oz/1 cup green beans,
  roughly chopped
15 walnuts, shelled (30 halves)
3 eggs
salt and ground black pepper
slices of rye bread or crisp matzos,
  to serve

1 Boil the eggs in a pan of water for 4–5 minutes. Drain, plunge into cold water and leave until cold, then shell.

2 Meanwhile, heat the oil in a pan, add the onions and fry until softened and lightly browned. Add the peas and beans and season with salt and pepper to taste. Continue to cook until the beans and peas are tender and the beans are no longer bright green.

3 Put the vegetables in a food processor, add the walnuts and eggs and process until the mixture forms a thick paste. Taste for seasoning and, if the mixture seems a bit dry, add a little more oil and mix in thoroughly. Serve with slices of rye bread or matzos.

Energy 309kcal/1277kJ; Protein 9g; Carbohydrate 11.1g, of which sugars 6.2g; Fat 25.9g, of which saturates 3.4g; Cholesterol 95mg; Calcium 64mg; Fibre 3.6g; Sodium 39mg.

MELON AND GRAPEFRUIT COCKTAIL

THIS PRETTY, COLOURFUL STARTER IS PERFECT FOR ALL THOSE OCCASIONS WHEN YOU DON'T HAVE MUCH TIME FOR COOKING, BUT WANT SOMETHING REALLY SPECIAL TO EAT.

Preparation: 8 minutes; Cooking: 0 minutes

SERVES FOUR

INGREDIENTS

1 small Ogen melon
1 small Charentais melon
2 pink grapefruit
45ml/3 tbsp orange juice
60ml/4 tbsp red vermouth
seeds from ½ pomegranate
mint sprigs, to garnish

1 Halve the melons lengthways and scoop out all the seeds. Cut into wedges and remove the skins, then cut across into large bitesize pieces. Set aside while you prepare the grapefruit.

2 Using a small sharp knife, cut the peel and pith from the grapefruit. Holding the fruit over a bowl to catch the juice, cut between the grapefruit membranes to release the segments.

3 Stir the orange juice and vermouth into the reserved grapefruit juice.

4 Arrange the melon pieces and grapefruit segments on four individual serving plates.

5 Spoon over the dressing, then scatter with the pomegranate seeds. Decorate with mint sprigs before serving.

COOK'S TIP
Handle the grapefruit segments gently – they can break up easily and the appearance of the dish will be spoiled.

Energy 111kcal/468kJ; Protein 2g; Carbohydrate 22.8g, of which sugars 22.8g; Fat 0.4g, of which saturates 0g; Cholesterol 0mg; Calcium 53mg; Fibre 2.1g; Sodium 85mg.

MELON, PINEAPPLE AND GRAPE COCKTAIL

A LIGHT FRESH FRUIT SALAD, WITH NO ADDED SUGAR, MAKES A REFRESHING AND SPEEDY APPETIZER THAT WAKES UP THE TASTEBUDS READY FOR THE REST OF THE MEAL.

Preparation: 6 minutes; Cooking: 0 minutes

SERVES FOUR

INGREDIENTS
½ melon
225g/8oz fresh pineapple
225g/8oz seedless white
  grapes, halved
120ml/4fl oz/½ cup white
  grape juice
fresh mint leaves, to garnish

COOK'S TIP
To save even more time, use a 225g/8oz can of pineapple chunks in natural juice. Drain the chunks, reserving the juice in a measuring jug. Make it up to the required quantity for pouring over the fruit with white grape juice.

1 Remove the seeds from the melon half and use a melon baller to scoop out even-size balls.

2 Using a sharp knife, cut the skin from the pineapple. Cut the fruit into bite-size chunks.

3 Combine all the fruits in a glass serving dish and pour over the white grape juice. Serve immediately or cover and chill until required. Garnish with mint leaves.

Energy 86kcal/366kJ; Protein 0.9g; Carbohydrate 21.4g, of which sugars 21.4g; Fat 0.3g, of which saturates 0g; Cholesterol 0mg; Calcium 31mg; Fibre 1.3g; Sodium 24mg.

SWEET AND SOUR CUCUMBER WITH FRESH DILL

THIS DISH IS HALF PICKLE, HALF SALAD, AND TOTALLY DELICIOUS SERVED AS A BRUNCH OR APPETIZER.
SERVE WITH THIN SLICES OF PUMPERNICKEL OR OTHER COARSE, DARK, FULL-FLAVOURED BREAD.

Preparation: 10–12 minutes; Cooking: 0 minutes

SERVES FOUR

INGREDIENTS
  1 large or 2 small cucumbers,
    thinly sliced
  3 onions, thinly sliced
  45ml/3 tbsp sugar
  75–90ml/5–6 tbsp white wine vinegar
    or cider vinegar
  30–45ml/2–3 tbsp water
  30–45ml/2–3 tbsp chopped
    fresh dill
  salt

COOK'S TIP
This salad can be kept in the refrigerator
for up to a week.

1 In a bowl, mix together the sliced cucumber and onion, season with salt and toss together until thoroughly combined. Leave to stand in a cool place for 5–10 minutes.

2 Add the sugar, vinegar, water and chopped dill to the cucumber mixture. Toss together until well combined, then chill for a few hours, or until ready to serve.

Energy 89kcal/375kJ; Protein 2g; Carbohydrate 20.7g, of which sugars 18.3g; Fat 0.4g, of which saturates 0g; Cholesterol 0mg; Calcium 63mg; Fibre 2.3g; Sodium 9mg.

TABBOULEH

THIS IS A WONDERFULLY REFRESHING, TANGY SALAD OF SOAKED BULGUR WHEAT AND MASSES OF FRESH MINT, PARSLEY AND SPRING ONIONS. IT CAN BE SERVED AS AN APPETIZER OR AS A SIDE DISH.

Preparation: 30 minutes; Cooking: 0 minutes

SERVES FOUR TO SIX

INGREDIENTS
  250g/9oz/1½ cups bulgur wheat
  1 large bunch spring onions
    (scallions), thinly sliced
  1 cucumber, finely chopped or diced
  3 tomatoes, chopped
  1.5–2.5ml/¼–½ tsp ground cumin
  1 large bunch fresh parsley, chopped
  1 large bunch fresh mint, chopped
  juice of 2 lemons, or to taste
  60ml/4 tbsp extra virgin olive oil
  salt
  olives, lemon wedges, tomato wedges,
    cucumber slices and mint sprigs, to
    garnish (optional)
  cos or romaine lettuce and natural
    (plain) yogurt, to serve (optional)

1 Pick over the bulgur wheat to remove any dirt. Place it in a bowl, cover with cold water and leave to soak for about 25 minutes. Tip the bulgur wheat into a sieve and drain well, shaking to remove any excess water, then return to the bowl.

2 Add the spring onions to the bulgur wheat, then mix and squeeze together with your hands to combine.

3 Add the cucumber, tomatoes, cumin, parsley, mint, lemon juice, oil and salt to the bulgur wheat and toss to combine.

4 Heap the tabbouleh on to a bed of lettuce and garnish with olives, lemon and tomato wedges, cucumber slices and mint sprigs, if you like. Serve with a bowl of natural yogurt, if you like.

VARIATION
Use couscous soaked in boiling water in place of the bulgur wheat and use chopped fresh coriander (cilantro) instead of parsley.

Energy 204kcal/848kJ; Protein 4.3g; Carbohydrate 24.8g, of which sugars 3.3g; Fat 10.3g, of which saturates 1.4g; Cholesterol 0mg; Calcium 91mg; Fibre 2.6g; Sodium 18mg.

QUAIL'S EGGS WITH HERBS

FOR AL FRESCO EATING OR LIGHT ENTERTAINING, THIS PLATTER OF CONTRASTING TASTES AND TEXTURES IS PERFECT FOR A RELAXED ATMOSPHERE. THE PRETTY EGGSHELLS ADD EXTRA APPEAL TO THE DISH.

Preparation: 10 minutes; Cooking: 10–15 minutes

SERVES SIX

INGREDIENTS

1 large Italian focaccia or 2–3 Indian
  parathas or other flatbreads
olive oil, for brushing and dipping
1 large garlic clove, finely chopped
small handful of fresh mixed herbs,
  such as coriander (cilantro), mint,
  parsley and oregano, chopped
18–24 quail's eggs
30ml/2 tbsp mayonnaise
30ml/2 tbsp sour cream
5ml/1 tsp chopped capers
5ml/1 tsp finely chopped shallot
225g/8oz fresh beetroot (beet),
  cooked in water or cider, peeled and
  sliced
½ bunch spring onions (scallions),
  trimmed and halved lengthways
60ml/4 tbsp red onion or tamarind
  and date chutney
coarse sea salt
mixed peppercorns, roughly ground

1 Preheat the oven to 190ºC/375ºF/
Gas 5. Brush the bread with olive oil,
sprinkle with garlic, mixed herbs and
seasoning, and bake for 10–15 minutes,
or until golden. Keep warm.

2 Meanwhile, put the quail's eggs into
a pan of cold water. Bring the water to
the boil and cook for 5 minutes. Lift out
of the pan using a slotted spoon and
place in a bowl of cold water. Leave
to cool.

3 Make the mayonnaise dip. Mix
together the mayonnaise, sour cream,
capers, shallot and seasoning. Peel the
eggs or leave the guests to shell their
own, and arrange in a serving dish.

4 Cut the bread into wedges and serve
with the eggs and mayonnaise dip,
along with dishes of beetroot, spring
onions and chutney. Serve with bowls of
coarse salt, ground peppercorns and
olive oil for dipping.

Energy 248kcal/1044kJ; Protein 10.8g; Carbohydrate 29g, of which sugars 9.1g; Fat 10.9g, of which saturates 2.8g; Cholesterol 197mg; Calcium 98mg; Fibre 1.9g; Sodium 301mg.

BAKED EGGS WITH CREAMY LEEKS

THIS SIMPLE BUT ELEGANT APPETIZER CAN ALSO BE MADE WITH OTHER VEGETABLES SUCH AS SPINACH PURÉE OR RATATOUILLE. IT IS PERFECT FOR LAST-MINUTE ENTERTAINING OR QUICK DINING.

Preparation: 10 minutes; Cooking: 20 minutes

SERVES FOUR

INGREDIENTS

15g/½ oz/1 tbsp butter, plus extra
    for greasing
225g/8oz small leeks, thinly sliced
75–90ml/5–6 tbsp whipping cream
freshly grated nutmeg
4 small/medium eggs
a few sage leaves
sunflower oil
salt and ground black pepper

VARIATION

For a slightly different result, beat the eggs with the remaining cream and seasoning in step 4 and spoon over the leeks. Bake as normal.

1 Preheat the oven to 190°C/375°F/ Gas 5. Generously butter the base and sides of four ramekins.

2 Melt the butter in a frying pan and cook the leeks for 3–5 minutes over medium heat, stirring frequently, until softened but not browned.

3 Add 45ml/3 tbsp of the cream and cook over a gentle heat for 5 minutes, until the leeks are very soft and the cream has thickened a little. Season with salt, pepper and nutmeg.

4 Place the ramekins in a small roasting tin and divide the leeks among them. Break an egg into each, spoon over the remaining cream and add some pepper.

5 Pour boiling water into the tin to come about halfway up the sides of the dishes. Transfer the tin to the oven and bake for about 10 minutes, until just set.

6 While the eggs are baking, fry the sage leaves in a little oil until crisp and scatter over the top of the eggs to serve.

Energy 219Kcal/905kJ; Protein 9g; Carbohydrate 2g, of which sugars 2g; Fat 19g, of which saturates 10g; Cholesterol 261mg; Calcium 61g; Fibre 1.2g; Sodium 100mg

WALNUT AND GOAT'S CHEESE BRUSCHETTA

*THE COMBINATION OF TOASTED WALNUTS AND MELTING GOAT'S CHEESE IS LOVELY IN THIS SIMPLE
LUNCHTIME SNACK, WHICH CAN BE SERVED WITH A DRESSED SALAD IF THE OCCASION CALLS FOR IT.*

Preparation: 5 minutes; Cooking: 3–5 minutes

SERVES FOUR

INGREDIENTS

50g/2oz/½ cup walnut pieces
4 thick slices walnut bread
120ml/4fl oz/½ cup French dressing
200g/7oz chèvre or other semi-soft
  goat's cheese

COOK'S TIP
Walnut bread is sold in most large
supermarkets and makes an interesting
alternative to ordinary crusty bread,
although a freshly baked loaf of the
latter is fine if speciality breads are not
available. If using crusty bread, try to
find a slender loaf to slice, so that the
portions are not too wide. If you can only
buy a large loaf, cut the slices in half
to make neat, chunky pieces.

1 Preheat the grill (broiler). Spread out
the walnut pieces on a baking sheet.
Lightly toast them, shivering the baking
sheet once or twice so that they cook
evenly, then remove and set aside.

2 Put the walnut bread on a foil-lined
grill rack and toast on one side. Turn
the slices over and drizzle each with
15ml/1 tbsp of the dressing.

3 Cut the goat's cheese into twelve
slices and place three on each piece of
bread. Grill (broil) for about 3 minutes,
until the cheese is melting and
beginning to brown.

4 Transfer the bruschetta to serving
plates, sprinkle with the toasted walnuts
and drizzle with the remaining French
dressing. Serve the bruschetta
immediately with salad leaves.

Energy 558kcal/2321kJ; Protein 16.7g; Carbohydrate 25.6g, of which sugars 2.2g; Fat 37.2g, of which saturates 12.7g; Cholesterol 47mg; Calcium 137mg; Fibre 1.2g; Sodium 841mg

PEARS WITH BLUE CHEESE AND WALNUTS

SUCCULENT PEARS FILLED WITH BLUE CHEESE AND WALNUT CREAM LOOK PRETTY ON COLOURFUL
LEAVES AND MAKE A GREAT APPETIZER. THEY ARE QUITE RICH, SO KEEP THE MAIN COURSE SIMPLE.

Preparation: 8–10 minutes; Cooking: 0 minutes

SERVES SIX

INGREDIENTS
115g/4oz fresh cream cheese
75g/3oz Stilton or other mature blue
  cheese, such as Roquefort
30–45ml/2–3 tbsp single
  (light) cream
115g/4oz/1 cup roughly
  chopped walnuts
6 ripe pears
15ml/1 tbsp lemon juice
mixed salad leaves, such as frisée,
  oakleaf lettuce and radicchio
6 cherry tomatoes
sea salt and ground black pepper
walnut halves and sprigs of fresh
  flat leaf parsley, to garnish
For the dressing
juice of 1 lemon
a little finely grated lemon rind
a pinch of caster (superfine) sugar
60ml/4 tbsp olive oil

1 Mash the cream cheese and blue cheese together in a mixing bowl with a good grinding of black pepper, then blend in the cream to make a smooth mixture. Add 25g/1oz/¼ cup of the chopped walnuts and mix to distribute evenly.

2 Peel and halve the pears and scoop out the core from each. Put the pears into a bowl of water with the 15ml/ 1 tbsp lemon juice to prevent them from browning. Make the dressing by whisking the ingredients together with salt and pepper to taste.

3 Arrange a bed of salad leaves on six plates – shallow soup plates are ideal – add a cherry tomato to each and sprinkle over the remaining chopped walnuts.

4 Drain the pears well and pat dry with kitchen paper, then turn them in the prepared dressing and arrange, hollow side up, on the salad leaves.

5 Divide the blue cheese filling among the 12 pear halves and spoon the dressing over the top. Garnish each filled pear half with a walnut half and a sprig of flat leaf parsley before serving.

COOK'S TIP
You need small pears that are perfectly ripe for this recipe. Comice or Bartlett pears would be ideal.

Energy 322kcal/1332kJ; Protein 5.1g; Carbohydrate 15.7g, of which sugars 15.7g; Fat 26.9g, of which saturates 10.2g; Cholesterol 30mg; Calcium 109mg; Fibre 3.7g; Sodium 218mg

TOMATO AND MOZZARELLA TOASTS

THESE RESEMBLE MINI PIZZAS AND ARE GOOD WITH DRINKS BEFORE A DINNER PARTY. YOU CAN PREPARE
THEM SEVERAL HOURS IN ADVANCE AND POP THEM IN THE OVEN JUST AS YOUR GUESTS ARRIVE.

Preparation: 3 minutes; Cooking: 7 minutes

SERVES SIX TO EIGHT

INGREDIENTS
 3 sfilatini (thin ciabatta)
 about 250ml/8 fl oz/1 cup sun-dried
 tomato purée (paste)
 3 x 150g/5oz packets mozzarella
 cheese, drained and chopped
 about 10ml/2 tsp dried oregano or
 mixed herbs
 30–45ml/2–3 tbsp olive oil
 ground black pepper

COOK'S TIP
Mozzarella can also be bought as tiny
balls. If you prefer to use these, just
halve them and place on top of the
tomato purée.

1 Preheat the oven to 220°C/425°F/
Gas 7. Also preheat the grill (broiler).
Cut each sfilatino on the diagonal into
12–15 slices, discarding the ends. Grill
(broil) until lightly toasted on both sides.
Spread sun-dried tomato purée on one
side of each slice of toast. Arrange the
mozzarella over the tomato purée.

2 Put the toasts on baking sheets,
sprinkle with herbs and pepper to taste
and drizzle with oil. Bake for 5 minutes,
or until the mozzarella has melted and
is bubbling. Leave the toasts to settle
for a few minutes before serving.

Energy 227kcal/947kJ; Protein 13.3g; Carbohydrate 10.9g, of which sugars 4.8g; Fat 14.8g, of which saturates 8.2g; Cholesterol 33mg; Calcium 230mg; Fibre 1.2g; Sodium 365mg.

SALAD LEAVES ᵂᴵᵀᴴ GORGONZOLA

CRISPY FRIED PANCETTA MAKES A TASTY ADDITION AND CONTRASTS WELL IN TEXTURE AND FLAVOUR WITH THE SOFTNESS OF MIXED SALAD LEAVES AND THE SHARP TASTE OF GORGONZOLA.

Preparation: 5 minutes; Cooking: 5 minutes

SERVES FOUR

INGREDIENTS

225g/8oz pancetta rashers (strips),
   any rinds removed, coarsely chopped
2 large garlic cloves, roughly chopped
75g/3oz rocket (arugula) leaves
75g/3oz radicchio leaves
50g/2oz/ ½ cup walnuts, roughly
   chopped
115g/4oz Gorgonzola cheese
60ml/4 tbsp olive oil
15ml/1 tbsp balsamic vinegar
salt and ground black pepper

VARIATIONS
If pancetta is not available, use
unsmoked streaky (fatty) bacon instead.
You could also try chorizo, cut thinly, for
extra flavour.

1 Put the chopped pancetta and garlic
in a non-stick or heavy-based frying pan
and heat gently, stirring constantly, until
the pancetta fat runs. Increase the heat
and fry until the pancetta and garlic are
crisp. Try not to let the garlic brown or it
will acquire a bitter flavour. Remove the
pancetta and garlic with a slotted spoon
and drain on kitchen paper. Leave the
pancetta fat in the pan, off the heat.

2 Tear the rocket and radicchio leaves
into a salad bowl. Sprinkle over the
walnuts, pancetta and garlic. Add salt
and pepper and toss to mix. Crumble
the Gorgonzola on top.

3 Return the frying pan to medium heat
and add the oil and balsamic vinegar to
the pancetta fat. Stir until sizzling, then
pour over the salad. Serve at once, to
be tossed at the table.

Energy 448Kcal/1850kJ; Protein 17.7g; Carbohydrate 1g, of which sugars 0.9g; Fat 41.4g, of which saturates 12.4g; Cholesterol 58mg; Calcium 219mg; Fibre 1.2g; Sodium 1113mg

PRAWN COCKTAIL

THERE IS NO NICER STARTER THAN A GOOD, FRESH PRAWN COCKTAIL, WITH FIRM JUICY PRAWNS, CRISP
LETTUCE AND A PIQUANT SAUCE. THIS RECIPE SHOWS JUST HOW GOOD A PRAWN COCKTAIL CAN BE.

Preparation: 6–7 minutes; Cooking: 0 minutes

SERVES SIX

INGREDIENTS

  60ml/4 tbsp double (heavy) cream,
    lightly whipped
  60ml/4 tbsp mayonnaise, preferably
    home-made
  60ml/4 tbsp tomato ketchup
  5–10ml/1–2 tsp Worcestershire sauce
  juice of 1 lemon
  ½ cos lettuce or other crisp lettuce
  450g/1lb cooked peeled prawns
    (shrimp)
  salt, ground black pepper
    and paprika
  6 large whole cooked prawns (shrimp)
    in the shell, to garnish (optional)
  thinly sliced brown bread with butter
    and lemon wedges, to serve

1 Place the lightly whipped cream,
mayonnaise and tomato ketchup in a
small bowl and whisk lightly to combine.
Add Worcestershire sauce to taste, then
whisk in enough of the lemon juice to
make a really tangy sauce.

2 Finely shred the lettuce and fill six
individual glasses one-third full.

3 Stir the prawns into the sauce, then
check the seasoning and spoon the
prawn mixture generously over the
lettuce. If you like, drape a whole
cooked prawn over the edge of each
glass and sprinkle each of the cocktails
with ground black pepper and/or
paprika. Serve immediately, with thinly
sliced brown bread with butter and
lemon wedges.

COOK'S TIP
Partly peeled prawns make a pretty
garnish. To prepare, carefully peel the
body shell from the prawns and leave the
tail 'fan' for decoration.

Energy 194kcal/805kJ; Protein 13.9g; Carbohydrate 4.2g, of which sugars 4g; Fat 13.6g, of which saturates 4.6g; Cholesterol 167mg; Calcium 80mg; Fibre 0.4g; Sodium 384mg.

CRAB SALAD WITH ROCKET

THIS COLOURFUL AND FRESH-TASTING APPETIZER IS AN INTERESTING WAY TO USE CRAB MEAT. THE
CAPERS AND PEPPERY ROCKET LEAVES ADD A ZING TO THE DISH.

Preparation: 6–7 minutes; Cooking: 0 minutes

SERVES SIX

INGREDIENTS

  white and brown meat from 4 small
    fresh dressed crabs, about 450g/1lb
  1 small red (bell) pepper, seeded and
    finely chopped
  1 small red onion, finely chopped
  30ml/2 tbsp drained capers
  30ml/2 tbsp chopped fresh coriander
    (cilantro)
  grated rind and juice of 2 lemons
  Tabasco sauce, to taste
  salt and ground black pepper
  lemon rind strips, to garnish
For the rocket (arugula) salad
  40g/1½oz rocket leaves
  30ml/2 tbsp sunflower oil
  15ml/1 tbsp fresh lime juice

1 Put the white and brown crab meat,
red pepper, onion, capers and chopped
coriander in a bowl. Add the lemon
rind and juice and toss gently to mix
together. Season with a few drops of
Tabasco sauce, according to taste,
and a little salt and pepper.

2 Divide the rocket leaves among four
plates. Mix together the oil and lime
juice in a small bowl. Dress the rocket
leaves, then pile the crab salad on top
and serve garnished with lemon rind.

COOK'S TIP
If the dressed crabs are really small, pile
the salad back into the shells to serve.

Energy 106kcal/443kJ; Protein 14.2g; Carbohydrate 2.1g, of which sugars 2g; Fat 4.6g, of which saturates 0.6g; Cholesterol 54mg; Calcium 114mg; Fibre 0.7g; Sodium 431mg.

LIGHT BITES AND LUNCHES

It's lunchtime, or time for a snack, and you need something quick. Rather than just making a sandwich, why not create a dish that will make a memorable pause in the day, without taking up too much time? For something ready in just five minutes, try Golden Gruyère and Basil Tortillas or Mexican Tortas. If you enjoy eggs, choose from Anchovy and Quail's Egg Bruschetta or Egg and Bacon Caesar Salad. If you fancy fish, try Focaccia with Sardines and Roast Tomatoes or Breaded Sole Batons, but if you need a meat fix in the middle of the day, Pork on Lemon Grass Sticks, Steak Ciabatta with Hummus and Salad, Mexican Tacos or Pan-fried Chicken Liver Salad might do the trick. Many people enjoy a salad for lunch, and the following can all be prepared in 15 minutes or less: Goat's Cheese Salad, Wilted Spinach with Rice and Dill, Orange, Onion and Olive Salad and Tomato, Mozzarella and Red Onion Salad, along with some warm salads with meat: Warm Chorizo and Spinach Salad and Asparagus, Bacon and Leaf Salad. Lunch will never be the same again.

GOLDEN GRUYÈRE AND BASIL TORTILLAS

TORTILLA FLIP-OVERS ARE A GREAT INVENTION. ONCE YOU'VE TRIED THIS RECIPE, YOU'LL WANT TO EXPERIMENT WITH DIFFERENT FILLINGS, AND LEFTOVERS WILL NEVER GO TO WASTE AGAIN.

Preparation: 1–2 minutes; Cooking: 4 minutes

SERVES TWO

INGREDIENTS
  15ml/1 tbsp olive oil
  2 soft flour tortillas
  115g/4oz Gruyère cheese,
    thinly sliced
  a handful of fresh basil leaves
  salt and ground black pepper

VARIATION

These crisp tortillas make excellent snacks to share with friends on a night in. If you have a few slices of ham or salami in the refrigerator, add these to the tortillas – or simply prepare a mixture of the two to satisfy a range of palates.

1 Heat the oil in a frying pan over a medium heat. Add one of the tortillas, and heat through for 1 minute.

2 Arrange the Gruyère cheese slices and basil leaves on top of the tortilla and season with salt and pepper.

3 Place the remaining tortilla on top to make a sandwich and flip the whole thing over with a metal spatula. Cook for a few minutes, until the underneath is golden.

4 Slide the tortilla sandwich on to a chopping board or plate and cut into wedges. Serve immediately.

Energy 354kcal/1474kJ; Protein 16.4g; Carbohydrate 15g, of which sugars 0.4g; Fat 24.6g, of which saturates 13.3g; Cholesterol 56mg; Calcium 453mg; Fibre 0.6g; Sodium 486mg

COURGETTE RISSOLES

THIS IS AN INGENIOUS WAY OF TRANSFORMING BLAND-TASTING COURGETTES INTO A DISH THAT CAPTIVATES EVERYONE WHO TRIES IT. SERVE THE RISSOLES WITH A TOMATO AND ONION SALAD.

Preparation: 5–6 minutes; Cooking: 14 minutes

SERVES THREE TO FOUR

INGREDIENTS

500g/1¼lb courgettes (zucchini)
120ml/4fl oz/½ cup extra virgin
    olive oil
1 large onion, finely chopped
2 spring onions (scallions), green and
    white parts finely chopped
1 garlic clove, crushed
3 medium slices proper bread
    (not from a pre-sliced loaf)
2 eggs, lightly beaten
200g/7oz feta cheese, crumbled
50g/2oz/½ cup freshly grated Greek
    Graviera or Italian Parmesan cheese
45–60ml/3–4 tbsp finely chopped
    fresh dill or 5ml/1 tsp dried oregano
50g/2oz/½ cup plain
    (all-purpose) flour
salt and ground black pepper
lemon wedges, to serve

1 Bring a pan of lightly salted water to the boil. Slice the courgettes into 4cm/1½in lengths and drop them into the boiling water. Cover and cook for about 10 minutes, or until very soft. Drain in a colander until they are cool enough to handle.

2 Heat 45ml/3 tbsp of the olive oil in a frying pan, add the onion and spring onions and sauté until translucent. Add the garlic, then, as soon as it becomes aromatic, take the pan off the heat.

3 Squeeze the courgettes with your hands, to extract as much water as possible, then place them in a large bowl. Add the fried onion and garlic mixture and mix well.

4 Toast the bread, cut off and discard the crusts, then break up the toast and crumb it in a food processor. Add the crumbs to the courgette mixture, with the eggs, feta, and grated Graviera or Parmesan.

5 Stir in the dill or oregano and add salt and pepper to taste. Mix well, using your hands to squeeze the mixture and make sure that all the ingredients are combined evenly. If the courgette mixture seems too wet, add a little flour.

6 Take about a heaped tablespoon of the courgette mixture, roll it into a round ball and press it lightly to make the typical rissole shape. Make more rissoles in the same way.

7 Coat the rissoles lightly in the flour and dust off any excess. Heat the remaining olive oil in a large non-stick frying pan and fry the rissoles, in batches if necessary, until they are crisp and brown, turning them over once or twice during cooking.

8 Drain the rissoles on a double layer of kitchen paper and serve on a warmed platter or on individual plates, with the lemon wedges for squeezing.

Energy 528kcal/2194kJ; Protein 22g; Carbohydrate 28.8g, of which sugars 7.9g; Fat 36.9g, of which saturates 13g; Cholesterol 143mg; Calcium 436mg; Fibre 3g; Sodium 1001mg

GRILLED AUBERGINE IN HONEY AND SPICES

THE COMBINATION OF HOT, SPICY, SWEET AND FRUITY FLAVOURS IN THIS MOROCCAN DISH WILL HAVE
EVERYONE ASKING FOR THE RECIPE. SERVE AS AN APPETIZER OR FOR A LIGHT SECOND COURSE.
Preparation: 2 minutes; Cooking: 15 minutes

SERVES FOUR

INGREDIENTS
2 aubergines (eggplants)
olive oil, for frying
2–3 garlic cloves, crushed
5cm/2in piece fresh root ginger,
   peeled and grated
5ml/1 tsp ground cumin
5ml/1 tsp harissa
75ml/5 tbsp clear honey
juice of 1 lemon
salt

COOK'S TIP
Grilled blood oranges make an excellent
quick accompaniment to this dish. Dip
the halves or quarters in icing sugar and
grill until just about to blacken. Then
thread on to metal skewers.

1 Preheat the grill (broiler) or a griddle
pan. Cut the aubergines lengthways into
thick slices.

2 Brush each aubergine slice with olive
oil and cook in a pan under the grill or
in a griddle pan. Turn the slices so that
they are lightly browned on both sides.

3 Meanwhile, in a wide frying pan, fry
the garlic in a little olive oil for a few
seconds, then stir in the ginger, cumin,
harissa, honey and lemon juice.

4 Add enough water to thin the mixture,
then add the aubergine slices. Cook for
about 10 minutes, or until they have
absorbed all the sauce.

5 Add a little extra water, if necessary,
season to taste with salt, and serve at
room temperature, with chunks of fresh
bread to mop up the juices.

Energy 168kcal/701kJ; Protein 1g; Carbohydrate 16.5g, of which sugars 16.3g; Fat 11.4g, of which saturates 1.7g; Cholesterol 0mg; Calcium 11mg; Fibre 2g; Sodium 4mg

WATERMELON AND FETA SALAD

THE COMBINATION OF SWEET WATERMELON WITH SALTY FETA CHEESE IS INSPIRED BY TURKISH
TRADITION. THE SALAD MAY BE SERVED PLAIN AND LIGHT, ON A LEAFY BASE, OR WITH A VINAIGRETTE.

Preparation: 5 minutes; Cooking: 0 minutes

SERVES FOUR

INGREDIENTS
  4 slices watermelon, chilled
  130g/4½oz feta cheese, preferably
    sheep's milk feta, cut into bitesize
    pieces
  handful of mixed seeds, such as
    lightly toasted pumpkin seeds and
    sunflower seeds
  10–15 black olives

1 Cut the rind off the watermelon and
remove as many seeds as possible. Cut
the flesh into triangular-shaped chunks.

2 Mix the watermelon, feta cheese,
mixed seeds and black olives together
in a serving bowl.

3 Cover the bowl with clear film (plastic
wrap) and chill the salad for 30 minutes
before serving.

COOK'S TIP
The best choice of olives for this recipe
are plump black Mediterranean ones,
such as kalamata, other shiny, brined
varieties or dry-cured black olives.

Energy 211Kcal/884kJ; Protein 8g; Carbohydrate 16g, of which sugars 15g; Fat 13g, of which saturates 5g; Cholesterol 23mg; Calcium 145mg; Fibre 1.1g; Sodium 700mg

WHITEFISH SALAD WITH TOASTED BAGELS

A TRADITIONAL DELI FAVOURITE, SMOKED WHITEFISH MAKES A SUPERB SALAD. IF YOU CAN'T FIND IT, USE SMOKED HALIBUT, BUT DON'T PASS UP THE BAGELS, WHICH ARE THE PERFECT ACCOMPANIMENT.

Preparation: 8–10 minutes; Cooking: 0 minutes

SERVES FOUR TO SIX

INGREDIENTS

1 smoked whitefish or halibut,
  skinned and boned
2 celery sticks, chopped
½ red, white or yellow onion
  or 3–5 spring onions
  (scallions), chopped
45ml/3 tbsp mayonnaise
45ml/3 tbsp sour cream
juice of ½–1 lemon
1 round lettuce
ground black pepper
5–10ml/1–2 tsp chopped fresh
  parsley, to garnish
toasted bagels, to serve

1 Break the smoked fish into bitesize pieces. In a bowl, combine the chopped celery, onion or spring onion, mayonnaise and sour cream, and add lemon juice to taste.

2 Fold the fish into the mixture and season with pepper. Arrange the lettuce leaves on serving plates, then spoon the smoked fish salad on top. Sprinkle with parsley and serve with bagels.

Energy 108kcal/450kJ; Protein 7.8g; Carbohydrate 1.6g, of which sugars 1.3g; Fat 7.9g, of which saturates 1.9g; Cholesterol 22mg; Calcium 29mg; Fibre 0.4g; Sodium 64mg

ANCHOVY AND QUAIL'S EGG BRUSCHETTA

QUAIL'S EGGS TASTE MARVELLOUS WITH THE ANCHOVIES AND MILD RED ONION SLICES, ESPECIALLY WHEN THE MIXTURE IS PILED ON TOASTED CIABATTA WHICH HAS BEEN RUBBED WITH FRESH GARLIC.

Preparation: 15 minutes; Cooking: 3–5 minutes

SERVES FOUR TO SIX

INGREDIENTS

    50g/2oz anchovy fillets in salt
    milk, for soaking
    12 quail's eggs
    2–3 garlic cloves
    1 ciabatta or similar loaf
    coarse salt
    1 red onion, halved and thinly sliced
    10–15ml/2–3 tsp cumin seeds,
      roasted and ground
    a small bunch of flat leaf parsley,
      roughly chopped
    30–45ml/2–3 tbsp olive oil

1 Soak the anchovies in milk for 15 minutes to reduce the salty flavour.

2 Meanwhile, put the quail's eggs in a pan of cold water. Bring to the boil and cook for 2 minutes, then drain and plunge into cold water.

3 Remove the skin from the garlic cloves, halve, and crush using a pestle and mortar.

4 Preheat the grill (broiler) on the hottest setting. Slice the loaf of bread horizontally in half and toast the cut sides until golden.

5 Rub the toasted bread all over with the crushed garlic and sprinkle with a little salt. Don't overdo this, as the anchovies will be quite salty.

6 Cut each piece of bread into four or six equal pieces. Drain the quail's eggs, shell them and cut them in half. Drain the anchovy fillets. Pile the onion slices, quail's egg halves and anchovy fillets on the pieces of bread. Sprinkle liberally with the ground roasted cumin and chopped parsley and serve immediately.

Energy 181kcal/761kJ; Protein 8.8g; Carbohydrate 18.2g, of which sugars 1.7g; Fat 8.6g, of which saturates 1.6g; Cholesterol 100mg; Calcium 87mg; Fibre 1g; Sodium 543mg

FOCACCIA WITH SARDINES AND ROAST TOMATOES

FRESH SARDINES HAVE A LOVELY FLAVOUR AND TEXTURE, ARE CHEAP TO BUY AND COOK QUICKLY.

Preparation: 3–4 minutes; Cooking: 15 minutes

SERVES FOUR

INGREDIENTS
  20 cherry tomatoes
  45ml/3 tbsp herb-infused olive oil
  12 fresh sardine fillets
  1 focaccia loaf
  salt and ground black pepper

VARIATIONS
This rather sumptuous topping tastes great on focaccia, but a split French stick would work just as well. If you happen to have some cold boiled potatoes in the refrigerator, slice them and fry them quickly in oil while the sardines are cooking. Abandon the bread and pile the sardines and tomatoes on top of the potatoes instead.

1 Preheat the oven to 190°C/375°F/Gas 5. Put the cherry tomatoes in a small roasting pan and drizzle 30ml/2 tbsp of the herb-infused olive oil over the top.

2 Season the tomatoes with salt and pepper and roast for 10–15 minutes, shaking the pan gently once or twice so that the tomatoes cook evenly on all sides. When they are tender and slightly charred, remove from the oven and set aside.

3 While the tomatoes are cooking, preheat the grill (broiler) to high. Brush the sardine fillets with the remaining oil and lay them on a baking sheet. Grill (broil) for 4–5 minutes on each side, until cooked through.

4 Split the focaccia in half horizontally and cut each piece in half to give four equal pieces. Toast the cut side under the grill. Top with the sardines and tomatoes and an extra drizzle of oil. Season with black pepper and serve.

Energy 301kcal/1262kJ; Protein 15.8g; Carbohydrate 27.6g, of which sugars 3.1g; Fat 15g, of which saturates 2.9g; Cholesterol 0mg; Calcium 106mg; Fibre 1.7g; Sodium 334mg

BREADED SOLE BATONS

CRISP, CRUMBED FISH STRIPS ARE ALMOST AS SPEEDY AS FISH FINGERS, BUT MUCH SMARTER.
Preparation: 10–12 minutes; Cooking: 6–7 minutes

SERVES FOUR

INGREDIENTS
   275g/10oz lemon sole fillets, skinned
   2 eggs
   115g/4oz/2 cups fine fresh
     breadcrumbs
   75g/3oz/¾ cup plain (all-purpose)
     flour
   salt and ground black pepper
   oil, for frying
   lemon wedges and tartare sauce,
     to serve

3 Dip the fish strips in the egg, turning to coat well. Place on a plate and then shake a few at a time in the bag of seasoned flour. Dip the fish strips in the egg again and then in the breadcrumbs, turning to coat well. Place on a tray in a single layer, not touching. Let the coating set for at least 5 minutes.

4 Heat 1cm/½in oil in a large frying pan over medium-high heat. When the oil is hot (a cube of bread will sizzle) fry the fish strips in batches for about 2–2½ minutes, turning once, taking care not to overcrowd the pan. Drain on kitchen paper and keep warm. Serve the fish with tartare sauce and lemon wedges.

1 Cut the fish fillets into long diagonal strips each measuring about 2cm/¾ in wide.

2 Break the eggs into a shallow dish and beat well with a fork. Place the breadcrumbs in another shallow dish. Put the flour in a large pastic bag and season with salt and ground black pepper.

Energy 334kcal/1405kJ; Protein 20.2g; Carbohydrate 36.9g, of which sugars 1g; Fat 12.9g, of which saturates 2.1g; Cholesterol 136mg; Calcium 90mg; Fibre 1.2g; Sodium 320mg.

STIR-FRIED NOODLES IN SEAFOOD SAUCE

*THIS CHINESE-STYLE PASTA DISH MAKES A PERFECT APPETIZER OR MAIN COURSE, COMBINING
NOODLES, VEGETABLES AND CRAB MEAT IN A COLOURFUL, TASTY AND QUICK DISH.*

Preparation: 10–12 minutes; Cooking: 6–7 minutes

SERVES SIX TO EIGHT AS AN APPETIZER,
FOUR AS A MAIN COURSE

INGREDIENTS

225g/8oz Chinese egg noodles
8 spring onions (scallions), trimmed
8 asparagus spears, plus extra
   steamed asparagus spears,
   to serve (optional)
30ml/2 tbsp vegetable oil
5cm/2in piece fresh root ginger,
   peeled and cut into very fine
   matchsticks
3 garlic cloves, chopped
60ml/4 tbsp oyster sauce
450g/1lb cooked crab meat (all
   white, or two-thirds white and
   one-third brown)
30ml/2 tbsp rice wine vinegar
15–30ml/1–2 tbsp light soy sauce,
   to taste

1 Put the noodles in a large pan, cover with lightly salted boiling water, place a lid on top and leave for 3–4 minutes, or for the time suggested on the packet. Drain, separate with a fork and set aside.

2 Cut off the green spring onion tops and slice them thinly. Set aside. Cut the white parts into 2cm/¾in lengths and quarter them lengthways. Cut the asparagus spears on the diagonal into 2cm/¾in pieces.

3 Heat the oil in a pan or wok until very hot, then add the ginger, garlic and white spring onion batons. Stir-fry over high heat for 1 minute. Add the oyster sauce, crab meat, rice wine vinegar and soy sauce to taste. Stir-fry for about 2 minutes, until the crab and sauce are hot. Add the noodles and toss until heated through. At the last moment, toss in the spring onion tops and serve with a few extra asparagus spears, if you like.

Energy 192kcal/811kJ; Protein 14.3g; Carbohydrate 23g, of which sugars 3.2g; Fat 5.5g, of which saturates 1.1g; Cholesterol 49mg; Calcium 83mg; Fibre 1.2g; Sodium 617mg.

BUCKWHEAT NOODLES WITH SMOKED SALMON

YOUNG PEA SPROUTS ARE AVAILABLE FOR ONLY A SHORT TIME. YOU CAN SUBSTITUTE WATERCRESS, MUSTARD CRESS, YOUNG LEEKS OR YOUR FAVOURITE GREEN VEGETABLE OR HERB IN THIS DISH.

Preparation: 8–10 minutes; Cooking: 6–7 minutes

SERVES FOUR

INGREDIENTS
225g/8oz buckwheat or soba noodles
15ml/1 tbsp oyster sauce
juice of ½ lemon
30–45ml/2–3 tbsp light olive oil
115g/4oz smoked salmon, cut into
 fine strips
115g/4oz young pea sprouts
2 ripe tomatoes, peeled, seeded and
 cut into strips
15ml/1 tbsp snipped chives
salt and ground black pepper

COOK'S TIP
To keep the cost of this dish down, use a packet of smoked salmon trimmings instead of cutting up more expensive slices. It will taste just the same.

1 Cook the buckwheat or soba noodles in a large pan of boiling water, following the directions on the packet. Drain, then tip into a colander and rinse under cold running water. Drain well, shaking the colander to extract any remaining water.

2 Tip the noodles into a large bowl. Add the oyster sauce and lemon juice and season with pepper to taste. Moisten with the olive oil.

3 Add the smoked salmon, pea sprouts, tomatoes and chives. Mix well and serve at once.

Energy 341kcal/1437kJ; Protein 16.2g; Carbohydrate 47.6g, of which sugars 3.6g; Fat 10.9g, of which saturates 1.2g; Cholesterol 10mg; Calcium 28mg; Fibre 3.5g; Sodium 547mg.

MEXICAN TORTAS

THE GOOD THING ABOUT HOLLOWING OUT A BREAD ROLL IS THAT YOU CAN PACK IN MORE FILLING.
THIS MEXICAN SNACK USES ROAST PORK AND REFRIED BEANS BUT EXPERIMENTING IS EXPECTED.

Preparation: 5–6 minutes; Cooking: 0 minutes

SERVES FOUR

INGREDIENTS

   2 fresh jalapeño chillies
   juice of ½ lime
   2 French bread rolls or 2 pieces
     French bread
   75g/3oz/⅔ cup canned refried beans
   150g/5oz roast pork
   2 small tomatoes, sliced
   115g/4oz Cheddar or Monterey Jack
     cheese, sliced
   a small bunch of fresh coriander
     (cilantro)
   30ml/2 tbsp crème fraîche

1 Cut the chillies in half, scrape out
the seeds, then cut the flesh into thin
strips. Put it in a bowl, pour in the lime
juice and leave to stand.

VARIATION
Sliced chicken carved from the rotisserie
is another popular Mexican torta filler.

2 If using rolls, slice them in half and
remove some of the crumb so that they
are slightly hollowed. If using French
bread, slice each piece in half
lengthways.

3 Set the top of each piece of bread or
roll aside and spread the bottom halves
with a nice thick layer of the refried
beans. Make sure the paste is evenly
spread, as it will help to hold the next
layer in place.

4 Cut the pork into thin shreds and put
these on top of the refried beans. Top
with the tomato slices. Drain the
jalapeño strips and put them on top of
the tomato slices. Add the cheese and
sprinkle with coriander leaves.

5 Turn the top halves of the bread or
rolls over so that the cut sides are
uppermost, and spread these with
crème fraîche. Sandwich back together
again and serve.

Energy 307kcal/1285kJ; Protein 22.8g; Carbohydrate 18.2g, of which sugars 2.9g; Fat 15.8g, of which saturates 9.4g; Cholesterol 78mg; Calcium 271mg; Fibre 2g; Sodium 485mg

PORK ᴏɴ LEMON GRASS STICKS

THESE MAKE A SUBSTANTIAL SNACK, EITHER ON THEIR OWN OR AS PART OF A BARBECUE MENU. THE
LEMON GRASS STICKS NOT ONLY ADD A SUBTLE FLAVOUR BUT ARE ALSO A GOOD TALKING POINT.

Preparation: 6 minutes; Cooking: 6–8 minutes

SERVES FOUR

INGREDIENTS
  300g/11oz/1½ cups minced
    (ground) pork
  4 garlic cloves, crushed
  4 fresh coriander (cilantro) roots,
    finely chopped
  2.5ml/½ tsp granulated sugar
  15ml/1 tbsp soy sauce
  salt and ground black pepper
  8 x 10cm/4in lengths lemon
    grass stalk
  sweet chilli sauce, to serve

VARIATION
Slimmer versions of these pork sticks are
perfect for parties. The mixture will be
enough for 12 lemon grass sticks if you
use it sparingly.

1 Place the minced pork, crushed garlic,
chopped coriander root, sugar and soy
sauce in a large bowl. Season with salt
and pepper to taste and mix well.

2 Divide into eight portions and mould
each one into a ball. It may help to
dampen your hands before shaping the
mixture, to prevent it from sticking.

3 Stick a length of lemon grass halfway
into each ball, then press the meat
mixture around the lemon grass to
make a shape like a chicken leg.

4 Cook the pork sticks under a hot grill
(broiler) for 3–4 minutes on each side,
until golden and cooked through. Serve
with the chilli sauce for dipping.

Energy 132kcal/552kJ; Protein 14.7g; Carbohydrate 2g, of which sugars 1.6g; Fat 7.3g, of which saturates 2.7g; Cholesterol 50mg; Calcium 10mg; Fibre 0.2g; Sodium 317mg

STEAK CIABATTA WITH HUMMUS AND SALAD

PACKED WITH GARLICKY HUMMUS AND A MUSTARD-SEASONED DRESSING ON THE CRUNCHY SALAD,
THESE STEAK SANDWICHES ARE JUST RIGHT FOR LUNCH ON THE PATIO.

Preparation: 5 minutes; Cooking: 6–9 minutes

SERVES FOUR

INGREDIENTS

  3 garlic cloves, crushed to a
    paste with enough salt to season
    the steaks
  30ml/2 tbsp extra virgin olive oil
  4 sirloin steaks, 2.5cm/1in thick,
    total weight about 900g/2lb
  2 romaine lettuce hearts
  4 small ciabatta breads
  salt and ground black pepper
For the dressing
  10ml/2 tsp Dijon mustard
  5ml/1 tsp cider or white wine vinegar
  15ml/1 tbsp olive oil
For the hummus
  400g/14oz can chickpeas, drained
    and rinsed
  45ml/3 tbsp tahini
  2 garlic cloves, crushed
  juice of 1 lemon
  30ml/2 tbsp water

1 To make the hummus, place the chickpeas in a large bowl and mash to a paste. Add the tahini, garlic, lemon juice, salt and pepper. Stir in the water. Mash together well.

2 Make a dressing by mixing the mustard and vinegar in a jar. Add the oil and season to taste. Shake well.

3 Mix the garlic and oil in a dish. Add the steaks and rub the mixture into both surfaces.

4 Preheat the grill (broiler). Cook the steaks on a rack in a grill pan. For rare meat, allow 2 minutes on one side and 3 minutes on the second side. For medium steaks, allow 4 minutes on each side. Transfer to a plate, cover and rest for 2 minutes.

5 Dress the lettuce. Split each ciabatta and heat on the grill rack for a minute. Fill with hummus, the steaks and leaves. Cut each in half and serve immediately, just as they are.

Energy 765kcal/3210kJ; Protein 69.8g; Carbohydrate 55.2g, of which sugars 2.8g; Fat 30.8g, of which saturates 7.4g; Cholesterol 115mg; Calcium 222mg; Fibre 6.7g; Sodium 783mg

STEAK AND BLUE CHEESE ON CIABATTA

MANY PEOPLE PREFER THEIR STEAKS COOKED QUITE RARE IN THE CENTRE, BUT THEY ARE STILL DELICIOUS IF COOKED A LITTLE LONGER. ADD A COUPLE OF MINUTES TO THE COOKING TIME IF NECESSARY.

Preparation: 2–3 minutes; Cooking: 12–14 minutes

SERVES TWO

INGREDIENTS
1 part-baked ciabatta bread
2 ribeye steaks, about
   200g/7oz each
15ml/1 tbsp olive oil
115g/4oz Gorgonzola cheese, sliced
salt and ground black pepper

1 Bake the ciabatta according to the instructions on the packet. Remove from the oven and leave to rest while you cook the steak.

2 Heat a griddle pan until hot. Brush the steaks with the olive oil and lay them on the griddle pan. Cook for 2–3 minutes on each side, depending on the thickness of the steaks.

3 Remove the steaks and set them aside to rest. Meanwhile, cut the loaf in half and split each half horizontally.

4 Cut the steaks in half lengthways so each is only half as thick as before. Moisten the bread with the pan juices then make into sandwiches using the steak and cheese. Season well and serve.

COOK'S TIP
Part-baked bread cooks in about 8 minutes in a hot oven, but if even that is too long, just warm a regular baked ciabatta or French stick.

Energy 767kcal/3221kJ; Protein 66g; Carbohydrate 52g, of which sugars 3.1g; Fat 34.2g, of which saturates 15.8g; Cholesterol 161mg; Calcium 410mg; Fibre 2.3g; Sodium 1360mg

MEXICAN TACOS

READY-MADE TACO SHELLS MAKE PERFECT EDIBLE CONTAINERS FOR SHREDDED SALAD, MEAT FILLINGS, GRATED CHEESE AND SOUR CREAM. THIS IS AN EXCELLENT CHOICE FOR A QUICK SUPPER.

Preparation: 8 minutes; Cooking: 8 minutes

SERVES FOUR

INGREDIENTS

15ml/1 tbsp olive oil
250g/9oz lean minced (ground) beef
  or turkey
2 garlic cloves, crushed
5ml/1 tsp ground cumin
5–10ml/1–2 tsp mild chilli powder
8 ready-made taco shells
½ small iceberg lettuce, shredded
1 small onion, thinly sliced
2 tomatoes, chopped in chunks
1 avocado, stoned (pitted) and sliced
60ml/4 tbsp sour cream
125g/4oz/1 cup crumbled queso
  blanco or anejado, or grated
  Cheddar or Monterey Jack cheese
salt and ground black pepper

1 Heat the oil in a frying pan. Add the meat, with the garlic and spices, and brown over a medium heat, stirring frequently to break up any lumps. Season, cook for 5 minutes, then set aside to cool slightly.

2 Meanwhile, warm the taco shells according to the instructions on the packet. Do not let them get too crisp. Spoon the lettuce, onion, tomatoes and avocado slices into the taco shells. Top with the sour cream followed by the minced beef or turkey mixture.

COOK'S TIP
Stir-fried strips of turkey, chicken or pork are excellent instead of the minced beef or turkey.

3 Sprinkle the crumbled or grated cheese into the tacos and serve immediately. Tacos are eaten with the fingers, so have plenty of paper napkins to hand.

Energy 497Kcal/2067kJ; Protein 25.4g; Carbohydrate 19.4g, of which sugars 3.8g; Fat 35.1g, of which saturates 14.3g; Cholesterol 74mg; Calcium 305mg; Fibre 3.6g; Sodium 511mg

ROAST CHICKEN PITTA POCKETS

FAMILIES OFTEN HAVE TO EAT IN RELAYS: A PARENT IS GOING TO BE HOME LATE; ONE CHILD HAS A MUSIC LESSON; ANOTHER IS OFF TO THE SKATE PARK. THIS SERVE-ANYTIME SNACK WILL SUIT THE LOT.

Preparation: 12–14 minutes; Cooking: 2 minutes

MAKES SIX

INGREDIENTS

1 small cucumber, peeled and diced
3 tomatoes, peeled, seeded
    and chopped
2 spring onions (scallions), chopped
30ml/2 tbsp olive oil
a small bunch of flat leaf parsley,
    finely chopped
a small bunch of mint,
    finely chopped
½ preserved lemon, finely chopped
45–60ml/3–4 tbsp tahini
juice of 1 lemon
2 garlic cloves, crushed
6 pitta breads
½ small roast chicken or
    2 large roast chicken breasts,
    cut into strips
salt and ground black pepper

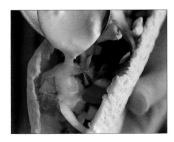

1 Place the cucumber in a strainer over a bowl, sprinkle with a little salt and leave for 5 minutes to drain. Rinse well and drain again, then place in a bowl with the tomatoes and spring onions. Stir in the olive oil, parsley, mint and preserved lemon. Season well.

2 In a small bowl, mix the tahini with the lemon juice, then thin the mixture down with a little water to the consistency of thick double (heavy) cream. Beat in the garlic and season.

COOK'S TIP
The chicken in these pitta breads can be hot or cold – either roast a small bird specially or use up the leftovers from a large roast chicken.

3 Preheat the grill (broiler) to hot. Lightly toast the pitta breads well away from the heat source until they puff up. (Alternatively, lightly toast the breads in a toaster.) Open the breads and stuff them liberally with the chicken and salad. Drizzle a generous amount of tahini sauce into each one and serve with any extra salad.

Energy 337kcal/1419kJ; Protein 21g; Carbohydrate 43.5g, of which sugars 4.4g; Fat 9.9g, of which saturates 1.5g; Cholesterol 35mg; Calcium 182mg; Fibre 3.5g; Sodium 369mg

GOAT'S CHEESE SALAD

YOU NEED A SOFT GOAT'S CHEESE WITH PLENTY OF FLAVOUR FOR THIS SALAD.
Preparation: 8–10 minutes; Cooking: 0 minutes

SERVES FOUR

INGREDIENTS

    175g/6oz mixed salad leaves, such as
      lamb's lettuce, rocket (arugula),
      radicchio, frisée or cress
    a few fresh large-leafed herbs, such
      as chervil and flat leaf parsley
    15ml/1 tbsp toasted hazelnuts,
      roughly chopped
    15–20 goat's cheese balls or cubes
For the dressing
    30ml/2 tbsp hazelnut oil, olive oil
      or sunflower oil
    5–10ml/1–2 tsp sherry vinegar or
      good wine vinegar, to taste
    salt and ground black pepper

1 Tear up any large salad leaves. Put
all the leaves into a large salad bowl
with the fresh herbs and most of the
toasted, chopped nuts (reserve a few
for the garnish).

2 To make the dressing, whisk the
hazelnut, olive or sunflower oil and
vinegar together, and then season to
taste with salt and pepper.

VARIATIONS
Toasted flaked (sliced) almonds could
replace the hazelnuts (teamed with extra
virgin olive oil). Stronger-flavoured
cheeses work well with walnuts and
walnut oil.

3 Just before serving, toss the salad in
the dressing and divide it among four
serving plates. Arrange the drained
goat's cheese balls or cubes over the
leaves, sprinkle over the remaining
chopped nuts and serve.

Energy 215kcal/893kJ; Protein 11.4g; Carbohydrate 1.5g, of which sugars 1.4g; Fat 18.3g, of which saturates 9.6g; Cholesterol 47mg; Calcium 84mg; Fibre 0.6g; Sodium 302mg

WILTED SPINACH WITH RICE AND DILL

THIS IS A DELICIOUS DISH THAT CAN BE MADE IN VERY LITTLE TIME.
Preparation: 5 minutes; Cooking: 15 minutes

SERVES SIX

INGREDIENTS

675g/1½lb fresh spinach, trimmed
  of any hard stalks
105ml/7 tbsp extra virgin olive oil
1 large onion, chopped
juice of ½ lemon
150ml/¼ pint/⅔ cup water
115g/4oz/generous ½ cup long
  grain rice
45ml/3 tbsp chopped fresh dill, plus
  extra sprigs to garnish
salt and ground black pepper

1 Thoroughly wash the spinach in cold water and drain. Repeat four or five times until the spinach is completely clean and free of grit, then drain it completely in a colander. Brush off the excess water with kitchen paper.

2 Heat the olive oil in a large pan and sauté the onion until translucent. Add the spinach and stir for a few minutes to coat it with the oil.

3 As soon as the spinach looks wilted, add the lemon juice and the measured water and bring to the boil. Add the rice and half of the dill, then cover and cook gently for about 10 minutes, or until the rice is cooked to your taste. If it looks too dry, add a little hot water.

4 Spoon into a serving dish and sprinkle the sprigs of dill over the top. Serve hot or at room temperature.

COOK'S TIP
This dish is ideal to accompany fried or barbecued fish or chickpea rissoles. It can also be eaten as a first course.

Energy 325Kcal/1,343kJ; Protein 7.8g; Carbohydrate 29.9g, of which sugars 5.6g; Fat 19.2g, of which saturates 2.7g; Cholesterol 0mg; Calcium 327mg; Fibre 4.8g; Sodium 242mg

ORANGE, ONION AND OLIVE SALAD

THIS IS A REFRESHING MOROCCAN SALAD FOR A LIGHT SUMMER LUNCH OR TO FOLLOW A RICH MAIN DISH, SUCH AS A TAGINE OF LAMB, OR TO LIGHTEN ANY SPICY MEAL.

Preparation: 15 minutes; Cooking: 0 minutes

SERVES SIX

INGREDIENTS
5 large oranges
90g/3½oz/scant 1 cup black olives
1 red onion, thinly sliced
1 large fennel bulb, thinly sliced,
  feathery tops reserved
15ml/1 tbsp chopped fresh mint,
  plus a few extra sprigs
15ml/1 tbsp chopped fresh coriander
  (cilantro), plus a few extra sprigs
2.5ml/½ tsp orange flower water
For the dressing
60ml/4 tbsp olive oil
10ml/2 tsp lemon juice
2.5ml/½ tsp ground toasted
  coriander seeds
salt and ground black pepper

1 Peel the oranges with a sharp knife, making sure you remove all the white pith, and cut them into 5mm/¼in slices. Remove any pips and work over a bowl to catch all the orange juice. Set the juice aside.

2 Stone the olives, if wished. In a bowl, toss the orange slices, onion and fennel together with the olives, chopped mint and fresh coriander.

3 Make the dressing. In a bowl or jug (pitcher), whisk together the olive oil, 15ml/1 tbsp of the reserved fresh orange juice and the lemon juice. Add the ground toasted coriander seeds and season to taste with a little salt and pepper. Whisk thoroughly to mix.

4 Toss the dressing into the salad and leave to stand for 30–60 minutes.

5 Drain off any excess dressing and place the salad on a serving dish. Scatter with the herbs and fennel tops, and sprinkle with the orange flower water.

Energy 582kcal/2473kJ; Protein 15.2g; Carbohydrate 114.7g, of which sugars 114.5g; Fat 10.4g, of which saturates 1.3g; Cholesterol 0mg; Calcium 646mg; Fibre 24.1g; Sodium 408mg.

TOMATO, MOZZARELLA AND ONION SALAD

SWEET TOMATOES AND THE HEADY SCENT OF BASIL CAPTURE THE ESSENCE OF SUMMER IN THIS SIMPLE SALAD. VINE-RIPENED TOMATOES USUALLY HAVE THE BEST FLAVOUR.

Preparation: 15 minutes; Cooking: 0 minutes

SERVES SIX

INGREDIENTS
5 large ripe tomatoes, peeled if liked
2 buffalo mozzarella cheeses,
  drained and sliced
1 small red onion, chopped
For the dressing
½ small garlic clove, peeled
15g/½oz fresh basil
30ml/2 tbsp chopped fresh flat leaf
  parsley
25ml/5 tsp small capers in brine,
  rinsed
2.5ml/½ tsp mustard
75–90ml/5–6 tbsp extra virgin olive
  oil
5–10ml/1–2 tsp balsamic vinegar
ground black pepper
fresh basil leaves and parsley sprigs,
  to garnish

1 First make the dressing. Put the garlic, basil, parsley, half the capers and the mustard in a food processor or blender and process briefly to chop. Then, with the motor running, gradually pour in the olive oil through the feeder tube to make a smooth purée with a dressing consistency. Add the balsamic vinegar to taste and season with pepper.

2 Slice the tomatoes. Arrange the tomato and mozzarella slices on a plate. Scatter the onion over and season with a little pepper.

3 Drizzle the dressing over the salad, then scatter the basil leaves, parsley sprigs and remaining capers on top. Leave for 10–15 minutes before serving.

Energy 232kcal/960kJ; Protein 10.3g; Carbohydrate 3.6g, of which sugars 3.3g; Fat 19.7g, of which saturates 8.3g; Cholesterol 29mg; Calcium 206mg; Fibre 1.4g; Sodium 208mg.

Egg ᴀɴᴅ Bacon Caesar Salad

Caesar Cardini invented the classic Caesar salad in 1924 at his restaurant in Tijuana, Mexico. The essentials are crisp lettuce, crunchy garlic croûtons and a creamy dressing.

Preparation: 10 minutes; Cooking: 15–16 minutes

2 Preheat the oven to 190°C/375°F/ Gas 5. Cut the bread into bitesize squares or chunks and toss them with the oil and garlic. Season to taste with salt and pepper.

3 Turn out on to a baking sheet. Bake for 10–14 minutes, stirring once or twice, until golden brown all over.

4 Meanwhile, for the dressing, bring a pan of water to the boil and add the egg, then boil it for 90 seconds. Plunge the egg into cold water and shell it into a food processor or blender.

SERVES SIX AS AN APPETIZER OR
FOUR AS A LIGHT MAIN COURSE

INGREDIENTS
  12–18 quail's eggs
  3 x 1cm/½in thick slices white bread
  45ml/3 tbsp olive oil
  1 large garlic clove, finely chopped
  3–4 Little Gem (Bibb) lettuces or 2
    larger cos or romaine lettuces
  115g/4oz thinly sliced prosciutto,
    San Daniele or Serrano ham
  40–50g/1½–2oz Parmesan
    cheese, grated
  salt and ground black pepper
For the dressing
  1 large egg
  1–2 garlic cloves, chopped
  4 anchovy fillets in oil, drained
  120ml/4fl oz/½ cup olive oil
  lemon juice or white wine vinegar

1 Place the quail's eggs in a pan, cover with cold water, then bring to the boil and boil for 2 minutes. Plunge the eggs into cold water, then part-shell them. Leave them to cool.

5 Add the garlic and anchovy fillets and process to mix. With the motor still running, gradually add the olive oil in a thin stream. When all the oil is incorporated and the dressing is creamy, add 10–15ml/2–3 tsp lemon juice or wine vinegar and season to taste with salt and pepper.

6 Trim the lettuces, cutting the Little Gem lettuces into quarters or separating the larger lettuces into leaves. Place in a large salad bowl.

7 Grill the ham for 2–3 minutes on each side, or until crisp.

8 Toss the dressing into the lettuce with 25g/1oz of the Parmesan. Add the croûtons. Cut the quail's eggs in half and add them to the salad. Crumble the ham into large pieces and scatter it over the salad with the remaining cheese.

Energy 331kcal/1374kJ; Protein 14.6g; Carbohydrate 7.8g, of which sugars 1.9g; Fat 27.2g, of which saturates 5.8g; Cholesterol 209mg; Calcium 153mg; Fibre 0.9g; Sodium 519mg.

CHOPPED EGGS <u>AND</u> ONIONS

QUICK AND EASY TO MAKE, THIS IS A SPEEDY LUNCH. YOU COULD EVEN PACK IT UP AND TAKE IT TO WORK, ALTHOUGH THE AROMA OF EGGS AND ONION MIGHT NOT PROVE IRRESISTIBLE TO EVERYONE.

Preparation: 3–4 minutes; Cooking: 12 minutes

SERVES FOUR TO SIX

INGREDIENTS

8–10 eggs
6–8 spring onions (scallions) and/or
  1 yellow or white onion, very finely
  chopped, plus extra to garnish
60–90ml/4–6 tbsp mayonnaise
mild French wholegrain mustard,
  to taste (optional)
15ml/1 tbsp chopped fresh parsley
salt and ground black pepper
rye toasts or crackers, to serve

COOK'S TIP
Holding a freshly boiled egg under cold running water helps to prevent the yolk from acquiring a greenish tinge where it meets the white.

1 Put the eggs in a large pan and pour in cold water to cover. Heat the water. When it boils, reduce the heat and simmer the eggs for 10 minutes. Stir the eggs twice so they cook evenly.

2 Drain the eggs, hold them under cold running water, then remove the shells, dry the eggs and chop roughly.

3 Place the chopped eggs in a large bowl. Add the onions, season with salt and pepper and mix well. Add enough mayonnaise to bind the mixture together. Stir in the mustard, if using, and the chopped parsley, or sprinkle the parsley on top to garnish. If you have time, chill the mixture before serving with rye toasts or crackers.

Energy 170kcal/706kJ; Protein 8.7g; Carbohydrate 0.5g, of which sugars 0.5g; Fat 15.1g, of which saturates 3.2g; Cholesterol 261mg; Calcium 48mg; Fibre 0.3g; Sodium 140mg

WARM CHORIZO AND SPINACH SALAD

SPANISH CHORIZO SAUSAGE CONTRIBUTES AN INTENSE SPICINESS TO ANY INGREDIENT WITH WHICH IT IS COOKED. IN THIS HEARTY SALAD, SPINACH HAS SUFFICIENT FLAVOUR TO COMPETE WITH THE CHORIZO.

Preparation: 2–3 minutes; Cooking: 3 minutes

SERVES FOUR

INGREDIENTS

225g/8oz baby spinach leaves
90ml/6 tbsp extra virgin olive oil
150g/5oz chorizo sausage,
  very thinly sliced
30ml/2 tbsp sherry vinegar
salt and ground black pepper
warm crusty bread, to serve

VARIATIONS

• Watercress or rocket (arugula) could be used instead of the spinach, if you prefer.
• For an added dimension, use a flavoured olive oil – rosemary, garlic or chilli oil would work perfectly.

1 Pour the oil into a large frying pan and add the sausage. Cook gently for 3 minutes, until the sausage slices start to shrivel slightly and colour.

2 Add the spinach leaves and remove the pan from the heat. Toss the spinach in the warm oil until it just starts to wilt. Add the sherry vinegar and a little seasoning. Toss briefly, then serve warm.

Energy 273Kcal/1127kJ; Protein 8g; Carbohydrate 2g, of which sugars 2g; Fat 26g, of which saturates 6g; Cholesterol 0mg; Calcium 96mg; Fibre 1.2g; Sodium 300mg

ASPARAGUS, BACON AND LEAF SALAD

AS AN ACCOMPANIMENT, THIS EXCELLENT SALAD TURNS A PLAIN ROAST CHICKEN OR SIMPLE GRILLED FISH INTO AN INTERESTING MEAL, OR MAKES AN APPETIZING FIRST COURSE OR LIGHT LUNCH.

Preparation: 5 minutes; Cooking: 6 minutes

SERVES FOUR

INGREDIENTS
    500g/1¼lb medium asparagus spears
    130g/4½oz thin-cut smoked back
    (lean) bacon
    250g/9oz frisée lettuce leaves or
    mixed leaf salad
    100ml/3½fl oz/scant ½ cup
    French dressing

COOK'S TIP
A wide range of different salad leaves is readily available – frisée has feathery, curly, slightly bitter-tasting leaves and is a member of the chicory family. Frisée leaves range in colour from yellow-white to yellow-green.

1 Trim off any tough stalk ends from the asparagus and cut the spears into three, setting the tender tips aside. Heat a 1cm/½in depth of water in a frying pan until simmering. Reserve the asparagus tips and cook the remainder of the spears in the water for about 3 minutes, until almost tender. Add the tips and cook for 1 minute more. Drain and refresh under cold, running water.

2 Dry-fry the bacon until golden and crisp and then set it aside to cool slightly. Use kitchen scissors to snip it into bitesize pieces. Place the frisée or mixed leaf salad in a bowl and add the bacon.

3 Add the asparagus and a little black pepper to the salad. Pour the dressing over and toss the salad lightly, then serve before the leaves begin to wilt.

Energy 239Kcal/989kJ; Protein 13g; Carbohydrate 5g, of which sugars 5g; Fat 19g, of which saturates 4g; Cholesterol 19mg; Calcium 54mg; Fibre 2.7g; Sodium 800mg.

PAN-FRIED CHICKEN LIVER SALAD

THIS FLORENTINE SALAD USES VIN SANTO, A DELICIOUS SWEET DESSERT WINE FROM TUSCANY, BUT THIS IS NOT ESSENTIAL — ANY DESSERT WINE WILL DO, OR A SWEET OR CREAM SHERRY.

Preparation: 4 minutes; Cooking: 6 minutes

SERVES FOUR

INGREDIENTS

75g/3oz fresh baby spinach leaves, washed and dried
75g/3oz lollo rosso leaves, washed dried and torn into pieces
75ml/5 tbsp olive oil
15g/ ½oz/1 tbsp butter
225g/8oz chicken livers, trimmed and thinly sliced
45ml/3 tbsp vin santo
50–75g/2–3oz fresh Parmesan cheese, shaved into curls
salt and ground black pepper

1 Put the spinach and lollo rosso leaves into a large bowl, season with salt and ground black pepper to taste and toss gently to mix.

2 Heat 30ml/2 tbsp of the oil with the butter in a large heavy frying pan. When foaming, add the chicken livers and toss over medium to high heat for 5 minutes, or until the livers are browned on the outside but still pink in the centre. Remove the pan from the heat.

3 Remove the livers from the pan with a slotted spoon, drain them on kitchen paper, then place on top of the salad leaves.

4 Return the pan to medium heat, add the remaining oil and the vin santo and stir until sizzling. Pour the hot dressing over the leaves and livers and toss to coat. Put the salad in a serving bowl and sprinkle over the Parmesan shavings. Serve at once.

COOK'S TIP
If you can't find baby spinach leaves, you can use older spinach, but discard any tough leaves along with the stalks and tear the remainder up into pieces.

Energy 277kcal/1146kJ; Protein 16g; Carbohydrate 0.7g, of which sugars 0.6g; Fat 22.5g, of which saturates 6.9g; Cholesterol 234mg; Calcium 220mg; Fibre 0.8g; Sodium 255mg

PARSLEY AND ROCKET SALAD

BEING LIGHT BUT FULL OF FLAVOUR, THIS MAKES A WELL-ROUNDED FIRST COURSE; IT IS ALSO GOOD SERVED ALONGSIDE RARE ROAST BEEF. USE PARMIGIANO REGGIANO TO ENSURE THIS SALAD IS SPECIAL.

Preparation: 10 minutes; Cooking: 12–17 minutes

SERVES SIX

INGREDIENTS
- 1 garlic clove, halved
- 115g/4oz good white bread, cut into 1cm/½in thick slices
- 45ml/3 tbsp olive oil, plus extra for shallow frying
- 75g/3oz rocket (arugula) leaves
- 75g/3oz baby spinach
- 25g/1oz flat leaf parsley, leaves only
- 45ml/3 tbsp salted capers, rinsed and dried
- 40g/1½oz Parmesan cheese, pared into shavings

For the dressing
- 25ml/5 tsp black olive paste
- 1 garlic clove, finely chopped
- 5ml/1 tsp Dijon mustard
- 75ml/5 tbsp olive oil
- 10ml/2 tsp balsamic vinegar
- ground black pepper

1 First make the dressing. Whisk the black olive paste, garlic and mustard together in a bowl. Gradually whisk in the olive oil, then the vinegar. Adjust the seasoning with black pepper – the dressing should be sufficiently salty.

2 Heat the oven to 190°C/375°F/Gas 5. Rub the halved garlic clove over the bread and tear the slices into bitesize croutons. Toss them in the oil and place on a small baking sheet. Bake for 10–15 minutes, stirring once, until golden brown. Cool on kitchen paper.

3 Mix the rocket, spinach and parsley in a large salad bowl.

4 Heat a shallow layer of olive oil in a frying pan. Add the capers and fry briefly until crisp. Scoop out straight away and drain on kitchen paper.

5 Toss the dressing and croutons into the salad and divide it among 6 bowls or plates. Scatter the Parmesan shavings and the fried capers over the top and serve immediately.

COOK'S TIP
Use a swivel-action or fixed-blade potato peeler to cut thin shavings from a block of Parmigiano Reggiano – some supermarkets sell tubs of ready-shaved cheese. It is easier to make shavings if you choose a relatively young cheese rather than an older, drier and much harder Parmesan.

Energy 219kcal/909kJ; Protein 5.1g; Carbohydrate 10g, of which sugars 1g; Fat 17.9g, of which saturates 3.6g; Cholesterol 7mg; Calcium 155mg; Fibre 1.1g; Sodium 303mg.

SHELLFISH AND
FISH DISHES

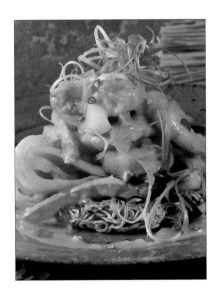

Fish dishes are usually quick to cook, often taking only minutes in the case of prawns (shrimp)
and scallops. Other dishes may take slightly longer, especially if they are baked, but there is still
a wide range here of exciting and tasty fish dishes that will be on the table within half an
hour. For prawn dishes try Sizzling Prawns, Pan-fried Prawns in Garlic, Prawn and New
Potato Salad, Curried Prawns in Coconut Milk or Satay Prawns; or mix them with scallops
in Garlicky Scallops and Prawns. Delicate sole may be served with chive butter, wild
mushrooms or lemon butter sauce. Ever-popular cod appears in a variety of dishes, including
Roast Cod with Pancetta and Mexican-style Cod, while haddock features in Haddock in Cider
Sauce and Omelette Arnold Bennett. Other inspiring dishes include classic Fishcakes, Seafood
Risotto, Sweet and Sour Fish, Red Snapper Burritos, Trout with Crunchy Peppercorns,
Malaysian Steamed Trout Fillets, Hot Smoked Salmon, Seared Tuna with Spicy Watercress
Salad, Grilled Swordfish Skewers and Monkfish with Pimiento and Cream Sauce.

SAUTÉED SCALLOPS

SCALLOPS GO WELL WITH ALL SORTS OF SAUCES, BUT SIMPLE COOKING IS THE BEST WAY TO ENJOY THEIR DELICATE, FRESH-FROM-THE-SEA FLAVOUR.

Preparation: 1 minute; Cooking: 5 minutes

SERVES TWO

INGREDIENTS
  450g/1lb shelled scallops
  25g/1oz/2 tbsp butter
  30ml/2 tbsp dry white vermouth
  15ml/1 tbsp finely chopped fresh
    parsley
  salt and ground black pepper

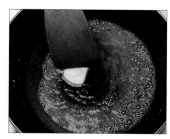

1 Rinse the scallops under cold running water to remove any sand or grit. Drain them well and pat dry using kitchen paper. Spread them out and season them lightly with salt and pepper.

2 In a frying pan large enough to hold the scallops in one layer, heat half the butter until it begins to colour. Sauté the scallops for 3–5 minutes, turning until golden brown on both sides and just firm to the touch. Remove to a serving platter and cover to keep hot.

3 Add the vermouth to the hot frying pan, swirl in the remaining butter, stir in the parsley and pour the sauce over the scallops. Serve immediately.

Energy 378kcal/1588kJ; Protein 52.5g; Carbohydrate 8.4g, of which sugars 0.7g; Fat 13.5g, of which saturates 7.4g; Cholesterol 132mg; Calcium 84mg; Fibre 0.4g; Sodium 485mg.

GARLICKY SCALLOPS AND PRAWNS

SCALLOPS AND PRAWNS PROVIDE A HEALTHY MEAL IN NEXT TO NO TIME. THIS METHOD OF COOKING COMES FROM FRANCE AND IS POPULAR IN PROVENCE.

Preparation: 1 minute; Cooking: 4–5 minutes

SERVES TWO TO FOUR

INGREDIENTS
  6 large shelled scallops
  6–8 large raw prawns (jumbo shrimp),
    peeled
  plain (all-purpose) flour, for dusting
  30–45ml/2–3 tbsp olive oil
  1 garlic clove, finely chopped
  15ml/1 tbsp chopped fresh basil
  30–45ml/2–3 tbsp lemon juice
  salt and ground black pepper

COOK'S TIP

Like oysters, scallops are traditionally best when there is an 'r' in the month. Frozen scallops are available, but their quality is not as good as the fresh ones.

1 Rinse the scallops under cold running water to remove any sand or grit. Drain, then pat dry using kitchen paper. Cut them in half crossways. Season the scallops and prawns with salt and pepper and dust lightly with flour. Heat the oil in a large frying pan over high heat and add the scallops and prawns.

2 Reduce the heat slightly and cook for 2 minutes, then turn the scallops and prawns and add the garlic and basil, shaking the pan to distribute them evenly. Cook for a further 2 minutes, until the scallops are golden and just firm to the touch. Sprinkle over the lemon juice and toss to blend. Serve at once.

Energy 159kcal/664kJ; Protein 16.4g; Carbohydrate 2.9g, of which sugars 0.2g; Fat 9.2g, of which saturates 1.4g; Cholesterol 72mg; Calcium 51mg; Fibre 0.4g; Sodium 140mg.

STIR-FRIED PRAWNS WITH TAMARIND

THE SOUR, TANGY FLAVOUR THAT IS CHARACTERISTIC OF MANY THAI DISHES COMES FROM TAMARIND.
FRESH TAMARIND PODS CAN BE BOUGHT, BUT IT IS MUCH EASIER TO USE A BLOCK OF TAMARIND PASTE.

Preparation: 8 minutes; Cooking: 10–12 minutes

SERVES FOUR TO SIX

INGREDIENTS

6 dried red chillies
30ml/2 tbsp vegetable oil
30ml/2 tbsp chopped onion
30ml/2 tbsp palm sugar (jaggery) or
   light muscovado (brown) sugar
30ml/2 tbsp chicken stock or water
15ml/1 tbsp Thai fish sauce
90ml/6 tbsp tamarind juice, made
   by mixing tamarind paste with
   warm water
450g/1lb raw prawns (shrimp), peeled
15ml/1 tbsp fried chopped garlic
30ml/2 tbsp fried sliced shallots

1 Heat a wok or large frying pan, but do not add any oil at this stage. Add the dried chillies and dry-fry them by pressing them against the surface of the wok or pan with a spatula, turning them occasionally. Do not let them burn. Set them aside to cool slightly.

2 Add the oil to the wok or pan and reheat. Add the chopped onion and cook over medium heat, stirring occasionally, for 2–3 minutes, until softened and golden brown.

3 Add the sugar, stock or water, fish sauce, dry-fried red chillies and the tamarind juice, stirring constantly until the sugar has dissolved. Bring to the boil, then lower the heat slightly.

4 Add the prawns, garlic and shallots. Toss over the heat for 3–4 minutes, until the prawns are cooked. Transfer to a warmed dish or individual bowls.

COOK'S TIP
Leave a few prawns (shrimp) in their shells for a garnish, if you like.

Energy 112kcal/469kJ; Protein 13.4g; Carbohydrate 5.5g, of which sugars 5.2g; Fat 4.1g, of which saturates 0.5g; Cholesterol 146mg; Calcium 65mg; Fibre 0.2g; Sodium 321mg.

SIZZLING PRAWNS

WHEN YOU LASH OUT AND BUY A LUXURY ITEM LIKE THESE LARGE PRAWNS, YOU WANT TO BE SURE THEY TASTE GREAT. THIS RECIPE IS SWIFT, SIMPLE AND ALWAYS A SURE-FIRE SUCCESS.

Preparation: 2–3 minutes; Cooking: 5 minutes

SERVES FOUR

INGREDIENTS
  1–2 dried chillies (to taste)
  60ml/4 tbsp olive oil
  3 garlic cloves, finely chopped
  16 large raw prawns (jumbo shrimp),
    in the shell
  salt and ground black pepper
  French bread, to serve

VARIATION
Another great way to serve the prawns (shrimp) is in a warm lime and sweet chilli dressing. Use garlic to flavour the oil, but remove it before frying the prawns. Let the oil for frying cool slightly, then whisk in fresh lime juice and a little sweet chilli sauce. Spoon over the prawns.

1 Split the chillies lengthways and discard the seeds. It is best to do this with a knife and fork, because the seeds, in particular, contain hot capsaicin, which can be very irritating to the eyes, nose and mouth.

2 Heat the oil in a large frying pan and stir-fry the garlic and chilli for 1 minute, until the garlic begins to turn brown.

3 Add the whole prawns and stir-fry for 3–4 minutes, coating them well with the flavoured oil.

4 Remove from the heat and divide the prawns among four dishes. Spoon over the flavoured oil and serve immediately. (Remember to provide a plate for the heads and shells, plus plenty of napkins for messy fingers.)

Energy 124kcal/511kJ; Protein 5.7g; Carbohydrate 0g, of which sugars 0g; Fat 11.2g, of which saturates 1.6g; Cholesterol 63mg; Calcium 26mg; Fibre 0g; Sodium 62mg

SOFT-SHELL CRABS WITH CHILLI AND SALT

IF FRESH SOFT-SHELL CRABS ARE UNAVAILABLE, YOU CAN BUY FROZEN ONES IN ORIENTAL SUPERMARKETS.
ALLOW TWO SMALL CRABS PER SERVING, OR ONE IF THEY ARE LARGE.

Preparation: 6 minutes; Cooking: 6–14 minutes

SERVES FOUR

INGREDIENTS
8 small soft-shell crabs, thawed if
   frozen
50g/2oz/½ cup plain (all-purpose)
   flour
60ml/4 tbsp groundnut (peanut) or
   vegetable oil
2 large fresh red chillies, or 1 green
   and 1 red, seeded and thinly sliced
4 spring onions (scallions) or a small
   bunch of garlic chives, chopped
sea salt and ground black pepper
To serve
   shredded lettuce, mooli (daikon) and
   carrot
   light soy sauce

COOK'S TIP
If you can't locate any mooli, use
celeriac instead.

1 Pat the crabs dry with kitchen paper. Season the flour with pepper and coat the crabs lightly with the mixture.

2 Heat the oil in a shallow pan until very hot, then put in the crabs (you may need to do this in two batches). Fry for 2–3 minutes on each side, until the crabs are golden brown but still juicy in the middle. Drain the cooked crabs on kitchen paper and keep hot.

3 Add the sliced chillies and spring onions or garlic chives to the oil remaining in the pan and cook gently for about 2 minutes. Sprinkle over a generous pinch of salt, then spread the mixture on to the crabs.

4 Mix the shredded lettuce, mooli and carrot together. Arrange on plates, top each portion with two crabs and serve, with light soy sauce for dipping.

Energy 306kcal/1280kJ; Protein 37.6g; Carbohydrate 10g, of which sugars 0.5g; Fat 13g, of which saturates 1.5g; Cholesterol 144mg; Calcium 262mg; Fibre 0.5g; Sodium 1101mg.

DEVILLED WHITEBAIT

SERVE THESE DELICIOUSLY CRISP LITTLE FISH WITH LEMON WEDGES AND THINLY SLICED BROWN BREAD
AND BUTTER, AND EAT THEM WITH YOUR FINGERS.

Preparation: 3 minutes; Cooking: 6–9 minutes

SERVES FOUR

INGREDIENTS
oil for deep-frying
150ml/¼ pint/⅔ cup milk
115g/4oz/1 cup plain (all-purpose)
   flour
450g/1lb whitebait, thawed if frozen
   and dried thoroughly on kitchen
   paper
salt, freshly ground black pepper and
   cayenne pepper

1 Heat the oil in a large pan or deep-fryer. Put the milk in a shallow bowl and spoon the flour into a plastic bag. Season the flour with salt, pepper and a little cayenne.

2 Dip a handful of the whitebait into the bowl of milk, drain them well, then pop them into the paper bag. Shake gently to coat them evenly in the seasoned flour. Repeat until all the fish have been coated. This is the easiest method of flouring whitebait, but don't add too many at once, or they will stick together

3 Heat the oil to 190°C/375°F or until a cube of stale bread, dropped into the oil, browns in 20 seconds. Add a batch of whitebait, preferably in a chip basket, and fry for 2–3 minutes, until crisp and golden brown. Drain and keep hot while you fry the rest. Sprinkle with more cayenne and serve very hot.

Energy 656kcal/2718kJ; Protein 24.4g; Carbohydrate 6.6g, of which sugars 0.1g; Fat 59.4g, of which saturates 0g; Cholesterol 0mg; Calcium 1075mg; Fibre 0.3g; Sodium 288mg.

PRAWNS FRIED IN GARLIC AND VERMOUTH

ALTHOUGH EXPENSIVE, THIS IS A VERY QUICK AND SIMPLE DISH, IDEAL FOR AN IMPROMPTU SUPPER WITH FRIENDS. SERVE WITH HOT CRUSTY ITALIAN BREAD TO SCOOP UP THE JUICES.

Preparation: 2–3 minutes; Cooking: 5–8 minutes

SERVES FOUR

INGREDIENTS

   60ml/4 tbsp extra virgin olive oil
   32 large raw prawns (jumbo shrimp),
     in their shells
   4 garlic cloves, finely chopped
   120ml/4fl oz/ ½ cup Italian dry
     white vermouth
   45ml/3 tbsp passata (bottled strained
     tomatoes)
   salt and ground black pepper
   chopped fresh flat leaf parsley,
     to garnish
   crusty bread, to serve

COOK'S TIP

If you want to serve this dish but need to keep the cost down, halve the number of prawns (shrimp) and serve it as an appetizer instead.

1 Heat the olive oil in a large heavy frying pan until just sizzling. Add the prawns and toss over a medium to high heat until their shells just begin to turn pink. Sprinkle the garlic over the prawns in the pan and toss again, then add the vermouth and let it bubble, tossing the prawns constantly so that they cook evenly and absorb the flavours of the garlic and vermouth.

2 Keeping the pan on the heat, add the passata, with salt and pepper to taste. Stir until the prawns are thoroughly coated in the sauce. Serve at once, sprinkled with the parsley and accompanied by plenty of hot crusty bread.

Energy 219Kcal/911kJ; Protein 19.9g; Carbohydrate 1.3g, of which sugars 1.3g; Fat 11.7g, of which saturates 1.7g; Cholesterol 219mg; Calcium 92mg; Fibre 0.1g; Sodium 243mg

THAI STEAMED MUSSELS IN COCONUT MILK

AN IDEAL DISH FOR INFORMAL ENTERTAINING, MUSSELS STEAMED IN COCONUT MILK AND FRESH AROMATIC HERBS ARE QUICK AND EASY TO PREPARE AND GREAT FOR A RELAXED DINNER WITH FRIENDS.

Preparation: 10 minutes; Cooking: 6–7 minutes

SERVES FOUR

INGREDIENTS

1.6kg/3½lb mussels
15ml/1 tbsp sunflower oil
6 garlic cloves, roughly chopped
15ml/1 tbsp finely chopped fresh
  root ginger
2 large red chillies, seeded and
  finely sliced
6 spring onions (scallions),
  finely chopped
400ml/14fl oz/1⅔ cups coconut milk
45ml/3 tbsp light soy sauce
2 limes
5ml/1 tsp caster (superfine) sugar
a large handful of chopped
  coriander (cilantro)
salt and ground black pepper

3 Grate the rind of the limes into the ginger mixture, then squeeze both fruit and add the juice to the wok with the coconut milk, soy sauce and sugar. Stir to mix.

4 Bring the mixture to the boil, then add the mussels. Return to the boil, cover and cook briskly for 5–6 minutes, or until all the mussels have opened. Discard any unopened mussels.

5 Remove the wok from the heat and stir in the chopped coriander. Season the mussels well with salt and pepper. Ladle into warmed bowls and serve immediately.

COOK'S TIP
For an informal supper with friends, take the wok straight to the table. There's something utterly irresistible about eating straight from the pan.

1 Scrub the mussels in cold water. Scrape off any barnacles with a knife, then pull out and discard the fibrous "beard" visible between the hinge on any of the shells. Discard any mussels that are not tightly closed, or which fail to close when tapped sharply.

2 Heat a wok over a high heat and then add the oil. Stir in the garlic, ginger, chillies and spring onions and stir-fry for 30 seconds.

COOK'S TIP
The best-flavoured mussels are blue or European mussels from cold British waters. They are inexpensive, so don't be afraid to buy more than you need!

Energy 160kcal/679kJ; Protein 21.5g; Carbohydrate 6.7g, of which sugars 6.7g; Fat 5.5g, of which saturates 1g; Cholesterol 48mg; Calcium 272mg; Fibre 0.2g; Sodium 630mg

LEMON GRASS PRAWNS ON NOODLE CAKE

THIS DELICIOUSLY LIGHT AND FRAGRANT PRAWN CURRY LOOKS GOOD ENOUGH FOR A DINNER PARTY BUT TAKES VERY LITTLE TIME TO PREPARE. THE CRISP NOODLE CAKE ADDS AN UNUSUAL TOUCH.

Preparation: 10 minutes; Cooking: 15 minutes

SERVES FOUR

INGREDIENTS

300g/11oz thin egg noodles
60ml/4 tbsp vegetable oil
500g/1¼ lb raw king prawns (jumbo
  shrimp), peeled and de-veined
2.5ml/ ½ tsp ground coriander
15ml/1 tbsp ground turmeric
2 garlic cloves, finely chopped
2 slices fresh root ginger,
  finely chopped
2 lemon grass stalks, finely chopped
2 shallots, finely chopped
15ml/1 tbsp tomato purée (paste)
250ml/8fl oz/1 cup coconut cream
15–30ml/1–2 tbsp fresh lime juice
15–30ml/1–2 tbsp Thai fish sauce
4–6 kaffir lime leaves (optional)
1 cucumber, peeled, seeded and cut
  into 5cm/2in batons
1 tomato, seeded and cut into strips
2 red chillies, seeded and
  finely sliced
salt and ground black pepper
finely sliced spring onions (scallions),
  and a few coriander (cilantro) sprigs,
  to garnish

1 Cook the egg noodles in a pan of boiling water until just tender. Drain, rinse under cold running water and drain well.

2 Heat 15ml/1 tbsp of the oil in a large frying pan. Add the noodles, distributing them evenly, and fry for 4–5 minutes until crisp and golden. Turn the noodle cake over and fry the other side. Alternatively, make four individual cakes. Keep hot.

3 Toss the prawns with the spices, garlic, ginger and lemon grass. Season.

4 Heat the remaining oil in a large frying pan. Fry the shallots for 1 minute, then add the prawns and fry for 2 minutes more. Lift out the prawns.

5 Stir the tomato purée and coconut cream into the mixture remaining in the pan. Stir in lime juice to taste and season with the fish sauce. Bring the sauce to a simmer, return the prawns to the sauce, then add the kaffir lime leaves, if using, and the cucumber. Simmer gently until the prawns are cooked and the sauce is a nice coating consistency.

6 Add the tomato, stir until just warmed through, then add the chillies. Serve on top of the crisp noodle cake(s), garnished with sliced spring onions and coriander sprigs.

COOK'S TIP
When cooking egg noodles, it is a good idea to break them up with a fork as they begin to cook to ensure they cook evenly and that no clumps form.

Energy 517kcal/2178kJ; Protein 32.1g; Carbohydrate 59.8g, of which sugars 7.4g; Fat 18.3g, of which saturates 3.3g; Cholesterol 266mg; Calcium 154mg; Fibre 2.8g; Sodium 735mg.

SEAFOOD RISOTTO

MOST SUPERMARKETS NOW STOCK PACKS OF READY-PREPARED MIXED SEAFOOD SUCH AS PRAWNS, SQUID AND MUSSELS, WHICH ARE IDEAL FOR MAKING THIS QUICK AND EASY RISOTTO.

Preparation: 5 minutes; Cooking: 25 minutes

SERVES FOUR

INGREDIENTS
1 litre/1¾ pints/4 cups fish or
  shellfish stock
50g/2oz/¼ cup butter
2 shallots, chopped
2 garlic cloves, chopped
350g/12oz/1¾ cups risotto rice
150ml/¼ pint/⅔ cup dry white wine
2.5ml/½ tsp powdered saffron, or a
  pinch of saffron threads
400g/14oz mixed prepared seafood
30ml/2 tbsp freshly grated
  Parmesan cheese
salt and ground black pepper
30ml/2 tbsp chopped fresh flat leaf
  parsley, to garnish

1 Pour the fish or shellfish stock into a large saucepan. Bring it to the boil, then reduce the heat and keep it at a gentle simmer. The water needs to be hot when it is added to the rice.

2 Meanwhile, melt the butter in a heavy pan, add the shallots and garlic and cook over a low heat until soft but not coloured. Add the rice, stir well to coat the grains with butter, then pour in the wine. Cook over a medium heat, stirring occasionally, until the wine has been absorbed by the rice.

COOK'S TIP
It is essential to use risotto rice for this dish. You can buy arborio or carnaroli risotto rice in an Italian delicatessan or a large supermarket.

3 Add a ladleful of hot stock and the saffron and cook, stirring continuously, until the liquid has been absorbed. Add the seafood and stir well. Continue to add stock a ladleful at a time, waiting until each quantity has been absorbed before adding more (this will take about 20 minutes) until the rice is swollen and creamy but still al dente (it has a little bite in the middle).

VARIATION
Use peeled prawns (shrimp), or cubes of fish such as cod or salmon in place of the mixed prepared seafood.

4 Vigorously mix in the freshly grated Parmesan and season to taste, then sprinkle over the chopped parsley and serve at once.

Energy 404kcal/1693kJ; Protein 28.1g; Carbohydrate 56.3g, of which sugars 1.1g; Fat 3.9g, of which saturates 1.9g; Cholesterol 228mg; Calcium 200mg; Fibre 0.2g; Sodium 301mg.

PRAWN AND NEW POTATO STEW

NEW POTATOES WITH PLENTY OF FLAVOUR ARE ESSENTIAL FOR THIS STEW. FOR A REALLY EASY SUPPER DISH, SERVE WITH WARM, CRUSTY BREAD TO MOP UP THE DELICIOUS SAUCE, AND A GREEN SALAD.

Preparation: 3 minutes; Cooking: 18–23 minutes

SERVES FOUR

INGREDIENTS

- 675g/1½lb small new potatoes, scrubbed
- 15g/½oz/½ cup fresh coriander (cilantro), half finely choppped
- 350g/12oz jar good-quality tomato and chilli sauce
- 300g/11oz cooked peeled prawns (shrimp), thawed and drained if frozen

1 Cook the potatoes in lightly salted, boiling water for 10–15 minutes, until tender. Drain and return to the pan.

2 Add the chopped coriander to the pan with the tomato and chilli sauce and 90ml/6 tbsp water. Bring to the boil, reduce the heat, cover and simmer gently for 5 minutes.

3 Stir in the prawns and heat briefly until they are warmed through. Do not overheat or they will become tough and tasteless. Spoon into bowls and serve sprinkled with the remaining coriander.

Energy 271Kcal/1147kJ; Protein 22g; Carbohydrate 35g, of which sugars 6g; Fat 6g, of which saturates 2g; Cholesterol 219mg; Calcium 113mg; Fibre 2.9g; Sodium 1.5g

SEAFOOD AND SPRING ONION SKEWERS

IF YOU MAKE THESE SKEWERS QUITE SMALL, THEY ARE GOOD AS A CANAPÉ TO SERVE AT A DRINKS PARTY OR BEFORE DINNER, WITH THE TARTARE SAUCE OFFERED AS A DIP.

Preparation: 20 minutes; Cooking: 5–6 minutes

MAKES NINE

INGREDIENTS

675g/1½lb monkfish tail, filleted,
  skinned and membrane removed
1 bunch thick spring onions
  (scallions)
75ml/5 tbsp olive oil
1 garlic clove, finely chopped
15ml/1 tbsp lemon juice
5ml/1 tsp dried oregano
30ml/2 tbsp chopped fresh flat leaf
  parsley
12–18 small scallops or large raw
  prawns (shrimp)
75g/3oz/1½ cups fine fresh
  breadcrumbs
salt and ground black pepper

For the tartare sauce
2 egg yolks
300ml/½ pint/1¼ cups olive oil, or
  vegetable oil and olive oil mixed
15–30ml/1–2 tbsp lemon juice
5ml/1 tsp French mustard, preferably
  tarragon mustard
15ml/1 tbsp chopped gherkin or
  pickled cucumber
15ml/1 tbsp chopped capers
30ml/2 tbsp chopped fresh flat
  leaf parsley
30ml/2 tbsp snipped fresh chives
5ml/1 tsp chopped fresh tarragon

2 Make the tartare sauce. Whisk the egg yolks and a pinch of salt. Whisk in the oil, a drop at a time at first. When about half the oil is incorporated, add it in a thin stream, whisking all the time. Stop when the mayonnaise is very thick.

4 Mix the breadcrumbs and remaining parsley together. Toss the seafood and spring onions in the mixture to coat.

5 Preheat the grill (broiler). Drain the skewers and thread the monkfish, scallops or prawns and spring onions on to them. Drizzle with marinade then grill (broil) for 5–6 minutes in total, turning once and drizzling with the marinade, until the fish is just cooked. Serve immediately with the tartare sauce.

1 Cut the monkfish and spring onions into 18 pieces. Mix the oil, garlic, lemon juice, oregano and half the parsley with seasoning. Add the monkfish, scallops or prawns and spring onions, then marinate for 15 minutes.

3 Whisk in 15ml/1 tbsp of the lemon juice, then a little more oil. Stir in all the mustard, gherkin or cucumber, capers, parsley, chives and tarragon. Add more lemon juice and seasoning to taste. Soak 9 bamboo skewers in cold water.

Energy 385kcal/1597kJ; Protein 20.3g; Carbohydrate 7.7g, of which sugars 0.7g; Fat 30.5g, of which saturates 4g; Cholesterol 67mg; Calcium 43mg; Fibre 0.6g; Sodium 139mg.

PRAWN AND VEGETABLE BALTI

A DELICIOUS ACCOMPANIMENT TO OTHER BALTI DISHES. DOUBLE THE QUANTITIES IF SERVING IT SOLO.

Preparation: 3 minutes; Cooking: 7 minutes

SERVES FOUR

INGREDIENTS

175g/6oz cooked, peeled prawns
  (shrimp), thawed if frozen
30ml/2 tbsp corn oil
1.5ml/¼ tsp onion seeds
4–6 curry leaves
115g/4oz/1 cup frozen peas
115g/4oz/⅔ cup frozen sweetcorn
1 large courgette (zucchini), sliced
1 red (bell) pepper, seeded and
  roughly diced
5ml/1 tsp crushed coriander seeds
5ml/1 tsp crushed dried red chillies
15ml/1 tbsp lemon juice
salt
15ml/1 tbsp fresh coriander (cilantro)
  leaves, to garnish

1 Drain any excess liquid from the prawns if thawed and pat them dry on kitchen paper. Heat the oil with the onion seeds and curry leaves in a non-stick wok or frying pan.

2 Add the prawns to the wok or frying pan and stir-fry until any liquid has evaporated.

3 Add the vegetables and stir-fry for 3–5 minutes more.

4 Add the coriander seeds, dried red chillies and lemon juice. Toss over the heat for 1 minute, season to taste and serve, garnished with the fresh coriander leaves.

COOK'S TIP
Crush whole seeds in an electric spice grinder or a marble mortar and pestle.

Energy 165kcal/688kJ; Protein 11.9g; Carbohydrate 14.6g, of which sugars 7g; Fat 6.9g, of which saturates 0.9g; Cholesterol 85mg; Calcium 58mg; Fibre 2.9g; Sodium 163mg.

GREEN PRAWN CURRY

THIS POPULAR, FRAGRANT, CREAMY PRAWN CURRY TAKES VERY LITTLE TIME TO PREPARE.

Preparation: 3 minutes; Cooking: 8 minutes

SERVES FOUR TO SIX

INGREDIENTS

   30ml/2 tbsp vegetable oil
   30ml/2 tbsp green curry paste
   450g/1lb raw king prawns (jumbo
     shrimp), shelled and de-veined
   4 kaffir lime leaves, torn
   1 lemon grass stalk, bruised and
     chopped
   250ml/8fl oz/1 cup coconut cream
   30ml/2 tbsp Thai fish sauce
   ½ cucumber, seeded and cut into
     thin batons
   10–15 basil leaves
   sliced green chillies, to garnish

1 Heat the oil in a frying pan. Add the green curry paste and fry until bubbling and fragrant.

2 Add the prawns, kaffir lime leaves and lemon grass. Fry for about 2 minutes, until the prawns are pink.

3 Stir in the coconut cream and bring to a gentle boil. Simmer, stirring, for about 5 minutes or until the prawns are tender.

4 Stir in the fish sauce and cucumber. Add the basil leaves, then top with the green chillies and serve.

Energy 115kcal/481kJ; Protein 14.1g; Carbohydrate 4g, of which sugars 2.6g; Fat 4.8g, of which saturates 0.6g; Cholesterol 146mg; Calcium 107mg; Fibre 1.3g; Sodium 567mg.

PINEAPPLE CURRY WITH PRAWNS AND MUSSELS

THE DELICATE SWEET AND SOUR FLAVOUR OF THIS SEAFOOD CURRY COMES FROM THE PINEAPPLE.
ALTHOUGH IT MAY SEEM AN ODD COMBINATION, IT IS DELICIOUS.

Preparation: 15 minutes; Cooking: 10 minutes

SERVES FOUR TO SIX

INGREDIENTS
600ml/1 pint/2½ cups coconut milk
30ml/2 tbsp red curry paste
30ml/2 tbsp Thai fish sauce
15ml/1 tbsp sugar
225g/8oz raw king prawns (jumbo
   shrimp), shelled and de-veined
450g/1lb live mussels, cleaned,
   beards removed and any discarded
   that don't close when tapped
175g/6oz fresh pineapple, finely
   crushed or chopped
5 kaffir lime leaves
For the garnish
2 red chillies, chopped
fresh coriander (cilantro) leaves

1 In a large pan, bring half the coconut
milk to the boil. Heat, stirring, until
it separates.

2 Add the red curry paste and cook
until fragrant. Add the fish sauce and
sugar and continue to cook for about
1 minute.

3 Stir in the rest of the coconut milk
and bring back to the boil. Add the king
prawns, mussels and pineapple. Tear
the kaffir lime leaves into pieces and
stir them into the mixture.

4 Reheat until boiling, then lower the
heat and simmer for 3–5 minutes, until
the prawns are cooked and the mussels
have opened. Remove and discard any
mussels that have not opened. Spoon
into a serving dish, garnish with
chopped red chillies and coriander
leaves and serve.

Energy 96kcal/408kJ; Protein 11.8g; Carbohydrate 10.5g, of which sugars 10.5g; Fat 1.1g, of which saturates 0.3g; Cholesterol 92mg; Calcium 113mg; Fibre 0.4g; Sodium 239mg.

CURRIED PRAWNS IN COCONUT MILK

PRAWNS AND COCONUT ARE AN EXCELLENT COMBINATION THAT OCCURS THROUGHOUT MUCH EASTERN
COOKERY. THE ADDITION HERE OF CHERRY TOMATOES ADDS AN INTERESTING TWIST.

Preparation: 4 minutes; Cooking: 22 minutes

SERVES FOUR TO SIX

INGREDIENTS
600ml/1 pint/2½ cups coconut milk
30ml/2 tbsp yellow curry paste
   (see Cook's Tip)
15ml/1 tbsp Thai fish sauce
2.5ml/½ tsp salt
5ml/1 tsp sugar
450g/1lb raw king prawns (jumbo
   shrimp), shelled, tails left intact
   and deveined
225g/8oz cherry tomatoes
juice of ½ lime, to serve
For the garnish
2 red chillies, cut into strips
fresh coriander (cilantro) leaves

1 Put half the coconut milk into a pan
and bring to the boil over medium heat.

2 Add the yellow curry paste, stir until it
dissolves, then simmer for about 10
minutes. Add the fish sauce, salt, sugar
and remaining coconut milk. Simmer for
5 minutes more until the sauce thickens.

COOK'S TIP
To make yellow curry paste, blend 6–8
yellow chillies, 1 chopped lemon grass
stalk, 4 peeled shallots, 4 garlic cloves,
15ml/1 tbsp chopped fresh root ginger,
5ml/1 tsp coriander seeds, 5ml/1 tsp salt,
5ml/1 tsp mustard powder, 2.5ml/½ tsp
ground cinnamon, 15ml/1 tbsp light brown
sugar and 30ml/2 tbsp oil in a food
processor until a paste has been formed.

3 Add the prawns and cherry tomatoes.
Simmer very gently for about 5 minutes
until the prawns are pink and tender.

4 Serve sprinkled with lime juice and
garnished with chillies and fresh
coriander leaves.

Energy 116kcal/491kJ; Protein 14.2g; Carbohydrate 8.1g, of which sugars 6.8g; Fat 3.2g, of which saturates 0.5g; Cholesterol 146mg; Calcium 123mg; Fibre 1.5g; Sodium 278mg.

SATAY PRAWNS

THIS DELICIOUS DISH IS INSPIRED BY THE CLASSIC INDONESIAN SATAY. THE COMBINATION OF MILD PEANUTS, AROMATIC SPICES, SWEET COCONUT MILK AND ZESTY LEMON JUICE IN THE DIP IS DELICIOUS.

Preparation: 12 minutes; Cooking: 25 minutes

SERVES FOUR TO SIX

INGREDIENTS

    450g/1lb king prawns (jumbo shrimp),
       shelled, tails left intact and deveined
    25ml/1½ tbsp vegetable oil
For the peanut sauce
    25ml/1½ tbsp vegetable oil
    15ml/1 tbsp chopped garlic
    1 small onion, chopped
    3–4 red chillies, seeded and chopped
    3 kaffir lime leaves, torn
    1 lemon grass stalk, bruised and
       chopped
    5ml/1 tsp medium curry paste
    250ml/8fl oz/1 cup coconut milk
    1cm/½in piece cinnamon stick
    75g/3oz/⅓ cup crunchy peanut butter
    45ml/3 tbsp tamarind juice, made
       by mixing tamarind paste with
       warm water
    30ml/2 tbsp Thai fish sauce
    30ml/2 tbsp palm sugar (jaggery) or
       light muscovado (brown) sugar
    juice of ½ lemon
For the garnish
    ½ bunch fresh coriander (cilantro)
       leaves (optional)
    4 fresh red chillies, finely sliced
       (optional)
    spring onions (scallions),
       cut diagonally

1 Make the peanut sauce. Heat half the oil in a wok or large, heavy frying pan. Add the garlic and onion and cook over medium heat, stirring occasionally, for 3 minutes, until the mixture has softened but not browned.

2 Add the chillies, kaffir lime leaves, lemon grass and curry paste. Stir well and cook for a further 2–3 minutes, then stir in the coconut milk, cinnamon stick, peanut butter, tamarind juice, fish sauce, sugar and lemon juice. Cook, stirring constantly, until well blended.

3 Bring to the boil, then reduce the heat to low and simmer gently for 15 minutes, until the sauce thickens. Stir occasionally with a wooden spoon to prevent the sauce from sticking to the base of the wok or frying pan.

4 Meanwhile, pan-fry the prawns, then thread on to skewers. Alternatively, thread the prawns on to skewers and brush with a little oil. Cook under a preheated grill (broiler) for 2 minutes on each side, until they turn pink and are firm to the touch.

5 Remove the cinnamon stick from the sauce and discard. Arrange the skewered prawns on a warmed platter, garnish with spring onions and coriander leaves and sliced red chillies, if you like, and serve with the sauce.

Energy 219kcal/913kJ; Protein 16.6g; Carbohydrate 10.1g, of which sugars 9g; Fat 12.7g, of which saturates 2.4g; Cholesterol 146mg; Calcium 98mg; Fibre 1.2g; Sodium 414mg.

PRAWNS WITH ALMOND AND TOMATO SAUCE

GROUND ALMONDS ADD AN INTERESTING TEXTURE TO THE CREAMY, PIQUANT SAUCE THAT ACCOMPANIES THESE SUCCULENT SHELLFISH.

Preparation: 12 minutes; Cooking: 18–20 minutes

SERVES SIX

INGREDIENTS
1 dried chilli
30ml/2 tbsp vegetable oil
1 onion, chopped finely
3 garlic cloves, crushed
8 plum tomatoes
5ml/1 tsp ground cumin
120ml/4fl oz/½ cup chicken stock
130g/4½oz/generous 1 cup ground almonds
175ml/6fl oz/¾ cup crème fraîche
½ lime
900g/2lb cooked, peeled prawns (shrimp)
salt
For the garnish
fresh coriander (cilantro)
spring onion (scallion) strips
To serve
cooked rice
warmed tortillas

1 Place the dried chilli in a heatproof bowl and pour boiling water over to cover. Leave to soak for 10 minutes until softened. Drain, remove the stalk, then slit the chilli and scrape out the seeds with a small sharp knife. Chop the flesh roughly and set it aside.

2 Meanwhile, heat the oil in a frying pan and fry the onion and garlic over a low heat until softened.

3 Cut a cross in the base of each tomato. Place them in a heatproof bowl and cover with boiling water. After 30 seconds, lift them out and plunge them into a bowl of cold water. Drain.

4 Skin and seed the tomatoes. Chop the flesh into 1cm/½ in cubes and add them to the onion mixture in the frying pan, with the chopped chilli. Stir in the ground cumin and cook for 10 minutes, stirring occasionally.

5 Tip the mixture into a food processor or blender. Add the stock and process on high speed until smooth.

6 Pour the mixture into a large pan, then add the ground almonds and stir over a low heat for 2–3 minutes. Stir in the crème fraîche until it has been incorporated completely.

7 Squeeze the juice from the lime into the sauce and stir it in. Season with salt to taste, then increase the heat and bring the sauce to simmering point.

8 Add the prawns to the sauce and heat until warmed through. Serve on a bed of hot rice garnished with the coriander and spring onion strips. Offer warm tortillas separately.

Energy 416kcal/1732kJ; Protein 32.7g; Carbohydrate 7.1g, of which sugars 6.2g; Fat 28.7g, of which saturates 9.6g; Cholesterol 325mg; Calcium 199mg; Fibre 3.1g; Sodium 307mg.

GRILLED SOLE WITH CHIVE BUTTER

THE BEST WAY OF TRANSFORMING SIMPLE GRILLED FISH INTO A LUXURY DISH IS BY TOPPING IT WITH A FLAVOURED BUTTER. THIS ONE, FLAVOURED WITH LEMON GRASS AND LIME, IS A WINNER.

Preparation: 3–4 minutes; Cooking: 10 minutes

SERVES FOUR

INGREDIENTS

115g/4oz/½ cup unsalted (sweet)
   butter, softened, plus extra, melted
5ml/1 tsp diced lemon grass
pinch of finely grated lime rind
1 kaffir lime leaf, very finely
   shredded (optional)
45ml/3 tbsp chopped chives or
   chopped chive flowers, plus extra
   chives or chive flowers to garnish
2.5–5ml/½–1 tsp Thai fish sauce
4 sole, skinned
salt and ground black pepper
lemon or lime wedges, to serve

COOK'S TIP
Finer white fish fillets, such as plaice,
can be cooked in this way, but reduce
the cooking time slightly.

1 Cream the butter with the lemon
grass, lime rind, lime leaf, if using, and
chives or chive flowers. Season to taste
with Thai fish sauce, salt and pepper.

2 Chill the butter mixture to firm it a
little, then form it into a roll and wrap in
foil or clear film (plastic wrap). Chill
until firm. Preheat the grill (broiler).

3 Brush the fish with melted butter.
Place it on the grill rack and season.
Grill (broil) for about 5 minutes on each
side, until firm and just cooked.

4 Meanwhile, cut the chilled butter into
thin slices and put these on the fish.
Garnish with chives and serve with
lemon or lime wedges.

Energy 349kcal/1447kJ; Protein 27.4g; Carbohydrate 0.5g, of which sugars 0.5g; Fat 26.3g, of which saturates 15g; Cholesterol 136mg; Calcium 49mg; Fibre 0g; Sodium 591mg

SOLE WITH WILD MUSHROOMS

IF POSSIBLE, USE CHANTERELLES FOR THIS DISH; THEIR GLOWING ORANGE COLOUR COMBINES REALLY WONDERFULLY WITH THE INTENSELY GOLDEN SAFFRON SAUCE.

Preparation: 10 minutes; Cooking: 18–20 minutes

SERVES FOUR

INGREDIENTS

4 Dover sole fillets, about 115g/4oz each, skinned and halved lengthways
50g/2oz/4 tbsp butter
500ml/17fl oz/generous 2 cups fish stock
150g/5oz/2 cups chanterelles, wiped clean and halved (or quartered if large)
a large pinch of saffron threads
150ml/¼ pint/⅔ cup double (heavy) cream
1 egg yolk
salt and ground white pepper
finely chopped fresh parsley
parsley sprigs, to garnish
boiled new potatoes, to serve

1 Preheat the oven to 200ºC/400ºF/Gas 6. Place the sole fillets on a chopping board with the skinned side uppermost. Season them with salt and white pepper, then roll them up. Use a little of the butter to grease a baking dish just large enough to hold all the sole fillets in a single layer, arrange the sole rolls in it, then pour over the fish stock. Cover tightly with foil and bake for 12–15 minutes, until cooked through.

2 Heat the remaining butter in a frying pan until foaming, and sauté the mushrooms for 3–4 minutes, until just tender. Season with salt and pepper and keep hot.

3 Lift the cooked sole fillets out of the cooking liquid and place them in a heated serving dish. Keep hot. Strain the liquid into a small saucepan, add the saffron, set over a very high heat and boil until reduced to about 250ml/8fl oz/1 cup. Stir in the cream then let the sauce bubble gently once or twice.

4 Lightly beat the egg yolk in a small bowl, pour on a little of the hot sauce and stir well. Stir the mixture into the remaining sauce in the pan and cook over a very low heat for 1–2 minutes, until slightly thickened. Season to taste. Stir the chanterelles into the sauce and pour it over the sole fillets. Sprinkle over the chopped parsley, garnish with the parsley sprigs and serve at once. Boiled new potatoes make the perfect accompaniment to this dish.

Energy 411kcal/1699kJ; Protein 24.7g; Carbohydrate 0.9g, of which sugars 0.8g; Fat 34.2g, of which saturates 19.5g; Cholesterol 191mg; Calcium 65mg; Fibre 0.4g; Sodium 213mg.

PAN-FRIED SOLE WITH LEMON BUTTER SAUCE

THE DELICATE FLAVOUR AND TEXTURE OF SOLE IS BROUGHT OUT IN THIS 10-MINUTE CLASSIC RECIPE, WHICH USES JUST A SIMPLE SAUCE TO COMPLEMENT THE FISH.

Preparation: 1 minute; Cooking: 9 minutes

SERVES TWO

INGREDIENTS
- 30–45ml/2–3 tbsp plain (all-purpose) flour
- 4 lemon or Dover sole fillets (see Cook's Tips)
- 45ml/3 tbsp olive oil
- 50g/2oz/¼ cup butter
- 60ml/4 tbsp lemon juice
- 30ml/2 tbsp rinsed bottled capers
- salt and ground black pepper

For the garnish
- fresh flat leaf parsley
- lemon wedges

1 Season the flour with salt and pepper. Coat the sole fillets evenly on both sides. Heat the oil with half the butter in a large shallow pan until foaming. Add two sole fillets and fry over a medium heat for 2–3 minutes on each side.

2 Lift out the sole fillets with a fish slice (metal spatula) and place on a warmed serving platter. Keep hot. Fry the remaining sole fillets in the same way, then and add them to the platter.

3 Remove the pan from the heat and add the lemon juice and remaining butter. Return the pan to a high heat and stir vigorously until the pan juices are sizzling and beginning to turn golden brown.

4 Remove from the heat and stir in the capers.

5 Arrange the sole fillets on two plates and pour the pan juices over them. Sprinkle with salt and pepper to taste.

6 Garnish with the parsley and lemon wedges. Serve at once.

COOK'S TIPS
- Lemon sole is used here because it is often easier to obtain and less expensive than Dover sole, but you can use whichever fish you choose.
- It is important to cook the pan juices to the right colour after removing the fish. If they are too pale they will taste insipid, but if they are too dark they may taste bitter. Take great care not to be distracted at this point so that you can watch the colour of the juices changing to a golden brown.

Energy 535kcal/2222kJ; Protein 35.9g; Carbohydrate 7.9g, of which sugars 0.3g; Fat 40.2g, of which saturates 15.8g; Cholesterol 173mg; Calcium 53mg; Fibre 0.3g; Sodium 342mg.

FRIED PLAICE <u>WITH</u> TOMATO SAUCE

THIS SIMPLE DISH IS PERENNIALLY POPULAR WITH CHILDREN. IT WORKS EQUALLY WELL WITH LEMON SOLE OR DABS, WHICH DO NOT NEED SKINNING, OR FILLETS OF HADDOCK AND WHITING.

Preparation: 5 minutes; Cooking: 14 minutes

SERVES FOUR

INGREDIENTS
25g/1oz/¼ cup plain (all-purpose) flour
2 eggs, beaten
75g/3oz/¾ cup dried breadcrumbs,
   preferably home-made
4 small plaice or flounder, skinned
25g/1oz/2 tbsp butter
30ml/2 tbsp sunflower oil
salt and ground black pepper
fresh basil leaves, to garnish
1 lemon, quartered, to serve
For the tomato sauce
30ml/2 tbsp olive oil
1 red onion, finely chopped
1 garlic clove, finely chopped
400g/14oz can chopped tomatoes
15ml/1 tbsp tomato purée (paste)
15ml/1 tbsp torn fresh basil leaves

1 First make the tomato sauce. Heat the olive oil in a large pan, add the finely chopped onion and garlic and cook for about 2–3 minutes, until softened.

2 Stir in the chopped tomatoes and tomato purée and simmer for 10 minutes, or until the fish is ready to be served, stirring occasionally.

3 Meanwhile, spread out the flour in a shallow dish, pour the beaten eggs into another and spread out the breadcrumbs in a third.

4 Season the fish with salt and pepper. Hold a fish in your left hand and dip it first in flour, then in egg and finally in the breadcrumbs, patting the crumbs on with your dry right hand. Aim for an even coating that is not too thick. Shake off any excess crumbs and set aside while you prepare the frying pans.

5 Heat the butter and oil in two large frying pans until foaming. Fry the fish for about 5 minutes on each side, until golden brown and cooked through. Drain on kitchen paper. Season the tomato sauce, stir in the basil and serve with the fish, garnished with basil leaves. Offer lemon wedges separately.

Energy 417kcal/1738kJ; Protein 28.1g; Carbohydrate 17.7g, of which sugars 4.9g; Fat 26.4g, of which saturates 3.1g; Cholesterol 0mg; Calcium 113mg; Fibre 1.6g; Sodium 349mg

HALIBUT WITH SAUCE VIERGE

SAUCE VIERGE CAN BE SERVED EITHER AT ROOM TEMPERATURE OR, AS IN THIS DISH, SLIGHTLY WARM.
Preparation: 4 minutes; Cooking: 5–6 minutes

SERVES TWO

INGREDIENTS

3 large ripe beefsteak tomatoes,
   peeled, seeded and chopped
2 shallots or 1 small red onion, finely
   chopped
1 garlic clove, crushed
90ml/6 tbsp chopped mixed fresh
   herbs, such as parsley, coriander
   (cilantro), basil, tarragon, chervil or
   chives
120ml/4fl oz/½ cup extra virgin olive
   oil, plus extra for greasing
4 halibut fillets or steaks
   (175-200g/6–7oz each)
salt and ground black pepper
green salad, to serve

1 To make the sauce vierge, mix together the tomatoes, shallots or onion, garlic and herbs in a bowl. Stir in the oil and season with salt and ground black pepper. Cover the bowl with clear film (plastic wrap) and leave the sauce to stand at room temperature while you grill the fish.

2 Preheat the grill (broiler). Line a grill (broiling) pan with foil and brush the foil lightly with oil.

3 Season the fish with salt and pepper. Place the fish on the foil and brush with a little extra oil. Grill (broil) for 5–6 minutes until the flesh is opaque and the top lightly browned.

4 Meanwhile, transfer the sauce to a pan and heat it gently for a few minutes. Serve the fish with the sauce and a salad.

COOK'S TIPS
• To peel the tomatoes, put a cross in the base of each one. Place them in a heatproof bowl and cover with boiling water. After 30 seconds, lift them out and plunge them into a bowl of cold water. Drain then remove the skins.
• If time permits, leave the sauce to stand for up to an hour before heating it to serve with the fish.

Energy 791kcal/3311kJ; Protein 89.3g; Carbohydrate 10.6g, of which sugars 9.7g; Fat 43.9g, of which saturates 6.5g; Cholesterol 140mg; Calcium 230mg; Fibre 4.9g; Sodium 276mg.

MACKEREL <u>WITH</u> MUSTARD <u>AND</u> LEMON

MACKEREL MUST BE REALLY FRESH TO BE ENJOYED. LOOK FOR BRIGHT, FIRM-LOOKING FISH.

Preparation: 5 minutes; Cooking: 10–12 minutes

SERVES FOUR

INGREDIENTS
    4 fresh mackerel, about 275g/10oz
      each, gutted and cleaned
    175–225g/6–8oz young
      spinach leaves
For the mustard and lemon butter
    115g/4oz/½ cup butter, melted
    30ml/2 tbsp wholegrain mustard
    grated rind of 1 lemon
    30ml/2 tbsp lemon juice
    45ml/3 tbsp chopped fresh parsley
    salt and ground black pepper

1 Cut off the mackerel heads just behind the gills, using a sharp knife, then slit the belly so that each fish can be opened out flat.

2 Place the fish skin-side up. With the heel of your hand, press along the backbone to loosen it.

3 Turn the fish the right way up and pull the bone away. Cut off the tail and cut each fish in half lengthways. Wash and pat dry.

4 Fold the mackerel back again. Score the skin three or four times, then season the fish.

5 To make the mustard and lemon butter, mix together the melted butter, mustard, lemon rind and juice, parsley and seasoning.

6 Place the mackerel on a grill (broiling) pan. Brush a little of the butter over the mackerel and grill (broil) for 5 minutes each side, basting occasionally, until cooked through.

7 Arrange the spinach leaves around a large plate. Place the mackerel on top. Heat the remaining flavoured butter until sizzling and pour over the mackerel. Serve at once.

Energy 785kcal/3253kJ; Protein 49.8g; Carbohydrate 1.2g, of which sugars 1.1g; Fat 64.5g, of which saturates 23.3g; Cholesterol 194mg; Calcium 116mg; Fibre 1.3g; Sodium 502mg.

HERRING FILLETS IN OATMEAL WITH APPLES

FRESH HERRINGS MAKE AN INEXPENSIVE AND TASTY SUPPER FISH. COATING THEM IN OATMEAL BEFORE FRYING GIVES THEM A CRISP OUTER EDGE THAT CONTRASTS WELL WITH THE TENDER APPLE SLICES.

Preparation: 3–4 minutes; Cooking: 6 minutes

SERVES FOUR

INGREDIENTS
8 herring fillets
seasoned flour, for coating
1 egg, beaten
115g/4oz/1 cup fine pinhead oatmeal
  or oatflakes
oil, for frying
2 eating apples
25g/1oz/2 tbsp butter

1 Wash the fish and pat dry with kitchen paper. Skin the fillets and check that all bones have been removed.

2 Toss the herring fillets in the seasoned flour, then dip them in the beaten egg and coat them evenly with the oatmeal or oatflakes.

3 Heat a little oil in a heavy frying pan and fry the fillets, a few at a time, until golden brown. Drain on kitchen paper and keep warm.

4 Core the apples, but do not peel. Slice them quite thinly. In another pan, melt the butter and fry the apple slices gently until just softened. Serve the apple with the coated fish fillets.

VARIATIONS
• Mackerel fillets can be cooked in the same way.
• A fruit sauce – apple, gooseberry or rhubarb – could be served instead of the sliced apples. Cook 225g/8oz of your preferred fruit with 90ml/6 tbsp cold water until just softened. Purée and serve with the fish.
• Try serving this with crisp grilled (broiled) bacon slices or follow the fruit theme by wrapping strips of bacon around pitted prunes that have been soaked in port, then grilling (broiling) the bacon rolls.
• Poached nectarine slices would also be a good accompaniment.

Energy 566kcal/2361kJ; Protein 35.6g; Carbohydrate 24.3g, of which sugars 3.4g; Fat 37g, of which saturates 9.9g; Cholesterol 146mg; Calcium 128mg; Fibre 2.6g; Sodium 270mg

SARDINE FRITTATA

IT MAY SEEM ODD TO COOK SARDINES IN AN OMELETTE, BUT THEY ARE SURPRISINGLY DELICIOUS THIS WAY. SERVE WITH CRISP SAUTÉED POTATOES AND THINLY SLICED CUCUMBER CRESCENTS.

Preparation: 10 minutes; Cooking: 12 minutes

SERVES FOUR

INGREDIENTS

4 fat sardines, cleaned, filleted and
   with heads removed, thawed if frozen
juice of 1 lemon
45ml/3 tbsp olive oil
6 large (US extra large) eggs
30ml/2 tbsp chopped fresh parsley
30ml/2 tbsp snipped fresh chives
1 garlic clove, chopped
salt and ground black pepper
paprika

1 Open out the sardines and sprinkle the fish with lemon juice, a little salt and paprika. Heat 15ml/1 tbsp of the olive oil in a frying pan and fry the sardines for 1–2 minutes on each side to seal them. Drain on kitchen paper, trim off the tails and set aside.

2 Separate the eggs. In a bowl, beat the yolks lightly with the parsley, chives and a little salt and pepper. Whisk the whites in a separate bowl with a pinch of salt until fairly stiff.

3 Preheat the grill (broiler) to medium-high. Heat the remaining olive oil in a frying pan, add the garlic and cook over low heat, until just golden. Gently mix the egg yolks and whites together and ladle half the mixture into the pan. Cook gently until just beginning to set on the base, then lay the sardines on the frittata and sprinkle with paprika. Pour over the remaining egg mixture and cook, until the frittata has browned underneath and is starting to set on top.

4 Put the pan under the grill (broiler) and cook until the top of the frittata is golden. Cut into wedges and serve at once with sautéed potatoes and sliced cucumber.

COOK'S TIP
It is important to use a frying pan with a handle that can safely be used under the grill. If your frying pan has a wooden handle, protect it with foil.

Energy 342kcal/1422kJ; Protein 28.9g; Carbohydrate 0.2g, of which sugars 0.2g; Fat 25.3g, of which saturates 6g; Cholesterol 285mg; Calcium 137mg; Fibre 0.4g; Sodium 220mg.

CLASSIC FISH AND CHIPS

QUINTESSENTIALLY ENGLISH, THIS IS FISH AND CHIPS AS IT SHOULD BE COOKED, WITH TENDER FLAKES OF FISH IN A CRISP BATTER, AND DOUBLE-DIPPED CHIPS THAT ARE CHUNKIER THAN NORMAL FRIES.

Preparation: 5 minutes; Cooking: 14–15 minutes

SERVES FOUR

INGREDIENTS
    450g/1lb potatoes
    groundnut (peanut) oil,
      for deep-frying
    4 x 175g/6oz cod fillets, skinned
      and any tiny bones removed
For the batter
    75g/3oz/⅔ cup plain
      (all-purpose) flour
    1 egg yolk
    10ml/2 tsp oil
    175ml/6fl oz/¾ cup water
    salt

1 To make the chips, cut the potatoes into 5mm/¼in thick slices. Then cut the slices into 5mm/¼in fingers or chips. Rinse the chips thoroughly in cold water, drain them well and then dry them thoroughly in a clean dish towel.

2 Heat the oil in a deep fat fryer to 180°C/350°F. Add the chips in the basket to the fryer and cook for 3 minutes. Lift out and shake off excess fat.

3 To make the batter, sift the flour into a bowl. Add a pinch of salt. Make a well in the middle of the flour and place the egg yolk in this. Add the oil and a little of the water. Mix the yolk with the oil and water, then add the remaining water and incorporate the surrounding flour to make a smooth batter. Cover and set aside until ready to use.

4 Reheat the oil in the fryer and cook the chips again for about 5 minutes, until they are golden and crisp. Drain on kitchen paper and season with salt. Keep hot in a low oven while you cook the pieces of fish.

COOK'S TIP
Use fresh rather than frozen fish for the very best texture and flavour. If you have to use frozen fish, thaw it thoroughly and make sure it is dry before coating with batter. Partially-frozen fish is unlikely to cook in the middle, despite the high cooking temperatures reached during deep-frying.

5 Dip the pieces of fish fillet into the batter and turn them to make sure they are evenly coated. Allow any excess batter to drip off before carefully lowering the fish into the hot oil.

6 Cook the fish for 5 minutes, turning once, if necessary, so that the batter browns evenly. The batter should be crisp and golden. Drain on kitchen paper. Serve at once, with lemon wedges and the chips.

VARIATIONS
• Although cod is the traditional choice for fish and chips, other white fish can be used: haddock is a popular alternative. Rock salmon, sometimes sold as huss or dogfish, also has a good flavour. Pollock or hoki are also suitable. Thin fillets, such as plaice or sole, tend to be too thin and can be overpowered by the batter. An egg and breadcrumb coating is more suitable for thin fish.
• To coat fish with egg and breadcrumbs, dip the fillets in seasoned flour, then in beaten egg and finally in fine, dry white breadcrumbs. Repeat a second time if the fish is to be deep-fried.
• Chunky chips are traditional with thick battered fish. Cut the potatoes into thick fingers to make chunky chips and allow slightly longer for the second frying.

Energy 645kcal/2700kJ; Protein 32.6g; Carbohydrate 54.3g, of which sugars 0.7g; Fat 34.5g, of which saturates 4.2g; Cholesterol 0mg; Calcium 130mg; Fibre 3.4g; Sodium 294mg

ROAST COD WITH PANCETTA

THICK COD STEAKS WRAPPED IN PANCETTA AND ROASTED MAKE A SUPERB SUPPER DISH WHEN SERVED ON A BED OF BUTTER BEANS, WITH SWEET AND JUICY ROASTED CHERRY TOMATOES ON THE SIDE.

Preparation: 8 minutes; Cooking: 14 minutes

SERVES FOUR

INGREDIENTS

200g/7oz/1 cup canned butter (lima)
beans
90ml/6 tbsp fruity olive oil
8 thin slices of pancetta
4 thick cod steaks, skinned
8 fresh sage leaves
12 cherry tomatoes on the vine
salt and ground black pepper
parsely sprigs, to garnish

VARIATIONS
You can use cannellini beans for this recipe, and streaky (fatty) bacon instead of pancetta. It is also good made with halibut, hake, haddock or salmon.

1 Drain and rinse the beans thoroughly, tip into a pan, season, then stir in 30ml/2 tbsp of the olive oil. Heat gently and keep warm.

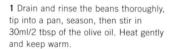

2 Preheat the oven to 200ºC/400ºF/ Gas 6. Wrap two slices of pancetta around the edge of each cod steak, tying it on with kitchen string or securing it with a wooden cocktail stick. Insert a sage leaf between each slice of the pancetta and the cod. Season the fish with salt and pepper.

3 Heat a heavy frying pan, add 15ml/1 tbsp of the remaining oil and seal the cod steaks two at a time for 1 minute on each side. Transfer them to an ovenproof dish and roast in the oven for 5 minutes.

4 Add the tomatoes to the dish and drizzle over the remaining olive oil. Roast for 5 minutes more, until the cod steaks are cooked but still juicy. Serve them on a bed of butter beans with the roasted tomatoes. Garnish with parsley.

Energy 386kcal/1611kJ; Protein 44.2g; Carbohydrate 9.9g, of which sugars 2.8g; Fat 19g, of which saturates 2.9g; Cholesterol 104mg; Calcium 57mg; Fibre 3.4g; Sodium 575mg.

MEXICAN-STYLE COD

THIS COLOURFUL MEXICAN DISH, WITH ITS CONTRASTING CRUNCHY TOPPING AND TENDER FISH
FILLING, CAN BE MADE WITH ANY WHITE FISH SUCH AS COLEY OR HADDOCK.

Preparation: 8 minutes; Cooking: 22 minutes

SERVES FOUR TO SIX

INGREDIENTS
450g/1lb cod fillets
225g/8oz smoked cod fillets
300ml/½ pint/1¼ cups fish stock
50g/2oz/¼ cup butter
1 onion, sliced
2 garlic cloves, crushed
1 green and 1 red (bell) pepper,
  seeded and diced
2 courgettes (zucchini), diced
115g/4oz/⅔ cup drained canned or
  thawed frozen corn kernels
2 ripe tomatoes, peeled and
  chopped
juice of 1 lime
Tabasco sauce
salt, ground black pepper and
  cayenne pepper
For the topping
75g/3oz tortilla chips
50g/2oz/½ cup grated Cheddar
  cheese
For the garnish
coriander (cilantro) sprigs
lime wedges

3 Melt the butter in a pan, add the onion and garlic and cook over low heat, until soft.

4 Add the peppers, stir and cook for 2 minutes. Stir in the courgettes and cook for 3 minutes more, until tender.

5 Stir in the corn and tomatoes, then add lime juice and Tabasco to taste. Season with salt, black pepper and cayenne. Cook for a couple of minutes to heat the corn and tomatoes, then stir in the fish.

6 Transfer to a dish that can safely be used under the grill (broiler). Preheat the grill.

7 Make the topping by crushing the tortilla chips, then mixing in the grated cheese. Add cayenne pepper to taste and sprinkle over the fish. Place the dish under the grill until the topping is crisp and brown. Garnish with coriander sprigs and lime wedges.

1 Lay the fish in a shallow pan and pour over the stock. Bring to the boil, lower the heat, cover and poach for about 8 minutes, until the flesh flakes easily when tested with a sharp knife.

2 Leave to cool slightly, then remove the skin, separate the flesh into large flakes and keep hot.

Energy 307kcal/1284kJ; Protein 26.4g; Carbohydrate 19.4g, of which sugars 8.3g; Fat 14g, of which saturates 7g; Cholesterol 78mg; Calcium 119mg; Fibre 3g; Sodium 760mg.

BAKED COD WITH HOLLANDAISE SAUCE

SIMPLY COOKED FRESH FISH NEEDS LITTLE ASSISTANCE OTHER THAN A SPOONFUL OF CLASSIC HOLLANDAISE SAUCE. THIS RECIPE ALSO INCLUDES SOME VARIATIONS TO THE CLASSIC SAUCE.

Preparation: 8 minutes; Cooking: 15–20 minutes

SERVES FOUR

INGREDIENTS
  4 cod steaks or cutlets
  a little olive oil
  a squeeze of lemon juice
  15ml/1 tbsp fresh white breadcrumbs
  15ml/1 tbsp roughly ground
    hazelnuts
  salt and ground black pepper
  a few sprigs of dill, to garnish
  chips, to serve
For the hollandaise sauce
  30ml/2 tbsp lemon juice
  2 egg yolks
  115g/4oz/½ cup butter, melted and
    cooled slightly

1 Preheat the oven to 200ºC/400ºF/ Gas 6. Brush both sides of the cod with oil and lemon juice. Season, then mix together the breadcrumbs, nuts and seasoning and press on to the fish. Place on a baking tray and bake for 15–20 minutes.

2 Meanwhile, prepare the hollandaise sauce. Simmer the lemon juice with 30ml/2 tbsp water in a small pan for a couple of minutes until reduced by at least half. Cool slightly.

3 Whisk in the egg yolks, then, over a very gentle heat, add the butter in a slow stream, whisking all the time. Keep whisking until glossy and thick, then season to taste. Keep warm over a pan of hot water, until ready to serve.

4 Top the fish with the sauce and garnish with dill. Serve with chips.

VARIATIONS
• To make anchovy sauce, whisk in 2–3 mashed anchovy fillets and keep whisking until they dissolve. Season with pepper after adding the anchovy.
• To make herb sauce, whisk in 30ml/2 tbsp finely chopped fresh dill and leave to stand 5–10 minutes before serving.
• To make tomato hollandaise sauce, stir in 30ml/2 tbsp very finely chopped plum tomatoes and add extra pepper to taste.

Energy 449kcal/1865kJ; Protein 39.2g; Carbohydrate 3.3g, of which sugars 0.4g; Fat 31g, of which saturates 16.3g; Cholesterol 254mg; Calcium 45mg; Fibre 0.3g; Sodium 328mg.

POACHED FISH IN SPICY TOMATO SAUCE

A SELECTION OF WHITE FISH FILLETS ARE USED IN THIS MIDDLE-EASTERN DISH: COD, HADDOCK, HAKE OR HALIBUT ARE ALL GOOD. SERVE WITH FLAT BREADS, SUCH AS PITTA, AND A SPICY TOMATO RELISH.

Preparation: 2 minutes; Cooking: 10 minutes

SERVES EIGHT

INGREDIENTS

600ml/1 pint/2½ cups fresh
   tomato sauce
2.5–5ml/½–1 tsp harissa
60ml/4 tbsp chopped fresh coriander
   (cilantro) leaves
1.5kg/3¼lb mixed white fish fillets,
   cut into chunks
salt and ground black pepper

COOK'S TIP
Harissa is a chilli paste spiced with
cumin, garlic and coriander. It is fiery
and should be used with care until you
are familiar with the flavour. Start by
adding a small amount and then add
more after tasting the sauce.

1 Heat the tomato sauce with the
harissa and coriander in a large pan. Add
seasoning to taste and bring to the boil.
Remove the pan from the heat.

2 Add the fish to the hot sauce. Return
to the heat and bring the sauce to the
boil again. Reduce the heat and simmer
very gently for about 5 minutes, or until
the fish flakes easily. Taste the sauce
and adjust the seasoning, adding more
harissa if necessary. Serve hot or warm.

Energy 219kcal/923kJ; Protein 36.2g; Carbohydrate 6.7g, of which sugars 3.2g; Fat 5.5g, of which saturates 1.5g; Cholesterol 94mg; Calcium 46mg; Fibre 1.4g; Sodium 370mg.

FISHCAKES

WELL-MADE FISHCAKES ARE ALWAYS A TREAT AND THEY CAN BE MADE WITH SALMON OR ANY FRESH OR SMOKED WHITE FISH, OR A COMBINATION. THEY ALSO MAKE A LITTLE FISH GO A LONG WAY.

Preparation: 10 minutes; Cooking: 20 minutes

SERVES FOUR

INGREDIENTS
    450g/1lb fresh salmon
    wedge of lemon
    small bay leaf
    parsley sprigs
    25g/1oz/2 tbsp butter
    1 onion, finely chopped
    450g/1lb mashed potatoes
    30ml/2 tbsp chopped fresh parsley
    pinhead oatmeal, to coat
    butter and oil, for frying
    ground black pepper

COOK'S TIP

To make the mashed potato, cook the potatoes in boiling salted water for about 20 minutes until tender, then drain well. Add a little milk and mash until smooth.

1 Rinse the fish and cut it into medium-size pieces. Put it into a pan with the lemon, bay leaf, a few of the parsley sprigs and enough cold water to cover. Bring slowly to the boil, then reduce the heat and simmer gently for 5–7 minutes. Remove the fish and drain well.

2 When cool enough to handle, flake the flesh and discard the skin and bones. Melt the butter in a large pan, add the onion and cook gently for a few minutes, until softened but not coloured. Add the flaked fish, mashed potato and parsley. Season to taste with pepper.

3 Turn the mixture on to a work surface generously covered with pinhead oatmeal. Divide in half, and then quarter each piece. Form into eight flat cakes and coat them with the oatmeal.

4 Heat a little butter and an equal quantity of oil in a heavy frying pan, add the fishcakes (in batches, if necessary) and fry until golden on both sides. Drain and serve immediately, garnished with the remaining parsley sprigs.

COOK'S TIPS
• Don't include more potato than fish, or the fishcakes will lack flavour.
• Parsley sauce is the traditional accompaniment to fishcakes.

Energy 1520kcal/6336kJ; Protein 101.2g; Carbohydrate 82.0g, of which sugars 13.2g; Fat 89.6g, of which saturates 34.4; Cholesterol 332mg; Calcium 2401mg; Fibre 7.2g; Sodium 552mg

FILO-WRAPPED FISH

THIS DELICIOUS DISH COMES FROM JERUSALEM, WHERE WHOLE FISH ARE WRAPPED IN FILO PASTRY AND THEN BAKED BEFORE BEING SERVED WITH A ZESTY TOMATO SAUCE.

Preparation: 10 minutes; Cooking: 20–25 minutes

SERVES THREE TO FOUR

INGREDIENTS

1 lemon
30ml/2 tbsp olive oil, plus extra for
  brushing
1 onion, chopped
2 celery sticks, chopped
1 green (bell) pepper, diced
5 garlic cloves, chopped
400g/14oz fresh or canned tomatoes,
  chopped
120ml/4fl oz/½ cup passata (bottled
  strained tomatoes)
30ml/2 tbsp chopped fresh flat
  leaf parsley
2–3 pinches of ground allspice or
  ground cloves
cayenne pepper, to taste
pinch of sugar
about 130g/4½oz filo pastry
  (6–8 large sheets)
450g/1lb salmon or cod steaks or
  fillets
salt and ground black pepper

1 Heat the olive oil in a pan, add the chopped onion, celery and pepper and fry for about 5 minutes, until the vegetables are softened. Add the garlic and cook for a further 1 minute, then add the tomatoes and passata and cook until the tomatoes are of a sauce consistency.

2 Stir the parsley into the sauce, then season with allspice or cloves, cayenne pepper, sugar and salt and ground black pepper.

3 Preheat the oven to 200°C/400°F/Gas 6. Take a sheet of filo pastry, brush with a little olive oil and cover with a second sheet. Place a piece of fish on top of the pastry, towards the bottom edge, then top with 1–2 spoonfuls of the sauce, spreading it evenly.

COOK'S TIP
Buy whichever fish is in season and looks freshest on the day of purchase.

4 Roll the fish in the pastry, taking care to enclose the filling completely. Arrange on a baking sheet and repeat with the remaining fish and pastry. You should have about half the sauce remaining, to serve with the fish.

5 Bake for 10–15 minutes, or until golden. Meanwhile, reheat the remaining sauce if necessary. Serve immediately with the fish.

Energy 509Kcal/2135kJ; Protein 36.2g; Carbohydrate 37.2g, of which sugars 10.4g; Fat 25.1g, of which saturates 4.2g; Cholesterol 75mg; Calcium 137mg; Fibre 5g; Sodium 192mg

HADDOCK <u>IN</u> CIDER SAUCE

FIRST-CLASS FISH DOESN'T NEED ELABORATE TREATMENT. THE CIDER SAUCE SERVED WITH THE HADDOCK IS BASED ON THE POACHING LIQUID, ENRICHED BY JUST A WHISPER OF CREAM.

Preparation: 2 minutes; Cooking: 13 minutes

SERVES FOUR

INGREDIENTS

675g/1½lb haddock fillet
1 medium onion, thinly sliced
1 bay leaf
2 parsley sprigs
10ml/2 tsp lemon juice
450ml/¾ pint/2 cups dry (hard) cider
25g/1oz/¼ cup cornflour (cornstarch)
30ml/2 tbsp single (light) cream
salt and ground black pepper

VARIATION

Try cod or hake or another white fish with firm flesh instead of haddock.

1 Cut the haddock fillet into four equal portions and place in a pan big enough to hold them neatly in a single layer. Add the onion, bay leaf, parsley and lemon. Season with salt.

2 Pour in most of the cider, reserving 30ml/2 tbsp for the sauce. Cover and bring to the boil, reduce the heat and simmer for 10 minutes, or until the fish is just cooked.

3 Strain 300ml/½ pint/1¼ cups of the cooking liquid into a measuring jug (cup). Cover the pan containing the fish and remove from the heat. In a small pan, mix the cornflour with the reserved cider, then gradually whisk in the measured cooking liquid and bring to the boil. Whisk until smooth and thick.

4 Whisk in more of the cooking liquid, if necessary, to make a pouring sauce. Remove the pan from the heat, stir in the cream and season to taste with salt and ground black pepper.

5 To serve, remove any skin from the fish, arrange on individual hot serving plates and pour the sauce over. Serve with a selection of vegetables.

Energy 216kcal/918kJ; Protein 32.5g; Carbohydrate 9.4g, of which sugars 3.5g; Fat 2.5g, of which saturates 1.1g; Cholesterol 65mg; Calcium 43mg; Fibre 0.1g; Sodium 127mg

OMELETTE ARNOLD BENNETT

CONTRIVING TO BE CREAMY AND FLUFFY AT THE SAME TIME, THIS SMOKED HADDOCK SOUFFLÉ
OMELETTE IS DELICIOUS. NO WONDER THE AUTHOR ARNOLD BENNETT LOVED IT SO MUCH.

Preparation: 2 minutes; Cooking: 12 minutes

SERVES TWO

INGREDIENTS

   175g/6oz smoked haddock fillet
     (preferably undyed if available)
   50g/2oz/4 tbsp butter, diced
   175ml/6fl oz/¾ cup whipping or
     double (heavy) cream
   4 eggs, separated
   40g/1½oz/⅓ cup mature (sharp)
     Cheddar cheese, grated
   ground black pepper
   watercress, to garnish

1 Put the haddock in a shallow pan
with water to cover and poach over
a medium heat for 8–10 minutes or
until the fish flakes easily when tested
with the tip of a knife. Drain well.

2 Remove the skin and any bones from
the haddock fillet and discard. Carefully
flake the flesh using a fork.

3 Melt half the butter with 60ml/4 tbsp
of the cream in a fairly small non-stick
pan, then add the flaked fish and stir
together gently. Cover the pan and
remove from the heat. Preheat the
grill (broiler).

4 Mix the egg yolks with 15ml/1 tbsp
of the cream. Season with pepper, then
stir into the fish. Mix the cheese and
the remaining cream. Whisk the egg
whites until stiff, then fold into the fish
mixture. Heat the remaining butter in an
omelette pan, add the fish mixture and
cook until browned underneath. Pour
the cheese mixture over and grill (broil)
until bubbling. Garnish and serve.

Energy 821kcal/3396kJ; Protein 36.1g; Carbohydrate 2.6g, of which sugars 2.6g; Fat 74g, of which saturates 42.6g; Cholesterol 577mg; Calcium 280mg; Fibre 0g; Sodium 1123mg

SMOKED HADDOCK WITH MUSTARD CABBAGE

THIS SIMPLE DISH OF POACHED HADDOCK IN A LEMON SAUCE WITH CABBAGE AND TOMATOES TAKES JUST THIRTY MINUTES TO MAKE AND IS QUITE DELICIOUS. SERVE IT WITH NEW POTATOES.

Preparation: 6 minutes; Cooking: 24 minutes

2 Meanwhile put the haddock in a large shallow pan with the milk, onion and bay leaves. Add the lemon slices and peppercorns. Bring to simmering point, cover and poach for 8–10 minutes, until the fish flakes easily when tested with the tip of a sharp knife. Take the pan off the heat and set aside until needed. Preheat the grill (broiler).

3 Cut the tomatoes in half horizontally, season them with salt and pepper and grill (broil) until lightly browned. Drain the cabbage, refresh under cold water and drain again.

SERVES FOUR

INGREDIENTS
1 Savoy or pointu cabbage
675g/1½lb undyed smoked
   haddock fillet
300ml/½ pint/1¼ cups milk
½ onion, peeled and sliced into rings
2 bay leaves
½ lemon, sliced
4 white peppercorns
4 ripe tomatoes
50g/2oz/¼ cup butter
30ml/2 tbsp wholegrain mustard
juice of 1 lemon
salt and ground black pepper
30ml/2 tbsp chopped fresh parsley,
   to garnish

1 Cut the cabbage in half, remove the central core and thick ribs, then shred the cabbage. Cook in a pan of lightly salted boiling water, or steam over boiling water for about 10 minutes, until just tender. Leave in the pan or steamer until required.

4 Melt the butter in a shallow pan, add the cabbage and toss over the heat for 2 minutes. Mix in the mustard and season to taste, then tip the cabbage into a warmed serving dish.

5 Drain the haddock. Skin and cut the fish into four pieces. Place on top of the cabbage with some onion rings and tomato halves. Pour on the lemon juice, then sprinkle with parsley and serve.

Energy 319kcal/1340kJ; Protein 36.1g; Carbohydrate 14.2g, of which sugars 13.7g; Fat 13.1g, of which saturates 7.3g; Cholesterol 90mg; Calcium 146mg; Fibre 4.2g; Sodium 1512mg.

HADDOCK WITH FENNEL BUTTER

FRESH FISH TASTES FABULOUS COOKED IN A SIMPLE HERB BUTTER. HERE THE LIQUORICE FLAVOUR OF FENNEL COMPLEMENTS THE HADDOCK BEAUTIFULLY TO MAKE A SIMPLE DISH FIT FOR A DINNER PARTY.

Preparation: 4 minutes; Cooking: 18–23 minutes

SERVES FOUR

INGREDIENTS

675g/1½ lb haddock fillet, skinned
and cut into 4 portions
50g/2oz/¼ cup butter
1 lemon
45ml/3 tbsp coarsely chopped fennel

COOK'S TIPS

• If you can buy only small haddock fillets, fold them in half before baking, or use cod as an alternative.
• Serve tiny new potatoes and a herb salad with the fish to make a light, summery main course.

1 Preheat the oven to 220ºC/425ºF/ Gas 7. Season the fish on both sides with salt and pepper. Melt one-quarter of the butter in a frying pan, preferably non-stick, and cook the fish over a medium heat briefly on both sides.

2 Transfer the fish to a shallow ovenproof dish. Cut four wafer-thin slices from the lemon and squeeze the juice from the remainder over the fish. Place the lemon slices on top and then bake for 15–20 minutes, or until the fish is cooked.

3 Meanwhile, melt the remaining butter in the frying pan and add the fennel and a little seasoning.

4 Transfer the cooked fish to plates and pour the cooking juices into the herb butter. Heat gently for a few seconds, then pour the herb butter over the fish. Serve immediately.

Energy 220Kcal/921kJ; Protein 29g; Carbohydrate 1g, of which sugars 1g; Fat 11g, of which saturates 7g; Cholesterol 81mg; Calcium 123mg; Fibre 0.3g; Sodium 200mg

GRILLED HAKE <u>WITH</u> LEMON <u>AND</u> CHILLI

NOTHING COULD BE SIMPLER THAN PERFECTLY GRILLED FISH WITH A DUSTING OF CHILLI AND LEMON RIND. THIS IS AN IDEAL MEAL FOR THOSE OCCASIONS WHEN SOMETHING LIGHT IS CALLED FOR.

Preparation: 2 minutes; Cooking: 6–8 minutes

SERVES FOUR

INGREDIENTS

4 hake fillets, each 150g/5oz
30ml/2 tbsp olive oil
finely grated rind and juice of
1 lemon
15ml/1 tbsp crushed chilli flakes
salt and ground black pepper

VARIATION
Any firm white fish can be cooked in this simple, low-fat way. Try cod, halibut or hoki. If you haven't got any chilli flakes, brush the fish with chilli oil instead of olive oil.

1 Preheat the grill (broiler) to high. Brush the hake fillets all over with the olive oil and place them skin side up on a baking sheet.

2 Grill (broil) the fish for 4–5 minutes, until the skin is crispy, then carefully turn the fillets over in the pan, using a metal spatula.

3 Sprinkle the fillets with the lemon rind and chilli flakes and season with salt and ground black pepper.

4 Grill the fillets for a further 2–3 minutes, or until the hake is cooked through. (Test using the point of a sharp knife; the flesh should flake.) Squeeze over the lemon juice just before serving.

Energy 188kcal/786kJ; Protein 27g; Carbohydrate 0.1g, of which sugars 0.1g; Fat 8.8g, of which saturates 1.2g; Cholesterol 35mg; Calcium 22mg; Fibre 0g; Sodium 150mg

HOKI STIR-FRY

ANY FIRM WHITE FISH, SUCH AS MONKFISH, HAKE OR COD, CAN BE USED FOR THIS STIR-FRY. VARY THE VEGETABLES ACCORDING TO WHAT IS AVAILABLE, BUT TRY TO INCLUDE AT LEAST THREE COLOURS.

Preparation: 7–8 minutes; Cooking: 9–10 minutes

SERVES FOUR TO SIX

INGREDIENTS
675g/1½ lb hoki fillet, skinned
pinch of five-spice powder
2 carrots, cut diagonally into slices
   as thin as mangetouts
115g/4oz/1 cup small mangetouts
   (snow peas)
115g/4oz asparagus spears, trimmed
   and cut in half crossways
4 spring onions (scallions)
45ml/3 tbsp groundnut (peanut) oil
2.5cm/1in piece fresh root ginger,
   peeled and cut into thin slivers
2 garlic cloves, finely chopped
300g/11oz beansprouts
8–12 small baby corn cobs
15–30ml/1–2 tbsp light soy sauce
salt and ground black pepper

1 Cut the hoki into thin strips and season with salt, pepper and five-spice powder.

2 Trim the mangetouts. Trim the spring onions and cut the green and white parts diagonally into 2cm/¾in pieces.

3 Heat a wok, then pour in the oil. As soon as it is hot, add the ginger and garlic. Stir-fry for 1 minute, then add the white parts of the spring onions and cook for 1 minute more.

COOK'S TIP
When adding the oil to the hot wok, drizzle it around the inner rim like a necklace. The oil will run down to coat the entire surface of the wok. Swirl the wok to make sure the coating is even.

4 Add the hoki strips and stir-fry for 2–3 minutes, until all the pieces of fish are opaque. Add the beansprouts. Toss them around to coat them in the oil, then put in the carrots, mangetouts, asparagus and corn. Continue to stir-fry for 3–4 minutes, by which time the fish should be cooked, but all the vegetables will still be crunchy. Add soy sauce to taste, toss everything quickly together, then stir in the green parts of the spring onions. Serve immediately.

Energy 183kcal/764kJ; Protein 22.4g; Carbohydrate 5g, of which sugars 3.8g; Fat 8.2g, of which saturates 1.1g; Cholesterol 0mg; Calcium 49mg; Fibre 2.3g; Sodium 295mg.

SEA BASS WITH PARSLEY AND LIME BUTTER

THE DELICATE BUT FIRM, SWEET FLESH OF SEA BASS GOES BEAUTIFULLY WITH CITRUS FLAVOURS. SERVE WITH ROAST FENNEL AND SAUTÉED DICED POTATOES.

Preparation: 2–3 minutes; Cooking: 9–10 minutes

SERVES SIX

INGREDIENTS

50g/2oz/¼ cup butter
6 sea bass fillets, about
  150g/5oz each
grated rind and juice of 1 large lime
30ml/2 tbsp chopped fresh parsley
salt and ground black pepper

1 Heat the butter in a large frying pan and add three of the sea bass fillets, skin side down. Cook for 3–4 minutes, or until the skin is crisp and golden. Flip the fish over and cook for a further 2–3 minutes, or until cooked through.

2 Remove the fillets from the pan with a metal spatula. Place each on a serving plate and keep them warm. Cook the remaining fish in the same way and transfer to serving plates.

3 Add the lime rind and juice to the pan with the parsley, and season with salt and black pepper. Allow to bubble for 1–2 minutes, then pour a little over each fish portion and serve immediately.

Energy 213Kcal/890kJ; Protein 29g; Carbohydrate 0g, of which sugars 0g; Fat 11g, of which saturates 5g; Cholesterol 138mg; Calcium 199mg; Fibre 0.1g; Sodium 200mg

SWEET AND SOUR FISH

WHEN FISH SUCH AS RED MULLET OR SNAPPER IS COOKED IN THIS WAY THE SKIN BECOMES CRISP, WHILE THE FLESH, WHICH IS SEALED INSIDE, REMAINS MOIST AND JUICY.

Preparation: 8 minutes; Cooking: 18–25 minutes

SERVES FOUR TO SIX

INGREDIENTS
  1 large or 2 medium fish, such as
    snapper or mullet, heads removed
  20ml/4 tsp cornflour (cornstarch)
  120ml/4fl oz/½ cup vegetable oil
  15ml/1 tbsp chopped garlic
  15ml/1 tbsp chopped fresh
    root ginger
  30ml/2 tbsp chopped shallots
  225g/8oz cherry tomatoes
  30ml/2 tbsp red wine vinegar
  30ml/2 tbsp sugar
  30ml/2 tbsp tomato ketchup
  15ml/1 tbsp Thai fish sauce
  45ml/3 tbsp water
  salt and ground black pepper
For the garnish
  coriander (cilantro) leaves
  shredded spring onions (scallions)

1 Rinse and dry the fish. Score the skin diagonally on both sides, then coat the fish lightly all over with 15ml/1 tbsp of the cornflour. Shake off any excess.

2 Heat the oil in a wok or large frying pan. Add the fish and cook over medium heat for 6–7 minutes. Turn the fish over and cook for 6–7 minutes more, until it is crisp and brown.

COOK'S TIP
The sweet and sour sauce, with its colourful cherry tomatoes, complements the fish beautifully.

3 Remove the fish with a metal spatula or fish slice and keep warm on a large platter. Pour off all but 30ml/2 tbsp of the oil from the wok or pan and reheat. Add the garlic, ginger and shallots and cook over medium heat, stirring occasionally, for 3–4 minutes, until golden.

4 Add the cherry tomatoes and cook until they burst open. Stir in the vinegar, sugar, tomato ketchup and fish sauce. Lower the heat and simmer gently for 1–2 minutes, then taste and adjust the seasoning, adding more vinegar, sugar and/or fish sauce, if necessary.

5 In a cup, mix the remaining 5ml/1 tsp cornflour to a paste with the water. Stir into the sauce. Heat, stirring, until it thickens. Pour the sauce over the fish, garnish with coriander leaves and shredded spring onions and serve.

Energy 233kcal/969kJ; Protein 21.9g; Carbohydrate 6.3g, of which sugars 3g; Fat 13.5g, of which saturates 1.6g; Cholesterol 54mg; Calcium 16mg; Fibre 0.5g; Sodium 335mg.

GRILLED RED MULLET <u>WITH</u> ROSEMARY

THIS RECIPE IS VERY SIMPLE — THE TASTE OF GRILLED RED MULLET IS SO GOOD IN ITSELF THAT IT NEEDS VERY LITTLE PREPARATION TO BRING OUT THE FLAVOUR.

Preparation: 10 minutes; Cooking: 10–12 minutes

SERVES FOUR

INGREDIENTS
  4 red mullet, cleaned, about
    275g/10oz each
  4 garlic cloves, cut into thin slivers
  75ml/5 tbsp olive oil
  30ml/2 tbsp balsamic vinegar
  10ml/2 tsp very finely chopped
    fresh rosemary
  ground black pepper
  coarse sea salt
For the garnish
  rosemary sprigs
  lemon wedges

VARIATION
Red mullet are extra delicious cooked on the barbecue. If possible, enclose them in a basket grill so that they are easy to turn over.

1 Cut three diagonal slits in both sides of each fish. Push the garlic slivers into the slits. Place the fish in a single layer in a shallow dish. Whisk the oil, vinegar and rosemary in a bowl and add ground black pepper to taste.

COOK'S TIP
Eight minutes is the minimum time for marinating, but if you can leave the fish for longer the flavour will be more intense.

2 Pour the vinaigrette mixture over the fish, cover with clear film (plastic wrap) and set aside for at least 8 minutes. Lift the fish out of the dish and put it on the rack of a grill (broiling) pan. Reserve the marinade for basting.

3 Grill (broil) the fish for 5 minutes on each side, turning once and brushing with the marinade. Serve hot, sprinkled with coarse sea salt and garnished with rosemary sprigs and lemon wedges.

Energy 280kcal/1168kJ; Protein 26.4g; Carbohydrate 0g, of which sugars 0g; Fat 19.5g, of which saturates 2g; Cholesterol 0mg; Calcium 99mg; Fibre 0g; Sodium 138mg.

RED SNAPPER BURRITOS

FISH MAKES A GREAT FILLING FOR A TORTILLA, ESPECIALLY WHEN IT IS SUCCULENT RED SNAPPER MIXED WITH RICE, CHILLI, TOMATOES, ALMONDS AND CHEESE.

Preparation: 5 minutes; Cooking: 25 minutes

SERVES EIGHT

INGREDIENTS

- 3 red snapper or any white fish fillets
- 90g/3½oz/½ cup long grain white rice
- 30ml/2 tbsp vegetable oil
- 1 small onion, finely chopped
- 5ml/1 tsp ground achiote seed
- 1 dried chilli, seeded and ground or 2.5ml/½ tsp chilli powder
- 200g/7oz can chopped tomatoes
- 75g/3oz/¾ cup flaked (sliced) almonds
- 150g/5oz/1¼ cups grated Monterey Jack or mild Cheddar cheese
- 8 x 20cm/8in wheat flour tortillas

1 Grill (broil) the fish on an oiled rack for about 5 minutes, turning once. When cool, remove the skin and flake the fish into a bowl. Set it aside. Meanwhile, put the rice in a pan, pour over cold water, cover and bring to the boil. Drain, rinse and drain again.

2 Heat the oil and fry the onion until soft. Stir in the ground achiote and the chilli, and cook for 5 minutes.

3 Add the rice, stir to coat all the grains in the flavoured oil, then stir in the tomatoes, flaked fish and almonds. Cook over a medium heat until the juice is absorbed and the rice is tender. Stir in the cheese and remove from the heat. Warm the tortillas.

4 Spread out the tortillas and divide the filling among them. Shape each burrito by folding the sides of the tortilla over the filling, then bringing the bottom up and the top down to form a neat parcel. Secure each burrito with a cocktail stick (toothpick) until ready to serve.

Energy 224kcal/935kJ; Protein 17.1g; Carbohydrate 11.3g, of which sugars 1.7g; Fat 11.9g, of which saturates 4.6g; Cholesterol 41mg; Calcium 172mg; Fibre 1.1g; Sodium 178mg.

TROUT <u>WITH</u> CRUNCHY PEPPERCORNS

BLACK, GREEN AND PINK PEPPERCORNS ADD COLOUR AND TEXTURE TO THIS DISH AND PROVIDE AN
EXPLOSION OF TASTE IN THE MOUTH WHEN CRUNCHED. PESTO MASH IS THE PERFECT ACCOMPANIMENT.

Preparation: 5 minutes; Cooking: 25 minutes

SERVES FOUR

INGREDIENTS
   60ml/4 tbsp mixed peppercorns
   4 trout fillets, each about 200g/7oz,
     skinned
   60ml/4 tbsp olive oil
   juice of 1 lemon
   mashed potato with pesto, to serve
For the garnish
   basil sprigs and lemon wedges

1 Place the mixed peppercorns in a
mortar and crush them lightly with a
pestle until about half are broken.

COOK'S TIP
Stir a large spoonful of pesto into the
mashed potato just before serving,
leaving green swirls in the creamy potato.

2 Press one-quarter of the peppercorns
on to one side of each trout fillet, using
the back of a spoon.

3 Heat the oil in a griddle pan. Place
the fish in the pan, coated side up, and
fry for 2–3 minutes, using a metal
spatula to press the peppercorns further
into the fish as it cooks.

4 Using the spatula, turn the trout fillets
over and cook for 2–3 minutes more,
until cooked right through. Turn the
fillets over again in the pan and sprinkle
with the lemon juice.

5 Place each fish on a bed of pesto
mash on an individual plate and garnish
with the basil sprigs and lemon wedges.

Energy 323kcal/1347kJ; Protein 39.2g; Carbohydrate 0g, of which sugars 0g; Fat 18.7g, of which saturates 1.6g; Cholesterol 0mg; Calcium 34mg; Fibre 0g; Sodium 114mg.

CHEESE AND HERB-TOPPED TROUT

FOR THIS SIMPLE YET SOPHISTICATED SUPPER DISH, SUCCULENT STRIPS OF FILLETED TROUT ARE TOPPED WITH A MIXTURE OF PARMESAN CHEESE, PINE NUTS, HERBS AND BREADCRUMBS.

Preparation: 12 minutes; Cooking: 12 minutes

SERVES FOUR

INGREDIENTS
  50g/2oz/1 cup fresh white
    breadcrumbs
  50g/2oz Parmesan cheese, finely
    grated
  25g/1oz/⅓ cup pine nuts, chopped
  15ml/1 tbsp chopped fresh parsley
  15ml/1 tbsp chopped fresh coriander
    (cilantro)
  30ml/2 tbsp olive oil
  4 thick trout fillets, each about
    225g/8oz
  40g/1½oz/3 tbsp butter
  juice of 1 lemon
  salt and ground black pepper
  lemon wedges, to garnish
To serve
  steamed asparagus tips
  steamed baby carrots

1 In a mixing bowl, combine the breadcrumbs, Parmesan, pine nuts, parsley and coriander. Add the oil.

2 Cut each trout fillet into two strips. Firmly press the breadcrumb mixture on to the top of each strip of trout.

3 Preheat the grill (broiler) to high. Grease the grill (broiling) pan with 15g/ ½oz of the butter. Melt the remaining butter in a pan and add the lemon juice.

4 Place the breadcrumb-topped fillets on the greased grill pan and pour the lemon butter over.

5 Grill (broil) the trout for 10 minutes or until the fillets are just cooked. Place two trout strips on each plate, garnish with lemon wedges and serve with steamed asparagus and carrots.

VARIATIONS
• It isn't essential to use pine nuts in the stuffing. Almonds would work well, or you could try hazelnuts.
• If you don't have any fresh coriander (cilantro), increase the amount of fresh parsley.
• Dried peaches or apricots could be chopped finely and added to the stuffing, with perhaps a little finely grated lemon rind to enhance the fruity flavour.

Energy 524kcal/2185kJ; Protein 51.3g; Carbohydrate 10.3g, of which sugars 0.9g; Fat 31.1g, of which saturates 8.9g; Cholesterol 34mg; Calcium 214mg; Fibre 1g; Sodium 422mg.

MALAYSIAN STEAMED TROUT FILLETS

THIS SIMPLE DISH CAN BE PREPARED EXTREMELY QUICKLY, AND IS SUITABLE FOR ANY FISH FILLETS.
SERVE IT ON A BED OF NOODLES ACCOMPANIED BY RIBBONS OF COLOURFUL VEGETABLES.

Preparation: 10 minutes; Cooking: 10–15 minutes

SERVES FOUR

INGREDIENTS

8 pink trout fillets of even thickness,
   about 115g/4oz each, skinned
45ml/3 tbsp coconut cream
grated rind and juice of 2 limes
45ml/3 tbsp chopped fresh coriander
   (cilantro)
15ml/1 tbsp sunflower or groundnut
   (peanut) oil
2.5–5ml/½–1 tsp chilli oil
salt and ground black pepper
For the garnish
   lime slices and coriander sprigs

1 Cut four rectangles of greaseproof
(waxed) paper, about twice the size of
the trout fillets. Place a fillet on each
piece and season lightly.

2 Mix together the coconut, lime rind
and chopped coriander and spread a
quarter of the mixture over each trout
fillet. Sandwich another trout fillet on
top. Mix the lime juice with the oils,
adjusting the quantity of chilli oil to your
own taste, and drizzle the mixture over
the trout 'sandwiches'.

3 Prepare a steamer. Fold up the edges
of the paper and pleat them over the
trout to make parcels, making sure they
are well sealed. Place in the steamer
and steam over simmering water for
10–15 minutes, depending on the
thickness of the trout fillets. Serve at
once, garnished with lime and coriander.

Energy 241kcal/1005kJ; Protein 25.1g; Carbohydrate 0.9g, of which sugars 0.9g; Fat 15.3g, of which saturates 7g; Cholesterol 0mg; Calcium 21mg; Fibre 0.2g; Sodium 75mg.

TROUT WITH TAMARIND AND CHILLI SAUCE

TROUT IS A VERY ECONOMICAL FISH, BUT CAN TASTE RATHER BLAND. THIS SPICY THAI-INSPIRED SAUCE REALLY GIVES IT A ZING. IF YOU LIKE YOUR FOOD VERY SPICY, ADD AN EXTRA CHILLI.

Preparation: 10 minutes; Cooking: 10–12 minutes

SERVES FOUR

INGREDIENTS
    4 trout, about 350g/12oz each
    6 spring onions (scallions), sliced
    60ml/4 tbsp soy sauce
    15ml/1 tbsp sunflower oil
    30ml/2 tbsp chopped fresh coriander
      (cilantro) and 1 sliced red chilli,
      to garnish
For the sauce
    50g/2oz tamarind pulp
    105ml/7 tbsp boiling water
    2 shallots, roughly chopped
    1 red chilli, seeded and chopped
    1cm/½in piece fresh root ginger,
      peeled and chopped
    5ml/1 tsp soft brown sugar
    45ml/3 tbsp Thai fish sauce

1 Clean the trout and slash diagonally four or five times on each side with a sharp knife. Place in a shallow dish.

2 Fill the cavities with spring onions and douse each fish with soy sauce. Carefully turn the fish over to coat both sides with the sauce. Sprinkle on any remaining spring onions and set aside.

3 Make the sauce. Put the tamarind pulp in a small bowl and pour on the boiling water. Mash with a fork until soft. Tip into a food processor or blender, add the shallots, chilli, ginger, sugar and fish sauce and whizz to a coarse pulp.

4 Heat the oil in a large frying pan or wok and fry the trout, one at a time if necessary, for about 5 minutes on each side, until the skin is crisp and browned and the flesh cooked. Put on warmed plates and spoon over some sauce. Sprinkle with the coriander and serve with the remaining sauce.

Energy 329kcal/1384kJ; Protein 47.9g; Carbohydrate 8.1g, of which sugars 6.3g; Fat 11.9g, of which saturates 2.5g; Cholesterol 192mg; Calcium 96mg; Fibre 1.2g; Sodium 978mg.

SALMON WITH HOLLANDAISE AND ASPARAGUS

THIS SUMMERY DISH IS LIGHT AND COLOURFUL. ASPARAGUS MAKES THE IDEAL ACCOMPANIMENT FOR SALMON WHEN IT IS IN SEASON IN EARLY SUMMER, AND HOLLANDAISE SAUCE COMPLEMENTS THEM BOTH.

Preparation: 10 minutes; Cooking: 10–12 minutes

3 Whisk in the remaining butter, no more than 10g/¼oz/1½ tsp at a time, until the sauce is shiny and has the consistency of thick cream. Season with salt and pepper.

4 Heat a ridged griddle pan or grill (broiler) until very hot. Brush the salmon with olive oil, sprinkle with the lemon juice and season with salt and black pepper. Cook the fish on the griddle or under a grill for 3–5 minutes on each side, depending on the thickness of the fish. Avoid over-cooking: the fish should be seared on the outside, moist and succulent within.

5 Melt the butter in a separate large pan and gently reheat the asparagus in it for 1–2 minutes before serving with the fish, hollandaise sauce and new potatoes.

COOK'S TIP
If the hollandaise sauce separates, remove it from the heat and beat in 15ml/1 tbsp cold water.

VARIATION
Blender hollandaise: this version is an easier substitute (and if it doesn't work you can rescue it by heating it over hot water): put 3 egg yolks into a blender with 30ml/2 tbsp lemon juice and seasoning. Blend for a few seconds. Heat 115g/4oz/½ cup butter until very hot, and then run the blender at high speed and gradually add the butter in a thin stream. Blend for about 30 seconds until thick.

SERVES FOUR

INGREDIENTS
bunch of 20 asparagus spears, woody ends trimmed
4 salmon portions, such as fillets or steaks, about 200g/7oz each
15ml/1 tbsp olive oil
juice of ½ lemon
25g/1oz/2 tbsp butter
salt and ground black pepper
boiled new potatoes, to serve
For the hollandaise sauce
45ml/3 tbsp white wine vinegar
6 peppercorns
1 bay leaf
3 egg yolks
175g/6oz/¾ cup butter, softened

1 Peel the lower stems of the asparagus. Stand in a deep pan with the tips up and cook in salted boiling water for about 1 minute, or until just beginning to become tender. Remove from the pan and cool quickly under cold running water to prevent further cooking. Drain.

2 To make the hollandaise sauce: in a small pan, boil the vinegar and 15ml/1 tbsp water with the peppercorns and bay leaf until reduced to 15ml/1 tbsp. Leave to cool. Cream the egg yolks with 15g/½oz/1 tbsp of the butter and a pinch of salt. Strain the vinegar into the eggs and set the bowl over a pan of boiling water. Remove from the heat.

Per portion Energy 834Kcal/3449kJ; Protein 46.5g; Carbohydrate 2.8g, of which sugars 2.7g; Fat 7.7g, of which saturates 31.6g; Cholesterol 358mg; Calcium 102mg; Fibre 2.1g; Sodium 401mg

TORTILLA CONES WITH SMOKED SALMON

SOPHISTICATED YET SIMPLE, THESE SALMON-FILLED TORTILLAS ALWAYS GO DOWN WELL. MAKE THEM SLIGHTLY AHEAD OF TIME, OR JUST SET OUT THE INGREDIENTS FOR A DIY PICNIC SNACK.

Preparation: 8 minutes; Cooking: 0 minutes

MAKES EIGHT

INGREDIENTS
115g/4oz/½ cup soft white
  (farmer's) cheese
30ml/2 tbsp roughly chopped
  fresh dill
juice of 1 lemon
1 small red onion
15ml/1 tbsp drained bottled capers
30ml/2 tbsp extra virgin olive oil
30ml/2 tbsp roughly chopped fresh
  flat leaf parsley
115g/4oz smoked salmon
8 small wheat flour tortillas
salt and ground black pepper
lemon wedges, for squeezing

3 Cut the smoked salmon into short, thin strips and add to the red onion mixture. Toss to mix. Season to taste with plenty of black pepper.

COOK'S TIP
If you use salted capers in this dish, rather than the unsalted variety, rinse them thoroughly before using.

4 Spread a little of the soft cheese mixture on each tortilla and top with the smoked salmon mixture.

5 Roll up the tortillas into cones and secure with wooden cocktail sticks (toothpicks). Arrange on a serving plate and add some lemon wedges, for squeezing. Serve immediately.

1 Place the soft cheese in a bowl and mix in half the chopped dill. Add a little salt and pepper and a dash of the lemon juice to taste. Reserve the remaining lemon juice in a separate mixing bowl.

2 Finely chop the red onion. Add the onion, capers and olive oil to the lemon juice in the mixing bowl. Add the chopped flat leaf parsley and the remaining dill and stir gently to mix the ingredients.

VARIATION
Tortilla cones can be filled with a variety of delicious ingredients. Try soft cheese with red pesto and chopped sun-dried tomatoes, or mackerel pâté with slices of cucumber.

Energy 154kcal/645kJ; Protein 6.7g; Carbohydrate 14.5g, of which sugars 0.7g; Fat 8.1g, of which saturates 3.3g; Cholesterol 18mg; Calcium 50mg; Fibre 0.8g; Sodium 383mg

HOT SMOKED SALMON

THIS IS A FANTASTIC WAY OF SMOKING SALMON ON A BARBECUE IN NO TIME AT ALL. THE MOJO MAKES A MILDLY SPICY COMPANION.
Preparation: 5 minutes; Cooking: 11–13 minutes, plus soaking

SERVES 6

INGREDIENTS
  6 salmon fillets, each about
    175g/6oz, with skin
  15ml/1 tbsp sunflower oil
  salt and ground black pepper
  2 handfuls hickory wood chips,
    soaked in cold water for as much
    time as you have available,
    preferably 30 minutes
For the mojo
  1 ripe mango, diced
  4 drained canned pineapple
    slices, diced
  1 small red onion, finely chopped
  1 fresh long mild red chilli, seeded
    and finely chopped
  15ml/1 tbsp good-quality sweet
    chilli sauce
  grated rind and juice of 1 lime
  leaves from 1 small lemon basil
    plant or 45ml/3 tbsp fresh
    coriander (cilantro) leaves,
    shredded or chopped

1 First, make the mojo by putting the mango, diced pineapple, chopped onion, and seeded and chopped chilli together in a bowl.

2 Add the chilli sauce, lime rind and juice, and the herb leaves. Stir to mix well. Cover tightly and leave in a cool place until needed.

3 Rinse the salmon fillets and pat dry, then brush each with a little oil.

4 Place the fillets skin side down on a lightly oiled grill rack over medium-hot coals. Cover the barbecue with a lid or tented heavy-duty foil and cook the fish for 3–5 minutes.

5 Drain the hickory chips into a colander and sprinkle about a third of them as evenly as possible over the coals. Carefully drop them through the slats in the grill racks, taking care not to scatter the ash as you do so.

6 Replace the barbecue cover and continue cooking for a further 8 minutes, adding a small handful of hickory chips twice more during this time. Serve the salmon hot or cold, with the mojo.

COOK'S TIP
When sweet pineapples are in season, you may prefer to use fresh ones in the mojo. You will need about half a medium pineapple. Slice off the skin, remove the core and cut the flesh into chunks.

Energy 364kcal/1519kJ; Protein 35.9g; Carbohydrate 7.8g, of which sugars 7.4g; Fat 21.2g, of which saturates 3.6g; Cholesterol 88mg; Calcium 58mg; Fibre 1.3g; Sodium 82mg

SEARED TUNA WITH SPICY WATERCRESS SALAD

TUNA STEAKS ARE WONDERFUL SEARED AND SERVED SLIGHTLY RARE WITH A PUNCHY SAUCE. IN THIS RECIPE A WATERCRESS SALAD IS SERVED JUST WARM AS A BED FOR THE TENDER FISH.

Preparation: 6 minutes; Cooking: 10 minutes

SERVES FOUR

INGREDIENTS

30ml/2 tbsp olive oil
5ml/1 tsp harissa
5ml/1 tsp clear honey
4 x 200g/7oz tuna steaks
salt and ground black pepper
lemon wedges, to serve
For the salad
30ml/2 tbsp olive oil
a little butter
25g/1oz fresh root ginger, peeled and thinly sliced
2 garlic cloves, finely sliced
2 fresh green chillies, seeded and thinly sliced
6 spring onions (scallions), cut into bitesize pieces
2 large handfuls watercress
1 lemon, cut into 4 wedges

1 Mix the olive oil, harissa, honey and salt, and rub it over the tuna steaks.

VARIATION

Prawns (shrimp) and scallops can be cooked in the same way. The shellfish will just need to be cooked through briefly – too long and they will become rubbery.

2 Heat a frying pan, grease it with a little oil and sear the tuna steaks for about 2 minutes on each side. They should still be pink on the inside.

3 Keep the tuna warm while you quickly prepare the salad: heat the olive oil and butter in a heavy pan. Stir in the ginger, garlic, chillies and spring onions, cook until the mixture begins to colour, then add the watercress. As soon as the watercress begins to wilt, toss in the lemon juice and season well with salt and plenty of ground black pepper.

4 Tip the warm salad on to a serving dish or individual plates. Slice the tuna steaks and arrange on top of the salad. Serve immediately with lemon wedges for squeezing over.

COOK'S TIP

Harissa is a North African spice paste based on chillies, garlic, coriander and cumin seeds. It is sold in tubes, like tomato purée (paste), or jars, or can be made fresh.

Energy 389kcal/1630kJ; Protein 49.2g; Carbohydrate 1.6g, of which sugars 1.6g; Fat 20.8g, of which saturates 4.2g; Cholesterol 56mg; Calcium 123mg; Fibre 1g; Sodium 120mg.

TONNO CON PISELLI

THIS ITALIAN-JEWISH DISH OF FRESH TUNA AND PEAS IS ESPECIALLY ENJOYED AT PASSOVER, WHICH
FALLS IN SPRING. USING A BOUGHT SAUCE KEEPS THE PREPARATION DOWN TO AN ABSOLUTE MINIMUM.

Preparation: 5 minutes; Cooking: 22 minutes

SERVES FOUR

INGREDIENTS

350g/12oz tuna steaks
600ml/1 pint/2½ cups fresh tomato
  sauce
350g/12oz/3 cups fresh shelled or
  frozen peas
45ml/3 tbsp chopped fresh flat
  leaf parsley
lemon wedges, to garnish

VARIATIONS

• This recipe works well with other types
and cuts of fish. Use tuna fillets in place
of the steaks or try different fish steaks,
such as salmon or swordfish.

• Chickpeas can be used instead of peas
for a more hearty dish.

1 Preheat the oven to 190ºC/375ºF/
Gas 5. Sprinkle the tuna steaks on each
side with salt and plenty of freshly
ground black pepper and place in a
shallow ovenproof dish, in a single layer.

2 Put the tomato sauce into a small
pan and bring to the boil, stirring
continuously to prevent it sticking.

3 Add the peas and parsley. Pour the
sauce and peas evenly over the fish
steaks in the ovenproof dish and bake
in the preheated oven, uncovered, for
about 20 minutes, or until tender.

4 Serve the fish, sauce and peas
immediately, straight from the dish,
with lemon wedges.

Energy 329kcal/1379kJ; Protein 30g; Carbohydrate 23g, of which sugars 8g; Fat 14g, of which saturates 4g; Cholesterol 40mg; Calcium 83mg; Fibre 6.8g; Sodium 600mg.

WARM SWORDFISH AND ROCKET SALAD

SWORDFISH IS ROBUST ENOUGH TO TAKE THE SHARP FLAVOURS OF ROCKET AND PECORINO CHEESE.
THE FISH CAN BE DRY, SO DON'T SKIP THE MARINATING STAGE UNLESS YOU'RE REALLY PUSHED.

Preparation: 7 minutes; Cooking: 8–12 minutes

SERVES FOUR

INGREDIENTS

4 swordfish steaks, about
    175g/6oz each
75ml/5 tbsp extra virgin olive oil,
    plus extra for serving
juice of 1 lemon
30ml/2 tbsp finely chopped
    fresh parsley
115g/4oz rocket (arugula) leaves,
    stalks removed
115g/4oz Pecorino cheese
salt and ground black pepper

1 Lay the swordfish steaks in a shallow dish. Mix 60ml/4 tbsp of the olive oil with the lemon juice. Pour over the fish. Season, sprinkle with parsley and turn the fish to coat. Cover the dish and leave to marinate for 5 minutes.

2 Heat a ridged griddle pan or the grill (broiler) until very hot. Take the fish out of the marinade and pat it dry with kitchen paper. Grill (broil) two steaks at a time for 2–3 minutes on each side until the swordfish is just cooked through, but still juicy.

3 Meanwhile, put the rocket leaves in a bowl and season with a little salt and plenty of pepper. Add the remaining 15ml/1 tbsp olive oil and toss well.

4 Place the swordfish steaks on four individual plates and arrange a little pile of salad on each steak. Shave the Pecorino over the top. Serve extra olive oil separately so it can be drizzled over the swordfish.

VARIATION
Tuna, shark or marlin steaks would be equally good in this recipe.

Energy 452kcal/1880kJ; Protein 43.6g; Carbohydrate 0.5g, of which sugars 0.4g; Fat 30.6g, of which saturates 9.5g; Cholesterol 101mg; Calcium 401mg; Fibre 0.6g; Sodium 581mg

GRIDDLED SWORDFISH <u>WITH</u> ROASTED TOMATOES

SLOW-ROASTING THE TOMATOES IS A GREAT TECHNIQUE WHEN YOU ARE ENTERTAINING AS THEY NEED NO LAST-MINUTE ATTENTION, BUT A MUCH QUICKER WAY IS SIMPLY TO GRILL THEM INSTEAD.

Preparation: 4 minutes; Cooking: 12 minutes, plus 3 hours if slow-roasting tomatoes

SERVES FOUR

INGREDIENTS

- 1kg/2¼lb large vine or plum tomatoes, peeled, halved and seeded
- 5–10ml/1–2 tsp ground cinnamon
- a pinch of saffron threads
- 15ml/1 tbsp orange flower water
- 60ml/4 tbsp olive oil
- 45–60ml/3–4 tbsp sugar
- 4 x 225g/8oz swordfish steaks
- rind of ½ preserved lemon, finely chopped
- a small bunch of fresh coriander (cilantro), finely chopped
- a handful of blanched almonds
- a knob (pat) of butter
- salt and ground black pepper

1 Preheat the oven to 110°C/225°F/ Gas ¼. Place the tomatoes on a baking sheet. Sprinkle with the cinnamon, saffron and orange flower water.

2 Trickle half the oil over, being sure to moisten every tomato half, and sprinkle with sugar. Place the tray in the bottom of the oven and cook the tomatoes for about 3 hours, then turn the oven off and leave them to cool. Alternatively, place under a medium grill (broiler) for 10 minutes.

VARIATION

If swordfish steaks are not available, use tuna or shark steaks.

3 Brush the remaining olive oil over the swordfish steaks and season with salt and pepper. Lightly oil a pre-heated cast-iron griddle and cook the steaks for 3–4 minutes on each side. Sprinkle the chopped preserved lemon and coriander over the steaks towards the end of the cooking time.

4 In a separate pan, fry the almonds in the butter until golden and sprinkle them over the tomatoes. Serve the steaks immediately with the tomatoes.

Energy 405kcal/1696kJ; Protein 42.3g; Carbohydrate 7.8g, of which sugars 7.8g; Fat 23g, of which saturates 5.2g; Cholesterol 98mg; Calcium 27mg; Fibre 2.5g; Sodium 330mg

GRILLED SWORDFISH SKEWERS

THIS DELICIOUS SKEWERED AND GRILLED SWORDFISH DISH IS COOKED WITH OLIVE OIL, GARLIC AND OREGANO. IN GREECE IT IS KNOWN AS SOUVLAKIA.

Preparation: 10 minutes; Cooking: 8–10 minutes

SERVES FOUR

INGREDIENTS
 2 red onions, quartered
 2 red or green (bell) peppers,
  quartered and seeded
 20–24 thick cubes of swordfish,
  675–800g/1½–1¾lb in total
 lemon wedges, to garnish
For the basting sauce
 75ml/5 tbsp extra virgin olive oil
 1 garlic clove, crushed
 large pinch of dried oregano
 salt and ground black pepper

1 Carefully separate the onion quarters in pieces, each composed of two or three layers. Slice each pepper quarter in half widthways, or into thirds if you have very large peppers.

2 Make the souvlakia by threading five or six pieces of swordfish on to each of four long metal skewers, alternating with pieces of the pepper and onion. Lay the souvlakia across a grill (broiling) pan or roasting tray and set aside while you make the basting sauce.

3 Whisk the olive oil, crushed garlic and oregano in a bowl. Add salt and pepper, and whisk again. Brush the souvlakia generously on all sides with the basting sauce.

4 Preheat the grill (broiler) to the highest setting, or prepare a barbecue. Slide the grill pan or roasting tray underneath the grill or transfer the skewers to the barbecue, making sure that they are not too close to the heat and that the heat is evenly distributed under them all.

5 Cook for 8–10 minutes, turning the skewers several times and brushing them with the basting sauce to increase the flavours, until the fish is cooked and the peppers and onions have begun to scorch around the edges.

6 Serve the souvlakia immediately with a salad of cucumber, red onion and fresh olives and garnished with one or two wedges of lemon.

COOK'S TIP
Many fishmongers will prepare the swordfish for you, and cut it into cubes for you too. But if you prefer to do this yourself, or you are buying the swordfish whole, you will need approximately 800g/ 1¾lb swordfish. The cubes should be fairly big – about 5cm/2in square – as they shrink in size when they cook. If you have larger cubes of swordfish, you may need to increase the cooking time slightly to ensure the fish is cooked through. If in doubt, cut a large cube open to check.

Energy 363Kcal/1,511kJ; Protein 32.2g; Carbohydrate 11.5g, of which sugars 9.6g; Fat 21.2g, of which saturates 3.6g; Cholesterol 69mg; Calcium 33mg; Fibre 2.5g; Sodium 225mg

CHARGRILLED SWORDFISH WITH SPICY SAUCE

SWORDFISH IS A PRIME CANDIDATE FOR GRILLING (BROILING), AS LONG AS IT IS NOT OVERCOOKED.
IT TASTES WONDERFUL WITH A TOMATO SAUCE, HERE ENLIVENED WITH SOME CHILLI AND LIME.
Preparation: 5 minutes; Cooking: 15–17 minutes

SERVES FOUR

INGREDIENTS

4 tomatoes
45ml/3 tbsp olive oil
15ml/1 tsp chilli powder
grated rind and juice of 1 lime
4 swordfish steaks, about
    225g/8oz each
2.5ml/½ tsp salt
2.5ml/½ tsp ground black pepper
175ml/6fl oz/¾ cup crème fraîche
fresh flat leaf parsley, to garnish
chargrilled vegetables, to serve

COOK'S TIP
Chargrilled vegetables are now available
frozen, so you can use them to save
preparation time. Just stir-fry or roast the
vegetables then serve with the fish.

1 Cut a cross in the base of each
tomato. Place them in a heatproof bowl
and pour over boiling water to cover.
After 30 seconds, lift the tomatoes out
on a slotted spoon and plunge them
into a bowl of cold water. Drain. The
skins will have begun to peel back from
the crosses.

2 Remove all the skin from the
tomatoes, then cut them in half and
squeeze out the seeds. Using a serrated
knife, chop the tomato flesh into
1cm/½ in pieces.

3 Heat 15ml/1 tbsp of the oil in a small
pan and add the chilli powder with the
lime rind and juice. Cook for 2–3
minutes, then stir in the tomatoes. Cook
for 10 minutes, stirring the mixture
occasionally, until the tomato is soft
and pulpy.

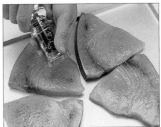

4 Brush the swordfish steaks with the
remaining olive oil and season them
well. Barbecue or grill (broil) for 3–4
minutes or until just cooked, turning
once. Meanwhile, stir the crème fraîche
into the sauce, heat it through gently
and pour over the swordfish steaks.
Garnish with parsley and serve with
chargrilled vegetables.

Energy 502kcal/2089kJ; Protein 42.2g; Carbohydrate 4.2g, of which sugars 4g; Fat 35.3g, of which saturates 15.2g; Cholesterol 142mg; Calcium 42mg; Fibre 1g; Sodium 311mg.

SKATE WITH BLACK BUTTER

SKATE CAN BE QUITE INEXPENSIVE AND THIS CLASSIC DISH IS PERFECT FOR A FAMILY SUPPER. SERVE IT WITH STEAMED LEEKS AND PLAIN BOILED POTATOES.

Preparation: 0 minutes; Cooking: 15–17 minutes

SERVES FOUR

INGREDIENTS

4 skate wings, about 225g/8oz each
60ml/4 tbsp red wine vinegar or
  malt vinegar
30ml/2 tbsp drained capers in
  vinegar, chopped if large
30ml/2 tbsp chopped fresh parsley
150g/5oz/²⁄₃ cup butter
salt and ground black pepper

COOK'S TIP
Despite the title of the recipe, the butter should be a rich golden brown. It should never be allowed to blacken, or it will taste unpleasantly bitter.

1 Put the skate wings in a large, shallow pan, cover with cold water and add a pinch of salt and 15ml/1 tbsp of the red wine or malt vinegar.

2 Bring to the boil, skim the surface, then lower the heat and simmer gently for about 10–12 minutes, until the skate flesh comes away from the bone easily. Carefully drain the skate and peel off the skin.

3 Transfer the skate to a warmed serving dish, season with salt and pepper and sprinkle over the capers and parsley. Keep hot.

4 In a small pan, heat the butter until it foams and turns a rich nutty brown. Pour it over the skate. Pour the remaining vinegar into the pan and boil until reduced by about two-thirds. Drizzle over the skate and serve.

MONKFISH ^{WITH} PIMIENTO ^{AND} CREAM SAUCE

THIS RECIPE COMES FROM SPAIN, WHERE PIMIENTOS (SPANISH RED PEPPERS) ARE USED TO MAKE A SPICY SAUCE. HERE, RED PEPPERS ARE USED WITH A LITTLE CHILLI AND CREAM FOR A MELLOW PINK SAUCE.

Preparation: 5 minutes; Cooking: 25–30 minutes

SERVES FOUR

INGREDIENTS
2 large red (bell) peppers
1kg/2¼lb monkfish tail or
  900g/2lb halibut
plain (all-purpose) flour, for dusting
30ml/2 tbsp olive oil
25g/1oz/2 tbsp butter
120ml/4fl oz/½ cup dry white wine
  or dry vermouth
½ dried chilli, seeded and chopped
8 raw king prawns (jumbo shrimp), in
  the shell
150ml/¼ pint/⅔ cup double
  (heavy) cream
salt and ground black pepper
fresh flat leaf parsley, to garnish

1 Preheat the grill (broiler) to high and cook the peppers for 8–12 minutes, turning occasionally, until they are soft and the skins blackened. Leave, covered, until cool enough to handle. Skin and discard the stalks and seeds. Put the flesh into a blender, strain in the juices and purée.

2 Meanwhile, cut the monkfish or halibut into eight steaks. Season well and dust with flour.

3 Heat the oil and butter in a large frying pan and fry the fish for 3 minutes on each side. Remove to a warm dish.

4 Add the wine or vermouth and chilli to the pan and stir to deglaze the pan. Add the prawns and cook them briefly, then lift out and set aside.

5 Boil the sauce to reduce by half, then strain into a small jug (pitcher). Add the cream to the pan and boil briefly to reduce. Return the sauce to the pan, stir in the puréed peppers and check the seasonings. Pour the sauce over the fish and serve garnished with the cooked prawns and parsley.

Energy 518kcal/2163kJ; Protein 50.2g; Carbohydrate 10.7g, of which sugars 10.3g; Fat 27.4g, of which saturates 13.7g; Cholesterol 140mg; Calcium 74mg; Fibre 2.3g; Sodium 115mg.

POULTRY
DISHES

Chicken is the most incredibly versatile ingredient. It can be roasted, baked, steamed, grilled and fried; it is delicious hot, warm and cold and it goes equally well with lemon in a Greek dish, soy sauce in a Chinese dish or tandoori paste in an Indian dish. It also cooks very quickly. So, the only problem regarding chicken is how to choose which half-hour recipe to cook. If you like spicy chicken dishes, choose from Fiery Chicken Wings, Tandoori Chicken Kebabs, Crispy Five-spice Chicken or Curried Chicken Noodles. If you prefer a Mediterranean flavour, try Chicken Livers in Sherry, Pan-fried Chicken with Pesto, Italian Chicken with Peas or Risotto with Chicken and Prosciutto. Chicken is not the only form of poultry, of course, and both turkey (often beaten out into escalopes for super-fast cooking) and duck can be used to create delicious meals such as Turkey Rolls in Gazpacho, Turkey and Cranberry Bundles and Turkey with Marsala, and Gingered Duck with Tamari, Skewered Duck with Poached Eggs and Marmalade and Soy Roast Duck.

CHICKEN WITH LEMON AND GARLIC

CHICKEN STRIPS SPICED WITH PAPRIKA MAKE AN UNUSUAL COURSE FOR FOUR, AND ONLY NEED TO BE COOKED AT THE LAST MOMENT. SERVE THEM AS A MAIN COURSE WITH FRIED POTATOES.

Preparation: 3 minutes; Cooking: 3–5 minutes

SERVES TWO TO FOUR

INGREDIENTS

   2 skinless chicken breast fillets
   30ml/2 tbsp olive oil
   1 shallot, finely chopped
   4 garlic cloves, finely chopped
   5ml/1 tsp paprika
   juice of 1 lemon
   30ml/2 tbsp chopped fresh parsley
   salt and ground black pepper
   fresh flat leaf parsley, to garnish
   lemon wedges, to serve

VARIATION

For a variation on this dish, try using strips of turkey breast or pork fillet. They need slightly longer cooking. The whites of spring onions (scallions) can replace shallots, and the chopped green tops can be used instead of parsley.

1 Remove the little fillet from the back of each breast portion. If the breast still looks fatter than a finger, bat it with a rolling pin to make it thinner. Slice all the chicken meat into strips.

2 Heat the oil in a large frying pan. Stir-fry the chicken strips with the shallot, garlic and paprika over a high heat for about 3 minutes until cooked through.

3 Add the lemon juice and parsley and season with salt and pepper to taste. Serve hot with lemon wedges, garnished with flat leaf parsley.

COOK'S TIP

Chicken breast fillets have a little fillet strip that easily becomes detached. Collect these in a bag or container in the freezer for this dish.

Energy 139kcal/580kJ; Protein 18.6g; Carbohydrate 1.5g, of which sugars 1.1g; Fat 6.5g, of which saturates 1g; Cholesterol 53mg; Calcium 33mg; Fibre 0.8g; Sodium 50mg

CHICKEN LIVERS <u>IN</u> SHERRY

THIS DELICIOUS LITTLE TAPAS DISH IS PARTICULARLY GOOD EATEN WITH BREAD OR ON TOAST. FOR A MORE ELEGANT PRESENTATION, SERVE PILED ON TOP OF LITTLE RICE TORTITAS.

Preparation: 3–4 minutes; Cooking: 5 minutes

SERVES FOUR

INGREDIENTS

225g/8oz chicken livers, thawed if
   frozen
15ml/1 tbsp olive oil
1 small onion, finely chopped
2 small garlic cloves, finely chopped
5ml/1 tsp fresh thyme leaves
30ml/2 tbsp sweet oloroso sherry
30ml/2 tbsp crème fraîche or double
   (heavy) cream
2.5ml/½ tsp paprika
salt and ground black pepper
fresh thyme, to garnish

1 Trim any green spots and sinews from the chicken livers. Heat the oil in a frying pan and fry the onion, garlic, chicken livers and thyme for 3 minutes.

2 Stir the sherry into the livers, add the crème fraîche and cook briefly. Season with salt, pepper and paprika, garnish with thyme and serve immediately.

Energy 119kcal/494kJ; Protein 10.3g; Carbohydrate 1.5g, of which sugars 1.1g; Fat 7.1g, of which saturates 2.8g; Cholesterol 222mg; Calcium 13mg; Fibre 0.2g; Sodium 46mg.

FIERY CHICKEN WINGS WITH BLOOD ORANGES

THIS IS A GREAT RECIPE FOR THE BARBECUE – IT IS QUICK AND EASY, AND BEST EATEN WITH THE
FINGERS. THE ORANGES CAN BE COOKED SEPARATELY OR WITH THE WINGS.

Preparation: 3 minutes; Cooking: 10 minutes

SERVES FOUR

INGREDIENTS
  60ml/4 tbsp fiery harissa
  30ml/2 tbsp olive oil
  16–20 chicken wings
  4 blood oranges, quartered
  icing (confectioners') sugar
  a small bunch of fresh coriander
    (cilantro), chopped
  salt

COOK'S TIP
Try making your own harissa if you have a
blender. You will need 6–8 dried red
chillies, 2 crushed garlic cloves, 2.5ml/
½ tsp salt, 5ml/1 tsp ground cumin,
2.5ml/½ tsp ground coriander and 120ml/
4fl oz/1 cup olive oil. Blend to a paste.
To store, spoon into a jar and cover with
olive oil. It will keep for 1 month.

1 Mix the harissa with the olive oil in a
small bowl, or, if using home-made
harissa, simply measure the required
amount into a bowl. Add a little salt and
stir to combine. Brush this mixture over
the chicken wings so that they are well
coated. Cook the wings on a hot
barbecue or under a hot grill (broiler)
for 5 minutes on each side.

2 Once the wings begin to cook, dip the
orange quarters lightly in icing sugar
and grill (broil) them for a few minutes,
until they are slightly burnt but not
blackened. If you thread them on to
skewers, it will be easier to turn them
under the heat. Serve the chicken wings
immediately with the oranges, sprinkled
with a little chopped fresh coriander.

Energy 658kcal/2758kJ; Protein 61.9g; Carbohydrate 21.8g, of which sugars 20.7g; Fat 36.7g, of which saturates 10.1g; Cholesterol 264mg; Calcium 163mg; Fibre 2.6g; Sodium 866mg

CHICKEN SALAD WITH HAZELNUT DRESSING

THIS WARM SALAD COMBINES PAN-FRIED CHICKEN, SPINACH, TOMATOES AND SPRING ONIONS WITH A LIGHT AND TASTY NUTTY DRESSING – A TASTY LUNCH READY IN LESS THAN 20 MINUTES.

Preparation: 8 minutes; Cooking: 10 minutes

SERVES FOUR

INGREDIENTS
- 45ml/3 tbsp olive oil
- 30ml/2 tbsp hazelnut oil
- 15ml/1 tbsp white wine vinegar
- 1 garlic clove, crushed
- 15ml/1 tbsp chopped fresh mixed herbs
- 225g/8oz baby spinach leaves
- 250g/9oz cherry tomatoes, halved
- 1 bunch spring onions (scallions), chopped
- 2 cooked chicken breast fillets, skinned and cut into thin strips
- salt and ground black pepper

VARIATION

This salad can also be served cold, if you need to make it in advance or have some cooked chicken breast to use up.

1 First make the dressing. Place 30ml/ 2 tbsp of the olive oil, the hazelnut oil, vinegar, garlic and herbs in a small bowl or jug (pitcher) and whisk together until thoroughly mixed. Set aside.

2 Trim any long stalks from the spinach leaves, then place in a large serving bowl with the tomatoes and spring onions, and toss together to mix.

3 Heat the remaining 15ml/1 tbsp olive oil in a large frying pan, add the chicken and fry over a high heat for 7–10 minutes, or until cooked through and lightly browned.

4 Scatter the chicken pieces over the salad, give the dressing a quick whisk to blend, then drizzle it over the salad and gently toss all the ingredients together to mix. Season to taste and serve immediately.

Energy 292kcal/1218kJ; Protein 20.9g; Carbohydrate 13.8g, of which sugars 10.3g; Fat 17.4g, of which saturates 2.8g; Cholesterol 56mg; Calcium 120mg; Fibre 2.1g; Sodium 163mg.

STIR-FRIED CHICKEN WITH THAI BASIL

ON THE TABLE IN UNDER 10 MINUTES – YOU CAN'T SAY BETTER THAN THAT. THIS THAI-INSPIRED STIR-FRY IS TASTY, COLOURFUL AND FULL OF FLAVOUR, PERFECT FOR ANY DAY OF THE WEEK.

Preparation: 2–3 minutes; Cooking: 5–7 minutes

SERVES FOUR

INGREDIENTS

4 skinless chicken breast fillets
2 red (bell) peppers
30ml/2 tbsp garlic-infused olive oil
1 small bunch fresh Thai basil
salt and ground black pepper

COOK'S TIP

Thai basil, sometimes called holy basil, has purple-tinged leaves and a more pronounced, slightly aniseedy flavour than the usual varieties. It is available in most Asian food stores but if you can't find any, use a handful of ordinary basil instead. Serve this fragrant stir-fry with plain steamed rice or boiled noodles and soy sauce on the side.

1 Using a sharp knife, slice the chicken breast portions into strips. Halve the peppers, remove the seeds, then cut each piece of pepper into strips.

2 Heat a wok or large frying pan. Add the oil. When it is hot, add the chicken and toss over the heat for 2 minutes.

3 Add the red peppers and continue to stir-fry the mixture over a high heat for about 3 minutes, until the chicken is golden and cooked through. Season with salt and ground black pepper.

4 Roughly tear up the basil leaves, add to the chicken and peppers and toss briefly to combine. Serve immediately.

Energy 211kcal/892kJ; Protein 37.8g; Carbohydrate 6.9g, of which sugars 5.4g; Fat 3.7g, of which saturates 0.8g; Cholesterol 105mg; Calcium 67mg; Fibre 1.4g; Sodium 97mg

CRÈME FRAÎCHE AND CORIANDER CHICKEN

THIS IS AN ANY-OCCASION MAIN COURSE DISH THAT CAN BE TURNED AROUND IN MINUTES. BE GENEROUS WITH THE CORIANDER LEAVES, AS THEY HAVE A WONDERFUL FRAGRANT FLAVOUR.

Preparation: 8 minutes; Cooking: 8 minutes

SERVES FOUR

INGREDIENTS

6 skinless, boneless chicken
thigh portions
60ml/4 tbsp crème fraîche
1 small bunch fresh coriander
(cilantro), roughly chopped
15ml/1 tbsp sunflower oil
salt and ground black pepper

COOK'S TIP

This recipe uses boneless chicken thighs, but boneless breast portions can be used instead. Simply cut into bitesize pieces and cook in the frying pan for 5–6 minutes, until just tender.

1 Using a sharp cook's knife or cleaver, cut each chicken thigh into three or four pieces.

2 Heat the oil in a large frying pan, add the chicken and cook for about 6 minutes, turning occasionally.

3 Add the crème fraîche to the pan and stir until melted, then allow the mixture to bubble for 1–2 minutes. Add the chopped coriander to the chicken and stir to combine. Season with salt and ground black pepper to taste, and serve immediately.

Energy 249kcal/1041kJ; Protein 32.1g; Carbohydrate 0.7g, of which sugars 0.6g; Fat 13.1g, of which saturates 5.6g; Cholesterol 174mg; Calcium 44mg; Fibre 0.6g; Sodium 143mg

SOY SAUCE AND STAR ANISE CHICKEN

ALTHOUGH THE CHICKEN COOKS QUICKLY, IT DOES BENEFIT FROM BEING MARINATED FIRST. THIS ONLY TAKES A MOMENT AND THERE'LL BE NO LAST-MINUTE WORK TO DO WHEN GUESTS ARRIVE.

Preparation: 3–4 minutes; Cooking: 16 minutes, plus marinating time (optional)

SERVES FOUR

INGREDIENTS
- 4 skinless chicken breast fillets
- 2 whole star anise
- 45ml/3 tbsp olive oil
- 30ml/2 tbsp soy sauce
- ground black pepper

1 Put the chicken breast fillets in a shallow, non-metallic dish and add the star anise.

2 In a small bowl, whisk together the oil and soy sauce and season with black pepper to make a marinade.

3 Pour the marinade over the chicken and stir to coat each breast fillet all over. Cover the dish with clear film (plastic wrap) and set aside for as much time as you have. If you are able to make it ahead, leave the chicken in the marinade for around 6–8 hours as the flavour will be improved. Place the covered dish in the refrigerator.

4 Cook the chicken under the grill (broiler), turning occasionally. It will need about 8 minutes on each side. Serve immediately.

VARIATION
If you prefer, cook on a barbecue. When the coals are dusted with ash, spread them out evenly. Remove the chicken breasts from the marinade and cook for 8 minutes on each side, spooning over the marinade from time to time, until the chicken is cooked through.

Energy 237kcal/992kJ; Protein 36.2g; Carbohydrate 0.6g, of which sugars 0.6g; Fat 9.9g, of which saturates 1.6g; Cholesterol 105mg; Calcium 9mg; Fibre 0g; Sodium 624mg

CRUMBED CHICKEN WITH GREEN MAYONNAISE

THE CONTRAST BETWEEN CRISP CRUMB AND TENDER CHICKEN IS WHAT MAKES THIS SO SUCCESSFUL. CAPER MAYONNAISE IS TRADITIONAL BUT MAYO FLAVOURED WITH WASABI WOULD BE GOOD TOO.

Preparation: 4 minutes; Cooking: 12 minutes

SERVES FOUR

INGREDIENTS

4 skinless chicken breast fillets,
  each weighing about 200g/7oz
juice of 1 lemon
5ml/1 tsp paprika
plain (all-purpose) flour, for dusting
1–2 eggs
dried breadcrumbs, for coating
about 60ml/4 tbsp olive oil
salt and ground black pepper
lemon wedges (optional), to serve

For the mayonnaise
120ml/4fl oz/½ cup mayonnaise
30ml/2 tbsp pickled capers, drained
  and chopped
30ml/2 tbsp chopped fresh parsley

1 Skin the chicken fillets. Lay them outside down and, with a sharp knife, cut horizontally, almost through, from the rounded side. Open them up like a book. Press gently, to make a roundish shape the size of a side plate. Sprinkle with lemon juice and paprika.

2 Set out three shallow bowls. Sprinkle flour over one, seasoning it well. Beat the egg with a little salt and pour into the second. Sprinkle the third with dried breadcrumbs. Dip the fillets first into the flour on both sides, then into the egg, then into the breadcrumbs to coat them evenly.

3 Put the mayonnaise ingredients in a bowl and mix well to combine.

4 Heat the oil in a heavy frying pan over a high heat. Fry the breast portions two at a time, turning after 3 minutes, until golden on both sides. Add more oil for the second batch if needed. Serve immediately, with the mayonnaise and lemon wedges, if using.

Energy 582kcal/2428kJ; Protein 51.5g; Carbohydrate 10.3g, of which sugars 0.8g; Fat 37.6g, of which saturates 6g; Cholesterol 210mg; Calcium 43mg; Fibre 0.5g; Sodium 369mg

PAN-FRIED CHICKEN WITH PESTO

WARM PESTO ACCOMPANYING PAN-FRIED CHICKEN MAKES A DELICIOUSLY QUICK MEAL. SERVE WITH BABY CARROTS AND CELERY, BRAISED IN STOCK IN A SEPARATE PAN WHILE THE CHICKEN IS COOKING.

Preparation: 2–3 minutes; Cooking: 18 minutes

SERVES FOUR

INGREDIENTS
15ml/1 tbsp olive oil
4 chicken breast fillets, skinned
fresh basil leaves, to garnish
For the pesto
90ml/6 tbsp olive oil
50g/2oz/½ cup pine nuts
50g/2oz/⅔ cup freshly grated
  Parmesan cheese
50g/2oz/1 cup fresh basil leaves
15g/½oz/¼ cup fresh parsley
2 garlic cloves, crushed
salt and ground black pepper

1 Heat the 15ml/1 tbsp oil in a frying pan. Add the chicken breasts and cook gently for about 15 minutes, turning several times until they are tender, lightly browned and thoroughly cooked.

2 Meanwhile, to make the pesto, place all the ingredients in a food processor and process until smooth and well mixed.

3 Remove the chicken from the pan, cover and keep hot. Reduce the heat slightly, then add the pesto to the pan and cook gently, stirring constantly, for a few minutes, or until the pesto has warmed through.

4 Put the cooked chicken on a plate, pour the warm pesto over the top, then garnish with basil leaves and serve immediately.

Energy 480kcal/1998kJ; Protein 43.2g; Carbohydrate 1g, of which sugars 0.9g; Fat 33.8g, of which saturates 6.4g; Cholesterol 118mg; Calcium 192mg; Fibre 1.1g; Sodium 232mg

CHICKEN STUFFED WITH HAM AND CHEESE

A CLASSIC THAT IS PERENNIALLY POPULAR, THIS CONSISTS OF BREASTS OF CHICKEN STUFFED WITH SMOKED HAM AND GRUYÈRE, THEN COATED IN EGG AND BREADCRUMBS AND FRIED UNTIL GOLDEN.

Preparation: 6–8 minutes; Cooking: 10–12 minutes

SERVES FOUR

INGREDIENTS

4 skinless, boneless chicken breast
  portions, about 130g/4½oz each
4 very thin smoked ham slices,
  halved and rind removed
about 90g/3½oz Gruyère cheese,
  thinly sliced
plain (all-purpose) flour, for coating
2 eggs, beaten
75g/3oz/¾ cup natural-coloured
  dried breadcrumbs
5ml/1 tsp dried thyme
75g/3oz/6 tbsp butter
60ml/4 tbsp olive oil
salt and ground black pepper
mixed leaf salad, to serve

3 Spoon the flour for coating into a shallow bowl. Pour the beaten eggs into another shallow bowl and mix the breadcrumbs with the thyme and seasoning in a third bowl.

4 Toss each stuffed breast in the flour, then coat in egg and breadcrumbs, shaking off any excess.

5 Place half the butter and half the oil in one pan, and the remaining half measures in the other, and heat separately

COOK'S TIP

If you are able to prepare these portions in advance, cover the crumbed breasts and chill them for about 1 hour in the refrigerator to set the coating. It's certainly a tip worth remembering for when you have more time on a recipe.

6 When the fat stops foaming, gently slide in the coated breasts, two in each pan. Shallow fry over a medium-low heat for about 5 minutes each side, turning over carefully with a spatula. Drain on kitchen paper for a few seconds to soak up the excess fat. Serve immediately with the mixed leaf salad.

1 Slit the chicken breasts about three-quarters of the way through, then open them up and lay them flat. Place a slice of ham on each cut side of the chicken, trimming to fit if necessary so that the ham does not hang over the edge.

2 Top with the Gruyère slices, making sure that they are well within the ham slices. Fold over the chicken and reshape, pressing well to seal and ensuring that no cheese is visible.

VARIATION
Instead of Gruyère, try one of the herb-flavoured hard cheeses, such as Double Gloucester with Chives.

Energy 599kcal/2496kJ; Protein 41.8g; Carbohydrate 14.8g, of which sugars 0.8g; Fat 41.5g, of which saturates 18.4g; Cholesterol 220mg; Calcium 222mg; Fibre 0.4g; Sodium 698mg

HONEY MUSTARD CHICKEN

THIS DISH IS SIMPLICITY ITSELF: MAKE A SIMPLE MARINADE, BRUSH IT OVER SOME CHICKEN THIGHS AND COOK FOR HALF AN HOUR FOR A TASTY RESULT. SERVE WITH A CHUNKY TOMATO AND RED ONION SALAD.

Preparation: 2 minutes; Cooking: 25–30 minutes

SERVES FOUR

INGREDIENTS
   8 chicken thighs
   60ml/4 tbsp wholegrain mustard
   60ml/4 tbsp clear honey
   salt and ground black pepper

1 Preheat the oven to 190°C/375°F/ Gas 5. Put the chicken thighs in a single layer in a roasting pan.

COOK'S TIP
Chicken thighs have a rich flavour, but if you want to cut down on fat, use four chicken breast portions instead and cook for 20–25 minutes.

2 Mix together the mustard and honey, season with salt and ground black pepper to taste and brush the mixture all over the chicken thighs.

3 Cook for 25–30 minutes, brushing the chicken with the pan juices occasionally, until cooked through. (To check the chicken is cooked through, skewer it with a sharp knife; the juices should run clear.)

Energy 244Kcal/1028kJ; Protein 27g; Carbohydrate 12g, of which sugars 12g; Fat 10g, of which saturates 2g; Cholesterol 130mg; Calcium 33mg; Fibre 0.7g; Sodium 400mg

CHICKEN BITKI

THIS CHICKEN DISH IS FROM POLAND, WHERE CHICKENS HAVE A GAMEY FLAVOUR AKIN TO GUINEA FOWL. COMBINED WITH MUSHROOMS, THE CHICKEN MAKES DELICIOUS MEATBALLS.

Preparation: 10 minutes; Cooking: 15–17 minutes

MAKES 12

INGREDIENTS

15g/½oz/1 tbsp butter
115g/4oz flat mushrooms, finely chopped
50g/2oz/1 cup fresh white breadcrumbs
350g/12oz skinless chicken or guinea fowl breast fillets, minced or finely chopped
2 eggs, separated
1.5ml/¼ tsp grated nutmeg
30ml/2 tbsp plain (all-purpose) flour
45ml/3 tbsp oil
salt and freshly ground black pepper

To serve
green salad
grated pickled beetroot (beet)

1 Melt the butter in a pan and fry the mushrooms for 5 minutes until the juices have evaporated. Allow to cool.

2 Mix the breadcrumbs, chicken, egg yolks, nutmeg, salt and pepper and cooked mushrooms well in a large bowl.

3 In a clean large bowl, whisk the egg whites until stiff. Stir half into the chicken mixture, then fold in the rest.

4 Scrape the mixture out on to the work surface and shape into 12 even meatballs, about 7.5cm/3in long and 2.5cm/1in wide. Roll in the flour to coat.

5 Heat the oil in a frying pan and fry the bitki for 10 minutes, turning until evenly golden brown and cooked through.

6 Serve hot with a green salad and pickled beetroot.

Energy 118kcal/493kJ; Protein 10.6g; Carbohydrate 5.2g, of which sugars 0.2g; Fat 6.2g, of which saturates 1.3g; Cholesterol 60mg; Calcium 16mg; Fibre 0.3g; Sodium 69mg.

STUFFED CHICKEN IN BACON COATS

*A SIMPLE CREAM CHEESE AND CHIVE FILLING FLAVOURS THESE CHICKEN BREASTS AND THEY ARE
BEAUTIFULLY MOIST WHEN COOKED IN THEIR BACON WRAPPING.*

Preparation: 5 minutes; Cooking: 25–30 minutes

SERVES FOUR

INGREDIENTS

4 skinless chicken breast fillets, each
weighing about 175g/6oz
115g/4oz/½ cup cream cheese
15ml/1 tbsp snipped chives
8 rindless unsmoked bacon rashers
(strips)
15ml/1 tbsp olive oil
ground black pepper
jacket potatoes and green salad,
to serve

1 Preheat the oven to 200ºC/400ºF/
Gas 6. Using a very sharp knife,
carefully make a horizontal slit from the
side into each chicken breast.

2 To make the filling, beat together the
cream cheese and chives in a bowl.
Divide the filling into four portions and,
using a teaspoon, fill each slit with some
of the cream cheese. Push the sides of
the slit together to keep the filling in.

3 Wrap each breast in two rashers of
bacon and place in an ovenproof dish.
Drizzle the oil over the chicken and bake
for 25–30 minutes, brushing occasionally
with the oil. Season with pepper and
serve at once.

Energy 457kcal/1908kJ; Protein 52.2g; Carbohydrate 0g, of which sugars 0g; Fat 27.6g, of which saturates 13g; Cholesterol 180mg; Calcium 40mg; Fibre 0g; Sodium 1058mg.

SOUTHERN FRIED CHICKEN

*THIS IS A LOW-FAT INTERPRETATION OF THE ORIGINAL DEEP-FRIED DISH, WHICH IS NOW AN
INTERNATIONAL FAST FOOD FAVOURITE. SERVE WITH POTATO WEDGES TO COMPLETE THE MEAL.*

Preparation: 5 minutes; Cooking: 25 minutes

SERVES FOUR

INGREDIENTS

15ml/1 tbsp paprika
30ml/2 tbsp plain (all-purpose) flour
4 skinless chicken breast fillets, each
weighing about 175g/6oz
30ml/2 tbsp sunflower oil
salt and ground black pepper
For the corn cakes
200g/7oz corn kernels
350g/12oz mashed potato, cooled
25g/1oz/2 tbsp butter
To serve
150ml/¼ pint/⅔ cup sour cream
15ml/1 tbsp snipped chives
potato wedges

COOK'S TIP

To make the mashed potato, cook the
potatoes in boiling salted water for about
20 minutes until tender, then drain well.
Add a little milk and mash until smooth.

1 Mix the paprika and flour together on
a plate. Coat each chicken breast in the
seasoned flour.

2 Heat the oil in a large frying pan and
add the floured chicken breasts. Cook
over high heat, until a golden brown
colour on both sides. Reduce the heat
and continue cooking for a further 20
minutes, turning once or twice, or until
the chicken is cooked right through.

3 Meanwhile, make the corn cakes.
Stir the corn kernels into the cooled
mashed potato and season with plenty
of salt and pepper to taste. Using lightly
floured hands, shape the mixture into
12 even-size round cakes, each about
5cm/2in in diameter.

4 Melt the butter in another large frying
pan and cook the corn cakes for 3
minutes on each side, or until golden
and heated through. Meanwhile, mix
together the sour cream with the chives
in a small bowl to make a dip.

5 When the chicken breasts and corn
cakes are cooked, use a slotted spoon
to transfer the corn cakes from the
frying pan to serving plates followed by
the chicken breasts, which should be
placed on top. Serve at once with potato
wedges, offering the sour cream with
chives on the side.

Energy 448kcal/1878kJ; Protein 46.5g; Carbohydrate 20.4g, of which sugars 3.4g; Fat 20.6g, of which saturates 9.2g; Cholesterol 158mg; Calcium 61mg; Fibre 1.8g; Sodium 738mg.

GREEK-STYLE CHICKEN WITH FENNEL SEEDS

THE SAUCE FOR THE CHICKEN IS BASED ON AVGOLEMONO, AN EXQUISITE EGG AND LEMON MIXTURE
WHICH IS ONE OF GREECE'S GIFTS TO GOOD COOKS EVERYWHERE. IT TASTES GREAT WITH THE FENNEL.
Preparation: 3–4 minutes; Cooking: 15 minutes

SERVES FOUR

INGREDIENTS
  4 skinless chicken breast fillets
  plain (all-purpose) flour, for dusting
  30–45ml/2–3 tbsp olive oil
  1–2 onions, chopped
  ¼ fennel bulb, chopped (optional)
  15ml/1 tbsp chopped fresh parsley,
    plus extra to garnish
  7.5ml/1½ tsp fennel seeds
  75ml/5 tbsp dry Marsala
  120ml/4fl oz/½ cup chicken stock
  300g/11oz/2¼ cups petits pois
    (baby peas)
  juice of 1½ lemons
  2 egg yolks
  salt and ground black pepper

1 Season the chicken with salt and pepper, then dust generously with flour. Shake off the excess flour; set aside.

2 Heat 15ml/1 tbsp oil in a pan, add the onions, fennel (if using), parsley and fennel seeds. Cook for 3 minutes.

3 Add the remaining oil and the chicken to the pan and cook over a high heat for 5–6 minutes on each side, until lightly browned and cooked through. Remove from the pan and set aside.

4 Deglaze the pan by pouring in the Marsala and cooking over a high heat until reduced to about 30ml/2 tbsp, then pour in the stock. Add the peas and return the chicken and onion mixture to the pan. Cook over a very low heat while you prepare the egg mixture.

5 In a bowl, beat the lemon juice and egg yolks together, then slowly add about 120ml/4fl oz/½ cup of the hot liquid from the chicken and peas, stirring well to combine.

6 Return the mixture to the pan and cook over a low heat, stirring, until the mixture thickens slightly. (Do not allow the mixture to boil or the eggs will curdle and spoil the sauce.) Serve the chicken immediately, sprinkled with a little extra chopped fresh parsley.

Energy 301kcal/1260kJ; Protein 41.6g; Carbohydrate 10.4g, of which sugars 3.3g; Fat 8.4g, of which saturates 1.5g; Cholesterol 105mg; Calcium 34mg; Fibre 4.3g; Sodium 96mg

CHICKEN ᵂᴵᵀᴴ PROSCIUTTO ᴬᴺᴰ CHEESE

IN THIS ITALIAN DISH, CHICKEN IS FILLED WITH PROSCIUTTO AND BASIL AND TOPPED WITH A SLICE
OF FONTINA CHEESE BEFORE IT IS BAKED. THE RESULT IS ABSOLUTELY WONDERFUL.

Preparation: 3 minutes; Cooking: 25 minutes

SERVES FOUR

INGREDIENTS
   2 thin slices of prosciutto
   4 part-boned chicken breast portions,
    skinned
   4 sprigs of basil
   30ml/2 tbsp olive oil
   15g/½ oz/1 tbsp butter
   120ml/4fl oz/½ cup dry white wine
   2 thin slices of Fontina cheese
   salt and ground black pepper
   young salad leaves, to serve

1 Preheat the oven to 200°C/400°F/
Gas 6. Lightly oil a baking dish.

2 Using a very sharp knife, carefully
make a horizontal slit from the side into
each chicken breast.

3 Cut the prosciutto slices in half
crossways. Place them in the centre of
each chicken breast with a basil sprig.

VARIATION
Instead of Fontina cheese you could use
a Swiss mountain cheese, such as
Gruyère or Emmenthal. Ask for the cheese
to be sliced thinly at the delicatessen
counter or buy pre-sliced packs.

4 Heat the oil and butter in a wide,
heavy frying pan until foaming. Cook the
chicken breasts over medium heat for
1–2 minutes on each side, until they
change colour. Transfer to the baking
dish. Add the wine to the pan juices,
stir until sizzling, then pour over the
chicken and season to taste.

5 Top each chicken breast with a half
slice of Fontina. Bake for 20 minutes, or
until the chicken is cooked through.
Serve hot, with young salad leaves.

Energy 470kcal/1959kJ; Protein 49.7g; Carbohydrate 0.3g, of which sugars 0.3g; Fat 26.8g, of which saturates 14.1g; Cholesterol 164mg; Calcium 381mg; Fibre 0g; Sodium 536mg.

CHICKEN ^{WITH} TOMATOES ^{AND} OLIVES

CHICKEN BREASTS OR TURKEY, VEAL OR PORK ESCALOPES CAN BE FLATTENED FOR QUICK AND EVEN COOKING. YOU CAN BUY THEM READY-PREPARED IN FRANCE, BUT THEY ARE EASY TO DO AT HOME.

Preparation: 5 minutes; Cooking: 5 minutes

SERVES FOUR

INGREDIENTS

4 skinless chicken breasts fillets,
  each weighing 150–175g/5–6oz
1.5ml/ ¼ tsp cayenne pepper
75–105ml/5–7 tbsp extra virgin
  olive oil
6 ripe plum tomatoes, peeled if
  necessary (see Cook's Tip), seeded
  and chopped
1 garlic clove, finely chopped
16–24 stoned (pitted) black olives
small handful of fresh basil leaves
salt

1 Carefully remove the fillets (the long finger-shaped muscle on the back of each breast) and reserve for another use.

2 Place each chicken breast between two sheets of clear film (plastic wrap) and pound with the flat side of a meat hammer or roll out with a rolling pin to flatten to about 1cm/½in thick. Season with the cayenne pepper.

3 Heat 45–60ml/3–4 tbsp of the olive oil in a large heavy frying pan over a medium-high heat. Add the flattened chicken breasts and cook for 3–4 minutes until golden brown and just cooked, turning them once. Transfer the chicken to warmed serving plates and season with a little salt. Keep the chicken hot.

4 Wipe out the frying pan and return to the heat. Add another 30–45ml/2–3 tbsp of olive oil and fry the garlic for 1 minute until golden and fragrant. Stir in the olives, cook for a further 1 minute, then stir in the tomatoes. Shred the basil leaves and stir into the olive and tomato mixture, then spoon it over the chicken and serve at once.

COOK'S TIP

If the tomato skins are at all tough, remove them by cutting a cross in the base of each tomato with a knife, then plunging them into boiling water for about 30 seconds then into a bowl of cold water. The skins should then simply peel off.

Energy 360kcal/1502kJ; Protein 37.5g; Carbohydrate 4.7g, of which sugars 4.7g; Fat 21.3g, of which saturates 3.4g; Cholesterol 105mg; Calcium 49mg; Fibre 3g; Sodium 1229mg.

CAJUN-SPICED CHICKEN

A SPICY COATING CONTAINING CAYENNE, PAPRIKA AND CUMIN TRANSFORMS PLAIN CHICKEN BREASTS INTO A MEAL TO REMEMBER, WITH VERY LITTLE PREPARATION OR COOKING.

Preparation: 4 minutes; Cooking: 10–15 minutes

SERVES SIX

INGREDIENTS

6 medium skinless chicken
  breast fillets
75g/3oz/⅓ cup butter
5ml/1 tsp garlic powder
10ml/2 tsp onion powder
5ml/2 tsp cayenne pepper
10ml/2 tsp paprika
1.5ml/¼ tsp ground cumin
5ml/1 tsp dried thyme
7.5ml/1½ tsp each salt and ground
  black pepper
salad leaves and pepper strips,
  to serve

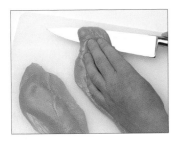

1 Slice each chicken breast in half horizontally, making two pieces of about the same thickness. Flatten them slightly with the heel of your hand.

2 Put the butter in a small pan and melt over a low heat. Do not let it brown.

VARIATION

For Cajun-spiced Fish, substitute six white fish fillets for the chicken. Do not slice the fish fillets in half, but season as for the chicken breasts and cook for about 2 minutes on one side and 1½–2 minutes on the other, until the fish flakes easily when tested with the tip of a sharp knife.

3 Mix the remaining ingredients in a bowl. Brush the chicken on both sides with a little of the melted butter. Sprinkle evenly with the seasoning mix.

4 Heat a large heavy-based frying pan over a high heat for about 5–8 minutes, until a drop of water sprinkled on the surface sizzles.

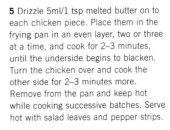

5 Drizzle 5ml/1 tsp melted butter on to each chicken piece. Place them in the frying pan in an even layer, two or three at a time, and cook for 2–3 minutes, until the underside begins to blacken. Turn the chicken over and cook the other side for 2–3 minutes more. Remove from the pan and keep hot while cooking successive batches. Serve hot with salad leaves and pepper strips.

Energy 256kcal/1071kJ; Protein 36.2g; Carbohydrate 0.9g, of which sugars 0.6g; Fat 12g, of which saturates 7g; Cholesterol 132mg; Calcium 12mg; Fibre 0.1g; Sodium 166mg.

WARM CHICKEN AND VEGETABLE SALAD

Succulent cooked chicken pieces are combined with vegetables in a light chilli dressing to make a quick, tasty and colourful salad with a difference.

Preparation: 7 minutes; Cooking: 10 minutes

SERVES SIX

INGREDIENTS
    50g/2oz mixed salad leaves
    50g/2oz baby spinach leaves
    50g/2oz watercress
    30ml/2 tbsp chilli sauce
    30ml/2 tbsp dry sherry
    15ml/1 tbsp light soy sauce
    15ml/1 tbsp tomato ketchup
    10ml/2 tsp olive oil
    8 shallots, finely chopped
    1 garlic clove, crushed
    350g/12oz skinless chicken breast
      fillets, cut into thin strips
    1 red (bell) pepper, seeded and sliced
    175g/6oz/1½ cups mangetouts
      (snow peas)
    400g/14oz can baby corn, drained
      and halved
    275g/10oz cooked brown rice
    salt and ground black pepper
    fresh flat leaf parsley sprig, to garnish

1 Tear any large salad leaves into smaller pieces. Arrange, with the spinach leaves, on a serving dish. Add the watercress and toss to mix.

2 In a small bowl, mix together the chilli sauce, dry sherry, light soy sauce and tomato ketchup and set aside.

3 Heat the oil in a large non-stick frying pan or wok. Add the shallots and garlic and stir-fry over medium heat for 1 minute.

4 Add the chicken and stir-fry for 3–4 minutes, then add the pepper, mangetouts, baby corn and rice and stir-fry for 2–3 minutes more.

5 Pour in the chilli sauce mixture and stir-fry for 2–3 minutes, until hot and bubbling. Season to taste. Spoon the chicken mixture over the salad leaves, toss together to mix and serve immediately, garnished with a fresh flat leaf parsley sprig.

VARIATIONS
Use other lean meat, such as turkey breast, or lean cuts of beef or pork, in place of the chicken. You could also use prawns (shrimp). If using cooked prawns, add them to the pan with the chilli sauce so they are not overcooked.

Energy 198kcal/832kJ; Protein 19.7g; Carbohydrate 23.2g, of which sugars 7.1g; Fat 2.9g, of which saturates 0.5g; Cholesterol 41mg; Calcium 77mg; Fibre 3.5g; Sodium 1053mg.

TANDOORI CHICKEN KEBABS

THIS DISH ORIGINATES FROM THE PLAINS OF THE PUNJAB AT THE FOOT OF THE HIMALAYAS. THERE, FOOD IS TRADITIONALLY COOKED IN CLAY OVENS KNOWN AS TANDOORS — HENCE THE NAME.

Preparation: 18 minutes; Cooking: 10–12 minutes

SERVES FOUR

INGREDIENTS

4 skinless chicken breast fillets,
  about 175g/6oz each
15ml/1 tbsp lemon juice
45ml/3 tbsp tandoori paste
45ml/3 tbsp natural (plain) yogurt
1 garlic clove, crushed
30ml/2 tbsp chopped fresh coriander
  (cilantro)
1 small onion, cut into wedges and
  separated into layers
a little oil, for brushing
salt and ground black pepper
fresh coriander sprigs, to garnish
pilau rice and naan bread, to serve

COOK'S TIP
You can make your own tandoori paste if
you like, but the bought product is a
boon to the busy cook.

1 Chop the chicken breasts into 2.5cm/
1in cubes, place in a bowl and add the
lemon juice, tandoori paste, yogurt,
garlic, coriander and seasoning. Mix
well. Cover and set aside for 15 minutes.

2 Preheat the grill (broiler). Thread
alternate pieces of chicken and onion
on to four skewers (pre-soaked in water
if wooden).

3 Brush the onion with a little oil, lay
the kebabs on a grill (broiling) rack and
cook under a high heat for 10–12
minutes, turning once. Garnish the
kebabs with fresh coriander and serve
at once with pilau rice and naan bread.

Energy 207kcal/871kJ; Protein 36.9g; Carbohydrate 3.2g, of which sugars 0.9g; Fat 5.2g, of which saturates 0.9g; Cholesterol 105mg; Calcium 59mg; Fibre 1.9g; Sodium 124mg.

STIR-FRIED CHICKEN WITH BASIL AND CHILLI

THIS QUICK AND EASY CHICKEN DISH IS AN EXCELLENT INTRODUCTION TO THAI CUISINE. THAI BASIL, SOMETIMES KNOWN AS HOLY BASIL, HAS A UNIQUE, PUNGENT FLAVOUR THAT IS BOTH SPICY AND SHARP.

Preparation: 5–7 minutes; Cooking: 15 minutes

SERVES FOUR TO SIX

INGREDIENTS
45ml/3 tbsp vegetable oil
4 garlic cloves, thinly sliced
2–4 fresh red chillies, seeded and
  finely chopped
450g/1lb skinless chicken breast
  fillets, diced
45ml/3 tbsp Thai fish sauce
10ml/2 tsp dark soy sauce
5ml/1 tsp sugar
10–12 Thai basil leaves
2 fresh red chillies, seeded and
  finely chopped and about 20
  deep-fried Thai basil leaves,

COOK'S TIP
Before fying Thai basil leaves, first make sure that the leaves are completely dry or they will splutter when added to the oil.

1 Heat the oil in a wok or large frying pan. Add the garlic and chillies and stir-fry over a medium heat for 1–2 minutes.

2 Add the chicken to the wok or pan and stir-fry until it changes colour.

3 Stir in the Thai fish sauce, soy sauce and sugar. Continue to stir-fry the mixture for 3–4 minutes, or until the chicken is fully cooked with the sauce.

4 Stir in the Thai basil leaves.

5 Spoon the entire mixture on to a warm serving platter or individual serving dishes and garnish with the sliced chillies and deep-fried Thai basil.

Energy 135kcal/566kJ; Protein 18.3g; Carbohydrate 1.1g, of which sugars 1g; Fat 6.4g, of which saturates 1g; Cholesterol 53mg; Calcium 21mg; Fibre 0.4g; Sodium 167mg.

CHICKEN WITH LEMON SAUCE

SUCCULENT CHICKEN WITH A REFRESHING CREAMY CITRUS SAUCE CONTAINING LEMON JUICE AND LIME CORDIAL IS A SURE WINNER, PARTICULARLY ON A HOT SUMMER'S DAY.

Preparation: 5 minutes; Cooking: 20 minutes, plus marinating time

SERVES FOUR

INGREDIENTS
- 4 small skinless chicken breast fillets
- 5ml/1 tsp sesame oil
- 15ml/1 tbsp dry sherry
- 2.5ml/½ tsp salt and 1.5ml/¼ tsp ground white pepper
- 1 egg white, lightly beaten
- 30ml/2 tbsp cornflour (cornstarch)
- 15ml/1 tbsp vegetable oil

For the sauce
- 45ml/3 tbsp fresh lemon juice
- 30ml/2 tbsp lime cordial
- 45ml/3 tbsp caster (superfine) sugar
- 10ml/2 tsp cornflour
- 90ml/6 tbsp cold water
- 1.5ml/¼ tsp salt

For the garnish
- chopped coriander (cilantro) leaves
- lemon wedges

1 Place the chicken in a shallow bowl. Mix the sesame oil with the sherry and add the salt and pepper. Pour over the chicken, cover and marinate for 15 minutes.

2 Mix together the egg white and cornflour. Add the mixture to the chicken and turn to coat thoroughly. Heat the vegetable oil in a non-stick frying pan or wok and fry the chicken fillets for about 15 minutes, or until the fillets are cooked through and golden brown on both sides.

3 Meanwhile, make the sauce. Combine all the ingredients in a small pan. Bring to the boil over a low heat, stirring constantly until the sauce is smooth and has thickened slightly.

4 Cut the chicken into pieces and arrange on a warm serving plate. Pour the sauce over the chicken, garnish with the coriander leaves and lemon wedges and serve.

Energy 281kcal/1189kJ; Protein 36.9g; Carbohydrate 22.1g, of which sugars 15.2g; Fat 5.2g, of which saturates 0.9g; Cholesterol 105mg; Calcium 16mg; Fibre 0g; Sodium 111mg.

SPICY CHICKEN STIR-FRY

THE CHICKEN IS MARINATED IN AN AROMATIC BLEND OF SPICES AND THEN STIR-FRIED WITH CRISP VEGETABLES. IF YOU FIND IT TOO SPICY, SERVE WITH A SPOONFUL OF SOUR CREAM OR YOGURT.

Preparation: 10 minutes; Cooking: 20 minutes

SERVES FOUR

INGREDIENTS

2.5ml/½ tsp ground turmeric
2.5ml/½ tsp ground ginger
5ml/1 tsp each salt and ground
  black pepper
10ml/2 tsp ground cumin
15ml/1 tbsp ground coriander
15ml/1 tbsp caster (superfine) sugar
450g/1lb chicken breast fillet,
  skinned
1 bunch spring onions (scallions)
4 celery sticks
2 red (bell) peppers
1 yellow (bell) pepper
175g/6oz courgettes (zucchini)
175g/6oz mangetouts (snow peas)
  or sugar snap peas
about 45ml/3 tbsp sunflower oil
15ml/1 tbsp lime juice
15ml/1 tbsp clear honey

1 Mix together the turmeric, ginger, salt, pepper, cumin, coriander and sugar in a bowl until well combined.

2 Cut the chicken into bitesize strips. Add to the spice mixture and stir to coat the chicken pieces thoroughly. Set aside.

3 Prepare the vegetables. Cut the spring onions, celery and peppers into 5cm/2in long, thin strips. Cut the courgettes at a slight angle into thin rounds and trim the mangetouts or sugar snap peas.

4 Heat 30ml/2 tbsp of the oil in a large frying pan or wok. Stir-fry the chicken in batches until cooked through and golden brown, adding a little more oil if necessary. Remove from the pan and keep warm.

5 Add a little more oil to the pan and cook the onions, celery, peppers and courgettes over medium heat for about 8–10 minutes, or until beginning to soften and turn golden. Add the mangetouts or sugar snap peas and cook for a further 2 minutes.

6 Return the chicken to the pan, with the lime juice and honey. Cook for 2 minutes. Adjust the seasoning and serve immediately.

Energy 295kcal/1237kJ; Protein 31.5g; Carbohydrate 19.6g, of which sugars 18.8g; Fat 10.5g, of which saturates 1.6g; Cholesterol 79mg; Calcium 72mg; Fibre 4.4g; Sodium 95mg.

CHICKEN CHOW MEIN

CHOW MEIN IS ARGUABLY THE BEST KNOWN CHINESE NOODLE DISH IN THE WEST. THE COMBINATION OF EGG NOODLES WITH VEGETABLES AND MEAT OR FISH IN A SOY-BASED SAUCE IS UNBEATABLE.

Preparation: 6–7 minutes; Cooking: 14 minutes

SERVES FOUR

INGREDIENTS

350g/12oz egg noodles
225g/8oz skinless chicken breast
  fillets
45ml/3 tbsp soy sauce
15ml/1 tbsp rice wine or dry sherry
15ml/1 tbsp dark sesame oil
60ml/4 tbsp vegetable oil
2 garlic cloves, finely chopped
50g/2oz mangetouts (snow peas),
  trimmed
115g/4oz beansprouts
50g/2oz ham, finely shredded
4 spring onions (scallions), finely
  chopped
salt and ground black pepper

1 Cook the noodles in a large pan of boiling lightly salted water until tender.

2 Meanwhile, slice the chicken into fine strips about 5cm/2in in length. Place in a bowl and add 10ml/2 tsp of the soy sauce, the rice wine or sherry and the sesame oil.

3 Heat half the vegetable oil in a wok or large frying pan over high heat. When it starts smoking, add the chicken mixture. Stir-fry for 2 minutes, then transfer the chicken to a plate and keep it hot.

4 Wipe the wok clean and heat the remaining oil. Stir in the garlic, mangetouts, beansprouts and shredded ham. Stir-fry for 2–3 minutes over high heat.

5 Drain the noodles, rinse them under cold water, then drain them again. Pat them dry with kitchen paper and add to the wok. Continue to stir-fry until the noodles are heated through. Add the remaining soy sauce and season with salt and ground black pepper. Return the chicken and any juices to the noodle mixture, add the chopped spring onions and give the mixture a final stir. Serve at once.

Energy 593kcal/2494kJ; Protein 31.1g; Carbohydrate 69.7g, of which sugars 4.4g; Fat 22.6g, of which saturates 2.7g; Cholesterol 44mg; Calcium 44mg; Fibre 3.4g; Sodium 995mg.

CRISPY FIVE-SPICE CHICKEN

STRIPS OF CHICKEN FILLET, WITH A SPICED RICE FLOUR COATING, BECOME DELICIOUSLY CRISP AND GOLDEN WHEN FRIED. THEY MAKE A GREAT MEAL WHEN SERVED ON STIR-FRIED VEGETABLE NOODLES.

Preparation: 5 minutes; Cooking: 10–12 minutes

SERVES FOUR

INGREDIENTS

200g/7oz thin egg noodles
30ml/2 tbsp sunflower oil
2 garlic cloves, very thinly sliced
1 fresh red chilli, seeded and sliced
½ red (bell) pepper, very
   thinly sliced
2 carrots, peeled and cut into
   thin strips
300g/11oz Chinese broccoli or
   Chinese greens, roughly sliced
45ml/3 tbsp hoisin sauce
45ml/3 tbsp soy sauce
5ml/1 tsp caster (superfine) sugar
4 skinless chicken breast fillets,
   cut into strips
2 egg whites, lightly beaten
115g/4oz/1 cup rice flour
15ml/1 tbsp five-spice powder
salt and ground black pepper
vegetable oil, for frying

1 Cook the noodles according to the packet instructions, drain and set aside.

2 Heat the sunflower oil in a wok, then add the garlic, chilli, red pepper, carrots and broccoli or greens and stir-fry over a high heat for 2–3 minutes.

3 Add the sauces and sugar to the wok and cook for a further 2–3 minutes. Add the drained noodles, toss to combine, then remove from the heat, cover and keep warm.

4 Dip the chicken strips into the egg white. Combine the rice flour and five-spice powder in a shallow dish and season. Add the chicken strips to the flour mixture and toss to coat.

5 Heat about 2.5cm/1½in oil in a clean wok. When hot, shallow-fry the chicken for 3–4 minutes until crisp and golden.

6 To serve, divide the noodle mixture between warmed plates or bowls and top each serving with the chicken.

VARIATION
Instead of the vegetables listed above for the stir-fry, try a mixture of mangetouts (snow peas), baby corn, orange (bell) peppers, spring onions (scallions) and celery.

Energy 574kcal/2419kJ; Protein 49.6g; Carbohydrate 68g, of which sugars 9.4g; Fat 12.3g, of which saturates 2.5g; Cholesterol 120mg; Calcium 83mg; Fibre 5.1g; Sodium 1210mg

SPICY FRIED NOODLES WITH CHICKEN

THIS IS A WONDERFULLY VERSATILE DISH AS YOU CAN ADJUST IT TO INCLUDE YOUR FAVOURITE INGREDIENTS — JUST AS LONG AS YOU KEEP A BALANCE OF FLAVOURS, TEXTURES AND COLOURS.

Preparation: 6 minutes; Cooking: 8–10 minutes

SERVES FOUR

INGREDIENTS
225g/8oz egg thread noodles
60ml/4 tbsp vegetable oil
2 garlic cloves, finely chopped
175g/6oz pork fillet (tenderloin),
  sliced into thin strips
1 skinless chicken breast fillet (about
  175g/6oz), sliced into thin strips
115g/4oz/1 cup peeled cooked
  prawns (shrimp)
45ml/3 tbsp fresh lemon juice
45ml/3 tbsp Thai fish sauce
30ml/2 tbsp soft light brown sugar
2 eggs, beaten
½ fresh red chilli, seeded and
  finely chopped
50g/2oz/⅔ cup beansprouts
60ml/4 tbsp roasted peanuts, chopped
3 spring onions (scallions), cut into
  5cm/2in lengths and shredded
45ml/3 tbsp chopped fresh
  coriander (cilantro)

1 Cook the noodles in a large pan of boiling water, then leave for 5 minutes.

2 Meanwhile, heat 45ml/3 tbsp of the oil in a wok or large frying pan, add the garlic and cook for 30 seconds. Add the pork and chicken and stir-fry until lightly browned, then add the prawns and stir-fry for 2 minutes.

3 Stir in the lemon juice, then add the fish sauce and sugar. Stir-fry until the sugar has dissolved.

4 Drain the noodles and add to the wok or pan with the remaining 15ml/1 tbsp oil. Toss all the ingredients together.

5 Pour the beaten eggs over the noodles and stir-fry until almost set, then add the chilli and beansprouts.

6 Divide the roasted peanuts, spring onions and coriander leaves into two equal portions, add one portion to the pan and stir-fry for about 2 minutes.

7 Transfer the noodles to a serving platter. Sprinkle on the remaining roasted peanuts, spring onions and chopped coriander and serve immediately.

COOK'S TIP
Store beansprouts in the refrigerator and use within a day of purchase, as they tend to lose their crispness and become slimy and unpleasant quite quickly. The most commonly used beansprouts are sprouted mung beans, but you could use other types of beansprouts instead.

Energy 605kcal/2537kJ; Protein 39.8g; Carbohydrate 52.1g, of which sugars 11.5g; Fat 27.9g, of which saturates 5.5g; Cholesterol 226mg; Calcium 83mg; Fibre 3.1g; Sodium 1052mg

CURRIED CHICKEN NOODLES

CHICKEN OR PORK CAN BE USED TO PROVIDE THE PROTEIN IN THIS TASTY DISH. IT IS SO QUICK AND EASY TO PREPARE AND COOK, IT MAKES THE PERFECT SNACK FOR BUSY PEOPLE.

Preparation: 5 minutes; Cooking: 10 minutes

SERVES TWO

INGREDIENTS

30ml/2 tbsp vegetable oil
10ml/2 tsp magic paste
1 lemon grass stalk, finely chopped
5ml/1 tsp Thai red curry paste
90g/3½oz skinless chicken breast
  fillet or pork fillet (tenderloin),
  sliced into slivers
30ml/2 tbsp light soy sauce
400ml/14fl oz/1⅔ cups coconut milk
2 kaffir lime leaves, rolled into
  cylinders and thinly sliced
250g/9oz medium egg noodles
90g/3½oz Chinese leaves (Chinese
  cabbage), shredded
90g/3½oz spinach or watercress
  (leaves), shredded
juice of 1 lime
small bunch fresh coriander
  (cilantro), chopped

1 Heat the oil in a wok or large, heavy frying pan. Add the magic paste and lemon grass and stir-fry over a low to medium heat for 4–5 seconds, until they give off their aroma.

2 Stir in the curry paste, then add the chicken or pork. Stir-fry over a medium to high heat for 2 minutes, until the chicken or pork is coated in the paste and seared on all sides.

3 Add the soy sauce, coconut milk and sliced lime leaves. Bring to a simmer, then add the noodles. Simmer for 4 minutes. Add the Chinese leaves and watercress. Stir, then add the lime juice. Spoon into a warmed bowl and sprinkle with coriander.

COOK'S TIP
Magic paste, a blend of garlic, coriander (cilantro) root, garlic and white pepper, is sold in Asian stores.

Energy 702kcal/2965kJ; Protein 28.7g; Carbohydrate 101.6g, of which sugars 14.2g; Fat 23g, of which saturates 4.9g; Cholesterol 69mg; Calcium 187mg; Fibre 4.7g; Sodium 1564mg.

MILD GREEN CHICKEN AND FRUIT CURRY

THE ADDITION OF COCONUT MILK CREATES A RICH SAUCE THAT IS SWEET WITH DRIED AND FRESH FRUIT AND FRAGRANT WITH HERBS. THE FRESH CORIANDER MAKES THE SAUCE GREEN.

Preparation: 10 minutes; Cooking: 17 minutes

SERVES FOUR

INGREDIENTS

4 garlic cloves, chopped
15ml/1 tbsp chopped fresh
  root ginger
2–3 chillies, chopped
½ bunch fresh coriander (cilantro)
  leaves, roughly chopped
1 onion, chopped
juice of 1 lemon
pinch of cayenne pepper
2.5ml/½ tsp curry powder
2.5ml/½ tsp ground cumin
2–3 pinches of ground cloves
large pinch of ground coriander
3 chicken breast fillets or thighs,
  skinned and cut into bitesize pieces
30ml/2 tbsp vegetable oil
2 cinnamon sticks
250ml/8fl oz/1 cup chicken stock
250ml/8fl oz/1 cup coconut milk
15–30ml/1–2 tbsp sugar
1–2 bananas
¼ pineapple, peeled and chopped
handful of sultanas (golden raisins)
handful of raisins or currants
2–3 sprigs of fresh mint, thinly sliced
juice of ¼–½ lemon
salt

1 Purée the garlic, ginger, chillies, fresh coriander, onion, lemon juice, cayenne pepper, curry powder, cumin, cloves, ground coriander and salt in a food processor.

2 Toss together the chicken pieces with about 15–30ml/1–2 tbsp of the spice mixture and set aside.

3 Heat the oil in a wok or frying pan, then add the remaining spice mixture and cook over medium heat, stirring, for 5 minutes, or until the paste is lightly browned.

4 Stir the chicken, cinnamon sticks, stock, coconut milk and sugar into the pan, bring to the boil, then reduce the heat and simmer for 10 minutes.

5 Meanwhile, thickly slice the bananas. Stir all the fruit into the curry and cook for 1–2 minutes. Stir in the mint and lemon juice. Check the seasoning and add more salt, spice and lemon juice if necessary. Serve immediately.

Energy 412kcal/1746kJ; Protein 38.6g; Carbohydrate 49.2g, of which sugars 48g; Fat 8.2g, of which saturates 1.3g; Cholesterol 105mg; Calcium 115mg; Fibre 3.8g; Sodium 185mg.

CHICKEN OMELETTE DIPPERS

HAVE YOU GOT A RELUCTANT EATER IN THE FAMILY? NOT ANY MORE. CHILDREN LOVE THESE PROTEIN-PACKED CHICKEN OMELETTE ROLLS. YOU MIGHT HAVE TO RATION THE KETCHUP DIP, HOWEVER.

Preparation: 3 minutes; Cooking: 16 minutes

SERVES FOUR

INGREDIENTS

- 1 skinless chicken thigh, about 115g/4oz, boned and cubed
- 40ml/8 tsp butter
- 1 small onion, chopped
- ½ carrot, diced
- 2 shiitake mushrooms, stems removed and chopped
- 15ml/1 tbsp finely chopped fresh parsley
- 225g/8oz/2 cups cooked long grain white rice
- 30ml/2 tbsp tomato ketchup, plus extra to serve
- 6 eggs, lightly beaten
- 60ml/4 tbsp milk
- 2.5ml/½ tsp salt, plus extra to season ground black pepper

1 Season the chicken. Melt 10ml/2 tsp butter in a frying pan. Fry the onion for 1 minute, then add the chicken and fry until cooked. Add the mushrooms and carrot, stir-fry over a medium heat until soft, then add the parsley. Set aside. Wipe the pan with kitchen paper.

2 Melt 10ml/2 tsp butter in the frying pan, add the rice and stir well. Mix in the fried ingredients, ketchup and black pepper. Stir well, adding salt to taste. Keep the mixture warm.

3 Beat the eggs with the milk in a bowl. Stir in the salt, and add pepper. Melt 5ml/1 tsp of the remaining butter in an omelette pan. Pour in a quarter of the egg mixture and stir it briefly with a fork, then allow it to set for 1 minute. Top with a quarter of the rice mixture.

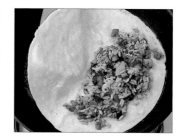

4 There are two ways of shaping the omelette. Either just flip it over the filling, then cut in half to make wedges, or roll the omelette around the filling and cut in half. Keep the filled omelette hot in a low oven while cooking three more. Serve two wedges or rolls per person, with a bowl of ketchup for dipping.

VARIATION
A mixture of tomato ketchup and chutney makes a tasty alternative dipping sauce.

Energy 316kcal/1322kJ; Protein 18g; Carbohydrate 21.5g, of which sugars 3.7g; Fat 18.4g, of which saturates 8.1g; Cholesterol 338mg; Calcium 80mg; Fibre 0.5g; Sodium 322mg

CHICKEN FRIED RICE

THIS STIR-FRY IS BASED ON COOKED RICE, SO IS IDEAL FOR USING UP YESTERDAY'S LEFTOVERS. ANY RICE WILL DO, BUT JASMINE HAS THE BEST FLAVOUR, ESPECIALLY IF COOKED IN COCONUT MILK.

Preparation: 4–5 minutes; Cooking: 10–12 minutes

SERVES FOUR

INGREDIENTS

- 30ml/2 tbsp groundnut (peanut) oil
- 1 small onion, finely chopped
- 2 garlic cloves, chopped
- 2.5cm/1in piece fresh root ginger, peeled and grated
- 225g/8oz skinless chicken breast fillets, cut into 1cm/½in dice
- 450g/1lb/4 cups cold cooked white long grain rice
- 1 red (bell) pepper, seeded and sliced
- 115g/4oz/1 cup drained canned whole kernel corn
- 5ml/1 tsp chilli oil
- 5ml/1 tsp hot curry powder
- 2 eggs, beaten
- salt
- spring onion (scallion) shreds, to garnish

2 Push the onion mixture to the sides of the wok, where it will kep warm but not cook, add the chicken to the centre and stir-fry for 2 minutes. Add the rice and toss well. Stir-fry over a high heat for about 3 minutes more, until the chicken is cooked through.

3 Stir in the sliced red pepper, corn, chilli oil and curry powder, with salt to taste. Toss over the heat for 1 minute. Stir in the beaten eggs and cook for 1 minute more, while the eggs lightly cook. Garnish with the spring onion shreds and serve.

1 Heat the oil in a wok. Add the onion and stir-fry over a medium heat for 1 minute, then add the garlic and ginger and stir-fry for 2 minutes more.

COOK'S TIP

If you don't have any cold cooked rice in the refrigerator, you can still make this stir-fry if you have a couple of pouches of instant or express long grain or basmati rice in the cupboard. This type of rice cooks in under 2 minutes. For a stir-fry, the rice should be cold, so spread it out on a baking sheet after cooking and fan it to cool it quickly.

Energy 356kcal/1500kJ; Protein 21g; Carbohydrate 46.4g, of which sugars 6.3g; Fat 10.9g, of which saturates 2.5g; Cholesterol 135mg; Calcium 46mg; Fibre 1.4g; Sodium 150mg

SPICED CHICKEN RISOTTO WITH MINT

A CLASSIC RISOTTO MUST BE STIRRED FOR AROUND 20 MINUTES, WHICH CAN BE A LABOUR OF LOVE,
BUT WHEN ROMANCE IS THE LAST THING ON YOUR MIND, THIS QUICK VERSION IS A GOOD ALTERNATIVE.
Preparation: 3–5 minutes; Cooking: 15–17 minutes

SERVES FOUR

INGREDIENTS
  250g/9oz skinless chicken breast
    fillets, diced
  3 garlic cloves, chopped
  5ml/1 tsp ground turmeric
  30–45ml/2–3 tbsp olive oil
  2 medium carrots, diced
  seeds from 6–8 cardamom pods
  500g/1¼lb/2½ cups long grain rice
  250g/9oz tomatoes, chopped
  750ml/1¼ pints/3 cups
    chicken stock
For the lemon and mint relish
  3 tomatoes, diced
  1 bunch or large handful fresh
    mint, chopped
  5–8 spring onions (scallions),
    thinly sliced
  juice of 2 lemons
  salt

1 Mix the diced chicken with half the
garlic and the turmeric. Heat a little of
the oil in a pan, add the chicken and
fry until the chicken has cooked
through thoroughly. Remove from the
pan and set aside.

2 Add the remaining oil, garlic and
cardamom seeds with the carrots
and rice. Stir-fry for 1–2 minutes.

3 Add the tomatoes and chicken stock
to the pan and bring to the boil. Cover
and simmer for about 10 minutes.

4 Meanwhile, make the relish by
mixing all the ingredients in a bowl.

5 When the rice is almost cooked, fork
in the chicken and heat through. Serve
with the relish.

VARIATIONS
• Use the same quantity of pumpkin or
butternut squash in place of the carrots.
• To make a vegetarian version, omit the
chicken and add a drained 400g/14oz
can of chickpeas to the rice just before
the end of cooking.

Energy 600kcal/2511kJ; Protein 26g; Carbohydrate 105.9g, of which sugars 5.3g; Fat 7.4g, of which saturates 1.1g; Cholesterol 44mg; Calcium 73mg; Fibre 1.8g; Sodium 55mg

RISOTTO WITH CHICKEN AND PROSCIUTTO

THIS IS A CLASSIC COMBINATION OF CHICKEN AND RICE, COOKED WITH PROSCIUTTO, WHITE WINE AND PARMESAN CHEESE TO PROVIDE A COMFORTING AND FILLING MEAL.

Preparation: 5 minutes; Cooking: 25 minutes

SERVES SIX

INGREDIENTS

30ml/2 tbsp olive oil
225g/8oz skinless chicken breast
  fillets, cut into 2.5cm/1in cubes
1 onion, finely chopped
1 garlic clove, finely chopped
450g/1lb/2⅓ cups risotto rice
120ml/4fl oz/½ cup dry white wine
1.5ml/¼ tsp saffron threads
1.75 litres/3 pints/7½ cups
  simmering chicken stock
50g/2oz prosciutto, cut into
  thin strips
25g/1oz/2 tbsp butter, cubed
25g/1oz/⅓ cup freshly grated
  Parmesan cheese, plus extra
  to serve
salt and freshly ground black pepper
flat leaf parsley, to garnish

4 When the rice is three-quarters cooked, add the prosciutto and continue cooking until the rice is just tender and the risotto creamy. This should take about 20 minutes in all.

5 Add the butter and the Parmesan and stir in well. Season with salt and pepper to taste. Serve the risotto hot, sprinkled with a little more Parmesan, and garnished with parsley.

1 Heat the oil in a frying pan over a moderately high heat. Add the chicken cubes and cook, stirring, until they start to turn white.

2 Reduce the heat to low and add the onion and garlic. Cook, stirring, until the onion is soft. Stir in the rice. Sauté for 1–2 minutes, stirring constantly, until all the rice grains are coated in oil.

3 Add the wine and cook, stirring, until the wine has been absorbed. Stir the saffron into the simmering stock, then add ladlefuls of stock to the rice, allowing each ladleful to be absorbed before adding the next.

Energy 418kcal/1744kJ; Protein 17.9g; Carbohydrate 60.9g, of which sugars 0.8g; Fat 9.5g, of which saturates 3.8g; Cholesterol 44mg; Calcium 72mg; Fibre 0.1g; Sodium 194mg.

TURKEY ROLLS WITH GAZPACHO SAUCE

COOK THESE WONDERFUL TURKEY ROLLS, WITH THEIR SPICY SAUSAGE CENTRES, ON THE BARBECUE OR UNDER THE GRILL (BROILER). THE COOL, FRESH GAZPACHO SAUCE IS THE PERFECT ACCOMPANIMENT.

Preparation: 8 minutes; Cooking: 10–12 minutes

SERVES FOUR

INGREDIENTS

  4 turkey breast steaks
  15ml/1 tbsp red pesto or
    tomato purée (paste)
  4 small chorizo sausages
  salt and ground black pepper
For the gazpacho sauce
  1 green (bell) pepper, seeded and
    chopped
  1 red (bell) pepper, seeded and
    chopped
  7.5cm/3in piece of cucumber
  1 tomato
  1 garlic clove, chopped
  15ml/1 tbsp red wine vinegar
  45ml/3 tbsp olive oil

1 To make the gazpacho sauce, place the peppers, cucumber, tomato, garlic, and vinegar in a food processor. Pour in 30ml/2 tbsp of the oil and process until almost smooth. Season to taste with salt and pepper and set aside.

2 If the turkey breast steaks are quite thick, place them between two sheets of clear film (plastic wrap) and beat them with the side of a rolling pin, to flatten them slightly.

3 Spread the pesto over the turkey, put a chorizo on each piece and roll up firmly. Preheat the barbecue or grill (broiler).

4 Slice the rolls thickly and thread them on to skewers. Brush with the remaining oil and barbecue or grill (broil) for 10–12 minutes, turning once. Serve with the gazpacho sauce.

Energy 421kcal/1762kJ; Protein 39g; Carbohydrate 13.1g, of which sugars 7.9g; Fat 24.1g, of which saturates 7.4g; Cholesterol 112mg; Calcium 47mg; Fibre 2.1g; Sodium 502mg.

TURKEY CUTLETS WITH OLIVES

THE MILD FLAVOUR OF TURKEY IS PEPPED UP WITH GARLIC AND CHILLI, THEN SERVED IN A TASTY
TOMATO AND OLIVE SAUCE. THIS IS A USEFUL DISH FOR QUICK AND EASY ENTERTAINING.
Preparation: 6 minutes; Cooking: 12 minutes

SERVES FOUR

INGREDIENTS
90ml/6 tbsp olive oil
1 garlic clove, peeled and lightly
  crushed
1 dried chilli, lightly crushed
500g/1¼lb boneless turkey breast,
  cut into 5mm/¼in thick slices
120ml/4fl oz/½ cup dry white wine
4 tomatoes, peeled, seeded and cut
  into thin strips
about 24 black olives, pitted
6–8 fresh basil leaves, torn
salt and ground black pepper

1 Heat 60ml/4 tbsp of the olive oil in a
large frying pan. Add the garlic and
dried chilli and cook over low heat, until
the garlic is golden: do not allow to burn.

2 Increase the heat to medium. Add the
turkey slices to the pan and cook them
for about 2 minutes on both sides, until
lightly browned. Season with salt and
pepper. Using a metal spatula, transfer
the turkey to a warmed dish.

COOK'S TIP
All olives start off green and then mature
into darker fruit, black olives being the
most mature. The varieties kept as table
olives and for cooking are preserved by
various methods, including dry-curing in
salt and preserving in brine. Often they
are flavoured with aromatics, such as
garlic, herbs and chillies. Any type of
black olive can be used in this recipe.

3 Remove the garlic and chilli from the
pan and discard. Add the wine, tomato
strips and olives to the pan. Cook over
medium heat for 3–4 minutes, scraping
any meat residue from the pan bottom.

4 Return the turkey to the pan and
sprinkle with the basil. Heat through for
about 30 seconds before transferring to
a warmed serving dish.

Energy 266Kcal/1117kJ; Protein 35.8g; Carbohydrate 9.8g, of which sugars 4.1g; Fat 8.3g, of which saturates 2.5g; Cholesterol 86mg; Calcium 43mg; Fibre 2.1g; Sodium 761mg.

TURKEY BURGERS

MINCED TURKEY MAKES DELICIOUSLY LIGHT BURGERS, WHICH ARE IDEAL FOR SUMMER MEALS. THE RECIPE IS A FLAVOURFUL VARIATION ON A CLASSIC BURGER.

Preparation: 4 minutes; Cooking: 20–24 minutes, plus chilling time

SERVES SIX

INGREDIENTS

675g/1½lb minced (ground) turkey
1 small red onion, finely chopped
grated rind and juice of 1 lime
small handful of fresh thyme leaves
15–30ml/1–2 tbsp olive oil
salt and ground black pepper

COOK'S TIP
Serve the burgers in split and toasted buns or pieces of crusty bread, with chutney, salad leaves and chunky chips.

VARIATION
Try replacing the minced (ground) turkey with lamb, pork or beef.

1 Mix together the turkey, onion, lime rind and juice, thyme and seasoning. Cover and chill for up to 4 hours to allow the flavours to infuse, then divide the mixture into six equal portions and shape into round burgers.

2 Preheat a griddle pan. Brush the burgers with oil, then place them in the pan and cook for 10–12 minutes. Turn the burgers over, brush with more oil and cook for 10–12 minutes on the second side, or until cooked through.

Energy 155Kcal/651kJ; Protein 26g; Carbohydrate 1g, of which sugars 1g; Fat 5g, of which saturates 1g; Cholesterol 79mg; Calcium 11mg; Fibre 0.1g; Sodium 100mg

TURKEY AND CRANBERRY BUNDLES

A ROAST TURKEY INVARIABLY LEAVES LOTS OF LEFTOVERS AND SO IMAGINATIVE USES FOR COOKED
TURKEY ARE ALWAYS WELCOME. THESE BUNDLES ARE DELICIOUS AND QUICK TO PREPARE.

Preparation: 10 minutes; Cooking: 20 minutes

SERVES SIX

INGREDIENTS

   450g/1lb cooked turkey, cut
    into chunks
   115g/4oz/1 cup diced Brie
   30ml/2 tbsp cranberry sauce
   30ml/2 tbsp chopped fresh parsley
   9 sheets filo pastry, 45 x 28cm/18 x
    11in each, thawed if frozen
   50g/2oz/¼ cup butter, melted
   salt and ground black pepper
   green salad, to serve

1 Preheat the oven to 200⁰C/400⁰F/
Gas 6. Mix the diced turkey and Brie,
the cranberry sauce and chopped parsley
in a bowl. Season with salt and pepper.

VARIATIONS
These little parcels can be made with a
variety of fillings and are great for using
up left-over cooked meats.
• To make Ham and Cheddar Bundles,
replace the turkey with ham and use
Cheddar in place of the Brie. A fruit-
flavoured chutney would make a good
alternative to the cranberry sauce.
• To make Chicken and Stilton Bundles,
use cooked chicken in place of the turkey
and white Stilton instead of Brie. Replace
the cranberry sauce with mango chutney.

2 Cut the filo sheets in half widthways
and trim to make 18 squares. Layer
three pieces of pastry together, brushing
them with a little melted butter so that
they stick together. Repeat with the
remaining filo squares to give six pieces.

3 Divide the turkey mixture among the
pastry, making neat piles on each piece.
Gather up the pastry to enclose the
filling in neat bundles. Place on a
baking sheet, brush with a little melted
butter and bake for 20 minutes, or until
the pastry is crisp and golden. Serve hot
or warm with a green salad.

Energy 304kcal/1274kJ; Protein 27.3g; Carbohydrate 16.6g, of which sugars 3.9g; Fat 14.3g, of which saturates 8.5g; Cholesterol 95mg; Calcium 91mg; Fibre 0.8g; Sodium 204mg.

TURKEY ESCALOPES WITH CAPERS

A STAPLE OF BISTRO COOKING, THESE THIN SLICES OF POULTRY OR MEAT, CALLED ESCALOPES, COOK VERY QUICKLY AND CAN BE SERVED WITH ALL KINDS OF INTERESTING SAUCES.

Preparation: 6 minutes; Cooking: 4 minutes

SERVES TWO

INGREDIENTS
  4 thin turkey breast escalopes,
    weighing about 75g/3oz each
  1 large unwaxed lemon
  2.5ml/ ½ tsp chopped fresh sage
  60–75ml/4–5 tbsp extra virgin
    olive oil
  50g/2oz/ ½ cup fine dry breadcrumbs
  15ml/1 tbsp capers, rinsed and
    drained
  salt and ground black pepper
For the garnish
  sage leaves
  lemon wedges

1 Place the turkey escalopes between two sheets of clear film (plastic wrap) and pound with the flat side of a meat hammer or roll with a rolling pin to flatten to about 5mm/¼in.

2 With a vegetable peeler, remove four pieces of lemon rind. Cut them into thin julienne strips, cover with clear film and set aside. Grate the remainder of the lemon rind and squeeze the lemon. Put the grated rind in a large shallow dish and add the sage, salt and pepper. Stir in 15ml/1 tbsp of the lemon juice, reserving the rest, and about 15ml/1 tbsp of the olive oil, then add the turkey, turn to coat and set aside.

3 Place the breadcrumbs in another shallow dish and dip the escalopes in the crumbs, coating both sides. In a heavy frying pan heat 30ml/2 tbsp of the olive oil over a high heat, add the escalopes and cook for 2–3 minutes, turning once, until golden. Transfer to two warmed plates and keep warm.

4 Wipe out the pan, add the remaining oil, the lemon julienne and the capers, stirring, and heat through. Spoon a little sauce over the turkey and garnish with sage leaves and lemon wedges.

Energy 476kcal/1990kJ; Protein 39.3g; Carbohydrate 20g, of which sugars 1.2g; Fat 27.1g, of which saturates 4.6g; Cholesterol 151mg; Calcium 90mg; Fibre 1.7g; Sodium 355mg.

TURKEY WITH YELLOW PEPPER SAUCE

THIS COMBINATION OF GARLIC CREAM CHEESE AND A YELLOW PEPPER AND ORANGE SAUCE TRANSFORMS HUMBLE TURKEY ESCALOPES INTO A MEMORABLE MEAL IN NO TIME AT ALL.

Preparation: 6–8 minutes; Cooking: 12 minutes

SERVES FOUR

INGREDIENTS
30ml/2 tbsp olive oil
2 large yellow (bell) peppers, seeded
  and chopped
1 small onion, chopped
15ml/1 tbsp freshly squeezed
  orange juice
300ml/½ pint/1¼ cups
  chicken stock
4 turkey escalopes
75g/3oz Boursin or garlic
  cream cheese
16 fresh basil leaves
25g/1oz/2 tbsp butter
salt and ground black pepper
To serve
  freshly cooked tagliatelle
  black olives

1 To make the sauce, heat half the oil in a pan and gently fry the peppers and onion until beginning to soften. Add the orange juice and stock and cook until very soft. Meanwhile, lay the turkey escalopes between sheets of clear film (plastic wrap) and beat them out lightly.

VARIATIONS
• Chicken breast fillets or veal escalopes could be used in place of the turkey.
• Stir some sun-dried tomato purée (paste) or red pesto into the cheese before spreading it.
• For an impressive effect, divide the sauce ingredients and make half with yellow pepper and half with red, then swirl them together on the plate.

2 Spread the turkey escalopes with the Boursin or garlic cream cheese. Chop half the basil and sprinkle on top, then roll up, tucking in the ends like an envelope. Secure with half a cocktail stick (toothpick).

3 Heat the remaining oil and the butter in a frying pan and fry the escalopes for 7–8 minutes, turning them frequently, until golden and cooked.

4 While the escalopes are cooking, press the pepper mixture through a sieve, or blend until smooth, then strain back into the pan. Season to taste and warm through, or serve cold, with the escalopes, garnished with the remaining basil leaves.

Energy 316kcal/1312kJ; Protein 22.1g; Carbohydrate 6.8g, of which sugars 6.2g; Fat 22.4g, of which saturates 10.5g; Cholesterol 117mg; Calcium 37mg; Fibre 1.6g; Sodium 188mg.

STIR-FRIED TURKEY WITH BROCCOLI

FOR A DELICIOUS MEAL WITHOUT BREAKING THE BANK, TURKEY IS AN EXCELLENT CHOICE. IT IS RELATIVELY INEXPENSIVE, HAS LITTLE WASTE AND TASTES GREAT IN A STIR-FRY LIKE THIS ONE.

Preparation: 8 minutes; Cooking: 8 minutes

SERVES FOUR

INGREDIENTS

115g/4oz broccoli florets
4 spring onions (scallions)
5ml/1 tsp cornflour (cornstarch)
45ml/3 tbsp oyster sauce
15ml/1 tbsp dark soy sauce
120ml/4fl oz/½ cup chicken stock
10ml/2 tsp lemon juice
45ml/3 tbsp groundnut (peanut) oil
450g/1lb turkey steaks, cut into
   strips about 5mm x 5cm/¼ x 2in
1 small onion, chopped
2 garlic cloves, crushed
10ml/2 tsp grated fresh root ginger
115g/4oz/1½ cups fresh shiitake
   mushrooms, sliced
75g/3oz baby corn, halved
   lengthways
15ml/1 tbsp sesame oil
salt and ground black pepper
egg noodles, to serve

1 Divide the broccoli florets into smaller sprigs and cut the stalks into thin diagonal slices.

2 Finely chop the white parts of the spring onions and slice the green parts into thin shreds.

3 Put the cornflour in a bowl. Stir in the oyster sauce to make a thin paste, then add the soy sauce, stock and lemon juice. Stir and set aside.

4 Heat a wok until it is hot, add 30ml/ 2 tbsp of the groundnut oil and swirl it around. Add the turkey and stir-fry for about 2 minutes, or until the strips are golden and crispy at the edges, and cooked through. Remove the turkey and keep the pieces warm.

5 Add the remaining groundnut oil to the wok and stir-fry the chopped onion, garlic and ginger over a medium heat for about 1 minute. Increase the heat to high, add the broccoli, mushrooms and corn and stir-fry for 2 minutes.

6 Return the turkey to the wok, then add the cornflour mixture with the chopped spring onion and seasoning. Cook, stirring, for about 1 minute, or until the sauce has thickened. Stir in the sesame oil. Serve immediately on a bed of egg noodles with the finely shredded spring onion sprinkled on top.

COOK'S TIP
For speed and convenience, use straight-to-wok noodles and toss them with the turkey stir-fry until heated through.

Energy 255kcal/1065kJ; Protein 30.3g; Carbohydrate 5.8g, of which sugars 5g; Fat 12.4g, of which saturates 2.4g; Cholesterol 64mg; Calcium 30mg; Fibre 1.7g; Sodium 725mg

TURKEY WITH MARSALA CREAM SAUCE

MARSALA MAKES A VERY RICH AND TASTY SAUCE. THE ADDITION OF LEMON JUICE GIVES IT A SHARP EDGE, WHICH HELPS TO OFFSET THE RICHNESS CONTRIBUTED BY THE BUTTER AND CREAM.

Preparation: 6 minutes; Cooking: 12 minutes

SERVES SIX

INGREDIENTS
6 turkey breast steaks
45ml/3 tbsp plain (all-purpose) flour
30ml/2 tbsp olive oil
25g/1oz/2 tbsp butter
60ml/4 tbsp lemon juice
175ml/6fl oz/¾ cup dry Marsala
175ml/6fl oz/¾ cup double
   (heavy) cream
salt and ground black pepper
For the garnish
   lemon wedges
   chopped fresh parsley
To serve
   mangetouts (snow peas)
   green beans

1 Put each turkey steak between two sheets of clear film (plastic wrap) and pound with a rolling pin to flatten and stretch the meat. Cut each in half, cutting away and discarding any sinew.

2 Put the flour in a shallow bowl. Season well and coat the meat.

COOK'S TIPS
• You can save a lot of time by cooking the turkey in an electric frying pan, which will hold considerably more pieces than a standard frying pan.
• Cook the mangetouts (snow peas) and beans while the sauce is heating. They will only need a few minutes.

3 Heat the oil and butter in a deep, heavy frying pan until sizzling. Add as many pieces of turkey as the pan will hold and sauté over a medium heat for 2–3 minutes on each side until crispy and tender. Lift the pieces of turkey out with tongs, transfer to a warmed serving dish and keep hot. Repeat with the remaining turkey.

4 Lower the heat. Mix the lemon juice and Marsala together, add to the pan and raise the heat. Bring to the boil, stirring in the sediment, then add the cream. Simmer, stirring constantly, until the sauce is reduced and glossy. Taste for seasoning. Spoon over the turkey, garnish with the lemon wedges and parsley and serve immediately with the mangetouts and green beans.

Energy 326kcal/1355kJ; Protein 25.3g; Carbohydrate 3.5g, of which sugars 1g; Fat 19.9g, of which saturates 12.2g; Cholesterol 106mg; Calcium 26mg; Fibre 0.1g; Sodium 85mg

DUCK <u>AND</u> SESAME STIR-FRY

FOR A SPECIAL FAMILY MEAL THAT IS A GUARANTEED SUCCESS, THIS IS IDEAL. IT TASTES FANTASTIC AND COOKS FAST, SO YOU'LL BE EATING IN NO TIME.

Preparation: 3 minutes; Cooking: 5–7 minutes

SERVES FOUR

INGREDIENTS
    250g/9oz boneless duck meat
    15ml/1 tbsp sesame oil
    15ml/1 tbsp vegetable oil
    4 garlic cloves, finely sliced
    2.5ml/½ tsp dried chilli flakes
    15ml/1 tbsp Thai fish sauce
    15ml/1 tbsp light soy sauce
    120ml/4fl oz/½ cup water
    1 head broccoli, cut into small florets
    coriander (cilantro) and 15ml/1 tbsp
        toasted sesame seeds, to garnish

VARIATION
Pak choi (bok choy) or Chinese flowering cabbage can be used instead of broccoli.

1 Cut all the duck meat into bitesize pieces. Heat the oils in a wok or large, heavy frying pan and stir-fry the garlic over a medium heat until it is golden brown – do not let it burn. Add the duck to the pan and stir-fry for a further 2 minutes, until the meat begins to brown.

2 Stir in the chilli flakes, fish sauce, soy sauce and water. Add the broccoli and continue to stir-fry for about 2 minutes, until the duck is just cooked through.

3 Serve on warmed plates, garnished with coriander and sesame seeds.

Energy 165kcal/686kJ; Protein 17.4g; Carbohydrate 2.3g, of which sugars 2g; Fat 10.6g, of which saturates 1.8g; Cholesterol 69mg; Calcium 72mg; Fibre 2.9g; Sodium 345mg

GINGERED DUCK WITH TAMARI AND MIRIN

DUCK TAKES VERY LITTLE TIME TO COOK ON A GRIDDLE AND TASTES GREAT WITH A TAMARI AND MIRIN GLAZE. IT LOOKS PRETTY ON ITS BED OF PANCAKES, WITH A DELICATE CUCUMBER GARNISH.

Preparation: 4–5 minutes; Cooking: 13 minutes

SERVES FOUR

INGREDIENTS
4 large duck breast fillets, total
   weight about 675g/1½lb
5cm/2in piece fresh root ginger,
   finely grated
½ large cucumber
12 Chinese pancakes
6 spring onions (scallions),
   finely shredded
For the sauce
105ml/7 tbsp tamari
105ml/7 tbsp mirin
25g/1oz/2 tbsp sugar
salt and ground black pepper

1 Make four slashes in the skin of each duck breast fillet, then lay them skin-side up on a plate. Squeeze the grated ginger over the duck to extract every drop of juice; discard the pulp. Generously rub the juice all over the duck, especially into the slashes.

2 Peel the cucumber in strips, then cut it in half, scoop out the seeds and chop the flesh. Set aside in a bowl.

3 To make the sauce, mix the tamari, mirin and sugar in a heavy pan and heat gently together until the sugar has dissolved. Increase the heat and simmer for 4–5 minutes, or until the sauce has reduced by about one-third and become syrupy.

4 Heat a griddle on the stove over a high heat until a few drops of water sprinkled on to the surface evaporate instantly. Sear the duck breasts, placing them skin-side down.

5 When the fat has been rendered, and the skin is nicely browned, remove the duck from the pan. Drain off the fat and wipe the pan clean with kitchen paper. Reheat it, return the duck flesh side down, and cook over a medium heat for about 3 minutes.

6 Brush on a little of the sauce, turn the duck over, brush the other side with sauce and turn again. This should take about 1 minute, by which time the duck should be cooked rare – you'll know because, when pressed, there should be some give in the flesh. Remove from the pan and let the duck rest for a few minutes before slicing each breast across at an angle.

7 Meanwhile, wrap the pancakes in foil and warm them in a steamer for about 3 minutes. Serve with the duck, sauce, spring onions and cucumber.

COOK'S TIP
To cook on the barbecue, position the duck on the grill rack over a large drip tray. Cook over hot coals, covered with a lid or tented heavy-duty foil.

Energy 436kcal/1829kJ; Protein 38g; Carbohydrate 23.3g, of which sugars 11g; Fat 21.6g, of which saturates 2.2g; Cholesterol 186mg; Calcium 113mg; Fibre 0.7g; Sodium 1615mg

SKEWERED DUCK WITH POACHED EGGS

THIS COMBINATION OF MARINATED DUCK, CHANTERELLE MUSHROOMS AND POACHED EGGS IS QUITE DELICIOUS, AND CAN EASILY BE PREPARED WITHIN HALF AN HOUR.

Preparation: 8 minutes; Cooking: 11 minutes

SERVES FOUR

INGREDIENTS

3 skinless duck breast fillets, thinly sliced
30ml/2 tbsp soy sauce
30ml/2 tbsp balsamic vinegar
30ml/2 tbsp groundnut (peanut) oil
25g/1oz/2 tbsp unsalted (sweet) butter
1 shallot, finely chopped
115g/4oz/1½ cups chanterelle mushrooms
4 eggs
50g/2oz mixed salad leaves
salt and ground black pepper
extra virgin olive oil, to serve

1 Toss the duck in the soy sauce and balsamic vinegar. Cover and marinate for 8–10 minutes. Meanwhile, soak 12 bamboo skewers in water to help prevent them from burning during cooking.

2 Meanwhile, melt the butter in a frying pan and cook the finely chopped shallot until softened but not coloured. Add the chanterelle mushrooms and cook over a high heat for about 5 minutes, stirring occasionally. Leave the pan over a low heat while you cook the duck.

3 Preheat the grill (broiler). Thread the duck slices on to the skewers, pleating them neatly. Place on a grill (broiling) pan and drizzle with half the oil.

4 Grill (broil) for 3–5 minutes, then turn the skewers and drizzle with the remaining oil. Grill for a further 3 minutes, or until the duck is cooked through and golden.

5 Poach the eggs while the duck is cooking. Half fill a frying pan with water, add salt and heat until simmering. Break the eggs one at a time into a cup before tipping carefully into the water. Poach the eggs gently for about 3 minutes, or until the whites are set. Use a slotted spoon to transfer the eggs to a warm plate and trim off any untidy white.

6 Arrange the salad leaves on serving plates, then add the chanterelles and skewered duck. Carefully add the poached eggs. Drizzle with olive oil and season with ground black pepper, then serve at once.

COOK'S TIPS
• If you haven't got time to thread the duck strips on to skewers, simply stir-fry in a little oil for a few minutes until crisp and cooked through, then sprinkle over the salad leaves with the mushrooms.
• To save time and simplify matters, soft boil the eggs rather than poaching them.

Energy 269kcal/1125kJ; Protein 29.3g; Carbohydrate 1.8g, of which sugars 1.3g; Fat 18.2g, of which saturates 6.3g; Cholesterol 327mg; Calcium 53mg; Fibre 0.7g; Sodium 412mg

STIR-FRIED DUCK WITH PINEAPPLE

*THE FATTY SKIN ON DUCK MAKES IT IDEAL FOR STIR-FRYING: AS SOON AS THE DUCK IS ADDED
TO THE HOT PAN THE FAT RUNS, CREATING DELICIOUS CRISP SKIN AND TENDER FLESH WHEN COOKED.*

Preparation: 5 minutes; Cooking: 10 minutes

SERVES FOUR

INGREDIENTS
- 250g/9oz fresh sesame noodles
- 2 duck breasts, thinly sliced
- 3 spring onions (scallions),
  cut into strips
- 2 celery sticks, cut into
  matchstick strips
- 1 fresh pineapple, peeled, cored and
  cut into strips
- 300g/11oz carrots, peppers,
  beansprouts and cabbage, shredded
- 90ml/6 tbsp plum sauce

1 Bring a pan of water to the boil and add the noodles. Cook for approximately 3 minutes then drain over the pan using a colander. Set aside.

2 Meanwhile, heat a wok. Add the duck and stir-fry for 2 minutes, until crisp. Drain off all but 30ml/2 tbsp of the fat. Add the spring onions and celery and stir-fry for 2 minutes. Remove the ingredients from the wok and set aside.

3 Add the pineapple strips and mixed vegetables and stir-fry for 2 minutes.

4 Add the cooked noodles to the wok with the plum sauce, then replace the duck mixture.

5 Stir-fry the duck mixture for about 2 minutes more, or until the noodles and vegetables are hot and the duck is cooked through. Serve at once.

COOK'S TIP
Fresh sesame noodles can be bought from large supermarkets – you'll find them in the chiller cabinets alongside fresh pasta. If they aren't available use fresh egg noodles instead and cook according to the instructions on the packet. For extra flavour, add a little sesame oil to the cooking water.

Energy 455Kcal/1927kJ; Protein 28.3g; Carbohydrate 69g, of which sugars 22.6g; Fat 11g, of which saturates 1.4g; Cholesterol 110mg; Calcium 81mg; Fibre 5.7g; Sodium 143mg.

DUCK WITH PLUM SAUCE

*THIS IS AN UPDATED VERSION OF AN OLD ENGLISH DISH, WHICH WAS TRADITIONALLY SERVED IN THE
LATE SUMMER AND EARLY AUTUMN WHEN VICTORIA PLUMS ARE BEAUTIFULLY RIPE.*

Preparation: 3 minutes; Cooking: 27 minutes

SERVES FOUR

INGREDIENTS
  4 duck quarters
  1 large red onion, finely chopped
  500g/1¼lb ripe plums, stoned
  and quartered
  30ml/2 tbsp redcurrant jelly
  salt and ground black pepper

COOK'S TIP
It is important that the plums used in
this dish are very ripe, otherwise the
mixture will be too dry and the sauce
extremely tart.

VARIATIONS
• If you can't locate red onions, then use
a white onion instead.
• Fine-cut orange marmalade makes a
tangy alternative to the redcurrant jelly.

1 Prick the duck skin all over with a
fork to release the fat during cooking
and help give a crisp result, then place
the portions in a heavy frying pan, skin
sides down.

2 Cook the duck pieces for 7 minutes
on each side, or until golden brown and
cooked right through. Remove the duck
from the frying pan using tongs, and
keep warm.

3 Pour away all but 30ml/2 tbsp of the
duck fat, then stir-fry the onion for
3 minutes, or until golden. Add the
plums and cook for a further 5 minutes,
stirring frequently. Add the redcurrant
jelly and mix well.

4 Replace the duck portions and cook
for a further 5 minutes, or until
thoroughly reheated. Season with salt
and pepper to taste before serving.

Energy 608kcal/2515kJ; Protein 15.1g; Carbohydrate 17.4g, of which sugars 17g; Fat 53.5g, of which saturates 14.5g; Cholesterol 0mg; Calcium 35mg; Fibre 2.2g; Sodium 102mg.

MARMALADE ᴬᴺᴰ SOY ROAST DUCK

SWEET-AND-SOUR FLAVOURS, SUCH AS MARMALADE AND SOY SAUCE, COMPLEMENT THE RICH TASTE OF DUCK BEAUTIFULLY WHILE ALSO CUTTING THROUGH ITS RICHNESS.

Preparation: 5 minutes; Cooking: 20–25 minutes

SERVES SIX

INGREDIENTS

  6 duck breast portions
  45ml/3 tbsp fine-cut marmalade
  45ml/3 tbsp light soy sauce
  salt and ground black pepper

1 Preheat the oven 190⁰C/375⁰F/ Gas 5. Place the duck breasts skin side up on a grill (broiler) rack and place in the sink. Pour boiling water all over the duck. This shrinks the skin and helps it to crisp during cooking. Pat the duck dry with kitchen paper and transfer to a roasting pan.

2 Combine the marmalade and soy sauce, and brush over the duck. Season with a little salt and some black pepper and roast for 20–25 minutes, basting occasionally with the marmalade mixture in the pan.

3 Remove the duck breasts from the oven and leave to rest for 5 minutes.

4 Slice the duck breasts and serve drizzled with any juices left in the pan.

COOK'S TIP
Serve these robustly flavoured duck breast portions with simple accompaniments such as steamed sticky rice and lightly cooked pak choi (bok choi).

Energy 273Kcal/1144kJ; Protein 32g; Carbohydrate 8g, of which sugars 7g; Fat 13g, of which saturates 4g; Cholesterol 144mg; Calcium 20mg; Fibre 0g; Sodium 700mg

MEAT MEALS

Forget slow-cooking casseroles or roasted joints of meat — when you're in a hurry you need a
meat dish that takes minimal cooking as well as minimal preparation. Beef can be prepared
quickly in many different ways: pan-fried, such as Steak with Warm Tomato Salsa, Pepper
Steaks with Chive Butter and Calf's Liver with Crisp Onions; stir-fried, such as Beef
Stroganoff and Beef Strips with Orange and Ginger; or made into hamburgers. Thin cuts of
veal also cook extremely quickly, in dishes such as Veal with Anchovies and Mozzarella and
Pan-fried Veal Chops. Pork is also highly versatile: just as tasty in a sweet-and-sour sauce as
in a dish such as Pork with Camembert Sauce, Lemon Grass and Ginger Pork Burgers and
Pork and Pineapple Coconut Curry. Finally, tender new-season lamb can be cooked in a trice:
try Lamb Steaks with Redcurrant Glaze, Barbecued Lamb with Red Pepper Salsa, Kofta Lamb
Burgers, Lamb Chops with Mint Vinaigrette and Skewered Lamb with Cucumber Raita. All
these main courses can be rustled up in no time.

PAN-FRIED STEAKS WITH WHISKY AND CREAM

A GOOD STEAK IS ALWAYS A POPULAR CHOICE FOR DINNER, AND TOP QUALITY MEAT PLUS TIMING ARE THE KEYS TO SUCCESS. CHOOSE SMALL, THICK STEAKS RATHER THAN LARGE, THIN ONES IF YOU CAN.

Preparation: 0 minutes; Cooking: 8 minutes

SERVES FOUR

INGREDIENTS
4 x 225–350g/8–12oz sirloin steaks,
  at room temperature
5ml/1 tsp oil
15g/½oz/1 tbsp butter
50ml/2fl oz/¼ cup whisky
300ml/½ pint/1¼ cups double
  (heavy) cream
salt and ground black pepper

1 Dry the steaks with kitchen paper and season with pepper. Heat a cast-iron frying pan, or other heavy pan, over high heat. When it is very hot, add the oil and butter. Add the steaks to the foaming butter, one at a time, to seal the meat quickly.

2 Lower the heat to moderate and continue to cook the steaks, allowing 3–4 minutes for rare, 4–5 minutes for medium or 5–6 minutes for well-done steaks.

3 To test if the timing is right, press down gently in the middle of the steak: soft meat will be rare; when there is some resistance but the meat underneath the outside crust feels soft, it is medium; if it is firm to the touch, the steak is well done.

COOK'S TIPS
• Turn the steaks only once during cooking to seal in the juices.
• Serve with fried onions and mushrooms, peas and chips (French fries).

4 When the steaks are cooked to your liking, transfer them to warmed plates and keep warm. Pour off the fat from the pan and discard. Add the whisky and stir around to scrape off all the sediment from the base of the pan.

5 Allow the liquid to reduce a little, then add the cream and simmer over a low heat for a few minutes, until the cream thickens. Season to taste, pour the sauce around or over the steaks, as you prefer, and serve immediately.

Energy 806kcal/3345kJ; Protein 65.9g; Carbohydrate 1.3g, of which sugars 1.3g; Fat 56.5g, of which saturates 32.6g; Cholesterol 251mg; Calcium 51mg; Fibre 0g; Sodium 232mg

BEEF WITH BLUE CHEESE SAUCE

CELEBRATIONS CALL FOR SPECIAL DISHES, AND THIS ONE IS MORE SPECIAL THAN MOST. ROQUEFORT CHEESE, CREAM AND FILLET STEAK IS A RICH COMBINATION, SO KEEP THE REST OF THE MEAL SIMPLE.

Preparation: 2 minutes; Cooking: 8 minutes

SERVES FOUR

INGREDIENTS
  25g/1oz/2 tbsp butter
  30ml/2 tbsp olive oil
  4 fillet steaks (beef tenderloins), cut
    5cm/2in thick, about 150g/5oz each
  salt and coarsely ground black pepper
  fresh flat leaf parsley, to garnish
  roast potatoes and Mediterranean
    vegetables, to serve
For the blue cheese sauce
  30ml/2 tbsp brandy
  150ml/5fl oz/⅔ cup double
    (heavy) cream
  75g/3oz Roquefort cheese, crumbled

COOK'S TIP
Adding oil to the butter for frying means you can cook at a higher heat, essential for searing the meat.

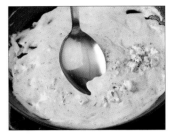

1 Heat the butter and oil together in a heavy frying pan, over a high heat. Season the steaks well. Fry them for 1 minute on each side, to sear them.

2 Lower the heat slightly and cook for a further 2–3 minutes on each side, or according to your taste. Remove the steaks to a warm plate.

3 Reduce the heat and add the brandy, stirring to incorporate the pan juices. Add the cream and boil to reduce a little.

4 Add the crumbled cheese and mash it into the sauce using a spoon. Taste for seasoning. Serve in a small sauce jug (pitcher), or poured over the steaks. Garnish the beef with parsley.

Energy 573kcal/2374kJ; Protein 36.3g; Carbohydrate 0.7g, of which sugars 0.7g; Fat 45.4g, of which saturates 24.4g; Cholesterol 170mg; Calcium 117mg; Fibre 0g; Sodium 341mg

STEAK WITH WARM TOMATO SALSA

A TANGY SALSA OF TOMATOES, SPRING ONIONS AND BALSAMIC VINEGAR MAKES A COLOURFUL TOPPING FOR CHUNKY, PAN-FRIED STEAKS COOKED JUST THE WAY YOU LIKE THEM.

Preparation: 2–3 minutes; Cooking: 8 minutes

SERVES TWO

INGREDIENTS
  2 steaks, about 2cm/¾in thick
  4 large plum tomatoes
  2 spring onions (scallions)
  30ml/2 tbsp balsamic vinegar

1 Trim any excess fat from the steaks, then season on both sides with salt and pepper. Heat a non-stick frying pan and cook the steaks for about 3 minutes on each side for medium rare. Cook for a little longer if you like your steak well cooked.

2 Meanwhile, put the tomatoes in a heatproof bowl, cover with boiling water and leave for 1–2 minutes.

3 When the tomato skins start to split, drain and peel them, then halve them and scoop out the seeds. Dice the tomato flesh.

4 When the steaks are cooked to your taste, remove from the pan with a fish slice, to drain off any excess oil, and transfer them to plates. Keep the steaks warm on a very low oven temperature while you prepare the salsa.

5 Thinly slice the spring onions and add them to the cooking juices in the frying pan with the diced tomato, balsamic vinegar, 30ml/2 tbsp water and a little seasoning. Stir briefly until warm, scraping up any meat residue. Spoon the salsa over the steaks to serve.

COOK'S TIP
Choose rump (round), sirloin or fillet steak (beef tenderloin). If you prefer to grill (broil) the steak, the timing will be the same as the recipe, though you must take into account the thickness of the meat.

Energy 207kcal/872kJ; Protein 33.9g; Carbohydrate 3.4g, of which sugars 3.4g; Fat 6.5g, of which saturates 2.7g; Cholesterol 89mg; Calcium 17mg; Fibre 1.2g; Sodium 100mg

HOME-MADE BURGERS WITH RELISH

MAKING YOUR OWN BURGERS MEANS YOU CONTROL WHAT GOES INTO THEM. THESE ARE FULL OF FLAVOUR AND ALWAYS PROVE POPULAR. THE TANGY RATATOUILLE RELISH IS VERY EASY TO MAKE.

Preparation: 6 minutes; Cooking: 14 minutes

SERVES FOUR

INGREDIENTS
  2 shallots, chopped
  450g/1lb lean minced (ground) beef
  30ml/2 tbsp chopped parsley
  30ml/2 tbsp tomato ketchup
  1 garlic clove, crushed
  1 fresh green chilli, seeded and
    finely chopped
  15ml/1 tbsp olive oil
  400g/14oz can ratatouille
  4 burger buns
  lettuce leaves
  salt and ground black pepper, to taste

1 Put the shallots in a bowl with boiling water to cover. Leave for 1–2 minutes, then slip off the skins and chop the shallots finely.

2 Mix half the shallots with the beef in a bowl. Add the chopped parsley and tomato ketchup, with salt and pepper to taste. Mix well with clean hands. Divide the mixture into four. Knead each portion into a ball, then flatten it into a burger.

3 Make a spicy relish by cooking the remaining shallot with the garlic and green chilli in the olive oil for 2–3 minutes, until softened.

4 Add the canned ratatouille to the pan containing the vegetables. Bring to the boil, then simmer for 5 minutes.

VARIATION
Set these burgers on individual plates with spicy corn relish on the side. To make the relish, heat 30ml/2 tbsp oil in a pan and fry 1 onion, 2 crushed garlic cloves and 1 seeded red chilli until soft. Add 10ml/2 tsp garam masala and cook for 2 minutes, then mix in a 320g/11¼oz can whole kernel corn and the grated rind and juice of 1 lime.

5 Meanwhile, preheat the grill (broiler) and cook the burgers for about 5 minutes on each side, until browned and cooked through. Meanwhile, split the burger buns. Arrange lettuce leaves on the bun bases, add the burgers and top with warm relish and the bun tops.

Energy 484kcal/2021kJ; Protein 27.9g; Carbohydrate 30.2g, of which sugars 7.7g; Fat 28.8g, of which saturates 9.3g; Cholesterol 68mg; Calcium 120mg; Fibre 2.2g; Sodium 473mg

STEAK WITH PICKLED WALNUT SAUCE

THIS IS A TRADITIONAL SCOTTISH WAY OF COOKING BEEF, WHICH MAKES IT GO A LITTLE FURTHER USING ONIONS. FILLET MIGNONS ARE THE SMALL PIECES FROM THE END OF THE FILLET.

Preparation: 2 minutes; Cooking: 15–20 minutes

SERVES FOUR

INGREDIENTS
    15ml/1 tbsp vegetable oil
    75g/3oz/6 tbsp butter
    8 slices of beef fillet (fillet mignon)
    4 onions, sliced
    15ml/1 tbsp pickled walnut juice
    salt and ground black pepper

1 Heat the oil and half the butter in a frying pan and cook the steaks for 4–5 minutes on each side until almost done. Keep the steaks warm while you cook the onions.

2 Once you have taken the steaks out of the pan, melt the remaining butter then add the sliced onions. Increase the heat and stir to brown and soften the onions, scraping the base of the pan.

3 Add the pickled walnut juice and cook for a few minutes. Season to taste with salt and ground black pepper. Serve the beef on warmed plates and spoon the onions and juices over.

Energy 1960kcal/8144kJ; Protein 173.6g; Carbohydrate 24.4g, of which sugars 17.2g; Fat 130.4g, of which saturates 68g; Cholesterol 668mg; Calcium 124mg; Fibre 4.4g; Sodium 876mg.

CORNED BEEF AND EGG HASH

THIS IS TRADITIONAL FAMILY FARE AT ITS VERY BEST. WARM AND COMFORTING, AND MADE IN MINUTES, IT WILL BECOME A FIRM FAVOURITE VERY QUICKLY.

Preparation: 4–5 minutes; Cooking: 12–15 minutes

SERVES FOUR

INGREDIENTS

30ml/2 tbsp vegetable oil
25g/1oz/2 tbsp butter
1 onion, finely chopped
1 green (bell) pepper, seeded
 and diced
2 large firm boiled potatoes, diced
350g/12oz can corned beef, cubed
1.5ml/¼ tsp grated nutmeg
1.5ml/¼ tsp paprika
4 eggs
salt and ground black pepper
parsley, deep-fried in oil, to garnish
sweet chilli sauce or tomato sauce,
 to serve

COOK'S TIP

Put the can of corned beef into the refrigerator to chill for about half an hour before using – it will firm up and be much easier to cut into cubes.

1 Heat the oil and butter together in a large frying pan. Add the onion and fry for 3–4 minutes until softened.

2 In a bowl, mix together the green pepper, potatoes, corned beef, nutmeg and paprika. Season well. Add to the pan and toss gently to distribute the cooked onion. Press down lightly and fry without stirring on a medium heat for about 3–4 minutes until a golden brown crust has formed on the underside.

3 Stir the mixture through to distribute the crust, then repeat the frying twice, until the mixture is well browned.

4 Make four wells in the hash and carefully crack an egg into each. Cover and cook gently for about 4–5 minutes until the egg whites are set.

5 Sprinkle with deep-fried parsley and cut into quarters. Serve hot with sweet chilli sauce or tomato sauce.

Energy 421kcal/1758kJ; Protein 30.9g; Carbohydrate 17g, of which sugars 5.4g; Fat 26.2g, of which saturates 10.6g; Cholesterol 277mg; Calcium 65mg; Fibre 1.7g; Sodium 871mg

RUSSIAN HAMBURGERS

THESE TASTY HAMBURGERS CAN BE MADE VERY QUICKLY AND YET STILL TASTE DIVINE. SERVE THEM SOLO, WITH A TOMATO SAUCE AND VEGETABLES, OR JUST SLIDE THEM INTO BUNS.

Preparation: 6 minutes; Cooking: 12–14 minutes

SERVES FOUR

INGREDIENTS
2 thick slices white bread,
  crusts removed
45ml/3 tbsp milk
450g/1lb finely minced (ground)
  beef, lamb or veal
1 egg, beaten
30ml/2 tbsp plain (all-purpose) flour
30ml/2 tbsp sunflower oil
salt and ground black pepper
tomato sauce, pickled vegetables and
  crispy fried onions, to serve

VARIATION
These burgers are quite plain. For extra flavour, add freshly grated nutmeg to the mixture, or a little chopped onion fried in oil.

1 Cut the bread into chunks and crumb in a food processor, or by using a metal grater. Put the breadcrumbs in a bowl and spoon over the milk. Leave to soak for 3 minutes.

2 Add the minced meat, egg, salt and pepper and mix all the ingredients together thoroughly.

3 Divide the mixture into four equal portions and shape into ovals, each about 10cm/4in long and 5cm/2in wide. Coat each with the flour.

4 Heat the oil in a frying pan and fry the burgers for 6–7 minutes on each side. Serve with a tomato sauce, pickled vegetables and fried onions.

Energy 384kcal/1597kJ; Protein 26g; Carbohydrate 13g, of which sugars 1g; Fat 25.7g, of which saturates 9g; Cholesterol 116mg; Calcium 56mg; Fibre 0.4g; Sodium 183mg

BEEF STROGANOFF

THIS IS ONE OF THE MOST FAMOUS FAST MEAT DISHES, CONSISTING OF TENDER STRIPS OF STEAK IN A TANGY SOUR CREAM SAUCE. SERVE IT WITH CHIPS OR ON A BED OF NOODLES.

Preparation: 3 minutes; Cooking: 12 minutes

SERVES FOUR

INGREDIENTS
450g/1lb fillet steak (beef tenderloin)
  or rump (round) steak, trimmed and
  tenderized with a rolling pin or
  meat mallet
15ml/1 tbsp sunflower oil
25g/1oz/2 tbsp butter
1 onion, sliced
15ml/1 tbsp plain (all-purpose) flour
5ml/1 tsp tomato purée (paste)
5ml/1 tsp Dijon mustard
5ml/1 tsp lemon juice
150ml/¼ pint/⅔ cup sour cream
salt and ground black pepper
fresh herbs, to garnish

1 Using a sharp cook's knife, cut the tenderized steak into thin strips, about 5cm/2in long. Heat the oil and half the butter in a frying pan and fry the beef over a high heat for 2 minutes, or until browned. Remove with a slotted spoon, leaving any juices behind.

2 Melt the remaining butter in the pan and gently fry the onion for 8 minutes, until soft. Stir in the flour, tomato purée, mustard, lemon juice and sour cream. Return the beef to the pan and stir until the sauce is bubbling. Season well and garnish with fresh herbs.

Energy 308kcal/1282kJ; Protein 26.5g; Carbohydrate 5.8g, of which sugars 2.5g; Fat 20.1g, of which saturates 10.2g; Cholesterol 102mg; Calcium 50mg; Fibre 0.4g; Sodium 124mg

GREEN BEEF CURRY <u>WITH</u> THAI AUBERGINES

THIS IS A VERY QUICK CURRY SO IT IS ESSENTIAL THAT YOU USE GOOD-QUALITY MEAT. SIRLOIN IS RECOMMENDED, BUT TENDER RUMP OR EVEN FILLET STEAK COULD BE USED INSTEAD.

Preparation: 2 minutes; Cooking: 16 minutes

SERVES FOUR TO SIX

INGREDIENTS
    450g/1lb beef sirloin
    15ml/1 tbsp vegetable oil
    45ml/3 tbsp Thai green curry paste
    600ml/1 pint/2½ cups coconut milk
    4 kaffir lime leaves, torn
    15–30ml/1–2 tbsp Thai fish sauce
    5ml/1 tsp palm sugar (jaggery) or
      light muscovado (brown) sugar
    150g/5oz small Thai aubergines
      (eggplants), halved
    a small handful of fresh Thai basil
    2 fresh green chillies, to garnish

1 Trim off any excess fat from the beef. Using a sharp knife, cut it into long, thin strips. This is easiest to do if it is well chilled. Set it aside.

2 Heat the oil in a large, heavy pan or wok. Add the curry paste and cook for 1–2 minutes, until it is fragrant.

3 Stir in half the coconut milk, a little at a time. Cook, stirring frequently, for about 5–6 minutes, until an oily sheen appears on the surface of the liquid.

4 Add the beef to the pan with the kaffir lime leaves, Thai fish sauce, sugar and aubergine halves. Cook for 2–3 minutes, then stir in the remaining coconut milk.

5 Bring back to a simmer and cook until the meat and aubergines are tender. Stir in the Thai basil just before serving.

6 To prepare the garnish, slit the fresh green chillies and scrape out the pith and seeds. Shred the chillies finely and sprinkle over the curry.

GREEN CURRY PASTE
To make the green curry paste, put 15 fresh green chillies, 2 chopped lemon grass stalks, 3 sliced shallots, 2 garlic cloves, 15ml/1 tbsp chopped galangal, 4 chopped kaffir lime leaves, 2.5ml/ ½ tsp grated kaffir lime rind, 5ml/1 tsp chopped coriander (cilantro) root, 6 black peppercorns, 5ml/1 tsp each roasted coriander and cumin seeds, 15ml/1 tbsp sugar, 5ml/1 tsp salt and 5ml/1 tsp shrimp paste into a food processor and process until smooth. Gradually add 30ml/2 tbsp vegetable oil, processing after each addition.

Energy 147kcal/619kJ; Protein 18.2g; Carbohydrate 6.4g, of which sugars 6.3g; Fat 5.6g, of which saturates 1.9g; Cholesterol 38mg; Calcium 36mg; Fibre 0.5g; Sodium 341mg

ESCALOPES OF VEAL WITH CREAM SAUCE

THIS QUICK, EASY DISH IS DELICIOUS SERVED WITH BUTTERED TAGLIATELLE AND LIGHTLY STEAMED GREEN VEGETABLES. IT WORKS JUST AS WELL WITH TURKEY ESCALOPES.

Preparation: 2–3 minutes; Cooking: 15–17 minutes

SERVES FOUR

INGREDIENTS
    15ml/1 tbsp plain (all-purpose) flour
    4 veal escalopes (US scallops),
        about 75–115g/3–4oz each
    30ml/2 tbsp sunflower oil
    1 shallot, chopped
    150g/5oz/2 cups oyster
        mushrooms, sliced
    30ml/2 tbsp Marsala or
        medium-dry sherry
    200ml/7fl oz/scant 1 cup crème
        fraîche or sour cream
    30ml/2 tbsp chopped fresh tarragon
    salt and ground black pepper

COOK'S TIP
If they are too thick, flatten the escalopes (US scallops) with a rolling pin. It'll help to cut down the cooking time.

1 Season the flour and use to dust the veal, then set the meat aside.

2 Heat the oil in a large frying pan and cook the shallot and mushrooms for 5 minutes. Add the escalopes and cook over a high heat for about 1½ minutes on each side. Pour in the Marsala or sherry and cook until reduced by half.

3 Remove the escalopes from the pan. Stir the crème fraîche, tarragon and seasoning into the juices in the pan and simmer gently for 3–5 minutes, or until the sauce is thick and creamy.

4 Return the escalopes to the pan and heat through for 1 minute before serving with the sauce, noodles and broccoli.

Energy 377kcal/1567kJ; Protein 25.1g; Carbohydrate 5.9g, of which sugars 2.5g; Fat 27.5g, of which saturates 14.9g; Cholesterol 108mg; Calcium 45mg; Fibre 0.8g; Sodium 75mg

PEPPER STEAKS WITH CHIVE BUTTER

A RICH BRANDY SAUCE PROVIDES THE FINISHING TOUCH TO THESE STEAKS DRESSED WITH CRUSHED PEPPERCORNS AND TOPPED WITH A SLICE OF CHIVE BUTTER.

Preparation: 4 minutes; Cooking: 12 minutes

SERVES FOUR

INGREDIENTS
 4 fillet (beef tenderloin) or sirloin
    beef steaks, about 115–175g/
    4–6oz each
 45ml⅓ tbsp olive oil
 15ml/1 tbsp black and white
    peppercorns, coarsely crushed
 1 garlic clove, halved
 50g/2oz/¼ cup butter
 30ml/2 tbsp brandy
 250ml/8fl oz/1 cup ready-made
    jellied beef stock
 salt and ground black pepper
 tied chive bundles, to garnish
 boiled new potatoes, to serve
For the chive butter
 50g/2oz/¼ cup butter
 45ml/3 tbsp snipped fresh chives
 salt and ground black pepper

1 Make the chive butter. Beat the butter until soft, add the chives and season with salt and pepper. Beat until well mixed, then shape into a roll, wrap in foil and chill.

2 Brush the steaks with a little olive oil and press crushed peppercorns on to both sides.

3 Rub the cut surface of the garlic over a frying pan. Melt the butter in the remaining oil. When hot, add the steaks and fry quickly, allowing 3½–4 minutes on each side for medium-rare. Lift out with tongs, place on a serving plate and keep hot while you make the sauce.

4 Add the brandy and stock to the pan, boil rapidly until reduced by half, then season with salt and pepper to taste. Slice the chive butter and put a piece on top of each steak. Spoon a little sauce on to each plate. Garnish each steak with a chive bundle and serve with a simple vegetable accompaniment, such as boiled new potatoes.

Energy 587kcal/2434kJ; Protein 40.3g; Carbohydrate 0.5g, of which sugars 0.5g; Fat 45.2g, of which saturates 20.9g; Cholesterol 155mg; Calcium 38mg; Fibre 0.6g; Sodium 268mg.

BEEF STRIPS WITH ORANGE AND GINGER

STIR-FRYING IS ONE OF THE BEST WAYS TO COOK WITH THE MINIMUM OF FAT. IT IS ALSO ONE OF THE QUICKEST WAYS TO COOK, PROVIDED YOU CHOOSE TENDER MEAT.

Preparation: 15 minutes; Cooking: 5 minutes, plus marinating

SERVES FOUR

INGREDIENTS
  450g/1lb lean beef rump (round)
    steak, fillet steak (beef tenderloin)
    or sirloin, cut into thin strips
  grated rind and juice of 1 orange
  15ml/1 tbsp light soy sauce
  5ml/1 tsp cornflour (cornstarch)
  2.5cm/1in piece of fresh root ginger,
    finely chopped
  15ml/1 tbsp sunflower oil
  1 large carrot, cut into thin strips
  2 spring onions (scallions), thinly
    sliced
  noodles or rice, to serve

1 Place the beef strips in a bowl and sprinkle over the orange rind and juice. If possible, leave to marinate for 10 minutes, or up to 30 minutes if you can spare the time.

2 Drain the liquid from the meat and set aside, then mix the meat with the soy sauce, cornflour and ginger, making sure the meat is evenly covered.

COOK'S TIPS
• Marinating the meat for longer will make it more tender, as the marinade will break down and tenderize the flesh.
• Just before serving, toss the stir-fry with 5ml/1 tsp sesame oil. If you haven't any sesame oil, use flavoured chilli oil, or a nut oil, such as hazelnut or walnut.

3 Heat the oil in a wok or large frying pan and add the beef. Stir-fry for 1 minute until lightly coloured, then add the carrot strips and stir-fry for another 2–3 minutes.

4 Stir in the spring onions and reserved liquid, then cook, stirring, until boiling and thickened. Serve hot with noodles or rice.

Energy 235kcal/981kJ; Protein 25.9g; Carbohydrate 3.1g, of which sugars 1.8g; Fat 13.3g, of which saturates 4.6g; Cholesterol 65mg; Calcium 13mg; Fibre 0.5g; Sodium 345mg.

THAI-STYLE RARE BEEF AND MANGO SALAD

RARE BEEF AND JUICY MANGOES — A MARRIAGE MADE IN HEAVEN. COME DOWN TO EARTH BY SERVING THE SALAD WITH A MIXTURE OF SLIGHTLY BITTER SALAD LEAVES IN A LEMON AND OIL DRESSING.

Preparation: 2 minutes; Cooking: 18 minutes; Marinating for 2 hours recommended

SERVES FOUR

INGREDIENTS
  450g/1lb sirloin steak
  45ml/3 tbsp garlic-infused olive oil
  45ml/3 tbsp soy sauce
  2 mangoes, peeled, stoned (pitted)
    and finely sliced
  ground black pepper

COOK'S TIP
This is a simplified version of the classic Thai beef salad, which usually comes with a vast array of chopped vegetables. If you want to add a complement to this delicious no-fuss version, set out little bowls of fresh coriander (cilantro) leaves, chopped spring onions (scallions) and peanuts, for sprinkling.

1 Put the steak in a shallow, non-metallic dish and pour over the oil and soy sauce. Season with pepper and turn the steaks to coat them in the marinade. Marinate for at least 10 minutes; longer if you can spare the time. Two hours in a covered bowl in the refrigerator would be ideal.

2 Heat a griddle until hot. Remove the steak from the marinade and place on the griddle. Cook for 3–5 minutes on each side, moving the steak halfway through if you want a criss-cross pattern.

3 Transfer the steak to a board and leave to rest for 2 minutes. Meanwhile, heat the marinade in a pan. Cook for a few seconds, then remove from the heat. Slice the steak thinly and arrange on four serving plates with the mangoes. Drizzle over the pan juices and serve with some salad leaves dressed with lemon and oil.

Energy 286kcal/1200kJ; Protein 27.4g; Carbohydrate 14.7g, of which sugars 14.4g; Fat 13.5g, of which saturates 3.5g; Cholesterol 57mg; Calcium 19mg; Fibre 2.6g; Sodium 615mg

CALF'S LIVER <u>WITH</u> CRISP ONIONS

SAUTÉED OR CREAMY MASHED POTATOES GO WELL WITH FRIED CALF'S LIVER. SERVE WITH A SALAD OF MIXED LEAVES AND FRESH HERBS, TO COMPLEMENT THE SIMPLE FLAVOURS OF THIS MAIN COURSE.

Preparation: 3–4 minutes; Cooking: 16 minutes

SERVES FOUR

INGREDIENTS
50g/2oz/¼ cup butter
4 onions, thinly sliced
5ml/1 tsp caster (superfine) sugar
4 slices calf's liver, each weighing
   about 115g/4oz
30ml/2 tbsp plain (all-purpose) flour
30ml/2 tbsp olive oil
salt and ground black pepper
parsley, to garnish

1 Melt the butter in a large, heavy-based pan with a lid. Add the onions and mix well to coat with butter. Cover the pan with a tight-fitting lid and cook gently for 10 minutes, stirring occasionally.

2 Stir in the sugar and cover the pan. Cook the onions for 8 minutes more, or until they are soft and golden. Increase the heat, remove the lid and stir the onions over a high heat until they are deep gold and crisp. Use a slotted spoon to remove the onions from the pan, draining off the fat.

3 Meanwhile, rinse the calf's liver in cold water and pat it dry on kitchen paper. Season the flour, put it on a plate and turn the slices of liver in it until they are lightly coated in flour.

COOK'S TIP
Take care not to cook the liver for too long as this may cause it to toughen.

4 Heat the oil in a large frying pan, add the liver and cook for about 2 minutes on each side, or until lightly browned and just firm. Arrange the liver on warmed plates, with the crisp onions. Garnish with parsley and serve with sautéed or mashed potatoes.

Energy 315kcal/1310kJ; Protein 22.7g; Carbohydrate 11.8g, of which sugars 4.4g; Fat 19.9g, of which saturates 8.5g; Cholesterol 452mg; Calcium 39mg; Fibre 1.3g; Sodium 160mg

VEAL ESCALOPES WITH LEMON

POPULAR IN ITALIAN RESTAURANTS, THIS DISH IS VERY SIMPLE TO MAKE AT HOME. WHITE VERMOUTH AND LEMON JUICE MAKE THE PERFECT SAUCE FOR THE DELICATELY FLAVOURED MEAT.

Preparation: 3–4 minutes; Cooking: 15 minutes

SERVES FOUR

INGREDIENTS

    4 veal escalopes (US scallops)
    30–45ml/2–3 tbsp plain
     (all-purpose) flour
    50g/2oz/¼ cup butter
    60ml/4 tbsp olive oil
    60ml/4 tbsp Italian dry white
     vermouth or dry white wine
    45ml/3 tbsp lemon juice
    salt and ground black pepper
    lemon wedges, grated lemon rind
     and fresh parsley, to garnish
    salad, to serve

VARIATIONS

• Use skinless chicken fillets instead of the veal. If they are thick, cut them in half before pounding.

• Substitute thin slices of pork fillet (tenderloin) for the veal and use orange juice instead of lemon.

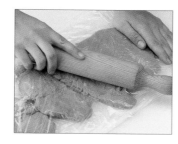

1 Put each veal escalope between two sheets of clear film (plastic wrap) and pound with the side of a rolling pin or the smooth side of a meat mallet until the slices are very thin.

2 Cut the pounded escalopes in half or quarters. Season the flour with a little salt and pepper and use it to coat the escalopes on both sides. Shake off any excess seasoned flour.

3 Melt the butter with half the oil in a large, heavy frying pan until sizzling. Add as many escalopes as the pan will hold. Cook over a medium to high heat for about 2 minutes on each side until lightly coloured. Remove with a spatula and keep hot. Add the remaining oil to the pan and cook the remaining veal escalopes in the same way.

4 Remove the pan from the heat and add the vermouth or wine and the lemon juice. Stir vigorously to mix well with the pan juices, then return the pan to the heat.

5 Return all the veal escalopes to the pan. Spoon the sauce over to coat the veal. Heat through for about 2 minutes, shaking the pan occasionally. Serve immediately with a salad, garnished with lemon wedges, lemon rind and a sprinkling of parsley.

Energy 360kcal/1498kJ; Protein 29g; Carbohydrate 4.8g, of which sugars 0.6g; Fat 23.5g, of which saturates 8.9g; Cholesterol 92mg; Calcium 16mg; Fibre 0.2g; Sodium 151mg

VEAL WITH ANCHOVIES AND MOZZARELLA

SCALOPPINE ARE THIN ESCALOPES OF VEAL CUT ACROSS THE GRAIN. FOR THIS DISH, THEY ARE ROLLED AROUND A RICH ANCHOVY, TOMATO AND MOZZARELLA FILLING AND SERVED WITH A MARSALA SAUCE.

Preparation: 6 minutes; Cooking: 12 minutes

SERVES SIX

INGREDIENTS

50g/2oz/¼ cup unsalted
  (sweet) butter
50g/2oz can anchovies
4 fresh tomatoes, peeled
  and chopped
30ml/2 tbsp chopped fresh flat
  leaf parsley
6 veal escalopes (US scallops), about
  100g/3¾oz each
200g/7oz mozzarella cheese, cut in
  thin slices
30ml/2 tbsp olive oil
175ml/6fl oz/¾ cup Marsala or
  medium dry sherry
30–45ml/2–3 tbsp whipping cream
salt and ground black pepper
fresh herbs, to garnish
cooked pasta, to serve

VARIATIONS
For a more defined flavour, try smoked mozzarella, Provolone or Bel Paese instead of regular mozzarella. If you prefer not to eat veal, substitute thinly sliced pork escalopes or turkey steaks. They will cook in roughly the same amount of time.

1 Melt half the butter in a small pan. Drain the anchovies and add them to the pan. Cook gently, stirring with a wooden spoon, until they break down to a pulp. Stir in the tomatoes and cook for about 3 minutes until they have softened and reduced. Transfer to a bowl, cool, then stir in the parsley.

2 Place each veal escalope in turn between two sheets of baking parchment or clear film (plastic wrap) and beat with a mallet or rolling pin until thin. Spread the escalopes out on a board and sprinkle with ground black pepper. Divide the anchovy and tomato mixture among them, leaving the edges free.

3 Top with the slices of cheese. Fold the long edges of each escalope towards the centre, then bring up the sides to form a neat parcel. Secure with kitchen string or cocktail sticks (toothpicks).

4 Heat the remaining butter with the oil in a large frying pan. Brown the rolled escalopes, then pour in the Marsala or sherry. Cook, uncovered, for 5 minutes or until the Marsala or sherry has reduced and thickened.

5 Transfer the rolls to a serving plate, stir the pan juices to incorporate any sediment, then pour in the cream. Reheat without boiling, then strain over the rolls. Garnish with fresh herbs and serve with tagliatelle, linguine or any other flat ribbon noodles.

Energy 367kcal/1529kJ; Protein 31.7g; Carbohydrate 4g, of which sugars 4g; Fat 22g, of which saturates 11.5g; Cholesterol 100mg; Calcium 161mg; Fibre 0.7g; Sodium 584mg

VEAL KIDNEYS WITH MUSTARD

IN FRANCE, WHERE THIS RECIPE ORIGINATED, VEAL KIDNEYS ARE EASILY FOUND, BUT THIS DISH IS EQUALLY DELICIOUS MADE WITH LAMB'S KIDNEYS IF YOU CAN'T BUY VEAL ONES.

Preparation: 15 minutes; Cooking: 10–12 minutes

SERVES FOUR

INGREDIENTS

2 veal kidneys or 8–10 lamb's
 kidneys, trimmed and
 membranes removed
25g/1oz/2 tbsp butter
15ml/1 tbsp vegetable oil
115g/4oz/1 cup button (white)
 mushrooms, quartered
60ml/4 tbsp chicken stock
30ml/2 tbsp brandy (optional)
175ml/6fl oz/ ¾ cup crème fraîche
 or double (heavy) cream
30ml/2 tbsp Dijon mustard
salt and ground black pepper
snipped fresh chives, to garnish

1 Cut the veal kidneys into pieces, discarding any fat. If using lamb's kidneys, remove the central core by cutting a V-shape from the middle of each kidney. Cut each kidney into three or four pieces.

2 In a large frying pan, melt the butter with the oil over a high heat and swirl to blend. Add the kidneys and sauté for 3–4 minutes, stirring frequently, until browned, then transfer them to a plate using a slotted spoon.

3 Add the mushrooms to the pan and sauté for 2–3 minutes until golden, stirring frequently. Pour in the chicken stock and brandy, if using, then bring to the boil and boil for 2 minutes.

4 Lower the heat, stir in the crème fraîche or double cream and cook for about 2–3 minutes until the sauce is slightly thickened. Stir in the mustard and season with salt and pepper, then add the kidneys and cook for 1 minute to reheat. Spoon into a serving dish, scatter over the chives and serve.

COOK'S TIP
Be sure not to cook the sauce too long once the mustard is added or it will lose its piquancy.

Energy 339kcal/1403kJ; Protein 19.3g; Carbohydrate 1.9g, of which sugars 1.6g; Fat 28.3g, of which saturates 16.3g; Cholesterol 328mg; Calcium 45mg; Fibre 0.3g; Sodium 440mg.

RAGOUT OF VEAL

FULL OF FLAVOUR, THIS VEAL, ONION AND PEPPER DISH IS QUICK AND EASY TO PREPARE. USE SMALL CUBES OF PORK FILLET RATHER THAN THE VEAL IF YOU PREFER.

Preparation: 3 minutes; Cooking: 17 minutes

SERVES FOUR

INGREDIENTS
450g/1lb veal fillet or loin
30ml/2 tbsp olive oil
10 –12 tiny onions, kept whole
1 yellow (bell) pepper, seeded and
cut in eight
1 orange or red (bell) pepper, seeded
and cut in eight
3 plum tomatoes, peeled and
quartered
4 fresh basil sprigs
30ml/2 tbsp dry martini or sherry
salt and ground black pepper

1 Trim off any fat and cut the veal into cubes. Heat the oil in a frying pan and gently fry the veal and onions until browned.

2 After a couple of minutes add the peppers and tomatoes. Fry for another 4 minutes.

3 Add half the basil leaves, roughly chopped, the martini or sherry, and seasoning. Cook, stirring frequently, for 10 minutes or until the meat is tender.

4 Sprinkle with the remaining basil leaves and serve hot.

Energy 294kcal/1225kJ; Protein 25.9g; Carbohydrate 13g, of which sugars 11.3g; Fat 14.7g, of which saturates 2.8g; Cholesterol 95mg; Calcium 38mg; Fibre 3g; Sodium 137mg.

PAN-FRIED VEAL CHOPS

VEAL CHOPS FROM THE LOIN ARE AN EXPENSIVE CUT AND ARE BEST COOKED QUICKLY AND SIMPLY SO THAT THEIR SUBTLE FLAVOUR AND TENDERNESS CAN BE ENJOYED AT THEIR FULL.

Preparation: 2 minutes; Cooking: 7–9 minutes

SERVES TWO

INGREDIENTS
  25g/1oz/2 tbsp butter, softened
  15ml/1 tbsp Dijon mustard
  15ml/1 tbsp chopped fresh basil
  olive oil, for brushing
  2 veal loin chops, 2.5cm/1in thick
    (about 225g/8oz each)
  ground black pepper
  fresh basil sprigs, to garnish

1 To make the basil butter, cream the butter with the mustard and chopped basil in a small bowl, then season with pepper.

2 Lightly oil a heavy frying pan or griddle. Set over a high heat until very hot but not smoking. Brush both sides of each chop with a little oil and season with a little pepper.

3 Place the chops in the pan or griddle and reduce the heat to medium. Cook for 4–5 minutes, then turn and cook for 3–4 minutes more until done as preferred (medium-rare meat will still be slightly soft when pressed, medium meat will be springy and well-done meat firm). Top each chop with half the basil butter and serve, garnished with basil.

VARIATION

The flavour of basil goes well with the veal, but rosemary or parsley in the herb butter would also work well.

Energy 349kcal/1459kJ; Protein 48.1g; Carbohydrate 0.8g, of which sugars 0.7g; Fat 17g, of which saturates 8.6g; Cholesterol 216mg; Calcium 26mg; Fibre 0g; Sodium 545mg.

VEAL ESCALOPES WITH TARRAGON

THESE THIN SLICES OF VEAL NEED LITTLE COOKING AND THE SAUCE IS MADE VERY QUICKLY AS WELL.

Preparation: 4 minutes; Cooking: 6 minutes

SERVES TWO

INGREDIENTS
  25g/1oz/2 tbsp butter, softened
  15ml/1 tbsp Dijon mustard
  15ml/1 tbsp chopped fresh basil
  olive oil, for brushing
  2 veal escalopes (US scallops),
    2.5cm/1in thick (about 225g/8oz
    each)
  ground black pepper
  fresh basil sprigs, to garnish

1 Place the veal escalopes between two sheets of clear film (plastic wrap) and pound with the flat side of a meat mallet or roll them with a rolling pin to flatten them out to about 5mm/¼in thickness. Season with salt and ground black pepper.

2 Melt the butter in a large frying pan over a medium-high heat. Add enough meat to the pan to fit easily in one layer (do not overcrowd the pan, cook in batches if necessary) and cook for 1½ –2 minutes, turning once. Each escalope should be lightly browned, but must not be overcooked. Transfer to a platter.

3 Add the brandy to the pan, then pour in the stock and bring to the boil. Add the tarragon and continue boiling until the liquid is reduced by half.

4 Return the veal to the pan with any accumulated juices and heat through. Serve immediately, garnished with tarragon sprigs.

Energy 342kcal/1436kJ; Protein 51.7g; Carbohydrate 0.8g, of which sugars 0.7g; Fat 14.7g, of which saturates 7.9g; Cholesterol 144mg; Calcium 17mg; Fibre 0g; Sodium 430mg.

CALF'S LIVER WITH HONEY

CALF'S LIVER IS THE PERFECT CHOICE FOR A QUICK MEAL, THOUGH LAMB'S LIVER IS ALSO FINE.
ALTHOUGH IT CAN BE BRAISED, IT IS AT ITS BEST WHEN SIMPLY FLASHED IN A HOT PAN.

Preparation: 2 minutes; Cooking: 4–5 minutes

SERVES FOUR

INGREDIENTS
  4 slices calf's liver (about 175g/6oz
    each and 1cm/½ in thick)
  plain (all-purpose) flour, for dusting
  25g/1oz/2 tbsp butter
  30ml/2 tbsp vegetable oil
  30ml/2 tbsp sherry vinegar or
    red wine vinegar
  30–45ml/2–3 tbsp chicken stock
  15ml/1 tbsp clear honey
  salt and ground black pepper
  watercress sprigs, to garnish

1 Wipe the liver slices with damp kitchen paper, then season both sides with a little salt and pepper and dust the slices lightly with flour, shaking off any excess.

2 In a large heavy frying pan, melt half of the butter with the oil over a high heat and swirl to blend thoroughly.

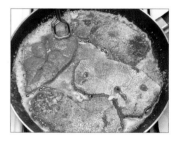

3 Add the liver slices to the pan and cook for 1–2 minutes until browned on one side, then turn and cook for a further 1 minute. Transfer to warmed plates and keep warm.

4 Stir the vinegar, stock and honey into the pan. Boil for about 1 minute, stirring constantly, then add the remaining butter, stirring until smooth. Spoon over the liver and garnish with watercress.

Energy 289kcal/1205kJ; Protein 32.1g; Carbohydrate 2.9g, of which sugars 2.9g; Fat 16.6g, of which saturates 5.8g; Cholesterol 661mg; Calcium 12mg; Fibre 0g; Sodium 163mg.

PORK IN SWEET AND SOUR SAUCE

THE COMBINATION OF SWEET AND SOUR FLAVOURS IS POPULAR IN VENETIAN COOKING, ESPECIALLY WITH MEAT AND LIVER. CRUSHED MIXED PEPPERCORNS ADD EXTRA BITE.

Preparation: 2–3 minutes; Cooking: 6 minutes

SERVES TWO

INGREDIENTS

1 whole pork fillet (tenderloin), about
  350g/12oz
25ml/1½ tbsp plain
  (all-purpose) flour
30–45ml/2–3 tbsp olive oil
250ml/8fl oz/1 cup dry white wine
30ml/2 tbsp white wine vinegar
10ml/2 tsp sugar
15ml/1 tbsp mixed peppercorns,
  coarsely ground
salt and ground black pepper
cooked broad (fava) beans tossed
  with grilled (broiled) bacon, to serve

1 Cut the pork diagonally into thin slices. Place between two sheets of clear film (plastic wrap) and pound lightly with a rolling pin to flatten them.

2 Spread out the flour in a shallow bowl. Season well and coat the meat. Alternatively, put the seasoned flour in a strong plastic bag, add the pork and shake to coat.

COOK'S TIP

Pork fillet (tenderloin) is not a cheap cut of meat but it cooks quickly to give a melting texture and so is worth the cost. If you use a cheaper cut of pork, you will find that it is tough after such a quick time in the frying pan.

3 Heat 15ml/1 tbsp of the oil in a wide heavy pan or frying pan and add as many slices of pork as the pan will hold. Fry over a medium to high heat for 2–3 minutes on each side until crisp and tender. Remove with a fish slice or metal spatula and set aside. Repeat with the remaining pork, adding more oil as necessary.

4 Mix the wine, vinegar and sugar in a measuring jug (cup). Pour into the pan and stir over a high heat until reduced. Stir in the peppercorns and return the pork to the pan. Spoon the sauce over the pork until it is evenly coated and heated through. Serve with cooked broad beans tossed with grilled (broiled) bacon.

Energy 440kcal/1839kJ; Protein 38.3g; Carbohydrate 11.8g, of which sugars 6.1g; Fat 18.1g, of which saturates 4.1g; Cholesterol 110mg; Calcium 37mg; Fibre 0.3g; Sodium 128mg.

PORK <u>WITH</u> CAMEMBERT SAUCE

WHEN IT COMES TO SPEEDY FEASTS, PORK FILLET IS AN EXCELLENT CHOICE. BEAUTIFULLY TENDER, IT NEEDS VERY LITTLE COOKING AND IS DELICIOUS SERVED WITH A CREAMY CHEESE SAUCE.

Preparation: 2 minutes; Cooking: 7–8 minutes

SERVES THREE TO FOUR

INGREDIENTS
350–450g/12oz–1lb pork fillet
   (tenderloin)
15g/½oz/1 tbsp butter
45ml/3 tbsp sparkling dry (hard)
   cider or dry white wine
120–175ml/4–6fl oz/ ½–¾ cup
   crème fraîche or whipping cream
15ml/1 tbsp chopped fresh mixed
   herbs, such as marjoram, thyme
   and sage
½ Camembert cheese (115g/4oz),
   rind removed (65g/2½ oz without
   rind), sliced
7.5ml/1½ tsp Dijon mustard
ground black pepper
fresh parsley, to garnish

1 Slice the pork fillet crossways into small steaks about 2cm/¾in thick. Place between two sheets of clear film (plastic wrap) and pound with the flat side of a meat mallet or roll with a rolling pin to flatten to a thickness of 1cm/½in. Sprinkle with pepper.

2 Melt the butter in a heavy frying pan over a medium-high heat until it begins to brown, then add the meat. Cook for 5 minutes, turning once, or until just cooked through and the meat is springy when pressed. Transfer to a warmed dish and cover to keep warm.

3 Add the cider or wine and bring to the boil, scraping the base of the pan. Stir in the cream and herbs and bring back to the boil.

4 Add the cheese and mustard and any accumulated juices from the meat. Stir until the cheese melts. Add a little more cream if needed and adjust the seasoning. Serve the pork with the sauce and garnish with parsley.

VARIATION
Any creamy cheese that is not too soft can be used instead of Camembert. Try Cambazola or Brie for a change, or perhaps a blue cheese for added flavour.

Energy 358kcal/1484kJ; Protein 25.3g; Carbohydrate 1.1g, of which sugars 1.1g; Fat 26.6g, of which saturates 16g; Cholesterol 121mg; Calcium 100mg; Fibre 0g; Sodium 307mg.

PORK AND PINEAPPLE SATAY

THIS VARIATION ON THE CLASSIC SATAY HAS ADDED PINEAPPLE, BUT KEEPS THE TRADITIONAL COCONUT AND PEANUT SAUCE. IT IS VERY EASY TO MAKE AND TASTES DELICIOUS.

Preparation: 5–8 minutes; Cooking: 15 minutes

SERVES FOUR

INGREDIENTS
500g/1¼lb pork fillet (tenderloin)
1 small onion, chopped
1 garlic clove, chopped
60ml/4 tbsp soy sauce
finely grated rind of ½ lemon
5ml/1 tsp ground cumin
5ml/1 tsp ground coriander
5ml/1 tsp ground turmeric
5ml/1 tsp dark muscovado sugar
  (molasses)
225g/8oz can pineapple chunks, or
  1 small fresh pineapple, peeled
  and diced
parsley, to garnish
For the satay sauce
175ml/6fl oz/¾ cup coconut milk
115g/4oz/⅓ cup crunchy
  peanut butter
1 garlic clove, crushed
10ml/2 tsp soy sauce
5ml/1 tsp dark muscovado sugar

1 Trim any fat from the pork fillet and cut it into 2.5cm/1in cubes. Place the meat in a large bowl.

2 Place the onion, garlic, soy sauce, lemon rind, spices and sugar in a blender or food processor. Add two pieces of pineapple and process until the mixture is well combined and almost smooth.

3 Add the paste to the pork, tossing well to coat evenly. Thread the pieces of pork on to bamboo skewers, with the remaining pineapple chunks. Preheat the grill (broiler) or light the barbecue.

COOK'S TIP
If you cannot buy coconut milk, look out for creamed coconut in a block. Stir a 50g/2oz piece in 150ml/¼ pint/¾ cup boiling water until dissolved. Alternatively, use 150ml/¼ pint/¾ cup coconut cream.

4 To make the satay sauce, pour the coconut milk into a small pan and stir in the peanut butter. Stir in the remaining sauce ingredients and heat gently on the hob or over the barbecue, stirring until smooth and hot. Cover and keep warm.

5 Cook the pork and pineapple skewers under the grill (broiler) or on a medium-hot barbecue for 10–12 minutes, turning occasionally, until golden brown and thoroughly cooked. Garnish with parsley and serve with the satay sauce.

Energy 373kcal/1560kJ; Protein 33.8g; Carbohydrate 15.2g, of which sugars 13g; Fat 20.1g, of which saturates 5.5g; Cholesterol 79mg; Calcium 41mg; Fibre 2.1g; Sodium 415mg.

LEMON GRASS AND GINGER PORK BURGERS

LEMON GRASS LENDS A FRAGRANT CITRUS FLAVOUR TO PORK AND IS ENHANCED BY THE FRESH ZING OF GINGER. SERVE THE BURGERS IN BURGER BUNS WITH TOMATO, CRISP LETTUCE AND SOME CHILLI SAUCE.

Preparation: 5 minutes; Cooking: 6–8 minutes

SERVES FOUR

INGREDIENTS
    450g/1lb/2 cups minced
    (ground) pork
    15ml/1 tbsp grated fresh root ginger
    1 lemon grass stalk, outer layers
    discarded and centre part
    chopped finely
    30ml/2 tbsp sunflower oil
    salt and ground black pepper
To serve
    juicy tomatoes, thickly sliced
    crisp lettuce leaves
    chilli sauce

COOK'S TIP
Chilling the burgers helps them to maintain their shape.

1 Put the pork in a bowl and stir in the ginger and chopped lemon grass. Season with salt and pepper. Shape the mixture into four burgers and chill for about 20 minutes.

2 Heat the oil in a large, non-stick frying pan and add the burgers. Fry for 3–4 minutes on each side over a gentle heat, until cooked through. Remove from the pan with a metal spatula and drain on kitchen paper, then serve with sliced tomato, lettuce and chilli sauce.

Energy 234kcal/974kJ; Protein 21.6g; Carbohydrate 0g, of which sugars 0g; Fat 16.4g, of which saturates 4.7g; Cholesterol 74mg; Calcium 8mg; Fibre 0g; Sodium 74mg.

PAN-FRIED GAMMON <u>WITH</u> CIDER

GAMMON AND CIDER ARE A DELICIOUS COMBINATION, SINCE THE SWEET, TANGY FLAVOUR OF CIDER COMPLEMENTS THE GAMMON PERFECTLY. SERVE WITH MUSTARD MASHED POTATOES.

Preparation: 1 minute; Cooking: 7–10 minutes

SERVES FOUR

INGREDIENTS
4 gammon (smoked or cured ham) steaks, 225g/8oz each
150ml/¼ pint/⅔ cup dry (hard) cider
45ml/3 tbsp double (heavy) cream
30ml/2 tbsp sunflower oil
salt and ground black pepper
flat leaf parsley, to garnish
mustard mashed potatoes, to serve

COOK'S TIP
Cooking gammon (smoked or cured ham) in a liquid is a good way of ensuring it stays moist and soft-textured.

1 Heat the oil in a large frying pan until hot. Neatly snip the rind on the gammon steaks to stop them curling up and add them to the pan.

2 Cook the steaks for 3–4 minutes on each side, then pour in the cider. Allow to boil for a couple of minutes, then stir in the cream and cook for 1–2 minutes, or until thickened. Season with salt and pepper, and serve immediately.

Energy 429kcal/1784kJ; Protein 39.6g; Carbohydrate 1.2g, of which sugars 1.2g; Fat 28.4g, of which saturates 10.1g; Cholesterol 67mg; Calcium 24mg; Fibre 0g; Sodium 1985mg.

PORK WITH MARSALA AND JUNIPER

ALTHOUGH MOST FREQUENTLY USED IN DESSERTS, SICILIAN MARSALA GIVES SAVOURY DISHES A RICH, FRUITY AND ALCOHOLIC TANG, BRINGING OUT THE FLAVOUR OF THE PORK PERFECTLY.

Preparation: 4 minutes; Cooking: 15 minutes

SERVES FOUR

INGREDIENTS

25g/1oz/½ cup dried cep or
  porcini mushrooms
4 pork escalopes (US scallops)
10ml/2 tsp balsamic vinegar
8 garlic cloves
15g/½ oz/1 tbsp butter
45ml/3 tbsp Marsala
several fresh rosemary sprigs
10 juniper berries, crushed
salt and ground black pepper
noodles and green vegetables,
  to serve

1 Put the dried mushrooms in a bowl and just cover with hot water. Leave to stand. Bring a small pan of water to the boil and add the garlic cloves. Cook for 10 minutes until soft. Drain, put the garlic in a bowl and set aside.

COOK'S TIPS
• Use good quality butcher's pork, which won't be overwhelmed by the intense flavour of the sauce.
• Juniper berries are the principal flavouring for gin. When added to meat, they impart a gamey flavour.

2 Meanwhile, place the pork escalopes on a board, brush with 5ml/1 tsp of the vinegar and add a generous and even grinding of salt and black pepper.

3 Melt the butter in a large frying pan. Add the pork and fry quickly until browned on the underside. Turn the meat over and cook for another minute.

4 Add the Marsala and rosemary to the pan. Drain the dried mushrooms, saving the juices, and add them to the mixture. Stir in 60ml/4 tbsp of the mushroom juices, then add the garlic cloves, juniper berries and remaining vinegar.

5 Simmer the mixture gently for about 3 minutes until the pork is cooked. Season lightly and serve hot with noodles and vegetables.

Energy 282kcal/1176kJ; Protein 32.2g; Carbohydrate 0.9g, of which sugars 0.9g; Fat 15.3g, of which saturates 8g; Cholesterol 118mg; Calcium 13mg; Fibre 0g; Sodium 175mg.

PORK SCHNITZEL

THIS CROATIAN DISH PROVIDES A HEARTY MEAL CONTAINING STRONG FLAVOURS. THE SCHNITZELS ARE TASTY IN THEMSELVES, BUT THE RICH BACON AND MUSHROOM SAUCE ROUNDS THE DISH OFF PERFECTLY.

Preparation: 10 minutes; Cooking: 16–22 minutes

SERVES FOUR

INGREDIENTS

4 pork leg steaks or escalopes (US scallops), about 200g/7oz each
60ml/4 tbsp olive oil
115g/4oz chicken livers, chopped
1 garlic clove, crushed
plain (all-purpose) flour, seasoned, for coating
salt and freshly ground black pepper
15ml/1 tbsp chopped fresh parsley to garnish

For the sauce

1 onion, thinly sliced
115g/4oz streaky (fatty) bacon, thinly sliced
175g/6oz/2 cups mixed wild mushrooms, sliced
120ml/4fl oz/½ cup olive oil
5ml/1 tsp ready-made mustard
150ml/¼ pint/⅔ cup white wine
120ml/4fl oz/½ cup sour cream
250ml/8fl oz/1 cup double (heavy) cream
salt and freshly ground black pepper

1 Place the pork between 2 sheets of clear film (plastic wrap) and flatten with a meat mallet or rolling pin until about 15 x 10cm/6 x 4in. Season well.

2 Heat half the oil in a frying pan and cook the chicken livers and garlic for 1–2 minutes. Remove, drain on kitchen paper and leave to cool.

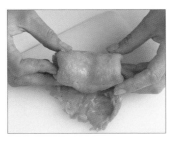

3 Divide the livers evenly between the four prepared pork steaks and roll up into neat parcels. Secure with cocktail sticks (toothpicks) or string before rolling lightly in the seasoned flour.

4 Heat the remaining oil and gently fry the schnitzels for 6–8 minutes on each side, or until golden brown. Drain on kitchen paper and keep warm.

5 Meanwhile, to make the sauce, fry the onion, bacon and mushrooms in the oil for 2–3 minutes, then add the mustard, white wine and sour cream. Stir to simmering point, then add the double cream and season.

6 Arrange the schnitzels on plates with a little of the sauce spooned around and the rest poured into a serving jug (pitcher). Garnish with the parsley.

COOK'S TIP
If you like, replace the pork with veal or chicken and cook in the same way.

Energy 1025kcal/4242kJ; Protein 55.3g; Carbohydrate 3.8g, of which sugars 3.4g; Fat 85g, of which saturates 34.3g; Cholesterol 358mg; Calcium 87mg; Fibre 0.7g; Sodium 554mg.

OMELETTE WRAPS

Cut open these neat parcels to reveal the flavoursome pork filling. They are perfect for an impromptu supper and are so easy to make that you won't mind offering seconds.

Preparation: 2–4 minutes; Cooking: 16–18 minutes

SERVES FOUR

INGREDIENTS

30ml/2 tbsp vegetable oil
2 garlic cloves, finely chopped
1 small onion, finely chopped
225g/8oz/2 cups minced (ground) pork
30ml/2 tbsp Thai fish sauce
5ml/1 tsp sugar
2 tomatoes, peeled and chopped
15ml/1 tbsp chopped fresh coriander (cilantro)
ground black pepper
sprigs of coriander and fresh red chillies, sliced, to garnish
For the omelettes
5–6 eggs
15ml/1 tbsp Thai fish sauce
30ml/2 tbsp vegetable oil

1 Heat the oil in a wok, add the garlic and onion, and fry for 2 minutes until soft. Add the pork and fry for about 8 minutes until lightly browned.

2 Stir in the fish sauce, sugar, tomatoes and black pepper; simmer until slightly thickened. Mix in the fresh coriander.

3 To make the omelettes, whisk together the eggs and fish sauce.

4 Heat 15ml/1 tbsp of the oil in an omelette pan or wok. Add half the beaten egg mixture and tilt the pan to spread the egg into a thin, even sheet.

5 Cook until the omelette is just set, then spoon half the filling into the centre. Fold into a neat square parcel by bringing the opposite sides of the omelette towards each other – first the top and bottom, then the right and left sides.

6 Slide the parcel on to a warm serving dish, folded side down. Repeat with the rest of the oil, eggs and filling to make a second omelette parcel. Garnish with sprigs of coriander and red chillies. Cut each omelette in half to serve.

COOK'S TIP

For a milder flavour, discard the seeds and membrane of the chillies, where most of their heat resides. Always wash your hands after handling chillies.

Energy 319kcal/1327kJ; Protein 20.7g; Carbohydrate 3.8g, of which sugars 3.4g; Fat 25g, of which saturates 5.7g; Cholesterol 323mg; Calcium 55mg; Fibre 0.7g; Sodium 147mg

PORK WITH CREAM AND APPLE SAUCE

TENDER NOISETTES OF PORK IN A CREAMY LEEK AND APPLE SAUCE MAKE A GREAT DINNER PARTY DISH.
USE THE SAME WHITE WINE AS THE ONE YOU PLAN TO SERVE WITH THE MEAL, OR TRY CIDER.

Preparation: 2 minutes; Cooking: 18 minutes

SERVES FOUR

INGREDIENTS

30ml/2 tbsp plain (all-purpose) flour
4 noisettes of pork, firmly tied
25g/1oz/2 tbsp butter
4 baby leeks, finely sliced
5ml/1 tsp mustard seeds,
  coarsely crushed
150ml/¼ pint/⅔ cup dry white wine
2 eating apples
150ml/¼ pint/⅔ cup double
  (heavy) cream
30ml/2 tbsp chopped fresh parsley
salt and ground black pepper
To serve
  red cabbage
  fried polenta

1 Place the flour in a bowl and add plenty of seasoning. Turn the noisettes in the flour mixture to coat them lightly.

2 Melt the butter in a heavy frying pan and cook the noisettes for 1 minute on each side.

3 Add the sliced leeks to the pan and cook for 3 minutes. Stir in the mustard seeds. Pour in the wine. Cook gently for 10 minutes, turning the pork occasionally. Peel, core and slice the apples.

VARIATION

Use thin slices of pork fillet (tenderloin) for even faster cooking.

4 Add the sliced apples and double cream and simmer for 3 minutes, or until the pork is fully cooked and the sauce is thick, rich and creamy. Taste for seasoning, then stir in the chopped parsley and serve at once.

Energy 415kcal/1724kJ; Protein 23.1g; Carbohydrate 8.8g, of which sugars 4.4g; Fat 29.5g, of which saturates 17.2g; Cholesterol 128mg; Calcium 45mg; Fibre 1.3g; Sodium 119mg

PORK AND PINEAPPLE COCONUT CURRY

THE HEAT OF THIS CURRY BALANCES OUT ITS SWEETNESS TO MAKE A FRAGRANT DISH. IT TAKES LITTLE TIME TO COOK, SO IS IDEAL FOR A QUICK SUPPER BEFORE GOING OUT FOR THE EVENING.

Preparation: 3 minutes; Cooking: 17 minutes

SERVES FOUR

INGREDIENTS

400ml/14fl oz coconut milk
10ml/2 tsp Thai red curry paste
400g/14oz pork loin steaks,
  trimmed and thinly sliced
15ml/1 tbsp Thai fish sauce
5ml/1 tsp palm sugar (jaggery) or
  light muscovado (brown) sugar
15ml/1 tbsp tamarind juice, made
  by mixing tamarind paste with
  warm water
2 kaffir lime leaves, torn
½ medium pineapple
1 fresh red chilli, seeded and
  finely chopped

1 Pour the coconut milk into a bowl and let it settle, so that the cream rises to the surface. Scoop the cream into a measuring jug (cup). You should have about 250ml/8fl oz/1 cup. If necessary, add a little of the coconut milk.

2 Pour the coconut cream into a large pan and bring it to the boil.

3 Cook the coconut cream for about 8 minutes, until the cream separates, stirring frequently to prevent it from sticking to the base of the pan. Peel and chop the pineapple.

4 Ladle a little of the coconut cream into a bowl and stir in the red curry paste. Return the mixture to the pan and stir until well mixed. Cook, stirring occasionally, for about 3 minutes, until the paste is fragrant.

5 Add the sliced pork and stir in the fish sauce, sugar and tamarind juice. Cook, stirring constantly, for 2–3 minutes, until the sugar has dissolved and the pork is no longer pink.

6 Add the remaining coconut milk and the lime leaves. Bring to the boil, then stir in the pineapple. Reduce the heat and simmer gently for 3 minutes, or until the pork is fully cooked. Sprinkle over the chilli and serve.

Energy 187kcal/790kJ; Protein 22.2g; Carbohydrate 15.3g, of which sugars 15.3g; Fat 4.5g, of which saturates 1.6g; Cholesterol 63mg; Calcium 55mg; Fibre 1.2g; Sodium 449mg

SWEET AND SOUR PORK THAI-STYLE

IT WAS THE CHINESE WHO ORIGINALLY CREATED SWEET AND SOUR COOKING, BUT THE THAIS ALSO DO IT VERY WELL. THIS VERSION HAS A FRESHER AND CLEANER FLAVOUR THAN THE CHINESE VERSION.

Preparation: 6 minutes; Cooking: 13 minutes

SERVES FOUR

INGREDIENTS

350g/12oz lean pork
30ml/2 tbsp vegetable oil
4 garlic cloves, thinly sliced
1 small red onion, sliced
30ml/2 tbsp Thai fish sauce
15ml/1 tbsp sugar
1 red (bell) pepper, seeded and diced
½ cucumber, seeded and very
  thinly sliced
2 plum tomatoes, cut into wedges
115g/4oz piece fresh pineapple,
  cut into small chunks
2 spring onions (scallions), cut into
  short lengths
ground black pepper
To garnish
  coriander (cilantro) leaves
  spring onions (scallions), shredded

1 Cut the pork into thin strips. This is easier to do if you freeze it for 30 minutes first.

2 Heat the oil in a wok or large frying pan. Add the garlic. Cook over a medium heat until golden, then add the pork and stir-fry for 4–5 minutes. Add the onion slices and toss to mix.

3 Add the fish sauce, sugar and ground black pepper to taste. Toss the mixture over the heat for 3–4 minutes more.

4 Stir in the red pepper, cucumber, tomatoes, pineapple and spring onions. Stir-fry for 3–4 minutes more, then spoon into a bowl. Garnish with the coriander and spring onions and serve.

Energy 211kcal/885kJ; Protein 20g; Carbohydrate 12.4g, of which sugars 11.8g; Fat 9.4g, of which saturates 2g; Cholesterol 55mg; Calcium 29mg; Fibre 1.8g; Sodium 68mg

FRIED PORK WITH SCRAMBLED EGG

WHEN YOU NEED A TASTY MEAL BEFORE GOING OUT FOR THE EVENING, THIS QUICK-TO-PREPARE AND EASY-RICE DISH, WITH JUST A LITTLE MEAT, IS THE ANSWER.

Preparation: 5 minutes; Cooking: 12 minutes

SERVES FOUR

INGREDIENTS

2 x 250g/9oz sachets quick-cook rice
45ml/3 tbsp vegetable oil
1 onion, chopped
15ml/1 tbsp chopped garlic
115g/4oz pork, cut into small cubes
2 eggs, beaten
30ml/2 tbsp Thai fish sauce
15ml/1 tbsp dark soy sauce
2.5ml/½ tsp caster (superfine) sugar
For the garnish
4 spring onions (scallions),
   finely sliced
2 fresh red chillies, sliced
1 lime, cut into wedges

1 Cook the rice according to the instructions on the packet. Spread out and leave to cool.

2 Heat the oil in a wok or large frying pan. Add the onion and garlic and cook for about 2 minutes, until softened.

3 Add the pork to the softened onion and garlic. Stir-fry until the pork changes colour and is cooked.

4 Add the eggs and cook until scrambled into small lumps.

5 Add the rice and continue to stir and toss, to coat it with the oil and prevent it from sticking.

6 Stir in the fish sauce, soy sauce and sugar and mix well. Continue to fry until the rice is thoroughly heated. Spoon into warmed individual bowls and serve, garnished with sliced spring onions, chillies and lime wedges.

Energy 602kcal/2512kJ; Protein 18.8g; Carbohydrate 101.3g, of which sugars 1.1g; Fat 12.8g, of which saturates 2.2g; Cholesterol 113mg; Calcium 45mg; Fibre 0.2g; Sodium 323mg

PORK KEBABS <u>WITH</u> BBQ SAUCE

USE PORK FILLET FOR THESE KEBABS BECAUSE IT IS LEAN AND TENDER AND COOKS VERY QUICKLY.
THE KEBABS ARE GOOD SERVED WITH RICE, OR IN WARMED PITTA BREAD WITH LETTUCE.

Preparation: 3–4 minutes; Cooking: 10 minutes

SERVES FOUR

INGREDIENTS

500g/1¼lb lean pork fillet
(tenderloin)
8 large, thick spring onions
(scallions)
120ml/4fl oz/½ cup barbecue sauce
1 lemon, cut into wedges, to garnish

VARIATION

This is an unusual kebab recipe, in that the cubes of pork are threaded on to the skewers only after cooking. This is because the meat is regularly dipped in glaze, and it is easier to get an all-round coating if the cubes of pork are free. If you prefer to assemble the skewers first and cook them on the barbecue, do so. Use metal skewers, which will not char, and baste frequently with the sauce.

1 Cut the pork into 2.5cm/1in cubes. Cut the spring onions into 2.5cm/1in-long sticks.

2 Preheat the grill (broiler) to high. Oil the wire rack and spread out the pork cubes on it. Grill (broil) the pork until the juices drip, then dip the pieces in the barbecue sauce and put back on the grill. Grill until cooked through, repeating the dipping process twice more. Set aside and keep warm.

3 Trim the spring onions and gently grill until soft and slightly brown on the outside. Do not dip in the barbecue sauce. Thread about four pieces of pork and three spring onion pieces on to each of eight bamboo skewers.

4 Arrange the skewers on a platter. Squeeze a little lemon juice over each skewer. Serve immediately, offering the remaining lemon wedges separately.

Energy 192kcal/806kJ; Protein 27.6g; Carbohydrate 9.2g, of which sugars 8.8g; Fat 5.1g, of which saturates 1.8g; Cholesterol 79mg; Calcium 21mg; Fibre 0.6g; Sodium 578mg

BACON CHOPS WITH APPLE AND CIDER SAUCE

EITHER THICK BACON OR PORK CHOPS COULD BE USED IN THIS RECIPE, WHICH BRINGS THE
TRADITIONAL INGREDIENTS OF PORK AND APPLES TOGETHER IN AN ATTRACTIVE DISH.

Preparation: 5 minutes; Cooking: 20–25 minutes

SERVES FOUR

INGREDIENTS
  15ml/1 tbsp oil
  4 bacon chops
  1 or 2 cooking apples, peeled,
    cored and sliced
  knob (pat) of butter
  1 or 2 garlic cloves,
    finely chopped
  5ml/1 tsp sugar
  150ml/¼ pint/⅔ cup dry
    (hard) cider
  5ml/1 tsp cider vinegar
  15ml/1 tbsp wholegrain mustard
  10ml/2 tsp chopped fresh thyme
  salt and ground black pepper
  sprigs of thyme, to garnish
To serve
  mashed potatoes
  steamed buttered cabbage

1 Heat the oil in a large heavy frying pan over a medium heat, and cook the chops for 10–15 minutes, browning well on both sides. Remove the chops from the pan and keep warm.

2 Add the butter and apples to the frying pan and cook until the juices begin to turn brown.

3 Add the garlic and sugar, and cook for 1 minute, then stir in the cider, cider vinegar, mustard and chopped thyme. Boil for a few minutes until reduced to a saucy consistency. Season to taste.

4 Place the chops on warmed serving plates, spoon over the sauce, garnish with the thyme sprigs and serve.

Energy 1140Kcal/4760kJ; Protein 105.6g; Carbohydrate 26g, of which sugars 26gg; Fat 64.4g, of which saturates 21.6g; Cholesterol 160mg; Calcium 68mg; Fibre 3.2g; Sodium 536mg

BACON SALAD WITH CAMEMBERT DRESSING

FRIED APPLES AND BACON ARE PERFECT PARTNERS. HERE THEY ARE HEAPED OVER CRISP LETTUCE TO
MAKE AN IRRESISTIBLE SALAD. A WARM TANGY CHEESE DRESSING ADDS THE FINISHING TOUCH.

Preparation: 5 minutes; Cooking: 4–5 minutes

SERVES FOUR

INGREDIENTS
- 30ml/2 tbsp olive oil
- 50g/2oz diced streaky (fatty) bacon slices, preferably dry-cured, diced
- 1 eating apple, cored and chopped
- 2 small heads cos or romaine lettuce
- a squeeze of lemon juice
- salt and ground black pepper

For the dressing
- 150ml/¼ pint/⅔ cup sour cream
- 15ml/1 tbsp cider
- 50g/2oz Camembert or similar cheese, chopped
- a dash of cider vinegar

VARIATION

For a slightly tangier topping, replace the Camembert with a mild and creamy blue cheese, such as Cambozola.

1 Heat 15ml/1 tbsp of the olive oil in a large frying pan and add the diced streaky bacon. Cook over a medium heat until crisp and golden. Add the apple and cook gently for 1–2 minutes until golden brown and softened.

2 Tear the cos or romain lettuce carefully into bitesize pieces.

3 To make the dressing, heat the ingredients together in a small pan over a low heat until smooth and creamy.

4 Toss the lettuce with the remaining oil and the lemon juice, season, then divide among four plates. Heap the warm apple and bacon on top, then drizzle over the dressing.

Energy 190kcal/785kJ; Protein 5.9g; Carbohydrate 3.5g, of which sugars 3.5g; Fat 16.7g, of which saturates 8.4g; Cholesterol 42mg; Calcium 76mg; Fibre 0.5g; Sodium 244mg

WARM SALAD OF HAM AND NEW POTATOES

WITH A LIGHTLY SPICED NUTTY DRESSING, THIS WARM SALAD IS AS DELICIOUS AS IT IS FASHIONABLE,
AND AN EXCELLENT CHOICE FOR A CASUAL SUMMER SUPPER WITH FRIENDS.

Preparation: 3 minutes; Cooking: 15–17 minutes

SERVES FOUR

INGREDIENTS
    225g/8oz new potatoes, halved
       if large
    50g/2oz green beans
    115g/4oz baby spinach leaves
    2 spring onions (scallions), sliced
    4 eggs, hard-boiled and quartered
    50g/2oz cooked ham, cut into strips
    juice of ½ lemon
    salt and ground black pepper
For the dressing
    60ml/4 tbsp olive oil
    5ml/1 tsp ground turmeric
    5ml/1 tsp ground cumin
    50g/2oz/⅓ cup shelled hazelnuts

1 Cook the potatoes in boiling salted water for 10–15 minutes, or until tender. Meanwhile, cook the beans in boiling salted water for 2 minutes.

2 Drain the potatoes and beans. Toss with the spinach and spring onions.

3 Arrange the hard-boiled egg quarters on the salad and sprinkle the strips of ham over the top. Drizzle with the lemon juice and season with plenty of salt and pepper.

4 Heat the dressing ingredients in a large frying pan and continue to cook, stirring frequently, until the nuts turn golden. Pour the hot, nutty dressing over the salad and serve immediately.

VARIATION
An even quicker salad can be made by using a 400g/14oz can of mixed beans and pulses instead of the potatoes. Drain and rinse the beans and pulses, then drain again.

Energy 318kcal/1319kJ; Protein 12.4g; Carbohydrate 11g, of which sugars 2.2g; Fat 25.4g, of which saturates 4g; Cholesterol 198mg; Calcium 106mg; Fibre 2.3g; Sodium 268mg

CRUNCHY SALAD <u>WITH</u> BLACK PUDDING

*HIGHLY FLAVOURED BLACK PUDDING IS A SPICY SAUSAGE ENRICHED WITH BLOOD. THIS PUTS SOME
PEOPLE OFF, WHICH IS A PITY AS IT HAS A GREAT FLAVOUR. IT IS THE STAR OF THIS SIMPLE SALAD.*

Preparation: 4 minutes; Cooking: 8–12 minutes

SERVES FOUR

INGREDIENTS
250g/9oz black pudding
(blood sausage), sliced
1 focaccia loaf, plain or flavoured
with sun-dried tomatoes, garlic
and herbs, cut into chunks
45ml/3 tbsp olive oil
1 cos or romaine lettuce, torn into
bitesize pieces
250g/9oz cherry tomatoes, halved
For the dressing
juice of 1 lemon
90ml/6 tbsp olive oil
10ml/2 tsp French mustard
15ml/1 tbsp clear honey
30ml/2 tbsp chopped fresh herbs,
such as coriander (cilantro),
chives and parsley
salt and ground black pepper

1 Dry-fry the black pudding in a large, non-stick frying pan for 5–10 minutes, or until browned and crisp, turning occasionally. Remove the black pudding from the pan using a slotted spoon and drain on kitchen paper. Set the black pudding aside and keep warm.

VARIATION
If black pudding (blood sausage) isn't your thing, try this recipe with spicy chorizo or kabanos sausages instead. Cut them into thick diagonal slices before cooking. Use a similar type of crusty bread, such as ciabatta, for the croûtons, if you prefer.

2 Cut the focaccia into chunks. Add the oil to the juices in the frying pan and cook the focaccia cubes in two batches, turning often, until golden on all sides. Lift out the focaccia chunks and drain on kitchen paper.

3 Mix together all the focaccia, black pudding, lettuce and cherry tomatoes in a large bowl. Mix together the dressing ingredients and season with salt and pepper. Pour the dressing over the salad. Mix well and serve at once.

Energy 641kcal/2674kJ; Protein 15.1g; Carbohydrate 55g, of which sugars 8.1g; Fat 41.6g, of which saturates 9.4g; Cholesterol 43mg; Calcium 196mg; Fibre 3.2g; Sodium 1001mg

HOME-MADE VENISON SAUSAGES

VENISON SAUSAGES HAVE AN EXCELLENT FLAVOUR, A MUCH LOWER FAT CONTENT THAN MOST SAUSAGES AND THEY'RE EASY TO MAKE IF YOU FORGET ABOUT SAUSAGE SKINS AND JUST SHAPE THE MIXTURE.

Preparation: 5 minutes; Cooking: 12 minutes

MAKES 1.4KG/3LB

INGREDIENTS
  900g/2lb finely minced
    (ground) venison
  450g/1lb finely minced
    (ground) belly of pork
  15ml/1 tbsp salt
  10ml/2 tsp ground black pepper
  1 garlic clove, crushed
  5ml/1 tsp dried thyme
  1 egg, beaten
  plain (all-purpose) flour, for dusting
  oil, for frying
To serve
  fried onions
  grilled (broiled) tomatoes
  grilled (broiled) field (portabello)
    mushrooms

1 Combine all the sausage ingredients, except the flour and oil, in a bowl. Take a small piece of the mixture and fry it in a little oil in a heavy frying pan, then taste to check the seasoning for the batch. Adjust if necessary.

2 Form the mixture into chipolata-size sausages using floured hands.

3 Heat the oil in a large, heavy frying pan and shallow-fry the sausages for 10 minutes or until they are golden brown and cooked right through.

4 If you use a large pan, you'll be able to fry some onion rings alongside the sausages. At the same time, grill (broil) mushrooms and halved tomatoes to serve on the side.

COOK'S TIP
If you find yourself with more sausages than you need for one meal, freeze the surplus in an airtight container for no more than a month. Be sure to thaw the sausages completely before cooking.

Energy 1747kcal/7356kJ; Protein 302.4g; Carbohydrate 0g, of which sugars 0g; Fat 65.3g, of which saturates 17.6g; Cholesterol 924mg; Calcium 105mg; Fibre 0g; Sodium 880mg

FLAMENCO EGGS

THIS ADAPTABLE DISH IS A SWIRL OF RED, GREEN, YELLOW AND WHITE. YOU CAN USE DIFFERENT VEGETABLES, BUT SHOULD ALWAYS INCLUDE THE CHORIZO FOR ITS FLAVOUR.

Preparation: 4–5 minutes; Cooking: 15 minutes

SERVES FOUR

INGREDIENTS
    30ml/2 tbsp olive oil
    115g/4oz diced smoked bacon
      or pancetta
    2 chorizos, cubed
    1 onion, chopped
    2 garlic cloves, finely chopped
    1 red and 1 green (bell) pepper,
      seeded and chopped
    500g/1¼lb tomatoes, chopped
    15–30ml/1–2 tbsp fino sherry
    45ml/3 tbsp chopped parsley
    8 large (US extra large) eggs
    salt, paprika and cayenne pepper
For the garlic crumbs
    4 thick slices stale bread
    oil, for frying
    2 garlic cloves, bruised

1 Preheat the oven to 180°C/350°F/Gas 4. Warm four individual baking dishes.

2 Heat the oil in a large pan and fry the diced bacon and chorizo until they yield their fat. Add the onion and garlic and cook gently until softened, stirring.

3 Add the peppers and tomatoes and cook to reduce, stirring occasionally. Add some paprika and stir in the sherry.

COOK'S TIP
The chorizo and vegetable mixture mustn't be too dry, so add a little more sherry if necessary.

4 Divide the vegetable mixture evenly among the baking dishes. Sprinkle with parsley. Swirl the eggs together with a fork (without overmixing) and season well with salt and cayenne. Pour over the vegetable mixture.

5 Bake the eggs and vegetables for 8 minutes, or until the eggs are just set.

6 Meanwhile make the garlic crumbs. Cut the crusts off the bread and reduce to crumbs in a food processor, or use a hand grater.

7 Heat plenty of oil in a large frying pan over a high heat, add the garlic cloves for a few moments to flavour it, then remove and discard them. Throw in the breadcrumbs and brown quickly, scooping them out on to kitchen paper with a slotted spoon. Season with a little salt and paprika, then sprinkle them around the edge of the eggs, when ready to serve.

Energy 597kcal/2485kJ; Protein 27.3g; Carbohydrate 28g, of which sugars 11.1g; Fat 42.4g, of which saturates 11.7g; Cholesterol 429mg; Calcium 163mg; Fibre 3.2g; Sodium 1116mg

LAMB STEAKS WITH REDCURRANT GLAZE

GOOD AND MEATY, BUT THIN ENOUGH TO COOK QUICKLY, LAMB LEG STEAKS ARE A GOOD CHOICE FOR THE COOK SHORT ON TIME. THE REDCURRANT AND ROSEMARY GLAZE LOOKS GORGEOUS.

Preparation: 2–3 minutes; Cooking: 10 minutes

SERVES FOUR

INGREDIENTS
  4 large fresh rosemary sprigs
  4 lamb leg steaks
  75ml/5 tbsp redcurrant jelly
  30ml/2 tbsp raspberry or
    red wine vinegar

1 Reserve the tips of the rosemary and finely chop the remaining leaves. Rub the chopped rosemary, salt and pepper all over the lamb.

2 Preheat the grill (broiler). Heat the redcurrant jelly gently in a small pan with 30ml/2 tbsp water and a little seasoning. Stir in the vinegar.

3 Place the lamb steaks on a foil-lined grill (broiling) rack and brush with a little of the redcurrant glaze. Cook under the grill for about 5 minutes on each side, until deep golden, brushing frequently with more redcurrant glaze.

4 Transfer the lamb to warmed plates. Tip any juices from the foil into the remaining glaze and heat through gently. Pour the glaze over the lamb and serve with peas and new potatoes, garnished with the reserved rosemary sprigs.

COOK'S TIP
This is a good recipe for the barbecue. Wait until the fierce heat has subsided and the coals are dusted with white ash, then place the rosemary-rubbed steaks directly on the grill rack. Brush frequently with the glaze as they cook. If you grow your own rosemary, try sprinkling some over the coals. As the oil in the herb warms, the scent of rosemary will perfume the air.

Energy 362kcal/1518kJ; Protein 34.4g; Carbohydrate 13g, of which sugars 13g; Fat 19.6g, of which saturates 9.1g; Cholesterol 133mg; Calcium 16mg; Fibre 0g; Sodium 156mg

BARBECUED LAMB <u>WITH</u> RED PEPPER SALSA

VIBRANT RED PEPPER SALSA BRINGS OUT THE BEST IN SUCCULENT LAMB STEAKS TO MAKE A DISH THAT LOOKS AS GOOD AS IT TASTES. SERVE A SELECTION OF SALADS AND CRUSTY BREAD WITH THE LAMB.

Preparation: 3 minutes; Cooking: 4–10 minutes; Marinating for 24 hours recommended

SERVES SIX

INGREDIENTS
  6 lamb steaks
  about 15g/½oz/½ cup fresh
    rosemary sprigs
  2 garlic cloves, sliced
  60ml/4 tbsp olive oil
  30ml/2 tbsp maple syrup
  salt and ground black pepper
For the salsa
  200g/7oz red (bell) peppers,
    roasted, peeled, seeded
    and chopped
  1 garlic clove, crushed
  15ml/1 tbsp chopped chives
  30ml/2 tbsp extra virgin olive oil
  fresh flat leaf parsley, to garnish

1 Place the lamb steaks in a dish and season with salt and pepper. Pull the leaves off the rosemary and sprinkle them over the meat.

2 Add the slices of garlic, then drizzle the olive oil and maple syrup over the top. Cover and chill until ready to cook. If you have time, the lamb can be left to marinate in the fridge for up to 24 hours.

3 Make sure the steaks are liberally coated with the marinating ingredients, then cook them over a hot barbecue for 2–5 minutes on each side. The cooking time depends on the heat of the barbecue coals and the thickness of the steaks as well as the result required – rare, medium or well cooked.

4 While the lamb steaks are cooking, mix together all the ingredients for the salsa in a bowl. Serve the salsa spooned on to the plates with the meat or in a small serving dish on the side. Garnish the lamb with sprigs of flat leaf parsley and serve with a cool, crisp salad – iceberg lettuce would be ideal.

Energy 390kcal/1627kJ; Protein 44.1g; Carbohydrate 2.1g, of which sugars 2g; Fat 22.8g, of which saturates 6.8g; Cholesterol 158mg; Calcium 33mg; Fibre 0.5g; Sodium 106mg

LAMB'S KIDNEYS WITH MUSTARD SAUCE

This piquant recipe is simple and flexible, so the exact amounts of any one ingredient are unimportant. It makes a tasty first course but would be equally suitable as a supper dish.

Preparation: 5 minutes; Cooking: 5 minutes

SERVES FOUR

INGREDIENTS
4–6 lamb's kidneys
butter, for frying
Dijon mustard or other mild mustard,
   to taste
250ml/8fl oz/1 cup white wine
5ml/1 tsp chopped fresh mixed
   herbs, such as rosemary, thyme,
   parsley and chives
1 small garlic clove, crushed
about 30ml/2 tbsp single
   (light) cream
salt and ground black pepper
fresh parsley, to garnish

COOK'S TIP
Look for kidneys that are firm, with a rich, even colour. Avoid those with dry spots or a dull surface.

1 Skin the kidneys and slice them horizontally. Remove the cores with scissors, and then wash them thoroughly in plenty of cold water. Drain and pat dry with kitchen paper.

2 Heat a little butter in a heavy frying pan and cook the kidneys for about 1½ minutes on each side. Be careful not to overcook. Remove the kidneys from the pan and keep warm.

3 Add a spoonful of mustard to the pan with the wine, herbs and garlic. Simmer gently to reduce the liquid by about half, then add enough cream to make a smooth sauce.

4 Return the kidneys to the pan and reheat gently in the sauce. Don't let them cook any further, or the kidneys will be tough. Serve garnished with parsley, and with rice or a green salad.

Energy 154kcal/640kJ; Protein 13.6g; Carbohydrate 0.9g, of which sugars 0.8g; Fat 6.2g, of which saturates 3.5g; Cholesterol 211mg; Calcium 44mg; Fibre 0.6g; Sodium 159mg.

LIVER AND BACON CASSEROLE

THE TRICK WHEN COOKING LIVER IS TO SEAL IT QUICKLY, THEN SIMMER IT GENTLY AND BRIEFLY.
PROLONGED AND/OR FIERCE COOKING MAKES LIVER HARD AND GRAINY.
Preparation: 5 minutes; Cooking: 20 minutes

SERVES FOUR

INGREDIENTS
30ml/2 tbsp sunflower oil
225g/8oz rindless unsmoked
  back bacon rashers (strips),
  cut into pieces
2 onions, halved and sliced
175g/6oz/2⅓ cups chestnut
  mushrooms, halved
450g/1lb lamb's liver, trimmed
  and sliced
25g/1oz/2 tbsp butter
15ml/1 tbsp soy sauce
30ml/2 tbsp plain (all-purpose) flour
150ml/¼ pint/⅔ cup chicken stock
salt and ground black pepper

1 Heat the oil in a frying pan and fry the bacon until crisp. Add the onions to the pan and cook for about 10 minutes, stirring frequently, or until softened. Add the mushrooms to the pan and fry for a further 1 minute.

2 Use a slotted spoon to remove the bacon and vegetables from the pan and set aside. Add the liver to the pan and cook over a high heat for 3–4 minutes, turning once to seal the slices on both sides. Remove the liver from the pan and keep warm.

3 Melt the butter in the pan, add the soy sauce and flour and blend together. Stir in the stock and bring to the boil, stirring until thickened. Return the liver and vegetables to the pan and heat through for 1 minute. Season with salt and pepper to taste, and serve at once with boiled new potatoes and lightly cooked green beans.

Energy 431kcal/1796kJ; Protein 34.7g; Carbohydrate 12.3g, of which sugars 6.1g; Fat 27.4g, of which saturates 9.4g; Cholesterol 527mg; Calcium 46mg; Fibre 2g; Sodium 1259mg.

DEVILLED KIDNEYS ON BRIOCHE CROÛTES

THE TRICK WITH LAMB'S KIDNEYS IS NOT TO OVERCOOK THEM, SO THIS RECIPE IS A GIFT FOR THE
QUICK COOK. CREAM TAMES THE FIERY SAUCE, MAKING A MIXTURE THAT TASTES GREAT ON CROÛTES.

Preparation: 5 minutes; Cooking: 12–14 minutes

SERVES FOUR

INGREDIENTS
   8 mini brioche slices
   25g/1oz/2 tbsp butter
   1 shallot, finely chopped
   2 garlic cloves, finely chopped
   115g/4oz/1½ cups mushrooms,
      halved
   1.5ml/¼ tsp cayenne pepper
   15ml/1 tbsp Worcestershire sauce
   8 lamb's kidneys, halved and trimmed
   150ml/¼ pint/⅔ cup double
      (heavy) cream
   30ml/2 tbsp chopped fresh parsley

1 Preheat the grill (broiler) and toast the brioche slices until golden brown on both sides. Keep warm.

2 Melt the butter in a frying pan. Add the shallot, garlic and mushrooms and cook for 5 minutes, or until the shallot has softened. Stir in the cayenne pepper and Worcestershire sauce and simmer for 1 minute.

3 Add the kidneys to the pan and cook for 3–5 minutes on each side. Finally, stir in the cream and simmer for about 2 minutes, or until the sauce has heated through and has thickened slightly.

4 Remove the brioche croûtes from the wire rack and place on warmed plates. Top with the kidneys. Sprinkle with chopped parsley and serve with salad.

COOK'S TIPS
If you can't find mini brioches, you can use a large brioche instead. Slice it thickly and stamp out croûtes using a 5cm/2in round cutter. If you prefer, the brioche croûtes can be fried rather than toasted. Melt 25g/1oz/2 tbsp butter in a frying pan and fry the croûtes until crisp and golden on both sides.

Energy 575kcal/2412kJ; Protein 37.7g; Carbohydrate 40.7g, of which sugars 13.2g; Fat 30.3g, of which saturates 16.3g; Cholesterol 623mg; Calcium 122mg; Fibre 2g; Sodium 599mg

CUMIN AND CORIANDER-RUBBED LAMB

WHEN SUMMER SIZZLES, TURN UP THE HEAT A LITTLE MORE WITH THESE SPICY LAMB CHOPS.
IF YOU HAVE TIME, MARINATE THE CHOPS FOR AN HOUR OR MORE — THEY WILL TASTE EVEN BETTER.

Preparation: 3 minutes; Cooking: 10 minutes. 1 hour's marinating time recommended

SERVES FOUR

INGREDIENTS
30ml/2 tbsp ground cumin
30ml/2 tbsp ground coriander
30ml/2 tbsp olive oil
8 lamb chops
salt and ground black pepper

VARIATION
To make Ginger- and Garlic-rubbed
Pork, use pork chops instead of lamb
chops and substitute the cumin and
coriander with ground ginger and
crushed garlic. Increase the cooking time
to 7–8 minutes each side.

1 Prepare a barbecue or preheat the
grill (broiler). Mix the cumin, coriander
and oil in a bowl, beating with a spoon
until a smooth paste is formed. Season
with salt and pepper.

2 Rub the mixture all over the lamb
chops. Cook the chops for 5 minutes
on each side, until lightly charred on
the outside but still pink in the centre.
Serve immediately.

Energy 494kcal/2059kJ; Protein 55.6g; Carbohydrate 0g, of which sugars 0g; Fat 30.1g, of which saturates 12.6g; Cholesterol 220mg; Calcium 18mg; Fibre 0g; Sodium 150mg

KOFTA LAMB BURGERS

FOR A QUICK AND EASY SUPPER, SIMPLY SLIDE THESE SPICY LITTLE BURGERS INTO CONES MADE BY ROLLING WARMED TORTILLAS. A DOLLOP OF THICK YOGURT OR CRÈME FRAÎCHE WOULDN'T GO AMISS.

Preparation: 8 minutes; Cooking: 10 minutes

SERVES FOUR

INGREDIENTS

450g/1lb minced (ground) lamb
1–2 large slices French bread,
   very finely crumbed
½ bunch fresh coriander (cilantro),
   finely chopped
5 garlic cloves, chopped
1 onion, finely chopped
juice of ½ lemon
5ml/1 tsp ground cumin
5ml/1 tsp paprika
15ml/1 tbsp curry powder
a pinch each of ground cardamom,
   turmeric and cinnamon
15ml/1 tbsp tomato purée (paste)
cayenne pepper or chopped fresh
   chillies (optional)
1 egg, beaten (optional)
salt and ground black pepper
flat bread and salads, to serve

1 Put the lamb, crumbed bread, coriander, garlic, onion, lemon juice, spices, tomato purée, cayenne pepper or chillies and seasoning in a large bowl. Mix well. If the mixture does not bind together, add the beaten egg and a little more bread.

2 With wet hands, shape the mixture into four large or eight small burgers.

3 Heat a heavy non-stick frying pan, add the burgers and cook for about 10 minutes, until browned. Turn once or twice, but make sure that they do not fall apart. Serve hot with flat bread and salads.

VARIATION
Mix a handful of raisins or sultanas (golden raisins) into the meat mixture before shaping it into burgers.

Energy 298kcal/1249kJ; Protein 24.2g; Carbohydrate 16.5g, of which sugars 2.6g; Fat 15.5g, of which saturates 7.1g; Cholesterol 87mg; Calcium 57mg; Fibre 1.1g; Sodium 242mg

FRIED LAMB MEATBALLS

MEATBALLS COOK QUICKLY; THE ONLY FIDDLY BIT IS SHAPING THEM. MIXING EVERYTHING TOGETHER WITH YOUR HANDS IS VERY SATISFYING AND WILL HELP TO SPEED UP THE PROCESS TOO.

Preparation: 10–15 minutes; Cooking: 5 minutes

SERVES FOUR

INGREDIENTS
2 medium slices of bread,
    crusts removed
500g/1¼lb minced (ground) lamb
    or beef
1 onion
5ml/1 tsp each dried thyme
    and oregano
45ml/3 tbsp chopped fresh flat leaf
    parsley, plus extra to garnish
1 egg, lightly beaten
salt and ground black pepper
lemon wedges, to serve (optional)
For frying
25g/1oz/¼ cup plain
    (all-purpose) flour
30–45ml/2–3 tbsp vegetable oil

1 Soak the slices of bread in a shallow bowl of water for 5 minutes. While the bread is soaking, grate or very finely chop the onion.

2 Drain the bread. Using clean hands, squeeze it dry and put it in a large bowl. Add the meat, onion, dried herbs, parsley, egg, salt and pepper to the bread. Mix together, preferably using your hands, until well blended.

3 Shape the meat mixture into individual balls about the size of a walnut, and roll them in the flour to give them a light dusting, shaking off any excess coating.

4 Heat the oil in a large frying pan. When it is hot, add the meatballs and fry for about 5 minutes, turning them frequently, until they are cooked through and look crisp and brown.

5 Using a slotted spoon, lift out the meatballs and drain on a double sheet of kitchen paper, to get rid of the excess oil. Sprinkle with the remaining chopped parsley and serve with lemon wedges, if you like.

Energy 411kcal/1710kJ; Protein 28.4g; Carbohydrate 13g, of which sugars 1.5g; Fat 27.6g, of which saturates 9.7g; Cholesterol 123mg; Calcium 66mg; Fibre 1.1g; Sodium 192mg

PITTAS WITH SPICED LAMB KOFTAS

WHEN YOU ARE EATING ALFRESCO, A BITE IN THE HAND IS WORTH TWO ON THE PLATE. HARISSA GIVES THE LAMB KOFTAS A MILDLY FIERY FLAVOUR, EASILY TAMED BY A TRICKLE OF YOGURT.

Preparation: 10 minutes; Cooking: 10 minutes

SERVES FOUR

INGREDIENTS
    450g/1lb/2 cups minced
      (ground) lamb
    1 small onion, finely chopped
    10ml/2 tsp harissa paste
    8 pitta breads, salad vegetables,
      mint and yogurt, to serve
    salt and ground black pepper

1 Prepare a barbecue. Soak eight wooden skewers in cold water for 10 minutes.

2 Meanwhile, put the lamb in a large bowl and add the onion and harissa. Mix well to combine, and season with plenty of salt and pepper.

VARIATION
Instead of adding mint leaves and yogurt separately to the pittas, spoon in some tzatziki, made by mixing finely diced cucumber, spring onions (scallions) and crushed garlic with Greek (US strained plain) yogurt.

3 Divide the mixture into eight equal pieces and press on to the skewers in a sausage shape to make the koftas.

4 Cook the skewered koftas on the barbecue for about 10 minutes, turning occasionally, until cooked through.

5 Warm the pitta breads on the barbecue grill, then split. Place a kofta in each one, and remove the skewer. Add some cucumber and tomato slices, mint leaves and a drizzle of natural (plain) yogurt.

Energy 609kcal/2568kJ; Protein 35.3g; Carbohydrate 83.8g, of which sugars 5.4g; Fat 17g, of which saturates 7.3g; Cholesterol 87mg; Calcium 230mg; Fibre 3.8g; Sodium 737mg

SWEET AND SOUR LAMB

BUY LAMB LOIN CHOPS FROM YOUR BUTCHER AND ASK HIM TO FRENCH TRIM THEM FOR YOU. SERVE THE CHOPS IN THEIR MARINADE WITH STEAMED CARROTS AND GREEN BEANS.

Preparation: 3 minutes; Cooking: 8–10 minutes, plus chilling time

SERVES FOUR

INGREDIENTS
8 French-trimmed lamb
  loin chops
90ml/6 tbsp balsamic vinegar
30ml/2 tbsp caster
  (superfine) sugar
30ml/2 tbsp olive oil
salt and ground black pepper

1 Put the lamb chops in a shallow, non-metallic dish and drizzle over the balsamic vinegar.

2 Sprinkle with the sugar and season with salt and black pepper. Turn the chops to coat in the mixture, then cover with clear film (plastic wrap) and chill for 15–20 minutes.

3 Heat the olive oil in a large frying pan and add the chops, reserving the marinade. Cook for 3–4 minutes on each side.

4 Pour the marinade into the pan and leave to bubble for about 2 minutes, or until reduced slightly. Remove from the pan and serve immediately.

COOK'S TIP
Lamb loin chops are sold as a rack of lamb, which is also known as a guard of honour, but they are chined (have the back bone removed) to leave cutlets that can easily be separated. French-trimmed chops are those that have also had the skin removed.

Energy 258kcal/1077kJ; Protein 19.7g; Carbohydrate 7.9g, of which sugars 7.9g; Fat 16.7g, of which saturates 6g; Cholesterol 76mg; Calcium 12mg; Fibre 0g; Sodium 87mg.

LAMB CHOPS WITH MINT VINAIGRETTE

SERVING VINAIGRETTE SAUCES WITH MEAT CAME IN WITH NOUVELLE CUISINE AND STAYED. THIS ONE OFFERS A CLASSIC COMBINATION — LAMB AND MINT — IN A NEW STYLE.

Preparation: 4 minutes; Cooking: 6–7 minutes

SERVES FOUR

INGREDIENTS

8 loin lamb chops or 4 double loin
    chops, about 2cm/¾ in thick
coarsely ground black pepper
fresh mint, to garnish
sautéed potatoes, to serve
For the mint vinaigrette
30ml/2 tbsp white wine vinegar
2.5ml/½ tsp clear honey
1 small garlic clove, very
    finely chopped
60ml/4 tbsp extra virgin olive oil
20g/¾ oz/½ cup fresh mint leaves,
    finely chopped
1 ripe plum tomato, peeled, seeded
    and finely diced
salt and ground black pepper

1 To make the vinaigrette, put the vinegar, honey, garlic, salt and pepper in a small bowl and whisk thoroughly to combine.

2 Slowly whisk in the oil, then stir in the mint and tomato and set aside.

3 Put the lamb chops on a board and trim off any excess fat. Sprinkle with the pepper, pressing it on to both sides of the meat.

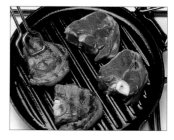

4 Lightly oil a heavy cast iron griddle and set over a high heat until very hot but not smoking. Place the chops on the griddle and reduce the heat to medium. Cook the chops for 6–7 minutes, turning once, or until done as preferred (medium-rare meat will still be slightly soft when pressed, medium will be springy and well-done firm). Serve the chops with the vinaigrette and sautéed potatoes, garnished with mint.

COOK'S TIP
The chops can also be cooked under a preheated grill (broiler) or barbecued over charcoal until done as you like. If barbecuing, put them in a hinged wire grill to make them easier to turn.

Energy 465kcal/1936kJ; Protein 39.6g; Carbohydrate 1.4g, of which sugars 1.2g; Fat 33.5g, of which saturates 12g; Cholesterol 152mg; Calcium 28mg; Fibre 0.3g; Sodium 175mg.

SKEWERED LAMB WITH CUCUMBER RAITA

LAMB IS THE MOST COMMONLY USED MEAT FOR TURKISH KEBABS, BUT LEAN BEEF OR PORK WORK EQUALLY WELL. FOR COLOUR, YOU CAN ALTERNATE PIECES OF PEPPER, LEMON OR ONIONS.

Preparation: 15 minutes; Cooking: 10 minutes

SERVES FOUR

INGREDIENTS
900g/2lb lean boneless lamb, cut
   into small chunks
1 large onion, grated
3 bay leaves
5 thyme or rosemary sprigs
grated rind and juice of 1 lemon
2.5ml/ ½ tsp caster (superfine) sugar
75ml/3fl oz/⅓ cup olive oil
salt and ground black pepper
sprigs of rosemary, to garnish
grilled lemon wedges, to serve
For the cucumber raita
½ cucumber, finely diced
1 green chilli, seeded and chopped
300ml/½ pint/1¼ cups Greek (US
   strained plain) yogurt
1.5ml/½ tsp salt
1.5ml/½ tsp ground cumin

1 To make the kebabs, put the lamb chunks in a bowl. Mix together the grated onion, herbs, lemon rind and juice, sugar and oil, then add salt and pepper and pour over the lamb.

2 Mix the ingredients together and leave to marinate in the fridge while you make the raita.

COOK'S TIP
If using wooden skewers, cover the tips with foil so they don't char. It's also a good idea to soak them in water for 30 minutes before threading them with food.

3 Place the cucumber in a bowl and stir in the chopped chilli.

4 Add the yogurt, salt and ground cumin. Preheat the grill (broiler).

5 Drain the meat and thread it on to skewers. Grill (broil) for 10 minutes until browned, turning twice. Garnish with the rosemary and grilled lemon wedges and serve with the raita.

Energy 589kcal/2455kJ; Protein 49.2g; Carbohydrate 12.3g, of which sugars 10.5g; Fat 38.7g, of which saturates 13.9g; Cholesterol 172mg; Calcium 188mg; Fibre 1.4g; Sodium 260mg.

VEGETARIAN DISHES

Gone are the days of nut roasts, dull salads and plenty of omelettes: the menu for vegetarians, or people who just happen to like eating meat- and fish-free food, has never been wider. Mushrooms appear in Balti Mushrooms in a Garlic Sauce, Mushroom Kedgeree and Mushroom Stroganoff; aubergines abound in Aubergine Rolls Stuffed with Ricotta, Aubergine, Mint and Couscous Salad and Aubergine and Sweet Potato Stew; and brightly coloured peppers adorn Frittata with Leeks and Red Pepper, Sweet Peppers Stuffed with Two Cheeses and Summer Vegetable Kebabs. The ever-versatile tofu makes an appearance in Stir-fried Crispy Tofu, Tofu and Pepper Kebabs and Tofu and Green Bean Red Curry, while protein in other forms appears in Cheese and Leek Sausages, Saffron Risotto with Parmesan, Corn and Cashew Nut Curry, Couscous with Halloumi, Fiorentina Pizza and Chickpea Tagine. What all these recipes have in common, apart from taking half an hour or less to prepare, is that they provide nutritious, colourful, varied and appealing vegetarian dishes.

BALTI MUSHROOMS IN A GARLIC SAUCE

THIS IS A SIMPLE AND DELICIOUS DISH — LIGHTLY SPICED MUSHROOMS IN A CREAMY SAUCE — WHICH COULD BE SERVED ON GRANARY TOAST OR WITH BASMATI RICE.

Preparation: 5 minutes; Cooking: 5 minutes

SERVES FOUR

INGREDIENTS
   350g/12oz/3 cups button (white)
     mushrooms
   45ml/3 tbsp olive oil
   1 bay leaf
   3 garlic cloves, roughly chopped
   2 green chillies, seeded and chopped
   225g/8oz/1 cup fromage frais
   15ml/1 tbsp chopped fresh mint
   15ml/1 tbsp chopped fresh coriander
     (cilantro)
   5ml/1 tsp salt
   fresh mint and coriander, to garnish

1 Unless they are very small, cut the mushrooms in half. Set them aside while you cook the garlic and chillies.

2 Heat the oil in a non-stick wok or balti pan, then add the bay leaf, garlic and chillies and cook for about 1 minute.

3 Add the mushrooms. Stir-fry for about 2 minutes, or longer if you like them well cooked and browned.

4 Remove from the heat and stir in the fromage frais followed by the mint, coriander and salt. Heat, stirring for 2 minutes, then transfer to a warmed serving dish, garnish with the mint and coriander leaves and serve at once.

Energy 153kcal/633kJ; Protein 5.4g; Carbohydrate 3.1g, of which sugars 2.8g; Fat 13.3g, of which saturates 4.4g; Cholesterol 5mg; Calcium 90mg; Fibre 1.5g; Sodium 28mg.

SPICED POTATOES AND TOMATOES

SUBSTANTIAL ENOUGH TO SERVE SOLO, THIS DISH CONSISTS OF DICED POTATOES COOKED GENTLY IN A FRESH TOMATO SAUCE WHICH IS FLAVOURED WITH CURRY LEAVES AND GREEN CHILLIES.

Preparation: 10 minutes; Cooking: 9–12 minutes

SERVES FOUR

INGREDIENTS

- 15ml/1 tbsp olive oil
- 2 onions, finely chopped
- 4 curry leaves
- 1.5ml/¼ tsp onion seeds
- 1 green chilli, seeded and chopped
- 4 tomatoes, sliced
- 5ml/1 tsp grated fresh root ginger
- 1 garlic clove, crushed
- 5ml/1 tsp chilli powder
- 5ml/1 tsp ground coriander
- salt
- 2 potatoes, diced
- 5ml/1 tsp lemon juice
- 15ml/1 tbsp chopped fresh
  coriander (cilantro)
- 4 hard-boiled eggs, to garnish

1 Heat the oil in a non-stick wok or frying pan and stir-fry the onions, curry leaves, onion seeds and chilli for about 1 minute.

2 Add the tomatoes and cook for about 2 minutes over a low heat, shaking the pan to prevent them from sticking.

3 Add the ginger, garlic, chilli powder, ground coriander and salt to taste. Continue to stir-fry for 1–2 minutes, then add the potatoes and cover the pan. Cook over a low heat for 5–7 minutes until the potatoes are tender.

4 Add the lemon juice and fresh coriander, and stir to mix together.

5 Shell the hard-boiled eggs, cut into quarters and add as a garnish to the finished dish.

Energy 163kcal/682kJ; Protein 7.5g; Carbohydrate 17.4g, of which sugars 8.2g; Fat 7.7g, of which saturates 1.7g; Cholesterol 143mg; Calcium 73mg; Fibre 3.1g; Sodium 73mg.

ASPARAGUS ROLLS WITH HERB BUTTER SAUCE

*FOR A TASTE SENSATION, TRY TENDER ASPARAGUS SPEARS WRAPPED IN CRISP FILO PASTRY. THE
BUTTERY HERB SAUCE DOESN'T TAKE LONG TO MAKE AND IS THE PERFECT ACCOMPANIMENT.*

Preparation: 5 minutes; Cooking: 12 minutes

SERVES TWO

INGREDIENTS
    4 sheets of filo pastry
    50g/2oz/¼ cup butter, melted
    16 young asparagus spears, trimmed
    mixed salad, to garnish
For the sauce
    2 shallots, finely chopped
    1 bay leaf
    150ml/¼ pint/⅔ cup dry white wine
    175g/6oz/¾ cup butter, melted
    15ml/1 tbsp chopped fresh herbs
    salt and ground black pepper
    snipped chives, to garnish

1 Preheat the oven to 200°C/400°F/
Gas 6. Grease a baking sheet. Brush
each filo sheet with melted butter. Fold
one corner of the sheet down to the
bottom edge to give a wedge shape.

2 Lay 4 asparagus spears on top at the
longest edge and roll up towards the
shortest edge. Using the remaining filo
and asparagus spears, make 3 more
rolls in the same way.

3 Lay the rolls on the prepared baking
sheet. Brush with the remaining melted
butter. Bake in the oven for 12 minutes
until golden.

4 Meanwhile, make the sauce. Put the
shallots, bay leaf and wine in a pan.
Cover and cook over a high heat until
the wine is reduced to about 45–60ml/
3–4 tbsp.

5 Strain the wine mixture into a
heatproof bowl. Whisk in the butter, a
little at a time, until the sauce is smooth
and glossy.

6 Stir in the herbs and add salt and
pepper to taste. Keep the sauce warm
over a pan of barely simmering water.
Serve the rolls on individual plates with
the mixed salad garnish. Serve the
butter sauce separately, sprinkled with a
few snipped chives.

VARIATIONS
Make miniature asparagus rolls for
parties. Cut smaller rectangles of filo and
roll around a single asparagus spear.
Serve hot with the suggested sauce, or
cold with a light mayonnaise. For a
quicker and more economical version,
use well-drained canned asparagus.

Energy 1050kcal/4340kJ; Protein 7.6g; Carbohydrate 34.7g, of which sugars 5.3g; Fat 93.6g, of which saturates 58.8g; Cholesterol 240mg; Calcium 114mg; Fibre 3.3g; Sodium 688mg.

COURGETTE PUFFS WITH MIXED LEAF SALAD

THIS UNUSUAL SALAD CONSISTS OF DEEP-FRIED COURGETTES, FLAVOURED WITH MINT AND SERVED WARM ON A BED OF SALAD LEAVES WITH A BALSAMIC DRESSING.

Preparation: 5 minutes; Cooking: 6 minutes

SERVES TWO TO THREE

INGREDIENTS

450g/1lb courgettes (zucchini)
75g/3oz/1½ cups fresh white
  breadcrumbs
1 egg
pinch of cayenne pepper
15ml/1 tbsp chopped fresh mint
oil for deep-frying
15ml/1 tbsp balsamic vinegar
45ml/3 tbsp extra virgin olive oil
200g/7oz mixed salad leaves
salt and ground black pepper

1 Trim the courgettes. Coarsely grate them and put into a colander. Squeeze out the excess water, then put the courgettes into a bowl.

2 Add the white breadcrumbs, egg, cayenne pepper and chopped fresh mint, with salt and pepper to taste. Mix well, with a wooden spoon or using clean hands.

3 Shape the courgette and breadcrumb mixture into balls, which should be about the size of walnuts.

4 Heat the oil for deep-frying to 180ºC/350ºF or until a cube of bread added to the oil browns in 30–40 seconds. Deep-fry the courgette balls in batches for 2 minutes. Drain on kitchen paper.

5 Whisk the vinegar and oil together and season well.

6 Put the salad leaves in a bowl and pour over the dressing. Toss lightly to coat the leaves evenly. Add the courgette puffs and toss lightly together. Serve at once, while the courgette puffs are still crisp.

Energy 314kcal/1307kJ; Protein 8.2g; Carbohydrate 23.2g, of which sugars 4.3g; Fat 21.6g, of which saturates 3.2g; Cholesterol 63mg; Calcium 98mg; Fibre 2.5g; Sodium 217mg.

CHEESE AND LEEK SAUSAGES

THESE ARE BASED ON THE WELSH SPECIALITY, WHICH ARE TRADITIONALLY MADE USING BREADCRUMBS. HOWEVER, ADDING MASHED POTATO LIGHTENS THE SAUSAGES AND MAKES THEM EASIER TO HANDLE.

Preparation: 10 minutes; Cooking: 15–20 minutes

SERVES FOUR

INGREDIENTS
  25g/1oz/2 tbsp butter or
    low-fat spread
  175g/6oz leeks or shallots,
    finely chopped
  90ml/6 tbsp cold mashed potato
  115g/4oz/2 cups fresh white or
    wholemeal (whole-wheat)
    breadcrumbs
  150g/5oz/1¼ cups grated Caerphilly,
    Lancashire or Cantal cheese
  30ml/2 tbsp chopped fresh parsley
  5ml/1 tsp chopped fresh sage
    or marjoram
  2 eggs, beaten
  pinch of cayenne pepper
  65g/2½ oz/⅔ cup dry white
    breadcrumbs
  oil, for shallow-frying
  salt and ground black pepper
For the tomato sauce
  15ml/1 tbsp olive oil
  1 red onion, finely chopped
  1 garlic clove, crushed
  400g/14oz can chopped tomatoes
  120ml/4fl oz/½ cup vegetable stock
    or white wine or a mixture
  15ml/1 tbsp chopped fresh parsley

1 Make the tomato sauce. Heat the oil in a small pan and fry the onion and garlic for 2–3 minutes until softened. Add the tomatoes, vegetable stock and/or wine, and parsley. Season well. Bring to the boil, then lower the heat and simmer for 10 minutes until slightly thickened, stirring.

2 Meanwhile, melt the butter and fry the leeks for 4–5 minutes, until softened but not browned. Tip into a bowl and add the mashed potato, fresh breadcrumbs, cheese, chopped fresh parsley and sage or marjoram. Mix well. Add sufficient beaten egg (about two-thirds of the quantity) to bind the mixture. Season well and add a good pinch of cayenne.

3 Shape the mixture into 12 sausage shapes. Dip in the remaining egg, then coat in the dry breadcrumbs.

4 Fry the sausages in shallow oil until golden brown on all sides. Drain on kitchen paper and serve with the tomato sauce.

VARIATIONS
• These sausages are also delicious served with garlic mayonnaise or a confit of slow-cooked red onions.
• The mixture can be shaped into burgers and served in burger buns with tomato relish, as a welcome variation on meat burgers for vegetarians and carnivores alike.

Energy 547kcal/2286kJ; Protein 21.5g; Carbohydrate 44.1g, of which sugars 6.5g; Fat 31.9g, of which saturates 14.9g; Cholesterol 151mg; Calcium 420mg; Fibre 3.4g; Sodium 744mg.

AUBERGINE ROLLS STUFFED WITH RICOTTA

THESE LITTLE ROLLS OF AUBERGINE WRAPPED AROUND A FILLING OF RICOTTA AND RICE MAKE AN
INSPIRED ADDITION TO A SUMMER BUFFET TABLE OR A GREEK- OR TURKISH-STYLE MEZE.

Preparation: 10 minutes; Cooking: 20 minutes

SERVES FOUR

INGREDIENTS

2 aubergines (eggplants)
olive oil or sunflower oil for
  shallow-frying
75g/3oz/scant ½ cup ricotta cheese
75g/3oz/scant ½ cup soft goat's
  cheese
225g/8oz/2 cups cooked long grain
  white rice
15ml/1 tbsp chopped fresh basil
5ml/1 tsp chopped fresh mint, plus
  mint sprigs, to garnish
salt and ground black pepper
For the tomato sauce
15ml/1 tbsp olive oil
1 red onion, finely chopped
1 garlic clove, crushed
400g/14oz can chopped tomatoes
120ml/4fl oz/½ cup vegetable stock
  or white wine or a mixture
15ml/1 tbsp chopped fresh parsley

1 Make the tomato sauce. Heat the oil in a small pan and fry the onion and garlic for 2–3 minutes until softened. Add the tomatoes, vegetable stock and/or wine, and parsley. Season well. Bring to the boil, then lower the heat and simmer for 10 minutes until slightly thickened, stirring.

COOK'S TIP
If you prefer to use less oil for the aubergines, brush each slice with a little oil, then grill (broil) until evenly browned.

2 Meanwhile, preheat the oven to 190ºC/375ºF/Gas 5. Slice the aubergines lengthways, discarding the two outer slices. Heat the oil in a large frying pan and fry the aubergine slices until they are golden brown on both sides. Drain on kitchen paper. Mix the remaining ingredients in a bowl. Season well.

3 Place a generous spoonful of the cheese and rice mixture at one end of each aubergine slice and roll up. Arrange the rolls side by side in a shallow ovenproof dish. Pour the tomato sauce over the top and bake for 10–15 minutes until heated through. Garnish with the mint sprigs and serve.

Energy 283kcal/1185kJ; Protein 8.9g; Carbohydrate 24.7g, of which sugars 6.7g; Fat 17.3g, of which saturates 6.6g; Cholesterol 25mg; Calcium 56mg; Fibre 3.3g; Sodium 125mg.

PEA AND MINT OMELETTE

SERVE THIS DELICIOUSLY LIGHT OMELETTE WITH CRUSTY BREAD AND A GREEN SALAD FOR A FRESH AND TASTY LUNCH. WHEN THEY ARE IN SEASON, USE FRESHLY SHELLED PEAS INSTEAD OF FROZEN ONES.

Preparation: 2 minutes; Cooking: 8–10 minutes

SERVES TWO

INGREDIENTS
50g/2oz/½ cup frozen peas
4 eggs
30ml/2 tbsp chopped fresh mint
a knob (pat) of butter
salt and ground black pepper

VARIATION
When young broad (fava) beans are in season, use them instead of peas. Shell the beans and cook them in boiling salted water for 3–4 minutes until just tender. Meanwhile, grill (broil) 3–4 rashers (strips) of bacon. Add the beans to the egg mixture instead of the peas and crumble the bacon over the omelette when it is almost cooked.

1 Break the eggs into a large bowl and beat with a fork. Season well with salt and pepper and set aside.

2 Cook the peas in a large pan of salted boiling water for 3–4 minutes until just tender. Drain well in a colander and add them to the eggs in the bowl. Stir in the chopped fresh mint and swirl with a spoon until thoroughly combined.

3 Heat the butter in a medium frying pan until foamy. Pour in the egg mixture and cook over a medium heat for 3–4 minutes, drawing in the cooked egg from the edges from time to time, until the mixture is nearly set.

4 Finish off cooking the omelette under a hot grill (broiler) until set and golden. Carefully fold the omelette over, cut it in half and serve immediately.

Energy 208kcal/865kJ; Protein 14.6g; Carbohydrate 3.3g, of which sugars 0.6g; Fat 15.7g, of which saturates 5.8g; Cholesterol 391mg; Calcium 79mg; Fibre 1.2g; Sodium 172mg

FRITTATA WITH LEEKS AND RED PEPPER

SIMILAR TO A QUICHE, BUT WITHOUT THE CRUST, THIS FRITTATA INCORPORATES A MIXTURE OF LIGHTLY SPICED VEGETABLES IN AN EGG CUSTARD. SLICES ARE EASY TO PACK FOR A PICNIC OR WORKING LUNCH.

Preparation: 5 minutes; Cooking: 14 minutes

SERVES THREE TO FOUR

INGREDIENTS
  30ml/2 tbsp olive oil
  1 large red (bell) pepper, seeded
    and diced
  2.5–5ml/½–1 tsp ground
    toasted cumin
  3 leeks, about 450g/1lb, thinly sliced
  150g/5oz small spinach leaves
  45ml/3 tbsp pine nuts, toasted
  5 large (US extra large) eggs
  15ml/1 tbsp chopped fresh basil
  15ml/1 tbsp chopped fresh flat
    leaf parsley
  salt and ground black pepper
  watercress, to garnish
  50g/2oz Parmesan cheese, grated,
    to serve

1 Heat a frying pan and add the oil. Add the red pepper and cook over a medium heat, stirring occasionally, for 3–4 minutes, until soft and beginning to brown. Add 2.5ml/½ tsp of the cumin and cook for another 1–2 minutes.

2 Stir in the leeks, then part-cover the pan and cook gently for about 5 minutes, until the leeks have softened and collapsed. Season with salt and ground black pepper.

3 Add the spinach. Cover the pan and leave the spinach to wilt in the steam for 2 minutes, then stir to mix it into the vegetables. Add the pine nuts and stir to mix well.

4 Preheat the grill (broiler). Beat the eggs with salt, pepper, the remaining cumin, basil and parsley. Add to the pan and cook over a gentle heat until the bottom of the omelette sets and turns golden brown. Pull the edges of the omelette away from the sides of the pan as it cooks and tilt the pan so that the uncooked egg runs underneath.

5 Flash the frittata under the hot grill to set the egg on top, but do not let it become too brown. Cut the frittata into wedges and serve warm, garnished with watercress and sprinkled with grated Parmesan.

VARIATION
A delicious way to serve frittata is to pack it into a slightly hollowed-out loaf and then drizzle it with a little extra virgin olive oil. Wrap tightly in clear film (plastic wrap) and leave to stand for 1–2 hours before cutting into thick slices. A frittata-filled loaf is ideal picnic fare.

Energy 323kcal/1342kJ; Protein 17.6g; Carbohydrate 7.1g, of which sugars 6.2g; Fat 25.3g, of which saturates 6g; Cholesterol 250mg; Calcium 281mg; Fibre 4.2g; Sodium 280mg

SPICY OMELETTE

THE ACCUSATION THAT EGG DISHES CAN BE A BIT BLAND COULD NEVER BE LEVELLED AT THIS SPICY,
VEGETABLE-RICH DISH. IT COMES FROM INDIA, WHERE IT IS OFTEN SERVED FOR BREAKFAST.

Preparation: 6–7 minutes; Cooking: 10 minutes

SERVES FOUR TO SIX

INGREDIENTS

30ml/2 tbsp vegetable oil
1 onion, finely chopped
2.5ml/½ tsp ground cumin
1 garlic clove, crushed
1 or 2 fresh green chillies,
   finely chopped
a few coriander (cilantro) sprigs,
   chopped, plus extra, to garnish
1 firm tomato, chopped
1 small potato, cubed and boiled
25g/1oz/¼ cup cooked peas
25g/1oz/¼ cup cooked corn,
   or drained canned corn
2 eggs, beaten
25g/1oz/¼ cup grated cheese
salt and ground black pepper

1 Heat the vegetable oil in a wok or
large frying pan, and fry the next nine
ingredients for 2–3 minutes until they
are well blended but the potato and
tomato are still firm. Season with salt
and ground black pepper.

2 Increase the heat and pour in the
beaten eggs. Reduce the heat, cover
and cook until the bottom of the
omelette is golden brown. Sprinkle
the omelette with the grated cheese.
Place under a hot grill (broiler) and
cook until the egg sets and the cheese
has melted.

3 Garnish the omelette with sprigs of
coriander and serve with salad for a
light lunch or supper.

VARIATION
You can use any vegetable with the
potatoes. Try adding thickly sliced
mushrooms instead of the corn.

Energy 93kcal/388kJ; Protein 4g; Carbohydrate 3.7g, of which sugars 1.2g; Fat 7.1g, of which saturates 1.9g; Cholesterol 67mg; Calcium 46mg; Fibre 0.6g; Sodium 104mg

WARM DRESSED SALAD WITH POACHED EGGS

SOFT POACHED EGGS, CHILLI, HOT CROÛTONS AND COOL, CRISP SALAD LEAVES MAKE A LIVELY AND UNUSUAL COMBINATION. THIS SIMPLE SALAD IS PERFECT FOR A MID-WEEK SUPPER.

Preparation: 2–3 minutes; Cooking: 10–12 minutes

SERVES TWO

INGREDIENTS
½ small loaf wholemeal
  (whole-wheat) bread
45ml/3 tbsp chilli oil
2 eggs
115g/4oz mixed salad leaves
45ml/3 tbsp extra virgin olive oil
2 garlic cloves, crushed
15ml/1 tbsp balsamic or
  sherry vinegar
50g/2oz Parmesan cheese, shaved
ground black pepper

1 Carefully cut the crust from the Granary loaf and discard. Cut the bread into neat slices and then into 2.5cm/1in cubes.

2 Heat the chilli oil in a large frying pan. Add the bread cubes and cook for about 5 minutes, tossing the cubes occasionally, until they are crisp and golden brown all over.

3 Meanwhile, bring a pan of water to the boil. Break each egg into a measuring jug (cup) and carefully slide into the water, one at a time. Gently poach the eggs for about 4 minutes until lightly cooked.

4 Divide the salad leaves between two plates. Remove the croûtons from the pan and arrange them over the leaves.

5 Wipe the pan clean with kitchen paper. Then heat the olive oil in the pan, add the garlic and vinegar and cook over high heat for 1 minute. Pour the warm dressing over the salads.

6 Place a poached egg on each salad. Top with thin Parmesan shavings and a little ground black pepper.

Energy 697kcal/2907kJ; Protein 25.9g; Carbohydrate 41.3g, of which sugars 2.8g; Fat 49g, of which saturates 11.5g; Cholesterol 215mg; Calcium 408mg; Fibre 6.3g; Sodium 914mg

SOUFFLÉ OMELETTE WITH MUSHROOMS

A SOUFFLÉ OMELETTE MAKES AN IDEAL MEAL FOR ONE, ESPECIALLY WITH THIS DELICIOUS FILLING,
BUT BE WARNED — WHEN OTHERS SMELL IT COOKING THEY ARE LIKELY TO DEMAND THEIR SHARE.

Preparation: 5 minutes; Cooking: 13–15 minutes

SERVES ONE

INGREDIENTS

2 eggs, separated
15g/½oz/1 tbsp butter
flat leaf parsley or coriander
  (cilantro) leaves, to garnish
For the mushroom sauce
15g/½oz/1 tbsp butter
75g/3oz/generous 1 cup button
  (white) mushrooms, thinly sliced
15ml/1 tbsp plain (all-purpose) flour
85–120ml/3–4fl oz/⅓–½ cup milk
5ml/1 tsp chopped fresh parsley
salt and ground black pepper

COOK'S TIP

For extra flavour, add a few drops of soy
sauce to the mushrooms.

1 To make the mushroom sauce, melt
the butter in a pan or frying pan and
add the sliced mushrooms. Fry gently
for 4–5 minutes, stirring occasionally.
The mushrooms will exude quite a
lot of liquid, but this will rapidly
be reabsorbed.

2 Stir in the flour, then gradually add
the milk, stirring all the time. Cook
until the sauce boils and thickens. Add
the parsley, if using, and season with
salt and pepper. Keep warm.

3 Make the omelette. Beat the egg yolks
with 15ml/1 tbsp water and season with
a little salt and pepper. Whisk the egg
whites until stiff, then fold into the egg
yolks. Preheat the grill (broiler).

4 Melt the butter in a large frying pan
and pour in the egg mixture. Cook over
a gentle heat for 2–4 minutes. Place the
frying pan under the grill and cook for
a further 3–4 minutes until the top is
golden brown.

5 Slide the omelette on to a warmed
serving plate, pour the mushroom sauce
over the top and fold the omelette in
half. Serve, garnished with parsley.

Energy 838kcal/3514kJ; Protein 45.5g; Carbohydrate 53.7g, of which sugars 42.1g; Fat 51.4g, of which saturates 28.3g; Cholesterol 497mg; Calcium 1150mg; Fibre 1.3g; Sodium 707mg

MEXICAN TORTILLA PARCELS

SEEDED GREEN CHILLIES ADD JUST A FLICKER OF FIRE TO THE SPICY TOMATO FILLING IN THESE
PARCELS, WHICH ARE PERFECT AS A MAIN COURSE, APPETIZER OR SNACK.

Preparation: 15 minutes; Cooking: 14–16 minutes

SERVES FOUR

INGREDIENTS
    675g/1½ lb tomatoes
    60ml/4 tbsp sunflower oil
    1 large onion, finely sliced
    1 garlic clove, crushed
    10ml/2 tsp cumin seeds
    2 fresh green chillies, seeded
        and chopped
    30ml/2 tbsp tomato purée (paste)
    1 vegetable stock (bouillon) cube
    200g/7oz can corn, drained
    15ml/1 tbsp chopped fresh
        coriander (cilantro)
    115g/4oz/1 cup grated
        Cheddar cheese
    8 wheat tortillas
    fresh coriander (cilantro), to garnish
To serve
    shredded lettuce
    sour cream

1 Peel the tomatoes: place them in a heatproof bowl, add boiling water to cover and leave for 30 seconds. Lift out with a slotted spoon and plunge into a bowl of cold water. Leave for 1 minute, then drain. Slip the skins off the tomatoes and chop the flesh.

2 Heat half the oil in a frying pan and fry the onion with the garlic and cumin seeds for 5 minutes, until the onion softens. Add the chillies and tomatoes, then stir in the tomato purée. Crumble the stock cube over, stir well and cook gently for 5 minutes, until the chilli is soft but the tomato has not completely broken down. Stir in the corn and fresh coriander and heat gently to warm through. Keep warm.

COOK'S TIP
Mexican wheat tortillas (sometimes described as wheatflour tortillas) are available in most supermarkets. They are handy to keep in the pantry as a wrapping for a variety of mixtures.

3 Sprinkle grated cheese in the middle of each tortilla. Spoon some tomato mixture over the cheese. Fold over one edge of the tortilla, then the sides and finally the remaining edge, to enclose the filling completely.

4 Heat the remaining oil in a frying pan and fry the filled tortillas for 1–2 minutes on each side until golden and crisp. Lift them out carefully with tongs and drain on kitchen paper. Garnish with coriander and serve immediately with shredded lettuce and sour cream.

Energy 576kcal/2424kJ; Protein 17.5g; Carbohydrate 79.3g, of which sugars 12.2g; Fat 22.5g, of which saturates 7.8g; Cholesterol 28mg; Calcium 339mg; Fibre 5g; Sodium 656mg.

FRIED BANANAS WITH EGG AND TOMATO RICE

ARROZ A LA CUBANA, GARNISHED WITH FRIED EGGS AND BANANAS, IS POPULAR IN THE CANARY ISLANDS AND CATALONIA. IT MAKES AN EASY AND SUBSTANTIAL SUPPER DISH.

Preparation: 4 minutes; Cooking: 16 minutes

SERVES FOUR

INGREDIENTS
850ml/28fl oz/3½ cups water
2 whole and 1 chopped garlic cloves
120ml/4fl oz/½ cup olive oil
300g/11oz/1½ cups long grain rice
15g/½ oz/1 tbsp butter
4 small bananas or 2 large bananas,
    halved lengthways
4 large (US extra large) eggs
salt and paprika
For the tomato sauce
30ml/2 tbsp olive oil
1 onion, chopped
2 garlic cloves, finely chopped
2 x 400g/14oz cans tomatoes
4 thyme or oregano sprigs
ground black pepper

VARIATION
For a non-vegetarian option, add bacon to the tomato sauce, or fry it and serve it with the eggs.

1 Put the measured water in a pan with the two whole garlic cloves and 15ml/1 tbsp of the oil. Bring to the boil, add the rice and cook for 10 minutes until the rice is cooked and the liquid has been absorbed.

2 Meanwhile, make the tomato sauce. Heat the oil in a pan, add the onion and garlic and fry gently, stirring, until soft. Stir in the tomatoes and herb sprigs and simmer gently for 5 minutes. Add seasoning to taste. Remove the herb sprigs and keep the sauce warm.

3 Heat a pan with 30ml/2 tbsp of the oil and gently fry the chopped garlic clove. Tip in the rice, stir, season well, then turn off the heat and cover the pan.

4 Heat the butter in a frying pan with 15ml/1 tbsp of the oil. Fry the bananas briefly on both sides. Keep them warm.

5 Add the remaining oil to the pan and fry the eggs over a medium-high heat, so that the edges turn golden. Season with salt and paprika. Serve with the rice, tomato sauce and fried bananas.

Energy 725kcal/3021kJ; Protein 14.5g; Carbohydrate 88.2g, of which sugars 25.9g; Fat 35.4g, of which saturates 7.5g; Cholesterol 198mg; Calcium 67mg; Fibre 3.2g; Sodium 112mg

STEWED VEGETABLES WITH HARD-BOILED EGG

THIS RICH-FLAVOURED AND SIMPLE SUMMER VEGETABLE DISH IS FROM THE POOREST AND HOTTEST PART OF SPAIN, LA MANCHA. IT MAY BE EATEN HOT, ALONE OR WITH SUCH THINGS AS FRIED HAM AND EGGS.

Preparation: 6 minutes; Cooking: 24 minutes

SERVES FOUR

INGREDIENTS

45–60ml/3–4 tbsp olive oil
2 Spanish (Bermuda) onions,
 thinly sliced
3 garlic cloves, finely chopped
3 large green (bell) peppers,
 seeded and chopped
3 large courgettes (zucchini),
 thinly sliced
5 large ripe tomatoes or 2 x 400g/
 14oz cans tomatoes, with juice
60ml/4 tbsp chopped fresh parsley
2 hard-boiled eggs, chopped
30–45ml/2–3 tbsp virgin olive oil
 (if serving cold)
salt and ground black pepper

1 Heat the oil in a large heavy pan or flameproof casserole and cook the onions and garlic gently, until soft.

2 Add the peppers, courgettes and tomatoes. Season and cook gently for 20 minutes until the flavours blend.

3 Stir in 30ml/2 tbsp parsley and serve hot, if wished, topped with chopped hard-boiled eggs and more parsley. To serve cold, check the seasoning, adding more if needed, and sprinkle with a little virgin olive oil before adding the parsley garnish.

Energy 278kcal/1152kJ; Protein 7g; Carbohydrate 28.6g, of which sugars 25g; Fat 15.7g, of which saturates 2.4g; Cholesterol 0mg; Calcium 93mg; Fibre 7.4g; Sodium 24mg.

STIR-FRIED CRISPY TOFU

VEGETARIAN GUESTS OFTEN DRAW THE SHORT STRAW AT DINNERS WHERE MEAT EATERS ARE IN THE MAJORITY. OFFER A DISH LIKE THIS ONE, AND THERE'LL BE ENVIOUS LOOKS FROM ACROSS THE TABLE.

Preparation: 3–4 minutes; Cooking: 12 minutes

SERVES ONE TO TWO

INGREDIENTS

> 250g/9oz deep-fried tofu cubes
> 30ml/2 tbsp groundnut (peanut) oil
> 15ml/1 tbsp Thai green curry paste
> 30ml/2 tbsp light soy sauce
> 2 kaffir lime leaves, rolled into
>   cylinders and thinly sliced
> 30ml/2 tbsp sugar
> 150ml/¼ pint/⅔ cup vegetable stock
> 250g/9oz asparagus, trimmed and
>   sliced into 5cm/2in lengths
> 30ml/2 tbsp roasted peanuts,
>   finely chopped

VARIATION

Substitute slim carrot batons, baby leeks or small broccoli florets for the asparagus, if you like.

1 Preheat the grill (broiler) to medium. Place the tofu cubes in a grill (broiling) pan and grill (broil) for 2–3 minutes, then turn them over and continue to cook until they are crisp and golden brown all over. Watch them carefully: they must not be allowed to burn.

2 Heat the oil in a wok or heavy frying pan. Add the green curry paste and cook over a medium heat, stirring constantly, for 1–2 minutes, until it gives off its aroma.

3 Stir the soy sauce, kaffir lime leaves, sugar and vegetable stock into the wok or pan and mix well. Bring to the boil over a high heat, then reduce the heat to low so that the curried stock is just simmering.

4 Add the asparagus and simmer gently for 5 minutes. Meanwhile, chop each piece of tofu into four, then add to the pan with the peanuts.

5 Toss to coat all the ingredients in the sauce, then spoon into a warmed dish and serve immediately.

Energy 551kcal/2287kJ; Protein 37.3g; Carbohydrate 7.8g, of which sugars 5.2g; Fat 41.4g, of which saturates 2.8g; Cholesterol 0mg; Calcium 1894mg; Fibre 3.1g; Sodium 1203mg

ENSALADILLA

ALSO KNOWN AS RUSSIAN SALAD, THIS MIXTURE OF COOKED AND RAW VEGETABLES IN A RICH GARLIC
MAYONNAISE MAKES A USEFUL VEGETARIAN MAIN COURSE. IT TASTES GOOD WITH HARD-BOILED EGGS.

Preparation: 10 minutes; Cooking: 8 minutes

SERVES FOUR

INGREDIENTS
8 new potatoes, scrubbed
   and quartered
1 large carrot, diced
115g/4oz fine green beans,
   cut into 2cm/¾ in lengths
75g/3oz/¾ cup peas
½ Spanish (Bermuda) onion, chopped
4 cornichons or small
   gherkins, sliced
1 small red (bell) pepper, seeded
   and diced
50g/2oz/½ cup pitted black olives
15ml/1 tbsp drained pickled capers
15ml/1 tbsp freshly squeezed
   lemon juice
30ml/2 tbsp chopped fresh fennel
   or parsley
salt and ground black pepper
For the aioli
2–3 garlic cloves, finely chopped
2.5ml/½ tsp salt
150ml/¼ pint/⅔ cup mayonnaise

2 Cook the potatoes and diced carrot in a pan of boiling lightly salted water for 5 minutes, until almost tender.

3 Add the beans and peas to the potatoes and carrot and cook for 2 minutes, or until all the vegetables are tender but the beans still retain some crunch. Drain and transfer to a bowl of iced water to cool quickly.

4 When cool, drain the vegetables, place them in a large bowl and add the onion, cornichons or gherkins, red pepper, olives and capers. Stir in the aioli and pepper and lemon juice to taste.

5 Toss the vegetables and aioli together until well combined, check the seasoning and chill well. Serve garnished with fennel or parsley.

1 Make the aioli. Put two or three garlic cloves, depending on their size, in a mortar. Add the salt and crush to a paste. Whisk or stir into the mayonnaise.

VARIATION
This salad is delicious using any combination of chopped, cooked vegetables. Use whatever is available.

Energy 395kcal/1636kJ; Protein 5.2g; Carbohydrate 25.6g, of which sugars 8.1g; Fat 30.9g, of which saturates 4.8g; Cholesterol 28mg; Calcium 68mg; Fibre 4.9g; Sodium 472mg

VEGETABLE AND SATAY SALAD

THIS TASTY SALAD CONTAINS BOTH COOKED AND UNCOOKED VEGETABLES ALONG WITH CHICKPEAS,
ALL DRESSED IN A SPICY SATAY SAUCE, MAKING A DELICIOUS SUMMER MAIN COURSE.

Preparation: 5 minutes; cooking: 12–14 minutes

SERVES FOUR

INGREDIENTS
  450g/1lb baby new potatoes
  1 small head cauliflower, broken into
    small florets
  225g/8oz green beans, trimmed
  400g/14oz can chickpeas, drained
  115g/4oz/2 cups watercress sprigs
  115g/4oz/2 cups beansprouts
  8 spring onions (scallions), sliced
For the dressing
  60ml/4 tbsp crunchy peanut butter
  150ml/¼ pint/⅔ cup hot water
  5ml/1 tsp chilli sauce
  10ml/2 tsp soft brown sugar
  5ml/1 tsp soy sauce
  5ml/1 tsp lime juice
  lime wedges, to garnish (optional)

1 Put the potatoes into a pan and add water to just cover. Bring to the boil and cook for 10–12 minutes or until the potatoes are just tender when pierced with the point of a sharp knife. Drain and refresh under cold running water. Drain the potatoes again.

2 Meanwhile, bring another pan of salted water to the boil. Add the cauliflower and cook for about 6 minutes, then add the beans and cook for 5 minutes more. Drain both vegetables, refresh under cold water and drain again.

3 Put the cauliflower and beans in a large bowl and add the chickpeas. Halve the potatoes and add. Toss lightly. Mix the watercress, beansprouts and spring onions. Divide among four plates and pile the cooked vegetables on top.

4 Put the peanut butter into a bowl and stir in the water. Add the chilli sauce, brown sugar, soy sauce and lime juice. Whisk well then drizzle the dressing over the salad. Serve at once, garnished with lime wedges, if you like.

Energy 364kcal/1530kJ; Protein 19.4g; Carbohydrate 45.8g, of which sugars 10.9g; Fat 12.7g, of which saturates 2.7g; Cholesterol 0mg; Calcium 161mg; Fibre 10.2g; Sodium 578mg.

MUSHROOM KEDGEREE

CRUNCHY, JUST-COOKED GREEN BEANS AND BROWN CAP MUSHROOMS ARE THE STAR INGREDIENTS IN
THIS VEGETARIAN VERSION OF AN OLD FISH-BASED FAVOURITE.

Preparation: 3–4 minutes; Cooking: 16 minutes

SERVES TWO TO THREE

INGREDIENTS
115g/4oz/scant ¾ cup basmati rice
3 eggs
175g/6oz green beans, trimmed
50g/2oz/¼ cup butter
1 onion, finely chopped
225g/8oz/2 cups brown cap
  mushrooms, quartered
30ml/2 tbsp single (light) cream
15ml/1 tbsp chopped fresh parsley
salt and ground black pepper

1 Wash the rice several times in a bowl of cold water. Drain thoroughly. Bring a pan of water to the boil, add the rice and cook for 10–12 minutes until the grains are just tender.

2 Meanwhile, half fill a second pan with water, add the eggs and bring to the boil. Lower the heat and simmer for 8 minutes. Drain the eggs, cool them under cold water, then remove the shells. Cut them into wedges.

3 Bring another pan of water to the boil and cook the green beans for 5 minutes. Drain, refresh under cold running water, then drain again.

4 Melt the butter in a large frying pan. Add the onion and mushrooms. Cook for 2–3 minutes over a moderate heat.

5 Drain the rice well and add it to the onion mixture with the beans. Stir lightly. Cook for about 2 minutes. Add the hard-boiled eggs to the pan.

VARIATION
Leave out the beans and cook two sliced celery sticks with the onion and mushrooms. Garnish with toasted almonds.

6 Stir in the cream and parsley, taking care not to break up the eggs. Reheat the kedgeree until hot, then serve.

Energy 385kcal/1600kJ; Protein 12.2g; Carbohydrate 34.7g, of which sugars 2.9g; Fat 22.1g, of which saturates 11.6g; Cholesterol 231mg; Calcium 78mg; Fibre 2.4g; Sodium 178mg.

S P I N A C H WITH R A I S I N S AND P I N E N U T S

LIGHTLY COOKED SPINACH WITH A LITTLE ONION, OLIVE OIL, RAISINS AND PINE NUTS IS A TYPICAL
ITALIAN-JEWISH COMBINATION. IT MAKES A TASTY AND QUICK-TO-PREPARE SUPPER DISH.
Preparation: 4 minutes; Cooking: 10 minutes

2 Meanwhile, steam or cook the spinach in a very large pan over a medium-high heat, with only the water that clings to the leaves after washing, for 1–2 minutes until the leaves are bright green and wilted. Remove from the heat and drain well. Leave to cool.

3 When the spinach has cooled, chop it roughly with a sharp knife.

4 Heat the oil in a frying pan over a medium-low heat, then lower the heat further and add the spring onions or onions. Fry for about 5 minutes, or until soft, then add the spinach, raisins and pine nuts. Raise the heat and cook for 2–3 minutes to warm through. Season with salt and ground black pepper to taste and serve hot or warm.

SERVES FOUR

INGREDIENTS
  60ml/4 tbsp raisins
  1kg/2¼ lb fresh spinach
  leaves, washed
  45ml/3 tbsp olive oil
  6–8 spring onions (scallions), thinly
  sliced or 1–2 small yellow or white
  onions, finely chopped
  60ml/4 tbsp pine nuts
  salt and ground black pepper

VARIATION
For a deeper flavour, add a finely chopped garlic clove. Fry with the spring onions (scallions) or onions.

1 Put the raisins in a small bowl and pour over boiling water to cover. Leave to stand for about 10 minutes until plumped up, then drain.

COOK'S TIP
Pine nuts can turn rancid quickly, so always buy them in small quantities. Freeze any leftover amounts for use in later dishes.

Energy 271kcal/1119kJ; Protein 9.6g; Carbohydrate 12g, of which sugars 11.7g; Fat 20.7g, of which saturates 2.1g; Cholesterol 0mg; Calcium 437mg; Fibre 6g; Sodium 357mg.

STUFFED CELERIAC

IN THIS ROMANIAN RECIPE, THE CELERIAC HAS A GARLIC STUFFING AND IS COOKED IN A MIXTURE OF
OLIVE OIL AND LEMON-FLAVOURED WATER, GIVING IT EXTRA ZEST.

Preparation: 10 minutes; Cooking: 15–20 minutes

SERVES FOUR

INGREDIENTS
   4 small celeriac, about 200–225g/
      7–8oz each
   juice of 2 lemons
   150ml/¼ pint/⅔ cup extra virgin
      olive oil
For the stuffing
   6 garlic cloves, finely chopped
   5ml/1 tsp black peppercorns,
      finely crushed
   60–75ml/4–5 tbsp chopped
      fresh parsley
   salt
For the garnish
   lemon wedges
   sprigs of flat leaf parsley

1 Peel the celeriac carefully with a
sharp knife and quickly immerse in a
bowl of water and the lemon juice until
ready to use.

2 Reserve the lemon water. Very
carefully scoop out the flesh of each
celeriac, leaving a shell about 2cm/¾in
thick in which to put the filling.

3 Working quickly, chop up the scooped-
out celeriac flesh and mix with the
garlic and peppercorns. Add the parsley
and season with salt.

4 Fill the shells with the stuffing and sit
them in a large pan, making sure they
remain upright throughout cooking.
Pour in the olive oil and enough lemon
water to come halfway up the celeriac.

5 Simmer very gently for 15–20 minutes
until the celeriac are tender and nearly
all the cooking liquid has been
absorbed. Serve the celeriac hot or cold
with their juices, and garnish with
lemon wedges and sprigs of parsley.

COOK'S TIPS
• Celeriac is a rather odd-looking root
vegetable that resembles an
underdeveloped head of celery and tastes
a bit like sweet nutty celery.
• It is necessary to add the lemon juice
to the water in order to help prevent the
peeled celeriac from discolouring.

Energy 251kcal/1033kJ; Protein 1.8g; Carbohydrate 3.5g, of which sugars 3.1g; Fat 25.7g, of which saturates 3.6g; Cholesterol 0mg; Calcium 123mg; Fibre 3.4g; Sodium 127mg

TOFU AND PEPPER KEBABS

A SIMPLE COATING OF GROUND, DRY-ROASTED PEANUTS PRESSED ON TO CUBED TOFU PROVIDES PLENTY OF ADDITIONAL FLAVOUR ALONG WITH THE PEPPERS. USE METAL OR BAMBOO SKEWERS.

Preparation: 6–8 minutes; Cooking: 10–12 minutes

SERVES FOUR

INGREDIENTS
  250g/9oz firm tofu
  50g/2oz/½ cup dry-roasted peanuts
  2 red and 2 green (bell) peppers
  60ml/4 tbsp sweet chilli
    dipping sauce

1 Pat the tofu dry on kitchen paper and then cut it into small cubes. Grind the peanuts in a blender or food processor and transfer to a plate.

COOK'S TIP
Don't forget to soak the bamboo skewers upright in a jar of water for about half an hour before using, so they don't scorch.

2 Preheat the grill (broiler) to medium. Using a sharp knife, halve and seed the red and green peppers, and cut them into large chunks. Turn the tofu cubes in the ground nuts to coat thoroughly on all sides.

3 Thread the chunks of pepper on to four large skewers with the tofu cubes and place on a foil-lined grill rack. Grill (broil) the kebabs, turning frequently, for 10–12 minutes, or until the peppers and peanuts are beginning to brown.

Energy 175kcal/730kJ; Protein 10g; Carbohydrate 12.9g, of which sugars 11.4g; Fat 9.6g, of which saturates 1.6g; Cholesterol 0mg; Calcium 339mg; Fibre 3.6g; Sodium 108mg

SWEET PEPPERS STUFFED <u>WITH</u> TWO CHEESES

THIS IS A DELICIOUS BARBECUE STARTER TO COOK BEFORE THE GRILL TASTES TOO STRONGLY OF MEAT.
ALTERNATIVELY, USE A DISPOSABLE BARBECUE FOR THESE TASTY PEPPERS.

Preparation: 5 minutes; Cooking: 12–14 minutes

SERVES FOUR

INGREDIENTS

4 sweet romano peppers, preferably
  in mixed colours, total weight about
  350g/12oz
90ml/6 tbsp extra virgin olive oil
200g/7oz mozzarella cheese
10 drained bottled sweet cherry
  peppers, finely chopped
115g/4oz ricotta salata
30ml/2 tbsp chopped fresh
  oregano leaves
24 black olives
2 garlic cloves, crushed
salt and ground black pepper
dressed mixed salad leaves and
  bread, to serve

1 Prepare a barbecue. Split the peppers lengthways and remove the seeds and membrane. Rub 15ml/1 tbsp of the oil all over the peppers. Place them hollow-side uppermost.

2 Slice the mozzarella and divide it equally among the pepper halves.

3 Sprinkle over the chopped cherry peppers, season lightly and crumble the ricotta salata over the top, followed by the oregano leaves and olives. Mix the garlic with the remaining oil and add a little salt and pepper. Spoon about half the mixture over the filling in the peppers.

4 Once the flames have died down, rake the coals to one side. Position a lightly oiled grill rack over the coals to heat. When the coals are medium-hot, or with a moderate coating of ash, place the filled peppers on the section of grill rack that is not over the coals.

5 Cover with a lid, or improvise with a wok lid or tented heavy-duty foil. Cook for 6 minutes, then spoon the remaining oil mixture over the filling, replace the lid and continue to grill for 6–8 minutes more, or until the peppers are lightly charred and the cheese has melted. Serve with a dressed green or leafy salad and bread.

VARIATION

The peppers can be cooked on a griddle if you prefer. It is a good idea to blanch them in boiling water before filling, to give them a head start.

Energy 371kcal/1532kJ; Protein 13.1g; Carbohydrate 6.6g, of which sugars 6.3g; Fat 32.6g, of which saturates 12.2g; Cholesterol 41mg; Calcium 203mg; Fibre 2g; Sodium 484mg

STUFFED SWEET PEPPERS

THIS IS AN UNUSUAL RECIPE IN THAT THE STUFFED PEPPERS ARE STEAMED RATHER THAN BAKED.
THE TECHNIQUE IS SPEEDY AND THE RESULT IS BEAUTIFULLY LIGHT AND TENDER.

Preparation: 5 minutes; Cooking: 15 minutes

SERVES FOUR

INGREDIENTS
3 garlic cloves, finely chopped
2 coriander (cilantro) roots,
  finely chopped
400g/14oz/3 cups
  mushrooms, quartered
5ml/1 tsp Thai red curry paste
1 egg, lightly beaten
15–30ml/1–2 tbsp light soy sauce
2.5ml/½ tsp sugar
3 kaffir lime leaves, finely chopped
4 yellow (bell) peppers, halved
  lengthways and seeded

VARIATIONS
Use red or orange (bell) peppers if you
prefer, or a combination of the two.

1 In a mortar or spice grinder pound or
blend the garlic with the coriander
roots. Scrape into a bowl.

2 Put the mushrooms in a food
processor and pulse briefly until they
are finely chopped. Add to the garlic
mixture, then stir in the curry paste,
egg, sauces, sugar and lime leaves.

3 Place the pepper halves in a single
layer in a steamer basket. Spoon the
mixture loosely into the pepper halves.

4 Bring the water in the steamer to the
boil, then lower the heat to a simmer.
Steam the peppers for 15 minutes, or
until the flesh feels tender when tested
with a knife tip. Serve hot.

Energy 89kcal/374kJ; Protein 5.1g; Carbohydrate 10.6g, of which sugars 9.9g; Fat 3.2g, of which saturates 0.8g; Cholesterol 48mg; Calcium 27mg; Fibre 3.5g; Sodium 563mg

MIXED BEAN AND TOMATO CHILLI

THE ONLY TALENT THIS DISH REQUIRES IS THE ABILITY TO OPEN A CAN, CHOP A CHILLI AND STIR A SAUCE. IT'S IDEAL FOR THOSE DAYS WHEN YOUR ENERGY LEVELS ARE ZERO AND YOU NEED FOOD FAST.

Preparation: 2–3 minutes; Cooking: 12 minutes

SERVES FOUR

INGREDIENTS

400g/14oz jar tomato and herb sauce
2 x 400g/14oz cans mixed beans,
  drained and rinsed
1 fresh red chilli
large handful of fresh coriander
  (cilantro), finely chopped
120ml/4fl oz/½ cup sour cream

1 Seed and thinly slice the chilli, then put it into a pan.

2 Pour the tomato sauce and mixed beans into a pan. Set some of the finely chopped coriander aside for the garnish and add the remainder to the tomato and bean mixture. Stir the contents of the pan for a few seconds to mix all the ingredients together.

3 Bring the mixture to the boil, then quickly reduce the heat, cover and simmer gently for 10 minutes. Stir the mixture occasionally and add a dash of water if the sauce starts to dry out.

4 Ladle the chilli into warmed individual bowls and top with sour cream. Sprinkle with coriander and serve.

VARIATIONS
This chilli is great just as it is, served with chunks of bread, but you may want to dress it up a bit occasionally. Try serving it over a mixture of long grain and wild rice, piling it into split pitta breads or using it as a filling for baked potatoes. Serve with yogurt or crème fraîche instead of sour cream.

COOK'S TIP
Treat chillies with caution and wash your hands in soapy water after touching them. The capsaicin they contain is a powerful irritant and will cause eyes to sting if it comes into contact with them.

Energy 309kcal/1302kJ; Protein 16.7g; Carbohydrate 43.7g, of which sugars 14.1g; Fat 8.7g, of which saturates 4.2g; Cholesterol 18mg; Calcium 193mg; Fibre 12.4g; Sodium 1202mg

MUSHROOM STROGANOFF

THIS CREAMY MIXED MUSHROOM SAUCE TASTES GREAT AND IS IDEAL FOR A DINNER PARTY.
SERVE IT WITH TOASTED BUCKWHEAT, BROWN RICE OR A MIXTURE OF WILD RICES.

Preparation: 3 minutes; Cooking: 15–17 minutes

SERVES FOUR

INGREDIENTS
    25g/1oz/2 tbsp butter
    900g/2lb/8 cups mixed mushrooms,
      cut into bitesize pieces
    350g/12oz/1¾ cups white long
      grain rice
    350ml/12fl oz/1½ cups white
      wine sauce
    250ml/8fl oz/1 cup sour cream
    chopped chives, to garnish

1 Melt the butter in a large, heavy pan
and add the mushrooms. Cook over a
medium heat until the mushrooms give
up their liquid. Continue cooking until
they are tender and beginning to brown.

2 Meanwhile, bring a large pan of lightly
salted water to the boil. Add the rice,
partially cover the pan and cook over a
medium heat for 13–15 minutes until
the rice is just tender.

3 Add the wine sauce to the cooked
mushrooms in the pan and bring to the
boil, stirring. Stir in the sour cream and
season to taste. Drain the rice well,
spoon on to warm plates, top with the
sauce and garnish with chives.

Energy 556kcal/2316kJ; Protein 13.3g; Carbohydrate 80.4g, of which sugars 7.2g; Fat 21.7g, of which saturates 11.4g; Cholesterol 51mg; Calcium 96mg; Fibre 2.5g; Sodium 897mg

CORN FRITTERS

Sometimes it is the simplest dishes that taste the best. These fritters, packed with corn, are easy to prepare and go well with everything from gammon to nut rissoles.

Preparation: 5 minutes; Cooking: 8 minutes

MAKES TWELVE

INGREDIENTS

3 corn cobs, total weight about
  250g/9oz
1 garlic clove, crushed
a small bunch of fresh coriander
  (cilantro), chopped
1 small fresh red or green chilli,
  seeded and finely chopped
1 spring onion (scallion),
  finely chopped
15ml/1 tbsp soy sauce
75g/3oz/¾ cup rice flour or plain
  (all-purpose) flour
2 eggs, lightly beaten
60ml/4 tbsp water
oil, for shallow-frying
salt and ground black pepper
sweet chilli sauce, to serve

1 Using a sharp knife, slice the kernels from the cobs using downward strokes. Rinse to remove any clinging debris from the cob and place in a bowl.

2 Add the garlic, chopped coriander, red or green chilli, spring onion, soy sauce, flour, beaten eggs and water to the corn and mix well. Season with salt and pepper to taste and mix again. The mixture should be firm enough to hold its shape, but not stiff.

3 Heat the oil in a large frying pan. Add spoonfuls of the corn mixture, gently spreading each one out with the back of the spoon to make a roundish fritter. Cook for 1–2 minutes on each side.

4 Drain the first batch of fritters on kitchen paper and keep hot on a foil-covered dish while frying more in the same way. Serve the fritters hot with sweet chilli sauce – arrange on a large plate around the sauce, if you like.

Energy 76kcal/314kJ; Protein 2.1g; Carbohydrate 7.6g, of which sugars 0.5g; Fat 4.1g, of which saturates 0.7g; Cholesterol 32mg; Calcium 14mg; Fibre 0.6g; Sodium 102mg

TOFU AND GREEN BEAN RED CURRY

THIS IS ONE OF THOSE VERSATILE RECIPES THAT SHOULD BE IN EVERY COOK'S REPERTOIRE. THIS VERSION USES GREEN BEANS, BUT OTHER TYPES OF VEGETABLE WORK EQUALLY WELL.

Preparation: 2–3 minutes; Cooking: 7 minutes

SERVES FOUR TO SIX

INGREDIENTS
600ml/1 pint/2½ cups coconut milk
15ml/1 tbsp Thai red curry paste
10ml/2 tsp palm sugar (jaggery)
  or honey
225g/8oz/3¼ cups button
  (white) mushrooms
115g/4oz green beans, trimmed
175g/6oz firm tofu, rinsed, drained
  and cut into 2cm/¾in cubes
4 kaffir lime leaves, torn
2 fresh red chillies, seeded
  and sliced
fresh coriander (cilantro) leaves,
  to garnish

1 Pour about one-third of the coconut milk into a wok or pan. Cook until it starts to separate and an oily sheen appears on the surface.

2 Add the red curry paste and palm sugar or honey to the coconut milk. Mix thoroughly, then add the mushrooms. Stir and cook for 1 minute.

3 Stir in the remaining coconut milk. Bring back to the boil, then add the green beans and tofu cubes. Simmer gently for 4–5 minutes more.

4 Stir in the kaffir lime leaves and sliced red chillies. Spoon the curry into a serving dish, garnish with the coriander leaves and serve immediately.

Energy 59kcal/250kJ; Protein 3.8g; Carbohydrate 7.5g, of which sugars 7.1g; Fat 1.8g, of which saturates 0.4g; Cholesterol 0mg; Calcium 188mg; Fibre 0.8g; Sodium 291mg

SIMPLE RICE SALAD

*SOMETIMES CALLED CONFETTI SALAD, THIS FEATURES BRIGHTLY COLOURED CHOPPED VEGETABLES
SERVED IN A WELL-FLAVOURED DRESSING. CHILL IT WELL IF YOU INTEND TO TAKE IT ON A PICNIC.*
Preparation: 6 minutes; Cooking: 10–12 minutes

SERVES SIX

INGREDIENTS
   275g/10oz/1½ cups long grain rice
   1 bunch spring onions (scallions),
     finely sliced
   1 green (bell) pepper, seeded and
     finely diced
   1 yellow (bell) pepper, seeded and
     finely diced
   225g/8oz tomatoes, peeled, seeded
     and chopped
   30ml/2 tbsp chopped fresh flat leaf
     parsley or coriander (cilantro)
For the dressing
   75ml/5 tbsp mixed olive oil and
     extra virgin olive oil
   15ml/1 tbsp sherry vinegar
   5ml/1 tsp strong Dijon mustard
   salt and ground black pepper

1 Cook the rice in a large pan of lightly salted boiling water for 10–12 minutes, until tender but still *al dente*. Be careful not to overcook it.

2 Drain the rice well in a sieve (strainer), rinse thoroughly under cold running water and drain again. Leave the rice to cool while you prepare the ingredients for the dressing.

3 Meanwhile, make the dressing by whisking all the ingredients together. Transfer the rice to a bowl and add half the dressing to moisten it and cool it further.

4 Add the spring onions, peppers, tomatoes and parsley or coriander with the remaining dressing, and toss well to mix. Season with salt and pepper to taste.

Energy 276kcal/1150kJ; Protein 4.6g; Carbohydrate 41.9g, of which sugars 5.2g; Fat 9.9g, of which saturates 1.4g; Cholesterol 0mg; Calcium 29mg; Fibre 1.7g; Sodium 8mg

STEWED OKRA WITH TOMATOES

THIS IS A FAVOURITE MIDDLE-EASTERN WAY TO PREPARE OKRA. ADD WEDGES OF LEMON AS A GARNISH SO THAT THEIR JUICE CAN BE SQUEEZED OVER THE VEGETABLES TO TASTE.

Preparation: 2 minutes; Cooking: 25 minutes

SERVES FOUR TO SIX

INGREDIENTS
400g/14oz can chopped tomatoes
  with onions and garlic
generous pinch each of ground
  cinnamon, cumin and cloves
90ml/6 tbsp chopped fresh coriander
  (cilantro) leaves
800g/1¾lb okra

1 Heat the tomatoes and the cinnamon, cumin and cloves with half the coriander in a pan, then season to taste with salt and freshly ground black pepper and bring to the boil.

2 Add the okra and cook, stirring constantly, for 1–2 minutes. Reduce the heat to low, then simmer, stirring occasionally, for 20 minutes, until the okra is tender.

3 Taste for spicing and seasoning, and adjust if necessary, adding more of any one spice, salt or pepper to taste. Stir in the remaining coriander. Serve hot, warm or cold.

Energy 56kcal/234kJ; Protein 4.5g; Carbohydrate 6.3g, of which sugars 5.6g; Fat 1.6g, of which saturates 0.5g; Cholesterol 0mg; Calcium 235mg; Fibre 6.4g; Sodium 20mg.

BARBECUED AUBERGINES WITH FETA

AUBERGINES TAKE ON A LOVELY SMOKY FLAVOUR WHEN GRILLED ON A BARBECUE. CHOOSE A GOOD QUALITY GREEK FETA CHEESE TO ADD THE BEST FLAVOUR TO THIS DISH.

Preparation: 5 minutes; Cooking: 25 minutes

SERVES SIX

INGREDIENTS
3 medium aubergines (eggplants)
400g/14oz feta cheese, drained
  and crumbled
a small bunch of coriander (cilantro),
  roughly chopped, plus extra for
  garnish
60ml/4 tbsp extra virgin olive oil
salt and ground black pepper

1 Prepare a barbecue. Cook the aubergines for 20 minutes, turning occasionally, until charred and soft. Remove from the barbecue and cut in half lengthways.

2 Carefully scoop the aubergine flesh into a bowl, reserving the skins. Mash the flesh roughly with a fork.

3 Stir the feta cheese into the mashed aubergine with the chopped coriander and olive oil. Season with salt and ground black pepper to taste.

4 Spoon the aubergine and feta mixture back into the skins and return to the barbecue for 5 minutes to warm through. Serve immediately garnished with coriander leaves.

COOK'S TIP
Be careful when scraping out the aubergine flesh, otherwise you might cut through the skin with the spoon, leaving a hole through which the filling could fall.

Energy 251kcal/1038kJ; Protein 11.6g; Carbohydrate 3.4g, of which sugars 3.2g; Fat 21.3g, of which saturates 10.3g; Cholesterol 47mg; Calcium 267mg; Fibre 2.4g; Sodium 965mg.

RATATOUILLE

A HIGHLY VERSATILE TOMATO AND MIXED VEGETABLE STEW FROM PROVENCE, RATATOUILLE IS DELICIOUS WARM OR COLD, ON ITS OWN OR WITH EGGS, PASTA, FISH OR MEAT, PARTICULARLY LAMB.

Preparation: 5 minutes; Cooking: 25 minutes

SERVES SIX

INGREDIENTS
900g/2lb ripe plum tomatoes
120ml/4fl oz/½ cup olive oil
2 onions, thinly sliced
2 red and 1 yellow (bell) pepper,
  seeded and cut into chunks
1 large aubergine (eggplant),
  cut into chunks
2 courgettes (zucchini), sliced
4 garlic cloves, crushed
2 bay leaves
15ml/1 tbsp chopped thyme
salt and ground black pepper

1 Plunge the tomatoes into boiling water for 30 seconds, then refresh in cold water. Peel away the skins and chop the flesh roughly.

2 Heat a little of the olive oil in a large, heavy pan and gently fry the onions for 4 minutes. Stir them constantly so that they do not brown. Cook them until they are just transparent.

3 Add the peppers to the fried onions and cook for a further 2 minutes. Using a slotted spoon, transfer the onions and peppers to a plate and set them aside.

4 Meanwhile, in a separate pan, add more oil and the aubergine and fry gently for 4 minutes. Add the remaining oil and courgettes, and fry for 3 minutes. Lift out the courgettes and aubergine and set them aside.

5 Add the garlic and tomatoes with the bay leaves and thyme, and some seasoning. Cook gently until the tomatoes have softened and are turning pulpy.

6 Return all the vegetables to the pan and cook gently, stirring frequently, for about 15 minutes, until fairly pulpy but retaining a little texture. Season to taste.

Energy 194kcal/806kJ; Protein 3.9g; Carbohydrate 14.6g, of which sugars 13.1g; Fat 13.7g, of which saturates 2.1g; Cholesterol 0mg; Calcium 49mg; Fibre 4.7g; Sodium 19mg.

SAFFRON RISOTTO ᴡɪᴛʜ PARMESAN

*THIS RISOTTO, COOKED WITH SAFFRON AND SCATTERED WITH CHEESE AND GREMOLATA, MAKES A
DELICIOUS LIGHT MEAL OR ACCOMPANIMENT TO A MEATY STEW OR CASSEROLE.*

Preparation: 5 minutes; Cooking: 25 minutes

SERVES FOUR

INGREDIENTS
5ml/1 tsp (or 1 sachet)
   saffron strands
15ml/1 tbsp boiling water
25g/1oz/2 tbsp butter
1 large onion, finely chopped
275g/10oz/1½ cups arborio
   (risotto) rice
150ml/¼ pint/⅔ cup dry white wine
1 litre/1¾ pints/4 cups simmering
   vegetable stock
salt and ground black pepper
Parmesan cheese shavings or grated
   Parmesan, to serve
For the gremolata
2 garlic cloves, crushed
60ml/4 tbsp chopped fresh parsley
finely grated rind of 1 lemon

1 Start by making the gremolata.
Combine the crushed garlic, chopped
parsley and grated lemon rind in a bowl.
Set aside while you make the risotto.

2 Put the saffron strands in a small
bowl. Pour over the boiling water and
leave to stand. Melt the butter in a
heavy pan and gently fry the onion for
3 minutes, until softened.

COOK'S TIP
Italian risottos have a distinctive creamy
texture that is achieved by using arborio
rice – a short grain rice that absorbs
plenty of stock while still retaining its
nutty texture.

3 Stir in the rice and cook, stirring all
the time, for about 2 minutes until it
becomes translucent. Add the wine and
saffron mixture and cook for several
minutes until the wine is absorbed.

4 Add 600ml/1 pint/2½ cups of the
stock to the pan and simmer gently
until the stock is absorbed, stirring
frequently.

5 Gradually add more stock, a ladleful
at a time, until the rice is tender.
(The rice might be tender and creamy
before you've added all the stock, so
add it slowly towards the end of the
cooking time.)

6 Season the risotto with salt and
pepper and transfer to a serving dish.
Scatter lavishly with shavings of
Parmesan cheese or grated Parmesan
and the gremolata.

Energy 310kcal/1295kJ; Protein 5.6g; Carbohydrate 56.4g, of which sugars 1.2g; Fat 5.7g, of which saturates 3.3g; Cholesterol 13mg; Calcium 39mg; Fibre 0.7g; Sodium 42mg.

SWEET PUMPKIN AND PEANUT CURRY

THIS HEARTY, SOOTHING CURRY IS PERFECT FOR AUTUMN OR WINTER EVENINGS. ITS CHEERFUL COLOUR ALONE WILL BRIGHTEN YOU UP — AND IT TASTES TERRIFIC TOO.

Preparation: 10 minutes; Cooking: 20 minutes

SERVES FOUR

INGREDIENTS

30ml/2 tbsp vegetable oil
4 garlic cloves, crushed
4 shallots, finely chopped
30ml/2 tbsp yellow curry paste
600ml/1 pint/2½ cups
    vegetable stock
2 kaffir lime leaves, torn
15ml/1 tbsp chopped fresh galangal
450g/1lb pumpkin, peeled, seeded
    and diced
225g/8oz sweet potatoes, diced
90g/3½ oz/scant 1 cup roasted
    peanuts, chopped
300ml/½ pint/1¼ cups coconut milk
90g/3½ oz/1½ cups chestnut
    mushrooms, sliced
15ml/1 tbsp soy sauce
30ml/2 tbsp mushroom ketchup
For the garnish
50g/2oz/⅓ cup pumpkin
    seeds, toasted
fresh green chilli flowers

1 Heat the oil in a large pan. Add the garlic and shallots and cook over a medium heat, stirring occasionally, for 3 minutes, until softened and golden. Do not let them burn.

2 Add the yellow curry paste and stir-fry over a medium heat for 30 seconds, until fragrant, then add the stock, lime leaves, galangal, pumpkin and sweet potatoes. Bring to the boil, stirring frequently, then reduce the heat to low and simmer gently for 12 minutes.

3 Add the peanuts, coconut milk and mushrooms. Stir in the soy sauce and fish sauce and simmer for 5 minutes more. Serve in individual bowls garnished with the seeds and chilli flowers.

COOK'S TIP
To make a chilli flower, hold a chilli by its stem and cut from the tip to the base, but only through the side facing you, all round to create the petals. Soak in iced water for an hour or two to make the petals open and curl.

Energy 306kcal/1279kJ; Protein 9.6g; Carbohydrate 24.5g, of which sugars 11.4g; Fat 19.6g, of which saturates 3.3g; Cholesterol 0mg; Calcium 160mg; Fibre 6.4g; Sodium 409mg.

CORN AND CASHEW NUT CURRY

A SUBSTANTIAL CURRY, THIS COMBINES ALL THE ESSENTIAL FLAVOURS OF SOUTHERN THAILAND. IT IS DELICIOUSLY AROMATIC, BUT THE FLAVOUR IS FAIRLY MILD.

Preparation: 6 minutes; Cooking: 24 minutes

SERVES FOUR

INGREDIENTS
30ml/2 tbsp vegetable oil
4 shallots, chopped
90g/3½ oz/scant 1 cup cashew nuts
5ml/1 tsp Thai red curry paste
400g/14oz potatoes, peeled and cut
    into chunks
1 lemon grass stalk, finely chopped
200g/7oz can chopped tomatoes
600ml/1 pint/2½ cups boiling water
200g/7oz/generous 1 cup drained
    canned whole kernel corn
4 celery sticks, sliced
2 kaffir lime leaves, rolled into
    cylinders and thinly sliced
15ml/1 tbsp tomato ketchup
15ml/1 tbsp light soy sauce
5ml/1 tsp palm sugar (jaggery) or
    light muscovado (brown) sugar
5ml/1 tsp mushroom ketchup
For the garnish
4 spring onions (scallions),
    thinly sliced
small bunch fresh basil, chopped

1 Heat the oil in a large, heavy pan or wok. Add the shallots and stir-fry over a medium heat for 2–3 minutes, until softened. Add the cashew nuts and stir-fry for a few minutes until golden.

2 Stir in the red curry paste. Stir-fry for 1 minute, then add the potatoes, lemon grass, tomatoes and boiling water.

3 Bring back to the boil, then reduce the heat to low, cover and simmer gently for 15 minutes, or until the potatoes are tender.

4 Stir the corn, celery, lime leaves, tomato ketchup, soy sauce, sugar and fish sauce into the pan or wok. Simmer for a further 5 minutes, until heated through, then spoon into warmed serving bowls. Sprinkle with the sliced spring onions and basil and serve.

COOK'S TIPS
• Rolling the lime leaves into cylinders before slicing produces very fine strips – a technique known as cutting *en chiffonnade*. Remove the central rib from the leaves before cutting them.
• The well-drained vegetables from this curry would make a very tasty filling for a pastry or pie. This may not be a Thai tradition, but it is a good example of fusion food.

Energy 298kcal/1245kJ; Protein 8.8g; Carbohydrate 27.6g, of which sugars 8.9g; Fat 17.7g, of which saturates 3.1g; Cholesterol 0mg; Calcium 33mg; Fibre 3.5g; Sodium 981mg.

LENTIL FRITTERS

*THESE SPICY FRITTERS FROM THE INDIAN SUBCONTINENT ARE DELICIOUS SERVED WITH A WEDGE OF
LEMON AND A SPOONFUL OF HOT, FRAGRANT CHUTNEY SUCH AS MINT.*

Preparation: 15 minutes; Cooking: 10–12 minutes

SERVES FOUR TO SIX

INGREDIENTS

250g/9oz/generous 1 cup red lentils,
  soaked overnight
3–5 garlic cloves, chopped
30ml/2 tbsp roughly chopped fresh
  root ginger
120ml/4fl oz/½ cup chopped fresh
  coriander (cilantro) leaves
2.5–5ml/½–1 tsp ground cumin
1.5–2.5ml/¼–½ tsp ground turmeric
large pinch of cayenne pepper or
  ½–1 fresh green chilli, chopped
120ml/4fl oz/½ cup gram flour
5ml/1 tsp baking powder
30ml/2 tbsp couscous
2 large or 3 small onions, chopped
vegetable oil, for frying
2.5ml/½ tsp each of salt and ground
  black pepper
lemon wedges, to garnish
hot fragrant chutney, to serve

1 Drain the lentils, reserving a little of
the soaking water. Put the chopped
garlic and ginger in a food processor or
blender and process until finely minced
(ground). Add the drained lentils,
15–30ml/1–2 tbsp of the reserved
soaking water and the chopped
coriander and process to form a purée.

2 Add the cumin, turmeric, cayenne or
chilli, salt and pepper, the gram flour,
baking powder and couscous to the
mixture and combine. The mixture
should form a thick batter. If it seems too
thick, add a spoonful of soaking water
and if it is too watery, add a little more
flour or couscous. Mix in the onions.

3 Heat the oil in a wide, deep frying
pan, to a depth of about 5cm/2in, until
it is hot enough to brown a cube of
bread in 30 seconds. Using two spoons,
form the mixture into two-bitesize balls
and slip each one gently into the hot oil.
Cook until golden brown on the
underside, then turn and cook the
second side until golden brown.

4 Remove the fritters from the hot oil
with a slotted spoon and drain well on
kitchen paper. Transfer the fritters to a
baking sheet and keep warm in the
oven until all the mixture is cooked.
Serve hot or at room temperature with
lemon wedges and chutney.

Energy 297kcal/1249kJ; Protein 12.9g; Carbohydrate 47.9g, of which sugars 5.2g; Fat 6.6g, of which saturates 0.7g; Cholesterol 0mg; Calcium 84mg; Fibre 4.4g; Sodium 25mg.

AUBERGINE, MINT AND COUSCOUS SALAD

PACKETS OF FLAVOURED COUSCOUS ARE AVAILABLE IN MOST SUPERMARKETS — YOU CAN USE
WHICHEVER YOU LIKE, BUT GARLIC AND CORIANDER IS PARTICULARLY GOOD FOR THIS RECIPE.

Preparation: 3 minutes; Cooking: 6 minutes

SERVES TWO

INGREDIENTS
   1 large aubergine (eggplant),
     cut into chunks
   30ml/2 tbsp olive oil
   115g/4oz packet couscous flavoured
     with garlic and coriander (cilantro)
   30ml/2 tbsp chopped fresh mint
   salt and ground black pepper

1 Preheat the grill (broiler) to high. Toss the aubergine chunks with the olive oil. Season with salt and pepper to taste and spread them on a non-stick baking sheet. Grill (broil) for 5–6 minutes, turning occasionally, until golden brown.

2 Meanwhile, prepare the flavoured couscous according to the instructions on the packet.

3 Stir the grilled aubergine and chopped fresh mint into the garlic and coriander couscous, toss thoroughly and serve immediately.

VARIATION
For extra colour and flavour, add tomato to the salad. Grill (broil) about six baby plum tomatoes alongside the aubergine (eggplant).

Energy 251kcal/1044kJ; Protein 4.8g; Carbohydrate 32.5g, of which sugars 2g; Fat 12.1g, of which saturates 1.7g; Cholesterol 0mg; Calcium 53mg; Fibre 2g; Sodium 5mg

SPICED LENTILS

THE COMBINATION OF LENTILS, TOMATOES AND CHEESE IS WIDELY USED IN MEDITERRANEAN COOKING.
THE TANG OF FETA CHEESE COMPLEMENTS THE SLIGHTLY EARTHY FLAVOUR OF THE ATTRACTIVE LENTILS.

Preparation: 2 minutes; Cooking: 20 minutes

SERVES FOUR

INGREDIENTS
250g/9oz/1½ cups Puy lentils
600ml/1 pint/2½ cups water
200g/7oz feta cheese
75ml/5 tbsp sun-dried tomato
 purée (paste)
small handful of fresh chervil
 or flat leaf parsley, chopped,
 plus extra to garnish

COOK'S TIPS
• True Puy lentils come from the region of France, Le Puy, which has a unique climate and volcanic soil in which the lentils thrive.
• Always pick over lentils very carefully before cooking them to remove any little stones that may be among them. The dark colour of Puy lentils means that the stones can be harder to find.

1 Place the lentils in a heavy pan with the measured water. Bring to the boil, reduce the heat and cover the pan. Simmer gently for about 20 minutes, until the lentils are just tender and most of the water has been absorbed.

2 Crumble half the feta cheese into the pan. Add the sun-dried tomato purée, chopped chervil or flat leaf parsley and a little salt and freshly ground black pepper. Heat through for 1 minute.

3 Transfer the lentil mixture and juices to warmed plates or bowls. Crumble the remaining feta cheese on top and sprinkle with the fresh herbs to garnish. Serve the lentils immediately.

Energy 339kcal/1427kJ; Protein 23.7g; Carbohydrate 38.6g, of which sugars 4.9g; Fat 11g, of which saturates 7g; Cholesterol 35mg; Calcium 221mg; Fibre 3.7g; Sodium 788mg.

SPICED CHICKPEA AND AUBERGINE STEW

THE INGREDIENTS HERE COMBINE TO MAKE A FIERY TOMATO AND AUBERGINE STEW THAT IS TYPICAL OF ISRAELI COOKING, FOR WHICH AUBERGINES AND ALL THINGS HOT AND SPICY ARE STAPLES.

Preparation: 10 minutes; Cooking: 20 minutes

SERVES FOUR TO SIX

INGREDIENTS

about 60ml/4 tbsp olive oil
1 large aubergine (eggplant) cut
   into bitesize chunks
2 onions, thinly sliced
3–5 garlic cloves, chopped
1–2 green (bell) peppers, thinly
   sliced or chopped
1–2 fresh hot chillies, chopped
4 fresh or canned tomatoes, diced
30–45ml/2–3 tbsp tomato purée
   (paste), if using fresh tomatoes
5ml/1 tsp ground turmeric
pinch of curry powder or
   ras al hanout
cayenne pepper, to taste
400g/14oz can chickpeas, drained
   and rinsed
juice of ½–1 lemon
30–45ml/2–3 tbsp chopped fresh
   coriander (cilantro) leaves
salt

2 Heat the remaining oil in the pan, add the onions, garlic, peppers and chillies and fry until softened. Add the diced tomatoes, tomato purée, if using, spices and salt, and cook, stirring, until the mixture is of a sauce consistency. Add a little water if necessary.

3 Add the chickpeas to the sauce and cook for about 5 minutes, then add the aubergine, stir to mix and cook for 5–10 minutes until the flavours are well combined. Add lemon juice to taste, then add the coriander leaves. Chill before serving.

1 Heat half the oil in a frying pan, add the aubergine chunks and fry until brown, adding more oil if necessary. When cooked, transfer the aubergine to a strainer, standing over a bowl, and leave to drain.

VARIATION
To make a Middle Eastern-style ratatouille, cut 2 courgettes (zucchini) and one red (bell) pepper into chunks. Add to the pan with the onions and garlic and continue as before.

Energy 201kcal/843kJ; Protein 7.1g; Carbohydrate 22.3g, of which sugars 10.4g; Fat 10g, of which saturates 1.4g; Cholesterol 0mg; Calcium 57mg; Fibre 5.9g; Sodium 175mg.

AUBERGINE AND SWEET POTATO STEW

INSPIRED BY THAI COOKING, THIS AUBERGINE AND SWEET POTATO STEW COOKED IN A COCONUT
SAUCE IS SCENTED WITH FRAGRANT LEMON GRASS, GINGER AND LOTS OF GARLIC.

Preparation: 8 minutes; Cooking: 22 minutes

SERVES SIX

INGREDIENTS
60ml/4 tbsp groundnut (peanut) oil
400g/14oz baby aubergines
 (eggplants), halved, or 2 standard
 aubergines, cut into chunks
225g/8oz Thai red shallots or other
 small shallots or pickling onions
5ml/1 tsp fennel seeds,
 lightly crushed
4–5 garlic cloves, thinly sliced
25ml/1½ tbsp finely chopped fresh
 root ginger
475ml/16fl oz/2 cups vegetable stock
2 stems lemon grass, outer layers
 discarded, finely chopped or minced
15g/½ oz fresh coriander (cilantro),
 stalks and leaves chopped separately
3 kaffir lime leaves, lightly bruised
2–3 small red chillies
45–60ml/3–4 tbsp Thai green
 curry paste
675g/1½ lb sweet potatoes, peeled
 and cut into thick chunks
400ml/14fl oz/1⅔ cups coconut milk
2.5–5ml/½–1 tsp light muscovado
 (brown) sugar
250g/9oz mushrooms, thickly sliced
juice of 1 lime, to taste
salt and ground black pepper
18 fresh Thai basil leaves or
 ordinary basil, to serve

1 Heat half the oil in a wide pan or deep, lidded frying pan. Add the aubergines and cook over a medium heat, stirring occasionally, until lightly browned on all sides. Remove from the pan and set aside.

2 Slice 4–5 of the shallots and set aside. Fry the remaining whole shallots in the oil remaining in the pan, adding a little more oil if necessary, until lightly browned. Set aside with the aubergines. Meanwhile, add the remaining oil to the pan and cook the sliced shallots, fennel seeds, garlic and ginger very gently until soft but not browned.

3 Add the vegetable stock, lemon grass, chopped coriander stalks and any roots, lime leaves and whole chillies. Bring to the boil, cover and simmer over a low heat for 5 minutes.

4 Stir in 30ml/2 tbsp of the curry paste and the sweet potatoes. Simmer gently for about 10 minutes, then return the aubergines and browned shallots to the pan and cook for a further 3 minutes.

5 Stir in the coconut milk and the sugar. Season to taste, then stir in the mushrooms and simmer for 5 minutes, or until all the vegetables are cooked. Stir in more curry paste and lime juice to taste, followed by the chopped coriander leaves. Adjust the seasoning and ladle the vegetables into warmed bowls. Scatter basil leaves over the vegetables and serve.

Energy 228kcal/960kJ; Protein 4.3g; Carbohydrate 34g, of which sugars 13.4g; Fat 9.3g, of which saturates 1.2g; Cholesterol 0mg; Calcium 130mg; Fibre 7.2g; Sodium 159mg.

SPICY PARSNIPS AND CHICKPEAS

THE SWEET FLAVOUR OF PARSNIPS GOES VERY WELL WITH THE SPICES IN THIS INDIAN-STYLE
VEGETABLE STEW. OFFER INDIAN BREADS TO MOP UP THE DELICIOUS SAUCE.

Preparation: 8 minutes; Cooking: 22–25 minutes

SERVES FOUR

INGREDIENTS
   7 garlic cloves, finely chopped
   1 small onion, chopped
   5cm/2in piece fresh root
      ginger, chopped
   2 green chillies, seeded and
      finely chopped
   450ml/¾ pint/scant 2 cups plus
      75ml/5 tbsp water
   60ml/4 tbsp groundnut (peanut) oil
   5ml/1 tsp cumin seeds
   10ml/2 tsp ground coriander seeds
   5ml/1 tsp ground turmeric
   2.5–5ml/½–1 tsp chilli powder or
      mild paprika
   50g/2oz cashew nuts, toasted and
      ground
   250g/9oz tomatoes, peeled and
      chopped
   400g/14oz can chickpeas, drained
      and rinsed
   900g/2lb parsnips, cut into chunks
   5ml/1 tsp ground roasted
      cumin seeds
   juice of 1 lime, to taste
   5ml/1 tsp salt
   ground black pepper
To serve
   fresh coriander (cilantro) leaves
   a few cashew nuts, toasted
   Indian breads
   natural (plain) yogurt

1 Set 10ml/2 tsp of the garlic aside, then place the remainder in a food processor or blender with the onion, ginger and half the chillies. Add the 75ml/5 tbsp water and process to make a smooth paste.

2 Heat the oil in a large, deep, frying pan and cook the cumin seeds for 30 seconds. Stir in the coriander seeds, turmeric, chilli powder or paprika and the ground cashew nuts. Add the ginger and chilli paste and cook, stirring frequently, until the water begins to evaporate.

3 Add the tomatoes and stir-fry until the mixture begins to turn red-brown in colour.

4 Mix in the chickpeas and parsnips with the main batch of water, the salt and plenty of black pepper. Bring to the boil, stir, then simmer, uncovered, for 15 minutes, until the parsnips are completely tender.

5 Reduce the liquid, if necessary, by boiling fiercely until the sauce is thick. Add the ground roasted cumin with more salt and/or lime juice to taste. Stir in the reserved garlic and green chilli, and cook for a further 1–2 minutes. Scatter the fresh coriander leaves and toasted cashew nuts over and serve straight away with Indian breads.

Energy 516kcal/2163kJ; Protein 18.6g; Carbohydrate 61.4g, of which sugars 19.6g; Fat 23.5g, of which saturates 3.4g; Cholesterol 0mg; Calcium 194mg; Fibre 17.5g; Sodium 89mg.

LEMONY COUSCOUS SALAD

THIS POPULAR SALAD MIXES OLIVES, ALMONDS AND COURGETTES WITH FLUFFY COUSCOUS AND ADDS A HERB, LEMON JUICE AND OLIVE OIL DRESSING. IT HAS A DELICIOUSLY DELICATE FLAVOUR.

Preparation: 10 minutes; Cooking: 0 minutes

SERVES FOUR

INGREDIENTS
275g/10oz/1⅔ cups couscous
550ml/18fl oz/2½ cups boiling
   vegetable stock
2 small courgettes (zucchini)
16–20 black olives
25g/1oz/¼ cup flaked (sliced)
   almonds, toasted
For the dressing
60ml/4 tbsp olive oil
15ml/1 tbsp lemon juice
15ml/1 tbsp chopped fresh
   coriander (cilantro)
15ml/1 tbsp chopped fresh parsley
a good pinch of ground cumin
a good pinch of cayenne pepper

1 Place the couscous in a bowl and pour over the boiling stock. Stir with a fork and then set aside for 10 minutes until all the stock has been absorbed and the couscous has fluffed up.

2 Meanwhile, trim the courgettes and cut them into pieces about 2.5cm/1in long. Slice into fine julienne strips with a sharp knife. Halve the black olives, discarding the pits.

3 Fluff up the couscous with a fork, then carefully mix in the courgettes, olives and almonds.

4 Whisk the olive oil, lemon juice, coriander, parsley, cumin and cayenne in a bowl. Stir into the salad and toss gently. Transfer to a large serving dish and serve.

Energy 319kcal/1322kJ; Protein 6.6g; Carbohydrate 36.9g, of which sugars 1.4g; Fat 16.9g, of which saturates 2.1g; Cholesterol 0mg; Calcium 68mg; Fibre 1.8g; Sodium 286mg

SUMMER VEGETABLE KEBABS WITH HARISSA

EATING IN THE GARDEN IS ONE OF THE PLEASURES OF SUMMER. THIS WOULD BE LOVELY FOR LUNCH OR AS AN APPETIZER FOR GUESTS TO NIBBLE WHILE WAITING FOR MORE FILLING BARBECUE FARE.

Preparation: 7 minutes; Cooking: 8–10 minutes

SERVES FOUR

INGREDIENTS
60ml/4 tbsp olive oil
juice of ½ lemon
1 garlic clove, crushed
5ml/1 tsp ground coriander
5ml/1 tsp ground cinnamon
10ml/2 tsp clear honey
2 aubergines (eggplants), part peeled
    and cut into chunks
2 courgettes (zucchini), cut
    into chunks
2–3 red or green (bell) peppers,
    seeded and cut into chunks
12–16 cherry tomatoes
4 small red onions, quartered
5ml/1 tsp salt
For the harissa and yogurt dip
450g/1lb/2 cups Greek (US strained
    plain) yogurt
30–60ml/2–4 tbsp harissa
a small bunch of fresh coriander
    (cilantro), finely chopped
a small bunch of mint, finely chopped
salt and ground black pepper

1 Preheat the grill (broiler) or prepare a barbecue. Mix the olive oil, lemon juice and garlic in a bowl. Add ground coriander, cinnamon, honey and salt.

2 Add the aubergine and courgette chunks, with the peppers, cherry tomatoes and onion quarters. Stir to mix, then thread a generous number of vegetable pieces on to skewers, so that they are just touching each other.

3 Cook the kebabs under the grill or over the coals, turning occasionally until the vegetables are browned all over.

4 Meanwhile, make the dip. Put the yogurt in a bowl and beat in harissa to taste. Add most of the coriander and mint, reserving a little to garnish, and season well with salt and pepper.

5 As soon as the kebabs are cooked, serve on a bed of couscous and sprinkle with the remaining fresh coriander. Spoon a little of the yogurt dip on the side, and put the rest in a small serving bowl.

COOK'S TIP
As well as being a quick-cook aid, metal skewers enhance presentation tremendously.

Energy 305kcal/1267kJ; Protein 9.9g; Carbohydrate 24.8g, of which sugars 22.6g; Fat 19.1g, of which saturates 6.6g; Cholesterol 16mg; Calcium 230mg; Fibre 5.2g; Sodium 181mg

MEXICAN TOMATO RICE

VERSIONS OF THIS DISH — A RELATIVE OF SPANISH RICE — ARE POPULAR ALL OVER SOUTH AMERICA.
IT IS A DELICIOUS MEDLEY OF RICE, TOMATOES, PEAS AND AROMATIC FLAVOURINGS.
Preparation: 3 minutes; Cooking: 17 minutes

SERVES FOUR

INGREDIENTS
    400g/14oz can chopped tomatoes in
      tomato juice
    30ml/2 tbsp vegetable oil, preferably
      olive oil
    ½ onion, roughly chopped
    2 garlic cloves, roughly chopped
    500g/1¼lb/2½ cups long grain rice
    750ml/1¼ pints/3 cups
      vegetable stock
    2.5ml/½ tsp salt
    3 fresh chillies
    150g/5oz/1 cup frozen peas
    ground black pepper

COOK'S TIP
The rice makes a good filling for red or
orange (bell) peppers, which have been
halved, seeded and steamed for about
15 minutes, until tender.

1 Pour the tomatoes and juice into a
food processor or blender, and process
until smooth.

2 Heat the oil in a large, heavy pan,
add the onion and garlic and cook over
a medium heat for 2 minutes until
softened. Stir in the rice and stir-fry for
1–2 minutes.

3 Add the tomato mixture and stir over
a medium heat for 3–4 minutes until all
the liquid has been absorbed.

4 Stir in the stock, salt, whole chillies
and peas. Bring to the boil. Cover and
simmer for about 6 minutes, stirring
occasionally, until the rice is just tender.

5 Remove the pan from the heat, cover
it with a tight-fitting lid and leave it to
stand in a warm place for 5 minutes.

6 Remove the chillies, fluff up the rice
lightly with a fork, and serve in warmed
bowls, sprinkled with black pepper.
The chillies can be used as a garnish,
if you like.

Energy 552kcal/2305kJ; Protein 12.7g; Carbohydrate 108.3g, of which sugars 4.8g; Fat 7g, of which saturates 1g; Cholesterol 0mg; Calcium 43mg; Fibre 3g; Sodium 10mg

COUSCOUS WITH HALLOUMI

COUSCOUS IS VERY OFTEN CONSIDERED A SIDE DISH, BUT HERE IT PLAYS A LEADING ROLE AND IS TOPPED WITH GRIDDLED SLICED COURGETTES AND HALLOUMI – A MILD CHEESE FROM CYPRUS.

Preparation: 5 minutes; Cooking: 10–12 minutes

SERVES FOUR

INGREDIENTS

30ml/2 tbsp olive oil, plus extra
  for brushing
1 large red onion, chopped
2 garlic cloves, chopped
5ml/1 tsp mild chilli powder
5ml/1 tsp ground cumin
5ml/1 tsp ground coriander
5 cardamom pods, bruised
3 courgettes (zucchini), sliced
  lengthways into ribbons
225g/8oz halloumi cheese, sliced
1 bay leaf
1 cinnamon stick
275g/10oz/1⅔ cups couscous
50g/2oz/¼ cup whole shelled
  almonds, toasted
1 peach, stoned (pitted) and diced
25g/1oz/2 tbsp butter
salt and ground black pepper
chopped fresh flat leaf parsley,
  to garnish

1 Heat the oil in a large heavy pan, add the onion and garlic and sauté for 3–4 minutes until the onion has softened, stirring occasionally.

2 Stir in the chilli powder, cumin, coriander and cardamom pods, and leave the pan over a low heat to allow the flavours to mingle.

3 Meanwhile, brush the courgettes lightly with oil and cook them on a hot griddle or under a hot grill (broiler) for 2–3 minutes, until tender and slightly charred.

4 Turn the courgettes over, add the halloumi and continue cooking for a further 3 minutes, turning the halloumi over once.

5 While the vegetables are cooking, pour 300ml/½ pint/1¼ cups water into a large pan and add the bay leaf and cinnamon stick. Bring to the boil, remove from the heat and immediately add the couscous. Cover and allow to swell for 2 minutes.

6 Add the couscous to the spicy onion mixture, with the almonds, diced peach and butter. Toss over the heat for 2 minutes, then remove the whole spices, arrange the couscous on a plate and season well. Top with the halloumi and courgettes. Sprinkle the parsley over the top and serve.

COOK'S TIP
Look out for packets of flavoured instant couscous at the supermarket. They are very quick and easy to cook, come in a range of flavours and taste delicious. A spiced version would work well in this recipe.

Energy 515kcal/2138kJ; Protein 19.9g; Carbohydrate 42.7g, of which sugars 6.1g; Fat 30.3g, of which saturates 12.5g; Cholesterol 46mg; Calcium 290mg; Fibre 2.9g; Sodium 264mg

MUSHROOM PILAFF

THIS DISH IS SIMPLICITY ITSELF. A HANDFUL OF HERBS IMPARTS AN AROMATIC FLAVOUR, AND THE RICE MAKES A SATISFYING MEAL THAT IS PERFECT FOR A QUICK AND EASY SUPPER.

Preparation: 5 minutes; Cooking: 22–25 minutes

SERVES FOUR

INGREDIENTS

30ml/2 tbsp vegetable oil
2 shallots, finely chopped
1 garlic clove, crushed
3 green cardamom pods
25g/1oz/2 tbsp butter
175g/6oz/2½ cups button (white)
   mushrooms, sliced
225g/8oz/generous 1 cup
   basmati rice
5ml/1 tsp grated fresh root ginger
good pinch of garam masala
450ml/¾ pint/scant 2 cups water
15ml/1 tbsp chopped fresh
   coriander (cilantro)
salt

1 Heat the oil in a flameproof casserole and fry the shallots, garlic and cardamoms for 3–4 minutes until the shallots are beginning to brown.

2 Add the butter, then the mushrooms and fry for 2–3 minutes.

3 Add the rice, ginger and garam masala. Stir-fry over a low heat for 2–3 minutes, then stir in the water and a little salt. Bring to the boil, then cover tightly and simmer very gently for 10 minutes.

4 Remove the casserole from the heat. Leave the pilaff to stand, covered, for 5 minutes to complete the cooking. Add the chopped coriander and fork it through the rice. Spoon into a serving bowl and serve at once.

Energy 582kcal/2409kJ; Protein 4.6g; Carbohydrate 46.3g, of which sugars 1.1g; Fat 41.8g, of which saturates 23.4g; Cholesterol 93mg; Calcium 22mg; Fibre 0.2g; Sodium 266mg.

CHICKPEA TAGINE

A TAGINE IS A TYPE OF MOROCCAN STEW ORIGINALLY PREPARED BY LONG SIMMERING OVER AN OPEN FIRE. A TAGINE CAN BE SAVOURY OR SWEET AND SOUR.

Preparation: 6 minutes; Cooking: 24 minutes

SERVES SIX TO EIGHT

INGREDIENTS

30ml/2 tbsp sunflower oil or extra virgin olive oil

1 large onion, chopped

1 garlic clove, crushed or chopped (optional)

400g/14oz can chopped tomatoes

200g/7oz fresh tomatoes, peeled, chopped and puréed

5ml/1 tsp ground cumin

350ml/12fl oz/1½ cups vegetable stock

2 x 400g/14oz cans chickpeas, drained

¼ preserved lemon

30ml/2 tbsp chopped fresh coriander (cilantro)

crusty bread, to serve

1 Heat the oil in a large pan or flameproof casserole and fry the onion and garlic, if using, for 8–10 minutes until golden.

2 Stir in the tomatoes and cumin, then pour over the stock and stir well. Cook for 10 minutes. Add the chickpeas and simmer, uncovered, for 3–4 minutes.

4 Rinse the preserved lemon and cut away the flesh and pith. Cut the peel into slivers and stir into the chickpeas along with the coriander.

5 Spoon into warmed bowls and serve immediately with crusty bread.

Energy 167kcal/704kJ; Protein 8.3g; Carbohydrate 21.5g, of which sugars 4.9g; Fat 6g, of which saturates 0.8g; Cholesterol 0mg; Calcium 64mg; Fibre 5.5g; Sodium 229mg.

SPICED VEGETABLE COUSCOUS

THIS TASTY VEGETARIAN MAIN COURSE IS EASY TO MAKE AND CAN BE PREPARED WITH ANY NUMBER OF YOUNG SEASONAL VEGETABLES SUCH AS SPINACH, LEEKS, PEAS OR CORN.

Preparation: 10 minutes; Cooking: 15 minutes

SERVES SIX

INGREDIENTS

45ml/3 tbsp olive oil
1 large onion, finely chopped
2 garlic cloves, crushed
15ml/1 tbsp tomato purée (paste)
2.5ml/½ tsp ground turmeric
2.5ml/½ tsp cayenne pepper
5ml/1 tsp ground coriander
5ml/1 tsp ground cumin
225g/8oz cauliflower florets
225g/8oz baby carrots, trimmed
1 red (bell) pepper, seeded and diced
225g/8oz courgettes (zucchini), sliced
400g/14oz can chickpeas, drained
   and rinsed
4 beefsteak tomatoes, peeled
   and sliced
45ml/3 tbsp chopped fresh coriander
   (cilantro)
sea salt and ground black pepper
coriander sprigs, to garnish
For the couscous
2.5ml/½ tsp salt
450g/1lb/2⅔ cups couscous
50g/2oz/¼ cup butter

1 Heat 30ml/2 tbsp oil in a large pan, add the onion and garlic and cook until soft and translucent. Stir in the tomato purée, turmeric, cayenne, coriander and cumin. Cook, stirring, for 2 minutes.

2 Add the cauliflower, baby carrots and pepper, with enough water to come halfway up the vegetables. Bring to the boil and cook for 5 minutes.

3 Add the courgettes, chickpeas and tomatoes and cook for 5 minutes. Stir in the fresh coriander and season. Lower the heat to a bare simmer.

4 Cook the couscous. Bring about 475ml/16fl oz/2 cups water to the boil in a large pan. Add the remaining olive oil and the salt. Remove from the heat and add the couscous, stirring. Allow to swell for 2 minutes.

5 Add the butter, and heat through gently, stirring to separate the grains.

6 Turn the couscous out on to a warm serving dish and place the cooked vegetables on top, pouring over any liquid. Garnish with coriander sprigs and serve immediately.

Energy 419kcal/1749kJ; Protein 12.9g; Carbohydrate 61.8g, of which sugars 11.8g; Fat 14.8g, of which saturates 1.9g; Cholesterol 0mg; Calcium 87mg; Fibre 6.7g; Sodium 178mg

SESAME-TOSSED ASPARAGUS WITH NOODLES

TENDER ASPARAGUS SPEARS TOSSED WITH SESAME SEEDS AND SERVED ON A BED OF CRISPY, DEEP-FRIED NOODLES MAKES A LOVELY DISH FOR CASUAL ENTERTAINING.

Preparation: 2–3 minutes; Cooking: 7–8 minutes

SERVES FOUR

INGREDIENTS
 15ml/1 tbsp sunflower oil
 350g/12oz thin asparagus
  spears, trimmed
 5ml/1 tsp salt
 5ml/1 tsp ground black pepper
 5ml/1 tsp golden caster (superfine) sugar
 30ml/2 tbsp Chinese cooking wine
  or sherry
 45ml/3 tbsp light soy sauce
 60ml/4 tbsp oyster sauce (see
  Cook's Tip)
 10ml/2 tsp sesame oil
 60ml/4 tbsp toasted sesame seeds
For the noodles
 50g/2oz dried bean thread noodles
  or thin rice noodles
 sunflower oil, for frying

1 First make the crispy noodles. Fill a wok one-third full of oil and heat to 180°C/350°F (or until a cube of bread, dropped into the oil, browns in 15 seconds). Add the noodles, small bunches at a time, to the oil; they will crisp and puff up in seconds. Using a slotted spoon, remove from the wok and drain on kitchen paper. Set aside.

COOK'S TIP
• Thin asparagus spears, called sprue, are often cheaper than fat stalks. Look for them at farmer's markets.
• A vegetarian version of oyster sauce is available from specialist Chinese food stockists.

2 Heat a clean wok over a high heat and add the sunflower oil. Add the asparagus and stir-fry for 3 minutes.

3 Put four bowls to warm so that they are ready for serving.

4 Add the salt, pepper, sugar and wine or sherry to the wok with the soy sauce and oyster sauce. Stir-fry for 2–3 minutes. Add the sesame oil, toss to combine and remove from the heat.

5 To serve, divide the crispy noodles between four warmed plates or bowls and top with the asparagus and juices. Sprinkle over the toasted sesame seeds and serve immediately.

Energy 131kcal/547kJ; Protein 4.6g; Carbohydrate 16.5g, of which sugars 6.9g; Fat 5.6g, of which saturates 0.6g; Cholesterol 0mg; Calcium 31mg; Fibre 2g; Sodium 1047mg

SESAME NOODLES

THIS IS ONE OF THOSE QUICK, COMFORTING DISHES THAT BECOME FAMILY FAVOURITES. CHILDREN LOVE ITS SWEET-SOUR FLAVOURS AND THERE ARE SHARP SPICES TO ADD ZING.

Preparation: 10 minutes; Cooking: 4 minutes

SERVES FOUR

INGREDIENTS
450g/1lb fresh egg noodles
½ cucumber, sliced lengthways, seeded and diced
4–6 spring onions (scallions)
a bunch of radishes, about 115g/4oz
225g/8oz mooli (daikon), peeled
115g/4oz/2 cups beansprouts, rinsed, then left in iced water and drained
60ml/4 tbsp groundnut (peanut) oil or sunflower oil
2 garlic cloves, crushed
45ml/3 tbsp toasted sesame paste
15ml/1 tbsp sesame oil
15ml/1 tbsp light soy sauce
5–10ml/1–2 tsp sweet chilli sauce, to taste
15ml/1 tbsp rice vinegar
120ml/4fl oz/½ cup vegetable stock
5ml/1 tsp sugar, or to taste
salt and ground black pepper
roasted cashew nuts, to garnish

1 Cook the fresh noodles in boiling water for 1 minute then drain well. Rinse the noodles in fresh water and drain again.

2 Place the cucumber in a colander or sieve (strainer), sprinkle with salt and leave to drain over a bowl for 10 minutes.

COOK'S TIP
Always check beforehand that guests do not have any nut allergies.

3 Meanwhile, cut the spring onions into fine shreds. Cut the radishes in half and slice finely. Coarsely grate the mooli. Rinse the cucumber, drain, pat dry and mix with all the vegetables in a salad bowl. Toss gently.

4 Heat half the oil in a wok or frying pan and stir-fry the noodles for about 1 minute. Using a slotted spoon, transfer the noodles to a large serving bowl and keep warm.

5 Add the remaining oil to the wok. When it is hot, fry the garlic to flavour the oil. Remove from the heat and stir in the sesame paste, with the sesame oil, soy and chilli sauces, vinegar and chicken stock.

6 Add a little sugar and season to taste. Warm through but do not overheat. Pour the sauce over the noodles and toss well. Garnish with the cashew nuts and serve with the vegetables.

Energy 633kcal/2658kJ; Protein 17.6g; Carbohydrate 84.5g, of which sugars 5.3g; Fat 27.2g, of which saturates 5g; Cholesterol 34mg; Calcium 139mg; Fibre 5.7g; Sodium 484mg

SWEET AND SOUR HOT VEGETABLE NOODLES

THIS NOODLE DISH HAS THE COLOUR OF FIRE, BUT ONLY THE MILDEST SUGGESTION OF HEAT. GINGER AND PLUM SAUCE GIVE IT ITS FRUITY FLAVOUR, WHILE LIME ADDS A DELICIOUS TANG.

Preparation: 10 minutes; Cooking: 18 minutes

SERVES FOUR

INGREDIENTS

130g/4½ oz dried rice noodles
30ml/2 tbsp groundnut (peanut) oil
2.5cm/1in piece fresh root ginger, sliced into thin batons
1 garlic clove, crushed
130g/4½ oz drained canned bamboo shoots, sliced into thin batons
2 medium carrots, sliced into batons
130g/4½ oz/1½ cups beansprouts
1 small white cabbage, shredded
30ml/2 tbsp mushroom ketchup
30ml/2 tbsp soy sauce
30ml/2 tbsp plum sauce
10ml/2 tsp sesame oil
15ml/1 tbsp palm sugar (jaggery) or light muscovado (brown) sugar
juice of ½ lime
90g/3½ oz mooli (daikon), sliced into thin batons
small bunch fresh coriander (cilantro), chopped
60ml/4 tbsp sesame seeds, toasted

1 Cook the noodles in a large pan of boiling water, following the instructions on the packet. Meanwhile, heat the oil in a wok or large frying pan and stir-fry the ginger and garlic for 2–3 minutes over a medium heat, until golden.

2 Drain the noodles and set them aside. Add the bamboo shoots to the wok, increase the heat to high and stir-fry for 5 minutes. Add the carrots, beansprouts and cabbage and stir-fry for a further 5 minutes, until they are beginning to char on the edges.

3 Stir in the sauces, sesame oil, sugar and lime juice. Add the mooli and coriander, toss to mix, then spoon into a warmed bowl, sprinkle with toasted sesame seeds and serve immediately.

COOK'S TIP
Use a large, sharp knife for shredding cabbage. Remove any tough outer leaves, if necessary, then cut the cabbage into quarters. Cut off and discard the hard core from each quarter, place flat side down, then slice the cabbage very thinly to make fine shreds.

Energy 256kcal/1072kJ; Protein 7.1g; Carbohydrate 42.2g, of which sugars 14.1g; Fat 6.4g, of which saturates 1g; Cholesterol 0mg; Calcium 136mg; Fibre 4.2g; Sodium 858mg.

VEGETABLE AND EGG NOODLE RIBBONS

SERVE THIS ELEGANT, COLOURFUL DISH WITH A TOSSED GREEN SALAD AS A LIGHT LUNCH. USE FRESH PASTA NOODLES FOR OPTIMUM SPEED AND MAXIMUM FLAVOUR.

Preparation: 3 minutes; cooking 7 minutes

SERVES FOUR

INGREDIENTS

1 large carrot, peeled
2 courgettes (zucchini)
50g/2oz/¼ cup butter
15ml/1 tbsp olive oil
6 fresh shiitake mushrooms,
  finely sliced
50g/2oz/½ cup frozen peas, thawed
350g/12oz fresh broad egg ribbon
  noodles
10ml/2 tsp chopped fresh mixed
  herbs, such as marjoram, chives
  and basil
salt and ground black pepper
25g/1oz Parmesan cheese,
  to serve (optional)

1 Using a vegetable peeler, carefully slice thin strips from the carrot and from the courgettes.

2 Heat the butter with the olive oil in a large frying pan. Stir in the carrots and shiitake mushrooms; fry for 2 minutes. Add the courgettes and peas and stir-fry until the courgettes are cooked, but still crisp. Season with salt and pepper.

3 Meanwhile, cook the noodles in a large saucepan of boiling water until just tender. Drain the noodles well and tip them into a bowl. Add the vegetables and toss gently to mix.

4 Sprinkle over the fresh herbs and season to taste. If using the Parmesan cheese, grate or shave it over the top. Toss lightly and serve.

Energy 500kcal/2100kJ; Protein 13.9g; Carbohydrate 68.1g, of which sugars 5.6g; Fat 21g, of which saturates 9.1g; Cholesterol 53mg; Calcium 62mg; Fibre 4.9g; Sodium 242mg.

BUCKWHEAT NOODLES WITH GOAT'S CHEESE

THIS GOOD, FAST SUPPER DISH COMBINES THE EARTHY FLAVOUR OF BUCKWHEAT WITH THE NUTTY, PEPPERY TASTE OF ROCKET LEAVES AND BOTH ARE OFFSET BY THE DELICIOUSLY CREAMY GOAT'S CHEESE.

Preparation and cooking: 8–10 minutes

SERVES FOUR

INGREDIENTS

350g/12oz buckwheat noodles
50g/2oz/¼ cup butter
2 garlic cloves, finely chopped
4 shallots, sliced
75g/3oz/¾ cup hazelnuts, lightly
  roasted and roughly chopped
large handful rocket (arugula) leaves
175g/6oz goat's cheese, crumbled
salt and ground black pepper

1 Bring a large pan of lightly salted water to a rolling boil and add the noodles. Cook until just tender.

2 Meanwhile, heat the butter in a large frying pan. Add the garlic and shallots and cook for 2–3 minutes, stirring all the time, until the shallots are soft. Do not let the garlic brown. Drain the noodles well.

3 Add the hazelnuts to the pan and fry for about 1 minute. Add the rocket leaves and, when they start to wilt, toss in the noodles and heat through.

4 Season with salt and pepper. Add the goat's cheese and serve immediately.

Energy 418kcal/1736kJ; Protein 14.4g; Carbohydrate 15g, of which sugars 2.9g; Fat 33.9g, of which saturates 15.2g; Cholesterol 67mg; Calcium 97mg; Fibre 2.2g; Sodium 342mg.

FIORENTINA PIZZA

AN EGG ADDS THE FINISHING TOUCH TO THIS CLASSIC ITALIAN SPINACH PIZZA; TRY NOT TO
OVERCOOK IT THOUGH, AS IT'S BEST WHEN THE YOLK IS STILL SLIGHTLY SOFT IN THE MIDDLE.

Preparation: 2 minutes; Cooking: 18 minutes

2 Preheat the oven to 220°C/425°F/ Gas 7. Brush the pizza base with half the remaining olive oil. Spread the pizza sauce evenly over the base, using the back of a spoon, then top with the spinach mixture. Sprinkle over a little freshly grated nutmeg.

3 Thinly slice the mozzarella and arrange over the spinach. Drizzle over the remaining oil. Bake for 10 minutes, then remove from the oven.

4 Make a small well in the centre of the pizza topping and carefully break the egg into the hole. Sprinkle over the grated Gruyère cheese and return the pizza to the oven for a further 5–10 minutes until crisp and golden. Serve immediately.

SERVES TWO TO THREE

INGREDIENTS
  45ml/3 tbsp olive oil
  1 small red onion, thinly sliced
  175g/6oz fresh spinach,
    stalks removed
  1 pizza base, about 25–30cm/
    10–12in in diameter
  1 small jar pizza sauce
  freshly grated nutmeg
  150g/5oz mozzarella cheese
  1 egg
  25g/1oz/¼ cup Gruyère
    cheese, grated

1 Heat 15ml/1 tbsp of the oil and fry the onion until soft. Add the spinach and fry until wilted. Drain any excess liquid.

VARIATION
A calzone is like a pizza but is folded in half to conceal the filling. Add the egg with the rest of the pizza topping, fold over the dough, seal the edges and bake for 20 minutes.

Energy 503kcal/2100kJ; Protein 20.8g; Carbohydrate 40.3g, of which sugars 5.9g; Fat 29.7g, of which saturates 10.9g; Cholesterol 101mg; Calcium 417mg; Fibre 2.8g; Sodium 668mg

FOUR CHEESE CIABATTA PIZZA

FEW DISHES ARE AS SIMPLE — OR AS SATISFYING — AS THIS PIZZA MADE BY TOPPING A HALVED LOAF OF CIABATTA. THIS IS THE SORT OF THING CHILDREN COULD MAKE TO GIVE MUM AND DAD A BREAK.

Preparation: 4 minutes; Cooking: 10–12 minutes

SERVES TWO

INGREDIENTS

1 loaf ciabatta bread
1 garlic clove, halved
30–45ml/2–3 tbsp olive oil
about 90ml/6 tbsp passata (bottled
strained tomatoes) or sugocasa
1 small red onion, thinly sliced
30ml/2 tbsp chopped pitted olives
about 50g/2oz each of four cheeses,
one mature/sharp (Parmesan or
Cheddar), one blue-veined
(Gorgonzola or Stilton), one mild
(Fontina or Emmental) and a goat's
cheese, sliced, grated or crumbled
pine nuts or cumin seeds, to sprinkle
salt and ground black pepper
sprigs of basil, to garnish

1 Preheat the oven to 200°C/400°F/ Gas 6. Split the ciabatta bread in half. Rub the cut sides with the garlic, then brush over the oil. Spread with the passata or sugocasa, then add the onion slices and olives. Season to taste with salt and black pepper.

2 Divide the cheeses between the ciabatta halves and sprinkle over the pine nuts or cumin seeds. Bake for 10–12 minutes, until bubbling and golden brown. Cut the pizza into slices and serve immediately, garnished with the sprigs of fresh basil.

Energy 782kcal/3265kJ; Protein 34g; Carbohydrate 55.8g, of which sugars 6.2g; Fat 47.4g, of which saturates 22.8g; Cholesterol 86mg; Calcium 756mg; Fibre 3.4g; Sodium 1952mg

CLASSIC MARINARA PIZZA

THE COMBINATION OF SIMPLE INGREDIENTS — FRESH GARLIC, GOOD-QUALITY OLIVE OIL AND A FRESH TOMATO SAUCE — GIVES THIS DELICIOUS PIZZA AN UNMISTAKABLY ITALIAN FLAVOUR.

Preparation: 10 minutes; Cooking: 20 minutes

SERVES TWO

INGREDIENTS
  60ml/4 tbsp extra virgin olive oil
    or sunflower oil
  2 x 375g/14oz chopped tomatoes
  4 garlic cloves, cut into slivers
  15ml/1 tbsp chopped
    fresh oregano
  salt and ground black pepper
For the pizza base
  225g/8oz/2 cups plain (all-purpose)
    white flour
  pinch of salt
  10ml/2 tsp baking powder
  50g/2oz/4 tbsp butter or
    hard margarine
  about 150ml/¼ pint/⅔ cup milk

1 Preheat the oven to 220ºC/425ºF/ Gas 7. Line a baking sheet with baking parchment. Sieve the flour, salt and baking powder into a bowl and rub the butter or hard margarine lightly into the flour with your fingertips until it resembles breadcrumbs.

2 Pour in enough milk to form a soft dough and knead. Roll the dough out to a circle about 25cm/10in in diameter.

3 Place the dough on the prepared baking sheet and make the edges slightly thicker than the centre.

4 Meanwhile, heat 30ml/2 tbsp of the oil in a pan. Add the plum tomatoes and cook, stirring frequently for about 5 minutes until soft.

5 Put the tomatoes into a sieve over a bowl and press with the back of a spoon. Alternatively, use a food processor or blender and beat until the tomatoes are smooth.

6 Brush the pizza base with half the remaining oil. Spoon over the tomatoes and sprinkle with garlic and oregano. Drizzle over the remaining oil and season with salt and pepper.

7 Bake for 15 minutes in the oven until the pizza is crisp and golden. Serve immediately.

Energy 860kcal/3606kJ; Protein 15.7g; Carbohydrate 102.1g, of which sugars 16.3g; Fat 46.2g, of which saturates 4g; Cholesterol 4mg; Calcium 273mg; Fibre 7g; Sodium 267mg.

BAKED HERB CRÊPES WITH TOMATO SAUCE

TURN LIGHT HERB CRÊPES INTO SOMETHING SPECIAL BY FILLING THEM WITH A SPINACH, CHEESE AND
PINE NUT FILLING, THEN BAKING AND SERVING THEM WITH A DELICIOUS TOMATO SAUCE.

Preparation: 10 minutes; Cooking: 20 minutes

SERVES FOUR

INGREDIENTS
   25g/1oz/½ cup chopped fresh herbs
   15ml/1 tbsp sunflower oil, plus extra
      for frying and greasing
   120ml/4fl oz/½ cup milk
   3 eggs
   25g/1oz/¼ cup plain
      (all-purpose) flour
   pinch of salt
For the sauce
   30ml/2 tbsp olive oil
   1 small onion, chopped
   2 garlic cloves, crushed
   400g/14oz can chopped tomatoes
   pinch of soft light brown sugar
For the filling
   450g/1lb fresh spinach, cooked
      and drained
   175g/6oz/¾ cup ricotta cheese
   25g/1oz/¼ cup pine nuts, toasted
   5 sun-dried tomato halves in olive
      oil, drained and chopped
   30ml/2 tbsp shredded fresh basil
   salt and ground black pepper
   grated nutmeg
   4 egg whites

1 To make the crêpes mixture, place
the herbs and oil in a food processor
and process until smooth. Add the milk,
eggs, flour and salt and process again
until smooth.

2 Meanwhile, make the sauce. Heat the
oil in a small pan, add the onion and
garlic, and cook gently for 5 minutes.
Stir in the tomatoes and sugar, and
cook for about 10 minutes until
thickened. Purée in a blender, then
sieve into a small pan and set aside.

3 To make the filling, put the spinach in
a bowl and add the ricotta, pine nuts,
tomatoes and basil. Season with salt,
nutmeg and pepper, and mix well.

4 Preheat the oven to 190ºC/375ºF/
Gas 5. Whisk the egg whites until they
are stiff and stand in peaks. Stir one-
third into the spinach mixture, then
gently fold in the rest.

5 To make the crêpes, heat a large
non-stick frying pan and add a very
small amount of oil. Pour out any
excess oil and pour in a ladleful of the
batter. Swirl around until the batter
covers the base evenly.

6 Cook the crêpe for 2 minutes, turn
over and cook for a further 1–2
minutes. Make three more crêpes in the
same way.

7 Place one crêpe at a time on a lightly
oiled baking sheet, add a spoonful of
filling and fold into quarters. Bake for
12 minutes until set.

8 Meanwhile, reheat the tomato sauce
gently, stirring occasionally. Serve with
the crêpes.

Energy 471kcal/1957kJ; Protein 24.4g; Carbohydrate 16.1g, of which sugars 10.9g; Fat 34.8g, of which saturates 13.4g; Cholesterol 192mg; Calcium 271mg; Fibre 3.9g; Sodium 294mg.

MAIN COURSE PASTA DISHES

From old favourites such as Macaroni Cheese and Spaghetti Carbonara to more sophisticated dishes such as Seafood Conchiglie and Warm Pasta Salad with Egg, Asparagus and Ham, pasta dishes have always been speedy to prepare – and delicious to eat. Most of the ingredients that accompany the pasta in these recipes can be cooked in the time it takes the pasta to boil, so there's no waiting around. For tomato-based dishes, try Linguine with Sun-dried Tomato Pesto, Tagliatelle with Tomatoes and Black Olives, Warm Penne with Fresh Tomatoes and Basil and Spaghetti with Tomatoes and Pancetta. For meat-based recipes, choose Fettucine with Ham and Peas, Tagliatelle with Prosciutto and Asparagus, Fusilli with Sausage or Pappardelle with Chicken and Mushrooms; for those based on fish choose from Spaghetti with Clams, Linguine with Crab, Orecchiette with Anchovies and Broccoli or Penne with Cream and Smoked Salmon; and for pasta dishes featuring cheese in the starring role, try Fettucine All'Alfredo, Ravioli with Four-cheese Sauce or Pasta with Roquefort and Salami.

MINTY COURGETTE LINGUINE

SWEET, MILD COURGETTES AND REFRESHING MINT ARE A GREAT COMBINATION AND ARE DELICIOUS
WITH PASTA. DRIED LINGUINE HAS BEEN USED HERE BUT YOU CAN USE ANY TYPE OF PASTA YOU LIKE.

Preparation: 5 minutes; Cooking: 12–15 minutes

<u>SERVES FOUR</u>

INGREDIENTS
   450g/1lb dried linguine
   4 small courgettes (zucchini), sliced
   1 small bunch of fresh mint, roughly
     chopped
   75ml/5 tbsp garlic-infused olive oil
   salt and ground black pepper

1 Cook the pasta in a large pan of lightly salted boiling water for 10–12 minutes.

2 Meanwhile, heat 45ml/3 tbsp of the oil in a large frying pan and add the courgettes. Fry for 2–3 minutes, stirring occasionally, until they are golden.

3 Drain the pasta well and toss with the courgettes and chopped mint. Season with salt and pepper, drizzle over the remaining oil and serve immediately.

Energy 536kcal/2261kJ; Protein 16.2g; Carbohydrate 86.3g, of which sugars 5.9g; Fat 16.4g, of which saturates 2.3g; Cholesterol 0mg; Calcium 86mg; Fibre 4.4g; Sodium 7mg.

SPAGHETTI WITH GARLIC AND OIL

IT DOESN'T GET MUCH SIMPLER THAN THIS: SPAGHETTI TOSSED WITH THE VERY BEST OLIVE OIL, WITH CHILLI FOR A HINT OF HEAT AND PLENTY OF PARSLEY FOR A CONTRASTING COOL, FRESH FLAVOUR.

Preparation: 1 minute; Cooking: 4–12 minutes

SERVES FOUR

INGREDIENTS
    400g/14oz fresh or dried spaghetti
    90ml/6 tbsp extra virgin olive oil
    2–4 garlic cloves, crushed
    1 dried red chilli
    1 small handful fresh flat leaf
      parsley, roughly chopped
    salt

1 Cook the pasta in a large pan of lightly salted boiling water. Dried pasta will take 10–12 minutes, fresh about 3 minutes. Fresh pasta is ready when it rises to the surface of the water.

2 Meanwhile, heat the oil very gently in a small frying pan. Add the crushed garlic and whole dried chilli and stir over a low heat until the garlic is just beginning to brown. Remove the chilli and discard.

3 Drain the pasta and tip it into a warmed large bowl. Pour on the oil and garlic mixture, add the parsley and toss vigorously until the pasta glistens. Serve immediately in warm bowls.

COOK'S TIPS
• Since the oil is such an important ingredient here, only use the very best cold-pressed extra virgin olive oil.
• Don't use salt in the oil and garlic mixture, because it will not dissolve sufficiently. This is why salt is recommended for cooking the pasta.
• In Rome, grated Parmesan is never served with this dish, nor is it seasoned with pepper.
• In summer, Romans use fresh chillies, which they grow in pots on their terraces and window ledges. As the chilli is mainly used for flavouring, you could use chilli oil instead.

Energy 498kcal/2097kJ; Protein 12.6g; Carbohydrate 75.3g, of which sugars 3.4g; Fat 18.3g, of which saturates 2.6g; Cholesterol 0mg; Calcium 27mg; Fibre 3.2g; Sodium 3mg

LINGUINE WITH SUN-DRIED TOMATO PESTO

TOMATO PESTO WAS ONCE A RARITY, BUT IS BECOMING INCREASINGLY POPULAR. TO MAKE IT, SUN-DRIED TOMATOES ARE USED INSTEAD OF BASIL. THE RESULT IS ABSOLUTELY DELICIOUS.

Preparation: 5 minutes; Cooking: 5–16 minutes

SERVES FOUR

INGREDIENTS
  25g/1oz/⅓ cup pine nuts
  25g/1oz/⅓ cup freshly grated
    Parmesan cheese
  50g/2oz/½ cup sun-dried tomatoes
    in olive oil
  1 garlic clove, roughly chopped
  60ml/4 tbsp olive oil
  350g/12oz fresh or dried linguine
  ground black pepper
  coarsely shaved Parmesan cheese,
    to serve
  basil leaves, to garnish

1 Put the pine nuts in a small non-stick frying pan and toss over a low to medium heat for 1–2 minutes or until lightly toasted and golden.

2 Tip the nuts into a food processor. Add the Parmesan, sun-dried tomatoes and garlic, with pepper to taste. Process until finely chopped.

3 With the machine running, gradually add the olive oil through the feeder tube until it has all been incorporated evenly and the ingredients have formed a smooth-looking paste.

4 Cook the pasta in a large pan of lightly salted boiling water. Dried pasta will take 10–12 minutes, fresh about 3 minutes. Drain well, reserving a little of the water. Tip the pasta into a warmed bowl, add the pesto and a few spoonfuls of the hot water and toss well. Serve immediately garnished with basil and hand round the Parmesan separately.

COOK'S TIP
You can make this pesto up to 2 days in advance and keep it in the refrigerator. Pour a thin film of olive oil over the pesto in a bowl, then cover the bowl tightly with clear film (plastic wrap).

Energy 503kcal/2114kJ; Protein 14.4g; Carbohydrate 66.7g, of which sugars 4.7g; Fat 21.7g, of which saturates 3.4g; Cholesterol 6mg; Calcium 102mg; Fibre 3g; Sodium 98mg.

PUMPKIN AND PARMESAN PASTA

THE SWEET FLAVOUR OF PUMPKIN IS NICELY BALANCED BY THE PARMESAN IN THIS CREAMY PASTA SAUCE, WHILE FRIED GARLIC BREADCRUMBS PROVIDE A WELCOME CRUNCH.

Preparation: 4 minutes; Cooking: 14 minutes

SERVES FOUR

INGREDIENTS

800g/1¾lb fresh pumpkin flesh,
  cut into small cubes
300g/11oz dried tagliatelle
65g/2½oz/5 tbsp butter
1 onion, sliced
115g/4oz rindless smoked back
  bacon, diced
15ml/1 tbsp olive oil
2 garlic cloves, crushed
75g/3oz/1½ cups fresh white
  breadcrumbs
150ml/¼ pint/⅔ cup single
  (light) cream
50g/2oz/⅔ cup freshly grated
  Parmesan cheese
freshly grated nutmeg
30ml/2 tbsp chopped fresh parsley
15ml/1 tbsp chopped fresh chives
salt and ground black pepper
sprigs of flat leaf parsley, to garnish

1 Bring two pans of lightly salted water to the boil. Place the pumpkin cubes in one pan and the pasta in the other. Cook for 10–12 minutes.

2 Meanwhile, heat one-third of the butter in a separate large pan. Fry the onion and bacon for 5 minutes.

3 Melt the remaining butter with the oil in a frying pan. Add the garlic and breadcrumbs. Fry gently until the crumbs are golden brown and crisp. Drain on kitchen paper and keep warm.

4 Drain the pumpkin and add it to the onion and bacon mixture, with the cream. Heat until the cream is just below boiling point.

5 Drain the pasta, add to the pan and heat through. Stir in the Parmesan, nutmeg, parsley, chives and seasoning. Serve sprinkled with the garlic breadcrumbs and garnished with parsley.

COOK'S TIP

Look out for tubs of diced bacon bits in the supermarket chiller. They're a real time-saver. If you find cubed pumpkin too, you're on to a winner.

Energy 691kcal/2897kJ; Protein 23.8g; Carbohydrate 76.6g, of which sugars 8.1g; Fat 34.2g, of which saturates 18.1g; Cholesterol 83mg; Calcium 293mg; Fibre 4.8g; Sodium 834mg

LEMON AND PARMESAN CAPELLINI

IN THIS RECIPE, CREAM IS THICKENED WITH PARMESAN AND FLAVOURED WITH LEMON TO MAKE A SUPERB SAUCE FOR PASTA. GRANARY BREAD MAKES THE PERFECT ACCOMPANIMENT.

Preparation: 5 minutes; cooking: 2–12 minutes

SERVES TWO

INGREDIENTS

  50g/2oz/¼ cup butter, softened
  1 garlic clove, crushed
  30ml/2 tbsp chopped fresh herbs
  ½ Granary baguette
  225g/8oz dried or fresh capellini
  250ml/8fl oz/1 cup single (light)
    cream
  75g/3oz Parmesan cheese, grated
  finely grated rind of 1 lemon
  salt and ground black pepper

1 Preheat the oven to 200ºC/400ºF/
Gas 6. Put the butter in a bowl and beat
with the garlic and herbs.

2 Cut the Granary baguette into thick
slices and spread them thickly with the
flavoured butter.

3 Reassemble the baguette. The garlic
herb butter will help to hold the slices
together. Wrap in foil, support on a
baking sheet and bake for 10 minutes.

4 Meanwhile, cook the pasta in a large
pan of lightly salted boiling water. Dried
pasta will take 10–12 minutes, fresh
about 3 minutes.

5 Pour the cream into another pan and
bring to the boil. Stir in the Parmesan
and lemon rind. The sauce should
thicken in 30 seconds or so.

6 Drain the pasta, return it to the pan
and toss with the sauce. Season to taste
and sprinkle with a little chopped fresh
parsley and more grated lemon rind, if
you like. Serve with the hot herb bread.

Energy 1219kcal/5111kJ; Protein 42.2g; Carbohydrate 133.7g, of which sugars 9.5g; Fat 61g, of which saturates 36.7g; Cholesterol 160mg; Calcium 803mg; Fibre 6.6g; Sodium 1145mg.

TAGLIATELLE <u>WITH</u> TOMATOES <u>AND</u> OLIVES

THE SUN-DRIED TOMATOES AND BLACK OLIVES ADD PUNGENCY TO THIS RUSTIC DISH, WHILE THE GRILLED FRESH TOMATOES GIVE IT A BIT OF BITE, WITH A REFRESHING CHANGE OF TEXTURE.

Preparation: 5 minutes; cooking: 10–12 minutes

SERVES FOUR

INGREDIENTS
45ml/3 tbsp olive oil
1 garlic clove, crushed
1 small onion, chopped
60ml/4 tbsp dry white wine
6 sun-dried tomatoes, chopped
30ml/2 tbsp chopped fresh parsley
50g/2oz/½ cup stoned (pitted) black
  olives, halved
450g/1lb fresh tagliatelle
4 tomatoes, halved
salt and ground black pepper
Parmesan cheese, to serve

1 Heat 30ml/2 tbsp of the oil in a pan. Add the garlic and onion and cook for 2–3 minutes, stirring occasionally. Add the wine, sun-dried tomatoes and the parsley. Cook for 2 minutes. Stir in the black olives, lower the heat and leave the sauce over a low heat.

COOK'S TIP
It is essential to buy Parmesan in a piece for this dish. Find a good source – fresh Parmesan should not be unacceptably hard – and shave or grate it yourself. The flavour will be much more intense than that of the ready-grated product.

2 Preheat the grill (broiler). Cook the pasta in a large pan of lightly salted boiling water for about 3 minutes.

3 Put the tomatoes on a baking sheet and brush with the remaining oil. Grill (broil) for 3–4 minutes.

4 When the pasta rises to the surface of the boiling water, it is ready. Drain it thoroughly, return it to the pan and toss with the sauce. Pile into a bowl and add the grilled tomatoes. Grind black pepper over the top and add Parmesan shavings.

Energy 508kcal/2151kJ; Protein 14.7g; Carbohydrate 88.5g, of which sugars 8.5g; Fat 12.1g, of which saturates 1.8g; Cholesterol 0mg; Calcium 50mg; Fibre 5.1g; Sodium 297mg.

PASTA <u>WITH</u> SUN-DRIED TOMATOES

THIS IS A LIGHT, MODERN PASTA DISH OF THE KIND SERVED IN FASHIONABLE RESTAURANTS. IT IS NOT ONLY QUICK AND EASY TO PREPARE, IT LOOKS STUNNING TOO — AND TASTES DELICIOUS.

Preparation: 3 minutes; Cooking: 13–15 minutes

SERVES FOUR TO SIX

INGREDIENTS

45ml/3 tbsp pine nuts
350g/12oz dried paglia e fieno (or two different colours of tagliatelle)
45ml/3 tbsp extra virgin olive oil
30ml/2 tbsp sun-dried tomato paste
2 pieces drained sun-dried tomatoes in olive oil, cut into very thin slivers
40g/1½oz radicchio leaves, finely shredded
4–6 spring onions (scallions), thinly sliced into rings
salt and ground black pepper

1 Put the pine nuts in a non-stick frying pan and toss over a low to medium heat for 1–2 minutes or until they are lightly toasted and golden. Remove from the pan and set aside.

2 Cook the pasta in two large pans of lightly salted water for 10–12 minutes, using one pan for each colour to keep.

COOK'S TIP
If you find the presentation too fussy, you can toss the tomato and radicchio mixture with the pasta in a large bowl before serving, then sprinkle the spring onions and toasted pine nuts on top.

3 While the pasta is cooking, heat 15ml/1 tbsp of the oil in a medium pan or frying pan. Add the sun-dried tomato paste and the sun-dried tomatoes, then stir in 2 ladlefuls of the water used for cooking the pasta. Simmer until the sauce is slightly reduced, stirring constantly.

4 Mix in the shredded radicchio, then taste and season if necessary. Keep on a low heat. Drain the paglia e fieno, keeping the colours separate, and return the pasta to the pans. Add about 15ml/1 tbsp oil to each pan and toss over a medium to high heat until the pasta is glistening with the oil.

5 Arrange a portion of green and white pasta in each of 4–6 warmed bowls, then spoon the sun-dried tomato and radicchio mixture in the centre. Sprinkle the spring onions and pine nuts over the top and serve immediately. Before eating, each diner should toss the sauce ingredients with the pasta.

Energy 309kcal/1302kJ; Protein 8.6g; Carbohydrate 44.9g, of which sugars 3.6g; Fat 11.8g, of which saturates 1.3g; Cholesterol 0mg; Calcium 23mg; Fibre 2.3g; Sodium 16mg

SPAGHETTI WITH LEMON

THIS IS THE DISH TO MAKE WHEN YOU RUSH HOME FOR A QUICK BITE TO EAT AND FIND THERE'S NOTHING IN THE HOUSE EXCEPT A LEMON, SOME GARLIC AND WHAT'S IN THE PANTRY.

Preparation: 2–3 minutes; Cooking: 15 minutes

SERVES FOUR

INGREDIENTS
350g/12oz dried spaghetti
90ml/6 tbsp extra virgin olive oil
juice of 1 large lemon
2 garlic cloves, cut into
  very thin slivers
salt and ground black pepper

COOK'S TIP
Spaghetti is the best type of pasta for this recipe, because the olive oil and lemon juice cling to its long thin strands. If you are out of spaghetti, use another dried long pasta shape instead, such as spaghettini, linguine or tagliatelle.

1 Cook the pasta in a large pan of lightly salted boiling water for 10–12 minutes, until tender, then drain well and return to the pan.

2 Pour the olive oil and lemon juice over the cooked pasta, sprinkle in the slivers of garlic and add seasoning to taste. Toss the pasta over a medium to high heat for 1–2 minutes. Serve immediately in four warmed bowls.

Energy 448kcal/1886kJ; Protein 10.5g; Carbohydrate 64.9g, of which sugars 3g; Fat 18.1g, of which saturates 2.5g; Cholesterol 0mg; Calcium 22mg; Fibre 2.6g; Sodium 3mg

FETTUCINE ALL'ALFREDO

THIS SIMPLE RECIPE WAS INVENTED BY A ROMAN RESTAURATEUR CALLED ALFREDO, WHO BECAME FAMOUS FOR SERVING IT WITH A GOLD FORK AND SPOON.

Preparation: 1–2 minutes; Cooking: 10–12 minutes

SERVES FOUR

INGREDIENTS
  50g/2oz/¼ cup butter
  200ml/7fl oz/scant 1 cup double
  (heavy) cream
  50g/2oz/⅔ cup freshly grated
  Parmesan cheese, plus
  extra to serve
  350g/12oz fresh fettucine
  salt and ground black pepper

1 Melt the butter in a large pan. Add the cream and bring it to the boil. Simmer for 5 minutes, stirring constantly, then add the Parmesan, with salt and ground black pepper to taste, and turn off the heat under the pan.

2 Cook the pasta in a large pan of lightly salted boiling water for about 3 minutes.

3 Turn on the heat under the pan of cream to low, add the cooked pasta all at once and toss until it is coated in the sauce. Taste for seasoning and serve immediately, with extra Parmesan cheese handed around separately.

Energy 697kcal/2912kJ; Protein 16.3g; Carbohydrate 65.8g, of which sugars 3.8g; Fat 42.8g, of which saturates 26g; Cholesterol 108mg; Calcium 199mg; Fibre 2.6g; Sodium 226mg

LINGUINE <u>WITH</u> ROCKET

THIS FASHIONABLE LUNCH IS VERY QUICK AND EASY TO MAKE AT HOME. ROCKET HAS AN EXCELLENT PEPPERY FLAVOUR THAT COMBINES BEAUTIFULLY WITH THE PARMESAN.

Preparation: 3–5 minutes; Cooking: 11–14 minutes

SERVES FOUR

INGREDIENTS

350g/12oz dried linguine
120ml/4fl oz/½ cup extra virgin
  olive oil
1 large bunch rocket (arugula), about
  150g/5oz, stalks removed, shredded
75g/3oz/1 cup freshly grated
  Parmesan cheese

1 Cook the pasta in a large pan of lightly salted boiling water for 10–12 minutes, then drain thoroughly.

2 Heat about 60ml/4 tbsp of the olive oil in the pasta pan, then add the drained pasta and rocket. Toss over a medium heat for 1–2 minutes, or until the rocket is just wilted, then remove the pan from the heat.

3 Transfer the pasta and rocket to a large, warmed bowl. Add half the freshly grated Parmesan and the remaining olive oil. Add a little salt and black pepper to taste.

4 Toss the mixture quickly to mix all the flavours together and ensure the pasta is well coated with the oil. Serve immediately, sprinkled with the remaining Parmesan.

COOK'S TIPS

• Fresh Parmesan keeps well in the refrigerator for up to a month, if wrapped in greaseproof paper.

• Linguine is an egg pasta and looks rather like flattened strands of spaghetti. Spaghetti, fettucine or pappardelle could be used instead.

• Dried pasta cooks in 10–12 minutes, but an even faster result can be obtained by using fresh pasta. Simply add it to a large pan of boiling, lightly salted water, making sure that all the strands are fully submerged, and cook for 2–3 minutes. The pasta is ready when it rises to the top of the pan and is tender to the taste, with a slight firmness in the centre.

Energy 573kcal/2404kJ; Protein 19g; Carbohydrate 65.4g, of which sugars 3.5g; Fat 28g, of which saturates 6.9g; Cholesterol 19mg; Calcium 311mg; Fibre 3.3g; Sodium 260mg

PASTA WITH TOMATOES AND GOAT'S CHEESE

ROASTING TOMATOES BRINGS OUT THEIR SWEETNESS, WHICH CONTRASTS PERFECTLY WITH THE SHARP TASTE AND CREAMY TEXTURE OF GOAT'S CHEESE.

Preparation: 2 minutes; Cooking: 20–25 minutes

SERVES FOUR

INGREDIENTS

  8 large ripe tomatoes
  450g/1lb/4 cups dried rigatoni
  200g/7oz firm goat's cheese,
    crumbled
  60ml/4 tbsp garlic-infused olive oil
  salt and ground black pepper

1 Preheat the oven to 190ºC/375ºF/Gas 5. Place the tomatoes in a roasting pan and drizzle over 30ml/2 tbsp of the oil. Season well with salt and pepper and roast for 20–25 minutes, or until soft and slightly charred.

2 Meanwhile, cook the pasta in a large pan of lightly salted boiling water for 10–12 minutes. Drain well and return to the pan.

3 Roughly mash the tomatoes with a fork, and stir the contents of the roasting pan into the pasta. Gently stir in the goat's cheese and the remaining oil and serve.

Energy 682kcal/2873kJ; Protein 25.6g; Carbohydrate 90.8g, of which sugars 11.2g; Fat 26.6g, of which saturates 11g; Cholesterol 47mg; Calcium 111mg; Fibre 5.5g; Sodium 324mg.

GARGANELLI PASTA WITH ASPARAGUS AND CREAM

WHEN FRESH ASPARAGUS IS ON SALE AT THE MARKET, THIS IS A WONDERFUL WAY TO SERVE IT. ANY TYPE OF PASTA CAN BE USED, BUT ONE THAT MIRRORS THE SHAPE OF THE ASPARAGUS WORKS BEST.

Preparation: 4–5 minutes; Cooking: 15 minutes

SERVES FOUR

INGREDIENTS

1 bunch fresh young asparagus,
    250–300g/9–11oz
350g/12oz/3 cups dried garganelli
25g/1oz/2 tbsp butter
200ml/7fl oz/scant 1 cup panna da
    cucina or double (heavy) cream
30ml/2 tbsp dry white wine
90–115g/3½–4oz/1–1⅓ cups freshly
    grated Parmesan cheese
30ml/2 tbsp chopped fresh mixed
    herbs, such as basil, flat leaf
    parsley, chervil, marjoram
    and oregano
salt and ground black pepper

4 Meanwhile, melt the butter in a heavy pan. Add the cream, with salt and pepper to taste, and bring to the boil. Simmer for a few minutes until the cream reduces and thickens.

5 Stir the asparagus, wine and about half the Parmesan into the sauce. Drain the pasta and return it to the clean pan. Add the sauce and herbs and toss. Serve with the remaining Parmesan.

1 Snap off and throw away the woody ends of the asparagus – after trimming, you should have about 200g/7oz asparagus spears. Cut the spears diagonally into pieces about the same length and shape as the garganelli.

2 Blanch the thicker asparagus pieces in a large pan of lightly salted boiling water for 2 minutes, the tips for 1 minute. Using a slotted spoon, transfer the blanched asparagus to a colander, rinse under cold water and set aside.

3 Bring the water in the pan back to the boil, add the pasta and cook for 10–12 minutes.

Energy 716kcal/2994kJ; Protein 22g; Carbohydrate 67g, of which sugars 5g; Fat 41.3g, of which saturates 24.8g; Cholesterol 104mg; Calcium 335mg; Fibre 3.6g; Sodium 298mg

PASTA WITH BROCCOLI AND ARTICHOKES

THIS COLOURFUL DISH LOOKS HIGHLY APPETIZING AND ITS COMBINATION OF PEPPER, ARTICHOKE HEARTS, BROCCOLI, PASTA AND OLIVES MAKES IT A WINNER.

Preparation: 5 minutes; cooking: 13 minutes

SERVES FOUR

INGREDIENTS

105ml/7 tbsp olive oil
1 red (bell) pepper, seeded and
  thinly sliced
1 onion, halved and thinly sliced
5ml/1 tsp dried thyme
45ml/3 tbsp sherry vinegar
450g/1lb/4 cups fresh or
  dried rigatoni
2 x 175g/6oz jars marinated artichoke
  hearts, drained and thinly sliced
150g/5oz cooked broccoli, chopped
20–25 black olives, pitted
  and chopped
30ml/2 tbsp chopped fresh parsley
salt and ground black pepper

1 Heat 30ml/2 tbsp of the oil in a non-stick frying pan. Add the red pepper and onion and cook over a low heat for 8–10 minutes, or until the vegetables are just soft, stirring occasionally.

2 Stir in the thyme and vinegar. Cook for 30 seconds, stirring, then set aside.

3 Meanwhile, cook the pasta in a large pan of lightly salted boiling water. Dried pasta will take 10–12 minutes, fresh about 3 minutes. Drain, then transfer to a serving large bowl. Add 30ml/2 tbsp of the oil and toss well to coat.

4 Add the artichokes, broccoli, olives, parsley, onion mixture and remaining oil to the pasta. Season with salt and pepper. Toss to blend. Leave to stand for at least 5 minutes before serving.

Energy 622kcal/2614kJ; Protein 16.4g; Carbohydrate 88.8g, of which sugars 8.6g; Fat 24.7g, of which saturates 3.5g; Cholesterol 0mg; Calcium 108mg; Fibre 6.8g; Sodium 624mg.

PASTA <u>WITH</u> SPRING VEGETABLES

THIS IS A REAL TASTE OF SPRING ON A PLATE — SEASONAL ASPARAGUS, FENNEL, LEEKS, BROCCOLI AND PEAS ARE ALL COMBINED WITH PASTA IN A HERBY CREAM SAUCE.

Preparation: 5 minutes; cooking: 15–17 minutes

SERVES FOUR

INGREDIENTS
115g/4oz/1 cup broccoli florets
115g/4oz baby leeks
225g/8oz asparagus, trimmed
1 small fennel bulb
115g/4oz/2 cups fresh or frozen peas
40g/1½ oz/3 tbsp butter
1 shallot, chopped
45ml/3 tbsp chopped fresh mixed
  herbs, such as parsley, thyme
  and sage
300ml/ ½ pint/1¼ cups
  double (heavy) cream
350g/12oz/3 cups dried penne
salt and ground black pepper
freshly grated Parmesan cheese,
  to serve

1 Divide the broccoli florets into tiny sprigs. Cut the leeks and asparagus diagonally into 5cm/2in lengths. Trim the fennel bulb and cut into wedges.

2 Cook all the vegetables in boiling salted water until just tender.

3 Remove the vegetables with a slotted spoon and keep hot. Melt the butter in a separate pan, add the chopped shallot and cook, stirring occasionally, until softened, but not browned. Stir in the herbs and cream and cook for a few minutes, until slightly thickened.

4 Meanwhile, cook the pasta in a large pan of lightly salted boiling water for 10–12 minutes. Drain well and add to the sauce with the vegetables. Toss gently and season with black pepper.

5 Serve the pasta at once with a generous sprinkling of freshly grated Parmesan.

Energy 810kcal/3377kJ; Protein 17.9g; Carbohydrate 73.1g, of which sugars 8.2g; Fat 51.5g, of which saturates 30.7g; Cholesterol 124mg; Calcium 142mg; Fibre 8.1g; Sodium 93mg.

PASTA <u>WITH</u> FRESH PESTO

BOTTLED PESTO IS A USEFUL INGREDIENT, BUT YOU CAN MAKE YOUR OWN IN LESS TIME THAN IT TAKES TO BOIL THE PASTA THAT ACCOMPANIES IT. ANY SPARE PESTO WILL KEEP FOR A FEW DAYS.

Preparation: 4 minutes; Cooking: 12–14 minutes

SERVES FOUR

INGREDIENTS

400g/14oz/3½ cups dried fusilli
50g/2oz/1⅓ cups fresh basil leaves,
  plus extra, to garnish
2–4 garlic cloves
60ml/4 tbsp pine nuts
120ml/4fl oz/½ cup extra virgin
  olive oil
115g/4oz/1⅓ cups freshly grated
  Parmesan cheese, plus extra
  to serve
25g/1oz/⅓ cup freshly grated
  Pecorino cheese
salt and ground black pepper

1 Cook the pasta in a large pan of lightly salted boiling water for 10–12 minutes.

2 Meanwhile, put the basil leaves, garlic and pine nuts in a blender or food processor. Add 60ml/4 tbsp of the olive oil. Process until the ingredients are finely chopped, scraping down the sides of the bowl twice.

3 With the motor running, slowly pour the remaining oil in a thin, steady stream through the feeder tube.

4 Scrape the mixture into a large bowl and beat in the cheeses with a wooden spoon. Taste and add salt and pepper if necessary.

5 Drain the pasta well, then add it to the bowl of pesto and toss to coat. Serve immediately, garnished with the fresh basil leaves. Hand shaved Parmesan around separately.

Energy 783kcal/3279kJ; Protein 27.9g; Carbohydrate 74.7g, of which sugars 3.9g; Fat 43.5g, of which saturates 10.9g; Cholesterol 35mg; Calcium 447mg; Fibre 3.2g; Sodium 385mg

FUSILLI <u>WITH</u> WILD MUSHROOMS

A VERY RICH DISH WITH AN EARTHY FLAVOUR AND LOTS OF GARLIC, THIS MAKES AN IDEAL MAIN COURSE FOR VEGETARIANS, ESPECIALLY IF IT IS FOLLOWED BY A CRISP GREEN SALAD.

Preparation: 8 minutes; Cooking: 12–14 minutes

SERVES FOUR

INGREDIENTS
½ x 275g/10oz jar wild mushrooms
in olive oil
25g/1oz/2 tbsp butter
225g/8oz/2 cups fresh wild
mushrooms, sliced if large
5ml/1 tsp finely chopped fresh thyme
5ml/1 tsp finely chopped fresh
marjoram or oregano, plus extra
herbs to serve
4 garlic cloves, crushed
350g/12oz/3 cups fresh or
dried fusilli
200ml/7fl oz/scant 1 cup panna
da cucina or double (heavy) cream
salt and ground black pepper

1 Drain about 15ml/1 tbsp of the oil from the mushrooms into a medium pan. Slice or chop the bottled mushrooms into bitesize pieces if they are large.

2 Add the butter to the oil in the pan and place over a low heat until sizzling. Add the bottled and fresh mushrooms, the chopped herbs and the garlic, with salt and pepper to taste. Simmer over a medium heat, stirring frequently, for about 10 minutes or until the fresh mushrooms are soft and tender. Meanwhile, cook the pasta in a large pan of lightly salted boiling water for 10–12 minutes.

3 As soon as the mushrooms are cooked, increase the heat to high and toss the mixture with a wooden spoon to drive off any excess liquid. Pour in the cream and bring to the boil, stirring, then taste and add more salt and pepper if needed.

4 Drain the pasta and tip it into a warmed bowl. Pour the sauce over the pasta and toss well. Serve immediately, sprinkled with extra fresh herb leaves.

Energy 1029kcal/4277kJ; Protein 13.6g; Carbohydrate 66.5g, of which sugars 4.3g; Fat 80.7g, of which saturates 47.1g; Cholesterol 188mg; Calcium 63mg; Fibre 3.7g; Sodium 360mg.

MACARONI CHEESE

RICH AND CREAMY, THIS IS A DELUXE VERSION OF THE HUMBLE MACARONI CHEESE. IT GOES WELL WITH EITHER A TOMATO AND BASIL SALAD OR A LEAFY GREEN SALAD.

Preparation: 5 minutes; Cooking: 25 minutes

SERVES FOUR

INGREDIENTS
250g/9oz/2¼ cups dried
    short-cut macaroni
50g/2oz/¼ cup butter
50g/2oz/½ cup plain
    (all-purpose) flour
600ml/1 pint/2½ cups milk
100ml/3½ fl oz/scant ½ cup panna
    da cucina or double (heavy) cream
100ml/3½ fl oz/scant ½ cup dry
    white wine
50g/2oz/½ cup grated Gruyère or
    Emmenthal cheese
50g/2oz Fontina cheese, diced small
50g/2oz Gorgonzola cheese, crumbled
75g/3oz/1 cup freshly grated
    Parmesan cheese
salt and ground black pepper

1 Preheat the oven to 200ºC/400ºF/Gas 6. Cook the pasta in a large pan of lightly salted boiling water for 10 minutes.

2 Meanwhile, gently melt the butter in a pan, add the flour and cook, stirring, for 1–2 minutes. Add the milk gradually, whisking vigorously after each addition. Stir in the cream, then the wine. Bring to the boil. Cook, stirring constantly, until the sauce thickens. Remove the pan from the heat.

3 Add the Gruyère or Emmenthal, Fontina, Gorgonzola and about one-third of the grated Parmesan to the sauce. Stir well to mix in the cheeses, then taste for seasoning and add salt and pepper if necessary.

4 Drain the pasta well and tip it into a baking dish. Pour the sauce over the pasta and mix well, then sprinkle the remaining Parmesan over the top. Bake for 15–20 minutes or until golden brown. Serve hot.

COOK'S TIP
Fontina is a mountain cheese with a slightly sweet, nutty flavour. If you can't get it, use Taleggio or simply double the quantity of Gruyère or Emmenthal.

Energy 791kcal/3306kJ; Protein 30.6g; Carbohydrate 63.8g, of which sugars 10g; Fat 45.5g, of which saturates 28.3g; Cholesterol 122mg; Calcium 701mg; Fibre 2.2g; Sodium 687mg.

PANSOTTI <u>WITH</u> WALNUT SAUCE

RECIPES DON'T COME MUCH EASIER THAN THIS. WALNUTS, GARLIC OIL AND CREAM MAKE A
STUNNINGLY SUCCESSFUL SAUCE FOR STUFFED PASTA. FOR SPEED AND FLAVOUR, USE FRESH PASTA.
Preparation: 4 minutes; Cooking: 4–5 minutes

SERVES FOUR

INGREDIENTS
   90g/3½oz/scant 1 cup shelled
      walnuts or walnut pieces
   60ml/4 tbsp garlic-flavoured olive oil
   120ml/4fl oz/½ cup double
      (heavy) cream
   350g/12oz fresh cheese and herb-
      filled pansotti or other stuffed pasta

1 Put the walnuts and garlic oil in a
food processor and process to a paste,
adding up to 120ml/4fl oz/½ cup warm
water through the feeder tube to
slacken the consistency. Spoon the
mixture into a large bowl and add the
cream. Beat well to mix, then season to
taste with salt and black pepper.

2 Cook the stuffed pasta in a large pan
of salted boiling water for 4–5 minutes,
or according to the instructions on the
packet. Meanwhile, put the walnut
sauce in a large warmed bowl and add
a ladleful of the water the pasta was
cooked in to thin it.

3 Drain the pasta and tip it into the
bowl of walnut sauce. Toss well, then
serve immediately.

COOK'S TIP
Walnuts become rancid quite quickly, so
you shouldn't store open packets in the
pantry for long periods. For a sauce like
this one, or anything else for which the
walnuts are ground, buy the more
economical walnut pieces.

VARIATION
Don't worry if you can't locate pansotti;
tortellini will work just as well. The best
place to buy the pasta for this recipe is a
specialist deli where pasta is made on
the premises.

Energy 702kcal/2931kJ; Protein 14.3g; Carbohydrate 66.1g, of which sugars 4g; Fat 44.1g, of which saturates 13g; Cholesterol 41mg; Calcium 58mg; Fibre 3.3g; Sodium 11mg

WARM PENNE WITH FRESH TOMATOES AND BASIL

WHEN YOU'RE HEADING OFF FOR A FAMILY BIKE RIDE OR A WALK ON THE BEACH, SOMETHING LIGHT AND FRESH, BUT WHICH KEEPS ENERGY LEVELS TOPPED UP OVER TIME, IS JUST WHAT YOU NEED.

Preparation: 2–3 minutes; Cooking: 12–14 minutes

SERVES FOUR

INGREDIENTS
   500g/1¼lb/5 cups dried penne
   5 very ripe plum tomatoes
   1 small bunch fresh basil
   60ml/4 tbsp extra virgin olive oil
   salt and ground black pepper

COOK'S TIP
If you cannot find ripe tomatoes, roast those you have to bring out their flavour. Put the tomatoes in a roasting pan, drizzle with oil and roast at 190°C/375°F/Gas 5 for 20 minutes, then mash roughly.

1 Cook the pasta in a large pan of lightly salted boiling water for 10–12 minutes. Meanwhile, roughly chop the tomatoes and tear up the basil leaves.

2 Drain the pasta thoroughly and return it to the clean pan. Toss with the tomatoes, basil and olive oil. Season with salt and freshly ground black pepper and serve immediately.

Energy 552kcal/2336kJ; Protein 16.3g; Carbohydrate 96.9g, of which sugars 8.3g; Fat 13.8g, of which saturates 2g; Cholesterol 0mg; Calcium 65mg; Fibre 5.5g; Sodium 19mg

TAGLIATELLE <u>WITH</u> VEGETABLE RIBBONS

NARROW STRIPS OF COURGETTE AND CARROT MINGLE WELL WITH TAGLIATELLE TO RESEMBLE COLOURED PASTA. SERVE WITH FRESHLY GRATED PARMESAN CHEESE HANDED ROUND SEPARATELY.

Preparation: 5 minutes; Cooking: 5 minutes

SERVES FOUR

INGREDIENTS

   2 large courgettes (zucchini)
   2 large carrots
   250g/9oz fresh egg tagliatelle
   60ml/4 tbsp garlic-flavoured olive oil
   salt and ground black pepper
To serve
   freshly grated Parmesan cheese

COOK'S TIP

Garlic-flavoured olive oil is used in this dish. Flavoured oils such as rosemary, chilli or basil are widely available and are a quick way of adding flavour to pasta.

1 With a vegetable peeler, cut the courgettes and carrots into long thin ribbons. Bring a large pan of salted water to the boil, then add the courgette and carrot ribbons. Bring the water back to the boil and boil for 30 seconds, then remove the vegetables with a slotted spoon and set aside.

2 Bring the water back to boiling point and cook the pasta for 3 minutes. Drain well and return it to the pan. Add the vegetable ribbons, garlic-flavoured oil and seasoning and toss over a medium to high heat until the pasta and vegetables are glistening with oil. Serve the pasta immediately.

Energy 397kcal/1663kJ; Protein 11.5g; Carbohydrate 52.4g, of which sugars 8.3g; Fat 17.1g, of which saturates 3.3g; Cholesterol 19mg; Calcium 80mg; Fibre 4.8g; Sodium 127mg.

SPAGHETTI WITH ANCHOVIES AND OLIVES

THE STRONG FLAVOURS OF THIS GUTSY RUSTIC PASTA DISH ARE TYPICAL OF SICILIAN CUISINE.
Preparation: 8 minutes; Cooking: 22–26 minutes

SERVES FOUR

INGREDIENTS
45ml/3 tbsp olive oil
1 large red (bell) pepper, seeded
  and finely chopped
1 small aubergine (eggplant),
  finely chopped
1 onion, finely chopped
8 ripe Italian plum tomatoes, peeled,
  seeded and finely chopped
2 garlic cloves, finely chopped
120ml/4fl oz/½ cup dry red or
  white wine
120ml/4fl oz/½ cup water
1 handful fresh herbs, such as basil,
  flat leaf parsley and rosemary
300g/11oz dried spaghetti
50g/2oz canned anchovies, roughly
  chopped, plus whole ones to garnish
12 pitted black olives
15–30ml/1–2 tbsp capers, to taste
salt and ground black pepper

1 Heat the oil in a pan and add all the finely chopped vegetables and garlic. Cook gently, stirring frequently, for 10–12 minutes until the vegetables are soft. Pour in the wine and measured water, add the fresh herbs and pepper to taste and bring to the boil. Lower the heat and simmer, stirring occasionally, for 10–12 minutes. Meanwhile, cook the pasta in a large pan of lightly salted boiling water for 10–12 minutes.

2 Add the chopped anchovies, olives and capers to the sauce, heat through for a few minutes and taste for seasoning. Drain the pasta and tip it into a warmed bowl. Pour the sauce over the pasta, toss well and serve immediately, garnished with the whole anchovies.

COOK'S TIP
If the anchovies are omitted, this makes a good sauce for vegetarians.

Energy 754kcal/3162kJ; Protein 42.7g; Carbohydrate 65.5g, of which sugars 11.8g; Fat 35.4g, of which saturates 5.4g; Cholesterol 79mg; Calcium 419mg; Fibre 5.6g; Sodium 4933mg.

SPAGHETTI WITH TUNA, OLIVES AND CHEESE

THIS RECIPE FROM CAPRI IS FRESH, LIGHT AND FULL OF FLAVOUR, SO SERVE IT AS SOON AS IT IS COOKED TO ENJOY ALL THE INGREDIENTS AT THEIR BEST.
Preparation: 8 minutes; Cooking: 15–17 minutes

SERVES FOUR

INGREDIENTS
300g/11oz dried spaghetti
30ml/2 tbsp olive oil
6 ripe Italian plum tomatoes, chopped
5ml/1 tsp sugar
50g/2oz jar anchovies in olive oil,
  drained, snipped with scissors
about 60ml/4 tbsp dry white wine
200g/7oz can tuna in olive oil,
  drained
50g/2oz/½ cup pitted black olives,
  quartered lengthways
125g/4½ oz mozzarella cheese,
  drained and diced
salt and ground black pepper
fresh basil leaves, to garnish

1 Cook the pasta in a large pan of lightly salted boiling water for 10–12 minutes. Meanwhile, heat the oil in a medium pan. Add the tomatoes, sugar and pepper to taste, and toss over a medium heat until the tomatoes soften and the juices run. Add the anchovies.

2 Add the wine, tuna and olives and stir until they are just evenly mixed into the sauce. Add the mozzarella and heat through without stirring. Taste and add salt if necessary. Drain the pasta and tip it into a warmed bowl. Pour the sauce over, toss gently and sprinkle with basil.

Energy 533kcal/2246kJ; Protein 29.6g; Carbohydrate 61.4g, of which sugars 8.3g; Fat 19.5g, of which saturates 6.4g; Cholesterol 43mg; Calcium 158mg; Fibre 4g; Sodium 566mg.

SPAGHETTI WITH CLAM SAUCE

THIS VENETIAN SPECIALITY IS ONE OF ITALY'S MOST FAMOUS PASTA DISHES, SOMETIMES TRANSLATED AS "WHITE CLAM SAUCE" TO DISTINGUISH IT FROM THAT OTHER CLASSIC, CLAMS IN TOMATO SAUCE.

Preparation: 10 minutes; Cooking: 10–12 minutes

SERVES FOUR

INGREDIENTS
350g/12oz dried spaghetti
1kg/2¼ lb fresh clams
60ml/4 tbsp olive oil
45ml/3 tbsp chopped fresh
 flat leaf parsley
120ml/4fl oz/½ cup dry white wine
2 garlic cloves
salt and ground black pepper

1 Scrub the clams under cold running water, discarding any that are open or that do not close when sharply tapped against the work surface.

2 Cook the pasta in a large pan of lightly salted boiling water for 10–12 minutes. Meanwhile, heat half the oil in a large pan, add the clams and 15ml/1 tbsp of the parsley and cook over a high heat for a few seconds. Pour in the wine, then cover tightly. Cook for about 5 minutes, shaking the pan frequently, until the clams have opened.

3 Use a slotted spoon to transfer the clams to a bowl. Discard any that have failed to open. Strain the liquid and set it aside. Put eight clams in their shells to one side for the garnish, then remove the rest from their shells with a fork.

4 Heat the remaining oil in the clean pan. Fry the whole garlic cloves over a medium heat until golden, crushing them with a wooden spoon. Remove the garlic with a slotted spoon and discard.

5 Add the shelled clams to the oil still in the pan, gradually add some of the strained liquid from the clams, then add plenty of pepper. Cook for 1–2 minutes, gradually adding more liquid as the sauce reduces. Add the remaining parsley and cook for 1–2 minutes.

6 Drain the pasta, add it to the pan and toss well. Serve in individual dishes, scooping the shelled clams from the bottom of the pan and placing some of them on top of each serving. Garnish with the reserved clams and serve.

Energy 519kcal/2187kJ; Protein 30.9g; Carbohydrate 67.7g, of which sugars 3.4g; Fat 13.5g, of which saturates 2g; Cholesterol 84mg; Calcium 142mg; Fibre 3.2g; Sodium 1508mg.

LINGUINE WITH CRAB

THIS RECIPE COMES FROM ROME. IT MAKES A VERY RICH AND TASTY FIRST COURSE ON ITS OWN, OR CAN BE SERVED FOR A LUNCH OR SUPPER WITH CRUSTY ITALIAN BREAD.

Preparation: 5 minutes; Cooking: 20 minutes

SERVES FOUR

INGREDIENTS
about 250g/9oz shelled crab meat
45ml/3 tbsp olive oil
1 small handful fresh flat leaf
   parsley, roughly chopped, plus extra
   to garnish
1 garlic clove, crushed
350g/12oz ripe Italian plum
   tomatoes, skinned and chopped
60–90ml/4–6 tbsp dry white wine
350g/12oz fresh or dried linguine
salt and ground black pepper

COOK'S TIP
The best way to obtain crab meat is to ask a fishmonger to remove it from the shell for you, or buy dressed crab from the supermarket. For this recipe you will need one large crab, and you should use both the white and dark meat.

1 Put the crab meat in a mortar and pound to a rough pulp with a pestle. If you do not have a mortar and pestle, use a sturdy bowl and the end of a rolling pin. Set aside.

2 Heat 30ml/2 tbsp of the oil in a large pan. Add the parsley and garlic, with salt and pepper to taste, and fry for a few minutes until the garlic begins to turn brown.

3 Add the tomatoes, crab meat and wine, cover the pan and simmer gently for 15 minutes, stirring occasionally.

4 Meanwhile, cook the pasta in a large pan of lightly salted boiling water. Dried pasta will take 10–12 minutes, fresh about 3 minutes. Drain it the moment it is al dente, and reserve a little of the cooking water.

5 Return the pasta to the clean pan, add the remaining oil and toss quickly over a medium heat until the oil coats it.

6 Add the tomato and crab mixture to the pasta and toss again, adding a little of the reserved cooking water if you think it necessary. Adjust the seasoning to taste.

7 Serve hot, in warmed bowls, sprinkled with parsley.

Energy 457kcal/1932kJ; Protein 22.8g; Carbohydrate 68g, of which sugars 6g; Fat 10.8g, of which saturates 1.5g; Cholesterol 45mg; Calcium 125mg; Fibre 3.9g; Sodium 359mg.

SPAGHETTI <u>WITH</u> SALMON <u>AND</u> PRAWNS

THIS IS A LOVELY FRESH-TASTING PASTA DISH, PERFECT FOR AN AL FRESCO MEAL IN SUMMER. SERVE IT AS A MAIN COURSE LUNCH WITH WARM CIABATTA OR FOCACCIA AND A DRY WHITE WINE.

Preparation: 10 minutes; Cooking: 15–20 minutes

SERVES FOUR

INGREDIENTS

300g/11oz salmon fillet
200ml/7fl oz/scant 1 cup dry
   white wine
a few fresh basil sprigs, plus extra
   basil leaves, to garnish
150ml/¼ pint/⅔ cup double (heavy)
   cream
6 ripe Italian plum tomatoes, peeled
   and finely chopped
350g/12oz dried spaghetti
115g/4oz/⅔ cup peeled cooked
   prawns (shrimp), thawed and
   thoroughly patted dry if frozen
salt and ground black pepper

1 Put the salmon skin side up in a wide shallow pan. Pour the wine over, then add the basil sprigs to the pan and sprinkle the fish with salt and pepper. Bring the wine to the boil, cover the pan and simmer gently for no more than 5 minutes. Using a fish slice (metal spatula), lift the fish out of the pan and set it aside to cool a little.

2 Add the cream and tomatoes to the liquid remaining in the pan and bring to the boil. Stir well, then lower the heat and simmer, uncovered, for 10–15 minutes. Meanwhile, cook the pasta in a large pan of lightly salted boiling water for 10–12 minutes.

3 Flake the fish into large chunks, discarding the skin and any bones. Add the fish to the sauce with the prawns, shaking the pan until the fish and shellfish are well coated. Taste the sauce for seasoning.

4 Drain the pasta and tip it into a warmed bowl. Pour the sauce over the pasta and toss to combine. Serve immediately, garnished with the basil.

COOK'S TIP
Check the salmon fillet carefully for small bones when you are flaking the flesh. Although the salmon is already filleted, you will always find a few stray "pin" bones. Pick them out carefully using tweezers or your fingertips.

Energy 701kcal/2941kJ; Protein 32.4g; Carbohydrate 70.4g, of which sugars 8.5g; Fat 30.6g, of which saturates 14.3g; Cholesterol 145mg; Calcium 94mg; Fibre 4g; Sodium 115mg.

SEAFOOD CONCHIGLIE

THIS IS A VERY SPECIAL MODERN DISH — A WARM SALAD COMPOSED OF SCALLOPS, PASTA AND FRESH ROCKET FLAVOURED WITH ROASTED PEPPER, CHILLI AND BALSAMIC VINEGAR.

Preparation: 8 minutes; Cooking: 10–12 minutes

SERVES FOUR

INGREDIENTS
  8 large fresh scallops
  300g/11oz/2¾ cups dried conchiglie
  15ml/1 tbsp olive oil
  15g/½ oz/1 tbsp butter
  120ml/4fl oz/½ cup dry white wine
  90g/3½ oz rocket (arugula) leaves,
    stalks trimmed
  salt and ground black pepper
For the vinaigrette
  60ml/4 tbsp extra virgin olive oil
  15ml/1 tbsp balsamic vinegar
  1 piece bottled roasted pepper,
    drained and finely chopped
  1–2 fresh red chillies, seeded and
    chopped
  1 garlic clove, crushed
  5–10ml/1–2 tsp clear honey, to taste

6 Drain the pasta and tip it into a warmed bowl. Add the rocket, scallops, the reduced cooking juices and the vinaigrette and toss well to combine. Serve immediately.

1 Cut each scallop into 2–3 pieces. If the corals are attached, pull them off and cut each piece in half. Season the scallops and corals with salt and pepper.

2 To make the vinaigrette, put all the ingredients in a measuring jug (cup) and whisk well.

3 Cook the pasta in a large pan of lightly salted boiling water for 10–12 minutes.

4 Meanwhile, heat the oil and butter in a non-stick frying pan until sizzling. Add half the scallops and toss over a high heat for 2 minutes. Remove with a slotted spoon and keep warm. Cook the remaining scallops in the same way.

5 Add the wine to the liquid remaining in the pan and stir over a high heat until the mixture has reduced to a few tablespoons. Remove from the heat and keep warm.

COOK'S TIPS
• Use only fresh scallops for this dish – they are available all year round in most fishmongers and from fish counters in supermarkets. Frozen scallops tend to be watery and tasteless, and often prove to be rubbery when cooked.
• For a more formal presentation, arrange the rocket leaves in a circle on each of four individual serving plates. Toss the pasta, scallops, reduced cooking juices and vinaigrette together and spoon into the centre of the rocket leaves.

Energy 485kcal/2039kJ; Protein 18.4g; Carbohydrate 59.3g, of which sugars 4.9g; Fat 18.9g, of which saturates 4.3g; Cholesterol 26mg; Calcium 72mg; Fibre 2.7g; Sodium 126mg.

ORECCHIETTE WITH ANCHOVIES AND BROCCOLI

WITH ITS ROBUST FLAVOURS, THIS DISH IS TYPICAL OF SOUTHERN ITALIAN AND SICILIAN COOKING.
ANCHOVIES, PINE NUTS, GARLIC AND PECORINO CHEESE ARE ALL VERY POPULAR INGREDIENTS.
Preparation: 5 minutes; Cooking: 14–16 minutes

SERVES FOUR

INGREDIENTS
   300g/11oz/2 cups broccoli florets
   40g/1½ oz/½ cup pine nuts
   350g/12oz/3 cups dried orecchiette
   60ml/4 tbsp olive oil
   1 small red onion, thinly sliced
   50g/2oz jar anchovies in olive oil
   1 garlic clove, crushed
   50g/2oz/⅔ cup freshly grated
     Pecorino cheese
   salt and ground black pepper

COOK'S TIPS
• Orecchiette (little ears) from Puglia are
a special type of pasta with a chewy
texture. You can get them in Italian
delicatessens, or use conchiglie instead.
• Serving some crusty Italian bread with
this dish makes it suitable for a light
lunch or supper.
• Be careful not to overcook the pine
nuts, as they will taste bitter.

1 Break the broccoli florets into small
sprigs and cut off the stalks. If the
stalks are large, chop or slice them.
Cook the florets and stalks in a pan of
boiling salted water for 2 minutes, then
drain and refresh under cold running
water. Leave to drain on kitchen paper.

2 Put the pine nuts in a dry non-stick
frying pan and toss over a low to
medium heat for 1–2 minutes or until
the nuts are lightly toasted and golden.
Remove and set aside.

3 Cook the pasta in a large pan of lightly
salted boiling water for 10–12 minutes.

4 Meanwhile, heat the oil in a frying
pan, add the red onion and fry gently,
stirring frequently, for about 5 minutes
until soft. Add the anchovies with their
oil, then add the garlic and fry over a
medium heat, stirring, for 1–2 minutes
until the anchovies form a paste.

5 Add the broccoli and plenty of
pepper and toss over the heat for a
minute or two until the broccoli is hot.
Taste for seasoning.

6 Drain the pasta and tip it into a warm
bowl. Add the broccoli mixture and
cheese and toss well to combine.
Sprinkle the pine nuts on top and serve.

Energy 572kcal/2403kJ; Protein 23.3g; Carbohydrate 66.6g, of which sugars 4.4g; Fat 25.4g, of which saturates 5.1g; Cholesterol 20mg; Calcium 253mg; Fibre 4.7g; Sodium 636mg.

PENNE WITH CREAM AND SMOKED SALMON

No supper dish could be simpler. Freshly cooked pasta is tossed with cream, smoked salmon and thyme to make a lovely, light dish that looks as good as it tastes.

Preparation: 2 minutes; Cooking: 10–12 minutes

SERVES FOUR

INGREDIENTS

350g/12oz/3 cups dried penne
115g/4oz thinly sliced
  smoked salmon
2–3 fresh thyme sprigs
25g/1oz/2 tbsp butter
150ml/¼ pint/⅔ cup double
  (heavy) cream
salt and ground black pepper

VARIATION

Substitute low-fat cream cheese for half the cream in the sauce for a less rich mixture that still tastes very good.

1 Cook the pasta in a large pan of lightly salted boiling water for 10–12 minutes, until tender but still firm to the bite.

2 Meanwhile, using kitchen scissors or a small, sharp knife, cut the smoked salmon into thin strips, each about 5mm/¼in wide, and place on a plate. Strip the leaves from the thyme sprigs.

3 Melt the butter in a large pan. Stir in the cream with a quarter of the salmon and thyme leaves, then season with pepper. Heat gently for 3–4 minutes, stirring constantly. Do not allow the sauce to boil. Taste for seasoning.

4 Drain the pasta and toss it in the cream and salmon sauce. Divide among four warmed bowls and top with the remaining salmon and thyme leaves.

Energy 573kcal/2403kJ; Protein 18.5g; Carbohydrate 65.5g, of which sugars 3.6g; Fat 28.2g, of which saturates 16.2g; Cholesterol 75mg; Calcium 47mg; Fibre 2.6g; Sodium 589mg

WARM PASTA SALAD WITH ASPARAGUS

TAGLIATELLE DRESSED WITH A CREAMY ASPARAGUS SAUCE IS THE BASIS FOR THIS SUSTAINING SALAD.
IF YOU'VE SPENT THE MORNING GARDENING OR PLAYING SPORT, THIS IS A GREAT QUICK LUNCH.

Preparation: 6 minutes; Cooking: 12 minutes

SERVES FOUR

INGREDIENTS
450g/1lb asparagus
450g/1lb dried tagliatelle
225g/8oz cooked ham, in 5mm/¼in-
  thick slices, cut into fingers
2 hard-boiled eggs, sliced
50g/2oz Parmesan cheese
salt and ground black pepper
For the dressing
50g/2oz cooked potato
75ml/5 tbsp olive oil
15ml/1 tbsp lemon juice
10ml/2 tsp Dijon mustard
120ml/4fl oz/½ cup vegetable stock

VARIATIONS
Use sliced chicken instead of the ham,
or thin slices of softer Italian cheese,
such as Fontina or Asiago.

1 Snap the asparagus spears and
discard the tough woody ends. Cut the
spears in half and cook the thicker
halves in boiling salted water for
12 minutes, adding the tips after
6 minutes.

2 Meanwhile, cook the pasta in a large
pan of lightly salted boiling water for
10–12 minutes.

3 Drain the asparagus. Reserve the tips.
Purée the remainder with the dressing
ingredients until smooth.

4 Drain the pasta, toss with the
asparagus sauce and cool slightly.
Divide among four pasta plates. Top
with the ham, hard-boiled eggs and
asparagus tips. Shave Parmesan cheese
over the top.

Energy 699kcal/2941kJ; Protein 35.4g; Carbohydrate 88.2g, of which sugars 6.6g; Fat 25.2g, of which saturates 6.3g; Cholesterol 140mg; Calcium 228mg; Fibre 5.3g; Sodium 852mg

FETTUCCINE ^{WITH} HAM ^{AND} PEAS

THIS SIMPLE DISH MAKES A VERY GOOD FIRST COURSE FOR SIX PEOPLE, OR A MAIN COURSE FOR THREE TO FOUR. DESPITE ITS SIMPLICITY, IT MAKES AN IDEAL IMPROMPTU SUPPER.

Preparation: 4 minutes; Cooking: 8–10 minutes

SERVES THREE TO SIX

INGREDIENTS

50g/2oz/¼ cup butter
1 small onion, finely chopped
200g/7oz/1¾ cups fresh or
    frozen peas
100ml/3½ fl oz/scant ½ cup
    chicken stock
2.5ml/½ tsp sugar
175ml/6fl oz/¾ cup dry white wine
350g/12oz fresh fettuccine
75g/3oz piece cooked ham, cut into
    bitesize chunks
115g/4oz/1⅓ cups freshly grated
    Parmesan cheese
salt and ground black pepper

COOK'S TIP
If you want to make this with dried pasta it will take a little longer, but if you start cooking the pasta before making the sauce, it won't take too much more time.

1 Melt the butter in a medium frying pan, add the onion and cook over a low heat for about 5 minutes until softened but not coloured. Add the peas, stock and sugar, with salt and pepper to taste.

2 Bring the mixture to the boil, then lower the heat and simmer for 3–5 minutes or until the peas are tender. Add the wine, increase the heat and boil until the wine has reduced.

3 Meanwhile, cook the pasta in a large pan of lightly salted boiling water for about 3 minutes. When it is almost ready, add the ham to the sauce, with about a third of the Parmesan. Heat through, stirring, then taste for seasoning.

4 Drain the pasta and tip it into a large warmed bowl. Pour the sauce over the pasta and toss well. Serve immediately, sprinkled with the remaining Parmesan.

Energy 414kcal/1738kJ; Protein 19.4g; Carbohydrate 48.6g, of which sugars 4g; Fat 15.1g, of which saturates 8.6g; Cholesterol 44mg; Calcium 259mg; Fibre 3.4g; Sodium 413mg.

LINGUINE WITH HAM AND MASCARPONE

MASCARPONE CHEESE MASQUERADES AS CREAM IN THIS SIMPLE YET DELICIOUS RECIPE. ITS THICK, UNCTUOUS CONSISTENCY MAKES IT PERFECT FOR SAUCES WHICH CLING BEAUTIFULLY TO THE PASTA.

Preparation: 5 minutes; Cooking: 5 minutes

SERVES SIX

INGREDIENTS
  25g/1oz/2 tbsp butter
  150g/5oz/¾ cup mascarpone
  90g/3½oz cooked ham, cut into
    thin strips
  30ml/2 tbsp milk
  45ml/3 tbsp freshly grated Parmesan
    cheese, plus extra to serve
  500g/1¼lb fresh linguine
  salt and ground black pepper

1 Melt the butter in a medium pan, add the mascarpone, ham and milk and stir well over a low heat until the mascarpone has melted. Add 15ml/1 tbsp of the grated Parmesan and plenty of pepper and stir well.

2 Cook the pasta in a large pan of lightly salted boiling water for about 3 minutes.

3 Drain the cooked pasta well and tip it into a warmed bowl. Pour the sauce over the pasta, add the remaining Parmesan and toss well.

4 Taste for seasoning and serve the pasta immediately, with more ground black pepper and extra grated Parmesan handed around separately.

COOK'S TIP
Have the water boiling, ready for the pasta, before you start making the sauce, because everything cooks very quickly.

Energy 413kcal/1745kJ; Protein 18.2g; Carbohydrate 62.9g, of which sugars 3.9g; Fat 11.6g, of which saturates 6.4g; Cholesterol 36mg; Calcium 119mg; Fibre 2.4g; Sodium 292mg.

FARFALLE WITH GORGONZOLA CREAM

SWEET AND SIMPLE, THIS SAUCE HAS A NUTTY TANG THAT COMES FROM THE BLUE CHEESE. IT IS ALSO GOOD WITH LONG PASTA, SUCH AS SPAGHETTI, TAGLIATELLE OR TRENETTE.

Preparation: 5 minutes; Cooking: 12–14 minutes

SERVES SIX

INGREDIENTS
  350g/12oz/3 cups dried farfalle
  175g/6oz Gorgonzola cheese, any
    rind removed, diced
  150ml/¼ pint/¾ cup panna da
    cucina or double (heavy) cream
  pinch of sugar
  10ml/2 tsp finely chopped fresh
    sage, plus fresh sage leaves (some
    whole, some shredded) to garnish
  salt and ground black pepper

1 Cook the pasta in a large pan of lightly salted boiling water for 10–12 minutes.

2 Meanwhile, put the Gorgonzola and cream in a medium pan. Add the sugar and plenty of ground black pepper and heat gently, stirring frequently, until the cheese has melted. Remove the pan from the heat.

3 Drain the cooked pasta well and return it to the pan in which it was cooked. Pour the sauce into the pan with the pasta.

4 Add the chopped sage to the pasta and toss over a medium heat until the pasta is evenly coated. Taste for seasoning, adding salt if necessary, then divide among four warmed bowls. Garnish each portion with sage and serve immediately.

Energy 423kcal/1773kJ; Protein 13.4g; Carbohydrate 43.7g, of which sugars 2.4g; Fat 22.9g, of which saturates 14.1g; Cholesterol 56mg; Calcium 169mg; Fibre 1.7g; Sodium 363mg.

TAGLIATELLE WITH PROSCIUTTO AND ASPARAGUS

THIS STUNNING DISH IS VERY EASY TO MAKE. SERVE IT FOR A SPECIAL OCCASION.

Preparation: 5 minutes; Cooking: 10–20 minutes

SERVES FOUR

INGREDIENTS

350g/12oz fresh or dried tagliatelle
25g/1oz/2 tbsp butter
15ml/1 tbsp olive oil
225g/8oz asparagus tips
1 garlic clove, chopped
115g/4oz prosciutto, sliced
 into strips
30ml/2 tbsp chopped fresh sage
150ml/¼ pint/⅔ cup single
 (light) cream
115g/4oz Double Gloucester
 cheese, grated
115g/4oz Gruyére cheese, grated
fresh sage leaves, to garnish

1 Cook the pasta in a large pan of lightly salted boiling water. Dried pasta will take 10–12 minutes, fresh about 3 minutes.

2 Meanwhile, melt the butter and oil in a frying pan and gently fry the asparagus for 3–4 minutes, or until almost tender.

3 Stir in the garlic and prosciutto and fry for 1 minute.

4 Stir in the chopped sage leaves and fry for a further 1 minute.

5 Pour in the cream and bring to the boil over a medium heat, stirring frequently, then tip in the grated cheeses. Simmer gently, stirring occasionally until thoroughly melted. Season to taste.

6 Drain the pasta thoroughly and tip it into a bowl. Add the sauce and toss to coat. Serve immediately, garnished with fresh sage.

Energy 727kcal/3046kJ; Protein 33.3g; Carbohydrate 67.2g, of which sugars 5.2g; Fat 36.7g, of which saturates 21.2g; Cholesterol 106mg; Calcium 499mg; Fibre 3.5g; Sodium 813mg.

RAVIOLI WITH FOUR-CHEESE SAUCE

THIS DISH HAS A SMOOTH EXTRA-CHEESY SAUCE THAT COATS THE PASTA VERY EVENLY.

Preparation: 8 minutes; Cooking: 10–12 minutes

SERVES FOUR

INGREDIENTS

350g/12oz dried ravioli
50g/2oz/¼ cup butter
50g/2oz/½ cup plain
  (all-purpose) flour
450ml/¾ pint/scant 2 cups milk
50g/2oz Parmesan cheese, grated
50g/2oz Edam cheese, grated
50g/2oz Gruyère cheese, grated
50g/2oz Fontina cheese, grated
salt and ground black pepper
chopped fresh flat leaf parsley,
  to garnish

1 Cook the pasta in a large pan of lightly salted boiling water for 10–12 minutes.

4 Bring the milk to the boil over a low heat, stirring constantly until thickened.

5 Stir the cheeses into the sauce until they are just beginning to melt. Remove the sauce from the heat and season with salt and pepper.

6 Drain the pasta thoroughly and turn it into a large warmed serving bowl. Pour over the sauce and toss to coat. Serve immediately, garnished with the chopped fresh parsley.

COOK'S TIP

If you cannot find all of the above cheeses, simply substitute your favourites. The aim is to have a total quantity of 225g/8oz cheese and to include Parmesan in the selection. Always buy Parmesan in the piece and grate it yourself. Using the ready grated cheese may save time, but the flavour will not be as good.

2 Meanwhile, melt the butter in a medium pan, stir in the flour and cook for 2 minutes, stirring.

3 Gradually stir in the milk until well blended, being careful to avoid any lumps forming.

Energy 520kcal/2174kJ; Protein 26.8g; Carbohydrate 37.7g, of which sugars 6.3g; Fat 29.7g, of which saturates 16.2g; Cholesterol 72mg; Calcium 704mg; Fibre 1.5g; Sodium 813mg.

SPAGHETTI CARBONARA

THIS ITALIAN CLASSIC, FLAVOURED WITH PANCETTA AND A GARLIC-AND-EGG SAUCE THAT COOKS AROUND THE HOT SPAGHETTI, IS POPULAR WORLDWIDE. IT MAKES A GREAT LAST-MINUTE SUPPER.

Preparation: 3 minutes; Cooking: 15–17 minutes

SERVES FOUR

INGREDIENTS

30ml/2 tbsp olive oil
1 small onion, finely chopped
1 large garlic clove, crushed
8 slices pancetta or rindless smoked
  streaky (fatty) bacon, cut into
  1cm/½in pieces
350g/12oz dried spaghetti
4 eggs
90–120ml/6–8 tbsp crème fraîche
60ml/4 tbsp freshly grated
  Parmesan cheese, plus extra
  to serve
salt and ground black pepper

1 Heat the oil in a large pan, add the onion and garlic and fry gently for about 5 minutes until softened.

2 Add the pancetta or bacon to the pan. Cook for 10 minutes, stirring often.

3 Meanwhile, cook the spaghetti in a large pan of lightly salted boiling water for 10–12 minutes.

4 Put the eggs, crème fraîche and grated Parmesan in a bowl. Stir in plenty of black pepper, then beat together well.

5 Drain the pasta thoroughly, tip it into the pan with the pancetta or bacon and toss well to mix.

6 Turn off the heat under the pan, then immediately add the egg mixture and toss thoroughly so that it cooks lightly and coats the pasta.

7 Season to taste, then divide the pasta among four warmed bowls and sprinkle with ground black pepper. Serve immediately, with extra grated Parmesan handed around separately.

VARIATION
You can replace the crème fraîche with double (heavy) cream or sour cream, if you prefer.

Energy 708kcal/2966kJ; Protein 30.7g; Carbohydrate 66.6g, of which sugars 4.2g; Fat 37.5g, of which saturates 15.5g; Cholesterol 261mg; Calcium 250mg; Fibre 2.8g; Sodium 824mg

SPAGHETTI WITH TOMATOES AND PANCETTA

THIS SAUCE COMES FROM UMBRIA. IT IS A FRESH, LIGHT SAUCE IN WHICH THE TOMATOES ARE COOKED FOR A SHORT TIME, SO IT SHOULD BE MADE ONLY WITH FLAVOURSOME SUMMER TOMATOES.

Preparation: 10 minutes; Cooking: 20 minutes

SERVES FOUR

INGREDIENTS
350g/12oz ripe Italian plum tomatoes
150g/5oz pancetta or rindless
  streaky (fatty) bacon, diced
30ml/2 tbsp olive oil
1 onion, finely chopped
350g/12oz fresh or dried spaghetti
2–3 fresh marjoram sprigs,
  leaves stripped
salt and ground black pepper
shredded fresh basil, to garnish
freshly grated Pecorino cheese,
  to serve

1 With a sharp knife, cut a cross in the bottom (flower) end of each plum tomato. Bring a medium pan of water to the boil and remove from the heat. Plunge a few of the tomatoes into the water, leave for 30 seconds or so, then lift them out with a slotted spoon and set aside. Repeat with the remaining tomatoes, then peel off the skin and finely chop the flesh.

2 Put the pancetta or bacon in a medium pan with the oil. Stir over a low heat until the fat runs.

COOK'S TIP
Do try to find pancetta. Bacon can be substituted but the sauce will not taste precisely the same. You can buy ready diced pancetta in packets in supermarkets. Alternatively, you can buy it thinly sliced, sometimes cut from a roll (arrotolata), and dice it yourself.

3 Add the onion and stir to mix. Cook gently for about 10 minutes, stirring. Add the tomatoes, with salt and pepper to taste. Stir well and cook, uncovered, for about 10 minutes.

3 Meanwhile, cook the pasta in a large pan of lightly salted boiling water. Dried pasta will take 10–12 minutes, fresh about 3 minutes.

5 Remove the sauce from the heat, stir in the marjoram and taste for seasoning. Drain the pasta and tip it into a warmed bowl. Pour the sauce over the pasta and toss well. Serve immediately, sprinkled with shredded basil. Hand around the grated Pecorino so people can serve themselves.

Energy 473kcal/1992kJ; Protein 17.2g; Carbohydrate 68.7g, of which sugars 6.5g; Fat 16.2g, of which saturates 4.1g; Cholesterol 24mg; Calcium 34mg; Fibre 3.6g; Sodium 484mg.

PENNE WITH TOMATO AND CHILLI SAUCE

THIS IS ONE OF ROME'S MOST FAMOUS PASTA DISHES – PENNE TOSSED IN A TOMATO SAUCE FLAVOURED WITH CHILLI. MAKE THE SAUCE AS HOT AS YOU LIKE BY ADDING MORE CHILLIES TO TASTE.

Preparation: 8 minutes; Cooking: 17–22 minutes, plus 15–20 minutes soaking

SERVES FOUR

INGREDIENTS
  25g/1oz dried porcini mushrooms
  90g/½oz/7 tbsp butter
  150g/5oz pancetta or rindless
    smoked streaky (fatty) bacon, diced
  1–2 dried red chillies, to taste
  2 garlic cloves, crushed
  8 ripe Italian plum tomatoes, peeled
    and chopped
  a few fresh basil leaves, torn,
    plus extra to garnish
  350g/12oz/3 cups fresh or
    dried penne
  50g/2oz/⅔ cup freshly grated
    Parmesan cheese
  25g/1oz/⅓ cup freshly grated
    Pecorino cheese
  salt

1 Soak the dried mushrooms in warm water to cover for 15–20 minutes. Drain, then squeeze dry with your hands. Finely chop the mushrooms.

2 Melt 50g/2oz/4 tbsp of the butter in a medium pan or skillet. Add the pancetta or bacon and stir-fry over a medium heat until golden and slightly crispy. Remove the pancetta with a slotted spoon and set it aside.

3 Add the chopped mushrooms to the pan and cook in the same way. Remove and set aside with the pancetta or bacon. Crumble 1 dried chilli into the pan, add the garlic and cook, stirring, for a few minutes until the garlic turns golden.

4 Add the tomatoes and basil and some salt. Cook gently, stirring occasionally, for 10–15 minutes. Meanwhile, cook the pasta in a large pan of lightly salted boiling water. Dried pasta will take 10–12 minutes, fresh about 3 minutes.

5 Add the pancetta or bacon and the mushrooms to the tomato sauce. Taste for seasoning, adding the second chilli if you prefer a hotter flavour. If the sauce is too dry, add a little of the pasta water.

6 Drain the pasta and tip it into a warmed bowl. Dice the remaining butter, add it to the pasta with the cheeses, then toss until well coated. Pour the tomato sauce over the pasta, toss well and serve immediately, with a few basil leaves sprinkled on top.

Energy 689kcal/2889kJ; Protein 25.4g; Carbohydrate 71.2g, of which sugars 9.2g; Fat 35.7g, of which saturates 19g; Cholesterol 91mg; Calcium 267mg; Fibre 4.5g; Sodium 834mg.

FUSILLI WITH SAUSAGE

GETTING SAUSAGES, PASTA AND TOMATO SAUCE READY AT THE RIGHT MOMENT TAKES A BIT OF JUGGLING, BUT THE RESULT IS A DELICIOUS DISH THAT EVERY MEMBER OF THE FAMILY WILL LOVE.
Preparation: 4–5 minutes; Cooking: 12–15 minutes

SERVES FOUR

INGREDIENTS
400g/14oz spicy pork sausages
30ml/2 tbsp olive oil
1 small onion, finely chopped
2 garlic cloves, crushed
5ml/1 tsp paprika
5ml/1 tsp dried mixed herbs
5–10ml/1–2 tsp chilli sauce
1 large yellow (bell) pepper, seeded
  and cut into strips
400g/14oz can Italian plum tomatoes
250ml/8fl oz/1 cup vegetable stock
300g/11oz/2³/4 cups dried fusilli
salt and ground black pepper
freshly grated Pecorino cheese,
  to serve

1 Grill (broil) the sausages for 10–12 minutes until they are browned on all sides.

2 Meanwhile, heat the oil in a large pan, add the onion and garlic and cook for 3 minutes. Add the paprika, herbs and chilli sauce to taste, then the yellow pepper. Cook for 3 minutes more, stirring occasionally.

3 Pour in the canned tomatoes, breaking them up with a wooden spoon, then add salt and pepper to taste and stir well. Cook over a medium heat for 10–12 minutes, adding the vegetable stock gradually. At the same time, cook the pasta in a large pan of lightly salted boiling water for 10–12 minutes.

4 While the tomato sauce and pasta are cooking, drain the cooked sausages on kitchen paper, and, when cool enough to touch, cut each one diagonally into 1cm/½in pieces.

5 Add the sausage pieces to the sauce and mix well. Drain the pasta and add it to the pan of sauce. Toss well, then divide among four warmed bowls, sprinkled with the grated Pecorino.

Energy 709kcal/2970kJ; Protein 20.9g; Carbohydrate 72.2g, of which sugars 10.5g; Fat 39.5g, of which saturates 13.3g; Cholesterol 47mg; Calcium 74mg; Fibre 4.6g; Sodium 774mg

ELICHE WITH SAUSAGE AND RADICCHIO

*SAUSAGE AND RADICCHIO MAY SEEM ODD COMPANIONS, BUT THE COMBINATION OF THESE INGREDIENTS
IS REALLY DELICIOUS. THIS ROBUST AND HEARTY DISH MAKES A GOOD MAIN COURSE.*

Preparation: 5 minutes; Cooking: 20–22 minutes

SERVES FOUR

INGREDIENTS
    30ml/2 tbsp olive oil
    1 onion, finely chopped
    200g/7oz Italian pure pork sausage
    175ml/6fl oz/¾ cup tomato sauce
    6 tbsp dry white wine
    300g/11oz/2¾ cups eliche
    50g/2oz radicchio leaves
    salt and ground black pepper

1 Heat the olive oil in a large, deep pan. Add the finely chopped onion and cook over a low heat, stirring frequently, for about 5 minutes or until softened.

2 Snip the end off the sausage skin and squeeze the sausage meat into the pan. With a wooden spoon, stir the sausage meat to mix it with the oil and onion and break it up into small pieces.

3 Continue to fry the mixture, increasing the heat if necessary, until the sausage meat is brown all over and looks crumbly. Stir in the tomato sauce, then sprinkle in the wine, with salt and pepper to taste. Simmer over a low heat, stirring occasionally, for 10–12 minutes.

4 Meanwhile, cook the pasta in a large pan of lightly salted boiling water. Dried pasta will take 10–12 minutes, fresh about 3 minutes. Just before draining the pasta, add a ladleful or two of the cooking water to the sausage sauce and stir it in well. Taste the sauce to check the seasoning.

5 Finely shred the radicchio leaves. Drain the cooked pasta and turn it into the pan of sausage sauce. Add the shredded radicchio and toss well to combine everything thoroughly. Serve immediately.

COOK'S TIPS
• The best sausage to use is the one you can buy from Italian delicatessens called salsiccia puro suino. It is made from 100 per cent pure pork plus flavourings and seasonings.
• If you can get it, use the long, tapering radicchio di Treviso for this dish; otherwise the tightly furled, round radicchio can be used.

Energy 569kcal/2393kJ; Protein 17.9g; Carbohydrate 75.1g, of which sugars 7.7g; Fat 21.9g, of which saturates 6.3g; Cholesterol 34mg; Calcium 101mg; Fibre 4.2g; Sodium 563mg.

TORTELLINI <u>WITH</u> HAM

THIS IS A VERY EASY RECIPE THAT CAN BE MADE QUICKLY FROM STORE-CUPBOARD INGREDIENTS. IT IS THEREFORE IDEAL FOR AN AFTER-WORK SUPPER OR A THROWN-TOGETHER LUNCH.

Preparation: 5 minutes; Cooking: 12 minutes

SERVES FOUR

INGREDIENTS

2 tbsp olive oil
1 small onion, finely chopped
115g/4oz cooked ham, diced
150ml/¼ pint/⅔ cup passata
  (strained tomatoes)
100ml/3½fl oz/scant ½ cup panna
  da cucina or double (heavy) cream
250g/9oz tortellini alla carne
  (meat-filled tortellini)
75g/3oz/1 cup freshly grated
  Parmesan cheese
salt and ground black pepper

COOK'S TIP
Cartons of passata (strained tomatoes)
are handy for making quick sauces.

1 Heat the oil in a large pan, add the onion and cook over low heat, stirring frequently, for about 5 minutes, until softened. Add the ham and cook, stirring occasionally, until it darkens.

2 Add the passata to the pan along with 150ml/¼ pint/⅔ cup water. Stir well, then add salt and pepper to taste. Bring to the boil, lower the heat and simmer the sauce for a few minutes, stirring occasionally, until it has reduced slightly. Stir in the cream.

3 Meanwhile, cook the pasta in a large pan of lightly salted boiling water for about 3 minutes.

4 Drain the pasta well and add it to the sauce. Add a handful of grated Parmesan to the pan. Stir, toss well and taste for seasoning. Serve in warmed bowls, topped with the remaining Parmesan.

Energy 509kcal/2118kJ; Protein 19.9g; Carbohydrate 26.2g, of which sugars 4.1g; Fat 36.8g, of which saturates 17.5g; Cholesterol 85mg; Calcium 353mg; Fibre 1.9g; Sodium 696mg.

PASTA SALAD WITH ROQUEFORT AND SALAMI

THIS PASTA DISH IS EASY TO MAKE AND WOULD BE PERFECT FOR A PICNIC OR PACKED LUNCH.
TAKE THE DRESSING AND SALAD LEAVES SEPARATELY AND MIX EVERYTHING AT THE LAST MOMENT.

Preparation: 3–4 minutes; Cooking: 10–12 minutes

SERVES FOUR

INGREDIENTS

225g/8oz/2 cups dried fusilli
275g/10oz jar charcoal-roasted
  peppers in oil
115g/4oz/1 cup pitted black olives
4 sun-dried tomatoes in oil, drained
  and quartered
115g/4oz Roquefort cheese,
  crumbled
10 slices peppered salami, cut
  into strips
115g/4oz packet mixed leaf salad
30ml/2 tbsp white wine vinegar
30ml/2 tbsp chopped fresh oregano
2 garlic cloves, crushed
salt and ground black pepper

1 Cook the pasta in a large pan of lightly salted boiling water for 10–12 minutes.

VARIATION
Use chicken instead of the salami and cubes of Brie in place of the Roquefort.

2 Meanwhile, drain the peppers and reserve 60ml/4 tbsp of the oil for the dressing. Cut the peppers into long, fine strips and mix them with the olives, sun-dried tomatoes and Roquefort in a large bowl.

3 Drain the pasta thoroughly and rinse with cold water, then drain again. Stir it into the pepper mixture along with the peppered salami.

4 Divide the salad leaves among four individual bowls and spoon the pasta salad on top. Whisk the reserved oil with the vinegar, oregano, garlic and seasoning to taste. Spoon this dressing over the salad and serve at once.

Energy 429kcal/1797kJ; Protein 17.8g; Carbohydrate 46.7g, of which sugars 6.6g; Fat 20.3g, of which saturates 8.9g; Cholesterol 37mg; Calcium 188mg; Fibre 3.9g; Sodium 1341mg

PAPPARDELLE ^{WITH} CHICKEN ^{AND} MUSHROOMS

RICH AND CREAMY, THIS IS A GOOD SUPPER PARTY DISH. PAPPARDELLE ALWAYS LOOKS RATHER GLAMOROUS AND THE CREAMY CHICKEN AND MUSHROOM SAUCE SUITS IT BEAUTIFULLY.

Preparation: 7 minutes; Cooking: 16 minutes, plus soaking

SERVES FOUR

INGREDIENTS

15g/½oz dried porcini mushrooms
175ml/6fl oz/¾ cup warm water
25g/1oz/2 tbsp butter
1 small leek or 4 spring onions
 (scallions), chopped
1 garlic clove, crushed
1 small handful fresh Italian parsley,
 coarsely chopped
120ml/4fl oz/½ cup dry white wine
250ml/8fl oz/1 cup chicken stock
400g/14oz fresh or dried pappardelle
2 skinless chicken breast fillets,
 cut into thin strips
105ml/7 tbsp mascarpone
salt and ground black pepper
fresh basil leaves, shredded,
 to garnish

1 Put the dried mushrooms in a bowl. Pour in the warm water and allow to soak for 15–20 minutes. Turn into a fine sieve set over a bowl and squeeze the mushrooms with your hands to release as much liquid as possible. Set aside the strained soaking liquid until required. Chop the mushrooms finely.

VARIATIONS
• Add 1 cup sliced button (white) or cremini mushrooms with the chicken.
• Add blanched sprigs of broccoli before the mascarpone in Step 4.

2 Melt the butter in a medium pan, add the chopped mushrooms, garlic, parsley and leek or spring onions, with salt and pepper to taste. Cook over a low heat, stirring frequently, for about 5 minutes, then pour in the wine and stock and bring to the boil. Lower the heat and simmer for about 5 minutes or until the liquid has reduced and is thickened.

3 Meanwhile, cook the pasta in a large pan of lightly salted boiling water, adding the reserved soaking liquid from the mushrooms to the water. Dried pasta will take 10–12 minutes, fresh about 3 minutes.

4 Add the chicken strips to the sauce and simmer for 5 minutes or until just tender. Add the mascarpone a spoonful at a time, stirring well after each addition, then add one or two spoonfuls of the water used for cooking the pasta. Taste for seasoning.

5 Drain the pasta and turn it into a warmed large bowl. Add the chicken and sauce and toss well. Serve immediately, topped with the shredded basil leaves.

Energy 513kcal/2172kJ; Protein 34.2g; Carbohydrate 76.4g, of which sugars 5.4g; Fat 8.3g, of which saturates 3.9g; Cholesterol 68mg; Calcium 59mg; Fibre 4g; Sodium 53mg.

FARFALLE WITH CHICKEN AND TOMATOES

QUICK TO PREPARE AND EASY TO COOK, THIS TASTY DISH IS FULL OF COLOUR AND FLAVOUR.
SERVE IT FOR A MIDWEEK SUPPER, WITH A CRISP GREEN SALAD TO FOLLOW.

Preparation: 10 minutes; Cooking: 15–17 minutes

SERVES FOUR

INGREDIENTS
350g/12oz skinless chicken breast
  fillets, cut into bitesize pieces
60ml/4 tbsp Italian dry vermouth
10ml/2 tsp chopped fresh
  rosemary, plus 4 fresh rosemary
  sprigs, to garnish
15ml/1 tbsp olive oil
1 onion, finely chopped
90g/3½oz Italian salami, diced
275g/10oz/2½ cups dried farfalle
15ml/1 tbsp balsamic vinegar
400g/14oz can cherry tomatoes
good pinch of crushed dried
  red chillies
salt and ground black pepper

1 Put the pieces of chicken in a large bowl, pour in the dry vermouth and sprinkle with half the chopped rosemary and salt and pepper to taste. Stir well and set aside.

2 Heat the oil in a pan, add the onion and salami and fry over a medium heat for about 5 minutes, stirring frequently.

3 Cook the pasta in a large pan of lightly salted boiling water for 10–12 minutes.

4 Meanwhile, add the chicken and vermouth to the pan, increase the heat to high and fry for 3 minutes or until the chicken is white on all sides. Sprinkle the vinegar over the chicken.

5 Add the cherry tomatoes and dried chillies. Stir well and simmer for a few minutes more. Taste the sauce to check the seasoning.

6 Drain the pasta and turn it into the pan. Add the remaining chopped rosemary and toss to mix the pasta and sauce together. Serve immediately in warmed bowls, garnished with the rosemary sprigs.

COOK'S TIP
The tomatoes look good left whole, but if you prefer you can crush them with the back of a wooden spoon while they are simmering in the pan.

Energy 509kcal/2147kJ; Protein 33.1g; Carbohydrate 60.4g, of which sugars 7g; Fat 15.1g, of which saturates 4.5g; Cholesterol 73mg; Calcium 37mg; Fibre 3.4g; Sodium 508mg.

PENNE WITH CHICKEN, BROCCOLI AND CHEESE

CRISP-TENDER, LIGHTLY COOKED BROCCOLI GIVES THIS DISH COLOUR AND CRUNCH. IT IS ALSO AN EXCELLENT FOIL TO THE RICHNESS OF THE CREAMY GORGONZOLA CHEESE-AND-WINE SAUCE.

Preparation: 3–4 minutes; Cooking: 12–14 minutes

SERVES FOUR

INGREDIENTS

400g/14oz/3½ cups dried penne
115g/4oz/scant 1 cup broccoli
   florets, divided into tiny sprigs
50g/2oz/¼ cup butter
2 chicken breast fillets, skinned and
   cut into thin strips
2 garlic cloves, crushed
120ml/4fl oz/½ cup dry white wine
200ml/7fl oz/scant 1 cup panna da
   cucina or double (heavy) cream
90g/3½oz Gorgonzola cheese, rind
   removed, finely diced
salt and ground black pepper
freshly grated Parmesan cheese,
   to serve

1 Bring two pans of lightly salted water to the boil. Add the penne to one pan and cook over a medium heat for 10–12 minutes or until tender.

2 Meanwhile, plunge the broccoli into the second pan of salted boiling water. Bring back to the boil and boil for 2 minutes, then drain in a colander and refresh under cold running water. Shake well to remove the surplus water and set aside to drain completely.

VARIATION
Use leeks instead of broccoli if you prefer. Fry them with the chicken strips.

3 While the pasta is cooking, melt the butter in a large frying pan and add the chicken and garlic, with salt and pepper to taste. Stir well. Fry over a medium heat, stirring frequently, for 3 minutes, or until the chicken becomes white.

4 Pour the wine and cream over the chicken mixture in the pan, stir to mix, then simmer, stirring occasionally, for about 5 minutes, or until the sauce has reduced and thickened and the chicken is cooked through.

5 Add the broccoli, increase the heat and toss to heat it through and mix it with the chicken. Taste for seasoning.

6 Drain the pasta and add it to the sauce. Add the Gorgonzola and toss well. Serve in warmed bowls and sprinkle each portion with grated Parmesan.

Energy 951kcal/3982kJ; Protein 47.8g; Carbohydrate 80.2g, of which sugars 8.6g; Fat 48.8g, of which saturates 28.5g; Cholesterol 165mg; Calcium 324mg; Fibre 10.2g; Sodium 433mg

ON THE SIDE: VEGETABLES AND SIDE SALADS

With dishes ranging from Wilted Spinach with Rice and Dill and Masala Beans with Fenugreek to Cauliflower with Garlic Crumbs and Stir-fried Carrots with Mango and Ginger, vegetable dishes have never been so interesting. Crisp Broccoli with Soy Sauce and Sesame Seeds puts an end to overcooking this brassica, while Stir-fried Brussels Sprouts with Bacon will convert even the most confirmed sprout hater. When summer comes and thoughts turn to salads, try such delights as Warm Potato Salad with Bacon Dressing, Moroccan-style Vegetable Salad and Pink Grapefruit and Avocado Salad. For main salad dishes, choose from Warm Halloumi and Fennel Salad, Warm Broad Bean and Feta Salad and Halloumi and Grape Salad. And with speedy preparation and cooking, all these dishes will be on the table in no time.

SAUTÉED HERB SALAD WITH CHILLI AND LEMON

FIRM-LEAFED FRESH HERBS, SUCH AS FLAT-LEAF PARSLEY AND MINT TOSSED IN A LITTLE OLIVE OIL AND SEASONED WITH SALT, ARE FABULOUS WITH SPICY KEBABS OR STEAKS.

Preparation: 4–5 minutes; Cooking: 2 minutes

SERVES FOUR

INGREDIENTS
  1 large bunch of flat-leaf parsley
  1 large bunch of mint
  1 large bunch of fresh
    coriander (cilantro)
  1 bunch of rocket (arugula)
  1 large bunch of spinach leaves,
    about 115g/4oz
  60–75ml/4–5 tbsp olive oil
  2 garlic cloves, finely chopped
  1 fresh green or red chilli, seeded
    and finely chopped
  ½ preserved lemon, finely chopped
  salt and ground black pepper
  45–60ml/3–4 tbsp Greek
    (US strained plain) yogurt, to serve

1 Roughly chop the herbs and combine with the rocket and spinach. Heat the olive oil in a wide, heavy pan. Stir in the garlic and chilli, and fry until they begin to colour. Toss in the herbs and leaves and cook gently, until they begin to wilt.

2 Add the preserved lemon and season to taste. Serve warm with yogurt.

VARIATION
Flavour the yogurt with crushed garlic, if you like.

Energy 142kcal/585kJ; Protein 3.6g; Carbohydrate 3.1g, of which sugars 2.7g; Fat 12.9g, of which saturates 2.1g; Cholesterol 2mg; Calcium 216mg; Fibre 4.4g; Sodium 82mg

BROCCOLI WITH SOY SAUCE AND SESAME SEEDS

THE BEST WAY TO COOK BROCCOLI IS TO FRY IT QUICKLY IN A WOK, SO THAT THE RICH COLOUR AND CRUNCHY TEXTURE ARE RETAINED. SOY SAUCE AND SESAME SEEDS ADD TO THE FLAVOUR.

Preparation: 2 minutes; Cooking: 3–4 minutes

SERVES TWO

INGREDIENTS

225g/8oz purple-sprouting broccoli
15ml/1 tbsp sesame seeds
15ml/1 tbsp olive oil
15ml/1 tbsp soy sauce
salt and ground black pepper

VARIATION

Purple-sprouting broccoli has been used for this recipe. This vegetable is at its best when in season during early spring, so finding a good crop may not always be easy during the rest of the year. When it is not available, an ordinary variety of broccoli, such as calabrese, will also work very well. Or you could substitute the broccoli altogether for Chinese leaves, which offer just as much crunch.

1 Using a sharp knife, cut off and discard any thick stems from the broccoli and cut the broccoli into long, thin florets.

2 Spread out the sesame seeds in a small frying pan and dry-fry over a medium heat until toasted. Do not leave them unattended as they will readily burn if left just a fraction too long.

3 Heat the olive oil in a wok or large frying pan and add the broccoli. Stir-fry for 3–4 minutes, or until tender, adding a splash of water if the pan becomes too dry.

4 Add the soy sauce to the broccoli, then season with salt and ground black pepper to taste. Add sesame seeds, toss to combine and serve immediately.

Energy 135kcal/558kJ; Protein 6.6g; Carbohydrate 2.7g, of which sugars 2.3g; Fat 10.9g, of which saturates 1.7g; Cholesterol 0mg; Calcium 115mg; Fibre 3.5g; Sodium 545mg

CRISPY CABBAGE

LIKE SO MANY BRASSICAS, CABBAGE IS LOVELY WHEN CRISP AND HORRIBLE WHEN SOGGY. IN THIS RECIPE THE BALANCE IS JUST RIGHT, AND THE RESULT GOES VERY WELL WITH PORK OR HAM.

Preparation: 2–3 minutes; Cooking: 2–3 minutes

SERVES FOUR TO SIX

INGREDIENTS
1 medium green or
   small white cabbage
30–45ml/2–3 tbsp oil
salt and ground black pepper

VARIATION
For cabbage with a bacon dressing, fry 225g/8oz diced streaky (fatty) bacon in a pan. Set aside while cooking the cabbage. Remove the cabbage from the pan and keep warm with the bacon. Boil 15ml/1 tbsp wine or cider vinegar with the juices remaining in the pan. Bring to the boil and season with ground black pepper. Pour over the cabbage and bacon. This makes a versatile side dish, and is especially good with chicken.

1 Remove the central core from the cabbage as well as any coarse outside leaves and the central rib from the larger remaining leaves. Place the cabbage on a board and shred the leaves finely. Wash under cold running water, shake well and blot on kitchen paper to dry thoroughly.

2 Heat a wok or wide-based flameproof casserole over a fairly high heat. Heat the oil and add the cabbage. Stir-fry for 2–3 minutes, using one or two wooden spoons to keep the cabbage moving so that it cooks evenly but is still crunchy. Season with salt and pepper and serve immediately.

Energy 56kcal/230kJ; Protein 1.2g; Carbohydrate 4.2g, of which sugars 4.1g; Fat 3.8g, of which saturates 0.5g; Cholesterol 0mg; Calcium 41mg; Fibre 1.8g; Sodium 6mg

STIR-FRIED BRUSSELS SPROUTS <u>WITH</u> BACON

THIS IS A GREAT WAY OF COOKING BRUSSELS SPROUTS, HELPING TO RETAIN THEIR SWEET FLAVOUR AND CRUNCHY TEXTURE. STIR-FRYING GUARANTEES THAT THERE WILL NOT BE A SINGLE SOGGY SPROUT.

Preparation: 4 minutes; Cooking: 5 minutes

SERVES FOUR

INGREDIENTS
   450g/1lb Brussels sprouts, trimmed
    and washed
   30ml/2 tbsp sunflower oil
   2 streaky (fatty) bacon rashers
    (strips), finely chopped
   10ml/2 tsp caraway seeds,
    lightly crushed
   salt and ground black pepper

COOK'S TP
Save time on preparation by buying
diced bacon or diced pancetta, available
ready packaged at the supermarket,
which needs no further preparation.
Just tip it straight into the pan.

1 Using a sharp knife, carefully cut all
the Brussels sprouts into fine shreds.

2 Heat the oil in a wok or large frying
pan. Add the shredded sprouts and turn
quickly over the heat, season with salt
and ground black pepper, then remove
and set aside.

3 Use the the same wok or pan to cook
the chopped bacon. Stir-fry for 1–2
minutes until golden.

4 Return the seasoned sprouts to the
pan containing the bacon and stir in the
caraway seeds. Cook for a further 1–2
minutes, then serve immediately.

Energy 131kcal/545kJ; Protein 5.9g; Carbohydrate 4.6g, of which sugars 3.5g; Fat 10g, of which saturates 2g; Cholesterol 8mg; Calcium 30mg; Fibre 4.6g; Sodium 164mg

GREEN BEANS WITH TOMATOES

THIS RECIPE IS FULL OF THE FLAVOURS OF SUMMER. IT RELIES ON FIRST-CLASS INGREDIENTS, SO USE ONLY THE BEST RIPE PLUM TOMATOES AND GREEN BEANS THAT YOU CAN BUY.

Preparation: 5 minutes; Cooking: 25 minutes

SERVES FOUR

INGREDIENTS

30ml/2 tbsp olive oil
1 large onion, finely sliced
2 garlic cloves, finely chopped
6 large ripe plum tomatoes, peeled,
  seeded and coarsely chopped
150ml/¼ pint/⅔ cup dry white wine
450g/1lb green beans, sliced in
  half lengthways
16 pitted black olives
10ml/2 tsp lemon juice
salt and ground black pepper

COOK'S TIP

Green beans need little preparation and now that they are grown without the string, you simply trim either end.

1 Heat the oil in a large frying pan. Add the finely sliced onion and chopped garlic. Cook over a medium heat for about 5 minutes, stirring frequently and lowering the heat if necessary, until the onion has softened but not browned.

2 Add the chopped tomatoes, white wine, beans, olives and lemon juice, and cook over a gentle heat for a further 20 minutes, stirring occasionally, until the sauce has thickened and the beans are tender. Season with salt and pepper to taste and serve immediately.

Energy 162kcal/672kJ; Protein 4.2g; Carbohydrate 14.4g, of which sugars 11.6g; Fat 8g, of which saturates 1.3g; Cholesterol 0mg; Calcium 80mg; Fibre 5.4g; Sodium 298mg.

MASALA BEANS WITH FENUGREEK

THE SECRET OF THIS SUPER-FAST DISH IS THE SPICE MIXTURE THAT COATS THE VEGETABLES.
COOKING IS KEPT TO A MINIMUM SO THAT INDIVIDUAL FLAVOURS ARE STILL DETECTABLE.
Preparation: 4–5 minutes; Cooking: 10–12 minutes

SERVES FOUR

INGREDIENTS
    1 onion
    5ml/1 tsp ground cumin
    5ml/1 tsp ground coriander
    5ml/1 tsp sesame seeds
    5ml/1 tsp chilli powder
    2.5ml/½ tsp crushed garlic
    1.5ml/¼ tsp ground turmeric
    5ml/1 tsp salt
    30ml/2 tbsp vegetable oil
    1 tomato, quartered
    225g/8oz/1½ cups green
      beans, blanched
    1 bunch fresh fenugreek leaves,
      stems discarded
    60ml/4 tbsp chopped fresh
      coriander (cilantro)
    15ml/1 tbsp lemon juice

1 Roughly chop the onion. Mix together
the cumin and coriander, sesame seeds,
chilli powder, garlic, turmeric and salt.

2 Put the chopped onion and spice
mixture into a food processor or
blender, and process for 30–45 seconds
until you have a rough paste.

3 In a wok or large, heavy pan, heat
the oil over a medium heat and fry the
spice paste for about 5 minutes, stirring
the mixture occasionally.

VARIATION
Instead of fresh fenugreek, substitute
15ml/1 tbsp dried fenugreek, which is
available from Indian markets.

4 Add the tomato quarters, blanched
green beans, fresh fenugreek and
chopped coriander.

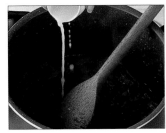

5 Stir-fry the contents of the pan for
about 5 minutes, then sprinkle in the
lemon juice and serve.

Energy 70kcal/289kJ; Protein 1.6g; Carbohydrate 2.7g, of which sugars 2.1g; Fat 6g, of which saturates 0.7g; Cholesterol 0mg; Calcium 47mg; Fibre 2g; Sodium 6mg

SPICED GREENS

HERE IS A REALLY GOOD WAY TO ENLIVEN YOUR GREENS, EXCELLENT FOR CRUNCHY CABBAGES BUT ALSO GOOD FOR KALE AND OTHER PURPLE SPROUTING LEAVES.

Preparation: 1 minute; Cooking: 5 minutes

SERVES FOUR

INGREDIENTS

  1 medium cabbage, or the equivalent
    in quantity of your chosen green
    vegetable
  15ml/1 tbsp groundnut (peanut) oil
  5ml/1 tsp grated fresh root ginger
  2 garlic cloves, grated
  2 shallots, finely chopped
  2 red chillies, seeded and freshly
    sliced
  salt and ground black pepper

1 Remove any tough outer leaves from the cabbage then quarter it and remove the core. Shred the leaves.

2 Pour the groundnut oil into a large pan and as it heats stir in the ginger and garlic. Add the shallots and as the pan becomes hotter add the chillies.

3 Add the greens and toss to mix. Cover the pan and reduce the heat to create some steam. Cook, shaking the pan occasionally, for about 3 minutes. Remove the lid and increase the heat to dry off the steam, season with salt and pepper and serve immediately.

Energy 77kcal/322kJ; Protein 2.6g; Carbohydrate 9.9g, of which sugars 9.4g; Fat 3.1g, of which saturates 0.5g; Cholesterol 0mg; Calcium 90mg; Fibre 3.9g; Sodium 13mg.

YOUNG VEGETABLES <u>WITH</u> TARRAGON

THIS IS ALMOST A SALAD, BUT THE VEGETABLES HERE ARE JUST LIGHTLY COOKED TO BRING OUT THEIR DIFFERENT FLAVOURS. THE TARRAGON ADDS A WONDERFUL DEPTH TO THIS BRIGHT, FRESH DISH.

Preparation: 5 minutes; Cooking: 10 minutes

SERVES FOUR

INGREDIENTS
5 spring onions (scallions),
  quartered lengthways
50g/2oz/½ cup butter
1 garlic clove, crushed
115g/4oz asparagus tips
115g/4oz mangetouts (snowpeas),
  trimmed
115g/4oz broad (fava) beans
2 Little Gem (Bibb) lettuces
5ml/1 tsp finely chopped
  fresh tarragon
salt and ground black pepper

COOK'S TIP
This dish is very succesful as a light accompaniment to fish and seafood.

1 In a large frying pan, fry the spring onions gently over a medium-low heat in half the butter with the garlic.

2 Add the asparagus tips, mangetouts and broad beans. Mix in, covering all the pieces with oil.

3 Just cover the base of the pan with water, season, bring to the boil and allow to simmer gently for a few minutes.

4 Cut the lettuces into quarters and add to the pan. Cook for 3 minutes then, off the heat, swirl in the remaining butter and the tarragon, and serve.

Energy 596kcal/2476kJ; Protein 18.8g; Carbohydrate 24.4g, of which sugars 12g; Fat 48g, of which saturates 29.2g; Cholesterol 116mg; Calcium 220mg; Fibre 14g; Sodium 356mg

BRAISED SWISS CHARD

SWISS CHARD (OR SPINACH BEET) IS LESS WELL KNOWN THAN SPINACH. FIRST USE THE LEAVES FOR A RECIPE SUCH AS THIS, THEN ON THE NEXT DAY COOK THE STALKS IN THE SAME WAY AS ASPARAGUS.

Preparation: 6 minutes; Cooking: 3–5 minutes

SERVES FOUR

INGREDIENTS
  900g/2lb Swiss chard or spinach
  15g/½ oz/1 tbsp butter
  a little freshly grated nutmeg
  sea salt and ground black pepper

1 Remove the stalks from the Swiss chard or spinach (and reserve the chard stalks, if you like, for another dish). Wash the leaves well and lift straight into a lightly greased heavy pan; the water clinging to the leaves will be all that is needed for cooking.

2 Cover with a tight-fitting lid and cook over medium heat for about 3–5 minutes, or until just tender, shaking the pan occasionally.

3 Drain well, then add the butter and nutmeg and season to taste. When the butter has melted, toss it into the Swiss chard and serve immediately.

COOK'S TIP
To cook the stalks, trim the bases, wash them and tie in bundles like asparagus. Add to a pan of boiling water, with a squeeze of lemon juice, and cook for about 20 minutes, or until tender but still slightly crisp. Drain and serve with some white sauce or fresh single (light) cream.

Energy 336kcal/1388kJ; Protein 25.2g; Carbohydrate 14.4, of which sugars 13.6g; Fat 19.6g, of which saturates 8.8g; Cholesterol 32mg; Calcium 153.2mg; Fibre 18.8g; Sodium 1352mg

BAKED COURGETTES WITH CHEDDAR

THIS EASY DISH MAKES A GREAT ACCOMPANIMENT TO A WIDE RANGE OF MAIN COURSES, OR IT CAN BE SERVED WITH SOME FRESH CRUSTY BREAD AS A LIGHT LUNCH OR SUPPER DISH FOR ONE OR TWO.

Preparation: 3 minutes; Cooking: 20 minutes

SERVES FOUR

INGREDIENTS
    4 courgettes (zucchini)
    30ml/2 tbsp grated farmhouse
      Cheddar cheese
    about 25g/1oz/2 tbsp butter
    salt and ground black pepper

COOK'S TIP

Any strong-flavoured farmhouse cheese will do for this dish, so look out for regional specialities to make a change. Coloured cheeses would look appealing.

1 Preheat the oven to 180ºC/350ºF/ Gas 4. Slice the courgettes in half, lengthways. Butter a shallow baking dish and arrange the courgettes, cut side up, inside the dish.

2 Sprinkle the cheese over the courgettes, and sprinkle over a few knobs (pats) of butter.

3 Bake for about 20 minutes, or until the courgettes are tender and the cheese is bubbling and golden brown. Serve immediately.

Energy 384kcal/1580kJ; Protein 15.2g; Carbohydrate 7.6g, of which sugars 7.2g; Fat 32g, of which saturates 20g; Cholesterol 84mg; Calcium 328mg; Fibre 3.6g; Sodium 372mg

BRAISED LETTUCE AND PEAS

THIS LIGHT VEGETABLE DISH IS BASED ON THE CLASSIC FRENCH METHOD OF BRAISING PEAS WITH LETTUCE AND SPRING ONIONS IN BUTTER, AND IS DELICIOUS SERVED WITH GRILLED FISH OR DUCK.

Preparation: 2–3 minutes; Cooking: 13 minutes

SERVES FOUR

INGREDIENTS

50g/2oz/¼ cup butter
4 Little Gem (Bibb) lettuces,
  halved lengthways
2 bunches spring onions (scallions),
  trimmed and cut into pieces
400g/14oz shelled peas
  (about 1kg/2¼lb in pods)
120ml/4fl oz/½ cup water
salt and ground black pepper

VARIATIONS

• For a splash of extra colour, and to add some crunch to the texture, braise about 250g/9oz baby carrots with the lettuce.
• Try a meatier alternative by cooking 115g/4oz chopped smoked bacon or pancetta in the butter in step 1. Use one bunch of spring onions (scallions) and stir in some chopped parsley.

1 Melt half the butter in a wide, heavy pan over a low heat. Add the lettuces and spring onions.

2 Turn the vegetables in the butter, then sprinkle with salt and plenty of ground black pepper. Cover the pan with a tight-fitting lid and cook the lettuces and spring onions very gently for 5 minutes, stirring once.

3 Add the peas and turn them in the buttery juices. Pour in the measurement water, then cover and cook over a gentle heat for a further 5 minutes. Uncover and increase the heat to reduce the liquid to a few tablespoons.

4 Stir in the remaining butter and adjust the seasoning. Transfer to a warmed serving dish and serve immediately.

Energy 191kcal/790kJ; Protein 8g; Carbohydrate 13.3g, of which sugars 4.2g; Fat 12.3g, of which saturates 6.9g; Cholesterol 27mg; Calcium 52mg; Fibre 5.7g; Sodium 81mg

CREAMY LEEKS WITH CHEESE

THIS IS QUITE A RICH ACCOMPANIMENT THAT COULD EASILY BE SERVED AS A MEAL IN ITSELF WITH BROWN RICE OR COUSCOUS. FOR A VERY QUICK SNACK, JUST SERVE IT ON TOAST.

Preparation: 3–4 minutes; Cooking: 12 minutes

SERVES FOUR

INGREDIENTS

4 large leeks or 12 baby leeks,
   trimmed and washed
15ml/1 tbsp olive oil
150ml/¼ pint/⅔ cup double
   (heavy) cream
75g/3oz mature (sharp) Cheddar or
   Monterey Jack cheese, grated
salt and ground black pepper

3 Transfer the creamy leeks to a shallow ovenproof dish and sprinkle with the cheese. Grill (broil) for 4–5 minutes, or until the cheese topping is golden brown and bubbling. Serve immediately.

VARIATIONS

• This recipe works well with all sorts of hard cheeses, from Parmesan and Gran Padano to Red Leicester, Double Gloucester and Caerphilly. Experiment with different flavours to suit your own tastes.

• For a more substantial dish, cook sliced button (white) mushroom with the leeks, or top the mixture with sliced cherry tomatoes before adding the cheese.

• To make the dish more appealing to meat lovers, add some diced smoky bacon or pancetta to the pan in step 1, after you have fried the leeks for a couple of minutes.

1 If using large leeks, slice them lengthways; leave baby ones intact. Heat the oil in a large frying pan and add the leeks. Season with salt and pepper and cook for about 4 minutes, stirring occasionally, until they become aromatic and the outsides start to turn golden.

2 Preheat the grill (broiler) to high. Pour the cream into the pan, drizzling it over the leeks, and stir until well combined. Lower the heat and allow to bubble gently for a few minutes, but do not overboil as the cream may begin to curdle.

Energy 322kcal/1330kJ; Protein 7.8g; Carbohydrate 5g, of which sugars 4g; Fat 29.8g, of which saturates 17.1g; Cholesterol 70mg; Calcium 193mg; Fibre 3.3g; Sodium 147mg

CURRIED RED CABBAGE SLAW

THREE SHADES OF RED COMBINE IN THIS FRESH, CRISP SLAW. EACH CONTRIBUTES A DIFFERENT TEXTURE AND FLAVOUR, FROM THE CRUNCH OF CABBAGE TO THE SATIN SMOOTHNESS OF PEPPER.

Preparation: 5 minutes; Cooking: 0 minutes; Chilling recommended

SERVES FOUR TO SIX

INGREDIENTS

½ red cabbage, thinly sliced
1 red (bell) pepper, chopped
 or very thinly sliced
½ red onion, chopped
60ml/4 tbsp red or white wine
 vinegar or cider vinegar
60ml/4 tbsp sugar, or to taste
120ml/4fl oz/½ cup Greek
 (US strained plain) yogurt or
 natural (plain) yogurt
120ml/4fl oz/½ cup mayonnaise,
 preferably home-made
1.5ml/¼ tsp curry powder
2–3 handfuls raisins
salt and ground black pepper

1 Put the cabbage, pepper and red onion in a bowl and toss to combine. In a small pan, heat the vinegar and sugar until the sugar has dissolved, then pour over the vegetables. Leave to cool slightly.

2 Combine the yogurt and mayonnaise, then mix into the cabbage mixture. Season to taste with curry powder, salt and ground black pepper, then mix in the raisins.

3 Chill the salad before serving, if you have time. Just before serving, drain off any excess liquid and briefly stir the slaw again.

VARIATION
If you prefer, ready-made low-fat mayonnaise can be used instead of the Greek yogurt and mayonnaise mixture. Stir the curry powder into the mayonnaise.

Energy 272kcal/1136kJ; Protein 3g; Carbohydrate 27.9g, of which sugars 27.5g; Fat 17.5g, of which saturates 3.4g; Cholesterol 15mg; Calcium 74mg; Fibre 2g; Sodium 120mg

BEETROOT WITH FRESH MINT

THE LOVELY, BRIGHT COLOUR OF BEETROOT CONTRASTS BEAUTIFULLY WITH THE DEEP GREEN OF MINT.
THE FLAVOURS WORK WELL TOGETHER, TOO, AND ARE ENHANCED BY THE SWEET BALSAMIC DRESSING.
Preparation: 3–4 minutes; Cooking: 0 minutes; Chilling recommended

SERVES FOUR

INGREDIENTS
4–6 cooked beetroot (beets)
5–10ml/1–2 tsp sugar
15–30ml/1–2 tbsp balsamic vinegar
juice of ½ lemon
30ml/2 tbsp extra virgin olive oil
1 bunch fresh mint, leaves stripped
   and thinly sliced
salt

VARIATIONS
• To make a spicy version, add harissa
to taste and substitute fresh coriander
(cilantro) for the mint.
• As an alternative, add a chopped onion
and some fresh dill.

1 Slice the beetroot or cut it into even-
size dice with a sharp knife. Put the
beetroot in a bowl. Add the sugar,
balsamic vinegar, lemon juice, olive oil
and a pinch of salt and toss together
to combine.

2 Add half the thinly sliced fresh mint
to the salad and toss lightly until well
combined. If you have time, chill
the salad for about 1 hour. Serve
garnished with the remaining thinly
sliced mint leaves.

Energy 90kcal/376kJ; Protein 1.9g; Carbohydrate 7.8g, of which sugars 6.7g; Fat 5.9g, of which saturates 0.8g; Cholesterol 0mg; Calcium 45mg; Fibre 1.2g; Sodium 69mg

STIR-FRIED CARROTS <u>WITH</u> MANGO <u>AND</u> GINGER

RIPE, SWEET MANGO TASTES WONDERFUL WITH CARROTS AND GINGER IN THIS SPICY VEGETABLE DISH, WHICH IS GOOD ENOUGH TO SERVE ON ITS OWN WITH YOGURT AND A SALAD.

Preparation: 6 minutes; Cooking: 4–5 minutes

SERVES FOUR TO SIX

INGREDIENTS

- 15–30ml/1–2 tbsp olive oil
- 2–3 garlic cloves, chopped
- 1 onion, chopped
- 25g/1oz fresh root ginger, peeled and chopped
- 5–6 carrots, sliced
- 30–45ml/2–3 tbsp shelled pistachio nuts, roasted
- 5ml/1 tsp ground cinnamon
- 5–10ml/1–2 tsp ras el hanout
- 1 small firm, ripe mango, peeled and coarsely diced
- a small bunch of fresh coriander (cilantro), finely chopped
- juice of ½ lemon
- salt

1 Heat the olive oil in a heavy frying pan or wok. Stir in the garlic, then the onion and ginger. Fry for 1 minute. Add the carrots, tossing them in the pan to make sure that they are mixed with the flavouring ingredients, and cook until they begin to brown.

2 Roughly chop the roasted pistachio nuts. Add to the pan with the ground cinnamon and ras el hanout, then gently mix in the diced mango. Sprinkle with the chopped coriander, season with salt and pour over the lemon juice. Toss to mix and serve immediately.

Energy 89kcal/371kJ; Protein 1.7g; Carbohydrate 8.2g, of which sugars 7.5g; Fat 5.7g, of which saturates 0.8g; Cholesterol 0mg; Calcium 23mg; Fibre 2.2g; Sodium 47mg

CARROT AND PARSNIP PURÉE

PURÉED VEGETABLES AREN'T JUST FOR THE UNDER FIVES. THEIR CREAMINESS APPEALS TO ALL AGES, AND THEY ARE IDEAL PARTNERS FOR CRISP VEGETABLES SUCH AS LIGHTLY COOKED GREEN BEANS.

Preparation: 3 minutes; Cooking: 15–17 minutes

SERVES SIX TO EIGHT

INGREDIENTS

350g/12oz carrots
450g/1lb parsnips
a pinch of freshly grated nutmeg
  or ground mace
15g/½oz/1 tbsp butter
about 15ml/1 tbsp single (light)
  cream or crème fraîche
a small bunch of parsley, chopped,
  plus extra to garnish
salt and ground black pepper

1 Peel the carrots and slice fairly thinly. Peel the parsnips and cut into bitesize chunks (they are softer and will cook more quickly than the carrots).

2 Boil the carrots and parsnips in separate pans of salted water until tender. Drain them well, then purée them together in a food processor, with the grated nutmeg or mace, a generous seasoning of salt and ground black pepper, and the butter. Whizz until smooth.

3 Transfer the purée to a bowl and beat in the cream or crème fraîche. Add the chopped parsley for extra flavour.

4 Transfer the carrot and parsnip purée to a warmed serving bowl, sprinkle with the remaining chopped parsley to garnish, and serve hot.

COOK'S TIP
• Any leftover purée can be thinned to taste with good-quality chicken or vegetable stock and heated to make a quick home-made soup.
• The carrots can be substituted altogether for a small sweet potato. Peel and dice finely. Boil the sweet potato a little ahead of the parsnips if possible.

Energy 71kcal/298kJ; Protein 1.5g; Carbohydrate 10.7g, of which sugars 6.6g; Fat 2.7g, of which saturates 1.4g; Cholesterol 5mg; Calcium 49mg; Fibre 4g; Sodium 31mg

CAULIFLOWER WITH EGG AND LEMON

ALTHOUGH CAULIFLOWER HAS SHRUGGED OFF ITS IMAGE AS THE VEGETABLE MOST PEOPLE LOVE TO HATE, IT STILL NEEDS A BIT OF A MAKEOVER NOW AND THEN.

Preparation: 2–3 minutes; Cooking: 12 minutes

SERVES FOUR

INGREDIENTS
  75–90ml/5–6 tbsp extra virgin
    olive oil
  1 medium cauliflower, divided into
    large florets
  2 eggs
  juice of 1 lemon
  5ml/1 tsp cornflour (cornstarch),
    mixed to a cream with a little
    cold water
  30ml/2 tbsp chopped fresh flat
    leaf parsley
  salt

VARIATION
This delightful, summery style of cooking cauliflower is popular in the Mediterranean. It works equally well with a close relative, broccoli. Divide the broccoli into small florets and cook for slightly less time than the cauliflower, until just tender.

1 Heat the olive oil in a large heavy pan, add the cauliflower florets and sauté over a medium heat until they start to brown.

2 Pour in enough hot water to almost cover the cauliflower, add salt to taste, then cover the pan and cook for 7–8 minutes until the florets are just soft. Remove the pan from the heat and leave to stand, covered, while you make the sauce.

3 Beat the eggs in a bowl, add the lemon juice and cornflour and beat until mixed. Beat in a few tablespoons of the hot liquid from the cauliflower.

4 Pour the egg mixture slowly over the cauliflower, then stir gently. Place the pan over a very gentle heat for 2 minutes to thicken the sauce, but do not allow to boil. Spoon into a warmed serving bowl, sprinkle with parsley and serve.

Energy 201kcal/833kJ; Protein 7g; Carbohydrate 4.4g, of which sugars 2.7g; Fat 17.5g, of which saturates 3g; Cholesterol 95mg; Calcium 51mg; Fibre 2.2g; Sodium 47mg

CAULIFLOWER WITH GARLIC CRUMBS

THIS METHOD OF COOKING CAULIFLOWER IS VERY SIMPLE AND IT MAKES A GREAT ACCOMPANIMENT TO ANY MEAT OR DAIRY MEAL. THE GARLIC BREADCRUMBS ADD BITE AND FLAVOUR.

Preparation: 5 minutes; Cooking: 10 minutes

SERVES FOUR TO SIX

INGREDIENTS

1 large cauliflower, cut into bitesize florets
pinch of sugar
90–120ml/6–8 tbsp olive or vegetable oil
130g/4½ oz/2¼ cups dry white or wholemeal (whole-wheat) breadcrumbs
3–5 garlic cloves, thinly sliced or chopped
salt and ground black pepper

3 Heat the remaining oil in the pan, then add the cauliflower, mashing and breaking it up a little as it lightly browns in the oil. (Do not overcook but just cook lightly in the oil.)

COOK'S TIP
In Jerusalem, this dish is often eaten with meat or fish wrapped in filo pastry, since the textures and flavours complement each other perfectly.

4 Add the garlic breadcrumbs to the pan and cook, stirring, until well combined and some of the cauliflower is still holding its shape. Season with salt and pepper and serve hot or warm.

1 Steam or boil the cauliflower in a pan of water, to which you have added the sugar and a pinch of salt, until just tender. Drain and leave to cool.

2 Heat 60–75ml/4–5 tbsp of the olive or vegetable oil in a pan, add the breadcrumbs and cook over a medium heat, tossing and turning, until browned and crisp. Add the garlic, turn once or twice, then remove from the pan and set aside.

Energy 204kcal/852kJ; Protein 5.5g; Carbohydrate 19.3g, of which sugars 2.7g; Fat 12.2g, of which saturates 1.7g; Cholesterol 0mg; Calcium 46mg; Fibre 2g; Sodium 172mg.

ARTICHOKES WITH GARLIC, LEMON AND OIL

THIS CLASSIC DISH OF FLORENCE IS SAID TO BE OF JEWISH ORIGIN. IT IS NOT ONLY DELICIOUS AS A SALAD BUT IT CAN ALSO BE ADDED TO ROASTED FISH, CHICKEN OR LAMB DURING COOKING.

Preparation: 10 minutes; Cooking: 17–22 minutes

SERVES FOUR

INGREDIENTS
    4 globe artichokes
    juice of 1–2 lemons, plus extra to
        acidulate water
    60ml/4 tbsp extra virgin olive oil
    1 onion, chopped
    5–8 garlic cloves, roughly chopped
        or thinly sliced
    30ml/2 tbsp chopped fresh parsley
    120ml/4fl oz/½ cup dry
        white wine
    120ml/4fl oz/½ cup vegetable
        stock or water
    salt and ground black pepper

COOK'S TIP
Placing trimmed artichokes in a bowl of acidulated water prevents them from discolouring.

1 Prepare the artichokes. Pull back and snap off the tough leaves. Peel the tender part of the stems and cut into bitesize pieces, then put in a bowl of acidulated water. Cut the artichokes into quarters and cut out the inside thistle heart. Add them to the bowl.

2 Heat the oil in a pan, add the onion and garlic and fry for 5 minutes until softened. Stir in the parsley and cook for a few seconds. Add the wine, stock and drained artichokes. Season with half the lemon juice, salt and pepper.

3 Bring the mixture to the boil, then lower the heat, cover and simmer for 10–15 minutes until the artichokes are tender. Lift the artichokes out with a slotted spoon and transfer to a serving dish.

4 Bring the cooking liquid to the boil and boil until reduced to about half its volume. Pour the mixture over the artichokes and drizzle over the remaining lemon juice. Taste for seasoning and cool before serving.

Energy 132kcal/543kJ; Protein 1.1g; Carbohydrate 1.5g, of which sugars 1.4g; Fat 11.4g, of which saturates 1.6g; Cholesterol 0mg; Calcium 79mg; Fibre 2g; Sodium 54mg.

CARAMELIZED SHALLOTS

SWEET, GOLDEN SHALLOTS ARE GOOD WITH ALL SORTS OF MAIN DISHES, INCLUDING POULTRY OR MEAT. THEY ALSO TASTE GOOD WITH ROASTED CHUNKS OF BUTTERNUT SQUASH OR PUMPKIN.

Preparation: 3 minutes; Cooking: 17 minutes

SERVES FOUR TO SIX

INGREDIENTS
50g/2oz/¼ cup butter
500g/1¼lb shallots or small onions,
   peeled with root ends intact
15ml/1 tbsp golden caster
   (superfine) sugar
30ml/2 tbsp red or white wine,
   Madeira or port
salt and ground black ppper

1 Heat the butter in a large frying pan and add the shallots or onions in a single layer. Cook gently, turning occasionally, for about 5 minutes, until they are lightly browned all over.

2 Sprinkle the sugar over the browned shallots and cook gently, turning the shallots in the juices, until the sugar begins to caramelize.

3 Pour the wine, Madeira or port over the caramelized shallots and increase the heat. Let the mixture bubble for 4–5 minutes.

4 Add 150ml/¼ pint/⅔ cup water and seasoning. Cover and cook for 5 minutes, then remove the lid and cook until the liquid evaporates and the shallots are tender and glazed. Adjust the seasoning before serving.

COOK'S TIP
Leaving the root ends of the shallots intact helps to ensure that they do not separate or unravel during cooking, but remain whole. They also look more presentable served in this way.

Energy 96kcal/399kJ; Protein 1.3g; Carbohydrate 5.4g, of which sugars 5.4g; Fat 7.5g, of which saturates 1.1g; Cholesterol 0mg; Calcium 22mg; Fibre 1.2g; Sodium 9mg

SPICY ROASTED VEGETABLES

OVEN ROASTING BRINGS OUT ALL THE FLAVOURS OF CHERRY TOMATOES, COURGETTES, ONION AND
RED PEPPERS. SERVE THEM HOT WITH MEAT OR FISH.

Preparation: 5 minutes; Cooking: 25 minutes

SERVES FOUR

INGREDIENTS

2–3 courgettes (zucchini)
1 Spanish (Bermuda) onion
2 red (bell) peppers
16 cherry tomatoes
2 garlic cloves, chopped
pinch of cumin seeds
5ml/1 tsp fresh thyme or
   4–5 torn fresh basil leaves
60ml/4 tbsp olive oil
juice of ½ lemon
5–10ml/1–2 tsp harissa or
   Tabasco sauce
fresh thyme sprigs, to garnish

COOK'S TIP

Harissa is a chilli paste, popular in
northern Africa. It can be bought in cans
and contains pounded chillies, garlic,
coriander, olive oil and seasoning.

1 Preheat the oven to 220ºC/425ºF/
Gas 7. Trim and halve the courgettes
and cut into long strips. Cut the onion
into thin wedges. Cut the peppers into
chunks, discarding the seeds and core.

2 Place these vegetables in a roasting
pan. Add the tomatoes, chopped
garlic, cumin seeds and thyme or
torn basil leaves.

3 Sprinkle with the olive oil and toss to
coat. Cook the mixture in the oven for
25 minutes until the vegetables are very
soft and have begun to char slightly
around the edges.

4 In a cup, mix the lemon juice with the
harissa or Tabasco sauce. Stir into the
vegetables, garnish with the thyme and
serve immediately.

Energy 163kcal/675kJ; Protein 3.7g; Carbohydrate 10.6g, of which sugars 9.9g; Fat 12g, of which saturates 1.8g; Cholesterol 0mg; Calcium 46mg; Fibre 3.2g; Sodium 10mg.

SPICED TURNIPS, SPINACH AND TOMATOES

SWEET BABY TURNIPS, TENDER BABY SPINACH AND RIPE PLUM TOMATOES MAKE TEMPTING PARTNERS IN THIS SIMPLE BUT VERY TASTY EASTERN MEDITERRANEAN VEGETABLE STEW.

Preparation: 8 minutes; Cooking: 22 minutes

SERVES SIX

INGREDIENTS

450g/1lb plum tomatoes
2 onions, sliced
60ml/4 tbsp olive oil
450g/1lb baby turnips, peeled
5ml/1 tsp paprika
2.5ml/½ tsp sugar
60ml/4 tbsp chopped fresh
 coriander (cilantro)
450g/1lb fresh young spinach
salt and ground black pepper

VARIATION

Try this with celery hearts instead of baby turnips. It is also good with fennel or drained canned artichoke hearts.

1 Plunge the tomatoes into a bowl of boiling water for 30 seconds or so, then refresh in a bowl of cold water. Drain, peel away the tomato skins and chop the flesh roughly.

2 Heat the olive oil in a large frying pan and gently fry the onion slices for about 5 minutes until golden. Ensure that they do not blacken.

3 Add the baby turnips, tomatoes and paprika to the pan with 60ml/4 tbsp water and cook until the tomatoes are pulpy. Cover the pan with a lid and continue cooking until the baby turnips have softened.

4 Stir in the sugar and coriander, then add the spinach and a little salt and ground black pepper. Cook the mixture for a further 2–3 minutes until the spinach has wilted. The dish can be served warm or cold.

Energy 140kcal/584kJ; Protein 4.1g; Carbohydrate 12.8g, of which sugars 11g; Fat 8.5g, of which saturates 1.2g; Cholesterol 0mg; Calcium 186mg; Fibre 5.1g; Sodium 125mg.

SQUASH AND NEW POTATOES WITH SOUR CREAM

THIS IS AN ISRAELI DISH OF FRESH VEGETABLES AND FRAGRANT DILL THAT ARE TOSSED IN A RICH,
BUTTERY SOUR CREAM SAUCE. IT LOOKS AND TASTES DELICIOUS.

Preparation: 5 minutes; Cooking: 14 minutes

SERVES FOUR

INGREDIENTS
400g/14oz mixed squash, such as
   green courgettes (zucchini), and
   small yellow squash
400g/14oz tiny, baby new potatoes
pinch of sugar
40–75g/1½–3oz/3–5 tbsp butter
2 bunches spring onions (scallions),
   thinly sliced
1 large bunch fresh dill, finely
   chopped
300ml/½ pint/1¼ cups sour cream
   or Greek (US strained plain) yogurt
salt and ground black pepper

COOK'S TIP
Choose small specimens of squash with
bright skins that are free of blemishes
and bruises.

1 Cut the squash into pieces about the same size as the potatoes. Put the potatoes in a pan and add water to cover, with the sugar and salt. Bring to the boil, then simmer for about 10 minutes, until almost tender. Add the squash and continue to cook until the vegetables are just tender, then drain.

2 Melt the butter in a large pan; fry the spring onions until just wilted, then gently stir in the dill and vegetables.

3 Remove the pan from the heat and stir in the sour cream or yogurt. Return to the heat and heat gently until warm. Season with salt and pepper and serve.

Energy 328kcal/1361kJ; Protein 6.7g; Carbohydrate 22.3g, of which sugars 7.3g; Fat 24.1g, of which saturates 14.8g; Cholesterol 66mg; Calcium 122mg; Fibre 2.7g; Sodium 107mg.

GRIDDLE POTATOES

THIS ATTRACTIVE DISH HAS TRADITIONALLY BEEN COOKED WITH LEFTOVER COOKED POTATOES THAT HAVE BEEN BOILED IN THEIR SKINS. IT MAKES A TASTY ACCOMPANIMENT TO GRILLED MEAT OR FISH.

Preparation: 10 minutes; Cooking: 8 minutes

SERVES FOUR TO SIX

INGREDIENTS
  2 onions, thinly sliced
  450–675g/1–1½lb whole cooked
    potatoes, boiled in their skins
  25g1oz butter and 15ml/ 1 tbsp oil,
    for shallow-frying
  salt and ground black pepper

1 Put the onions in a large pan and scald them briefly in boiling water. Refresh under cold water and drain well. Peel and slice the potatoes.

2 Put a mixture of butter and oil into a large, heavy frying pan and heat well.

3 When the fat is hot, fry the onion until tender. Add the potato slices and brown them together, turning the potato slices to brown as evenly as possible on both sides. Transfer to a warmed serving dish and season with salt and pepper. Serve very hot.

Energy 652Kcal/2724kJ; Protein 13.6g; Carbohydrate 105.6g, of which sugars 20g; Fat 22g, of which saturates 13.2g; Cholesterol 52mg; Calcium 194mg; Fibre 10.4g; Sodium 196mg

IRISH CHAMP

THIS TRADITIONAL DISH OF MASHED POTATOES FLAVOURED WITH ONION OR HERBS IS ESPECIALLY ASSOCIATED WITH NORTHERN IRELAND. TRY IT AS A SIDE DISH WITH GRILLED MEAT OR SAUSAGES.

Preparation: 8 minutes; Cooking: 15 minutes

SERVES TWO TO THREE

INGREDIENTS
675g/1½lb potatoes
1 bunch spring onions
   (scallions), chopped
about 300ml/½ pint/1¼ cups milk
salt and ground black pepper
butter, to serve

COOK'S TIP
Flavourings for champ include a wide range of greens – freshly chopped chives or parsley, onions or spring onions (scallions) and even green peas.

1 Peel, cut up and boil the potatoes in salted water for about 15 minutes until tender. Drain and return to the pan.

2 Meanwhile, simmer the spring onions for 5 minutes in the milk in a heavy pan. (Alternatively, bring the milk to boiling point on its own if you prefer the spring onions raw.)

3 Cover the potatoes with a clean cloth and dry them at the side of the stove for a few minutes before mashing them well. Beat in the boiling milk and spring onions. Working over the heat so that the champ is kept very hot, beat until the consistency is like well-creamed potatoes. Add more milk if necessary.

4 Season well with pepper and salt. To serve, divide the champ between heated bowls and make a well in the centre of each. Add a knob (pat) of butter. Dip the champ into the melting butter in the middle as you eat.

Energy 1002kcal/4245kJ; Protein 39.6g; Carbohydrate 199.8g, of which sugars 31.5g; Fat 10.5g, of which saturates 5.1g; Cholesterol 27mg; Calcium 651mg; Fibre 15.6g; Sodium 276mg

COLCANNON

THIS TRADITIONAL IRISH DISH IS ESPECIALLY ASSOCIATED WITH HALLOWEEN, WHEN IT IS LIKELY TO BE MADE WITH CURLY KALE. AT OTHER TIMES DURING THE WINTER GREEN CABBAGE IS MORE OFTEN USED.

Preparation: 5 minutes; Cooking: 10 minutes

SERVES THREE TO FOUR

INGREDIENTS
  450g/1lb potatoes, peeled
    and boiled
  450g/1lb curly kale or
    cabbage, cooked
  milk, if necessary
  50g/2oz/2 tbsp butter, plus extra
    for serving
  1 large onion, finely chopped
  salt and ground black pepper

1 Mash the potatoes. Chop the kale or cabbage, add it to the potatoes and mix. Stir in a little milk if the mash is too stiff.

2 Melt a little butter in a frying pan over a medium heat and add the onion. Cook for 3–4 minutes until softened. Remove and mix well with the potato and kale or cabbage.

3 Add the remainder of the butter to the hot pan. When very hot, turn the potato mixture on to the pan and spread it out. Fry until brown, then cut it roughly into pieces and continue frying until they are crisp and brown.

4 Serve in bowls or as a side dish, with plenty of butter.

COOK'S TIP
At Halloween, Colcannon would have a ring hidden in it – predicting marriage during the coming year for the person who found it.

Energy 1224kcal/5124kJ; Protein 21.6g; Carbohydrate 162.4g, of which sugars 54.4g; Fat 58.4g, of which saturates 35.2; Cholesterol 144mg; Calcium 416mg; Fibre 23.6g; Sodium 508mg

WARM POTATO SALAD BACON DRESSING

THIS TASTY SUMMER SALAD BECOMES A FAVOURITE WITH ALL WHO TRY IT. USE REAL NEW-SEASON POTATOES RATHER THAN ALL-YEAR "BABY" POTATOES, IF POSSIBLE, AND ALSO DRY-CURED BACON.

Preparation: 10 minutes; Cooking: 14–16 minutes

SERVES FOUR TO SIX

INGREDIENTS
900g/2lb small new potatoes
sprig of mint
15–30ml/1–2 tbsp olive oil
1 onion, chopped
175g/6oz streaky (fatty) or
  back (lean) bacon, diced
2 garlic cloves, crushed
30ml/2 tbsp chopped parsley
1 small bunch chives, chopped
15ml/1 tbsp wine vinegar
  or cider vinegar
15ml/1 tbsp wholegrain mustard
salt and ground black pepper

1 Scrape or rub off the skins from the new potatoes and cook in salted water with the mint for about 10 minutes, or until just tender. Drain and allow to cool a little, then turn into a salad bowl.

2 Heat the oil in a frying pan, then add the onion and cook gently until just softening. Add the diced bacon to the pan and cook for 3–5 minutes, until beginning to crisp up.

3 Add the garlic and cook for another minute or so, and then add the chopped herbs, the vinegar, mustard and seasoning to taste, remembering that the bacon may be salty.

4 Pour the dressing over the potatoes. Toss gently to mix, and serve warm.

VARIATION
Finely chopped spring onions (scallions) can replace the chopped chives and/or chopped parsley, if you like.

COOK'S TIP
Using superior ingredients makes this a special dish and it's ideal for a barbecue or party.

Energy 1056Kcal/4448kJ; Protein 53.2g; Carbohydrate 159.6g, of which sugars 22.4g; Fat 27.2g, of which saturates 6.8g; Cholesterol 56mg; Calcium 304mg; Fibre 16g; Sodium 2500mg

SPICY POTATO AND OLIVE SALAD

DELICIOUS WARM OR CHILLED, THIS NEW POTATO SALAD IS ENLIVENED WITH CUMIN AND CORIANDER, THEN DRESSED IN OLIVE OIL AND A FRUITY VINEGAR. IT TASTES GOOD WITH COLD ROAST PORK OR HAM.

Preparation: 5 minutes; Cooking: 10 minutes

SERVES FOUR

INGREDIENTS

  8 large new potatoes
  large pinch of salt
  large pinch of sugar
  3 garlic cloves, chopped
  15ml/1 tbsp vinegar of your choice,
    such as a fruit variety
  large pinch of ground cumin or whole
    cumin seeds
  pinch of cayenne pepper or hot
    paprika, to taste
  30–45ml/2–3 tbsp extra virgin
    olive oil
  30–45ml/2–3 tbsp chopped fresh
    coriander (cilantro) leaves
  10–15 dry-fleshed black
    Mediterranean olives

1 Chop the new potatoes into chunks. Put them in a pan, pour in water to cover and add the salt and sugar. Bring to the boil, then reduce the heat and boil gently for about 10 minutes, or until the potatoes are just tender. Drain well and leave in a colander to cool.

2 When cool enough to handle, slice the potato chunks and put them in a bowl.

3 Sprinkle the garlic, vinegar, cumin and cayenne or paprika over the salad. Drizzle with olive oil and sprinkle over coriander and olives.

Energy 238kcal/998kJ; Protein 4g; Carbohydrate 32.6g, of which sugars 2.9g; Fat 11.1g, of which saturates 1.7g; Cholesterol 0mg; Calcium 49mg; Fibre 3.2g; Sodium 448mg

ISRAELI CHOPPED VEGETABLE SALAD

THIS COLOURFUL AND REFRESHING SUMMER SALAD IS VERY POPULAR IN ISRAEL, WHERE IT IS OFTEN EATEN FOR BREAKFAST, BUT IT CAN BE ENJOYED AT ANY TIME OF THE DAY.

Preparation: 12 minutes; Cooking: 0 minutes

SERVES FOUR TO SIX

INGREDIENTS

1 each red, green and yellow (bell)
  pepper, seeded
1 carrot
1 cucumber
6 tomatoes
3 garlic cloves, finely chopped
3 spring onions (scallions),
  thinly sliced
30ml/2 tbsp chopped fresh coriander
  (cilantro) leaves
30ml/2 tbsp each chopped fresh dill,
  parsley and mint leaves
½–1 hot fresh chilli,
  chopped (optional)
45–60ml/3–4 tbsp extra virgin
  olive oil
juice of 1–1½ lemons
salt and ground black pepper

1 Using a sharp knife, finely dice the red, green and yellow peppers, carrot, cucumber and tomatoes and place them in a large mixing bowl.

2 Add the garlic, spring onions, coriander, dill, parsley, mint and chilli, if using, to the chopped vegetables and toss together to combine.

3 Pour the olive oil and lemon juice over the vegetables, season with salt and pepper to taste and toss together. Chill before serving.

VARIATION
This salad lends itself to endless variety: add olives, diced potatoes or beetroot (beet), omit the chilli, vary the herbs or use lime or lemon in place of the vinegar.

Energy 116kcal/485kJ; Protein 3g; Carbohydrate 12.2g, of which sugars 11.7g; Fat 6.5g, of which saturates 1.1g; Cholesterol 0mg; Calcium 43mg; Fibre 3.8g; Sodium 21mg.

MOROCCAN–STYLE VEGETABLE SALAD

THIS FRESH AND INVIGORATING SALAD HAS MOROCCAN ORIGINS. THE COMBINATION OF CRISP PEPPERS, MOIST CUCUMBER, SPICY CHILLI AND SOFT POTATOES IN A HERB DRESSING IS A WINNER.

Preparation: 12 minutes; Cooking: 0 minutes

SERVES FOUR TO SIX

INGREDIENTS

1 large cucumber, thinly sliced
2 cold, boiled potatoes, sliced
1 each red, yellow and green (bell)
  pepper, seeded and thinly sliced
300g/11oz/2⅔ cups pitted olives
½–1 hot fresh chilli, chopped
3–5 garlic cloves, chopped
3 spring onions (scallions), sliced
60–90ml/4–6 tbsp extra virgin olive oil
15–30ml/1–2 tbsp white wine vinegar
juice of ½ lemon, or to taste
15–30ml/1–2 tbsp chopped fresh
  mint leaves
15–30ml/1–2 tbsp chopped fresh
  coriander (cilantro) leaves
salt (optional)

1 Arrange the cucumber, potato and pepper slices and the pitted olives on a serving plate or in a dish.

2 Sprinkle the chopped fresh chilli over the salad and season with salt, if you like. (Olives tend to be very salty.)

3 Sprinkle the garlic, spring onions, olive oil, white wine vinegar and lemon juice over the salad. Chill before serving, sprinkled with the chopped mint leaves and coriander leaves.

Energy 205kcal/847kJ; Protein 2.2g; Carbohydrate 9.5g, of which sugars 6.7g; Fat 17.8g, of which saturates 2.7g; Cholesterol 0mg; Calcium 57mg; Fibre 3.9g; Sodium 150.3mg.

CUCUMBER AND WALNUT SALAD

THE COMBINATION OF CUCUMBERS, GARLIC AND THICK YOGURT WITH DILL AND WALNUTS MAKES THIS COOL CREAMY SALAD AN IDEAL AND QUICK DISH FOR A HOT SUMMER'S DAY.

Preparation: 8 minutes; Cooking: 0 minutes

SERVES SIX

INGREDIENTS

1 large cucumber
3–5 garlic cloves, finely chopped
250ml/8fl oz/1 cup sour cream or
120ml/4fl oz/½ cup Greek
(US strained plain) yogurt mixed
with 120ml/4fl oz/½ cup double
(heavy) cream
250ml/8fl oz/1 cup yogurt, preferably
thick Greek (US strained plain)
sheep's milk yogurt
2–3 large pinches of dried dill or
30–45ml/2–3 tbsp chopped
fresh dill
45–60ml/3–4 tbsp chopped walnuts
salt
sprig of dill, to garnish (optional)

1 Dice the cucumber finely and place it in a large mixing bowl.

COOK'S TIP
When made with very thick Greek yogurt, this appetizer can be shaped into balls and served on salad leaves.

2 Add the garlic, sour cream or yogurt and cream, yogurt, dill and salt. Mix together, then cover and chill.

3 To serve, pile the mixture into a bowl and sprinkle with walnuts. Garnish with dill, if you like.

Energy 263kcal/1085kJ; Protein 5g; Carbohydrate 5.8g, of which sugars 5.7g; Fat 24.6g, of which saturates 12.5g; Cholesterol 53mg; Calcium 141mg; Fibre 0.5g; Sodium 58mg.

MINT AND PARSLEY TAHINI SALAD

THE ALMOST DRY FLAVOUR OF TAHINI (A CREAMY SESAME SEED PASTE) COMBINES WONDERFULLY WITH FRESH HERBS AND SUBTLE SPICES IN THIS REFRESHING SUMMER SALAD OR LIGHT APPETIZER.

Preparation: 5 minutes; Cooking: 0 minutes

SERVES FOUR TO SIX

INGREDIENTS

115g/4oz/½ cup tahini
3 garlic cloves, chopped
½ bunch (about 20g/¾oz) fresh
mint, chopped
½ bunch (about 20g/¾oz) fresh
coriander (cilantro), chopped
½ bunch (about 20g/¾oz) fresh flat
leaf parsley, chopped
juice of ½ lemon, or to taste
pinch of ground cumin
pinch of ground turmeric
pinch of ground cardamom seeds
cayenne pepper, to taste
salt
To serve
extra virgin olive oil
warmed pitta bread
olives
raw vegetables

1 Combine the tahini with the chopped garlic, fresh herbs and lemon juice in a bowl. Taste and add a little more lemon juice, if you like. Stir in a little water if the mixture seems too dense and thick. Alternatively, place the ingredients in a food processor. Process briefly, then stir in a little water if required.

2 Stir in the cumin, turmeric and cardamom to taste, then season with salt and cayenne pepper.

3 To serve, spoon into a shallow bowl or on to plates and drizzle with olive oil. Serve with warmed pitta bread, olives and raw vegetables.

Energy 125kcal/516kJ; Protein 4.3g; Carbohydrate 0.9g, of which sugars 0.7g; Fat 11.6g, of which saturates 1.6g; Cholesterol 0mg; Calcium 180mg; Fibre 2.8g; Sodium 12mg.

PINK GRAPEFRUIT AND AVOCADO SALAD

SMOOTH, CREAMY AVOCADO, ZESTY PINK GRAPEFRUIT AND PEPPERY ROCKET ARE PERFECT PARTNERS IN THIS ATTRACTIVE, REFRESHING SALAD. THE CHILLI OIL ADDS A SPICY NOTE.

Preparation: 8 minutes; Cooking: 0 minutes

SERVES FOUR

INGREDIENTS
  2 pink grapefruit
  2 ripe avocados
  90g/3½ oz rocket (arugula)
  30ml/2 tbsp chilli oil
  salt and ground black pepper

COOK'S TIP
Avocados turn brown quickly when exposed to the air, but the acidic grapefruit juice will prevent this. Combine the ingredients as soon as the avocados have been sliced.

VARIATION
Pink grapefruit are tangy but not too sharp for this salad, but you could try large oranges for a sweeter flavour.

1 Slice the top and bottom off one of the grapefruit, then cut off all the peel and pith from around the side. Working over a small bowl to catch the juices, cut out the segments from between the membranes and place them in a separate bowl. Squeeze any juices remaining in the membranes into the juice bowl, then discard them. Repeat with the remaining grapefruit

2 Halve, stone (pit) and peel the avocados. Slice the flesh and add it to the grapefruit segments. Whisk a little salt and then the chilli oil into the grapefruit juice.

3 Pile the rocket leaves on to four serving plates and top with the grapefruit segments and avocado. Pour over the dressing and serve.

Energy 174kcal/719kJ; Protein 2.2g; Carbohydrate 6.8g, of which sugars 6g; Fat 15.4g, of which saturates 2.9g; Cholesterol 0mg; Calcium 62mg; Fibre 3.2g; Sodium 37mg.

SALAD OF WILD GREENS AND OLIVES

THIS SIMPLE SALAD TAKES ONLY A FEW MINUTES TO PUT TOGETHER. USE AS WIDE A VARIETY OF GREENS AS YOU CAN FIND, MATCHING SWEET FLAVOURS WITH A FEW BITTER LEAVES FOR ACCENT.

Preparation: 6 minutes; Cooking: 0 minutes

SERVES FOUR

INGREDIENTS

115g/4oz wild rocket (arugula)
1 packet mixed salad leaves
¼ white cabbage, thinly sliced
1 cucumber, sliced
1 small red onion, chopped
2–3 garlic cloves, chopped
3–5 tomatoes, cut into wedges
1 green (bell) pepper, seeded
and sliced
2–3 mint sprigs, sliced or torn
15–30ml/1–2 tbsp chopped fresh
parsley and/or tarragon or dill
pinch of dried oregano or thyme
45ml/3 tbsp extra virgin olive oil
juice of ½ lemon
15ml/1 tbsp red wine vinegar
15–20 black olives
salt and ground black pepper
cottage cheese, to serve

1 In a large salad bowl, put the rocket, mixed salad leaves, sliced white cabbage, sliced cucumber, chopped onion and chopped garlic. Toss gently with your fingers to combine the leaves and vegetables.

COOK'S TIP
Try to find mixed salad leaves that include varieties such as lamb's lettuce, purslane and mizuna.

2 Arrange the tomatoes, pepper, mint, fresh and dried herbs, salt and pepper on top of the greens and vegetables. Drizzle over the oil, lemon juice and vinegar, stud with the olives and serve with a bowl of cottage cheese.

VARIATION
This is traditionally served with labneh or yogurt cheese, but tastes good with cottage cheese too.

Energy 150kcal/619kJ; Protein 3.3g; Carbohydrate 10.4g, of which sugars 9.8g; Fat 10.7g, of which saturates 1.6g; Cholesterol 0mg; Calcium 106mg; Fibre 4.2g; Sodium 338mg

TURNIP SALAD IN SOUR CREAM

OFTEN NEGLECTED, TURNIPS MAKE AN UNUSUAL AND VERY TASTY ACCOMPANIMENT WHEN PREPARED IN THIS SIMPLE WAY. CHOOSE YOUNG, TENDER TURNIPS OF THE TYPE THE FRENCH CALL NAVETS.

Preparation: 5 minutes; Cooking: 0 minutes

SERVES FOUR

INGREDIENTS

2–4 young, tender turnips, peeled
¼–½ onion, finely chopped
2–3 drops white wine vinegar,
  or to taste
60–90ml/4–6 tbsp sour cream
salt and ground black pepper
chopped fresh parsley or paprika,
  to garnish

VARIATION
Crème fraîche or thick yogurt can be used instead of the sour cream, if you like.

1 Thinly slice or coarsely grate the turnips. Alternatively, thinly slice half the turnips and grate the ones that remain. Put in a bowl.

2 Add the onion, vinegar, salt and pepper, toss together then stir in the sour cream. Serve chilled, garnished with a sprinkling of parsley or paprika.

Energy 48kcal/198kJ; Protein 1.1g; Carbohydrate 4.1g, of which sugars 3.7g; Fat 3.2g, of which saturates 1.9g; Cholesterol 9mg; Calcium 42mg; Fibre 1.4g; Sodium 14mg

GREEN LEAF SALAD WITH CAPERS AND OLIVES

THE BEST TIME TO MAKE THIS REFRESHING SALAD IS IN THE SUMMER WHEN TOMATOES ARE AT THEIR SWEETEST AND FULL OF FLAVOUR. IT MAKES A COLOURFUL ADDITION TO THE TABLE.

Preparation: 10 minutes; Cooking: 0 minutes

SERVES FOUR

INGREDIENTS
  4 tomatoes
  ½ cucumber
  1 bunch spring onions (scallions),
    trimmed
  1 bunch watercress
  8 stuffed olives
  30ml/2 tbsp drained capers
For the dressing
  30ml/2 tbsp red wine vinegar
  5ml/1 tsp paprika
  2.5ml/½ tsp ground cumin
  1 garlic clove, crushed
  75 ml/5 tbsp olive oil
  salt and ground black pepper

1 Peel the tomatoes and finely dice the flesh. Put them in a salad bowl.

2 Peel the cucumber, dice it finely and add it to the tomatoes. Chop half the spring onions and add them to the salad bowl and mix lightly. Break the watercress into sprigs. Add to the tomato mixture, with the olives and capers.

3 To make the dressing, mix the wine vinegar, paprika, cumin and garlic in a bowl. Whisk in the oil and add salt and pepper to taste. Pour over the salad and toss lightly. Serve immediately with the remaining spring onions.

Energy 167kcal/692kJ; Protein 2.2g; Carbohydrate 4.3g, of which sugars 4.3g; Fat 15.8g, of which saturates 2.4g; Cholesterol 0mg; Calcium 72mg; Fibre 2.3g; Sodium 305mg.

CABBAGE SLAW WITH DATE AND APPLE

THREE TYPES OF CABBAGE ARE SHREDDED TOGETHER FOR SERVING RAW, SO THAT THE MAXIMUM AMOUNT OF VITAMIN C IS RETAINED. THIS CHEERFUL AND SPEEDY SALAD MAKES A VERY GOOD LIGHT LUNCH.

Preparation: 8 minutes; Cooking: 0 minutes

SERVES SIX TO EIGHT

INGREDIENTS
¼ small white cabbage
¼ small red cabbage
¼ small Savoy cabbage
175g/6oz/1 cup dried stoned (pitted)
  dates
3 eating apples
juice of 1 lemon
10ml/2 tsp caraway seeds
For the dressing
60ml/4 tbsp olive oil
15ml/1 tbsp cider vinegar
5ml/1 tsp clear honey
salt and ground black pepper

1 Remove the central core from the cabbage quarters as well as any coarse outside leaves and the central rib from the larger remaining leaves, then finely shred them and place the shredded cabbage in a large salad bowl.

2 Chop the dates and add them to the cabbage mixture.

3 Core the eating apples and slice them thinly into a mixing bowl. Add the lemon juice and toss together to prevent discoloration before adding them to the salad bowl.

4 To make the dressing, combine the oil, vinegar and honey in a screw-top jar. Add salt and pepper, then close the jar tightly and shake well. Pour the dressing over the salad, toss lightly, then sprinkle with the caraway seeds and toss again.

COOK'S TIPS
Support local orchards by looking out for different home-grown apples. Many delicious older varieties are grown by specialist farmers, who will willingly offer a taste to would-be buyers. Choose both green and red-skinned apples if possible, to add extra colour to the salad.

Energy 141kcal/595kJ; Protein 1.7g; Carbohydrate 22.1g, of which sugars 22g; Fat 5.7g, of which saturates 0.8g; Cholesterol 0mg; Calcium 42mg; Fibre 2.8g; Sodium 7mg.

SPROUTED SEED SALAD

IF YOU SPROUT BEANS, LENTILS AND WHOLE GRAINS, THIS INCREASES THEIR NUTRITIONAL VALUE, AND THEY MAKE A DELICIOUSLY CRUNCHY SALAD.

Preparation: 5 minutes; Cooking: 0 minutes

SERVES SIX TO EIGHT

INGREDIENTS
2 eating apples
115g/4oz/2 cups alfalfa sprouts
115g/4oz/2 cups beansprouts
115g/4oz/2 cups aduki beansprouts
¼ cucumber, sliced
1 bunch watercress, trimmed
1 carton mustard and cress, trimmed
For the dressing
150ml/¼ pint/⅔ cup low-fat
  natural (plain) yogurt
juice of ½ lemon
bunch of chives, snipped
30ml/2 tbsp chopped fresh herbs
ground black pepper

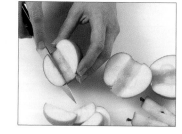

1 Core and slice the apples; mix with the other salad ingredients.

COOK'S TIP
Bean and seed sprouts will keep in the refrigerator salad drawer for a day or two.

2 Whisk the dressing ingredients in a measuring jug (cup). Drizzle the dressing over the salad and toss together just before serving.

Energy 38kcal/161kJ; Protein 2.9g; Carbohydrate 5.7g, of which sugars 4.9g; Fat 0.6g, of which saturates 0.2g; Cholesterol 0mg; Calcium 78mg; Fibre 1.6g; Sodium 26mg.

TURKISH SALAD

THIS SALAD IS A WONDERFUL COMBINATION OF TEXTURES AND FLAVOURS. THE SALTINESS OF THE CHEESE IS PERFECTLY BALANCED BY THE REFRESHING SALAD VEGETABLES.

Preparation: 8–10 minutes; Cooking: 0 minutes

SERVES FOUR

INGREDIENT

1 cos or romaine lettuce heart
1 green (bell) pepper
1 red (bell) pepper
½ cucumber
4 tomatoes
1 red onion
225g/8oz feta cheese, crumbled
handful of black olives, to garnish

For the dressing

45ml/3 tbsp olive oil
45ml/3 tbsp lemon juice
1 garlic clove, crushed
15ml/1 tbsp chopped fresh parsley
15ml/1 tbsp chopped fresh mint
salt and ground black pepper

1 Chop the lettuce into bitesize pieces. Seed the peppers, remove the cores and cut the flesh into thin strips. Chop the cucumber and slice or chop the tomatoes. Cut the onion in half, then slice finely.

2 Place the chopped lettuce, peppers, cucumber, tomatoes and onion in a large bowl. Scatter the feta over the top and toss lightly.

3 To make the dressing, whisk together the olive oil, lemon juice and garlic in a small bowl. Stir in the chopped fresh parsley and mint and season with salt and ground black pepper to taste.

4 Pour the dressing over the salad, toss lightly and serve at once, garnished with a handful of black olives.

Energy 273kcal/1133kJ; Protein 11.1g; Carbohydrate 11.2g, of which sugars 10.9g; Fat 20.7g, of which saturates 9.2g; Cholesterol 39mg; Calcium 242mg; Fibre 3.2g; Sodium 826mg.

PERSIAN SALAD

SOME OF THE SIMPLEST DISHES ARE ALSO THE MOST SUCCESSFUL. THIS SALAD IS MADE IN MINUTES AND HAS A CRISP, FRESH FLAVOUR. SERVE IT WITH COLD MEATS AND BAKED POTATOES.

Preparation: 5 minutes; Cooking: 0 minutes

SERVES TWO

INGREDIENTS

4 tomatoes
½ cucumber
1 onion
1 cos or romaine lettuce heart

For the dressing

30ml/2 tbsp olive oil
juice of 1 lemon
1 garlic clove, crushed
salt and ground black pepper

1 Cut the tomatoes and cucumber into small cubes. Finely chop the onion and tear the lettuce into bitesize pieces.

2 Place all the cut-up vegetables in a large salad bowl and mix lightly together.

3 To make the dressing, pour the olive oil into a small bowl. Add the lemon juice and garlic and whisk together well. Stir in salt to taste. Pour over the salad and toss lightly to mix. Sprinkle with black pepper and serve at once.

Energy 162kcal/671kJ; Protein 2.8g; Carbohydrate 11.2g, of which sugars 10.5g; Fat 12g, of which saturates 1.8g; Cholesterol 0mg; Calcium 50mg; Fibre 3.3g; Sodium 23mg.

WARM HALLOUMI AND FENNEL SALAD

HALLOUMI IS A ROBUST CHEESE THAT HOLDS ITS SHAPE WHEN COOKED ON A GRIDDLE OR BARBECUE.
DURING COOKING IT ACQUIRES THE DISTINCTIVE GRIDDLE MARKS THAT LOOK SO EFFECTIVE HERE.

Preparation: 13 minutes; Cooking: 6 minutes

SERVES FOUR

INGREDIENTS
    200g/7oz halloumi cheese,
      thickly sliced
    2 fennel bulbs, trimmed and
      thinly sliced
    30ml/2 tbsp roughly chopped
      fresh oregano
    45ml/3 tbsp lemon-infused olive oil
    salt and ground black pepper

COOK'S TIP
If you have time, chill the halloumi and
fennel mixture for about 2 hours before
cooking, so it becomes infused with
the dressing.

1 Put the halloumi, fennel and oregano
in a bowl and drizzle over the lemon-
infused oil. Season with salt and black
pepper to taste. (Halloumi is a fairly
salty cheese, so be very careful when
adding extra salt.)

2 Cover the bowl with clear film (plastic
wrap) and set aside for 10 minutes.

3 Place the halloumi and fennel on a
hot griddle pan or over the barbecue,
reserving the marinade, and cook
for about 3 minutes on each side,
until charred.

4 Divide the halloumi and fennel among
four serving plates and drizzle over the
reserved marinade. Serve immediately.

Energy 212kcal/876kJ; Protein 10g; Carbohydrate 1.4g, of which sugars 1.3g; Fat 18.6g, of which saturates 8.1g; Cholesterol 29mg; Calcium 199mg; Fibre 1.8g; Sodium 206mg

SPINACH AND ROAST GARLIC SALAD

SPINACH AND GARLIC GO WONDERFULLY TOGETHER, AND THIS SIMPLE COMBINATION OF WARM GARLIC AND COLD SPINACH LEAVES WITH CRUNCHY PINE NUTS MAKES A MEMORABLE SALAD.

Preparation: 3 minutes; Cooking: 15 minutes

SERVES FOUR

INGREDIENTS

  12 garlic cloves, unpeeled
  60 ml/4 tbsp extra virgin olive oil
  450g/1lb baby spinach leaves
  50g/2oz/½ cup pine nuts,
    lightly toasted
  juice of ½ lemon
  salt and ground black pepper

COOK'S TIP

Don't worry about the amount of garlic used in this salad. During roasting, it becomes sweet and subtle and loses its pungent taste.

1 Preheat the oven to 190°C/375°F/ Gas 5. Place the garlic in a small roasting pan, add 30 ml/2 tbsp of the oil and stir them around, then roast for about 15 minutes, until the garlic cloves are slightly charred around the edges.

2 While still warm, tip the garlic into a salad bowl. Add the spinach, pine nuts, lemon juice, remaining olive oil and a little salt. Toss well and add black pepper to taste. Serve immediately, inviting guests to squeeze the softened garlic purée out of the skin to eat.

Energy 225kcal/929kJ; Protein 5.9g; Carbohydrate 4.4g, of which sugars 2.4g; Fat 20.6g, of which saturates 2.3g; Cholesterol 0mg; Calcium 195mg; Fibre 3.1g; Sodium 158mg.

ASPARAGUS AND ORANGE SALAD

*A SIMPLE DRESSING OF OLIVE OIL AND SHERRY VINEGAR MINGLES WITH THE ORANGE AND TOMATO
FLAVOURS IN THIS ASPARAGUS-BASED SALAD WITH GREAT RESULTS.*

Preparation: 6 minutes; Cooking: 3–4 minutes

SERVES FOUR

INGREDIENTS

225g/8oz asparagus, trimmed and
   cut into 5cm/2in pieces
2 large oranges
2 well-flavoured ripe tomatoes,
   cut into eighths
50g/2oz romaine lettuce
   leaves, shredded
30ml/2 tbsp extra virgin olive oil
2.5ml/½ tsp sherry vinegar
salt and ground black pepper

1 Cook the asparagus in lightly salted,
boiling water for 3–4 minutes, until just
tender. Drain and refresh under cold
water. Set aside.

2 Grate the rind from half an orange
and reserve. Peel both oranges and cut
into segments, leaving the membrane
behind. Squeeze out the juice from the
membrane and reserve the juice.

COOK'S TIP
Sherry vinegar is golden brown with a
rounded and full flavour. It is matured in
wooden barrels in much the same way as
sherry itself.

3 Put the asparagus pieces, segments
of orange, tomatoes and lettuce into a
salad bowl. Mix together the olive oil
and sherry vinegar and add 15ml/1 tbsp
of the reserved orange juice and 5ml/
1 tsp of the grated orange rind, whisking
well to combine. Season with a little salt
and plenty of ground black pepper. Just
before serving, pour the dressing over
the salad and mix gently to coat.

Energy 106kcal/442kJ; Protein 3.1g; Carbohydrate 10g, of which sugars 10g; Fat 6.2g, of which saturates 0.9g; Cholesterol 0mg; Calcium 59mg; Fibre 3.1g; Sodium 12mg.

CAESAR SALAD

THIS IS A WELL-KNOWN AND MUCH ENJOYED SALAD INVENTED BY A CHEF CALLED CAESAR CARDINI.
BE SURE TO USE CRISP LETTUCE AND ADD THE VERY SOFT EGGS AT THE LAST MINUTE.

Preparation: 10 minutes; Cooking: 2 minutes

SERVES SIX

INGREDIENTS
175ml/6fl oz/¾ cup olive oil
115g/4oz French or Italian bread,
  cut into 2.5cm/1in cubes
1 large garlic clove, crushed
1 cos or romaine lettuce
2 eggs, boiled for 1 minute
120ml/4fl oz/½ cup lemon juice
50g/2oz/⅔ cup freshly grated
  Parmesan cheese
6 canned anchovy fillets, drained and
  finely chopped (optional)
salt and ground black pepper

1 Heat 50ml/2fl oz/¼ cup of the oil in a large frying pan. Add the bread cubes and garlic. Cook over a medium heat, stirring constantly, until the bread cubes are golden brown all over. Drain well on kitchen paper. Discard the garlic.

2 Tear large lettuce leaves into smaller pieces. Put all the lettuce in a bowl.

3 Add the remaining oil to the lettuce and season with salt and plenty of ground black pepper. Toss well to coat the leaves.

COOK'S TIP
Do not boil the eggs for longer than 1 minute: the whites should be milky, while the yolks remain raw. If you prefer to avoid lightly cooked eggs, substitute quartered hard-boiled eggs.

4 Break the eggs on top. Sprinkle with the lemon juice. Toss thoroughly again to combine.

5 Add the Parmesan cheese and anchovies, if using. Toss gently to mix.

6 Sprinkle the fried bread cubes on top and serve immediately.

VARIATION
For a tangier dressing, mix 30ml/2 tbsp white wine vinegar, 15ml/1 tbsp Worcestershire sauce, 2.5ml/½ tsp mustard powder, 5ml/1 tsp sugar, salt and pepper in a screw-top jar, then add the oil and shake well.

Energy 782kcal/3251kJ; Protein 49.6g; Carbohydrate 8.6g, of which sugars 1.2g; Fat 62.4g, of which saturates 15.6g; Cholesterol 1342mg; Calcium 354mg; Fibre 1g; Sodium 785mg.

WARM BROAD BEAN AND FETA SALAD

THIS RECIPE IS LOOSELY BASED ON A TYPICAL MEDLEY OF FRESH-TASTING GREEK SALAD INGREDIENTS – BROAD BEANS, TOMATOES AND FETA CHEESE. IT IS LOVELY SERVED WARM OR COLD.

Preparation: 2 minutes; Cooking: 4–5 minutes

SERVES FOUR TO SIX

INGREDIENTS

900g/2lb broad (fava) beans, shelled,
  or 350g/12oz frozen shelled beans
60ml/4 tbsp olive oil
175g/6oz plum tomatoes, halved,
  or quartered if large
4 garlic cloves, crushed
115g/4oz feta cheese,
  cut into chunks
45ml/3 tbsp chopped fresh dill,
  plus extra to garnish
12 black olives
salt and ground black pepper

1 Cook the fresh or frozen broad beans in boiling, salted water until just tender. Drain and set aside.

2 Meanwhile, heat the oil in a heavy frying pan and add the tomatoes and garlic. Cook over a high heat until the tomatoes are beginning to colour.

3 Add the feta to the pan and toss the ingredients together for 1 minute. Tip into a salad bowl and mix with the beans, dill, olives and salt and pepper. Serve garnished with chopped dill.

Energy 175kcal/727kJ; Protein 7.9g; Carbohydrate 8g, of which sugars 2g; Fat 12.6g, of which saturates 3.9g; Cholesterol 13mg; Calcium 109mg; Fibre 4.3g; Sodium 471mg.

HALLOUMI AND GRAPE SALAD

HALLOUMI, A FIRM-TEXTURED GREEK CHEESE, IS DELICIOUS FRIED. ITS SALTY FLAVOUR IS THE IDEAL FOIL FOR SWEET GRAPES AND MILD SALAD GREENS, WHICH TOGETHER MAKE A LOVELY LUNCH DISH.

Preparation: 2 minutes; cooking: 2–3 minutes

SERVES FOUR TO SIX

INGREDIENTS

150g/5oz mixed green salad leaves
75g/3oz/¾ cup each seedless green
  and black grapes
250g/9oz halloumi cheese
45ml/3 tbsp olive oil
fresh young thyme leaves and basil
  sprigs, to garnish
For the dressing
60ml/4 tbsp olive oil
15ml/1 tbsp lemon juice
2.5ml/½ tsp caster (superfine) sugar
salt and ground black pepper
15ml/1 tbsp chopped fresh thyme
  or dill

1 To make the dressing, whisk together the olive oil, lemon juice and sugar. Season with salt and pepper. Stir in the thyme or dill and set aside.

2 Toss together the salad leaves and the green and black grapes, then transfer to a large serving plate.

3 Thinly slice the cheese. Heat the oil in a large frying pan. Add the cheese and fry briefly until it turns golden on the underside. Turn the cheese with a fish slice (metal spatula) and cook the other side.

4 Arrange the cheese over the salad. Pour over the dressing and garnish with thyme and basil.

Energy 235kcal/973kJ; Protein 8g; Carbohydrate 2.8g, of which sugars 2.8g; Fat 21.4g, of which saturates 7.6g; Cholesterol 24mg; Calcium 160mg; Fibre 0.3g; Sodium 166mg.

DESSERTS, COOKIES AND BAKES

A dessert makes the perfect end to a meal, whether it is a casual family supper or a dinner party. If you think that desserts are just too time-consuming to make, especially on top of the rest of the meal, the contents of this chapter might make you think again. How about a Chocolate and Banana Fool (5 minutes), Blueberry Meringue Crumble (4 minutes) or Summer Berries in Warm Sabayon Glaze (11 minutes)? In very little extra time you could make Red Fruit Filo Baskets, Passion Fruit Soufflés, Summer Berry Sponge Tart or Portuguese Custart Tarts. Earlier in the day, nothing goes better with an afternoon cup of tea than a delicious home-made cake, such as Almond and Raspberry Roll, Chocolate and Prune Refrigerator Bars, White Chocolate Brownies, Chocolate and Pistachio Wedges and Pecan Toffee Shortbread. Your guests and family will be very impressed.

FRESH FRUIT SALAD

ORANGES ARE AN ESSENTIAL INGREDIENT FOR A SUCCESSFUL AND REFRESHING FRUIT SALAD, WHICH CAN INCLUDE ANY FRUIT IN SEASON. A COLOURFUL COMBINATION TAKES JUST MINUTES TO MAKE.

Preparation: 6 minutes; Cooking: 0 minutes

SERVES SIX

INGREDIENTS
    2 apples
    2 oranges
    2 peaches
    16–20 strawberries
    30ml/2 tbsp lemon juice
    15–30ml/1–2 tbsp orange
      flower water
    icing (confectioners') sugar,
      to taste (optional)

COOK'S TIP
The easiest way to remove the pith and peel from an orange is to cut a thin slice from each end of the orange first, using a sharp knife. It will then be easier to cut off the remaining peel and pith.

1 Peel and core the apples and cut into thin slices. Remove the pith and peel from the oranges and cut each one into segments. Squeeze the juice from the membrane and retain.

2 Blanch the peaches for 1 minute in boiling water. Peel and slice thickly.

3 Hull and halve the strawberries, and place all the fruit in a large bowl.

4 Blend together the lemon juice, orange flower water and any reserved orange juice. Taste and add a little icing sugar to sweeten, if you like. Pour the fruit juice over the salad and serve.

Energy 42kcal/180kJ; Protein 1.1g; Carbohydrate 9.8g, of which sugars 9.8g; Fat 0.1g, of which saturates 0g; Cholesterol 0mg; Calcium 28mg; Fibre 1.9g; Sodium 5mg

DRIED FRUIT SALAD

THIS DESSERT DOESN'T TAKE LONG TO PREPARE, BUT MUST BE MADE AHEAD OF TIME, TO ALLOW THE DRIED FRUIT TO PLUMP UP AND FLAVOURS TO BLEND. IT IS ALSO GOOD FOR BREAKFAST.

Preparation: 6 minutes; Cooking: 12 minutes; Make ahead

SERVES FOUR

INGREDIENTS
    115g/4oz/½ cup ready-to-eat dried
      apricots, halved
    115g/4oz/½ cup ready-to-eat dried
      peaches, halved
    1 pear
    1 apple
    1 orange
    115g/4oz/1 cup mixed raspberries
      and blackberries
    1 cinnamon stick
    50g/2oz/¼ cup caster
      (superfine) sugar
    15ml/1 tbsp clear honey
    30ml/2 tbsp lemon juice

1 Place the dried fruit in a large pan and add 600ml/1 pint/2½ cups water.

2 Peel and core the pear and apple, then dice. Remove peel and pith from the orange and cut into wedges. Add all the cut fruit to the pan with the raspberries and blackberries.

3 Pour in a further 150ml/¼ pint/⅔ cup water, the cinnamon, sugar and honey, and bring to the boil. Cover and simmer for 10 minutes, then remove the pan from the heat. Stir in the lemon juice. Leave to cool completely, then transfer the fruit and syrup to a bowl and chill for 1–2 hours before serving.

Energy 190kcal/811kJ; Protein 3.3g; Carbohydrate 46g, of which sugars 46g; Fat 0.5g, of which saturates 0g; Cholesterol 0mg; Calcium 75mg; Fibre 6g; Sodium 13mg

TROPICAL SCENTED FRUIT SALAD

WITH ITS SPECIAL COLOUR AND EXOTIC FLAVOUR, THIS FRESH FRUIT SALAD IS PERFECT AFTER A RICH MEAL. SERVE IT WITH WHIPPING CREAM FLAVOURED WITH FINELY CHOPPED PRESERVED STEM GINGER.

Preparation: 20 minutes; Cooking: 0 minutes

SERVES FOUR TO SIX

INGREDIENTS
  350–400g/12–14oz/3–3½ cups
    strawberries, hulled and halved
  6 oranges, peeled and segmented
  1–2 passion fruit
  120ml/4fl oz/½ cup medium dry or
    sweet white wine
  whipping cream flavoured with 15g/
    ½oz drained preserved stem ginger,
    to serve

VARIATION
For fabulous flavour and colour, try using three small blood oranges and three ordinary oranges.

1 Put the hulled and halved strawberries and peeled and segmented oranges into a serving bowl. Halve the passion fruit and use a teaspoon to scoop the flesh into the bowl.

2 Pour the wine over the fruit and toss gently. Cover and chill in the refrigerator until ready to serve with the flavoured whipping cream.

Energy 81kcal/342kJ; Protein 2g; Carbohydrate 15.6g, of which sugars 15.6g; Fat 0.2g, of which saturates 0g; Cholesterol 0mg; Calcium 75mg; Fibre 3g; Sodium 13mg.

MANGO STACKS <u>WITH</u> RASPBERRY COULIS

THIS MAKES A VERY HEALTHY YET STUNNING DESSERT — IT IS LOW IN FAT AND CONTAINS NO ADDED SUGAR. HOWEVER, IF THE RASPBERRIES ARE A LITTLE SHARP, ADD A PINCH OF SUGAR TO THE PURÉE.

Preparation: 10 minutes; Cooking: 5 minutes

SERVES FOUR

INGREDIENTS
   3 filo pastry sheets, thawed
      if frozen
   50g/2oz/¼ cup butter, melted
   2 small ripe mangoes
   115g/4oz/⅔ raspberries, thawed
      if frozen

1 Preheat the oven to 200⁰C/400⁰F/ Gas 6. Lay the filo sheets on a clean work surface and cut out four 10cm/4in rounds from each. Brush each round with the melted butter and lay the rounds on two baking sheets. Bake for 5 minutes, or until crisp and golden. Place on wire racks to cool.

2 Peel the mangoes, remove the stones and cut the flesh into thin slices. Put the raspberries in a food processor with 45ml/3 tbsp water and process to a purée. Place a pastry round on each of four serving plates. Top with a quarter of the mango and drizzle with a little of the raspberry purée. Repeat until all the ingredients have been used, ending with a layer of mango and a drizzle of raspberry purée.

COOK'S TIP
Always place a dishtowel or some clear film (kitchen wrap) over the filo sheets you are not working with to prevent them from drying out and becoming brittle.

Energy 186kcal/779kJ; Protein 2.2g; Carbohydrate 21.7g, of which sugars 11.9g; Fat 10.7g, of which saturates 6.7g; Cholesterol 27mg; Calcium 36mg; Fibre 3.1g; Sodium 79mg.

GRAPEFRUIT IN HONEY AND WHISKY

CREATE A SIMPLE YET ELEGANT DESSERT BY ARRANGING A COLOURFUL FAN OF PINK, RED AND WHITE GRAPEFRUIT SEGMENTS IN A SWEET WHISKY SAUCE. THIS DESSERT IS PERFECT AFTER A RICH MEAL.

Preparation: 4 minutes; Cooking: 14 minutes; Chilling recommended

SERVES FOUR

INGREDIENTS

   1 pink grapefruit
   1 red grapefruit
   1 white grapefruit
   50g/2oz/¼ cup sugar
   60ml/4 tbsp clear honey
   45ml/3 tbsp whisky
   mint leaves, to decorate

1 Cut a thin slice of peel and pith from each end of the grapefruit. Place the cut side down on a plate and cut off the peel and pith in strips. Remove any remaining pith. Cut out each segment leaving the membrane behind. Put the segments into a shallow bowl.

2 Put the sugar and 150ml/¼ pint/ ⅔ cup water into a heavy pan. Bring to the boil, stirring constantly, until the sugar has completely dissolved, then simmer, without stirring, for 10 minutes, until thickened and syrupy.

3 Heat the honey in a pan and boil until it becomes a slightly deeper colour and begins to caramelize. Remove the pan from the heat, add the whisky and, using a match or taper, carefully ignite, if you like, then pour the mixture into the sugar syrup.

VARIATION
The whisky can be replaced with brandy, Cointreau or Grand Marnier.

4 Bring the syrup to the boil, and pour over the grapefruit segments. Cover and leave until cold. To serve, put the grapefruit segments on to four serving plates, alternating the colours, pour over some of the syrup and decorate with the mint leaves.

Energy 154kcal/649kJ; Protein 1.1g; Carbohydrate 32.7g, of which sugars 32.7g; Fat 0.1g, of which saturates 0g; Cholesterol 0mg; Calcium 35mg; Fibre 1.6g; Sodium 6mg

CLEMENTINES <u>WITH</u> STAR ANISE

LOOKING DRAMATIC, WITH THE DARK STARS OF ANISE AGAINST THE SUNSHINE ORANGE CLEMENTINES, THIS IS A SIMPLY DELICIOUS DESSERT. IT TASTES BEST CHILLED, SO ALLOW TIME FOR THAT.

Preparation: 6–8 minutes; Cooking: 12 minutes; Chilling recommended

SERVES SIX

INGREDIENTS
    1 lime
    350ml/12fl oz/1½ cups sweet
       dessert wine, such as Sauternes
    75g/3oz/6 tbsp caster
       (superfine) sugar
    6 star anise
    1 cinnamon stick
    1 vanilla pod (bean)
    30ml/2 tbsp Cointreau or other
       orange liqueur
    12 clementines

VARIATION
Tangerines or seedless oranges can be used instead of clementines.

1 Thinly pare 1 or 2 strips of rind from the lime. Put them in a pan, with the dessert wine, sugar, star anise and cinnamon stick. Split the vanilla pod and add the seeds to the pan. Bring to the boil, then lower the heat and simmer for 10 minutes.

2 Remove the pan from the heat and leave to cool, then stir in the liqueur.

3 Peel the clementines. Cut some of them in half and place them all in a large dish. Pour over the wine and chill before serving.

Energy 149kcal/632kJ; Protein 0.9g; Carbohydrate 24.7g, of which sugars 24.7g; Fat 0.1g, of which saturates 0g; Cholesterol 0mg; Calcium 40mg; Fibre 1g; Sodium 12mg

CHOCOLATE AND BANANA FOOL

THIS DELICIOUS DESSERT HAS A LOVELY CITRUS FLAVOUR. IT IS QUITE RICH, SO IT IS A GOOD IDEA TO SERVE IT WITH SOME DESSERT BISCUITS, SUCH AS SHORTBREAD OR BISCOTTI.

Preparation: 3 minutes; Cooking: 2 minutes; Chilling recommended

SERVES FOUR

INGREDIENTS
115g/4oz plain (semisweet)
  chocolate, broken into
  small pieces
300ml/½ pint/1¼ cups ready-made
  fresh custard
2 bananas

COOK'S TIPS
Good-quality bought custard is ideal for this dessert. Don't be tempted to use anything but the best chocolate, though, or the flavour will be compromised. Look for a bar that contains at least 70 per cent cocoa solids. A flavoured chocolate such as pistachio or orange takes the dessert into another dimension.

1 Put the chocolate pieces in a heat-proof bowl and melt in the microwave on high power for 1–2 minutes. Stir, then set aside. If you do not have a microwave, put the chocolate in a heatproof bowl and place it over a pan of gently simmering water and leave until melted, stirring frequently to ensure all the pieces get melted.

2 Pour the custard into a bowl and gently fold in the melted chocolate to make a rippled effect.

3 Peel and slice the bananas and stir these into the chocolate and custard mixture. Spoon into four glasses. If you have time, chill for at least 30 minutes before serving.

Energy 268kcal/1127kJ; Protein 4.1g; Carbohydrate 42.1g, of which sugars 38.1g; Fat 9.6g, of which saturates 4.9g; Cholesterol 3mg; Calcium 81mg; Fibre 1.4g; Sodium 33mg

LEMON POSSET

THIS OLD-FASHIONED DESSERT WAS ONCE CONSIDERED A REMEDY FOR THE COMMON COLD. IT IS CERTAINLY WORTH SUFFERING A SNIFFLE IF IT MEANS YOU GET TO SAMPLE ITS SUPERB FLAVOUR.

Preparation: 2 minutes; Cooking: 8–10 minutes; Chilling recommended

SERVES FOUR

INGREDIENTS
600ml/1 pint/2½ cups double
  (heavy) cream
175g/6oz/scant 1 cup caster
  (superfine) sugar
grated rind and juice of
  2 unwaxed lemons

VARIATION
To intensify the lemon flavour of this lovely old dessert even more, swirl a spoonful of lemon curd or lemon cheese on the surface just before serving. Physalis make a suitable and very stylish accompaniment.

1 Pour the cream into a heavy pan. Add the sugar and heat gently until the sugar has dissolved, then bring to the boil, stirring constantly. Add the lemon juice and rind, reserving a little of the rind for decoration, and stir constantly over a medium heat until it thickens.

2 Pour the mixture into four heatproof serving glasses. Cool, then chill in the refrigerator until just set. Serve the posset decorated with a few strands of lemon rind, and with a selection of dessert biscuits (cookies), if you like. Rich, buttery shortbread is ideal.

Energy 917kcal/3801kJ; Protein 2.7g; Carbohydrate 48.5g, of which sugars 48.5g; Fat 80.6g, of which saturates 50.1g; Cholesterol 206mg; Calcium 98mg; Fibre 0g; Sodium 36mg

RHUBARB AND GINGER TRIFLES

CHOOSE A GOOD-QUALITY JAR OF RHUBARB COMPOTE FOR THIS RECIPE; TRY TO FIND ONE WITH LARGE, CHUNKY PIECES OF FRUIT. ALTERNATIVELY, USE WHOLE-FRUIT APRICOT JAM.

Preparation: 3–4 minutes; Cooking: 0 minutes

SERVES FOUR

INGREDIENTS
12 gingernut biscuits (gingersnaps)
50ml/2fl oz/¼ cup rhubarb compote
450ml/¾ pint/scant 2 cups extra
thick double (heavy) cream

1 Put the ginger biscuits in a plastic bag and seal. Bash the biscuits with a rolling pin until roughly crushed.

2 Set aside two tablespoons of crushed biscuits and divide the rest among four glasses.

3 Spoon the rhubarb compote on top of the crushed biscuits, then top with the cream. Place in the refrigerator and chill for about 30 minutes.

4 To serve, sprinkle the reserved crushed biscuits over the trifles and serve immediately.

Energy 695kcal/2874kJ; Protein 3.6g; Carbohydrate 27.1g, of which sugars 14.1g; Fat 64.3g, of which saturates 39.4g; Cholesterol 154mg; Calcium 98mg; Fibre 0.6g; Sodium 124mg

BLUEBERRY MERINGUE CRUMBLE

IMAGINE THE MOST APPEALING FLAVOURS OF A BLUEBERRY MERINGUE DESSERT — FRESH TANGY FRUIT, CRISP SUGARY MERINGUE AND VANILLA-SCENTED CREAM — ALL SERVED IN A TALL GLASS FOR EASY EATING.

Preparation: 4 minutes; Cooking: 0 minutes

SERVES THREE TO FOUR

INGREDIENTS
150g/5oz/1¼ cups fresh blueberries,
   plus extra to decorate
15ml/1 tbsp icing
   (confectioners') sugar
250ml/8fl oz/1 cup vanilla
   iced yogurt
200ml/7fl oz/scant 1 cup full cream
   (whole) milk
30ml/2 tbsp lime juice
75g/3oz meringues, lightly crushed

1 Put the blueberries and sugar in a blender or food processor with 60ml/4 tbsp water and blend until smooth, scraping the mixture down from the side once or twice, if necessary.

2 Transfer the purée to a small bowl and rinse out the blender or food processor bowl to get rid of any remaining blueberry juice.

COOK'S TIPS
• Buy good-quality meringues, not the brittle extra-sweet supermarket variety.
• The easiest way to crush the meringues is to put them in a plastic bag on a work surface and tap them gently with a rolling pin. Stop tapping the meringues as soon as they have crumbled into little bitesize pieces otherwise you'll just be left with tiny crumbs.

3 Put the iced yogurt, milk and lime juice in the blender and process until thoroughly combined. Add half of the crushed meringues and process again until smooth.

4 Carefully pour alternate layers of the milkshake, blueberry syrup and the remaining crushed meringues into tall glasses, finishing with a few chunky pieces of meringue.

5 Drizzle any remaining blueberry syrup over the tops of the meringues and decorate with a few extra blueberries. Serve immediately.

VARIATION
Iced yogurt is used to provide a slightly lighter note than ice cream, but there's nothing to stop you using ice cream instead, if you prefer.

Energy 164kcal/691kJ; Protein 6.2g; Carbohydrate 30.8g, of which sugars 30.8g; Fat 2.7g, of which saturates 1.6g; Cholesterol 8mg; Calcium 197mg; Fibre 1.2g; Sodium 96mg

BLACKCURRANT FOOL

THE STRONG FLAVOUR AND DEEP COLOUR OF THIS FRUIT MAKES IT ESPECIALLY SUITABLE FOR FOOLS AND ICES, ALTHOUGH THIS ADAPTABLE RECIPE CAN BE MADE USING OTHER SOFT FRUITS TOO.

Preparation: 5 minutes; Cooking: 5 minutes

SERVES SIX

INGREDIENTS
   350g/12oz/3 cups blackcurrants
   45ml/3 tbsp water
   about 175g/6oz/scant 1 cup caster
     (superfine) sugar
   5ml/1 tsp lemon juice
   300ml/½ pint/1¼ cups double
     (heavy) cream

VARIATION
To make an easy no-stir blackcurrant ice cream, turn the completed fool into a freezerproof container. Cover and freeze (preferably at the lowest setting). Transfer from the freezer to the refrigerator 10–15 minutes before serving to allow the ice cream to soften. Serve with whipped cream and biscuits.

1 Put the blackcurrants into a small pan with the measured water and cook over a low heat until soft. Remove from the heat, add the sugar according to taste and stir until dissolved.

2 Cool slightly, then liquidize (blend) to make a purée. Leave to cool completely. Add the lemon juice and stir well.

3 Whip the double cream until it is fairly stiff and, using a metal spoon, carefully fold it into the blackcurrant purée, losing as little volume as possible.

4 Turn the mixture into a serving dish or six individual serving glasses and leave to set. Chill in the refrigerator until ready to serve.

Energy 1516kcal/6324kJ; Protein 6g; Carbohydrate 140.8g, of which sugars 140.8g; Fat 107.6g, of which saturates 66.8g; Cholesterol 276mg; Calcium 300mg; Fibre 8.4g; Sodium 60mg

COOL CHOCOLATE FLOAT

CHOCOLATE MILKSHAKE AND SCOOPS OF CHOCOLATE AND VANILLA ICE CREAM ARE COMBINED HERE TO MAKE THE MOST MELTINGLY DELICIOUS DESSERT DRINK EVER. IT'S CLASS IN A GLASS.

Preparation: 6 minutes; Cooking: 2 minutes

SERVES TWO

INGREDIENTS

   115g/4oz plain (semisweet)
     chocolate, broken into pieces
   250ml/8fl oz/1 cup milk
   15ml/1 tbsp caster (superfine) sugar
   4 large scoops classic vanilla
     ice cream
   4 large scoops dark (bittersweet)
     chocolate ice cream
   a little lightly whipped cream
   grated chocolate or chocolate curls,
     to decorate

4 Using a dessertspoon, drizzle the chocolate milk over and around the ice cream in each glass, so that it dribbles down in swirls.

5 Top with lightly whipped cream and sprinkle over a little grated chocolate or some chocolate curls to decorate. Serve immediately.

1 Put the chocolate in a heavy pan and add the milk and sugar. Heat gently, stirring with a wooden spoon until the chocolate has melted and the mixture is smooth. Pour into a bowl and set in a larger bowl of iced water to cool quickly.

2 Blend the cooled chocolate mixture with half of both ice creams in a blender or food processor until the mixture resembles chocolate milk.

3 Scoop the remaining ice cream alternately into two tall glasses: vanilla then chocolate.

COOK'S TIP
You can experiment with all kinds of flavours of ice cream. Try substituting banana, coconut or toffee flavours for the chocolate and vanilla ice cream if you prefer. The health-conscious cook might prefer to substitute frozen yogurt, but make sure it is a creamy variety.

Energy 990kcal/4149kJ; Protein 17.7g; Carbohydrate 115.4g, of which sugars 110.4g; Fat 52.3g, of which saturates 32g; Cholesterol 83mg; Calcium 518mg; Fibre 1.5g; Sodium 262mg

WHISKY TRIFLE

THIS LUXURIOUSLY RICH TRIFLE IS MADE THE OLD-FASHIONED WAY, WITH REAL SPONGE CAKE, FRESH FRUIT AND RICH EGG CUSTARD, BUT WITH WHISKY RATHER THAN THE USUAL SHERRY FLAVOURING.

Preparation: 12 minutes; Cooking: 5 minutes

SERVES SIX TO EIGHT

INGREDIENTS
1 x 15–18cm/6–7in sponge cake
225g/8oz raspberry jam
150ml/¼ pint/⅔ cup whisky
450g/1lb ripe fruit, such as
  pears, bananas and strawberries
300ml/½ pint/1¼ cups
  whipping cream
flaked almonds, to decorate
For the custard
450ml/¾ pint/scant 2 cups
  full cream (whole) milk
1 vanilla pod (bean) or a few
  drops of vanilla essence (extract)
  (optional)
3 eggs
25g/1oz/2 tbsp caster (superfine)
  sugar

1 To make the custard, put the milk into a pan with the vanilla pod, if using, and bring almost to the boil. Remove the pan from the heat. Whisk the eggs and sugar together lightly. Remove the pod. Gradually whisk the milk into the egg mixture.

2 Rinse out the pan with cold water, return the mixture to it and stir over low heat until it thickens enough to cover the back of a wooden spoon; do not allow the custard to boil. Alternatively, for a very slow method of cooking, use a double boiler, or a bowl over a pan of boiling water.

3 Turn the custard into a mixing bowl and add the vanilla essence, if using. Cover the custard and set aside until ready to assemble the trifle.

4 Halve the sponge cake horizontally, spread with the raspberry jam and make a sandwich. Using a sharp knife, cut it into slices and use them to line the bottom and lower sides of a large glass serving bowl.

5 Sprinkle with the whisky. Peel and slice the fruit, then spread it out over the sponge to make an even layer. Pour the custard on top, cover with clear film (plastic wrap) to prevent a skin forming, and leave to cool and set. Chill until required. Before serving, whip the cream and spread it over the set custard. Decorate with the almonds.

VARIATION
Good-quality tinned fruit, such as peaches or pears, can be used instead of fresh fruit.

Energy 4260kcal/17754kJ; Protein 72.6g; Carbohydrate 348g, of which sugars 255.6g; Fat 259.2g, of which saturates 86.4g; Cholesterol 1026mg; Calcium 1164mg; Fibre 13.8g; Sodium 2016mg

PASSION FRUIT CREAMS

THESE DELICATELY PERFUMED CREAMS ARE LIGHT AND HAVE A FRESH FLAVOUR FROM THE PASSION FRUIT. THEY ARE STILL RICH, HOWEVER, SO THE PORTIONS ARE SMALL.
Preparation: 5 minutes; Cooking: 25–30 minutes

SERVES FIVE TO SIX

INGREDIENTS
  600ml/1 pint/2½ cups double
    (heavy) cream, or a mixture of
    single (light) and double
    (heavy) cream
  6 passion fruit
  30–45ml/2–3 tbsp vanilla sugar
  5 eggs

COOK'S TIPS
• Ripe passion fruit should look purple
and wrinkled – choose fruit that are
heavy for their size. When halved, the
fragrant, sweet juicy flesh with small
edible black seeds are revealed.
• These creams can be decorated with
mint or geranium leaves and served with
some cream.

1 Preheat the oven to 180°C/350°F/
Gas 4. Line the bases of six 120ml/4fl oz/
½ cup ramekins with rounds of baking
parchment and place them in a
roasting pan.

2 Heat the cream to just below boiling
point, then remove the pan from the
heat. Sieve the flesh of four passion
fruit and beat together with the sugar
and eggs. Whisk in the hot cream and
then ladle it into the ramekins.

3 Half fill the roasting pan with boiling
water. Bake the creams for 25–30
minutes, or until set, then leave to cool
before chilling.

4 Run a knife around the insides of the
ramekins, then invert them on to
serving plates, tapping the bases firmly.
Carefully peel off the baking parchment
and chill in the refrigerator until ready
to serve. Spoon on a little passion fruit
flesh just before serving.

Energy 585kcal/2414kJ; Protein 7.2g; Carbohydrate 8.5g, of which sugars 8.5g; Fat 58.4g, of which saturates 34.7g; Cholesterol 296mg; Calcium 77mg; Fibre 0.5g; Sodium 84mg.

POACHED PEARS IN SCENTED HONEY SYRUP

FRUIT HAS BEEN POACHED IN HONEY SINCE ANCIENT TIMES. DELICATE AND PRETTY TO LOOK AT,
THESE SCENTED PEARS PROVIDE AN EXQUISITE FINISHING TOUCH TO A MOROCCAN-STYLE MEAL.

Preparation: 3 minutes; Cooking: 27 minutes

SERVES FOUR

INGREDIENTS
45ml/3 tbsp clear honey
juice of 1 lemon
250ml/8fl oz/1 cup water
pinch of saffron threads
1 cinnamon stick
2–3 dried lavender heads
4 firm pears

1 Heat the honey and lemon juice in a heavy pan that will hold the pears snugly. Stir over a gentle heat until the honey has dissolved. Add the water, saffron threads, cinnamon stick and flowers from 1–2 lavender heads.

2 Bring the mixture to the boil, then reduce the heat and simmer gently for 5 minutes.

3 Peel the pears, leaving the stalks attached. Add the pears to the pan and simmer for 20 minutes, turning and basting at regular intervals, until they are tender. Leave the pears to cool in the syrup and serve at room temperature, decorated with a few lavender flowers.

Energy 93kcal/392kJ; Protein 0.5g; Carbohydrate 23.6g, of which sugars 23.6g; Fat 0.2g, of which saturates 0g; Cholesterol 0mg; Calcium 17mg; Fibre 3.3g; Sodium 6mg.

APRICOT PARCELS WITH HONEY GLAZE

THESE PARCELS CAN ALSO BE MADE WITH DRIED APRICOTS POACHED IN SYRUP AND THEN STUFFED, BUT FRESH FRUIT LENDS A JUICY TARTNESS TO THE OTHERWISE SWEET DISH.

Preparation: 10 minutes; Cooking: 20 minutes

SERVES SIX

INGREDIENTS
200g/7oz/1¾ cups blanched almonds, ground
115g/4oz/⅔ cup sugar
30 45ml/2–3 tbsp orange flower or rose water
12 apricots, slit and stoned (pitted)
3–4 sheets filo pastry, cut into 12 circles or squares
30ml/2 tbsp clear honey
double (heavy) cream, crème fraîche or natural (plain) yogurt, to serve

1 Preheat the oven to 180ºC/350ºF/ Gas 4. Using your hands, a blender or food processor, bind the almonds, sugar and orange flower water or rose water to a soft paste.

2 Take small walnut-size lumps of the paste and roll them into balls. Press a ball of paste into each slit apricot and gently squeeze the fruit closed. Place a stuffed apricot on a piece of filo pastry, fold up the sides to secure the fruit and twist the ends to form an open boat. Repeat with the remaining apricots and filo pastry.

3 Place the filo parcels in a shallow ovenproof dish and drizzle the honey over them. Bake for 20 minutes, until the pastry is crisp and the fruit has browned on top. Serve hot or cold with cream, crème fraîche, or a spoonful of natural yogurt.

COOK'S TIP

Roll or twist the filo parcels into any shape or size, just make sure you leave them open, so that the fruit and pastry benefit from the honey glaze.

Energy 361kcal/1517kJ; Protein 9.1g; Carbohydrate 41.6g, of which sugars 31.2g; Fat 18.9g, of which saturates 1.5g; Cholesterol 0mg; Calcium 120mg; Fibre 4.2g; Sodium 8mg.

ROAST PEACHES WITH AMARETTO

*THIS IS AN EXCELLENT DESSERT TO SERVE IN SUMMER, WHEN PEACHES ARE AT THEIR JUICIEST. THE
APRICOT AND ALMOND FLAVOUR OF THE AMARETTO LIQUEUR ENHANCES THE TASTE OF THE PEACHES.*
Preparation: 5 minutes; Cooking: 20–25 minutes

SERVES FOUR

INGREDIENTS
  4 ripe peaches
  45ml/3 tbsp Amaretto di Sarone
  45ml/3 tbsp clear honey
  crème fraîche or whipped cream,
    to serve

1 Preheat the oven 190ºC/375ºF/Gas 5.
Cut the peaches in half and prise out the
stones (pits) with the point of the knife.

2 Place the peaches cut side up in an
ovenproof dish. In a small bowl, mix the
amaretto liqueur with the honey and
drizzle over the halved peaches,
covering them evenly.

3 Bake the peaches for 20–25 minutes,
or until tender. Place two peach halves
on each serving plate and drizzle with
the pan juices. Serve immediately.

VARIATIONS
Nectarines work just as well as peaches
in this recipe. You could also try out
different liqueurs, such as Creme de
Framboise, which would add the flavour
of raspberries.

COOK'S TIP
You can cook these peaches over a
barbecue. Place them on sheets of foil,
drizzle over the liqueur, then scrunch the
foil around them to seal into parcels.
Cook for 15–20 minutes.

Energy 91kcal/387kJ; Protein 1.1g; Carbohydrate 16.4g, of which sugars 16.4g; Fat 0.1g, of which saturates 0g; Cholesterol 0mg; Calcium 8mg; Fibre 1.5g; Sodium 2mg.

PINEAPPLE AND RUM CREAM

WHEN PINEAPPLE IS HEATED, THE FLAVOUR INTENSIFIES AND THE GORGEOUS SWEET JUICES CARAMELIZE.
ADD RUM AND CREAM AND YOU HAVE A DREAM OF A SUMMER DESSERT.

Preparation: 4 minutes; Cooking: 4 minutes

SERVES FOUR

INGREDIENTS
25g/1oz/2 tbsp butter
115g/4oz pineapple, roughly chopped
45ml/3 tbsp dark rum
300ml/½ pint/1¼ cups double
(heavy) cream

VARIATIONS
Although a sumptuous dessert in its own right, this fruity alcoholic cream also works very well as a topping. Spoon over vanilla or rum-and-raisin ice cream for an extra special touch to a simple dessert. Peach slices, apple rings or halved bananas can also be used instead of pineapple pieces, if you prefer.

1 Heat the butter in a frying pan and add the pineapple. Cook over a moderate to high heat until the pineapple is starting to turn golden.

2 Add the rum and allow to bubble for 1–2 minutes, then remove and set aside. Pour the cream into a bowl and beat until soft. Fold the pineapple and rum mixture evenly through the cream, then spoon carefully into four glasses and serve immediately.

Energy 455kcal/1876kJ; Protein 1.4g; Carbohydrate 4.2g, of which sugars 4.2g; Fat 45.5g, of which saturates 28.3g; Cholesterol 116mg; Calcium 43mg; Fibre 0.4g; Sodium 55mg

SUMMER BERRIES IN WARM SABAYON GLAZE

THIS LUXURIOUS COMBINATION CONSISTS OF SUMMER BERRIES UNDER A LIGHT AND FLUFFY SAUCE
FLAVOURED WITH LIQUEUR. THE TOPPING IS LIGHTLY GRILLED TO FORM A CRISP, CARAMELIZED CRUST.
Preparation: 9 minutes; Cooking: 2 minutes

SERVES FOUR

INGREDIENTS
  450g/1lb/4 cups mixed summer
  berries, or soft fruit
  4 egg yolks
  50g/2oz/¼ cup vanilla sugar or
  caster (superfine) sugar
  120ml/4fl oz/½ cup liqueur, such as
  Cointreau, Kirsch or Grand Marnier,
  or a white dessert wine
  a little icing (confectioners') sugar,
  sifted, and mint leaves, to decorate
  (optional)

COOK'S TIP
If you prefer to omit the alcohol, use
grape, mango or apricot juice.

1 Arrange the fruit in four heatproof
ramekins. Preheat the grill (broiler).

2 Whisk the yolks in a large bowl with
the sugar and liqueur or wine. Place
over a pan of hot water and whisk
constantly until thick, fluffy and pale.

3 Pour equal quantities of the sauce
into each dish. Place under the grill for
1–2 minutes until just turning brown.
Dust the fruit with icing sugar and
sprinkle with mint leaves just before
serving, if you like. You could also add
an extra splash of liqueur.

Energy 235kcal/984kJ; Protein 3.9g; Carbohydrate 27.1g, of which sugars 27.1g; Fat 5.6g, of which saturates 1.6g; Cholesterol 202mg; Calcium 48mg; Fibre 1.3g; Sodium 18mg

FRUIT-FILLED SOUFFLÉ OMELETTE

THIS IMPRESSIVE DISH IS SURPRISINGLY QUICK AND EASY TO MAKE. THE CREAMY OMELETTE FLUFFS UP IN THE PAN, IS FLOPPED OVER TO ENVELOP ITS FRUIT FILLING AND THEN SLID OUT ON TO THE PLATE.

Preparation: 5 minutes; Cooking: 4–5 minutes

SERVES TWO

INGREDIENTS

75g/3oz/¾ cup strawberries, hulled
45ml/3 tbsp Kirsch, brandy
  or Cointreau
3 eggs, separated
30ml/2 tbsp caster (superfine) sugar
45ml/3 tbsp double (heavy)
  cream, whipped
a few drops of vanilla extract
25g/1oz/2 tbsp butter
icing (confectioners') sugar, sifted

3 Melt the butter in an omelette pan. When sizzling, pour in the egg mixture and cook until set underneath, shaking occasionally. Spoon on the strawberries and liqueur and, tilting the pan, slide the omelette so that it folds over.

4 Carefully slide the omelette on to a warm serving plate, spoon over the remaining liqueur, and serve dredged with icing sugar. Cut the omelette in half, transfer to two warmed plates and eat immediately.

1 Cut the strawberries in half and place in a bowl. Pour over 30ml/2 tbsp of the liqueur and set aside to macerate.

2 Beat the egg yolks and sugar together until pale and fluffy, then fold in the whipped cream and vanilla extract. Whisk the egg whites until stiff, then carefully fold in the yolks.

COOK'S TIP
You can give your omelette a professional look by marking sizzling grill lines on top. Protecting your hand with an oven glove, hold a long, wooden-handled skewer directly over a gas flame until it becomes very hot and changes colour. Sprinkle the top of the omelette with icing sugar, then place the hot skewer on the sugar, which will caramelize very quickly. Working quickly, before the skewer becomes too cold to caramelize the sugar, make as many lines as you like.

Energy 434kcal/1802kJ; Protein 10.2g; Carbohydrate 18.4g, of which sugars 18.4g; Fat 30.7g, of which saturates 16.4g; Cholesterol 343mg; Calcium 70mg; Fibre 0.4g; Sodium 189mg

FRUITY RICOTTA CREAMS

*RICOTTA IS AN ITALIAN SOFT CHEESE WITH A SMOOTH TEXTURE AND A MILD, SLIGHTLY SWEET FLAVOUR.
SERVED HERE WITH CANDIED FRUIT PEEL AND DELICIOUS CHOCOLATE, IT IS QUITE IRRESISTIBLE.*

Preparation: 15 minutes; Cooking: 0 minutes

SERVES FOUR

INGREDIENTS
350g/12oz/1½ cups ricotta
30–45ml/2–3 tbsp Cointreau or other
   orange liqueur
10ml/2 tsp grated lemon rind
30ml/2 tbsp icing
   (confectioner's) sugar
150ml/¼ pint/⅔ cup double
   (heavy) cream
150g/5oz candied peel, such as
   orange, lemon and citron,
   finely chopped
50g/2oz plain (semisweet) chocolate,
   finely chopped
chocolate curls, to decorate
amaretti, to serve (optional)

1 Using the back of a wooden spoon,
push the ricotta through a fine sieve
(strainer) into a large bowl.

2 Add the liqueur, rind and sugar and
beat until the mixture is light and smooth.

3 Whip the cream in a large bowl until it
forms soft peaks.

4 Gently fold the cream into the ricotta
mixture with the candied peel and
chopped chocolate.

5 Spoon the mixture into four glass
serving dishes and chill until ready to
serve. Decorate with chocolate curls and
serve with amaretti, if you like.

Energy 539kcal/2247kJ; Protein 9.4g; Carbohydrate 41.3g, of which sugars 41.2g; Fat 36.7g, of which saturates 22.6g; Cholesterol 89mg; Calcium 75mg; Fibre 2.1g; Sodium 115mg.

HOT FRUIT WITH MAPLE BUTTER

*BANANA, PAPAYA, MANGO AND PINEAPPLE ARE COATED WITH A MAPLE-SYRUP BUTTER AND GRILLED
UNTIL SOFT, PRODUCING A WONDERFUL AND UNUSUAL DESSERT.*

Preparation: 20 minutes; cooking: 10 minutes

SERVES FOUR

INGREDIENTS
1 large papaya, halved, seeds
   scooped out, halved and peeled
2 bananas, cut in half lengthways
115g/4oz/½ cup butter, diced
60ml/4 tbsp pure maple syrup
1 large mango, peeled and sliced
1 small pineapple, peeled and cubed
ground cinnamon, to decorate
   (optional)

COOK'S TIP
Be sure to use pure maple syrup for this
recipe, as imitations have little of the
taste of the real thing.

1 Put the butter and maple syrup in a
food processor and whizz until smooth
and creamy, scraping down the sides of
the processor bowl once or twice if
necessary. Scrape the maple butter into
a bowl and set it aside. (A hand-held
blender is ideal for the job, and then
you only need one bowl.)

2 Mix the bananas and papaya in a
gratin dish, cutting the papaya slices
into chunks if you prefer. Add the
mango and pineapple and mix gently.
Preheat the grill (broiler).

3 Grill (broil) the fruit under a medium
heat for 10 minutes or until tender,
turning it occasionally and brushing it
frequently with the maple butter.

4 Arrange the fruit on a warmed serving
platter and dot with the remaining
maple butter. Sprinkle over a little
ground cinnamon, if you like, and serve
the fruit piping hot.

Energy 405kcal/1692kJ; Protein 2g; Carbohydrate 47.8g, of which sugars 46.6g; Fat 24.2g, of which saturates 15.1g; Cholesterol 61mg; Calcium 56mg; Fibre 4.9g; Sodium 223mg.

BAKED BANANAS WITH ICE CREAM

BAKED BANANAS MAKE THE PERFECT PARTNERS FOR DELICIOUS VANILLA ICE CREAM TOPPED WITH A TOASTED HAZELNUT SAUCE. THIS IS QUICK AND EASY FOR TIMES WHEN ONLY SWEET TREATS WILL DO.

Preparation: 5 minutes; Cooking: 22 minutes

SERVES FOUR

INGREDIENTS
    4 large bananas, unpeeled
    15ml/1 tbsp lemon juice
    4 large scoops of vanilla ice cream
For the sauce
    25g/1oz/2 tbsp unsalted
      (sweet) butter
    50g/2oz/½ cup hazelnuts, toasted
      and roughly chopped
    45ml/3 tbsp golden (light corn) syrup
    30ml/2 tbsp lemon juice

1 Preheat the oven to 180°C/350°F/
Gas 4. Place the unpeeled bananas on
a baking sheet and brush them with the
lemon juice. Bake for about 20 minutes
until the skins are turning black and the
flesh gives a little when the bananas are
gently squeezed.

2 Meanwhile, make the sauce. Melt the
butter in a small pan. Add the hazelnuts
and cook gently for 1 minute. Add the
syrup and lemon juice and heat,
stirring, for 1 minute more.

3 To serve, slit each banana open with
a knife and open out the skins to reveal
the tender flesh. Transfer to serving
plates and serve with scoops of ice
cream. Pour the sauce over.

COOK'S TIP
If you are having a barbecue, cook the
bananas on the grill instead.

Energy 382Kcal/1598kJ; Protein 5.4g; Carbohydrate 49.4g, of which sugars 45.7g; Fat 18.6g, of which saturates 7.6g; Cholesterol 28mg; Calcium 88mg; Fibre 2.1g; Sodium 106mg

HONEY BAKED FIGS WITH HAZELNUT ICE CREAM

*FIGS BAKED IN A LEMON-GRASS SCENTED HONEY SYRUP HAVE THE MOST WONDERFUL FLAVOUR,
ESPECIALLY WHEN SERVED WITH A GOOD-QUALITY ICE CREAM DOTTED WITH ROASTED HAZELNUTS.*

Preparation: 4 minutes; Cooking: 16 minutes

SERVES FOUR

INGREDIENTS

    1 lemon grass stalk, finely chopped
    1 cinnamon stick, roughly broken
    60ml/4 tbsp clear honey
    200ml/7fl oz/scant 1 cup water
    75g/3oz/¾ cup hazelnuts
    8 large ripe dessert figs
    400ml/14fl oz/1⅔ cups good-quality
      vanilla ice cream
    30ml/2 tbsp hazelnut liqueur
      (optional)

3 Cut the figs into quarters, leaving them intact at the bases. Stand in a baking dish, pour the syrup over and cover tightly with foil and bake for 13–15 minutes until the figs are tender.

4 While the figs are baking, remove the ice cream from the freezer and let soften slightly. Chop the hazelnuts roughly and beat the softened ice cream briefly with an electric beater, then beat in the nuts.

5 To serve, puddle a little of the syrup from the figs on to each dessert plate. Arrange the figs on top and add a spoonful of ice cream. Spoon a little hazelnut liqueur over the ice cream if you like.

COOK'S TIP
If the hazelnut skins need to be removed, tip the nuts into a clean dish towel and rub them off.

1 Preheat the oven to 190°C/375°F/ Gas 5. Make the syrup by mixing the lemon grass, cinnamon stick, honey and measured water in a small pan. Heat gently, stirring until the honey has dissolved, then bring to the boil. Simmer for 2 minutes.

2 Meanwhile spread out the hazelnuts on a baking sheet and grill (broil) under a medium heat until golden brown. Shake the sheet occasionally, so that they are evenly toasted.

Energy 433kcal/1816kJ; Protein 7.8g; Carbohydrate 53.6g, of which sugars 52.1g; Fat 21.2g, of which saturates 7g; Cholesterol 24mg; Calcium 227mg; Fibre 4.2g; Sodium 88mg

RED FRUIT FILO BASKETS

FILO PASTRY IS AS LIGHT AS AIR AND MAKES A VERY ELEGANT DESSERT. THE FILLING OF SMOOTH
GREEK YOGURT AND JUICY SUMMER FRUITS PROVIDES THE PERFECT CONTRAST TO THE CRISP PASTRY.
Preparation: 8 minutes; cooking: 6–8 minutes

SERVES SIX

INGREDIENTS

3 sheets filo pastry
15ml/1 tbsp sunflower oil
175g/6oz/1½ cups soft fruits, such
    as redcurrants, strawberries
    and raspberries
250ml/8fl oz/1 cup Greek (US
    strained plain) yogurt
5ml/1 tsp icing (confectioners') sugar

1 Preheat the oven to 200°C/400°F/
Gas 6. Cut the sheets of filo pastry into
18 squares with sides about 10cm/4in
long. Cover the filo with clear film
(plastic wrap) to stop it drying out.

2 Brush each filo square very thinly with
oil, and then arrange the squares
overlapping in six small patty tins
(muffin pans), layering them in threes.
Bake for 6–8 minutes, until crisp and
golden. Lift the baskets out carefully
and leave them to cool for 5–10
minutes on a wire rack.

3 Reserve a few sprigs of redcurrants
on their stems for decoration and string
the rest. Stir into the yogurt with the
strawberries and raspberries.

4 Spoon the yogurt mixture into the filo
baskets. Decorate them with the
reserved sprigs of redcurrants and
sprinkle them with icing sugar to serve.

VARIATIONS
Other soft fruits can be used instead of
redcurrants, strawberries and raspberries. Try blueberries or blackberries
for a change, or use sliced bananas,
nectarines, peaches or kiwi fruit.

Energy 118kcal/492kJ; Protein 4.1g; Carbohydrate 13g, of which sugars 3.5g; Fat 6.3g, of which saturates 2.4g; Cholesterol 0mg; Calcium 85mg; Fibre 0.7g; Sodium 32mg.

APPLE SOUFFLÉ TURNOVER

APPLES SAUTÉED UNTIL THEY ARE SOFT AND SLIGHTLY CARAMELIZED MAKE A DELICIOUS AUTUMN FILLING FOR A SOUFFLÉD OMELETTE. THE BRANDING MARKS ADD THE FINISHING TOUCH.

Preparation: 3–4 minutes; cooking: 8 minutes

SERVES TWO

INGREDIENTS
4 eggs, separated
30ml/2 tbsp single (light) cream
15ml/1 tbsp caster (superfine) sugar
15g/½ oz/1 tbsp butter
icing (confectioner's) sugar,
    for dredging
For the filling
1 eating apple, peeled, cored
    and sliced
25g/1oz/2 tbsp butter
30ml/2 tbsp soft light brown sugar
45ml/3 tbsp single cream

1 To make the filling, sauté the apple slices in the butter and sugar until just tender. Stir in the cream and keep warm.

2 Beat the egg yolks with the cream and sugar. Whisk the egg whites until stiff, then fold into the yolk mixture. Preheat the grill (broiler).

3 Melt the butter in a large heavy frying pan, pour in the soufflé mixture and spread evenly. Cook until golden underneath, then brown the top under the grill.

4 Slide the turnover on to a plate, add the apple mixture, then fold over. Sift the icing sugar over thickly, then brand with a hot metal skewer. Cut in half and serve immediately.

Energy 469kcal/1952kJ; Protein 14.1g; Carbohydrate 27.5g, of which sugars 27.5g; Fat 34.8g, of which saturates 18.1g; Cholesterol 444mg; Calcium 107mg; Fibre 0.6g; Sodium 274mg.

WARM ZABAGLIONE

LIGHT AS AIR AND HIGHLY ALCOHOLIC, THIS WARM CUSTARD IS A MUCH-LOVED ITALIAN PUDDING.
IT IS TRADITIONALLY MADE WITH MARSALA, BUT MADEIRA OR SWEET SHERRY CAN BE USED INSTEAD.

Preparation: 8 minutes; Cooking: 5–7 minutes

2 Gradually add the Marsala, Madeira or sherry to the egg mixture, 15ml/ 1 tbsp at a time, whisking well after each addition.

3 Place the bowl over a pan of gently simmering water and continue to whisk for 5–7 minutes, until the mixture becomes thick; when the beaters are lifted they should leave a thick trail on the surface of the mixture. Do not be tempted to underbeat the mixture, as the zabaglione will be too runny and will be likely to separate.

4 Pour into four warmed, stemmed glasses and serve immediately with amaretti for dipping.

SERVES FOUR

INGREDIENTS
  4 egg yolks
  50g/2oz/¼ cup caster
    (superfine) sugar
  60ml/4 tbsp Marsala, Madeira or
    sweet sherry
  amaretti, to serve

VARIATION

To make a chocolate version of this dessert, whisk in 30ml/2 tbsp unsweetened cocoa powder with the wine or sherry and serve dusted with cocoa powder and icing (confectioners') sugar.

1 Place the egg yolks and sugar in a large heatproof bowl, and whisk with an electric beater until the mixture is pale and has thickened considerably.

COOK'S TIP

Zabaglione is also delicious served as a sauce with cooked fruit. Try serving it with poached pears, grilled (broiled) peaches or baked bananas to create a really special dessert.

Energy 131kcal/548kJ; Protein 3g; Carbohydrate 14.1g, of which sugars 14.1g; Fat 5.5g, of which saturates 1.6g; Cholesterol 202mg; Calcium 31mg; Fibre 0g; Sodium 12mg

SYRUPY BRIOCHE SLICES <u>WITH</u> ICE CREAM

KEEP A FEW INDIVIDUAL BRIOCHE BUNS IN THE FREEZER TO MAKE THIS SUPER DESSERT. FOR A SLIGHTLY TARTER TASTE, USE FINELY GRATED LEMON RIND AND JUICE INSTEAD OF ORANGE RIND.

Preparation: 4 minutes; Cooking: 9–10 minutes

SERVES FOUR

INGREDIENTS
  butter, for greasing
  finely grated rind and juice of
    1 orange, such as Navelina or
    blood orange
  50g/2oz/¼ cup caster
    (superfine) sugar
  90ml/6 tbsp water
  1.5ml/¼ tsp ground cinnamon
  4 brioche buns
  15ml/1 tbsp icing
    (confectioners') sugar
  400ml/14fl oz/1⅔ cups vanilla
    ice cream

1 Lightly grease a gratin dish and set aside. Put the orange rind and juice, sugar, water and cinnamon in a heavy pan. Heat gently, stirring constantly, until the sugar has dissolved, then boil rapidly, without stirring, for 2 minutes, until thickened and syrupy.

2 Remove the orange syrup from the heat and pour it into a shallow heatproof dish. Preheat the grill (broiler). Cut each brioche vertically into three thick slices. Dip one side of each slice in the hot syrup and arrange in the gratin dish, syrupy sides down. Reserve the remaining syrup. Grill (broil) the brioche until lightly toasted.

VARIATION
Substitute the same amount of ground cardamom for the cinnamon.

3 Using tongs, turn the brioche slices over and dust well with icing sugar. Grill for about 3 minutes more, or until they are just beginning to caramelize around the edges.

4 Transfer the hot brioche to serving plates and top with scoops of vanilla ice cream. Spoon the remaining syrup over them and serve immediately.

COOK'S TIP
You could also use slices of a larger brioche, rather than buns, or madeleines, sliced horizontally in half. These are traditionally flavoured with lemon or orange flower water, making them especially tasty.

Energy 399kcal/1681kJ; Protein 8.5g; Carbohydrate 65.5g, of which sugars 42.5g; Fat 12g, of which saturates 7.2g; Cholesterol 25mg; Calcium 174mg; Fibre 1.3g; Sodium 252mg

CRÊPES SUZETTE WITH COINTREAU BUTTER

THIN PANCAKES FILLED WITH COINTREAU-FLAVOURED BUTTER AND FLAMBÉED WITH COGNAC MAY BE A CLASSIC DISH, BUT THEY REMAIN JUST AS POPULAR AS EVER.

Preparation: 8–10 minutes; cooking: 14 minutes

SERVES SIX

INGREDIENTS
115g/4oz/1 cup plain
  (all-purpose) flour
2.5ml/½ tsp salt
2 eggs, beaten
300ml/½ pint/1¼ cups milk
oil, for frying
juice of 2 oranges
45ml/3 tbsp cognac
icing (confectioners') sugar,
  for dusting
strips of thinly pared orange rind,
  to decorate
For the orange butter
175g/6oz/¾ cup unsalted
  (sweet) butter
50g/2oz/¼ cup sugar
grated rind of 2 oranges
15ml/1 tbsp Cointreau

1 To make the orange butter, cream the butter with the sugar, orange rind and Cointreau. Set aside.

2 Sift the flour and salt into a bowl, make a well in the centre and beat in the eggs. Gradually stir in the milk and beat to a smooth batter. Pour into a measuring jug (cup). Heat the oil in a pan, pour in a little batter and make a thin pancake. Cook until the underside is golden, turn over and cook the other side. Slide out of the pan. Make at least five more pancakes.

3 Spread the pancakes with half the orange butter and fold into neat quarters.

4 Heat the rest of the orange butter in a frying pan with the orange juice, add all the folded pancakes and turn them carefully to heat them through. Push the pancakes to one side of the pan and pour in the cognac. Heat, then carefully set alight. When the flames die down, spoon the sauce over the pancakes. Serve immediately, dusted with icing sugar and decorated with strips of orange rind.

Energy 402kcal/1671kJ; Protein 5.9g; Carbohydrate 27.6g, of which sugars 13g; Fat 30.6g, of which saturates 16.8g; Cholesterol 129mg; Calcium 108mg; Fibre 0.6g; Sodium 224mg.

PASSION FRUIT SOUFFLÉS

IF YOU SHUN SOUFFLÉS BECAUSE YOU IMAGINE THEM TO BE DIFFICULT, TRY THESE DELIGHTFULLY EASY DESSERTS BASED ON BOUGHT CUSTARD. THEY ARE GUARANTEED TO RISE TO THE OCCASION.

Preparation: 3–4 minutes; Cooking: 8–10 minutes

SERVES FOUR

INGREDIENTS
  softened butter, for greasing
  200ml/7fl oz/scant 1 cup ready-made
    fresh custard
  3 passion fruit
  2 egg whites

1 Preheat the oven to 200°C/400°F/ Gas 6. Grease four 200ml/7fl oz/scant 1 cup ramekin dishes with the butter.

COOK'S TIP
Run the tip of the spoon handle around the inner rim of the soufflé mixture in each ramekin before baking to ensure even rising.

2 Pour the custard into a large mixing bowl. Cut the passion fruits in half. Using a teaspoon, carefully scrape out the seeds and juice from the halved passion fruit so that they drop straight on to the custard. Beat the mixture with a metal spoon until well combined, and set aside.

3 Whisk the egg whites until stiff, and fold a quarter of them into the custard. Carefully fold in the remaining egg whites, then spoon the mixture into the ramekin dishes. Place the dishes on a baking sheet and bake for 8–10 minutes, or until the soufflés are well risen. Serve immediately.

Energy 59kcal/249kJ; Protein 3.1g; Carbohydrate 8.8g, of which sugars 7.1g; Fat 1g, of which saturates 0g; Cholesterol 1mg; Calcium 48mg; Fibre 0.4g; Sodium 53mg

BLUEBERRY AND ORANGE CRÊPE BASKETS

IMPRESS YOUR GUESTS WITH THESE PRETTY, FRUIT-FILLED CRÊPES. WHEN BLUEBERRIES ARE OUT OF SEASON, REPLACE THEM WITH OTHER SOFT FRUIT, SUCH AS RASPBERRIES OR STRAWBERRIES.

Preparation: 5 minutes; cooking: 16–23 minutes

SERVES SIX

INGREDIENTS
150g/5oz/1½ cups plain
  (all-purpose) flour
pinch of salt
2 egg whites
200ml/7fl oz/scant 1 cup milk
150ml/¼ pint/⅔ cup orange juice
Greek (US strained plain) yogurt,
  crème fraîche or whipped cream,
  to serve
For the filling
4 oranges
225g/8oz/2 cups blueberries

1 Preheat the oven to 200ºC/400ºF/ Gas 6. To make the pancakes, sift the flour and salt into a bowl. Make a well in the centre of the flour and add the egg whites, milk and orange juice. Whisk hard, until all the liquid has been incorporated and the batter is smooth and bubbly. Pour it into a measuring jug (cup).

2 Lightly grease a heavy or non-stick pancake pan and heat until it is very hot. Pour in just enough of the batter to cover the base of the pan, swirling to cover the base evenly.

COOK'S TIPS
You'll need to work quickly to make this dessert in half an hour. If you can, make the batter ahead of time: it will improve on standing. Stir it before cooking the pancakes. Fill the pancake baskets seconds before serving, or they will absorb the fruit juice and start to soften.

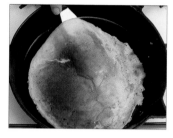

3 Cook for 1–2 minutes until the pancake has set and is brown underneath, then turn it over to cook the other side. Slide the pancake on to a sheet of kitchen paper, and then cook the rest of the batter, to make six pancakes in all.

4 Place six small ovenproof bowls or moulds on a baking sheet and drape the pancakes over them. Bake them in the oven for about 10 minutes, until they are crisp and set into shape. Carefully lift the "baskets" off the moulds.

5 Meanwhile, pare a thin piece of orange rind from one orange and cut it into fine strips. Blanch the strips in boiling water for 30 seconds, rinse them in cold water, drain them and set them aside.

6 Cut the peel and pith from all the oranges. Divide them into segments, catching the juice in a pan. Add the segments and blueberries to the pan and warm the mixture gently. Spoon the fruit into the baskets and scatter the shreds of rind on top. Serve immediately.

Energy 156kcal/662kJ; Protein 6.4g; Carbohydrate 32.2g, of which sugars 13.1g; Fat 1.1g, of which saturates 0.4g; Cholesterol 2mg; Calcium 133mg; Fibre 3.4g; Sodium 54mg.

CINNAMON AND APRICOT SOUFFLÉS

DON'T EXPECT THIS RECIPE TO BE DIFFICULT SIMPLY BECAUSE IT'S A SOUFFLÉ — IT REALLY COULDN'T BE EASIER, AND THE RESULTS ARE DELICIOUS. DUST WITH CINNAMON FOR THE FINISHING TOUCH.

Preparation: 10 minutes; cooking: 12–15 minutes

SERVES FOUR

INGREDIENTS
  melted butter, for greasing
  flour, for dusting
  3 eggs
  115g/4oz/½ cup apricot jam
  finely grated rind of ½ lemon
  5ml/1 tsp ground cinnamon, plus
    extra to decorate

1 Preheat the oven to 190ºC/375ºF/ Gas 5. Lightly grease four individual soufflé dishes and dust them lightly with flour.

2 Separate the eggs, placing the yolks in one bowl and the whites in a second, grease-free bowl. Add the apricot jam, grated lemon rind and cinnamon to the egg yolks.

3 Using a hand-held electric mixer, whisk the egg yolk mixture hard until it is thick and pale in colour. Whisk the egg whites with clean beaters until they are stiff enough to hold soft peaks.

4 Using a metal spoon or spatula, fold the egg whites evenly into the yolk mixture. Spoon into the prepared dishes. Bake the soufflés for 12–15 minutes, until well risen and lightly browned. Serve at once.

Energy 130kcal/550kJ; Protein 4.9g; Carbohydrate 19.8g, of which sugars 19.8g; Fat 4.2g, of which saturates 1.2g; Cholesterol 143mg; Calcium 25mg; Fibre 0g; Sodium 61mg.

HOT CHOCOLATE RUM SOUFFLÉS

LIGHT AS AIR, MELT-IN-THE-MOUTH SOUFFLÉS ARE ALWAYS IMPRESSIVE, YET THEY ARE OFTEN BASED ON THE SIMPLEST STORE-CUPBOARD INGREDIENTS. SERVE THEM AS SOON AS THEY ARE COOKED.

Preparation: 10 minutes; Cooking: 13–15 minutes

SERVES SIX

INGREDIENTS

50g/2oz/½ cup unsweetened
   cocoa powder
65g/2½ oz/5 tbsp caster (superfine)
   sugar, plus extra caster or icing
   (confectioners') sugar for dusting
30ml/2 tbsp dark rum
6 egg whites

1 Preheat the oven to 190°C/375°F/
Gas 3. Place a baking sheet in the oven.

COOK'S TIP
For an extra indulgent touch, serve the
soufflés with whipped cream flavoured
with dark rum and grated orange rind.

2 Mix 15ml/1 tbsp of the cocoa with
15ml/1 tbsp of the sugar in a bowl.
Grease six 250ml/8fl oz/1 cup ramekins.
Pour the cocoa and sugar mixture into
each of the dishes in turn, rotating them
so that they are evenly coated.

3 Mix the remaining cocoa powder with
the dark rum.

4 Whisk the egg whites in a clean,
grease-free bowl until they form stiff
peaks. Whisk in the remaining sugar.
Stir a generous spoonful of the whites
into the cocoa mixture to lighten it, then
fold in the remaining whites.

5 Divide the mixture among the dishes.
Place on the hot baking sheet, and
bake for 13–15 minutes, or until well
risen. Dust with caster or icing sugar
before serving immediately.

Energy 91kcal/386kJ; Protein 4.5g; Carbohydrate 12.3g, of which sugars 11.3g; Fat 1.8g, of which saturates 1.1g; Cholesterol 0mg; Calcium 18mg; Fibre 1g; Sodium 141mg.

APRICOT AND GINGER GRATIN

MADE WITH TANGY FRESH APRICOTS, THIS QUICK AND EASY DESSERT HAS A COMFORTING, BAKED CHEESECAKE-LIKE FLAVOUR. ITS DELICIOUS TASTE BELIES HOW SIMPLE IT IS TO MAKE.

Preparation: 8 minutes; Cooking: 18–20 minutes

SERVES FOUR

INGREDIENTS

    500g/1¼ lb apricots, halved and
      stoned (pitted)
    75ml/5 tbsp water
    75g/3oz/scant ½ cup caster
      (superfine) sugar
    200g/7oz/scant 1 cup cream cheese
    75g/3oz gingernut biscuits
      (gingersnaps), crushed to crumbs

1 Put the apricots in a pan with the sugar. Pour in the measurement water and heat until barely simmering. Cover and cook very gently for 8–10 minutes, until they are tender but still holding their shape. Preheat the oven to 200°C/400°F/Gas 6.

2 Drain the apricots, reserving the syrup, and place in a large dish or divide among four individual ovenproof dishes. Set aside 90ml/6 tbsp of the syrup and spoon the remainder over the fruit.

COOK'S TIP

For an even easier version, use a 400g/14oz can of apricots in juice.

3 Beat the cream cheese until softened, then gradually beat in the reserved syrup until smooth. Spoon the cheese mixture over the apricots. Sprinkle the biscuit crumbs over the cream cheese and juice mixture. Bake for 10 minutes, until the crumb topping is beginning to darken and the filling has warmed through. Serve immediately.

Energy 414kcal/1732kJ; Protein 3.8g; Carbohydrate 43.4g, of which sugars 35.3g; Fat 26.3g, of which saturates 16g; Cholesterol 48mg; Calcium 102mg; Fibre 2.4g; Sodium 216mg

AMARETTO SOUFFLÉ

*A DELICIOUSLY LIGHT SOUFFLÉ IS SANDWICHED BETWEEN TWO LAYERS OF CRUSHED AMARETTI TO GIVE
A SOPHISTICATED DESERT THAT IS FIT FOR A DINNER PARTY.*

Preparation: 5 minutes; cooking: 25 minutes

SERVES SIX

INGREDIENTS
  butter, for greasing
  105ml/7 tbsp caster (superfine) sugar
  6 amaretti, coarsely crushed
  90ml/6 tbsp Amaretto liqueur
  4 eggs, separated, plus 1 egg white
  30ml/2 tbsp plain (all-purpose) flour
  250ml/8fl oz/1 cup milk
  pinch of cream of tartar (if needed)
  icing (confectioners') sugar, for dusting

1 Preheat the oven to 200ºC/400ºF/
Gas 6. Thoroughly butter a 1.5 litre/2½
pint/6¼ cup soufflé dish and sprinkle it
with a little of the caster sugar.

2 Put the crushed amaretti in a bowl.
Sprinkle them with 30ml/2 tbsp of the
Amaretto liqueur and set aside.

3 Mix the egg yolks, flour and 30ml/
2 tbsp of the sugar.

4 Heat the milk in a heavy pan. When it
is almost boiling, stir it in to the egg and
flour mixture.

5 Pour the mixture back into the pan.
Put over a low heat and simmer gently
for 3–4 minutes or until thickened,
stirring occasionally. Remove from the
heat and gradually add the remaining
Amaretto liqueur, stirring all the time.

6 In a grease-free bowl, whisk the 5 egg
whites until they hold soft peaks. (If not
using a copper bowl, add the cream of
tartar as soon as the whites are frothy.)
Add the remaining sugar and continue
whisking until stiff.

7 Add about one-quarter of the whites
to the liqueur mixture and stir in with a
rubber spatula. Add the remaining
whites and fold in gently.

8 Spoon half of the mixture into the
prepared soufflé dish. Cover with a layer
of the moistened amaretti biscuits, then
spoon the remaining mixture on top.

9 Bake for 20 minutes or until the
soufflé is risen and lightly browned.
Sprinkle with sifted icing sugar and
serve immediately.

COOK'S TIP
Some people like soufflés to be
completely cooked while others prefer a
soft, creamy centre. The choice is up to
you. To check how cooked the middle is,
insert a thin skewer into the centre: it
will come out almost clean or with
some moist particles clinging to it when
it is done.

Energy 193kcal/814kJ; Protein 7.1g; Carbohydrate 30.7g, of which sugars 23.3g; Fat 5.6g, of which saturates 2g; Cholesterol 129mg; Calcium 96mg; Fibre 0.3g; Sodium 104mg.

CHOCOLATE SOUFFLÉS

THESE SOUFFLÉS ARE EASY TO MAKE AND CAN BE PREPARED IN ADVANCE IF IT'S MORE CONVENIENT —
THE FILLED DISHES CAN WAIT FOR UP TO ONE HOUR BEFORE BAKING.

Preparation: 10 minutes; cooking: 18–20 minutes

SERVES SIX

INGREDIENTS
  butter, for greasing
  45ml/3 tbsp caster (superfine) sugar,
    plus extra for sprinkling
  175g/6oz plain (semisweet)
    chocolate, chopped
  150g/5oz/²⁄₃ cup unsalted (sweet)
    butter, cut into small pieces
  4 large (US extra large) eggs,
    separated
  30ml/2 tbsp orange liqueur (optional)
  1.5ml/¼ tsp cream of tartar
  icing (confectioners') sugar,
    for dusting
For the white chocolate sauce
  90ml/6 tbsp whipping cream
  75g/3oz white chocolate, chopped
  15–30ml/1–2 tbsp orange liqueur
  grated rind of ½ orange

1 Generously butter six 150ml/¼ pint/
²⁄₃ cup ramekins. Sprinkle each with a
little caster sugar and tap out any excess.
Put the ramekins on a baking sheet.

2 In a heavy saucepan over a very low
heat, melt the chocolate and butter,
stirring until smooth. Remove from the
heat and cool slightly, then beat in the
egg yolks and orange liqueur, if using.
Set aside, stirring occasionally.

COOK'S TIP
Use chocolate with a high cocoa content
(at least 70 per cent) for this recipe to
obtain the best result.

3 Preheat the oven to 220°C/425°F/
Gas 7. In a clean grease-free bowl,
whisk the egg whites slowly until frothy.
Add the cream of tartar, increase the
speed and whisk until they form soft
peaks. Gradually sprinkle over the
sugar, 15ml/1 tbsp at a time, whisking
until the whites are stiff and glossy.

4 Stir one-third of the whites into the
cooled chocolate mixture to lighten it,
then pour the chocolate mixture over
the remaining whites. Using a rubber
spatula or large metal spoon, gently fold
the sauce into the whites. (Don't worry
about a few white streaks.) Spoon into
the prepared dishes and put them back
on the baking sheet. Bake for 10–12
minutes, until well risen.

5 Meanwhile, make the white chocolate
sauce. Put the chocolate and cream
into a small pan. Stir over a low heat
until melted and smooth. Remove from
the heat and stir in the liqueur and
orange rind, then pour into a serving
jug. Serve the soufflés as soon as they
are cooked, dusted with icing sugar and
accompanied by the sauce.

Energy 542kcal/2253kJ; Protein 7.1g; Carbohydrate 34.2g, of which sugars 33.9g; Fat 42.3g, of which saturates 25g; Cholesterol 198mg; Calcium 80mg; Fibre 0.7g; Sodium 218mg.

PORTUGUESE CUSTARD TARTS

CALLED PASTÉIS DE NATA IN PORTUGAL, THESE TARTS ARE TRADITIONALLY SERVED WITH A SMALL STRONG COFFEE AS A SWEET BREAKFAST DISH, BUT ARE EQUALLY DELICIOUS SERVED AS A DESSERT.

Preparation: 8 minutes; Cooking: 12–17 minutes

MAKES TWELVE

INGREDIENTS

225g/8oz ready-made puff pastry, thawed if frozen
175ml/6fl oz/¾ cup ready-made custard
30ml/2 tbsp icing (confectioners') sugar

COOK'S TIP
Fresh custard can be quickly made in the microwave. Mix together 25gl/1oz custard powder, 15g/½oz sugar and 17oz5ml/6 fl oz milk in a small bowl and microwave for 1 minute. Stir and microwave for a further 20–30 seconds to thicken.

1 Preheat the oven to 200ºC/400ºF/ Gas 6. Roll out the pastry and cut out twelve 13cm/5in rounds. Line a 12-hole patty tin (muffin pan) with the pastry rounds.

2 Line each pastry round with a circle of baking parchment and some baking beans or uncooked rice.

3 Bake the tarts for 10–15 minutes, or until the pastry is cooked through and golden. Remove the paper and baking beans or rice and set aside to cool.

4 Spoon the custard into the pastry cases and dust with the icing sugar. Place the tarts under a preheated hot grill (broiler) and cook until the sugar caramelizes. Remove from the heat and leave to cool before serving.

Energy 94kcal/395kJ; Protein 1.5g; Carbohydrate 11.9g, of which sugars 4.7g; Fat 4.9g, of which saturates 0g; Cholesterol 0mg; Calcium 26mg; Fibre 0g; Sodium 64mg.

SEMOLINA CAKE

HALVAS IS THE UNIVERSAL FAMILY TREAT, LOVED BY EVERYONE IN GREECE. IT TAKES VERY LITTLE TIME TO MAKE AND USES QUITE INEXPENSIVE INGREDIENTS.

Preparation: 5 minutes; Cooking: 8 minutes, plus standing

SERVES SIX TO EIGHT

INGREDIENTS
500g/1¼lb/2½ cups caster
  (superfine) sugar
1 litre/1¾ pints/4 cups cold water
1 cinnamon stick
250ml/8fl oz/1 cup olive oil
350g/12oz/2 cups coarse semolina
50g/2oz/½ cup blanched almonds
30ml/2 tbsp pine nuts
5ml/1 tsp ground cinnamon

COOK'S TIP
In Greece, this recipe would be made with extra virgin olive oil, but you may prefer the less dominant flavour of a light olive oil.

1 Put the sugar in a heavy pan, pour in the water and add the cinnamon stick. Bring to the boil, stirring until the sugar dissolves, then boil without stirring for about 4 minutes to make a syrup.

2 Meanwhile, heat the oil in a separate, heavy pan. When it is almost smoking, add the semolina gradually and stir continuously until it turns light brown.

3 Lower the heat, add the almonds and pine nuts and brown together for 2–3 minutes, stirring continuously. Take the semolina mixture off the heat and set aside. Remove the cinnamon stick from the hot syrup using a slotted spoon and discard it.

4 Protecting your hand with an oven glove or dishtowel, carefully add the hot syrup to the semolina mixture, stirring all the time. The mixture will hiss and spit at this point, so stand well away from it.

5 Return the pan to a gentle heat and stir until all the syrup has been absorbed and the mixture looks smooth. Remove the pan from the heat, cover it with a clean dishtowel and let it stand for 10 minutes so that any remaining moisture is absorbed.

6 Scrape the mixture into a 20–23cm/ 8–9in round cake tin (pan), preferably fluted, and set it aside. When it is cold, unmould it on to a platter and dust it all over with the ground cinnamon.

Energy 660kcal/2776kJ; Protein 6.8g; Carbohydrate 99.8g, of which sugars 65.7g; Fat 28.7g, of which saturates 3.6g; Cholesterol 0mg; Calcium 56mg; Fibre 1.5g; Sodium 10mg.

CORNFLAKE-TOPPED PEACH BAKE

MAKE THIS SIMPLE FAMILY PUDDING IN MINUTES, USING INGREDIENTS YOU'LL ALMOST CERTAINLY HAVE IN YOUR STORE CUPBOARD. THE COMBINATION OF SOFT FRUIT AND CRUNCHY TOPPING IS A WINNER.

Preparation: 2 minutes; cooking: 20 minutes

SERVES FOUR

INGREDIENTS
    400g/14oz can peach slices in juice
    30ml/2 tbsp sultanas (golden raisins)
    1 cinnamon stick
    strip of fresh orange rind
    25g/1oz/2 tbsp butter
    50g/2oz/1½ cups cornflakes
    15ml/1 tbsp sesame seeds

1 Preheat the oven to 200°C/400°F/ Gas 6. Drain the canned peach slices, reserving the juice, and then arrange them in a shallow ovenproof dish.

2 Place the peach juice, sultanas, cinnamon stick and orange rind in a pan and bring to the boil. Lower the heat and simmer for 3–4 minutes, to reduce the liquid by about half. Remove the cinnamon stick and orange rind and spoon the syrup over the peaches.

3 Melt the butter in a small pan and stir in the cornflakes and sesame seeds.

4 Spread the cornflake mixture over the fruit. Bake for about 15 minutes, or until the topping is crisp and golden. Serve hot.

Energy 176kcal/737kJ; Protein 2.5g; Carbohydrate 26.2g, of which sugars 16g; Fat 7.4g, of which saturates 3.6g; Cholesterol 13mg; Calcium 36mg; Fibre 1.4g; Sodium 177mg.

SUMMER BERRY SPONGE TART

WHEN SOFT FRUITS ARE IN SEASON, TRY MAKING THIS DELICIOUS SPONGE TART. SERVE WARM FROM THE OVEN WITH SCOOPS OF VANILLA ICE CREAM FOR A QUICK AND EASY SUMMER PUDDING.

Preparation: 10 minutes; cooking: 15 minutes

SERVES FOUR TO SIX

INGREDIENTS

softened butter, for greasing
450g/1lb/4 cups soft fruit, such as
  raspberries, blackberries,
  blackcurrants, redcurrants,
  strawberries or blueberries
2 eggs
about 50g/2oz/¼ cup caster
  (superfine) sugar
15ml/1 tbsp plain (all-purpose) flour
50g/2oz/½ cup ground almonds
  or hazelnuts
vanilla ice cream, to serve

1 Preheat the oven to 190°C/375°F/ Gas 5. Brush a 23cm/9in flan tin with softened butter and line the bottom with a circle of baking parchment. Scatter the fruit in the bottom of the tin, adding a little sugar if the fruit is tart.

COOK'S TIPS
• When time is short (or the soft fruit season has passed) use bottled fruits, but make sure they are well drained before use.
• To continue the almond theme, you could scatter some toasted almonds over the tart just before serving.

2 Whisk the eggs and sugar together for 3–4 minutes or until the whisk leaves a thick trail across the surface. Combine the flour and almonds or hazelnuts, then fold into the egg mixture with a spatula, retaining as much air as possible.

3 Pour the mixture over the top of the fruit base. Bake for about 15 minutes or until the sponge has set. Remove the tart from the tin and transfer to a serving plate. Serve warm with vanilla ice cream.

Energy 137kcal/574kJ; Protein 4.7g; Carbohydrate 15.7g, of which sugars 13.6g; Fat 6.6g, of which saturates 0.9g; Cholesterol 63mg; Calcium 50mg; Fibre 1.5g; Sodium 30mg.

PLUM AND ALMOND TART

THIS SIMPLE BUT DELICIOUS TART LOOKS LIKE SOMETHING FROM A FRENCH PATISSERIE. THOSE WHO ENJOY IT WON'T BELIEVE HOW LITTLE EFFORT IT TOOK TO PRODUCE.

Preparation: 8 minutes; Cooking: 20 minutes

SERVES FOUR

INGREDIENTS
   375g/13oz ready-rolled puff pastry,
     thawed if frozen
   115g/4oz marzipan
   6–8 plums, stoned (pitted) and sliced

1 Preheat the oven to 190ºC/375ºF/ Gas 5. Unroll the pastry on to a large baking sheet. Using a small, sharp knife, score a border 5cm/2in from the edge of the pastry all round, without cutting all the way through.

2 Roll out the marzipan into a rectangle, to fit just within the pastry border, then lay it on top of the pastry, pressing down lightly with the tips of your fingers.

3 Arrange the sliced plums on top of the marzipan and bake for 20 minutes, or until the pastry is risen and golden brown. Carefully transfer the tart to a wire rack to cool slightly, then cut into squares or wedges and serve.

Energy 478kcal/2003kJ; Protein 7.1g; Carbohydrate 58.1g, of which sugars 24.6g; Fat 26.7g, of which saturates 0.3g; Cholesterol 0mg; Calcium 79mg; Fibre 1.3g; Sodium 297mg.

ALMOND ᴬᴺᴰ RASPBERRY ROLL

A LIGHT AND AIRY GROUND ALMOND SPONGE CAKE IS ROLLED UP WITH A FRESH CREAM AND RASPBERRY FILLING FOR A DECADENT TEA-TIME TREAT OR DINNER PARTY DESSERT.

Preparation: 15 minutes; Cooking: 10–12 minutes

MAKES ONE 23CM/9IN LONG ROLL

INGREDIENTS
    3 eggs
    75g/3oz/6 tbsp caster
      (superfine) sugar
    50g/2oz/½ cup plain
      (all-purpose) flour
    30ml/2 tbsp ground almonds
    caster (superfine) sugar, for dusting
    250ml/8fl oz/1 cup double
      (heavy) cream
    225g/8oz/1⅓ cups fresh raspberries
    16 flaked almonds, toasted,
      to decorate

1 Preheat the oven to 200⁰C/400⁰F/Gas 6. Grease a 33 x 23cm/13 x 9in Swiss roll tin (jelly roll pan) and line with baking parchment. Grease the paper.

2 Whisk the eggs and sugar in a heatproof bowl until blended. Place the bowl over a pan of simmering water and whisk until thick and pale.

3 Whisk off the heat until cool. Sift over the flour and almonds, and fold them in to the mixture gently.

4 Transfer to the prepared tin and bake for 10–12 minutes, until risen and springy to the touch.

5 Invert the cake in its tin on to baking parchment dusted with caster sugar. Leave to cool, then remove the tin and lining paper.

6 Reserve a little cream, then whip the remainder until it holds its shape. Fold in all but 8 raspberries and spread the mixture over the cooled cake, leaving a narrow border. Roll the cake up and sprinkle with caster sugar.

7 Whip the reserved cream until it just holds its shape, and spoon or pipe a line along the top of the roll in the centre. Trim both ends of the roulade. Decorate the cream with the reserved raspberries and toasted flaked almonds.

Energy 2166Kcal/9012kJ; Protein 37.3g; Carbohydrate 133.9g, of which sugars 95g; Fat 169g, of which saturates 89.8g; Cholesterol 914mg; Calcium 446mg; Fibre 9.4g; Sodium 282mg.

CHOCOLATE AND PRUNE REFRIGERATOR BARS

WICKEDLY SELF-INDULGENT AND VERY EASY TO MAKE, THESE FRUITY CHOCOLATE BARS WILL KEEP FOR 2–3 DAYS IN THE REFRIGERATOR — IF THEY DON'T ALL GET EATEN AS SOON AS THEY ARE READY.

Preparation: 4–5 minutes; Cooking: 0 minutes; Chilling recommended

MAKES TWELVE BARS

INGREDIENTS
   250g/9oz good quality
   milk chocolate
   50g/2oz/¼ cup unsalted
   (sweet) butter
   115g/4oz digestive biscuits
   (graham crackers)
   115g/4oz/½ cup ready-to-eat prunes

1 Break the chocolate into small pieces and place in a heatproof bowl. Add the butter and melt in the microwave on high for 1–2 minutes. Stir to mix and set aside. (Alternatively, place the chocolate pieces and butter in a bowl over a pan of gently simmering water and leave until melted, stirring frequently.)

2 Put the biscuits in a plastic bag and seal, then bash into small pieces with a rolling pin. Alternatively, break up the biscuits in a food processor but do not let them become too fine. Use the pulse button.

3 Roughly chop the prunes and stir into the melted chocolate with the biscuits. Spoon the mixture into a 20cm/8in square cake tin (pan) and smooth out any lumps with the back of the spoon. Chill for 1–2 hours until set. Remove the cake from the refrigerator and, using a sharp knife, cut into 12 bars.

Energy 197kcal/826kJ; Protein 2.5g; Carbohydrate 21.7g, of which sugars 16.4g; Fat 11.8g, of which saturates 6.8g; Cholesterol 18mg; Calcium 59mg; Fibre 0.9g; Sodium 102mg

WHITE CHOCOLATE SNOWBALLS

THESE LITTLE SPHERICAL CAKES ARE PARTICULARLY POPULAR DURING THE CHRISTMAS SEASON.
THEY'RE SIMPLE TO MAKE, YET UTTERLY DELICIOUS AND BURSTING WITH CREAMY, BUTTERY FLAVOURS.
Preparation: 8 minutes; Cooking: 3 minutes

MAKES SIXTEEN

INGREDIENTS
200g/7oz white chocolate
25g/1oz/2 tbsp butter, diced
90g/3½ oz/generous 1 cup
  desiccated (dry unsweetened
  shredded) coconut
90g/3½ oz syrup sponge or
  Madeira cake, crumbled
icing (confectioner') sugar,
  for dusting

1 Break the chocolate into pieces and put in a heatproof bowl with the butter. Rest the bowl over a pan of gently simmering water and stir frequently until melted. Remove the bowl from the heat and set aside for a few minutes.

2 Meanwhile, put 50g/2oz/⅔ cup of the coconut on a plate and set aside. Add the cake to the melted chocolate with the remaining coconut. Mix well to form a chunky paste.

3 Take spoonfuls of the mixture and roll into balls about 2.5cm/1in in diameter and immediately roll them in the reserved coconut. Place the balls on baking parchment and leave to set.

COOK'S TIPS
• You'll need to shape the mixture into balls as soon as you've mixed in the coconut and cake; the mixture sets very quickly and you won't be able to shape it once it hardens.
• If you like, make them in advance of a special tea as they will keep well in the refrigerator for a few days.

Energy 133kcal/554kJ; Protein 1.6g; Carbohydrate 10.9g, of which sugars 9.7g; Fat 9.5g, of which saturates 6.6g; Cholesterol 3mg; Calcium 38mg; Fibre 0.8g; Sodium 46mg.

WHITE CHOCOLATE BROWNIES

THESE IRRESISTIBLE BROWNIES ARE PACKED FULL OF CREAMY WHITE CHOCOLATE AND JUICY DRIED FRUIT. THEY ARE BEST SERVED CUT INTO VERY SMALL PORTIONS AS THEY ARE INCREDIBLY RICH.

Preparation: 8 minutes; Cooking: 22 minutes

MAKES EIGHTEEN

INGREDIENTS
75g/3oz/6 tbsp unsalted (sweet)
butter, diced
400g/14oz white chocolate, chopped
3 eggs
90g/3½oz/½ cup golden caster
(superfine) sugar
10ml/2 tsp vanilla essence (extract)
90g/3½oz/¾ cup sultanas
(golden raisins)
coarsely grated rind of 1 lemon, plus
15ml/1 tbsp juice
200g/7oz/1¾ cups plain
(all-purpose) flour

1 Preheat the oven to 190ºC/375ºF/
Gas 5. Grease and line a 28 x 20cm/
11 x 8in shallow baking tin (pan) with
baking parchment.

2 Put the butter and 300g/11oz of the
chocolate in a bowl and place over a
pan of gently simmering water, stirring
frequently until melted.

3 Remove from the heat and beat in the
eggs and sugar, then add the vanilla
essence, sultanas, lemon rind and juice,
flour and the remaining chocolate.

4 Tip the mixture into the tin and
spread into the corners. Bake for about
20 minutes until slightly risen and the
surface is only just turning golden. The
centre should still be slightly soft. Leave
to cool in the tin.

5 Cut the brownies into small squares
and remove from the tin.

Energy 235Kcal/984kJ; Protein 4.3g; Carbohydrate 30.3g, of which sugars 21.8g; Fat 11.6g, of which saturates 6.6g; Cholesterol 47mg; Calcium 88mg; Fibre 0.4g; Sodium 65mg

CHOCOLATE FLORENTINES

THESE BIG, FLAT, CRUNCHY DELIGHTS ARE JUST LIKE TRADITIONAL FLORENTINES BUT USE TINY SEEDS INSTEAD OF NUTS. ROLLING THE EDGES IN MILK OR WHITE CHOCOLATE MAKES THEM A REAL TREAT.
Preparation: 10 minutes; Cooking: 10–12 minutes

MAKES TWELVE

INGREDIENTS
  50g/2oz/ ¼ cup unsalted
    (sweet) butter
  50g/2oz/ ¼ cup caster
    (superfine) sugar
  15ml/1 tbsp milk
  25g/1oz/scant ¼ cup pumpkin seeds
  40g/1½ oz/generous ¼ cup
    sunflower seeds
  50g/2oz/scant ½ cup raisins
  25g/1oz/2 tbsp multi-coloured glacé
    (candied) cherries, chopped
  30ml/2 tbsp plain (all-purpose) flour
  125g/4¼oz milk or white chocolate

1 Preheat the oven to 180ºC/350ºF/ Gas 4. Line two baking sheets with baking parchment and grease the paper well.

2 In a pan, melt the butter with the sugar, stirring, until the sugar has dissolved, then cook until bubbling. Remove the pan from the heat and stir in the milk, pumpkin and sunflower seeds, raisins, glacé cherries and flour. Mix well.

VARIATION
If you prefer, use plain (semisweet) or white chocolate to decorate the florentines. Or you could decorate 6 in each chocolate.

COOK'S TIP
Handle the florentines carefully when you roll their edges in the chocolate, as they are brittle and therefore fragile.

3 Spoon 6 teaspoonfuls of the mixture on to each baking sheet, spacing them well apart. Bake for 8–10 minutes until the florentines are turning dark golden. Using a metal spatula, push back their edges to neaten them. Leave on the baking sheets for about 5 minutes to allow them to firm up, then transfer to a wire rack to cool.

4 Break up the chocolate and put in a heatproof bowl set over a pan of gently simmering water. Heat, stirring frequently, until melted. Roll the edges of the florentines in the chocolate and leave to set on a clean sheet of baking parchment for about 1 hour.

Energy 159kcal/664kJ; Protein 2.3g; Carbohydrate 17.6g, of which sugars 14.8g; Fat 9.3g, of which saturates 4.3g; Cholesterol 11mg; Calcium 40mg; Fibre 0.6g; Sodium 38mg.

CHOCOLATE AND PISTACHIO WEDGES

THESE COOKIES ARE RICH AND GRAINY TEXTURED, WITH A STRONG CHOCOLATE FLAVOUR. THEY GO EXTREMELY WELL WITH VANILLA ICE CREAM AND ARE DELICIOUS WITH BANANAS AND CUSTARD.

Preparation: 10 minutes; Cooking: 15–20 minutes

MAKES SIXTEEN

INGREDIENTS
200g/7oz/scant 1 cup unsalted
  (sweet) butter, at room
  temperature, diced
90g/3½ oz/½ cup golden caster
  (superfine) sugar
250g/9oz/2¼ cups plain
  (all-purpose) flour
50g/2oz/½ cup unsweetened
  cocoa powder, plus extra for dusting
25g/1oz/¼ cup shelled pistachio
  nuts, finely chopped

1 Preheat the oven to 180ºC/350ºF/
Gas 4 and line a shallow 23cm/9in
round sandwich tin (pan) with baking
parchment.

2 Place the butter and sugar in a bowl
and beat until light and creamy. Sift
the flour and cocoa powder together,
then add the flour mixture to the
butter and work it in with your hands
until the mixture is smooth. Knead
until it is soft and pliable then press it
into the prepared tin.

3 Using the back of a tablespoon,
spread the mixture evenly in the tin.
Sprinkle the pistachio nuts over the
top and press them in gently. Prick
with a fork, then mark into 16
segments using a round-bladed knife.

4 Bake for about 15–20 minutes. Do
not allow to brown at all or the cookies
will taste bitter.

5 Remove the tin from the oven and
dust the surface with cocoa powder.
Cut through the marked sections with
a round-bladed knife and leave to
cool completely before removing them
from the tin.

COOK'S TIP
Pressing the pistachios into the mixture
prevents them getting over-browned.

Energy 188kcal/783kJ; Protein 2.4g; Carbohydrate 18.6g, of which sugars 6.3g; Fat 12g, of which saturates 7.1g; Cholesterol 27mg; Calcium 33mg; Fibre 1g; Sodium 115mg.

GIANT TRIPLE CHOCOLATE COOKIES

THESE COOKIES ARE PACKED WITH CHOCOLATE AND MACADAMIA NUTS. YOU WILL HAVE TO BE PATIENT WHEN THEY COME OUT OF THE OVEN, AS THEY ARE TOO SOFT TO MOVE UNTIL COMPLETELY COLD.

Preparation: 10 minutes; Cooking: 15 minutes

MAKES TWELVE LARGE COOKIES

INGREDIENTS
- 90g/3½ oz milk chocolate
- 90g/3½ oz white chocolate
- 300g/11oz dark (bittersweet) chocolate (minimum 70 per cent cocoa solids)
- 90g/3½ oz/7 tbsp unsalted (sweet) butter, at room temperature, diced
- 5ml/1 tsp vanilla essence (extract)
- 150g/5oz/¾ cup light muscovado (brown) sugar
- 150g/5oz/1¼ cups self-raising (self-rising) flour
- 100g/3½ oz/scant 1 cup macadamia nut halves

1 Preheat the oven to 180°C/350°F/ Gas 4. Line two baking sheets with baking parchment. Coarsely chop the milk and white chocolate and put them in a bowl.

2 Chop 200g/7oz of the dark chocolate into very large chunks, at least 2cm/ ½in in size. Set aside.

3 Break up the remaining dark chocolate and place in a heatproof bowl set over a pan of barely simmering water. Stir until melted and smooth. Remove from the heat and stir in the butter, then the vanilla essence and muscovado sugar.

4 Add the flour and mix gently. Add half the dark chocolate chunks, all the milk and white chocolate and the nuts and fold together.

5 Spoon 12 mounds on to the baking sheets. Press the remaining dark chocolate chunks into the top of each cookie. Bake for about 12 minutes until just beginning to colour. Cool on the baking sheets.

Energy 413Kcal/1727kJ; Protein 3.9g; Carbohydrate 48.4g, of which sugars 38.6g; Fat 24g, of which saturates 11.6g; Cholesterol 18mg; Calcium 69mg; Fibre 1.8g; Sodium 117mg

CHEWY FLAPJACK BARS

INSTEAD OF BUYING CEREAL BARS, MAKE THESE EASY AND FAR MORE TASTY VERSIONS. THEY WILL KEEP IN AN AIRTIGHT CONTAINER FOR UP TO FOUR DAYS BUT ARE USUALLY EATEN FAR QUICKER THAN THAT.

Preparation: 8 minutes; Cooking: 20 minutes

MAKES TWELVE

INGREDIENTS
270g/10oz jar apple sauce
115g/4oz/½ cup ready-to-eat dried
   apricots, chopped
115g/4oz/¾ cup raisins
50g/2oz/¼ cup demerara (raw) sugar
50g/2oz/⅓ cup sunflower seeds
25g/1oz/2 tbsp sesame seeds
25g/1oz/¼ cup pumpkin seeds
75g/3oz/scant 1 cup rolled oats
75g/3oz/⅔ cup self-raising
   (self-rising) wholemeal
   (whole-wheat) flour
50g/2oz/⅔ cup desiccated (dry
   unsweetened shredded) coconut
2 eggs

1 Preheat the oven to 200°C/400°F/
Gas 6. Grease a 20cm/8in square
shallow baking tin (pan) and line with
baking parchment.

2 Put the apple sauce in a large bowl
with the apricots, raisins, sugar and the
sunflower, sesame and pumpkin seeds
and stir together with a wooden spoon
until thoroughly mixed.

3 Add the oats, flour, coconut and eggs
to the fruit mixture and gently stir
together until evenly combined.

4 Turn the mixture into the tin and
spread to the edges in an even layer.
Bake for about 20 minutes or until
golden and just firm to the touch.

5 Leave to cool in the tin, then lift out
on to a board and cut into bars.

COOK'S TIP
Allow the baking parchment to hang over
the edges of the tin; this makes the
baked bars easier to remove.

Energy 194Kcal/816kJ; Protein 4.8g; Carbohydrate 28.9g, of which sugars 18.7g; Fat 7.4g, of which saturates 2.9g; Cholesterol 31mg; Calcium 52mg; Fibre 2.6g; Sodium 48mg

PECAN TOFFEE SHORTBREAD

COFFEE SHORTBREAD TOPPED WITH PECAN-STUDDED TOFFEE IS JUST DIVINE ... AND NUTS ARE VERY GOOD FOR YOU. CORNFLOUR GIVES A LIGHT TEXTURE, BUT ALL PLAIN FLOUR CAN BE USED INSTEAD.

Preparation: 10 minutes; Cooking: 20 minutes

MAKES TWENTY

INGREDIENTS
15ml/1 tbsp ground coffee
15ml/1 tbsp nearly boiling water
115g/4oz/½ cup butter, softened
30ml/2 tbsp smooth peanut butter
75g/3oz/scant ½ cup caster
(superfine) sugar
75g/3oz/⅔ cup cornflour (cornstarch)
185g/6½ oz/1⅔ cups plain
(all-purpose) flour
For the topping
175g/6oz/12 tbsp butter
175g/6oz/¾ cup soft light
brown sugar
30ml/2 tbsp golden (light corn) syrup
175g/6oz/1 cup shelled pecan nuts,
roughly chopped

4 Press into the base of the tin and prick all over with a fork. Bake for 20 minutes. To make the topping, put the butter, sugar and syrup in a pan and heat until melted. Bring to the boil.

5 Allow to simmer for 5 minutes, then stir in the chopped nuts. When the shortbread is baked, spread the topping over the base. Leave in the tin until cold, then cut into fingers. Remove from the tin and serve.

1 Preheat the oven to 180°C/350°F/ Gas 4. Lightly grease and line the base of a 18 x 28cm/7 x 11in tin (pan) with baking parchment.

2 Put the coffee in a bowl and pour the hot water over. Leave to infuse for 4 minutes, then strain through a fine sieve (strainer).

3 Meanwhile, cream the butter, peanut butter, sugar and coffee together until light. Sift the cornflour and flour together and mix in to make a smooth dough.

Energy 278Kcal/1160kJ; Protein 2.3g; Carbohydrate 25.7g, of which sugars 15g; Fat 19.2g, of which saturates 8.3g; Cholesterol 31mg; Calcium 29mg; Fibre 0.8g; Sodium 102mg

INDEX